Marketing Research in Ireland

Theory and Practice

THIRD EDITION

*Christine Domegan
and Declan Fleming*

D1332936

GILL & MACMILLAN

Gill & Macmillan Ltd
Hume Avenue
Park West
Dublin 12
with associated companies throughout the world
www.gillmacmillan.ie

© Christine Domegan and Declan Fleming 1999, 2003, 2007
978 07171 42002

Index compiled by Cover to Cover
Print origination in Ireland by Carole Lynch

The paper used in this book is made from the wood pulp of managed forests.
For every tree felled, at least one tree is planted, thereby renewing natural resources.

A CIP catalogue record is available for this book from the British Library.

In memory of Bridie Domegan.
CD

To Monique, Leah, Harry, Ross, Jade and Zach.
DF

Additional Resources for
Marketing Research in Ireland: Theory and Practice

Easy to use online support material for this book is available at
www.gillmacmillan.ie/lecturers

To access lecturer support material on our secure website:

1. Go to www.gillmacmillan.ie/lecturers

2. Log on using your username and password. If you don't have a password, register online and we will e-mail your password to you.

CONTENTS

ACKNOWLEDGMENTS

Special thanks are due to Dr Aidan Daly, Head of the Marketing Department, National University of Galway; Orla Murphy, Marketing Research Manager, Vodafone Ireland; and Rodger Jupp, Managing Director, Lansdowne Market Research, each of whom contributed in one way or another to the updated edition. To all our marketing colleagues who provided much needed and valuable Irish material; to Mary Greaney and the library staff, especially Trish Finnan, for their continual assistance and support; to our students for their feedback.

PART 1

INTRODUCTION TO MARKETING RESEARCH

CHAPTER 1

MARKETING RESEARCH INTRODUCED

CHAPTER OVERVIEW

▸ Introduction   ▸ What is Marketing Research?   ▸ Why is Marketing Research Essential?   ▸ Marketing Research in Ireland   ▸ Summary

INTRODUCTION

Ireland has produced numerous world leaders in many fields as diverse as music (U2), literature (Seamus Heaney) and entertainment (Colin Farrell, Pierce Brosnan). In business too, many Irish companies are world leaders — Baileys (cream liqueur), Kerry (food ingredients), Waterford Crystal, Glen Dimplex (electrical appliances) and Ryanair (low-fares European carrier). Ireland has internationally established brand names in Jameson, Guinness and Riverdance, among others. In lesser-known industries, Irish firms have also dominated or attained significant market positions. For example, Moffett Engineering for its Moffett Mounty, Lowe refrigeration for trade-fair refrigeration equipment, Bantry Bay Seafoods for mussels, and Dubarry for high-performance sailing shoes and boots. These firms know that to be this successful a business must direct all its efforts to giving customers what they want, while still earning a profit. The critical factor to attainment of such market dominance is the extensive use of *marketing research*.[1] To be truly marketing orientated, companies have to be information-orientated. As Feargal Quinn, founder of Superquinn, reminds us, 'the single most important skill you need to become truly customer-driven is the ability to listen (to the customer)'.[2] So, one of the first steps in marketing is to listen to the customer and gather marketing information, also known as *marketing research*.

This chapter introduces you to the concept of marketing research. Its purpose is to act as a precursor and prelude to an understanding and appreciation of the marketing research process, research tools and techniques. By the end of this chapter, you will be able to:

1. discuss the role of information and data in marketing;
2. define marketing research;
3. detail the role and functions of marketing research;

4. explain the hallmarks of good marketing research; and
5. discuss marketing research in Ireland.

WHAT IS MARKETING RESEARCH?

Marketing research is about generating and interpreting information to assist management with decision-making. It is the principal method for answering questions, such as: Who are my customers? Where do they shop? What do they want? What price will they pay? What do they think of me? Who are my competitors? What do my competitors offer?

So, marketing research is an activity that links the customers and competition to the company through timely, valid and reliable data. In this manner, marketing research is a function which supports and implements the marketing concept of customer satisfaction. It is 'the process of listening to the voice of the market and conveying it to management'.[3]

The idea of marketing research being an information-gathering process to assist with decision-making is encapsulated in the many formal definitions of marketing research that exist. Some are displayed in Box 1.1.

Box 1.1 Definitions of marketing research

'The formalised means of obtaining information to be used in making marketing decisions.'

The Marketing Institute of Ireland[4]

'The collection, analysis, interpretation and presentation of information obtained from individuals or groups of people in order to guide decisions on a wide range of matters, affecting consumers, either as buyers or as citizens.'

The Market Research Society (UK)[5]

'The function that links the consumer, customer and public to the marketer through information — information used to identify and define marketing opportunities and problems; generate, refine and evaluate marketing actions; monitor marketing performance; and improve understanding of marketing as a process. Marketing research specifies the information required to address these issues, designs the method for collecting information, manages and implements the data-collection process, analyses the results, and communicates the findings and their implications.'

The American Marketing Association[6]

Whatever definition of marketing research one chooses, there are several important characteristics inherent in the concept. Good marketing research must be *methodology-led, decision-driven* and *information-orientated.*

Firstly, marketing research is a *methodology-led* process that systematically and objectively investigates a problem or opportunity confronting marketing management. While no two research projects are ever identical, there is a single procedure for all researchers to follow. So, marketing research denotes a process or sequence of steps to gather facts and figures in an objective and accurate manner.

In other words, marketing research stresses *how* to gather accurate, timely, appropriate, valid and reliable information. It details the accepted method to generate useful data and results. Obtaining information appears deceptively simple — it is easy to walk down Grafton Street on a Monday afternoon and talk with the first twenty shoppers one meets, enquiring after their shopping patterns. This, however, excludes those working, travelling or eating in restaurants, attending college or collecting children from school, for example. The generated data could be misleading — it may not represent the shopping habits of all Dubliners or shoppers.

So, one critical methodology-led aspect of marketing research is about how to generate representative, objective and accurate data. The process of gathering information and the actual information collected has to be unbiased and untainted. This means that marketing research is scientific in nature. Special techniques are needed to ensure accurate, valid and reliable results. Great care is taken to ensure the research is free from error and that the research bears all the hallmarks of *validity* and *reliability.* These two terms, *validity* (measuring what we actually wanted to measure) and *reliability* (consistency in measurement) are the characteristics of good research.[7] When present, marketing research is free from error, objective in nature and scientific in character. This scientific nature is referred by Baker[8] as the 'look before you leap' phenomenon. The word 'research' means to search again, re-search what we think we already know. The term 'research' is used by all sciences and is not confined to marketing.

The second trait of marketing research is that it is *decision-driven.* The purpose of conducting research is to aid management decisions. Research is always undertaken with a specific decision in mind. The collected information should decrease the risk and uncertainty associated with a decision and, in this manner, improve management decision-making.

Specifically, marketing research is concerned with a particular decision — an opportunity or problem — facing a company at a point in time. Normally, a company has to make a strategic or tactical decision to rectify a problem. Some examples: sales are decreasing in the Cork region and the company does not know why; the firm is ready to launch a new advertising campaign, and wants to know how existing customers will perceive the potential new copy and message; the firm is already selling to multiples through a wholesaler in Britain and needs to make a decision about price points and margins to make more sales; or the company needs to decide whether to enter the Dutch market with its new range of slimming products.[9] In all of these cases, the decision is time-bound. As a result, marketing research has a definite beginning and a definite end.

Thirdly, marketing research is *information-orientated*. With the myriad of occasions that customers come into contact with the company and with the numerous activities that have to be undertaken to achieve customer satisfaction, it comes as no surprise to find that the marketing research process can be applied to a huge variety of marketing problems that can arise for a firm. Different types of marketing research project span all aspects of the macro and micro environment, and so marketing research studies are to be found in every context that links the company with its environment. In reality, marketing research can be applied to any industry sector, any product or service, any country or used by any firm, large or small. So, while the decision is action-orientated for the manager in question, marketing research is information-orientated for the investigator.

Box 1.2 Types of marketing research studies

Market research

What is the market size by value and volume? What are the trends? What is the market structure — breakdown by customer type, geography, distribution methods? Who are the competitors, what are their market shares and volumes? What are their strengths and weaknesses? What are their competitive edges or advantages?

Consumer research

Who are the customers and consumers? What is their profile? Why do they buy the product, what needs does the product meet, what product features are they interested in? Where do customers get information about the product? What are their attitudes to the product/service? How/where do they shop? What lifestyle do they have?

For example, consumer research informed Baileys,[10] producers of Sheridans liqueur, of the difficulties consumers had with the innovative packaging of the liqueur. The bottle is divided into two sections and early growth was hampered by concerns about how to pour the product (initially, Sheridans had two corks). This was upgraded to the 'perfect pour' cap, which delivers the dark liqueur and creamy top in the right combinations. However, further consumer research revealed that some people who liked the product were still a 'little apprehensive' about how to pour it, leading to the possible introduction of some form of twist cap.

Distribution research

What are all the potential distribution outlets for the product? What incentives work best for the different outlets? What is the best distribution system? What options are available if exporting? Which agent? What about shop assistants, what role do they play? How can they be assisted?

On this last point about the role of staff, one report[11] states that 'the majority of very satisfactory service incidents resulted from employees breaking the rules of their own organisations'.

Product/services research

How important is service, fast delivery, back-up facilities and warranties as part of the product? Is the quality right for the market segment? What could/should be added to the existing product to augment it? Is the packaging attractive?

Golden Vale,[12] for example, engaged in eighteen months of research prior to their launch of Cheestrings — cheese sticks that can be peeled into strings. The company's product research uncovered that fun and not flavour was the source of real appeal to young children when eating cheese.

The brand manager for Goodfella's pizzas at Green Isle Foods maintains that superior product quality, value for money, pricing appeal and relevant brand imagery are the three contributions to the success of Goodfella's pizzas, all unearthed by product, pricing and promotional research.[13]

Pricing research

How should prices be set? What constitutes value? What will the market bear? What are competitors charging? Should different customers be charged different prices?

Promotion research

What is the best way to promote the firm and its products? How much should be spent on promotions? Should you advertise on national radio, local radio, in print media or on the internet? How do you reach the target audience? How often should you talk with the target market? Should there be point-of-sale material? What makes our brand relevance distinctive and memorable? How does our brand fit with our image?

HB launched a new corporate identity as it was discovered, through promotional and consumer research, that their logo was becoming outdated. The new logo, a heart-shaped symbol in yellow and red with the HB letters underneath in blue, is intended to reflect consumer perceptions of ice cream — warmth and affection. The new logo was deemed necessary as the previous one reflected the fact that ice cream was traditionally regarded as a summer refreshment product, but is now becoming a year-round product. Promotional research, therefore, informed the company of the need to change their identity in line with the market.[14]

In cod's name, what became of Captain Birds Eye? Recent promotional research showed that pre-teens thought the old Captain Birds Eye was just that — old. 'These are kids that are very familiar with computer games and fast-moving action,' says Terry Byrne, marketing manager for Birds Eye. Hence the transformation from a Gilbert and Sullivan-type scenario to an Indiana Jones-inspired action hero, who roams the seabed in his space-age sea mobile accompanied by a Star Trek-type crew protecting the recipe for fish fingers from the piranha gang.[15]

WHY IS MARKETING RESEARCH ESSENTIAL?

One reason why marketing research is essential to firms is because marketing research provides answers to key questions, e.g. Who are my customers? What do they want? What price will they pay? What do they read? Where do they shop?

For example, the major banks in Ireland often conduct customer satisfaction surveys to investigate how satisfied customers are with their services. In a recent study, Bank of Ireland asked customers about their telephone services, staff friendliness, credit card facilities, opening hours, statements, and loan facilites.[16] This has resulted in initiatives such as 'Banking 365'. Another firm, Goodfella's Pizzas, before entering the Irish market, investigated when and why people eat pizzas — to find that Irish consumers associate pizzas with fun.[17]

Firms also engage in marketing research to reduce risk and uncertainty and so aid decision-making. Information helps management make better and more informed decisions about customer needs, the market, competitors and potential changes in the firm's offerings. Better information leads to better decisions, customer satisfaction and profitability. Good decision-making relies upon a sound information base. The value of information lies in its assistance in decision-making. In the face of intense competition, increasing service requirements of customers, shorter product life cycles and greater segmentation, an efficient and effective marketing information system enables marketing managers to make better-informed decisions. Managers can respond to changing environments and customer stimuli with greater speed. New opportunities can be capitalised upon, increasing profitability and market share. As put by Roger Jupp, Lansdowne Marketing Research,[18] 'Good research is equivalent to the lights on a car — you can see where you are going.' Managers can thus use information at:

- An operational level, e.g. a customer complaint has been received about late deliveries and management need information to diagnose the problem — was it a transport difficulty; traffic delays; or an incorrect delivery docket?

- A tactical level, e.g. sales-force management and measurement of sales levels, market share, brand awareness, preferred brands and brand loyalty are used to describe how effective the firm was in pursuing their marketing strategy. The managing director of the *Sunday World* maintains that marketing research informs the company of the variety of reasons why people buy and read newspapers. By fulfilling one of these requirements to the satisfaction of a reader, brand loyalty is established.[19]

- A strategic level, e.g. new target-market identification within the company to enhance performance or development of a sales forecast to help strategy-setting issues. To illustrate, the brand manager of Dairygold[20] food products maintains that the first step in the creation of a national brand, such as Sno Yogurt, was the comprehensive research looking into the potential of the market, the strengths and weaknesses of other brands, whether or not there was room for a new brand, and how best to penetrate the market. In a similar manner, Biosite Diagnostics Inc.,[21] prior to the introduction of a new product, Triage, engaged in market research to ascertain whether or not a market existed for the 'novel technology' they had produced. As a result, the company was able to identify one market out of five or six potential end-user segments. Thanks to this early marketing research, the firm chose the best market niche and selling strategy for its drug-testing device, and so used strategic marketing research as an antidote to the seduction of science!

Box 1.3
Examples of companies using marketing research

Extensive market research was conducted by a new regional newspaper before its launch in 2005. The research proved that there was a market for a newspaper that provided an alternative to what was already available. The research showed that consumers wanted a regional newspaper that would service a younger age group, that had an increased arts and leisure section, had increased supplements (e.g. motoring or wedding supplements), a larger property section and a more compact paper for ease of read.

Redmond O'Donoghue discussed research carried out by Waterford Crystal to identify consumers' opinions of the crystal brand. Although the response was favourable, it was noted that younger consumers were not suited to the classic design associated with traditional and excellent craftsmanship. The research indicated that younger consumers were more style-conscious, favouring minimalist designs of products with a practical use over those with a purely decorative function. It was at this point that Waterford Crystal brought John Rocha on board to design a range of contemporary crystal to attract younger customers, who were aware of the fashion designer from a fashion perspective. Rocha's designs would help to modernise the company and achieve new markets into which the company could expand. This move proved successful as the company has achieved huge profits, with the Rocha range contributing €20 million to overall sales and, with its inimitable style, it is easily distinguished from the classic Waterford brand.[22]

Supermacs, the well-known Irish fast-food brand, used consumer research when deciding to revamp its flagship store in Galway and its stores in Dublin. The marketing manager of Supermacs said, 'We do huge research with our customers and that is certainly part of it. We also want to give them something new and challenging regarding the content of our menus and how the stores are presented.'[23]

In summary, marketing research is essential because it can:

- identify problems in current marketing strategies;
- aid and improve management decision-making;
- reduce the business risk associated with a management decision;
- identify new opportunities;
- improve the firm's ultimate objective of profitability through customer satisfaction;
- act as the linkage between the firm, its environment and customers.

A word of caution: managers can suffer from three potential inertia difficulties where information is concerned. Firstly, too much information can result in information overload — managers experience 'paralysis by analysis'. Secondly, there is information deprivation — managers can 'drown in data, but lack information to make an informed decision'.[24] Thirdly, while marketing information can greatly enhance a manager's judgment about the marketing strategies, it never eliminates risk or uncertainty surrounding a decision. Information is not a substitute for management judgment.

MARKETING RESEARCH IN IRELAND

Marketing research in Ireland has developed enormously since the early 1960s, which was the founding period of two of the first indigenous market research agencies — Irish Marketing Surveys and Market Research Bureau of Ireland. Since that time, the number of companies has grown slowly but steadily, and now includes a range of companies operating as all-purpose, generalist market research agencies and many small organisations who specialise in particular market niches, for example, qualitative or online research. Thus, marketing research in Ireland is a well-developed industry, relative to the size of the economy. The current field of research companies includes multinationals such as AC Nielsen, who undertake a wide range of retail audits and are now responsible for measurement of the television audience in Ireland via the Nielsen TV ratings surveys. Lansdowne Market Research is the largest *ad hoc* research company, followed by Millward Brown IMS, TNS mrbi and Behaviour and Attitudes (these companies are frequently quoted in national newspapers). Most of the leading companies now have links with international partners in order to satisfy demand for co-ordinating research outside Ireland and to remain in continuous contact with developments in Europe and America.

Box 1.4 Marketing research associations and professional bodies

AAI	Association of Advertisers in Ireland	www.aai.ie
AEMRI	Association of European Market Research Institutes	www.aemri.org
AIMRO	Association of Irish Market Research Organisations	www.aimro.ie
AMA	American Marketing Association	www.marketingpower.com
EFAMRO	European Federation of Associations in Marketing	www.efamro.org
MRA	Marketing Research Association	www.mra-net.org
CMOR	Council for Marketing and Opinion Research	www.cmor.org
EMC	European Federation of Associations in Marketing	www.emc.be
ESOMAR	World Association of Opinion and Marketing Research	www.esomar.org
EPHMRA	European Pharmaceutical Marketing Research Association	www.ephmra.org
IAPI	Institute of Advertising Practitioners in Ireland	www.iapi.ie
MSI	Marketing Society Ireland	www.marketingsociety.ie
MRS	Market Research Society, UK	www.mrs.org.uk

The overall size of the industry was estimated at over €70 million in 2005 by AIMRO (the Association of Irish Market Research Organisations), which includes the ten largest market research companies in the Republic of Ireland. Europe has the largest research market in the world, 41% of the worldwide total of €18.6 billion

– a significant market by any standards. Traditionally, more than 80% of Irish research expenditure is of a domestic nature, with the remainder attributed to international research, either work commissioned in Ireland from clients abroad, or commissioned abroad by clients in Ireland.[25]

The profile of the Irish market research industry is broadly similar to the rest of Europe. The growth of the service economy and proliferation of marketing practices in such industries as financial services, telecommunications, the retail industry and media has led to a sharp increase in the importance of research for companies involved in these industries in recent years. Fast-moving consumer goods, the original life-blood of market research, represents a continuing important flow of business to market research agencies. It is estimated that 80% of market research expenditure is on consumer products and services,[26] the majority of which comes from manufacturers, followed by the service industry. Recent years have seen a much greater emphasis on customer satisfaction studies and also on brand and advertising tracking studies. The former is due to an enhanced understanding of the need to retain and defend the customer base against competitors' attention; the latter is driven by a higher priority on gaining more insight into media buying and advertising effectiveness. Both study types tend to be continuous, by virtue of their need to identify change.

Market research is not undertaken only by the largest companies in Ireland, but certainly, as in many other spheres, they constitute the largest buyers. This is, in part, a reflection of their substantially larger marketing budgets *vis-à-vis* small to medium enterprises. For the vast majority of smaller firms, market research is about assessing the firm's ability to match their resources with the customers' needs, in light of the environment within which they operate. Essentially, marketing research in Ireland for small firms is about:

- the market;
- the 'W' issues — What? When? Where? Why?;
- the effectiveness of the firm (versus competitors).

The particular types of projects undertaken are extremely diverse, as they now are throughout the world. The range of project types is just as diverse as the needs of the companies themselves. Usage and attitude surveys, providing market overviews and market share data, remain relevant, especially in the light of greater emphasis on truly understanding the image positioning occupied by specific brands *vis-à-vis* their competitors. Changes in customer profiles and penetration of brands remain a constant source of customer research, but these are often allied to more complex studies which look at issues such as customer segmentation into particular typologies or customer satisfaction. The Pareto principle (80/20 rule) has ensured a strong focus on identifying the most relevant and important customers, for the main buyers of market research. It has led to an emphasis on understanding the customer, in keeping

---

Box 1.5
Examples of marketing research studies
in Ireland

Dubarry 'Dubes'
Brand recognition
Attitude study
Bank of Ireland and AIB
Customer service analysis
Customer satisfaction
Communication research
Customer image
Thermo King
Customer perception feedback
Competitive profiling
Price positioning
Environmental changes and forces
Irish Life
Image studies
Segmentation research
Distribution research
Bord na Móna
Consumer buyer behaviour
Usage patterns
Vodafone
Advertising test
Switcher drivers
Segmentation
Customer satisfaction
Brand Image
Jury's Radisson
Tourism trends and changes
Customer satisfaction surveys

United Beverages
New product development
Brand name — Finches
Goodfella's
Pizza-buying behaviour
Market size
Brown Thomas
Corporate identity and positioning
Guinness
Test marketing — beer
Chanelle Veterinary
Awareness and image studies
Usage patterns
Effective promotional methods
Dairygold Food
Competitive analysis
Market studies, e.g. yoghurt
National Dairy Council
New product development
Häagen-Dazs
Market segmentation
Mars Ireland
Test market — celebrations
Iarnród Éireann
Customer satisfaction
Route studies

---

with the need to provide appropriate communications strategies to enhance customer retention, loyalty and satisfaction.

In the business-to-business arena, similar marketing philosophies have been applied in recent years; but it is fair to say that business-to-business research is probably of a lesser scale in Ireland than elsewhere, by virtue of the relative smallness of the economy. A greater need exists in larger markets such as the USA, Britain, Germany, etc. to understand business-to-business habits than appears to be the case in the Republic of Ireland.

Overall, the marketing research industry in Ireland is growing and varied. It has learned to apply online techniques, while maintaining a broad focus across industries. In so doing, the marketing research industry in Ireland continues to advise leading companies about their marketing decision-making processes.

SUMMARY

Good marketing practice requires a firm to be both customer-orientated and information-driven. Marketing research complements the marketing concept of customer satisfaction. Marketing research is an all-pervasive information activity that is necessary in implementing the marketing concept.

The purpose of this chapter has been to reflect upon what marketing research is — a valuable tool in the evaluation of different courses of action. Marketing research cannot make the decisions for managers, it is not a substitute for management decision-making. However, marketing research can help decrease the risk and uncertainty connected with many marketing decisions by delivering accurate and relevant information.

Marketing research is defined as the systematic planning, gathering, analysis and reporting of information to management to assist with a specific decision. A firm engages in marketing research because research improves decision-making. Marketing research also reduces risk and uncertainty. Marketing research is the strategic link between the firm, its customer and environment. We can conclude that marketing research is:

- a building block of marketing;
- a function in its own right;
- a management responsibility;
- an asset to be invested in;
- a source of competitive advantage or differentiation.

The marketing research industry is well developed in Ireland. First established in the 1960s, it embraces consumer and business-to-business research across a wide variety of sectors, with links to international partners. Valued at €70 million, it is set to continue to grow and advise leading companies about their marketing decision-making processes, through the provision of accurate, timely and relevant information.

KEY TERMS

Marketing concept	Customer satisfaction
Marketing research	Scientific approach
Methodology-led	Information intense

Uncertainty   Risk
Decision-making   Management function
Valid   Reliable
Decision-driven   Systematic

QUESTIONS

1. What is marketing?
2. Describe the role information plays in marketing research. How important is it?
3. What are the three levels at which managers utilise information?
4. Why is the management of information so important to decision-making?
5. What are the implications for information management over the next few years?
6. What is marketing research?
7. What are the main characteristics of marketing research?
8. How would you argue that some form of marketing research is needed in all organisations?
9. Does the type of marketing research a company needs depend on the nature of its customers? Why?
10. How would you describe the marketing research industry in Ireland?

PROBLEMS AND ASSIGNMENTS

1. How might the following use marketing research? Be specific:
    (a) A small sports shop.
    (b) A fast-food chain.
    (c) A major television network (RTÉ or UTV for example).
    (d) A computer firm.
    (e) A university.
    (f) Manchester United football club.
2. One of the key marketing trends of the 21st century is that organisations are trying to be more market-driven. What role should marketing research play in the process?
3. A marketing manager responsible for DVD games has received a copy of ten new books on this industry and five new industry reports prepared by industry consultants. These items total over 3,000 pages. 'All this data will be great help with the new games we are planning,' noted the analyst who delivered the documents. Comment on this quote, and describe how the manager should proceed.
4. The new president of an established company, selling a wide variety of equipment and supplies to the dairy industry, is facing a problem. The company is currently unprofitable and is, in the president's opinion, operating inefficiently. Some items

it manufactures, and many it wholesales to dairies, creameries, and similar plants. Because the industry is changing in several ways, survival will be more difficult in the future. In particular, many equipment companies are bypassing the wholesalers and are selling directly to dairies. In addition, many of the independent smaller dairies are being taken over by larger dairies. How might research help the new president make the right decisions?

5. You have received a report from a consultant hired by your firm — a life insurance company. The study is a survey of morale in the head office and covers the opinions of about 30 secretaries about 100 executives and actuaries. You are asked to comment on its quality. What would you look for?

6. Use a web browser to visit Ireland On Line at: http://www.iol.ie. What type of information can be accessed?

7. The owner of 22 fast-food restaurants was asked how he does marketing research. He answered that he did it by driving around. 'I stay up late. If it's midnight and I don't have anything else to do, I drive around town and look at the lines in front of places. I'll look at the rubbish and see if the guy's doing business. If he's got real clean rubbish bins and an empty car park, he's not doing any business. I also find out a lot by talking to my suppliers. I ask the bread guy how many boxes of buns the drive-in down the street is buying. Very few managers do that.' Is this manager conducting marketing research? Justify your answer.

8. Look through recent issues of newspapers and magazines to identify five examples of marketing research.

9. List one kind of marketing research that would be useful to each of the following organisations:
    (a) Your campus bookshop.
    (b) A major department store in your area.
    (c) A restaurant located near your campus.
    (d) A museum or heritage centre near you.
    (e) A nearby hospital.

10. Use the Internet to locate and examine:
    (a) ESOMAR's Code of Conduct.
    (b) The Market Research Society (UK) and its code of conduct.
    (c) Marketing associations in Ireland (name, address, phone, fax, etc.).
    (d) Marketing research firms in Ireland and other European countries, together with the facilities they offer to clients (via ESOMAR).

Case Study
Electronic Engineering Systems*

Karin Grieves has built up her small electronic engineering business over the past seven years. A successful operation, manufacturing electrical control devices for government departments, Grieves has hitherto relied upon her own extensive knowledge of government and tender procedures to outbid rival competitors.

Now, she is faced with some equipment adapted by one of her senior engineers while on a trip to the USA. The device basically is an automatic garage door-opening mechanism. A switch is activated on the garage door when a beam located on the garage forecourt passes through a small electronic package and the door opens. Grieves and the engineer have been using the device on their own garages and are quite happy that the device works well.

Grieves is keen to embrace the idea and is willing to spend a small amount of money to enter the market. She finds herself wondering who would be interested in buying the product and why. She is well aware that the device is unlikely to have extensive appeal to the mass market.

Questions
1. Discuss all the facts, figures and statistics, etc. you can think of that would be of value to Karin Grieves.
2. Discuss as many sources of information as possible that will provide this data.
3. Propose a marketing research study, detailing all the relevant stages, that you will undertake on behalf of Grieves to solve her dilemma.
4. Identify likely errors that would be of concern to you.

*This case was written by Christine Domegan. It is intended to be used as a basis for class discussion rather than to illustrate either effective or ineffective handling of an administrative situation.

Case Study
The Role of Social Marketing in Preventing Adolescent Drinking*

Underage drinking is seen as an epidemic problem and of major concern, especially when the repercussions of such activity are taken into consideration. One in four deaths in young men aged 15–29 in Europe are attributable to alcohol. In 1999 fifty-five thousand young people died in Europe from causes related to alcohol. Early alcohol consumption (i.e. by age 12) is associated with subsequent alcohol abuse and related problem behaviours in later adolescence. These include alcohol-related violence, injuries, drinking and driving, absenteeism from school or work and increased risk for using other drugs.

In almost all EU countries, nearly two-thirds of 15–16 year olds admit to having been drunk at least once in their lives. Those described as 'experienced drinkers' – having drunk alcohol forty times or more in their lifetime – rose in at least six of these countries between 1995 and 1999. A survey of 13–16 year old students undertaken in the UK indicated that 40% of males and 32% of females reported having consumed at least eleven units of alcohol on their last drinking occasion.

In Ireland, it is estimated that alcohol-related problems cost the Irish economy €2.65 billion in 2003. This represented 2.6% of GNP. Figures relating to Ireland's underage drinking culture are a major concern, while the extent and regularity of the use of alcohol among adolescents is an issue that cannot be ignored. The National Health and Lifestyle Survey in 2003 found that one in every four between the age of 10 and 16 years drank alcohol in the previous month of the study. Research has shown that adolescents get addicted more quickly than adults because their bodies are still growing and brain cells killed by alcohol are not replaced. This growth process continues until approximately 24 years of age. It takes an adult 5–15 years to become physically addicted to alcohol. It takes an adolescent just six months to two years to become addicted.

Understanding the Causes of Adolescent Drinking

The Commission on Liquor Licensing conducted a survey in 2003 on underage drinking in a sample of schools in Ireland. The survey involved extensive interviewing of school principals, teachers and some students. Part-time work was highlighted as a significant factor in underage drinking and lack of engagement in extra-curricular work. All schools cited part-time work as contributing to:

- more disposable income independent of parental monitoring;
- greater independence from parents and the consequent erosion of discipline;
- inappropriate socialising with older adult work colleagues; and
- impact on school work through fatigue and through demotivation (i.e. not seeing the point by virtue of having a comfortable income).

The shift away from childhood towards independence and adult roles is accompanied by a desire to be autonomous, free from supervision and to be granted more decision-making opportunities.

Teenage beliefs are acquired through a variety of ways, such as observation, vicarious learning and cultural stereotypes. One of the strongest predictors of 'intention to drink' and subsequent drinking behaviour among adolescents is the belief that alcohol aids social interaction. This belief is enhanced even further in a culture like Ireland's where having a drink is seen as both acceptable and quite normal. These cultural phenomena may help to explain alcohol use by young people in Ireland.

The marketing and advertising of alcohol to young people is a cause of major concern (National Alcohol Strategy Task Force on Alcohol Report, 2004). Numerous studies have found that exposure to and liking of alcohol advertisements affects whether young people will drink alcohol. An Irish study in 2001 of Irish teenage attitudes to alcohol advertising found that the advertisements served to promote and reinforce the alcohol beliefs expressed by the participants. This included that drinking alcohol is fun and that the use of alcohol improves mood and contributes to social and sexual success. Irish teenagers in this study perceived alcohol advertisements as widening their knowledge of alcohol use, normalising it and portraying it as a safe and risk-free activity.

Social Marketing to Prevent/Reduce Alcohol Use

The term social marketing refers to the application of marketing techniques to the solution of social and health problems. Social marketing provides a mechanism for tackling such problems by encouraging people to adopt healthier lifestyles. Messages aimed at curtailing drinking are among the most common public service announcements (PSAs) produced.

The use of fear appeals is perhaps the most common tactic for PSAs, with threats of physical harm including injury and death used more frequently than social threats (fear of looking stupid in front of one's peers, etc.). A fear appeal is a type of 'psychoactive' advertisement, which is capable of arousing fear in the viewer regarding the effect of the viewer's suboptimal lifestyle. How much fear should one arouse? Should one evoke just a little fear, lest people become so frightened that they tune out the painful message? Or should one try to scare them? Although the relationship between the amount of fear invoked by an advertisement and the attitude change has been investigated, results have been inconsistent. For instance, some research has found that invoking too much fear arouses intense feelings of anxiety, which causes individuals to avoid the advertisement.

Harm reduction is also worthy of further investigation. Harm reduction refers to programmes that are directed at decreasing the harmful consequences of drinking, without requiring abstinence as a necessary outcome. In the context of the social acceptance of drinking and smoking among adults, young people see abstinence messages as hypocritical and thus are likely to reject them.

Questions

1. What type of marketing information would assist in the formulation of a marketing strategy to combat adolescent drinking?
2. Having decided on the type of information required, where would you go in search of such information?
3. Devise a list of questions you wish to ask adolescents on their attitudes to advertisements aimed at curtailing the consumption of drink.

* This case study was written by Cian Long, a post-graduate student who completed his MBS in the Department of Management and Marketing in the Cork Institute of Technology, and Maurice Murphy, Lecturer in Marketing and Management in the Department of Management and Marketing in the Cork Institute of Technology. The case is based on Cian Long's MBS Thesis. It is intended to be used as a basis for class discussion rather than to illustrate either effective or ineffective handling of an administrative situation. 2006.

CHAPTER 2

THE MARKETING RESEARCH PROCESS

CHAPTER OVERVIEW

▸ Introduction ▸ The Marketing Research Process ▸ Additional Comments on the Marketing Research Process ▸ The Characteristics of Good Research ▸ Marketing Research Errors ▸ Online Marketing Research ▸ Ethics in Marketing Research ▸ ESOMAR Guidelines ▸ Summary

INTRODUCTION

The challenge for marketing managers is to obtain and use accurate information upon which to base good decisions, as we saw in Chapter 1. This may appear to be making an essentially simple process of gathering information into a very complicated and complex procedure. This is not so, as gathering information is not simple — not if you want that information to be accurate, objective, valid and reliable. Any manager can talk informally with several customers who just happen to be in the shop. But what about the customers who are not in the shop? What about their likes and dislikes, their complaints, their changing requirements? What about those people who are buying from competitors — Why? What are they buying? How could they buy from you? These types of questions and many others offer some insight into why gathering information must first be planned, and then collected. If the information is to assist with a decision about a problem or new opportunity, the manager must have complete confidence that the correct information was gathered in a reliable and accurate manner.

Enter marketing research. Marketing research is merely a label we give to a sequence of stages for gathering decision-making information using scientific techniques. This chapter is devoted to an overview of the stages involved in research, i.e. the marketing research process. That done, we turn our attention to the methodological and conceptual foundation underlying the process of good marketing research. To this end, we detail the terms *validity* and *reliability*, and examine the concept of error management. Lastly, the chapter describes marketing research and the technological and ethical trends that are affecting it. Having completed this chapter, you will be able to detail and describe:

1. the stages necessary to undertake a marketing research study;
2. the role of validity and reliability in marketing research;
3. how error can detract from the usefulness of marketing research;
4. error management;
5. technological developments in marketing research; and
6. ethics in marketing research.

The stages outlined in this chapter are used as a structure for the remainder of the book. Many of the concepts and terms raised here may be unfamiliar to you at this point. They are the tools and techniques of the marketing researcher and are repeated in more depth as we move through the book to facilitate your learning.

THE MARKETING RESEARCH PROCESS

The marketing research process refers to a set of stages that detail a number or sequence of tasks a researcher undertakes to gather and report valid and reliable information to assist with decision-making. Different authors categorise the various stages in marketing research differently. This arises due to the interrelated nature of marketing research activities. For the purposes of this book, we present the marketing research process as a set of seven stages that encapsulate the major concerns of the researcher in conducting a marketing research study. Each stage has both a conceptual dimension and activities facet for the investigator to consider. The following stages are overlapping and complementary to each other; they serve the purpose of providing a general structure for planning a research project. They are depicted in Figure 2.1.

Figure 2.1 The marketing research process

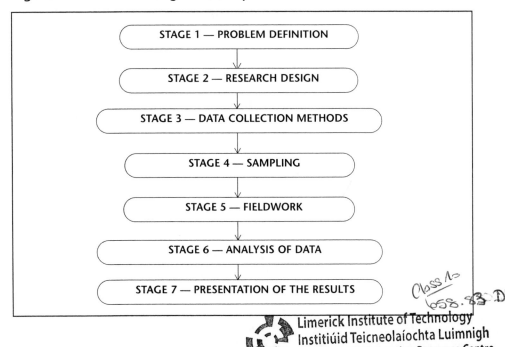

We now present a general discussion of the stages involved in any marketing research project, according to Figure 2.1. The above presentation of marketing research is adopted to capture the complexity and structure needed to understand the concept. Remember, many of the terms introduced here are explained in further detail in the relevant following chapters.

Stage 1 — Problem Definition

A research project is first concerned with correct and proper *problem definition*. This stage is essentially about the researcher deciding what information is needed to solve the problem on hand. The researcher has to determine the purpose of the study and why it is being undertaken. For example, the British Newspaper Society[1] initiated a study into the relative strengths of colour in advertising and, to this end, defined the objectives of the project as follows:

- to measure the difference in effectiveness between colour and mono advertising;
- to ascertain why some advertisements work more effectively than others;
- to develop an understanding of what elements within an advertisement will (a) make it more effective and (b) make the colour work harder.

Thus, the management decision has to be stated by the researcher as a question-and/or an information-oriented statement. This consists of a number of activities and involves the manager and researcher working closely to identify the problem.

In this manner, the tasks involved in problem definition: problem identification, clarification, formulation and objectives, are highly inter-related and dependent upon each other, as Figure 2.2 depicts. The marketing research problem or opportunity cannot be formulated without a tentative list of the information needs. To this end, a marketing information system (discussed in Chapter 3) is an important mechanism for accessing numerous sources and persons who can potentially help in defining the information needs of the project on hand.

Figure 2.2 Problem definition stages

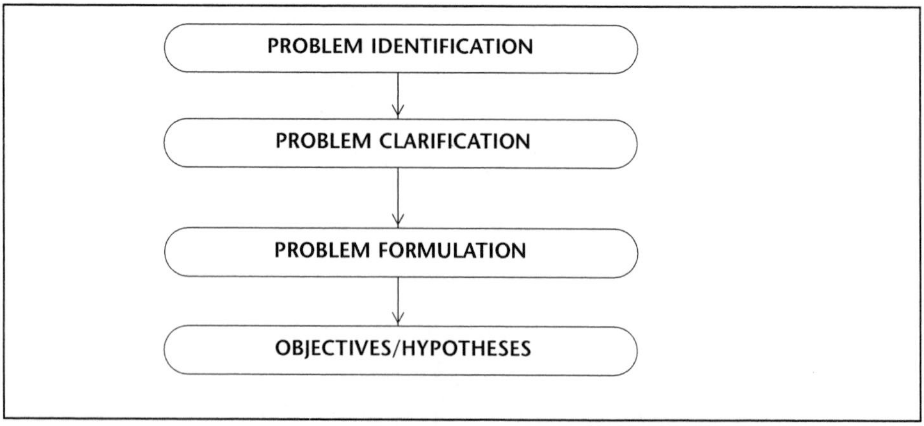

PROBLEM IDENTIFICATION

PROBLEM CLARIFICATION

PROBLEM FORMULATION

OBJECTIVES/HYPOTHESES

Problem definition ends with, and results in, either (a) a list of objectives or (b) a hypothesis. Objectives are broad statements of intent, while a hypothesis is a tentative answer to the question being considered. These are discussed in more detail in Chapter 3, as are all the individual aspects to this first stage in marketing research.

A decision at Stage 1, problem definition, automatically, directly and explicitly affects the remaining stages of research. While the stages of a marketing research study appear at face value to be mutually exclusive, they are highly dependent upon each other.

At some point early on in the research process, budget and costing have to be considered in light of required information and proposed methods for collecting the data. A research proposal may also be necessary, especially if the research is being undertaken by a research agency on behalf of the firm.

Box 2.1 Main components of a research proposal

A good research proposal will incorporate the following headings:

1. Background
A broad overview and introduction to the present situation, covering the firm, person requesting the research, an outline of the product/service, market segment, etc. to be researched. Problem/opportunity to be contextualised.

2. Research objectives
A clear statement of the research objectives and aims. The research question behind the objectives is discussed. The research can be expressed as a hypothesis.

3. Required information
A discussion of the needed qualitative and/or quantitative information and data, along with the decision facing management and potential outcomes. The decision implications of potential findings are examined. The research parameters agreed with management are presented, e.g. products, markets, topics and key issues.

4. Research methods
Based upon the (a) nature of the problem in hand; (b) time and resources; (c) size and nature of target groups and (d) nature of the decision, the researcher chooses the research techniques, in light of the accuracy and objectivity sought by management. The planned secondary and primary research is outlined.

5. Terms of reference
The researcher sets out clearly what is to be undertaken, the time frame, when, where and how he/she will report to management. The key assumptions with respect to the research are also given.

6. Schedule and Costs
All direct and indirect costs for the entire project are given, with breakdowns for each of the individual stages. Financial constraints are clearly outlined.

7. Presentation
The presentation has to be prepared with the client's needs clearly in mind. It will include a written report, presenting conclusion and recommendations, and one or more oral presentations.

In summary, finding the starting point for any marketing research project can be the most difficult part. Once the problem has been correctly identified and the information needs and objectives have been established, the research task gains momentum and starts to unfold.[2]

Stage 2 — Choose a Research Design
Choosing a research design is the second stage in marketing research. A research design is an overall blueprint, guideline, plan of action or framework for the rest of the research process to facilitate later decisions that need to be made. One way to classify the nature of the required information, and hence research designs in marketing research, is according to the three terms: *exploratory, descriptive* or *causal,* as shown in Figure 2.3.

Figure 2.3 Research designs

Exploratory research is research that aims to explore and to discover issues about the problem on hand, because very little is known about the situation by anyone inside or outside the firm. A research project is exploratory when there is uncertainty about the dimensions or characteristics of a problem or opportunity. Golden Vale[3] conducted a pan-European food research project, with the aim of the research being to find out more about the health benefits of Omega 3, the fish oil used by Golden Vale in its spread, Live. In this manner, you are 'putting your toe in the water'. This need by exploratory research to explore and discover means it is response-driven, i.e. it's the respondents' responses that matter to the investigator and not the questions posed by the researcher.

In contrast to this, you may already know a lot about the market and its behaviour, and you may want to describe this market or facets of it in more detail. You may want to categorise existing distribution outlets according to size, turnover, customer type and geographical spread. This kind of research is about quantifying some aspects of a market and so is referred to as *descriptive research.* Descriptive research is concerned with describing the associations between two or more variables, e.g. how advertising affects sales, how price and quality are related, the degree to which product usage varies with income. Alternatively, descriptive research could describe one phenomenon or variable in detail, such as brand loyalty. Thus, this type of research seeks to document the number of people who behave in a certain way or the number of units that have a certain characteristic. It is question-driven. Descriptive research is highly structured, formal, and mathematically based. For this reason, you will often hear that exploratory research generates data that is dubbed as 'soft' and descriptive research data is labelled as 'hard' data.

Causal research aims to establish *a cause and effect relationship* between two or more variables, for example, x causes y. Cadbury[4] test marketed three new chocolate assortments for the Christmas gift market: a high-class prestigious gift, a woman-to-woman gift, and a box of chocolates for men, in order to predict potential sales and the most likely new product to succeed. So, causal research describes a specific type of relationship between two or more variables. Therefore, the distinction between descriptive and causal research is one of degree, as both are dealing with quantifiable data.

Stage 3 — Planning the Data Collection Method(s) and Instrument(s)

With problem definition and research design already decided upon, the researcher is now in a position to decide how, when and where the required information is to be gathered. This stage of the marketing research process incorporates choosing a data collection method and relevant data collection instrument, in light of the problem and the research design.

Data can be collected from *secondary* sources or from *primary* sources. Secondary data is information that has already been collected by someone else for another reason, other than the one on hand. It can be either internal or external to the firm. For example, an internal source is a set of accounts or an invoice, whereas government-published figures are an example of external secondary data. Primary data is defined as data or information collected first-hand by the researcher to solve the specific problem/opportunity on hand.

Here, one comes across an important rule of marketing research. You always exhaust your secondary sources of data before planning to collect any primary data. In practice, this means that as a researcher, you first plan what information you need, and then check that the required information is not already in a written report that you could access in a library. If not, you again plan what primary research to conduct before actually gathering data from respondents. For example, as a furniture manufacturer wishing to export to the Swedish market, before going to Sweden to talk with potential customers (primary research), you would visit the Enterprise Ireland library in Sandymount, Dublin (or other sources) and consult a marketing report that they commissioned about the furniture market in Europe (secondary research).

However, in many cases, secondary sources of data are not sufficient to solve the problem. The marketing researcher then turns her/his attention to primary data collection methods.

The choice of primary data collection method is closely tied to the type of research design that is being pursued. Generally speaking, *focus groups*, *in-depth interviews* and *projective techniques* are generally, though not exclusively, associated with *exploratory research*. This is also referred to as qualitative data as it looks at *why* people buy/shop and *how* they feel. Food manufacturers often talk with small groups of seven to ten housewives to find out about their food concerns, changing opinions on nutrition and brand preferences. Medical companies conduct in-depth interviews with doctors to uncover their attitudes and opinions about new medical devices. Extensive exploratory research in Ireland convinced Murphy Brewery in Cork that the brand's traditional burgundy-coloured livery and counter mounts were too conservative and did not appeal to drinkers in the important 18–25 age category, now being targeted.[5] Likewise, Gilbeys, in a bid to increase their share of the Irish wine market by targeting 'middle of the road' wine consumers, conducted focus-group research which showed that independently minded wine consumers and connoisseurs make up about 20% of the Irish market. They discovered that these consumers don't want the 'hard sell' approach but want quality information and will pay up to €19 a bottle.[6] Focus groups were also used to identify the name and product positioning for a male contraceptive pill.[7] To utilise these data collection methods, data collection instruments or tools, such as a moderator's script, interviewer guidelines and tape recorders, are necessary.

Box 2.2 Specific research approaches for service business

A number of research approaches are uniquely applicable in people processing services simply because customers must be present during the service provision and can be summarized as:

Type of research	Qualitative/Quantitative	Frequency
Critical Incident Studies	Qualitative	Occasionally
Mystery Shopping	Both	Regularly
Trailer Calls	Both	Continuous
Mini-encounter Research	Both	Regularly
Brown Bag Chats	Both	Occasionally
Accompanied Shopper	Both	Regularly

Critical incident studies

Such studies involve researching critically poor or excellent service. They give customers the opportunity to tell their own story, and to describe best practice, poor practice and what should have happened in the case of fail points. The technique essentially focuses on behavioural aspects of employees' performance and the researcher acquires a very clear picture of desirable/undesirable employee behaviours and also of the strengths/weaknesses of the process in general, e.g. lack of signage, seating, queuing time, etc. Employees should also be surveyed to gather their views about the particular incident and to add balance to the findings from customers.

The following straightforward approach may be used to carry out a critical incident study. Select one customer at a time and go through the following broad questions but anticipate responses to each and prepare appropriate probe sub-questions.

1. Think of a time, if any, when as a customer you had a very satisfying experience with a [name the service] or an aspect of the service.
2. Tell me about it.
3. Right from the very start, what did the [staff member] do or say?
4. How did you feel?
5. [In the case of a poor experience.] What should have happened?

Mystery shopping

This form of research could be said to be particularly appropriate to people processing services. The researchers pretend to be different types of customers, and experience the reality of the service. Naturally, the researchers are unknown to service staff and operations management. The research must be objective and must compare experiences against agreed criteria. For example, researchers must have a checklist of issues against which to evaluate/grade their experiences. Service organisations should know mystery shopping is in use and staff in particular should be convinced of its value. Apart from being an excellent means of continuously monitoring service performance, it can be an excellent motivator, a way of keeping staff alert and of reinforcing service standards. Many service businesses publish mystery shopping findings on notice boards and staff newsletters, reward staff or departments with prizes and bonuses, and on occasion build it into staff compensation schemes.

Trailer calls/Accompanied shopper

As the name suggests, customers are 'trailed'; followed during or after the service experience. For example, customers may be asked in a restaurant when they're eating their starters, how satisfied they are and again when they've finished. Or customers may be asked about the service experience just after paying. Customers may be 'trailed' home by mail or telephone interview. One hotel uses trailer calls to validate and satisfy complainers. For example, if a guest at a checkout complains that people were very noisy on the corridor outside his room the previous night and demands a discount, trailer calls are used to survey people who stayed in adjoining rooms to assess their satisfaction with their stay in the hotel. If no one mentions unacceptable noise levels, then the complainer was either trying it on or a very light sleeper!

Mini-encounter research

This is a more specific application of trailer research and other techniques where researchers focus on a particular aspect of a service, e.g. queuing for the theatre or checkouts in a supermarket. The objective is through observation and discussion with customers to learn as much as possible about the satisfaction levels with that aspect of service.

Brown bag chats

This is a very informal research method but can be very useful for exploring customers' views that can be tested more methodically later. Basically it means selecting at random a small group of customers, inviting them for a cup of tea/coffee or a light lunch and chatting to them about the service or changes/additions being thought about. Naturally the 'chat' is pre-planned and follows an agenda of what the manager/researcher would like to find out from customers. It's a useful sounding board to find out customer satisfaction levels, experiences, information about competitors and reaction to new ideas.[8]

Surveys, either personal, telephone, postal or online are the data collection methods available to the researcher when conducting *descriptive research*. For example, Bank of Ireland and AIB regularly conduct personal interviews (CATI and CAPI) with customers to monitor the level of satisfaction with services and product offerings. These utilise the questionnaire as the main data collection instrument. The survey approach was also used to identify the value of the Internet as a marketing tool among Ireland's Top 500 companies.[9]

Computers can also be used to conduct CATI, computer-aided telephone interviews, or CAPI, computer-aided personal interviews. In these circumstances, the questionnaire is displayed on a screen, the responses are captured on the keyboard, the computer inserts the correct skip patterns and prepares the data for analysis.

Panels are made up of people, business firms or households who record their purchasing activities over a long period. The ever-changing children's market was monitored by use of school panels,[10] and Superquinn use consumer panels to identify ways of improving customer service and augmenting product ranges.[11] In Ireland, the two major types of panels are household and retail. Nielsen, a television audience measurement, is the most sophisticated measurement of household panels in Ireland.[12]

Observation is another data collection method suitable for descriptive research. Here, the researcher observes behaviour instead of asking a respondent about their behaviour. Retailers such as SuperValu and Brown Thomas utilise Electronic Point of Sale (EPoS) to observe sales of products and trends, and infer from this the purchasing behaviour of consumers.

Surveys, observations and panels provide the researcher with quantitative data – facts and figures about how many purchase a product.

Finally, the recognised data collection method for *causal research* is the *experiment*. As a method of gathering data, the experiment is characterised by manipulation of variables to establish the cause and effect relationship between variables. For example, to measure the effectiveness of a new educational intervention, a distant learning marketing course, the perceptions of the owner/managers of small Irish companies are examined before and after the course.[13]

The data collection instrument normally associated with surveys, observation, panels and experimentation is the *questionnaire*. By definition, a questionnaire is a structured list of questions asked of the respondent. Other instruments, such as interviewer checklists, can also be used.

This stage of the research process, primary data collection, is essentially concerned with *measurement*, measuring the amount of characteristic present or not present. To help us in measuring whether a person has a positive attitude, their consumption or usage rates or any of the other numerous variables that marketers are interested in, we have access to four mathematical measurement scales — the *nominal, ordinal, interval and ratio scales*. These measurement scales underlie all data collection instruments.

Figure 2.4 Data collection methods

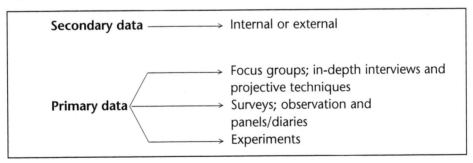

Secondary data ──────────→ Internal or external

Primary data
- → Focus groups; in-depth interviews and projective techniques
- → Surveys; observation and panels/diaries
- → Experiments

Stage 4 — Sampling

The fourth stage of a marketing research project centres around deciding who to talk to or observe, i.e. identifying who or what has the required information. The technical name given to this stage is *sampling* — choosing a small number of people or objects to represent the larger population or universe from which they are drawn. Many researchers like to consider this question before selecting a data collection method, as the form of the primary research can be influenced by who you are talking with. For example, if you are a toy manufacturer and wish to evaluate the best colour for your new product, you might give the toy in different colours to a group of children, similar to your expected target market, to play with, and observe which colour they favour. If the top five retail grocery buyers are the persons you identify as having the needed information, you may decide to e-mail or fax them a list of your questions, in light of the heavy demands placed upon their time.

The first stage in sampling is to decide upon whether a *sample* or *census* will be undertaken. The *population* of interest needs to be defined and a *sampling list* or frame of all the relevant parties and their unique characteristics, e.g. income, gender, etc. has to be generated.

At this point, the researcher has to choose a sampling method. *Probability* sampling uses a procedure that is based upon statistics, and so every unit within the population has a known chance of being selected as part of the sample. This use of statistics allows the researcher to be objective in selecting who to talk to, and so increases the validity of a study. Types of probability sampling include simple random sampling, systematic random sampling, stratified random sampling, cluster and area random sampling. For example, a paint manufacturer could use the electoral register (list of every single person over the age of 18 registered to vote) for simple random sampling, whereby x number of names are randomly chosen from the said list.

Non-probability sampling, an alternative form of sampling, is not based upon probability. It is therefore more subjective in character. It depends upon criteria such as the researcher's judgment, access to the population, cost and time constraints. It includes quota, convenience, purposeful and judgment, which are different types of non-probability sampling. For example, due to time and cost constraints, a local Dublin firm may conduct personal interviews with the first 100 people walking down Grafton Street on any given Saturday afternoon about a new coffee shop in the area — a convenience, non-probability sample.

As part of sampling, the *sample size* has to be decided upon too, i.e. how many people do you talk to or observe? Sample sizes can vary from one to many thousands and really depend on how confident the manager wants to be about the information collected. The confidence level is one way of expressing the desired accuracy of the sample — how closely the sample mirrors and reflects the population. Accuracy and confidence are measured under the concept of sampling error — the degree to which sample values vary from the population values. The general rule of thumb is that the more accuracy or confidence required in the collected data, the larger the sample size. The available budget will also influence the necessary sample size.

Having got to this point in the research process, the investigator has now planned out in advance all expected actions to acquire the needed information. The marketing research process now moves into the fifth stage.

Stage 5 — Fieldwork, Gathering the Required Information

Knowing who, what, where, how, and why, about the required information, the researcher commences the plan of action and physically collects the primary data. This is often referred to as *fieldwork*. This stage may incorporate the selection, training, controlling and evaluating of a field force, a team of researchers.

Stage 6 — Analysis of the Data

Once all fieldwork is completed, the data has to be translated into information to satisfy the objectives of the study. So the *analysis* stage of marketing research is about the processing or translation of data into information.

Prior to any detailed analysis, the data collection instruments and procedures will have to be checked for completeness and accuracy. This is data preparation and includes the functions of *editing* and *coding* the data. The data can then be entered into a computer for analysis. A computer package is used at this point, such as Minitab, SPSS or SAS. This is often referred to as *data reduction*.

With *qualitative data analysis*, the researcher is looking for patterns, themes and relationships between elements in the data. There are no statistical tests for significance in qualitative research studies. It is the responsibility of the researcher to determine and evaluate the relevance of what was observed. Aspects of qualitative data analysis would include locating individual words and phrases, creating alphabetic word lists, checking frequency of occurrence, attaching key words to segments of text, connecting words and exploring linkages between or among identified categories.

The analysis of qualitative data is aided by the availability of computer-aided qualitative data analysis software (represented by the acronym CAQDAS). Simple and cross tabulations, and frequency distributions, are the basic form of *quantative data analysis* in marketing research. Measures of central tendency or location, e.g. mean, mode, median and measures of dispersion, e.g. range and standard deviation, are also used to summarise the data in basic data analysis. Other data analysis techniques, such as significance testing, correlation, regression, factor analysis, cluster analysis and multidimensional scaling, lend richness and depth to the analysis phase.

We often refer to the type of analysis as *univariate, bivariate* or *multivariate analysis*. This refers to the number of variables concerned in the analysis. Univariate analysis denotes one variable, such as the average amount spent on beer by tourists visiting Ireland. Bivariate analysis examines two variables — for example, the relationship between price and quality; while multivariate analysis investigates a variety of variables, e.g. the market share for a particular brand of coffee is influenced by the price of the coffee, the competitors' price, the size of the jar, the competitors' jar size, special promotions, advertising and competitor advertising, shelf spacing and competitor shelf spacing, to name but a few. The National Dairy Council used factor analysis, a multivariate analysis technique, to establish an opening for a hard, white, low-fat cheddar cheese in the Irish market.[14] The actual choice of analytical technique will be dependent upon a number of issues — the problem; the required information; the nature of the collected information; whether the analysis is bivariate or multivariate in nature and whether the variables are dependent or independent. These and other analysis techniques used today are available on computer-based statistical packages used by other social sciences as well as marketing. SPSS and SAS are two of the computer-based packages widely available and used by marketing researchers worldwide. Computer-based analysis methods such as factor analysis are examined and described in depth in Part 4.

Stage 7 — Presentation of the Results and Findings

The final and remaining stage in any marketing research process is to communicate the findings and information to solve the problem/opportunity. This involves the researcher preparing and presenting a written report for the client.

To write such a report, the researcher must first understand the audience for the report. For example, most managers, of either small or large firms, do not want to hear about the pros and cons of the chosen data collection method. Such information is too technical for many managers. So, while this technical dimension to the study would be included in a report, it would not be the focal point. If the *raison d'être* of research is to assist with decision-making through the provision of information, then the marketing research report reflects this, by primarily discussing and explaining the findings and results, and not the methodology followed. The limitations of the study would also be acknowledged at this point — limitations are actual errors or shortcomings which occurred in reality. The validity and reliability implications for the study as a whole are thus documented.

Secondly, the written marketing research report follows the standardised reporting format used among the business and marketing community, unless otherwise specified by the manager in question. For example, all research reports have an executive summary — one or two pages of statements summarising the key/core findings of the research.

The presentation of results normally incorporates an oral presentation to the manager and other relevant decision-makers within the company. Again, the crux of the presentation is the findings and results of the research process and not the actual research process itself. This follows a generally accepted number of guidelines, as outlined in Chapter 15, and affords the manager a question and answer period.

ADDITIONAL COMMENTS ON THE MARKETING RESEARCH PROCESS

There are some hidden issues surrounding any basic marketing research model, such as the one above, which a researcher needs to be aware of.

1. In practice, the stages in any marketing research process are more interactive than the stage-by-stage model, presented in this chapter, tends to suggest. For

example, it is common for a researcher, while considering the data collection method best suited to the project on hand, to also think about sampling and fieldwork, as all three issues impact upon each other. The marketing research stages are very interdependent upon each other, and overlap.

2. Each stage in the marketing research process is, in reality, very complex. Each stage of the research process is fraught with difficulties and potential pitfalls. To illustrate, when doing survey work, it is possible that the respondent will not remember the required information (do you know how many pints you have consumed in the past year?), will not reveal the true answer (how much did you earn this year?), or will answer yes or no to make the researcher happy. These are merely examples of respondent error.

Figure 2.5 The marketing research process

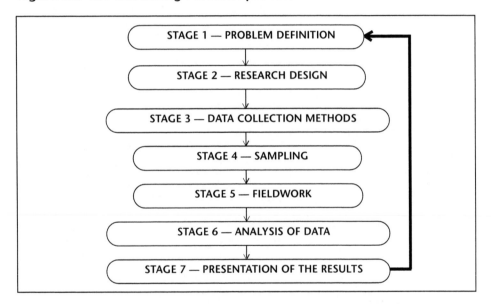

3. As presented, the marketing research stages seem very rigid; in practice they are much more fluid than first appears. Marketing research is not as linear as depicted by any model. To illustrate this point — firms can undertake an exploratory research and then turn around and use this to feed into a second descriptive research study. Given this, we can now introduce a feedback loop into our basic marketing research model, as shown in Figure 2.5.

4. Sometimes, secondary sources of data can supply enough information to solve the problem and thus allow the manager to make a decision. In this situation, you would then move to the analysis stage of the marketing research process and continue on from that point. A firm, having defined the information needs, may

locate and access a secondary source of data, a report or study, that provides answers to the problem on hand. By analysing the report and documented information within, the researcher may be in a position to write up the results and present them to the manager. This type of research is still a marketing research study, except that in these circumstances, no primary research was needed. So, our marketing research model looks like that presented in Figure 2.6.

Figure 2.6 The marketing research process

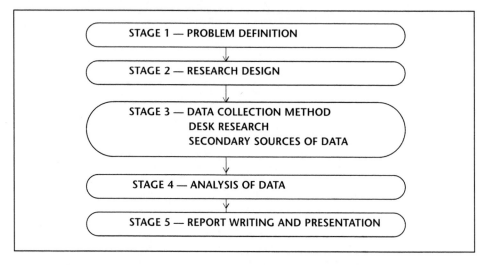

- STAGE 1 — PROBLEM DEFINITION
- STAGE 2 — RESEARCH DESIGN
- STAGE 3 — DATA COLLECTION METHOD
  DESK RESEARCH
  SECONDARY SOURCES OF DATA
- STAGE 4 — ANALYSIS OF DATA
- STAGE 5 — REPORT WRITING AND PRESENTATION

THE CHARACTERISTICS OF GOOD RESEARCH

An important question for an investigator to consider is, 'What makes for good marketing research?' To answer such a question, we must consider a web of factors. Firstly, management must be confident in the information gathered. Secondly, the collected information has to be in accordance with scientific principles. If the provided information is to be accurate and relevant, it has be valid and reliable. Thirdly, planning every stage is essential to good research. The nature of marketing research involves much planning, attention to detail and a scientific approach to information gathering. These factors translate into four key characteristics of good marketing research: systematic, objective, valid, and reliable.

Systematic

Marketing research has to be well organised, well thought out and planned in advance. As an approach to collecting relevant information, marketing research is a logical and defined method. Thus marketing research is, by definition, systematic.

Objective

The process of gathering information and the actual information collected has to be unbiased and untainted. There is great care taken to ensure the research is free from error (random and systematic error), and that the research bears all the hallmarks of validity and reliability. These two terms, validity (measuring what we actually wanted to measure) and reliability (consistency in measurement) are required of good research. When present, marketing research is free from systematic and random error and is therefore 'objective' in nature.

Valid

Results are valid when we have measured what we truly wanted to measure. This concept of validity underlies each and every stage of any marketing research process, and is considered necessary for the soundness of the research.

Reliable

Results are reliable when the measuring instruments used deliver consistent findings over time. It assists us in generalising the results from our study to other persons, objects, stores or entities.

Throughout the remainder of this book, the concepts of validity and reliability are given due consideration as they conceptually underlie every stage of the marketing research process. To manage for and ensure they are both present, we consider the likelihood of error detracting from our findings and results.

MARKETING RESEARCH ERRORS

Precautions must be taken at all times to guard against error, bias or shortcomings in the findings, as these detract from the research being valid and reliable. So, it is equally important for a researcher to consider what makes for poor research.

To understand error, we introduce the concept of measurement. Error is said to have occurred when our obtained measurement deviates from the real or true measurement. By virtue of the fact that the researcher is taking a measurement (M) of a characteristic (C), there is a distortion in the measurement of the true characteristic. So, instead of $M = C$, in reality $M = C + E$, where E is the amount of total error present. This error can come from random events (and so affect the reliability of the study) or it can surface from systematic error (thus bringing into question the validity of the research). However, on a more practical level, we can say that there are two general or broad types of error that can affect any marketing research. These are *systematic error* and *random error*. Systematic error is *bias* or shortcomings that detract from the accuracy and usefulness of the measurements. It occurs because of faults in the measurement procedure. Random error is *ad hoc* bias that results in an inconsistent measurement. Both can occur at any time during the research process. Systematic error is within the control of the researcher, while random error is not. To simplify a discussion of error and its effect on any research process, we will coincide our discussion of error with each of the marketing research stages and possible errors, as outlined in Table 2.1.

Table 2.1 Sources of error in marketing research

Marketing research stage	Source of errors	
	Systematic errors	**Random errors**
Problem definition	Informational error	Random error
Research design	Informational error	Random error
Data collection	Non-sampling error (Response error) (Non-response error) (Interviewer error) (Measurement error)	Random error
Sampling	Sampling error (Population error) (Frame error)	Random error
Analysis of data	Analysis error	Random error
Presentation of the results	Communication errors	Random error

Regardless of the classification system used to understand the impact of error in any given project, the tasks and activities undertaken in *each* stage of marketing research are aimed at reducing or eliminating total error, so as to increase the overall objectivity, validity and reliability of the project.

The remainder of this book presents a more in-depth understanding and examination of error in each of the stages in the marketing research process, along with the different management strategies used to eliminate or minimise error.

ONLINE MARKETING RESEARCH

The Internet is transforming the way marketing research is conducted at virtually every level.[15] It is the single most significant change affecting marketing research today. Online data collection, storage and retrieval systems deliver volumes of secondary data on market trends and the competitive environment. Online surveys have simplified and accelerated primary data collection. Virtual reality simulations now allow marketers to test new marketing ideas quickly, inexpensively and confidentially. The task of analysing marketing data is no longer relegated to research specialists. Increasingly, managers are using networked desktop computers, data analysis and data mining software, and Internet search engines to access and process marketing research information.[16]

More and more qualitative research is being conducted on the Internet. Online focus groups have become commonplace and are often the preferred research method for a wide range of scenarios rather than the traditional focus groups. The Internet enables the researcher to reach segments that are usually hard to access: doctors, lawyers, professional people, working mothers and others who lead busy lives and are not interested in taking part in traditional focus groups. They offer several advantages, including less time and low costs and can bridge the time and distance gap in recruiting respondents. Even indepth interviews and projective techniques are gaining popularity on the Internet. According to Edmondson, the traditional disadvantages of the Internet – eliciting less spontaneous responses, lack of interactivity between the respondent and the interviewer, and limited group dynamics – are being substantially overcome as the Internet becomes a way of life.[17]

The advantages of online research are self-evident. For example, the task of data entry, a costly and time-consuming process involved in traditional offline marketing research, is avoided as data is collected directly from respondents in electronic format. Fieldwork can be validated in real time, enabling greater levels of quality control (consistency checks, item response checks) and the ability to fine-tune surveys as they are being executed. Survey questions can be randomised, eliminating a potential source of response bias. In the online environment, there are fewer of the conventional research constraints, such as the difficulties in accessing multiple, geographically disparate physical sites.[18] The sheer quantity of data that can be collected using electronic methods is unprecedented.

Online Secondary Data

Nowhere is the effect of technology more evident than in secondary data. Web-sites, online databases, data mining, intranets, data warehousing and sophisticated search agents mean that more marketing research problems are being solved quickly and cost-efficiently through desk research alone, as discussed in Chapter 4.

Online Focus Groups

Online focus groups are useful in cases where the survey touches on sensitive topics and where respondents are difficult to recruit, have low incidence or are geographically dispersed. They have become more commonplace and more powerful when the majority of users have broadband Internet connections; in the short term, they may suffer from a certain lack of spontaneity caused by varying connection speeds.

Online Surveys, Observation & Panels

Researchers are finding that Internet surveys have many advantages over their paper, telephone or face-to-face alternatives – the two most important being that they are more cost-effective and faster to develop, test, administer and analyse. However, they are not suitable in all situations. Marketing researchers have a choice of carrying out a web-based survey or an email survey, each with their own advantages and disadvantages, as discussed in Chapter 6.

The Internet allows marketing researchers an incredible opportunity to observe the behaviour of their online customers and prospects. As consumers move through a website, every step of 'click' can be followed and recorded in detail, and subsequently analysed to provide rich insights.

The application of panel research on the Internet is commonly seen in the form of bulletin boards. These are a web-based form that allows respondents to submit messages as part of a discussion list. The advantage of bulletin boards is that messages are kept for participants until they are ready to read and reply to them. Many online bulletin board discussions involve up to twenty participants and last for a number of days, or even weeks.

Online Experimentation

As technology becomes more powerful and broadband fibre optic communications become available, the nature of the material that can be put on the web is changing. It is possible (but still expensive) to use the multimedia capabilities of the web to their true potential, combining elaborate multidimensional graphics, sound, photographs and live voice and video links to create a rich 'virtual' experience, allowing the use of experimental techniques.

Online Sampling

Online sampling is particularly suited to computer-orientated populations of interest, such as the software industry, education, music, books and other established online businesses. As the dominance of the Internet grows, so too will the ability to conduct virtual sampling. One word of warning as a researcher: you have to be very careful to ensure that the respondents you target online have consented to being contacted; otherwise you are guilty of 'spamming'. This is regarded as an unethical practice and can result in sanctions being taken against the guilty parties. This is further examined in Chapter 10.

Box 2.3 Internet marketing research

Consumers now live in a multimedia world. They are bombarded with sights, sounds and motion that subtly communicate a product's benefits. Multimedia is one new emerging method of conducting marketing research among the youth market on topics such as music, fashion and entertainment. Multimedia represents a new and powerful method of channelling information from teenagers to marketers. But today's computer-based techniques don't interact well with all consumers. Respondents need at least some level of comfort with a keyboard or mouse.

Marketing researchers, as they strive to find increasingly efficient design solutions for their clients, are attempting to keep pace with on-line technology. These efforts have led to on-line focus groups and surveys as well as greater interest overall in research and idea generation. Online research can provide the researcher with a solution that is sensitive to both budget and time constraints. Now thanks to innovations in technology, researchers know in real time what is happening in the marketplace.

There are three electronic primary data collection methods. These are: the World Wide Web, e-mail, and online discussion groups. HTML forms (also called web questionnaires) are accessible via the WWW or via an Intranet. E-mail questionnaires are essentially questionnaires which are written in ASCII format, or alternatively an e-mail with an attached HTML form. Unlike e-mail questionnaires which are quite restrictive in their potential size, format and design, web forms or questionnaires can potentially integrate colour, graphics, sound and video. Online discussion groups are text based and controlled by moderators. Only specified users are permitted to take part and the discussions are moderated in order to initiate dialogue from respondents.

For certain types of research (online focus group discussions) the Internet has some fervent supporters. With an online discussion, you have an immediate transcript, already in computer form, and the respondent can get involved from anywhere in the world. If the topic is about a sensitive subject, the respondents don't have to sit in front of other people and say what they are thinking. Sensitive topics such as birth control, health care and personal finance sometimes can be researched more candidly online than in person. However, it should also be noted that e-mail provides less anonymity to the respondent in that the receiver can, in most cases, identify the respondent.

In conventional surveys, the initial contact is made via telephone, post or person-to-person meeting. However, the principal method of communicating over the Internet is e-mail. With online surveys, respondents can choose either to answer the questionnaire on their screens and return it electronically, or print out paper copies, fill them out and return them by mail or fax.

Coupled with developments in software (e.g. SNAP, which combines questionnaire design, data collection and analysis), web surveys remove any errors that typically occur in surveying techniques that rely on human encoding of the collected data. Also a more recent development is that, instead of scrolling down a web page to answer a survey, questions will be shown to the respondent individually (or in sections) and the actual responses to questions will determine which questions will follow thereafter.

To date, many studies have looked at electronic primary data collection compared with conventional research methods such as postal or face-to-face interviewing. There is very little evidence to prove that electronic survey methods enjoy higher response rates when compared to other methods. However, there is evidence to show that a quicker response can be obtained from e-mail as opposed to postal surveys. There is also some evidence (although to a lesser extent) to show that responses to open-ended questions in e-mail surveys are higher than that of conventional postal surveys.

As a way of reaching certain target groups, such as anything to do with IT and technical people, business people, academics, early adopters and youth markets, the Internet can be quite useful. Yet, because household e-mail penetration is still low, it cannot be considered as a representative sample of Joe Public. A parallel is to be found in terms of the development of telephone interviewing in Europe, where twenty years ago a number of countries were waiting for the household penetration of telephones to reach critical mass before CATI was both viable and representative.

The sampling frame for electronic surveys is restricted to members of the population who have access to computer networks and to those who feel comfortable using them. As more and more organisations and individuals have access to and rely on computer-mediated communication, the opportunity for network, electronic, or online surveying will increase. When TVs and computers converge, we will become a truly 'wired' generation.

And as the online use population continues to rise and the profile more closely matches that of the general population, the results of these methods will be useful in extrapolating results to form conclusions about the general population.

Source: Adapted from: 'Electronic surveys – new methods of primary data collection', Competitive Paper, 27th EMAC Conference, May 1998; 'Fishing by the Net', *Marketing*, 22 August 1996, pp. 25 – 6; 'Online technology creates research tools', *Marketing News*, Vol. 30 No. 6; 'Virtual research exists, but how real is it?', *Marketing News*, 3 June 1996, Vol. 30 No. 12; 'Fountain of youth', *Marketing*, 14 September 1995, pp. 39 – 41; 'Multimedia research can improve NPD today', *Marketing News*, 3 June 1996, Vol. 30 No. 12; 'Technology forces changes in marketing research', *Marketing News*, 23 October 1995, Vol. 29 No. 22.

ETHICS IN MARKETING RESEARCH

The ethical concerns in marketing research have been the subject of an ongoing debate in the industry for a long time. The trends discussed above continue to fuel this debate. Professional marketing researchers and practitioners adhere to a strict 'code of conduct' to support those engaged in maintaining professional standards throughout the industry. Ethical issues cluster around the researcher's integrity, fair and just treatment of respondents and clients, and anonymity and confidentiality to respondents and clients alike.[20] For these reasons, reputable research companies require their interviewers to show a photo-identity card to respondents if asked, and provide a contact name and number for respondent access to a field controller or manager.[21] Such 'codes of conduct' are readily available from professional organisations such as the Marketing Society of Ireland, ICC/ESOMAR (International Code of Marketing and Social Research Practice; ESOMAR published their first code in 1948), the Market Research Society (UK) (Code of Conduct) and are in keeping with data protection and other relevant legislation (national and international).

The key principles of a 'code of conduct' for the industry are based upon the willing co-operation of the public and of business organisations — hence the over-riding need for research to be conducted with honesty, objectivity, with co-operation and respect for respondents. The general public is entitled to complete assurance that every research project is conducted with strict adherence to this code, and that their rights of privacy are respected. The information supplied by respondents cannot, without their express agreement, be supplied to other organisations. Wherever possible, respondents should be informed of the purpose of the research and the length of time needed to collect the information.[22] Thus, practices such as slugging (selling under the guise of market research) is unacceptable in the industry. For these reasons, ESOMAR state that 'marketing research must always be carried out objectively and in accordance with established scientific principles and must always conform to the national and international legislation which applies in those countries involved in a given research project'.

ESOMAR GUIDELINES

Responsibilities to the respondent

Specifically, ESOMAR guidelines of responsibilities to the respondent stress that marketing research should not in any way become confused with the range of activities carried out under the broad heading of 'direct marketing'. ESOMAR state that 'marketing research is not involved at any stage in collecting personal data for use in direct sales or promotional activities, directed at the individuals who participate in a research survey.' Hence, the following provisions are made under ESOMAR's code of conduct:[23]

- Respondents' cooperation in a marketing research project is entirely voluntary at all stages. They must not be misled when being asked for their cooperation.

- Respondents' anonymity must be strictly preserved. If the respondent, on request from the researcher, has given permission for data to be passed on in a form which allows that respondent to be personally identified, then:

1. The respondent must first have been told to whom the information would be supplied and the purposes for which it will be used.
2. The researcher must ensure that the information will not be used for any non-research purpose and that the recipient of the information has agreed to conform to the requirements of this Code.

- The researcher must take all reasonable precautions to ensure that respondents are in no way directly harmed or adversely affected as a result of their participation in a marketing research project.

- The researcher must take special care when interviewing children and young people. The informed consent of the parent or responsible adult must first be obtained for interviews with children.

- Respondents must be told (normally at the beginning of the interview) if observation techniques or recording equipment are being used, except where these are used in a public place. If a respondent so wishes, the record or relevant section of it must be destroyed or deleted. Respondents' anonymity must not be infringed by the use of such methods.

- Respondents must be enabled to check without difficulty the identity and bona fides of the researcher.

- Respondent cooperation is strictly on a voluntary basis. Respondents are entitled to withdraw from an interview at any stage or to refuse to cooperate in a research project. Interviewers should never lead respondents to believe they have no choice in their participation.

- Respondent confidentiality: the researcher will not use information to identify respondents without the permission of the respondent, except to those who check the data or are involved in processing the data. If such permission is given, the interviewer must record it at the time the permission is secured.

Responsibilities to the client/sponsor

The marketing researcher also has a professional and ethical responsibility to leverage their specific expertise to help clients answer their research questions. In this regard, researchers are responsible for the accurate collection, analysis and interpretation of research data. Researchers are ethically bound to ensure that each project is conducted according to the client's specifications. The research report needs to be able to describe how the research was done in enough detail so that another researcher could repeat the study. Researchers should also include any results or findings that may seem contradictory or unfavorable. To this end, ESOMAR guidelines state that:

- The researcher must inform the client if the work to be carried out for that client is to be combined or syndicated in the same project with work for other clients, but must not disclose the identity of such clients.

- The researcher must inform the client as soon as possible in advance when any part of the work for that client is to be subcontracted outside the researcher's own organisation (including the use of any outside consultants). On request, the client must be told the identity of any such subcontractor.

- The client does not have the right, without prior agreement between the parties involved, to exclusive use of the researcher's services or those of his organisation, whether in whole or in part. In carrying out work for different clients, however, the researcher must endeavour to avoid possible clashes of interest between the services provided to those clients.

- The following records remain the property of the client and must not be disclosed by the researcher to any third party without the client's permission:

  1. marketing research briefs, specifications and other information provided by the client;

  2. the research data and findings from a marketing research project (except in the case of syndicated or multi-client projects or services where the same data are available to more than one client).

- The client has no right to know the names or addresses of respondents, unless their explicit permission has been obtained by the researcher. The researcher must not disclose the identity of the client (provided there is no legal obligation to do so), or any confidential information about the latter's business, to any third party without the client's permission.

- The researcher must, on request, allow the client to arrange for checks on the quality of fieldwork and data preparation, provided that the client pays any additional costs involved in this.

- The researcher must provide the client with all appropriate technical details of any research project carried out for that client.

- When reporting on the results of a marketing research project, the researcher must make a clear distinction between the findings as such, the researcher's interpretation of these and any recommendations based on them.

- Where the client publishes any of the findings of a research project, the latter has a responsibility to ensure that these are not misleading. The researcher must be consulted and agree in advance the form and content of publication, and must take action to correct any misleading statements about the research and its findings.

Responsibilities to the general public

The researcher has a general responsibility not to intentionally abuse public confidence in marketing research. Marketing research information should not be used to intentionally mislead public opinion. ESOMAR uphold the following guidelines:

- Researchers must not, whether knowingly or negligently, act in any way that could bring discredit on the marketing research profession or lead to a loss of public confidence in it.

- Researchers must not make false claims about their skills and experience or about those of their organisation.

- Researchers must not unjustifiably criticise or disparage other researchers.

- Researchers must always strive to design research which is cost-efficient and of adequate quality, and then to carry this out to the specifications agreed with the client.

- Researchers must ensure the security of all research records in their possession.

- Researchers must not knowingly allow the dissemination of conclusions from a marketing research project which are not adequately supported by the data. They must always be prepared to make available the technical information necessary to assess the validity of any published findings.

- When acting in their capacity as researchers, the latter must not undertake any non-research activities, for example database marketing involving data about individuals which will be used for direct marketing and promotional activities. Any such non-research activities must always, in the way they are organised and carried out, be clearly differentiated from marketing research activities.

From an ethical perspective, the fact that the Internet is inexpensive to use and difficult to regulate means that it can be open to misuse by less experienced or less scrupulous researchers. The single most important ethical issue surrounding Internet research is that of 'Spam' – the term used to describe unsolicited email messages. The relatively low cost and high speed afforded by email means that researchers may be tempted to use unnecessarily large sample sizes and engage in waves of email reminders to respondents.[24] This is considered an abuse of the goodwill of Internet respondents and users in general.

Another Internet-specific ethical issue surrounds the nature of the technology itself. While there is a small security risk with personal interviews or telephone interviews, the anonymous nature of the Internet increases the risk of useful brand and market insights falling into the hands of competitors.[25] This could happen by unwittingly allowing competitors or their agents to participate in the research process, perhaps seeing prototypes or being told sensitive information or by a security breach occurring as a result of a computer hacking incident.

SUMMARY

There is a myriad of occasions when customers come into contact with a company. There are numerous activities undertaken by a firm in dealing with the customer. So it comes as no surprise to find that the marketing research can be applied to a huge variety of marketing problems facing a firm.

While no two marketing research projects are the same, there are common stages that always emerge to enable us to talk about a marketing research process.[26] This process consists of a number of generic stages, seven in total, which provide a general framework to follow when engaging in research. The seven stages in the marketing research process are overlapping and complementary as shown in Box 2.4.

Box 2.4 Summary of the marketing research process

Marketing research stage	Typical concerns
Problem definition	What decision has to be made? What are the problems facing management? What information is required?
Research design	What type of information is needed? How much is already known? Are we looking for insights or facts and figures? What is the aim of the study?
Data collection	What information exists within the firm? What information exists outside the firm? Do we need to gather the data ourselves? How? Where/when?
Sampling	Who has the necessary information? Where can we talk with them? How many people do we talk with?
Fieldwork	Over what time period do we visit people? How many researchers are needed? How much are they paid? Who will supervise them?
Analysis of data	How do we translate the raw data into a meaningful picture? What computer package will we use?
Presentation of findings	Who is the report for? What are their needs and interests? What do they expect in the report? How many copies of the report do they want? Is an oral presentation required?

The aim of these stages is to rid the research process of errors or mistakes that detract from the accuracy, relevance and confidence of the results. Thus, error management is an important dimension to any research investigation.

Technological developments, from CAFI, CAPI to databases, from web-sites to intranets, from online focus groups to on-line statistical packages, are dramatically reshaping the tools and techniques of the marketing research industry worldwide.

With this overview of the marketing research process completed, we are now ready to examine in detail each stage in its own right, starting with problem definition and choosing a research design in Chapter 3.

KEY TERMS

Objective	Exploratory research
Systematic	Planned
Marketing research	Measurement
Secondary data	Sampling error
Internal data source	Error
Validity	Reliability
Causal research	Descriptive research
Problem definition	Research design
Data collection	Analysis
Primary data	Sampling
Probability sampling	Non-probability sampling
Systematic error	Random error

QUESTIONS

1. Specify and briefly detail the seven stages involved in the marketing research process.
2. Why is accurately identifying the problem definition/opportunity so important to the subsequent six stages of the research process?
3. What are the three basic types of research design? In what circumstances would each be used?
4. What is the most popular type of data collection method and why? Why is there a growing trend towards qualitative research?
5. Which should be collected first: primary data or secondary data — and why?
6. What are the various data collection methods available to the researcher?
7. What role does sampling play in the whole research process?
8. What are the stages involved in sampling?
9. A major marketing research firm once declared one of its survey-based services to be 'free from all error, except sampling error'. Do you think this could be a true statement?

10. What is a non-sampling error?
11. What is meant by the term 'fieldwork'?
12. How might the choice of analytical technique depend on the previous stages of the research process?
13. Why is it important for the researcher to understand the audience for the report prior to writing and presenting it?
14. How might the various stages in the research process loop back to each other?
15. Name the types of error found in the research process and where they might occur within the process.
16. What are some of the trends in marketing research?
17. Detail the forces that are significantly affecting the Irish marketing research industry.

PROBLEMS AND ASSIGNMENTS

1. In Ireland, cars are polished more frequently when the owners do not have garages. Is the lack of a garage a good variable for predicting sales of car polish? Are there other hypotheses that might explain this finding?
2. You have been retained by a manufacturer of major appliances to investigate the probable colour preferences for ovens and refrigerators in 2007. What is the purpose of the research? Are there different purposes that might require different research approaches?
3. Give some hypothetical examples of situations when you would undertake (a) exploratory research; (b) descriptive research; and (c) causal research.
4. What are some management and accompanying research questions that might be useful to the following executives:
   (a) The president of a college sports club.
   (b) The production manager of a jeans factory.
   (c) The vice president of a software manufacturing firm.
5. Which research design seems appropriate for the following studies?
   (a) The manufacturer and marketer of flight simulators and other pilot training equipment wishes to forecast sales volume for the next five years.
   (b) A major food company researcher wishes to know what types of food are purchased in petrol court outlets to learn if the company can capitalise on this phenomenon.
   (c) A petroleum company is concerned with the increased costs of marketing regular leaded petrol and is considering dropping this product.
6. Examine a recent marketing research report in a local library (such as those reported in the business news). Identify the stages undertaken. Identify the sources of error that affected the study.

7. Read the business section of any national daily or Sunday paper for the past month to identify Irish companies that undertook or commissioned marketing research.
8. Select a well-known Irish consumer branded product. Conduct a database search in a local library to determine what has been published about the brand in Ireland.

Case Study
The 'Dubes' Phenomenon*

Michael Walsh, Marketing Director of Dubarry, smiled as he scrolled down the screen on his computer. He had googled the word 'Dubes' and was reading the comments from the wearers of his shoes from the Spin 1038 website.

'OMG dubes r like totally the best EVA like wot the hell r ya talking about? U goys r like total skobes if u don't wear dubes,' was a typical comment written in contemporary texting English. He thought back over the last seven years since he first noticed that one of his leading pairs of sailing shoes was being worn by a growing number of rugby-playing schoolboys in Dublin and being written about as a fashion item. Three to four years later, teenage girls adopted 'Dubes', wearing them with school uniforms and as casual wear. This phenomenon had spread across Ireland to all the major cities and towns. The dilemma he faced now was to estimate how large an order to place with his production plant for the autumn–winter 2006 season. The market for Dubes had grown by a factor of ten in the last few years and this had happened spontaneously without any significant promotion by Dubarry.

Dubes had appeared on google, linked to Dubarry, without any effort on the company's part.

Growth of Dubarry

Dubarry was founded in 1937 and quickly established a reputation as a high-quality footwear manufacturer, particularly of moccasin-constructed shoes. This expertise enabled the company to enter the international market in the 1970s as a sub-contract manufacturer. Since its establishment, the company has developed a heritage and expertise which combines the generations of skilled craftsmanship with the best of modern technology, resulting in constant innovation in products and the development of new markets.

In Ireland, Dubarry now sells a wide range of shoes for children, the youth market and the men's and ladies' market, meeting the footwear needs of most occasions.

Internationally, Dubarry has established a reputation as the world's leading producer of technical sailing shoes. The company's shoes now sell in most major international markets including Europe, the US, Japan and Australia. Dubarry has been the recipient of international awards for its sailing boots and shoes. The distinctive Dubarry non-slip, non-marking™ outsole design is one particular feature.

However the company's position internationally in the sailing-shoe market is based on many factors, including the quality of leathers used, the Gore-Tex® lining used in selected styles and the styling, which is reviewed annually. Key features of the company's performance leathers include water-resistance and dry-fast-dry-soft characteristics, which means that repeated wetting and drying out does not result in hardening or cracking of the leathers.

Dubarry was the first footwear manufacturer in Ireland or Britain to achieve the ISO 9001 International Standard for quality.

An indication of the worldwide reputation of Dubarry products is the fact that the company's flagship sailing-boot collection has become the footwear of choice for leading yachtsmen and crews competing in the America's Cup, Volvo Ocean Race, Vendee Globe, Admiral's Cup, Cowes Week and Cork Week.

Recently, Dubarry introduced its outdoor footwear collection due to the demand from many watersports enthusiasts to have a more rugged yet stylish product for their other outdoor pursuits.

This collection features a unique range of country/lifestyle boots suitable for a variety of uses, including equestrian, hunting, shooting, fishing, gardening and functional après-ski wear.

The 'Dubes' Line

The 'Dubes' line of sailing shoes, also commonly referred to as deck shoes, which had recently become a popular fashion item worn by teenagers, was known internally in the company by the sub-brand name Admirals. By 2005 Dubes had developed somewhat of a cult status. Not only had the young south Dublin (D4) market adopted these deck shoes, but in fact the name 'Dubes' had been established as the popular name for them. This had been further driven by a *Sunday Tribune* columnist, writing under the name of Ross O'Carroll-Kelly, who frequently referred to 'Dubes' in a way which made it clear that they are part of the uniform of today's 'with-it' teenagers. O'Carroll-Kelly has also written about 'Dubes' worn by characters in his recent novel, *The Curious Incident Of The Dog In The Nightdress*.

In an article in another Sunday newspaper, the *Sunday Independent*, headed 'Invasion of the Yummy Drummy Teen Clones', a glossary of current teen terms was given for the benefit of those not familiar with today's language. The glossary included terms such as pash (passion), ledge (as in legend), rentals (as in parentals, i.e. parents) and Dubes (Dubarry sailor-type deck shoes).

The term 'yummy drummies' in the article's title refers to the teens who shop at the Dundrum Shopping Centre in Dublin who are characterised in the article as girls from fee-paying schools with rich parents for whom conspicuous consumption is a way of life. One thirteen-year-old described Dundrum as 'the Holy Grail and sanctuary to so many Dublin teenagers'. She described the girls who go there as the 'infamous D4 girls who are always dressed to the nines with "Dubes", and always some nice designer top or polo, sporting the Ralph Lauren or Abercrombie logos'.

A recent advertisement for Jameson whiskey in *The Irish Times*, to coincide with a major rugby match between Leinster and Munster, gave a guide to Leinster supporters in the following terms: 'If you think it strange that someone would wear sunglasses as it buckets down with rain, then contemplate this: 20,000 pairs of deck shoes – and not a yacht in sight.' While the advert was a send-up of one group of supporters, it confirmed for Dubarry what their sales figures were telling them, that 'Dubes' were now an 'in' product, bought by teenagers and young adults, both male and female, in growing numbers.

The development of this market phenomenon had come about with very minimal promotion by Dubarry targeted at this segment. It was now generating its own publicity and Dubarry were increasing production of the line to keep up with demand.

Dubarry had very consciously decided not to put any significant promotion behind the Dubes brand and to avoid mass-market support in order to protect its exclusivity. The main support for the brand was a credit-card sized handout, distributed outside secondary schools in the larger Irish cities. This item focused on two pieces of communication: (1) how to tie the laces in a knot (headed 'Knot Ur Dubes') and (2) warning customers to beware of copies, of which there were some in the marketplace. Competing deck shoes sold for €40–€60, compared to Dubes' €100 retail price. In the summer of 2006, Dubarry introduced a limited edition of pink Dubes, retailing for €125 and supported by a small amount of PR. These sold out immediately. The market generated its own excitement via the Internet site Bebo for the limited edition and they were also referred to in Ross O'Carroll-Kelly's column.

Michael Walsh also held a promotion in the student bar at NUI Galway in February 2006 during rag week. This involved a competition to see who could make the perfect Dubarry knot. Prizes of Dubes were given to the winners.

Questions

1. Dubarry would now like to design a research project to determine the motivations behind the 'Dubes' phenomenon.
2. The company would also like to assess the potential market size for 'Dubes'. Michael Walsh had assembled data from the 2001 census to guide him on this. See *www.gillmacmillan.ie* for more information.

3. In terms of its general marketing strategy, Dubarry are wondering how to ensure that they respond adequately to this market potential.

*This case was written by Professor Jim Ward, NUI Galway. It is intended to be used as a basis for class discussion rather than to illustrate the effective or ineffective handling of an administrative situation. The case is based upon a real situation, though certain information has been disguised. © Jim Ward, 2006.

Case Study
Shellfish de la Mer – leading exporters of Irish crabmeat*

Background

Fishermen Richard Murphy and Peter O'Sullivan founded Shellfish de la Mer in 1987. According to an interview with Gearoid O'Rourke, Marketing Executive of Shellfish de la Mer, the company initially offered a white-fish product, so any crabs caught in their nets were thrown back to sea. When a restaurant owner who bought their white fish asked for crabmeat, they recognised a gap in the market. So, with family members, they set up their processing facility in Castletownbere, Co. Cork. The company brochure of 2006 states that Shellfish de la Mer employs over 100 staff in peak season in their 20,000 square foot site, producing 20,000 kg of seafood daily. With a new focus on the export market, and an emphasis on marketing and investment, the company achieved the award 'Irish Seafood Exporter of the Year' in 2004.

The Crab Product

Shellfish de la Mer was processing the claws of the crab and selling the rest as bait until 2003. When the facility was expanded, residual parts of the crab were processed. Today, even the crab shell forms a decorative part of the product range sold in Irish and European markets.

The company uses its own fishing fleet, so the quality and traceability of its product is guaranteed. Crabs are brought from boats, and passed through goods inwards to the process line. Here, the claw is removed from the body. The product is then pasteurised. Both claw and body are cooked separately in a conveyor cooker at 99 to 100 degrees. They are then cooled for the same length of time at a temperature of 5 to 7 degrees. The meat is separated into leg meat, red meat and white meat, while the claw is split into knuckles, thighs and toes. Products are all sold separately, but can also be combined to form mixed meat. Crab parts are processed manually, which retains flavour and quality better than the alternative machine method.

The Irish Market

Shellfish de la Mer supplies its product to direct, wholesale and retail markets in Ireland. The Irish customer demands timely delivery of fresh quality product. The company prides itself on its ability to provide products tailored to customer needs. Offering 100% traceability on all products and retaining ownership of its fishing fleet, production and Irish transportation provides reassurance of excellence in products and service.

Shellfish de la Mer supplies the hotel and restaurant sector directly with its crab meat and other seafood. The product supplied is fresh and bears the Shellfish de la Mer name. Due to transport costs, these sales have focused on the Munster region. This region has over 100 companies supplying fish products, but Richard and Peter believe that owning their fishing fleet is the advantage that places them among the top five fresh-fish providers in Munster. The wholesale market is also served with fresh product. The company must continually ensure that wholesalers selling to hotels and restaurants do not impact on their direct sales.

With increasing consumer demand for fish products, the company launched the 'Skipper's Choice' brand through the retail sector. Today, over fifteen products are branded 'Skipper's Choice' and include white fish and shellfish, as well as crabmeat. The market for 'Skipper's Choice' is defined as double-income couples aged between thirty and forty-five, and elderly customers. Products sold under this range are frozen, and include a 'Seafood Chowder Mix', 'Mouthwatering Crab Claws' and 'Pasteurised Crab Meat'. Seasonality is a factor; other products such as 'Local Peel Prawn' and 'Jumbo Prawn' have stronger sales at Christmas than at other periods. With competition from leading retail brands, Shellfish de la Mer must increase their market share in this sector, and this is a business priority.

The Overseas Market

Crabmeat constitutes over 70% of Shellfish de la Mer exports. In Europe, the company supplies products to the wholesale and grocery sectors, with transport outsourced from Irish transportation companies. The company's main European markets are France and Spain, and a dedicated sales representative is based in the Spanish market.

Wholesalers in France and Spain demand a fresh product. When a product leaves Castletownbere on Friday evening, it is available to these wholesalers on Monday morning. Initially, products were unbranded, but the company noticed that branding was becoming important to this market. All new packaging includes a small 'Shellfish de la Mer' label. Wholesale products include a half-kilo tub which is then sold to hotels and restaurants. These customers demand superior quality from wholesalers, so Shellfish de la Mer's product is attractive due to its traceability, quality and freshness.

The company's wholesale markets extend to Poland, where they supply a frozen product. The journey time from Castletownbere to Polish wholesalers is up to fifteen days, which has an impact on the product's thirty-day shelf life. The company is reliant on the quality of Irish transportation companies' onboard transport freezers. The challenge is to sustain their commitment to servicing markets in a cost-efficient way, without compromising their premium-quality product.

Within existing markets, Shellfish de la Mer noticed that wholesalers were supplying the retail sector as well as hotel and restaurant customers. So they decided to sell directly to the retail channel also and 'cut out the middleman'. They now supply larger supermarkets, such as Metro in France and Tesco in Poland. The retail sector also presents opportunities for new market entry. The company is evaluating other European countries, with a view to entering their markets through larger retailers. They recognise that success at retail level requires a greater understanding of the end consumer. Recently, the company researched consumer behaviour in Holland. Dutch consumers' high income, health-conscious attitude and search for convenience suggest they are ideal customers for a fish product. A marketing plan by Gearoid O'Rourke in 2006 showed that, in addition, these consumers tend to shop for food daily and travel by bicycle, so the freshness and neat packaging of the Shellfish de la Mer product suits their lifestyle.

As part of their desire to expand their business, the company recently accessed the Asian market. In May of 2006, in conjunction with three other seafood exporters, they successfully commenced exporting to Japan under an umbrella brand name 'Delicious Irish Shellfish'.

Conclusion

Through investment and a strong commitment to product and service quality, Shellfish de la Mer have expanded their market share domestically and overseas. They are growing their business through all channels of distribution. They continue to offer the 'Skipper's Choice' brand in the retail sector, and are placing more emphasis on including the 'Shellfish de la Mer' brand on products sold to wholesalers and direct customers. They also export under the 'Delicious Irish Shellfish' brand. An immediate challenge for the company is to develop a research strategy for their markets.

Questions

1. Develop a marketing research plan for Shellfish de la Mer, which will give them more information about their current domestic and export customers.
2. The company has two brands in Ireland: 'Shellfish de la Mer', and 'Skipper's Choice'. How would you measure channel and consumer attitudes towards these brands?

3. Shellfish de la Mer offers a tailored product to fit market needs and consumer behaviour. What research techniques would you advise the company to use to gain more insight into consumer behaviour in the Dutch market?

4. What secondary sources of data might the company use to assess the market attractiveness of other European countries?

*This case was written by Elaine Wallace, National University Ireland, Galway. It is intended to be used a basis for class discussion, rather than illustrating either effective or ineffective management practices. The case is based on a real situation. The author wishes to thank Richard Murphy, Peter O'Sullivan, Con Murphy and Gearoid O'Rourke for their kind permission to use the material in this case.

CHAPTER 3

PROBLEM DEFINITION AND RESEARCH DESIGN

CHAPTER OVERVIEW

▸ Introduction ▸ What is Problem Definition? ▸ Talks and Activities to Define the Problem ▸ Problem Definition Errors ▸ Problem Definition and the Marketing Information System ▸ Research Design Defined ▸ What Types of Research Designs Exist? ▸ How to Choose the Best Research Design ▸ Summary

INTRODUCTION

The basic nature of research, decision-making, information needs and the steps in marketing research have been discussed in the preceding chapters. We've also explained the concept of marketing research and where it fits into the overall information needs of an organisation. This discussion so far has been broad and general in tone, to introduce the reader to the area.

In this chapter, we detail the first two major steps of marketing research — *problem definition* and *research design*. The focus is now on the specific tasks and activities that cluster around defining the aims of the study. Regardless of the market, customers or difficulties facing the marketing manager, the investigator begins a research project by defining the problem. Correctly defined problems allow the investigator to anticipate activities, information requirements, data sources and likely errors. As management action is dependent upon research results, time taken at the problem definition step is time well spent. As the old adage goes: 'a problem well defined is a problem half solved'. By the end of this section, you will be able to:

1. explain what problem definition is;
2. undertake all the tasks and activities needed to complete problem definition;
3. choose a research design;
4. draw up a list of research objectives;
5. translate management decision needs into information requirements; and
6. develop hypotheses.

WHAT IS PROBLEM DEFINITION?

Problem definition is the first, initial step in any research project. The researcher questions what the problem is, what decision is necessary and what information is needed for management to make a decision. It is about examining the true problem, related decision and needed information.

Figure 3.1 Relationship between problem, information and decision

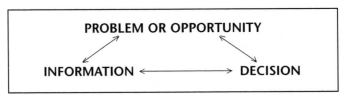

At this stage of the study, the investigator is querying what the purpose of the study is. Generally, a problem confronts the manager and he/she wants information to assist in making a more informed decision. Occasionally, there can be an opportunity presenting itself to the management team and the firm want information to capitalise upon the opportunity. In this sense, the title 'problem definition' is a misnomer, as it incorporates marketing opportunities facing a company. Correct, complete and thorough problem definition focuses the study and lends direction to the investigation and subsequent research steps. Problem definition translates the management decision and problem into research information needs.

So when a problem or opportunity occurs, information is needed to clarify the issue, and then information is sought on which to base a decision. Problem definition can be thought of as a needs assessment — what relevant information is missing at present? The ethos of problem definition is to be creative, investigative, probing and clear minded as to the information needs for decision-making.[1] More formally, problem definition is identification, clarification, formulation and definition of the specific marketing difficulty that necessitates decision-related information.

TASKS AND ACTIVITIES TO DEFINE THE PROBLEM

To uncover the true issues and the decision confronting managers, an intricate web of tasks and activities faces the researcher. Since most marketing decisions are complex, and numerous factors affect the outcome, careful investigation of the cause and symptoms is needed. Another old adage 'what comes out very much depends on what goes in' is relevant here — the greater the effort, the better the problem definition step and the better the whole project.

It is helpful to think of problem definition as having four sub-sections for the researcher to work through, to ensure adequate and correct problem definition.

These are identification, clarification, formulation and definition of the presented problem or opportunity facing the firm.

Figure 3.2 Problem definition

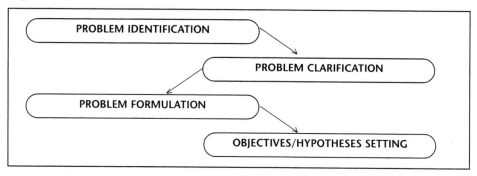

Each of these consists of distinct yet intertwined activities and duties for the researcher to complete, before moving on to any other research phase.

Box 3.1 Step one, problem definition, researcher activities and tasks

Problem identification
Dialogue with managers
Dialogue with relevant staff
Identify problem, decision, information needs
Identify *content* of decisions

Problem clarification
Immerse yourself in the background
Conduct a literature search, internal and external
Conduct a situational audit/ environmental audit
Determine what research exists within company
Talk with knowledgeable people
Clarify the *context* of the problem

Problem formulation
Isolate cause from symptoms
Differentiate between management decision and research decision
Undertake a problem audit
Determine the unit of analysis and relevant factors
Select appropriate analytical/theoretical model

Objectives/hypotheses setting
List outcomes of investigation
List research objectives
Phrase research questions to be answered
Write down the research hypothesis

Dialogue between management and the researcher marks the starting point for problem/opportunity identification. Management generally talk through their perception of the problem and the decisions they need to make with the researcher. The researcher has to understand how any gathered information will be used in the decision-making process to truly appreciate the kernel of the problem.

Generally speaking, managers have a feel for the problem/opportunity, but may not be able to communicate their exact information needs to the researcher. Managers have to be active participants at this point in the research process. Clearly, the greater the co-operation, discussion and commitment between management and researcher at this preparatory phase, the better the quality of the information supplied and decision made.

Some managers will want assistance with very specific problems. They will want very specific answers to specific questions. Typical examples include:

1. Of the three proposed package designs, which will result in the highest usage?
2. Should we offer a 20c discount or a token free gift to stimulate sales?
3. Which product features, freshness, convenience or nutrition will increase the probability of sales by 5%?

However, some studies will require more information before the problem can be identified. In such cases, specific questions have not been asked. Consider the situation where sales of a product are static — a lack of advertising, changing consumer tastes or competitive actions could all explain static sales.

So, problem identification leads to a management decision problem and a research problem. Such a distinction is necessary, as simply responding to information requests will not result in the needed answers. This aspect of problem definition identifies the content of the decision.

Box 3.2 Management decisions versus research problems

Management decision	*Research problem*
Develop a new advertisement	Evaluate effectiveness of alternative advertisements
Increase store traffic	Measure current customer satisfaction of store
Introduce new product	Forecast potential sales levels
Increase sales	Assess penetration level of existing outlets
Launch new product	Identify emerging consumer trends and changing tastes
Decrease costs	Determine non-price basis for competition

While managers may have a perspective on the problem, their insights may actually be limited. The *iceberg principle* operates here. The visible aspect of the presented problem is really only a small dimension of the real or true difficulty. Coupled with this, the scientific nature of the research process requires the researcher to be objective and exhaustive. So, the researcher moves into a clarification phase. To this end, the researcher must establish the *background* to the problem/opportunity. Much background information can be gleaned from reports, letters and documents, trade material and strategic plans. This is labelled as a *literature search*. It is first conducted in-house and then externally, making use of library facilities and the Internet. Once completed, the researcher turns her/his attention to experts to complete the problem clarification phase. Referred to as an *expert survey*, it usually requires the researcher to have discussions and meetings with knowledgeable persons related to the topic/problem. These can be personnel within the firm, such as production managers, accountants, delivery men and telephone receptionists and these can also be experts outside the company, e.g. trade associations, state bodies, government officials — to name but a few. The researcher, to provide a better appreciation of the problem/opportunity, combines the literature and expert survey. This phase of problem definition can be referred to as a *situational analysis*. It covers buyer behaviour and market characteristics that affect demand, coupled with competition and the micro and macro environment — the uncontrollable variables facing managers.

Box 3.3 Problem formulation in the Irish bottled gas market[2]

A company was considering entering the Irish bottled gas market. To decide if entry was feasible and, if so, to design a strategy to do this, the company managers wanted to know about the various market characteristics. In discussions with the researchers, this market entry problem turned into a need for information about end consumers, their current usage patterns, degree of brand loyalty and their perceptions of competitors. To this end, the researcher planned to gather information about:

- gas usage and consumption;
- brands used;
- bottle gas regulators;
- gas bottle physical characteristics;
- contents of gas bottles;
- stocking/storage of gas bottles;
- purchasing procedure;
- awareness of and attitude towards price;
- awareness of and interest in the origin of gas;
- purchasing criteria;
- safety concerns;
- reaction to the idea of a coalman-type delivery service.

At this point, the researcher will have developed a good understanding of the problem facing management, the related decision managers want to make and the necessary information to be supplied for a solution. This leads the researcher into the problem formulation element of problem definition. This is where the investigator is able to differentiate between the symptoms and the true cause of the problem. The researcher stands back from the problem and takes a broad perspective by setting the problem in an appropriate *analytical/theoretical* model to reflect and present all the variables of interest. The relevant model is drawn from the existing body of knowledge. Let's say you are the manager of a new 'paint-your-own-pottery' shop. The first of its kind in Ireland and Europe, the concept of painting your own pottery has taken America by storm. You are now faced with the challenge of promoting the shop. The 'Hierarchy of Effects' model states that you must first create awareness, then interest, followed by desire before a consumer will come to your shop to paint a piece of pottery. So, any research must measure and assess the current level of awareness, then interest, desire and action, in that order, so as to guide an effective promotional strategy.[3]

In this manner, the theory acts as a *problem audit*, as the model must capture all necessary variables impinging on the problem/opportunity and how they are related. The researcher must ensure that all important and necessary issues have been included. Failure to incorporate all issues results in inaccurate data and error. The problem audit requires the researcher to choose a *unit of analysis* — an entity to focus upon, at the micro level, from which to collect the necessary data. The unit of analysis in marketing is commonly the end consumer. For some products, e.g. children's toothpaste and cereals, the unit of analysis may be both the purchaser and the consumer, normally the mother and the child respectively. Other common units of analysis used much in marketing are retail buyers, retail stores, wholesalers, importers, agents, managers, advertisers, shop assistants, etc. (all people who may have valuable information about the consumer). A common mistake in considering the unit of analysis is to overlook the product, shelf spacing, price or an advertisement etc. as entities that may contain the much-needed information. Thus, the researcher has now determined the context of the problem, as well as the content.

Now the researcher is ready to define the problem. Problem definition results in a list of research objectives, and/or a research hypothesis. Research objectives are a statement of specific and limited information needs. There is one overall broad statement — referred to as the *primary objective*. This is divided into sub-components, namely *secondary objectives*. The relationship between the primary and secondary objectives operates upon the umbrella principle. The secondary objectives come together as a whole. The research objectives are specific, action-orientated statements of intent. The researcher, having prepared a list of needed information, evaluates the usefulness of the objectives by anticipating possible findings. This exercise in caution enables the researcher to weed out unrealistic aims and unnecessary goals (these can generate interesting information but are irrelevant to the problem on hand and a drain on limited resources).

Table 3.1 Marketing Problem Translated Into Research Objectives
Primary objective: to determine consumers' perceived need for an Internet banking service.

Marketing Problem	Research Question	Research Objectives
Should a national bank offer banking facilities via the Internet?	Are consumers aware of Internet banking? What are consumers' reactions to Internet banking?	To measure consumer attitudes and benefits about Internet banking facilities in Ireland.
How should the service be offered?	How do consumers react to service A? B? C? What are the perceived benefits of each service?	To obtain ratings and rankings from each form of service. To identify perceived benefits of and perceived objections to the system.
What market segment(s) should be the target market(s)?	Will consumers use the service? How often? Do the answers to the above questions differ depending on the demographic group? How can we profile consumers?	To measure purchase intentions; to estimate likelihood of usage. To compare using cross-tabulations – levels of awareness, evaluations, purchase intentions, etc. of men versus women, high-income versus low-income groups, young consumers versus old consumers.
What pricing strategy offers the best value proposition and return on investment?	Do potential customers think this product should be priced higher or lower than competitive offerings? Is the product perceived as good value?	To ascertain consumers' knowledge and expectation about prices. To learn how the price of this service is perceived relative to competitors' pricing. To determine the perceived value of the service.

Source: Adapted from *Exploring Market Research*, William G. Zikmund, 8th edition, 2003.

A research hypothesis is a tentative answer to the problem, or more specifically a research question. It requires empirical research to support or refute the proposition. It is an assertion as to the likely outcome. For example, a manager might question the most advantageous course of action — to run an advertisement during *Home and Away* or *Eastenders*? Given this, one research question might be 'Which programme has the highest viewership among 15- to 18-year-old teenagers?', while one hypothesis could read 'More 15- to 18-year-old teenagers watch *Eastenders* than *Home and Away*.'

To develop a hypothesis the researcher must identify the independent and dependent variables, coupled with the relationship between the two. Consider a manager who is reducing the price of his product. He will postulate the effect on sales, whether there will be a 2%, 3% or 5% increase in sales, or none as may be the case. Such an assumption or expectation is a hypothesis — a tentative statement about the expected outcome. In this case, the price decrease is the independent variable affecting the level of sales, which is the dependent variable. The independent variable comes before the dependent in time and alters the dependent variable in some manner.

Hypotheses are based upon and generated by management experience, literature reviews or insights. It is critical that these (like objectives) are in written form and agreed by all before proceeding with the remainder of the research process.

The final list of research objectives and/or hypotheses is presented to management to ensure that their interpretation of the problem is in keeping with the researcher's understanding of the information requirements. In this way, the project results will not surprise or disappoint the manager.

PROBLEM DEFINITION ERRORS

On the surface, problem definition appears easy — deceptively so as many firms often find out to their peril. The process of problem definition is slow and fraught with difficulties. The research process is only as good as the problem definition stage. Error can occur at any point — one major source of research error seriously affecting the scientific credibility of the project is poorly defined problems.

One of the biggest causes of incorrect or inappropriate problem definition occurs because of improper communication between the manager and researcher. Management tends to have a feeling for what's wrong, but cannot pinpoint exactly what the root cause of the problem is — akin to not being able to see the wood for the trees. Lack of communication results in vague goals at the outset of the study, giving rise to vague or ambiguous results at the end. Managers tend to think in terms of decisions and not the information needed to make an informed decision. Managers can and do have serious difficulties articulating the detailed data they need. The translation of the problem and decision into information requirements by the researcher is highly dependent upon good communication between all concerned. Close co-ordination and genuine dialogue between the researcher and managers can minimise such communication pitfalls. Conflict between management and researcher can be minimised. Managers can be too involved and have to guard against the professional knowing best. Managers as active participants are the best defence against improper definition of the problem. The researcher's perspective dictates that problem definition be approached as research-based decision-making.

Researchers should not assume that the presented difficulty is the true or real one. Problems are never taken at face value, often what the researcher sees first are the symptoms and not the cause of the difficulties. For example, the general trend evident across Europe is for problem definition to be more complex than ever before. As companies move into relationship marketing, networking, interactive marketing, and globalisation, distinguishing the marketing symptoms from the cause is increasingly difficult for managers and researcher alike. The boundaries between the firm and its environs are hazy and unclear. Given this, problem definition can seem limitless. So, it is critical for the investigator to continually probe to uncover the real problem.

Research produces data and information, not decisions. Management sometimes has greater expectations than research can deliver. Presenting the list of research objectives to managers can be a worthwhile exercise as it lays a common foundation as to expectations and potential findings. It ensures that the research process stays focused upon a solution and the necessary information needed to make a decision.

All of these issues — lack of communication, lack of co-operation, incorrect communication, ignorance of the role of research, and inappropriate time given to problem definition — can result in informational error. Worse still, problem definition error (or informational error) is carried throughout the entire project, tainting all subsequent steps. For this reason, we refer to it as systematic error. A mistake now by the researcher, for whatever reason, systematically affects all other phases and seriously threatens the validity of the research findings.

PROBLEM DEFINITION AND THE MARKETING INFORMATION SYSTEM

Before leaving the discussion of problem definition, it is worthwhile to note the role of the marketing information system in problem definition. Many of the tasks and activities in problem definition dictate that the investigator draw heavily upon the marketing information system within the company in question.

A marketing information system is a framework or structure for marketing information management. It is a system of processes, procedures and people to support marketing management. It generally incorporates the use of computers and software. It is about the collection, organisation, storage, communication and dissemination of information relevant to marketing managers.

Figure 3.3 Marketing information system and its components

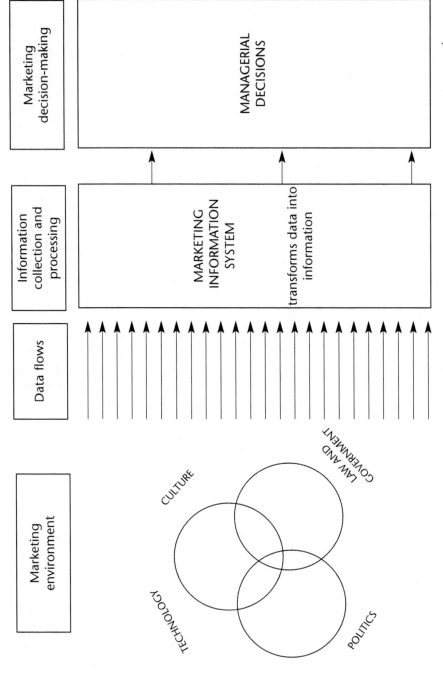

Source: J. Murray & A. O'Driscoll, *Managing Marketing, Concepts and Irish Cases*, Gill & Macmillan, 1993, p.134.[4]

An MkIS is an organised flow of information about customers, competitors and the company's performance in support of marketing decision-making. An MkIS is not about information automation, as the computer acronym says: GIGO — garbage in, garbage out. Rather, an MkIS is about information enhancement and management improvement.[5] It is designed to collect, gather, analyse, disseminate, store, retrieve and communicate both internal and external secondary marketing research and marketing intelligence data to marketing managers in order to improve decision-making. Thus, a marketing information system is charged with the responsibility of aiding and assisting marketing decision-making; filtering timely, accurate and relevant information and translating data into meaningful decision-related information. It enables the company to gather facts about the micro and macro environment within which the firm competes. In this manner, the marketing information system can be of immense value to an investigator grappling with problem definition.

The limitations of an MkIS are hard to imagine, apart from the time and cost necessary to manage it efficiently. However, the main drawback is the lack of information orientation in a firm, as this results in the trappings of an MkIS with no substance. MkISs have to assist management with decisions to be of use.

It can be very simple, such as an index card of customers, or very elaborate such as a network of computer databases. Larger Irish firms, such as Smurfit's, Kerry, Avonmore, Waterford, Superquinn, Bank of Ireland and AIB, to name but a few, have a complex and elaborate web of computers that constitute their MkIS. However, an MkIS can also be informal with basic or even no technology, as tends to be the case with many smaller Irish firms. When Aer Arran[6] began building an MkIS, customer names, addresses, phone numbers, usage patterns and complaints were initially held on an alphabetically sorted index card system. For smaller firms that are owner managed, once the basic elements or rudiments are present, the information link between the firm, the customer and environment can exist. So, while the degree of structure and formality of an MkIS can and does vary among Irish firms, the existence of an information flow and process is the kernel of the MkIS and the marketing attitude.[7, 8, 9]

RESEARCH DESIGN DEFINED

Closely allied to problem definition is the second step of the marketing research process — research design. Formulating the study goals is highly interrelated to the general information design of the study. Different problems lead to different research designs. Many research models subsume this step into problem definition and present them as one, as both are dependent on the amount of existing information about the problem. For the sake of simplicity, we consider the process of choosing a research design as a step in its own right. First, we discuss what a research design is.

A research design is a blueprint or overall action plan for the remaining marketing research study. It is a grand or master framework to guide the remaining steps of the research process — data collection, measurement, analysis and reporting. The research design is based on the nature of the information required by management. It dictates the scope and boundaries of the study.

The research design can only be chosen after the objectives have been finalised. It co-ordinates the methodology issues with the stated objectives and so acts as a guiding light for the researcher in deciding the when, where, how and why of information collection. It gives structure, order and logic to the remaining marketing research steps, in light of the study objectives. A research design is the bridge between the research objectives and the methodology used to fulfil these objectives.

While it is true that marketing problems are limitless and no two problems are the same, similarities do exist as to the type of information needed. The information type allows for the classification of a research project.

WHAT TYPES OF RESEARCH DESIGNS EXIST?

As noted in the previous chapter, a research design can be classified as exploratory, descriptive or causal in nature.

Figure 3.4 Research design continuum

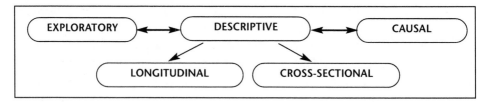

Exploratory research is about establishing trends, patterns and ranges of behaviour that are unknown. Exploratory research uncovers unknown and previously undocumented marketing variables. It aims to identify and establish the very existence of variables. For this reason, hypothesis generation is a feature of such research. An exploratory study is, by definition, a study exploring an area to understand it better. Flexibility, ingenuity and imagination are the traits of such research. This work is relatively non-mathematical and non-statistical in form. For this reason, exploratory research can be likened to Christopher Columbus charting new lands, or *Star Trek*, 'going where no man has gone before'. The researcher has the freedom to explore different avenues of interest and change the direction of enquiry. Such work often generates qualitative data which is inductive in character. This denotes the types of data collection methods likely to be used, e.g. literature review, expert survey, focus groups, in-depth interviews or projective techniques.

Exploratory research is especially useful in new product development, creative aspects of advertising, media selection and promotion in general: unearthing new segments, shifts in cultural values and changing attitudes.[10] This trend will continue as more human-orientated exploratory designs, for example ethnography, are being enabled in marketing research as a result of new technological tools.[11]

Box 3.4 Homeopathic remedies for pets and exploratory research

As a homeopathic manufacturer of medicines, the firm has recently had a number of enquiries about remedies for pets. Management decide to explore the idea of homeopathic remedies for pets as a possible new and emerging market.

To gain some insights and a basic understanding about an area that management know little about, they engage in exploratory research. This involves talking with leading vets in the area about their perceptions, experience and knowledge of homeopathic remedies for pets. Animal clubs and associations are contacted to learn of their experiences and needs. Finally, a number of groups of consumers are brought into the firm to hear first-hand from them about their use of alternative medicines for their pets.

In contrast, descriptive research quantifies known consumers, markets and known marketing issues. It measures the number and amount of a variable present. Quantitative research details the percentage or proportion of a characteristic present. It is heavily reliant on mathematics, statistics and probability theory. Quantitative research assumes prior knowledge exists, and background information is readily available. To this end, hypothesis testing is indicative of quantitative research.

Quantitative research is used to describe existing market segments, competitors and current marketing offerings. It lends itself well to evaluating and assessing various aspects of product, price, promotion and place.

Thus, descriptive data, as the name suggests, describes various facets of the problem on hand in mathematical terms. It requires a clear statement about the who, what, where, when, and how of the relevant issues. It is traditionally the most common form of research in marketing. Descriptive data can be further divided into either *longitudinal* or *cross-sectional* data. Longitudinal descriptive data is equivalent to a movie picture — describing the elements, variables and their relationship over a length of time. It incorporates repeated measurement of the relevant characteristics. Panels and EPoS (Electronic Point of Sales) are the data collection tools used. A cross-sectional study is like a snapshot — a description of variables and their association at one point in time. This is a once-off measurement — observation and surveys are utilised here.

Box 3.5 Entry into the pre-packed stuffing market and descriptive research

The family has been in the bakery business for three generations. As one of the largest suppliers to supermarkets all over the country, you are deciding whether to enter the pre-packed stuffing market. You require much information about all facets of the marketing mix. For example, some of the information will be concerned with:

(a) The actual market size — how many packs of pre-packed stuffing are sold each year? How much is the market valued at? By how much is the market increasing or decreasing on an annual basis? What are the market segments?
(b) The competitors — how many firms are already supplying the market? What is their market size? What are their strengths and weaknesses?
(c) The customer — what benefits are customers looking for when they buy such a product? What are the three most important features? Who are the customers: age, income, social class, lifestyle, and family life cycle?

Causal data proves a cause and effect relationship between two or more variables. It is the most demanding and rigorous of all research — the investigator must know, firstly, the exact variables, and also the effect they have on each other. The researcher must also be able to control outside factors and their influence on the variables being manipulated. Causal data can be collected *in a field or laboratory setting*, by utilising an experimental design. It is frequently associated with test marketing or simulated test marketing. Thus, this type of a research design is very demanding and rigorous.

First impressions tend to suggest that exploratory, descriptive and causal research are at odds with each other. In practice, they are not separate but complementary to each other. The Chinese idea of the yin and yang symbol captures the twinning essence of all three research designs. Exploratory research is often conducted before descriptive or causal work is undertaken.[12]

HOW TO CHOOSE THE BEST RESEARCH DESIGN

It is the researcher's responsibility to choose an appropriate research design for the study. Regrettably, there is no formula to help choose the best design. Equally, no one design is better than the other — it's really a question of which is best suited to the particular problem in hand. In practice, the information-based decision guides the choice of research design. That is, the aims of the study, to explore or describe or establish a cause and effect relationship, dictate the research design. Costs and timing are also borne in mind, as they influence the choice of design. So the choice of design is a matter of distinction and not absolute, as shown in Table 3.2.

Table 3.2 Choosing a research design

	Exploratory research	Descriptive research	Causal research
Data type	Qualitative	Qualitative or quantitative	Quantitative
Aims	To explore, chart, identify, define	To describe, quantify	To establish cause and effect
Nature of variables	Unknown Undocumented	Known associations and documented	Known exactly, Clearly supported
Degree of formality	Relatively little	Some to extensive	High mathematical content
Data	Literature review Expert survey Focus groups In-depth interviews Projective techniques	Literature review Surveys Observation Panels	Literature review Expert survey Experiments (Surveys) (Observation)
Sample size	Small	Small to large	Large
Question types	Probing Response driven	Some probing Interviewer driven	No probing
Hypothesis	Generates, Develops	Tests and/or Generates, Develops	Tests

Some concluding remarks about research designs include the following points:

Firstly, the selection of the wrong or inappropriate design is the biggest mistake made at this stage of the marketing research project. Such a research error arises due to poor problem definition. It results in systematic error throughout the remainder of the project. The validity content of the study is jeopardised if such an error occurs.

Secondly, information is growing exponentially, that is, all three types of research designs are utilised more than ever before by all industry sectors. Recent evidence[13, 14, 15] certainly suggests that this trend will continue in an effort to present a more holistic picture of consumers and markets.

Thirdly, new exploratory techniques such as games, time travel visualisations and role playing are all continuing to gain favour with Irish and European research firms alike — these are given detailed consideration in later chapters.

SUMMARY

In planning for a specific research project, the first step is problem definition. It is about defining the problem, the related problem and relevant information needed. It consists of problem identification, clarification, formulation and objective setting. It involves a multiplicity of interactive activities, for example, management discussions, literature review, situational audit, problem audit, and expert survey. It can draw heavily upon the marketing information system. The aim is to state the information needs of the decision as a list of objectives or hypotheses. It concludes with a list of research objectives and/or hypotheses.

Problem definition or informational error is the mistake most likely to occur. It is where the incorrect or improper definition has been made. To prevent such a threat to the validity of the study, it is vital that managers and researchers work closely to ensure correct definition of all issues.

The second step in marketing research is choosing a research design. A research design is a blueprint or framework for the methodological issues of the study. A research design can be either exploratory or descriptive or causal in character. The chosen research design is a function of the problem, the required information, the decision, the nature of the desired data and research concerns such as sample size, data collection methods and degree of formality.

KEY TERMS

Problem definition	Problem identification
Problem clarification	Problem formulation
Expert survey	Situational analysis
Marketing information system	Macro and micro environment
Secondary objectives	Primary objective
Hypothesis	Unit of analysis
Research design	Qualitative
Quantitative	Descriptive
Exploratory	Causal
Independent variable	Dependent variable
	Information error

QUESTIONS

1. What is problem definition and what are the four sub-sections of problem definition that the researcher should work through to ensure that the problem is accurately defined?
2. What is the starting point of problem definition?
3. Why is it important to define the marketing research problem appropriately?

4. What are the differences between research questions and hypotheses?
5. What is a situational analysis? What is involved in a literature search and an expert survey?
6. What is involved in formulating the problem?
7. What is the relationship between the primary objective and secondary objectives?
8. What is meant by the term 'research hypothesis'?
9. What trends are evident with relation to problem definition across Europe?
10. What is the biggest cause of incorrect problem definition?
11. Discuss the nature and role of research design in marketing research.
12. Define research design. What is its role within the overall research process?
13. Differentiate between the three basic types of research design. What are the characteristics of each and under what circumstances would each one be used?
14. If one is using both exploratory and descriptive research, which research design is normally undertaken first, and why?
15. How do the three categories of exploratory, descriptive and causal research design differ from each other?
16. What guides the choice of design that the researcher adopts?
17. What are the potential sources of error that can affect the beginning stages of any marketing research project?

PROBLEMS AND ASSIGNMENTS

1. How would you go about determining why market share for a particular brand has declined in the past year, i.e. what research design(s) would you use, and why?
2. In a research project for a chain of shoe stores, mothers of young children were asked the importance of various features of children's shoes and shoe outlets. Which type of error do you think would be most critical for the study?
3. Given the following decision problem, identify the research problems:
   (a) What pricing strategy to follow for a new product.
   (b) Whether to change the sales force compensation package.
   (c) Whether to increase in-store promotion of existing products.
4. Food Inc. is a chain of restaurants located in major cities in Ireland. Sales have been growing very slowly for the last two years. Management has decided to add some new items to the menu, but first they want to know more about their customers and their preferences.
   (a) List two hypotheses.
   (b) What kind of research design is appropriate, and why?
5. Propose one or more hypotheses for each of the following variable pairs, specify which is the independent variable and which the dependent variable.
   (a) The Consumer Price Index and the economic climate.
   (b) The level of worker output and the closeness of supervision of the worker.

    (c) The degree of personal friendship between customer and salespeople and the frequency of sales calls on the customer.

6. You have been hired by a group of hotel owners, restaurant owners and other business owners whose business benefits from tourism on one of the Aran Islands, just off the coast of Galway. They wish to learn how they can attract a larger number of college students to the islands during the Easter holidays. Define the marketing research problem.

7. You have been asked to determine how large corporations prepare for contract negotiations with labour unions. Since you know relatively little about this subject, how would you find out? Be as specific as possible.

8. A manufacturer of hand tools uses industrial agents to reach its major European markets. The company is considering a new automatic inventory control procedure. How would you proceed with an exploratory study in advance of a larger study of the dealers' reactions to this new procedure?

9. You have been hired by a local charity organisation to learn how they can increase the number of persons who volunteer to help with annual fund-raising activities. Define your research objectives.

10. You are the administrative assistant of a small hospital in a health board region. You and the hospital chief have just come from the general health board annual meeting of all hospital chiefs, where you were informed that your staff performance was unsatisfactory. You had sensed the tension among the staff but had not considered it unusual. The chief calls you into the office after the meeting and instructs you to investigate. Suggest at least three types of research that might be appropriate in this situation.

Case Study
Measuring Service Quality in Higher Education*

Jane O'Riordan has recently been appointed Senior Student Recruitment Officer at Ennis Institute of Technology (EIT). Jane was appointed to this position primarily due to the extensive experience she gained in student recruitment while working at Boston State College in the US. Her main responsibilities in her new role are to increase student enrolments and to improve student retention rates at EIT.

Established in 1965, EIT is currently the only third-level institution located in County Clare. With more than 4,600 students, the college offers a range of undergraduate and postgraduate programmes in the areas of Business & Management, Arts, Engineering & Computing, and Life & Health Sciences. EIT enjoys an excellent reputation in the Munster region amongst its various stakeholders due to the high calibre of both its teaching staff and graduates. The college is located on a modern campus on the edge of Ennis town with state-of-the-art facilities, including newly renovated computing and library services. EIT also provides health, welfare and counselling services, as well as sport and recreational facilities to support the teaching and learning environment.

Jane's first task in her new role is to develop a strategic plan outlining appropriate strategies to attract new students and to increase student retention over the next five years in EIT. In developing this plan, she examines demographical data from the Irish Department of Education and Science and the Central Statistics Office. The data pertaining to the third-level educational sector give Jane cause for concern as they indicate that the number of students entering third-level education will decline over the next five to ten years. This is due to the decline of the Irish birth rate, which is predicted to drop to 13 per thousand of the population by 2016 down from 23 per thousand in the 1970s. This will ultimately have an impact on the 16–19 age group which accounts for the vast majority of entry to tertiary education.[16] It is also predicted that the effects of the decline in student numbers will be more pronounced in some regional institutions than others due to regional dependence.[17]

In light of these demographic changes, Jane realises that immediate action needs to be taken by the college to prevent the knock-on effect on student numbers at EIT. She believes that improvements in the quality of the service provided to students are imperative for the continued success and future of EIT. Prior experience and research has taught her that a quality student experience can directly affect student satisfaction, resulting in positive word-of-mouth communication which will ultimately increase student intake.

Before improvements to service quality can be implemented in the college, Jane will need to measure EIT students' perceptions of the quality of the services currently provided in the college. While working as student retention and admissions officer at Boston State College, Jane conducted many research studies measuring service quality. One model she found particularly useful in her research was Hampton's model of service quality. Hampton developed a comprehensive set of service-quality dimensions as perceived by students in the US higher-education sector. This model, consisting of seven service-quality factors and thirty-six items, is presented in Table 3.3.

Table 3.3: Higher Education Quality Factors

1. *Quality of Education*

The quality of education students get here
The competence of most of the teachers in their own field
The chance to do well if you work hard
The chance your study fulfils your personal needs and prepares you for a future career
The appropriateness of requirements for your degree
The chance to develop your abilities and prepare for your career
The quality of material emphasised in courses

2. Teaching

The personal attention students get from teachers
Teachers' concern for students' needs and interest
The willingness of teachers to talk with students outside of class time
The way teachers talk to you when you ask for help
The chance to participate in class discussion about course materials
The chances of getting to know the professors

3. Social Life – Personal

Opportunities provided for men and women to get acquainted
The pressure to study
The availability of good places to live on or near campus
The chance to work on projects with members of the opposite sex
The friendliness of students and the opportunity to make close friends
The chance to meet people with the same interests as you have

4. Campus Facilities

The places provided for students to relax and lounge during the day
The amount and availability of library facilities
The cleanliness of most facilities used by students
The availability of good, quiet places to study
The concern here for the comfort of students outside of classes

5. Effort to Pass Courses

The amount of work required in most classes
The teachers' expectations as to the amount that students should study
The amount of time you must spend studying to get a passing grade
The difficulty in most of the courses
The pressure to study

6. Social Life – Campus

The activities and clubs you can join here
The chance to explore important ideas
The social events that are provided for the students here
The things you can do here and the opportunities for having a good time
The campus events that are provided for students

7. *Student Activities*

The interest that advisors take in the progress of their students
The availability and ability of most advisors to help students develop their course plans

Source: 'Gap Analysis of College Student Satisfaction as a Measure of Professional Service Quality', *Journal of Professional Services Marketing*, Vol. 9(1), 115–128.

The service-quality dimensions and associated items can then be used to create a questionnaire in which each item is rated by students using a seven-point Likert scale, ranging from strongly agree to strongly disagree.

Following extensive analysis of the relevant secondary data, Jane now sets about designing a research study to measure the students' perceptions of service quality at EIT. She will subsequently use the research findings to make recommendations to college management regarding improvements in service quality at EIT. She postulates that these improvements will have a positive effect on student retention and recruitment, thereby negating the effects of the demographic changes and safeguarding the future of EIT.

Questions

1. Given the situation affecting Ennis Institute of Technology, define the research problem and associated objectives.
2. Outline an appropriate research design for Jane's research.
3. Present a research proposal that incorporates the steps in the marketing research process that Jane should follow.

* This case was written by Martha Farrell and Sheila O'Mahony who are lecturers at the Institute of Technology, Tralee. It is intended to be used as a basis for class discussion rather than to illustrate the effective or ineffective handling of an administrative situation. The people and institutions referred to in the case are entirely fictitious. Some of the material used in the case is based on an MBS dissertation submitted by Martha Farrell in 2005. © Martha Farrell and Sheila O'Mahony.

Case Study
Babylux Limited*

Alice Casey works as an account manager with Communico Limited, an international marketing communications company. She is based in the Irish firm located in Dublin. The company has a broad range of clients operating in the FMCG sector primarily. Communico Ltd. offers media planning, advice and research, according to the client's needs. The company will also manage the implementation of a promotional campaign, if requested by the client.

Joe Lattin has recently established 'Babylux Limited'; a small- to medium-sized Irish firm operating in the baby care sector. Babylux currently produces a range of four different products for this sector. The product range includes baby shampoo, baby soaps, baby bath cleaner and moisturising lotion. Joe Lattin is confident that their product range is of high quality. Babylux uses a specialised process in the production of their products, making them particularly suitable for babies with sensitive skin or any skin allergies.

The baby care sector is extremely competitive in Ireland with a number of well-established companies providing a large range of baby care related products, including products similar to those produced by Babylux. These include companies such as Procter & Gamble, Lever Brothers and Johnson & Johnson. The products, which are competitively promoted, are available throughout supermarkets, department stores, baby shops and pharmacies. Promotions include extra free product, free samples, coupons, two-for-the-price-of-one, etc. The majority of these promotions are run in conjunction with co-operating retail outlets.

Joe Lattin knows that a strategic promotional campaign is critical to the future of his company. He himself is qualified in science and realises that he does not have enough experience to design or implement this type of campaign. Unfortunately, he cannot financially support a full-time marketing executive and therefore decides to approach a number of promotional agencies for advice. He has done some of his own research and knows that Bounty Services Ireland has a large database of mothers in Ireland. It is possible to buy this database, with a minimum requirement of 1,000 names. This company gives all mothers-to-be a free promotional pack both before and after the baby is born, containing free samples and coupons for sponsored baby care products. The database contains contact details for mothers with children up to six years of age. Joe has also found out that a 'mix of promotional tactics' is a more effective promotional strategy than relying on any one form of promotion.

Joe arranges a meeting with Alice Casey of Communico Limited. During the meeting he indicates his willingness to spend €100,000 on this campaign. He realises the limits of this budget, but is unable, as a start-up company, to allocate any more money towards promotion. Joe also informs Alice during the meeting that he would like this campaign to create awareness of his company but, more importantly, to gain trial for the company's products amongst Irish mothers. He feels this is necessary in order to establish a relationship with his target market. Alice agrees to get back to Joe within two weeks with a promotional campaign, clearly indicating a mix of promotional tactics and explaining why they have been chosen for this target market. As they leave, Joe simply asks Alice to 'check out the benefit of using coupons in particular'. She agrees and walks away.

Questions

1. Clarify the main issues that need to be addressed by Alice.
2. What information does Alice need before developing the promotional strategy for Joe and why?
3. How would you advise Alice to collect the information?
4. Clearly indicate the research design that you would use to solve these issues, and justify your design.

*This case study is written by Breda O'Dwyer. It is intended for use in research and discussion in the areas of promotions, consumer behaviour, segmentation and competitive analysis. The case is based upon real information, although certain information has been disguised.

PART 2

DATA COLLECTION METHODS

CHAPTER 4

SECONDARY SOURCES OF DATA

CHAPTER OVERVIEW

▶ Introduction   ▶ Desk Research and Secondary Data Defined
▶ Advantages and Disadvantages of Secondary Data   ▶ Conducting Desk
Research and Gathering Secondary Data   ▶ Classification of Secondary
Sources of Data   ▶ Internal Data   ▶ External Data   ▶ Government
▶ State-Sponsored Bodies   ▶ Directories   ▶ Trade Associations and
Professional Bodies   ▶ The Internet and Databases   ▶ EU and European
▶ Syndicated Services   ▶ Grey Material   ▶ Summary

INTRODUCTION

The central issue of the research process so far has been 'What information do we need?' The focus of this chapter is 'What information already exists?'

Very often, much information is close at hand and can be obtained with ease. Desk research is about collecting data already there, from existing published sources. It is the first step in the data collection phase of a research study. It is the next logical step once the problem is clearly defined. Desk research is concerned with secondary sources of data.

This chapter outlines the secondary sources of data in Ireland that can be used for desk research. *Be very mindful, given the tremendous amount of published information from official and other sources, of the dramatic changes that occur on a daily basis with respect to information sources, government bodies, the Internet and web sites, etc. Many of these information sources change or become redundant in a short space of time. As a result, the material presented in this chapter is not a fully comprehensive guide to every single source of secondary data. Rather, it provides an important starting point and framework for desk research.* So, by the end of this session, the reader will be able to:

1. distinguish between desk and field research, secondary and primary data;
2. detail the nature of secondary data;
3. describe the advantages and disadvantages of secondary data;

4. identify key Irish sources;
5. describe their use in marketing; and
6. conduct an efficient desk search.

DESK RESEARCH AND SECONDARY DATA DEFINED

A researcher conducts desk research to gather secondary data. Desk research is the systematic collection and analysis of secondary sources of data. Secondary data is data collected by another person for reasons other than the problem in hand. For example, when a researcher goes to a library and obtains population statistics, they are conducting desk research by gathering secondary data.

In contrast, a researcher is conducting field research when they talk to people such as consumers, product purchasers, shop managers or housewives. Field research generates primary data. Primary research is data collected first-hand by the investigator for the specific problem on hand. Field research is original data and is synonymous with primary data. Primary data is new data — unpublished and undocumented anywhere else, as captured by Figure 4.1.

Figure 4.1 Research and data types

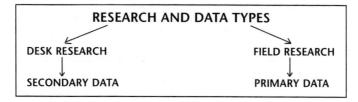

One of the biggest follies in marketing research is to collect primary data before exhausting secondary sources of data. On many occasions secondary data can provide inexpensive answers to posed research questions. The employment of secondary data can even rule out the need for costly primary data. It is assumed that all necessary desk research is completed before considering field research.

ADVANTAGES AND DISADVANTAGES OF SECONDARY DATA

The reasons behind such generally accepted practice lie in the advantages of secondary data over primary data. Secondary data is relatively cheaper than primary data to gather. It is less time-consuming and so is gathered faster than primary data. Against these advantages of secondary data, possible difficulties in using secondary data relate to the recency and origin of the data itself. A serious time lag can occur between the publication of the secondary data and the project on hand. In effect, such lack of recency renders the data obsolete. Table 4.1 presents the major advantages and disadvantages of secondary and primary data.

Table 4.1 Distinctions between secondary and primary data

	Secondary data	Primary data
Purpose	Collected for other reasons by others	Collected for specific problem in hand by researcher
Relevancy	Some to little	Complete
Objectivity	Unknown	High
Process	Easy to gather	Difficult to gather
Cost	Relatively cheap	Relatively expensive
Time required	Relatively little	Relatively a lot

A researcher should never assume that primary data will provide the absolute answer. In reality, primary data is the last resort to solving the problem. Secondary data is not to be underestimated. In such a situation, the investigator analyses the secondary data and writes up the results as displayed in figure 4.2.

Figure 4.2 The role of secondary data in the research process

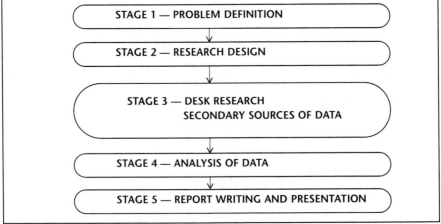

Once the decision has been made to collect secondary data, the data needs to be judged or evaluated before inclusion in the project.

Objectivity is used to evaluate desk research. This term refers to how scientifically the secondary data was originally collected. At some point, the secondary data being considered was primary data. To judge how valid and reliable the original research plan was, the following questions are asked of all secondary data:

- How was it collected?
- Why was it collected?
- When was it collected?

- Why was it published?
- How dependable is the data source?

Essentially, these questions are assessing the quality of the original data. They may highlight some problems or deficiency within the secondary data source. If these arise, the value and the effectiveness of the secondary data is queried. On occasion, it may be deemed inappropriate or even dangerous to utilise the data source.

The second criterion for judging secondary data relates to *comparability* with the current project. Specifically, measurement units and classification schemes being different can be a serious drawback to the use of the secondary source. For example, in Ireland we define a small firm as one employing fewer than 50 people. In many European countries, a small firm equates with 200 or fewer employees. As traditional boundaries are becoming blurred in domestic and international marketplaces, measurement units and their definitions are constantly changing. This detracts from the objectivity and comparability of data emanating from different sources and hence its usefulness to a marketing researcher.

The third criterion relates to the *time dimension* of the data. There can be a significant time lag between the data collection and data publication to the extent that the data is too dated for use. Such data is unhelpful or misleading and therefore should not be used. No information is better than poor or wrong information. One exception to this rule is when secondary data, while dated, can be adapted to account for its ageing. The Consumer Price Index is used to this effect in Ireland — it allows a researcher to account for the effects of inflation over time.

The fourth criterion is associated with multiple sources. It is very important when conducting secondary research to consult multiple sources of data. This means, instead of relying on one source of data to solve your research problem, it is best practice to consult five or six different sources before arriving at your conclusion.

In summary, secondary data fulfils a number of important roles in any research process. It:

- is a data source in its own right;
- can provide a solution to the problem;
- acts as background to primary data;
- can be a substitute to primary data; and
- aids in problem clarification (literature review).

CONDUCTING DESK RESEARCH AND GATHERING SECONDARY DATA

Often, it is an overabundance of information and not a lack of it which confronts the researcher at this point. The task is to sift through published sources, selecting those most pertinent to the study. Like all other steps in marketing research, the process of gathering secondary data is ordered and systematic. The researcher, to be exhaustive:

- goes from *internal to external* sources — that is from company documents such as invoices and customer letters to external reports and documents, e.g. government census data;
- goes from *general to specific* sources — the researcher starts with broad general issues and then to specific industry sources. This can be referred to as the *funnel effect*. Key search words and terms are also approached using the general-to-specific guideline. The help of an expert or librarian may be needed at this point, as one investigates more specific sources of data;
- is *methodical and logical* — to ensure effective use of resources and time, an ordered approach to potential sources is needed. A planned and careful approach minimises the likelihood of problems or deficiencies occurring in desk research;
- tries not to rely upon a single source of data — the old saying, 'two heads are better than one' applies to desk research — where possible, *two, three or more sources of data* are used. This is know as multiple data sources, as opposed to single data sources.
- *writes* everything down — at a later stage, you or another researcher may wish to refer to a minor point of information, so it is a time-saving device if there is a paper trail to follow.

Generally speaking, an effective, exhaustive research can be completed of all secondary data using an approach similar to the one described above. In calculating market size estimates or consumption rates, two or three sources will need to be combined. For example, the Census of Population, Household Budget Survey and the Consumer Price Index are necessary to determine the market size of many consumer products here in Ireland (we examine this issue at a later stage in this chapter).

In practice, one exception can arise, where the combination of sources does not give the desired information. In such circumstances, ingenuity and creativity are required in utilising the secondary data. Jane Williams[1] tells of an occasion when a firm wished to estimate the number of fire doors in Ireland. Unable to locate a source or sources of secondary data which quoted a figure, the firm in question used the number of fire signs in existence as an indication of the possible number of fire doors. Such an approach is not uncommon in Ireland. Assumptions, scenarios or lateral thinking are often required to calculate figures, etc. It is clearly important that there is a solid foundation for the assumptions and that the assumptions are explicitly documented in all calculations.

CLASSIFICATION OF SECONDARY SOURCES OF DATA

Secondary data can be classified broadly as either internal or external. This internal/external division refers to the origin of the data in the first instance — that is, whether the data was first conceived within the firm or outside.

Internal data is data already in existence within the firm. Accounting documents, sales reports, customer files, invoices and delivery dockets typify internal secondary data. Such secondary data can also be referred to as in-house data and historical data.

External data is data in existence outside the organisation. It consists of all published material, information and statistics from official, public and state bodies and other entities.

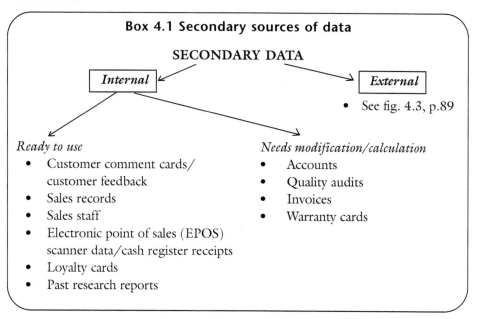

Box 4.1 Secondary sources of data

SECONDARY DATA

Internal

External
- See fig. 4.3, p.89

Ready to use
- Customer comment cards/ customer feedback
- Sales records
- Sales staff
- Electronic point of sales (EPOS) scanner data/cash register receipts
- Loyalty cards
- Past research reports

Needs modification/calculation
- Accounts
- Quality audits
- Invoices
- Warranty cards

INTERNAL DATA

Internal data may be obtained from the marketing or other functions. Examples of marketing data include output from the Marketing Information System (MkIS), salesforce data/reports, customer service data/reports, bar code scanner readings and Customer Relationship Management (CRM) systems. Data from other functions, e.g. accounting, includes sources such as finance, operations, web-site log files and research and development (R&D) data. For example, customer information held on a customer database can be a complementary force for marketing research[2] and can be used to:

- classify customers — gold, silver, bronze, according to the amount of business done with the firm;
- assess the probability of closing sale, e.g. 1–9 ranking, where 1 = signing within next day, 2 = within next week . . . ;
- determine the amount of purchase.

In the hotel industry, for example, hotel managers use reservations records and registration information to help in timing their advertising and sales calls. If most tourists book July and August holidays by February, advertising at Easter will be too late. Reservation records also provide information concerning the hotel's top producing travel agents and corporate clients. Hotel sales staff can phone, fax, or visit the travel agents or corporate clients to inform them of future promotional activities and identify new business opportunities. The salesperson can ascertain if the travel agent or corporate client has other needs that the hotel can satisfy, e.g. a conference that is just being planned, as highlighted in Table 4.2.[3]

Table 4.2 Internal records — customer information

Guest information

Guest information

Personal guest information
  Name
  Address
  Phone numbers: Work
                          Home
                          Mobile
                          E-mail
  Number in party
  Reason for trip
                          Business
                          Pleasure
                          Study
                          Other
  Name and address of employer
  Occupation

Types of tourism products/services purchased
  Single/double room/suite
  Restaurant
  Room service
  Spa

Details of trip
  Length of stay
  Method of arrival — car/bus/train/taxi/other

Method of payment
  Credit card/cash/cheque/bill to company

Membership of frequent guest programme

Salespeople come in contact with customers in the marketplace every day. They are used as information hounds — the ears and eyes of the firm. They pick up information on a continuous basis about customers, competitors and the marketplace. Sales records can keep the firm abreast of:

- competitor activity;
- market trends;
- customer problems;
- sales activities;
- sales expenses;
- trends in customer business;
- order status;
- potential new needs; and
- shifts in customer tastes.

Internal Data, Modification and Calculation

Many researchers and firms don't use the information already available in their own records. They tend to ignore such data. However, simple modification or recalculation enables the researcher to use existing organisational records. More data exists than people know of. In many cases, the researcher must 'dig and delve' to find data that answers the query on hand. This modification to data is needed as many firms have incomplete, inaccurate filing systems. Accounting data and records are used by marketing managers to:

- keep track of marketing expenses;
- relate performance to targets;
- analyse sales; and
- relate profits to sales.

Often, such historical data needs minor rearrangement to assist the marketing function. Here are some examples to demonstrate how a researcher can make company records work for them using profit and loss accounts and invoices.

Keeping Track of Marketing Expenses

Suppose your profit and loss statement for the last six months looks like Table 4.3.

Table 4.3 Profit and loss statement

Sales		€50,000
Expenses		
1. Rent	€4,000	
2. Supplies	€3,000	
3. Selling expenses	€5,000	
4. Salaries	€9,000	
5. Advertising	€1,000	
	€22,000	

Your only marketing costs are selling expenses and advertising. So, what information could you obtain from this profit and loss statement? Firstly, information might become more clearly visible if you rearrange the items as shown in Table 4.4.

Table 4.4 Analysis of profit and loss statement

2007 January–June		
Total costs/sales	Selling expenses/sales	Advertising/sales
€22,000/€50,000	€5,000/€50,000	€1,000/€50,000
(44%)	(10%)	(2%)

Having rearranged the data in your profit and loss statement, you can see that, in 2007, costs are 44% of sales, that selling expenses are 10% of sales and that advertising is 2% of sales. These figures can now be used as a basis for controlling future costs. For example, if your present advertising level is satisfactory at 2% of sales, then this figure could be used as a benchmark for your future advertising expenditure. If your selling expenses rise above 10% of sales, then you might try to cut back on costs. Of course, the figures quoted here are merely examples and should not be taken as recommended guidelines.

Relating Performance to Targets

From the accounts one can extract figures which will help to assess sales performance. However, it is essential that two things are done first: quantify benchmarks and set targets. A benchmark is merely a starting point which identifies how many sales you have now. Sales targets are the specific sales goals you anticipate your firm to achieve within a given time period, usually quarterly and/or annually.

Once benchmarks and targets are established, one can accurately measure progress. In this manner, a firm has the means of spotting trends; recognising problems, such as accounts that may have fallen in value; and identifying opportunities, such as fast-growing customers. Additionally, there is the information necessary for planning future action and handling questions.

So, what information do you need if you are to keep track of sales performance?

- total sales
- sales per region
- sales for each product or product group and
- sales for each salesperson.

Once this information is gathered, it is useful to display it on graphs or charts. Then one can see at a glance how a business is doing. Table 4.5 is an example of how one may want to organise sales data to help analyse sales performance.

Table 4.5 Sales analysis

	Target	Actual	Difference
Total sales	**€9,000**	**€7,000**	**€–2,000**
Sales by area			
Area 1	3,000	2,000	–1,000
Area 2	3,000	2,750	–250
Area 3	3,000	2,250	–750
Sales by product			
Product 1	4,000	3,500	–500
Product 2	3,000	2,000	–1,000
Product 3	2,000	1,500	–500

Relating Profit to Sales

Finally, a quick calculation of profit-to-sales ratio will help track trends in profitability. If this figure shows that sales are increasing but that the profit rate is falling, then it is time to look more closely at expenses or prices.

What You Can Learn From Invoices

- Do you know what your average sale is per customer?
- Do you know who are your top five customers? Your top ten?
- Can you say what is the average credit your customers take?
- What time of year do you make the most sales? By volume? By €?
- What is the monthly sales pattern for each product or product group?
- What is the geographic breakdown of your sales?
- How would you break down your overall sales into differing customer groups? (i.e. your firm's sales to different groups, such as builders, new home-buyers and engineering companies.)[4]

Marketing researchers may also be able to collect useful internal data from a company's own web-site. For example, systems can analyse web-site visitors to tell where they come from, which phrases they search with, what other pages they visit and whether they are first-time or returning visitors.

EXTERNAL DATA

There is also a large quantity of published information which is readily available, easy to consult and relatively inexpensive to gather. Such published information is external to a company. It is available from official sources, the government, trade bodies, the Internet and a myriad of other sources. This type of information is not gathered specifically for marketing purposes. To this end it will need to be adjusted.

Box 4.2 Data Mining – Gold nuggets in data files

Data mining is defined as the process of data selection, exploration and building models using vast data stores and software techniques to uncover previously unknown patterns, by identifying underlying rules and features in the data. What does this mean to the researcher?

The average large enterprise has terabytes of data on hand — customer information, supplier exchanges and internal company records that contain data. Within this mountain of data lie the 'golden nuggets' or 'insights' that can help solve business problems and propel new strategic initiatives. By putting on a miner's hat, you can better analyse the data you already have on hand and enrich your ability to increase revenues and reduce costs. Advances in both hardware and the capabilities of database management systems make data mining a more compelling proposition today.

The researcher can produce new knowledge to better inform decision makers before they act. They can build a model of the real world based on data collected from a variety of sources including corporate transactions, customer histories and demographics, even external sources such as credit bureaus. Data mining techniques are based upon advancing information technologies such as artificial intelligence methods, decision trees, rule induction methods, genetic algorithms and genetic programming, neural networks and clustering techniques.

New text mining capabilities enable the researcher to apply such analyses to text-based documents. With a rich suite of text-processing and analysis tools, the researcher can uncover underlying themes or concepts contained in large document collections, group documents into topical clusters, classify documents into predefined categories and integrate text data with structured data for enriched predictive modeling endeavors.

Data mining reaches across industries and business functions. For example, telecommunications, stock exchanges and credit card and insurance companies use data mining to detect fraud, optimise marketing campaigns, and identify the most profitable strategies. The medical industry uses data mining to predict the effectiveness of surgical procedures, medical tests and medications. Retailers use data mining to assess the effectiveness of coupons and special events, and predict which offers are most appropriate for different consumers. Here in Ireland, Bank of Ireland and Eircom are regarded as leaders in the data mining stakes. Linked closely to data mining is the idea of data warehousing. Data warehousing is a methodology that coordinates diverse databases into a unified block or storage of information, that can then be data mined.

Adapted from www.sas.com, 2002; *Business and Finance*, 'There's Gold in Them Thar Files-Computing', 31 August 1995; and Gargano, M and Raggad, B., 'Data Mining – a powerful information creating tool', *OCLC Systems and Services*, Vol.15, No.2, 1999, pp81–90; *Computerscope*, 'Mining Data for Digital Gold', 31 January 2004.

From a marketing perspective, this rich array of external information sources can be divided into seven main areas, as illustrated in Figure 4.3.

Figure 4.3 Secondary sources of data

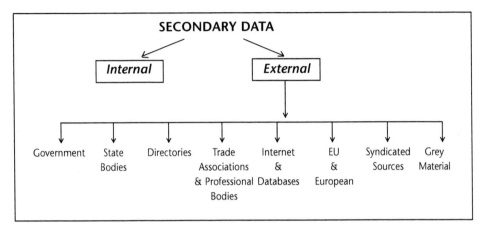

Having already discussed internal data sources, each of the major external data sources are now described. Remember, this discussion is meant as an indication of the wealth of information that is available to the marketing researcher in Ireland, rather than an exhaustive, finite listing of such!

1. GOVERNMENT

The Government constitutes one of the most important sources of external secondary data in Ireland. Vast amounts of data, from national to regional, and from urban to rural, are collected and published by the government. The government collects and publishes censuses, statistical information and other data generated in the normal course of operations, e.g. taxes collected and unemployment benefits paid.

Government data is generally of high quality. Such data tends to be readily available to the researcher at little or no cost. Its major value is in assessing the market size, market trends, consumption and expenditure patterns. Its main drawback relates to much of the data being aggregate in nature, i.e. it details product groups rather than brands; regions rather than towns. Coupled with this, the delay from time of collection to time of publication can be substantial, often two or more years. This can require the researcher to supplement the data to account for factors like inflation.

Government data can come from two broad sources, (a) the Central Statistics Office (CSO) and (b) government departments, as Figure 4.4 shows. The description here of the Central Statistics Office (CSO) and associated material draws heavily upon the CSO annual guide to CSO publications and information services.[5]

Figure 4.4 Government sources of secondary data

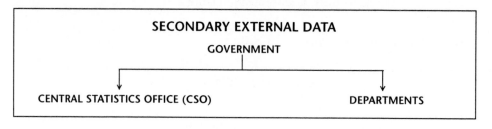

Central Statistics Office (CSO) (www.cso.ie)

The Central Statistics Office (CSO) is the largest gatherer of statistical information in the country. The CSO is the government agency charged with the responsibility of collecting, compiling and disseminating the results of its statistical enquiries. It publishes official Irish statistics. It is also responsible for the co-ordination of official statistics produced by other public authorities. General publications by the CSO fall under three main headings:

1. Statistical Yearbook (annually)

This yearbook is the most comprehensive source of statistical data published in Ireland. It contains statistics compiled by the Central Statistics Office, but also a considerable amount of statistical information compiled in the course of the administrative work of other government departments and state-sponsored bodies.

The yearbook is divided into eighteen sections giving detailed information on the following topics:

- Population
- Labour market
- Vital statistics
- Health and social conditions
- Education
- Justice and defence
- Economy
- Public finance and banking
- Agriculture, forestry and fishing
- Industry
- Building and construction
- Services and distribution
- External trade
- Travel
- Prices
- Earnings
- Households and
- Environment

Retrospective data is given in all sections. The abstract also includes an appendix which contains published statistics relating to Northern Ireland.

2. Statistical Bulletin (quarterly)
This bulletin is the formal publication medium for the detailed results of all the regular short-term CSO inquiries.

3. Economic Series (monthly)
This publication provides five years' retrospective data for over 160 principal short-term economic series in the following ten categories:

- Prices
- Industry
- Building and construction
- Agriculture
- External trade
- Distribution, transport and tourism
- Services
- Finance
- Labour
- Vital statistics

Other CSO statistics, publications and reports, invaluable for the marketing researcher in Ireland, cover the areas of agriculture, construction, demography and labour force, distribution and services and general industrial, economic and trade data – see Table 4.6 below.

Table 4.6 Examples of statistics and reports available from the CSO

Name	Description
Agriculture, Forestry and Fisheries	Crops and livestock survey
	Area, yield and production of crops
	Agriculture labour input
	Agricultural land sales
	Estimated output, input and income arising in agriculture
Building and Construction	Census of building and construction
	Earnings and hours worked
	Planning permissions
	Building and construction price index
	Building and construction materials wholesale price index

Name	Description
	House building cost index
	Index of employment
	House completions
	Number of new house and home improvement grants approved and paid
	Number of new loans approved
Demography	Census of population
	Population and migration estimates
	Population and labour force projections 2006–2036
	The demographic situation of the Traveller community in 1996
	Quarterly report on vital statistics
	Annual report on vital statistics
	Life tables
	Irish babies' names
Economic and Financial Statistics	National income and expenditure
	Quarterly national accounts
	Balance of international payments
	International investment position statistics
	Input–Output tables
	County incomes and regional GDP
	Public finance
	Monetary series
	Interest rates
	Government security yields
	Exchange rates
	Savings
Industry	Census of industrial production
	Industrial production and turnover indices
	Electricity – Output (giga watt hours per day) ESB generating stations
	Industrial employment
	Industrial earnings and hours worked
	Industrial productivity indicators
	Capital goods index for industry
	Output price index for manufacturing industries
	Wholesale price index for energy products purchased by industry

Name	Description
	PRODCOM product sales Industrial stocks Capital assets in industry
Labour	Quarterly national household survey Labour costs survey Survey of the structure of earnings Live register statistics Live register analysis Industrial disputes Number of redundancies notified
Services (including distribution)	Census of services including distribution Annual services inquiry Banking, insurance and building societies – employment and earnings Public sector employment and earnings Business of advertising agencies Earning in distribution and business services
Prices	Consumer price index Harmonised index of consumer prices Constant tax price index Import and export price (unit value) indices Average agricultural prices Price index of ordinary stocks and shares Wholesale price index
Trade	Trade statistics Availability of detailed trade statistics Availability of trade statistics complied by EU countries
Transport	Road freight transport survey Statistics of port traffic Vehicles licensed for the first time Railways – CIÉ rail services
Tourism and Travel	Tourism and travel Household travel survey Air traffic statistics Passenger movement by sea Cross-border passenger movement

In addition to these reports, the CSO, through their 'EirStat' data spreadsheet service, provide marketing researchers with spreadsheets containing raw data. This can be useful for carrying out analysis that is not facilitated by the reports produced by the CSO. Some of the more important CSO reports are presented below from a researcher's perspective.

Census of Population

The Census of Population is the largest statistical enquiry conducted by the Central Statistics Office. First undertaken in 1821, the census was merely a head count. It has now been expanded to the point where there are seven different sections to the census, all of interest to the marketing researcher. The most recent census was carried out on 23 April 2006.

The census questionnaire is issued to every household and to every other type of location where persons may be present on census night. In addition to the usual demographic questions on age, sex and marital status, topics such as religion, ability to speak the Irish language, usual residence, means of travel to work, education received, occupation, employment status and involvement in farming, were also covered. Full-time, part-time and duration of unemployment were covered. The household questions included the nature of occupancy of house or flat, the number of rooms, the year in which the house was built, water supply and sanitary facilities and the principal method of heating the household in winter time. The final census results include:

- Local population reports — a series of 32 reports for individual counties and county boroughs.
- Small Area Population Statistics (SAPS). This contains detailed classifications of:
  - (a) The population by age, sex and marital status.
  - (b) Households by type, size and by age, sex and marital status of the head of the household.
  - (c) Family units by size and age of youngest child.
  - (d) The population aged 15 years and over by principal economic status, age and sex.
  - (e) Persons at work by sex, employment status and broad industrial sector.
  - (f) Persons at work and unemployed by sex and occupational group.
  - (g) The entire population by socio-economic group and social class.

Detailed classifications by means of travel and distance travelled to work, education, ability to speak Irish, religion and housing characteristics, etc. are also provided for urban districts, rural districts, towns and district electoral divisions, under such heading as:

Volume 1 — Population by area.
Volume 2 — Ages and marital status.
Volume 3 — Household composition and family units.
Volume 4 — Usual residence and migration, birthplaces and nationalities.
Volume 5 — Principle economic status and industries.
Volume 6 — Occupations.
Volume 7 — Education, scientific and technological qualifications.
Volume 9 — Travel to work, school and college.
Volume 11 — An Ghaeilge/Irish language.

Other demographic publications include:

- Population and Labour Force Projections, 2001–2031.
- Quarterly Report on Vital Statistics.
- Life Tables.
- Irish Babies' Names.

Marketing Research Uses

Population data is used in marketing to estimate the market size and structure. It indicates whether a socio-economic or geographic market is growing or decreasing. Comparing previous years of census data will reveal if a target market is expanding or contracting. For example, a company in the Munster area manufacturing clothes for girls aged 5 to 9 wants to know the total relevant population. Total population in this category in 2002 was 36,379. In 2006, the total population of 5–9-year-olds was 38,826. This shows a significant drop in the size of this particular market segment and has serious implications for the marketing strategy pursued by the firm. The population census also provides a range of other useful information, such as:

- a demographic profile of target markets;
- trend data in the number of births, deaths, marriages, those emigrating, mobility patterns;
- distribution by social class;
- household composition;
- at local, regional or national level;
- employment status by occupational group;
- numbers at each level of education.

The biggest drawback to the use of the Census of Population is the time gap between the collection of data and its publication, with a lead time of three years in some cases.

Household Budget Survey

The large-scale national Household Budget Surveys cover 7,000–8,000 urban and rural households. The HBS provides estimates for household composition, accommodation facilities, weekly income, weekly expenditure (over 300 categories of goods and services are distinguished) and other miscellaneous items classified by various household characteristics, e.g. size, composition, gross income level, location, etc. To this end, it shows the actual amount of expenditure and the percentage of the total weekly budget spent on a named household item, such as bread, fish, meat, shoes, petrol and newspapers. It also indicates different patterns of spending in different categories of households, e.g. between urban and rural households and those on different incomes.

A large-scale national survey was conducted in 1994/95. The sampled households give a sufficiently representative picture for all of Ireland's households. Two detailed volumes are readily available — Volume 1 presents detailed results for all households and Volume 2 covers detailed results for urban and rural households. Such HBS results are on a harmonised basis with other EU member states to allow for comparisons — a very useful facility for Irish firms exporting and serving markets abroad. The last HBS was carried out over 2004 and 2005 and was made up of a sample of 7,644 Irish households.

The Household Budget Survey is a critical source of data on expenditure for a marketer. It enables a manager to estimate the level and trends in expenditure on individual products or services. In this capacity, market potential and market penetration targets can be realistically set. In practice, the HBS is used in conjunction with the Census of Population to estimate market sizes, market trends, consumption patterns and demand at local and national level, as shown in the worked example below.

Consumer Price Index

The Consumer Price Index (CPI) is designed to measure the change in the price of consumer goods and services. It is compiled monthly and is published in the monthly 'Economic Series' report and the quarterly 'Statistical Bulletin'. Data is collected from a representative panel of retail and service outlets nationwide and is based on a representative basket of goods and services. The quantity of each good and service in this basket is proportional to the average amount purchased by all private households in the country as determined by the Household Budget Survey (see above). Categories covered include: food, clothing, fuel & light, housing, consumer durables, alcohol and cigarettes.

The Consumer Price index is used by marketers to adjust market size estimates for the effects of retail price inflation. The indices are especially useful when considering monetary trends. For example, sales of a specific product may have increased from €100 in 2006 to €150 in 2008. This appears to be a 50% increase in the value of sales for this item. However, if prices rose by 20% during this period, then the increase in the value of sales in real terms was much less (allowing for inflation).

Estimating the Market Size

For many companies, especially those in the consumer goods field, market estimates can be found by using data published by the Central Statistics Office (CSO). An estimate of the market size can be calculated using three CSO publications:

- Household Budget Survey (HBS).
- Census of Population (CoP).
- Consumer Price Index (CPI).

Whether it be a national or a local market, most managers would like to be able to determine the size of the market to which they are selling. It is essential to have an estimate of market size in start-up situations so as to decide whether a venture is worthwhile. Established companies need to know market size to assist in planning. You cannot formulate financial projections or a marketing plan unless you can forecast sales, and, in order to forecast sales, you need to know market trends and the overall market size.

For example, according to the 1996 CoP (the last year for which data was available at the time of writing), the population of Cork City was 127,187. The CoP also tells us that there were 41,452 households in Cork City.

The 2004–2005 HBS tells us the average weekly household expenditure on a range of goods and services, with data broken down for urban and rural areas. For example, the average weekly expenditure for urban households on bread is as follows:

- White Bread €2.70
- Soda Bread €0.30
- Brown Bread €0.50
- Other Bread €1.38

Based on this data, it is possible to estimate the market size for the various types of bread in Cork City by multiplying the total number of households in Cork City by the average weekly expenditure in each product/service area. However, since the expenditure figures are based on data from 1999–2000, they need to be adjusted to take inflation into account.

According to the CPI, the rate of inflation for 2007 was 5% and, for the six months to June 2007, it was 4.4%. Therefore, the adjusted expenditure figures (up to June 2007) are:

- White Bread €2.96
- Soda Bread €0.33
- Brown Bread €0.55
- Other Bread €1.51

When we multiply these adjusted average household weekly spends in urban areas by the number of households in Cork City, we can estimate the weekly and annual value in 2007 of the Cork City market for bread. We should bear in mind that these figures are based on bread consumption rates in 2004–2005.

Table 4.7 Estimate of bread market size – average household consumption in Cork city, 2005

Weekly value (Euro)		Annual Value (Euro)
White Bread	122,698	6,380,296
Soda Bread	13,679	711,308
Brown Bread	22,799	1,185,548
Other Bread	62,592	3,254,784

This is a bottom-up approach to estimating the market size for a product or service — you focus upon consumption or usage. You could also, figures permitting, estimate the market size by examining production figures. This is a top-down approach to calculating market sizes, as shown in table 4.8.

Table 4.8 Estimating Irish Market Size

Top-down estimate	Bottom-up estimate
Total Irish Market (imports – exports + production) ↓	Usage by each household (Household Budget Survey) ↓
Percentage of Irish population in Dublin (CoP) ↓	Total number of households in Dublin (CoP/HBS) ↓
Estimate of Dublin market	Estimate of Dublin market

Quarterly National Survey

The Labour Force Survey is the definitive source of data on employment and unemployment. A sample of about 39,000 households is surveyed. The reports provide estimates of the total population classified by age, sex and planning region and of the population aged 15 and over classified by principal economic status (at work, unemployed, etc.), industrial group, occupational group, marital status, etc.

Annual Services Inquiry

Estimates of accounting and employment variables are provided by this survey of over 25,000 Irish service enterprises. Findings cover annual turnover, purchases, stocks, capital expenditure/disposal and employment/earnings estimates for the retail and wholesale trade. Real estate, renting and other selected services are covered, though not to the same level of detail as wholesale or retail.

Retail Sales Index (Monthly)

This series measures changes in both the value and volume levels of retail sales on a seasonally adjusted basis for thirteen types of retail businesses, for all businesses excluding garages and for all businesses combined.

Categories included in the volume index of retail sales:

- Grocery.
- Grocery with public house.
- Public house and off-licence.
- Tobacco, sweets and newspapers.
- Fresh meat.
- Garage and filling station.
- Chemist.
- Hardware.
- Electrical goods.
- Footwear.
- Drapery and apparel.
- Other non-food.
- Total retail sales, i.e. excluding garages and filling stations.
- Department stores: clothing and footwear, furniture, soft furnishings etc., and other goods and services.
- All businesses combined.

Marketing Research Uses

Using this data, it is possible to see, at a glance, the sales progress of particular product groups. This type of information can provide a basis for assessing a company's performance. For example, a shoe company can compare its monthly sales trends with that for the footwear industry overall to judge its performance. The Retail Index can also indicate product groups that are experiencing buoyancy, e.g. frozen pizzas, ice cream cakes and flavoured water drinks. It will also indicate those product groups in decline.

Advertising Agencies Inquiry

This annual series gives details of the gross amount charged by advertising agencies to clients for advertising space, production work and other work such as research and promotions. Information is also provided on the number of people engaged and the total wages and salaries paid.

Trade Statistics

The most detailed published trade statistics appear in the monthly Trade Statistics publication. This provides details for over 1,900 items classified according to the United Nations Standard International Trade Classification. Both quantity and value of imports of each type of product are given for each month, for the year to date and for the same period in the previous year. The December issue gives total figures for the full year. A breakdown of imports by country of origin is also included in each issue.

The monthly releases contain figures for total imports and exports. Cumulative data as well as data for the previous year are provided. Summary commodity and country analyses are also given. Some of the categories may be too broad or too narrow for the research purposes in hand, but it is possible to get a more detailed breakdown by visiting the CSO.

Marketing Research Uses

Such import figures provide information about customer demand and hence market size. In doing so, this data indicates import competition facing Irish companies and suggests opportunities for import substitution.

Import data can also be used in conjunction with production figures and export levels to estimate the market size for a product. Production, plus imports, minus exports, gives a market size estimate as shown in Table 4.7.

Industrial Production Index

This index monitors current trends in the volume of production by industrial establishments with three or more people. Seasonally adjusted and unadjusted indices are published for 49 industrial sectors and groupings. For each product group, the annual percentage change and that of the preceding month are given.

This data is used by marketers to benchmark a company's performance against the output of the industry.

Census of Industrial Production

This provides more comprehensive data on industrial production, but there is a greater time lag in the release of figures. The Census of Industrial Production is based on an annual survey of 5,000 industrial establishments known as local units. It details gross and net output overall, per establishment and per person. This is classified by industrial sector and broken down by region and company size.

Access to CSO Data

A huge variety of CSO data and information are accessible via the Internet. Since 1998, CSO publishes all statistical releases on the CSO website on the day of release. Since January 2003, all publications have been available on the CSO website. The website is www.cso.ie. It also provides valuable linkages to other EU and related sites and has a student section.

Information may also be easily obtained by phone. Detailed information is published in the quarterly Statistical Bulletin, the annual Statistical Yearbook and the reports on large-scale CSO inquiries. These may be purchased and are generally available in public and third-level institution libraries. The CSO also maintains a computerised data bank containing its principal economic and social statistics.

Provision of Special Analyses

Considerable volumes of *ad hoc* analyses not incorporated in published reports are provided on a fee basis on request.

CSO Library

The CSO library contains an extensive up-to-date collection of statistical and economic publications, including those of international organisations (i.e. EU, OECD, UN, and ILO). A large selection of statistical publications and yearbooks of other countries (e.g. all EU member states, other European countries, Canada, USA, Australia, New Zealand, South Africa, Japan, China, etc.) is also available for consultation. A number of statistical, economic and other journals are stocked, as are the annual reports of government departments and state-sponsored agencies.

The main library is located in the Cork office. A limited library service is being maintained in Dublin, comprising mainly national statistical publications and the publications of the principal international statistical organisations (e.g. EUROSTAT, OECD, UN). Both libraries are open to the public from 9.30 a.m. to 12.45 p.m. and 2.30 p.m. to 4.45 p.m., Monday to Friday.

Government Departments (*www.irlgov.ie*)

At present, there are fifteen government departments, each charged with responsibility for policy in their respective areas. In the course of operations, much data is generated and published and can be utilised by a researcher. It is also worth noting that much of this information is housed within a departmental library.

For example, the Department of Agriculture, Food and Forestry is responsible for the operation and implementation of EU schemes and regulations, the provision of grants for farm improvements, the operation of measures to improve livestock and horticultural production, the control and elimination of animal diseases, ensuring quality control in marketing and processing, and the formulation and operation of land policy. Much information pertaining to these topics can be accessed in the Department of Agriculture library.

Box 4.3 Government departments

DEPARTMENT	URL
Irish Government Website	www.irlgov.ie
Agriculture	www.agriculture.gov.ie
Arts, Sport, Tourism	www.arts-sport-tourism.gov.ie
Communications, Marine and Natural Resources	www.dcmnr.gov.ie
Department of Community, Rural and Gaeltacht Affairs	www.pobail.ie
Department of Defence	www.defence.ie
Education and Science	www.education.ie
Enterprise, Trade and Employment	www.entemp.ie
Department of the Environment, Heritage and Local Government	www.environ.ie
Department of Finance	www.finance.gov.ie
Foreign Affairs	www.foreignaffairs.gov.ie
Justice, Equality and Law Reform	www.justice.ie
Social and Family Affairs	www.welfare.ie
Tánaiste, Health and Children	www.dohc.ie
Taoiseach	www.taoiseach.gov.ie
Transport	www.transport.ie
Attorney General	www.attorneygeneral.ie
Ordnance Survey	www.osi.ie

---

2. STATE-SPONSORED BODIES

Many Irish state-sponsored bodies have a direct impact on the business world and so are important sources of information for marketing researchers. In addition to the regular and general releases and reports of state bodies, there are a number of special industry reports and occasional studies undertaken or commissioned on their behalf. The numerous Irish state bodies of interest to the marketing researcher are detailed in Table 4.9 below.

Table 4.9 Irish government agencies

Name	Description	URL
Bord Bia – Irish Food Board	International marketing support agency for the Irish food industry	www.bordbia.ie
Fáilte Ireland	Offical Irish Tourist Board	www.ireland.ie
Bord Iascaigh Mhara – Irish Sea Fisheries Board	Promotes sustainable development of coastal regions and Irish sea fish and aquaculture industry.	www.bim.ie
Border, Midland & Western Regional Assembly	Complements the services of the border, midland and western regional assembly by delivering up-to-date information and news.	www.bmwassembly.ie
County Enterprise Board	Central contact point web site for Ireland's 26 county enterprise boards.	www.enterpriseboards.ie
FÁS	Irish training and employment authority, provides a range of employment services to job seekers, community groups and employers.	www.fas.ie
Forfás	Policy advisory board for industrial development and science and technology in Ireland.	www.forfas.ie
IDA	Irish agency responsible for attracting internationally mobile industrial investment projects.	www.idaireland.com
Inter Trade Ireland	The trade and business development body	www.intertradeireland.com
Irish Government	Official Irish government website, covering all departments.	www.irlgov.ie
Irish Maritime Development Office	Ireland's agency dedicated to the promotion, assistance and development of the Irish Shipping and Shipping Services sector.	www.imdo.ie
Shannon Development	Responsible for supporting and promoting integrated development in the Shannon region.	www.shannon-dev.ie

Name	Description	URL
Teagasc	Agriculture and food development authority. Includes R&D facilities at National Food Centre and Dairy Research Centre.	www.teagasc.ie
Údarás na Gaeltachta	Promotes the development of Gaeltacht (native Irish-speaking). Supports job creation in manufacturing, natural resources and modern services.	www.udaras.ie

Some of the more relevant state bodies are discussed now to demonstrate the richness of data available to the marketing researcher.

Enterprise Ireland (www.enterprise-ireland.com)

Enterprise Ireland is the national organisation with responsibility for accelerating Ireland's national and regional development by helping Irish companies to develop and compete so that they can grow profitably in world markets.

Enterprise Ireland clients are primarily manufacturing and internationally traded services companies employing ten or more people, and new enterprises with the potential to grow rapidly. Enterprise Ireland assists clients by:

- providing the information needed to identify market opportunities;
- providing the knowledge and expertise required to profit from these opportunities;
- providing ways of working together with other Irish companies to achieve maximum impact on the marketplace;
- providing help to identify and evaluate the most appropriate sources of supply in Ireland (Professional Buyer Services).

The organisation has a network of thirteen offices in Ireland and 34 worldwide. Examples of reports published by Enterprise Ireland include:

- ITS 2007: Opportunities for Ireland's High-Technology Internationally Traded Services Sector to 2007.
- Doing Business in Japan – a Guide for Irish Technology Companies.
- Guide to British Markets.
- Shop Ireland in North America.
- Clothing and Textile Directory.
- Gifts, Tabletop and Jewellery Directory.

Enterprise Ireland has a Client Information Service with extensive information on products, markets and companies in both printed and electronic sources. Types of information available include:

1. Product and market information: market size; trends and developments; distribution channels; country profiles and company information.
2. Business news: business environment; sectoral issues and developments; company activities; government programmes.
3. Company information: who makes what; who owns what; company profiles by sector, size and location; credit/financial reports.
4. Standards and Technical information.
5. Trade Information: export/import procedures; documentation; tariffs and the Irish Exporter's Handbook.

The Client Information Service is primarily focused on Enterprise Ireland client companies, although the library at Glasnevin in Dublin is open to all callers. The library houses a wide range of marketing publications, overseas trade directories, industry directories, market statistics, specialist research reports, textbooks, booklets and information guides. An appointment is required for use of some information sources. Opening hours are 09.15 to 13.00 and 14.00 to 17.00, Monday to Friday.

Tourism Ireland Limited (www.tourismireland.com)

Tourism Ireland Limited is the tourism marketing company established on foot of the Good Friday Agreement by Bord Fáilte and the Northern Ireland Tourist Board. Tourism Ireland Ltd was formally incorporated on 11 December 2000. Its Memorandum and Articles of Association govern its operations and it is accountable to the North–South Ministerial Council. The organisation's role is to provide strategic leadership in international marketing and in the delivery of world-class marketing programmes through:

- Undertaking destination-marketing programmes to stimulate demand for visiting the island of Ireland;
- Facilitating and supporting business links to improve distribution of the Ireland tourism product to potential consumers; and
- Acting as an advocate for overseas consumers and trade to influence the quality of the tourism experience on the island of Ireland.

Fáilte Ireland (www.failteireland.com)

In November 2001, the government approved the creation of a National Tourism Development Authority to promote the development of sustainable tourist facilities and services, including the promotion of training, human resources and marketing skills.

Fáilte Ireland's mission is: '*To increase the contribution of tourism to the economy by facilitating the development of a competitive and profitable tourism industry.*' Fáilte Ireland's key role is to support and help the industry to meet the challenges facing the entire global tourism market and to sustain, or increase, the level of activity in the sector. It is primarily a catalyst of other people's activity. It supports the industry in its efforts to be more competitive and more profitable. As the State's tourism development authority, it is well placed to address some of the broader issues that need to be tackled if the industry is to grow and develop. Its emphasis is on strategic partnership, with all the interests in Irish tourism at national, local and regional levels working together towards a common goal.

Fáilte Ireland's range of supports and services provides those involved, or considering becoming involved, in Irish tourism with a one-stop-shop to meet their business or professional needs. Working in partnership with the industry, Fáilte Ireland aims to meet the industry's needs, leading and supporting Irish tourism in its next phase of development.

Its priorities for 2006 onwards are to develop and support regional tourism; develop the business tourism sector; improve enterprise competitiveness; encourage innovation and investment in new and existing products; promote sustainable development and champion 'tourism sensitive' public policies.

Fáilte Ireland Marketing Services

To demonstrate the extensive level of services and rich data and information sources offered to the marketing researcher from any of the state bodies (and indeed government departments, professional associations and trade bodies, directories, EU, etc.), we will now look to Fáilte Ireland and the detailed facilities available to industry providers and interested professionals, by way of example.

Tourism Marketing Services

The Tourism Marketing Services area provides effective marketing support and a comprehensive range of cost-efficient promotional opportunities for Irish product providers, marketing groups, tour operators, handling agents and other tourism interests, as well as visitor services to the consumer.

It provides leadership and direction to co-operative marketing groups and also undertakes product and niche marketing initiatives, such as the Festivals & Cultural Events Initiative and the Sports Tourism Initiative. An initiative to support the marketing effort and capability of small and medium-sized operators (SME) is also in place to provide a business advisory service, encourage start-ups in new and innovative product and service areas and advise in the formulation of e-business and e-marketing strategies.

Irish Trade Promotions

The Irish trade promotions section aims to provide industry partners with key information that will help them to devise a successful marketing plan for their product and to advise them on useful platforms for promoting their product, both at home and overseas.

Markets Publicity

Every year Fáilte Ireland's publicity section welcomes over 1,000 journalists, photographers, TV and radio crews from all over the world to Ireland with the main objective of creating a positive image of the country in the media overseas. Working closely with Tourism Ireland, regional colleagues and the Irish Travel Trade Partners throughout the industry via the Media Assistance Programme, their aims are to achieve the following objectives:

- Target leading media in the markets and develop themes to interest them.
- Invite selected journalists to come and experience the Irish lifestyle as well as a selection of our tourism products.
- Create stimulating tailor-made itineraries to meet the needs of each visit in line with the overall strategy of seasonal, regional and high-yield development.
- Send press-release material on Ireland's tourism products and events to market offices for inclusion in regular bulletins sent to media contacts in the markets.

Product Marketing

This section is responsible for the marketing of Ireland's special-interest activity products, and for liaising with Irish trade in these sectors in regard to overseas marketing. The section is also responsible for two specific initiatives – the Sports Tourism Initiative and the Festivals & Cultural Events Initiative. Key objectives of this section are:

- To ensure a co-ordinated and effective approach to the marketing of key activity and special-interest product areas.
- To increase business from activity and special-interest products with special emphasis on regional spread, high yield and season extension.
- To support Irish product providers to be more effective in their marketing efforts.
- To set up good channels of communication between Fáilte Ireland, Tourism Ireland Ltd, the Regional Tourism Authorities and trade so as to ensure co-ordination and integration of marketing efforts.
- To continue to support co-operative marketing groups where their overseas marketing activities contribute to Fáilte Ireland's marketing strategy for each product area.

Business Tourism

The Business Tourism Section is a specialist unit within the Product Marketing Division of Fáilte Ireland which focuses on the marketing of conferences and incentive travel in partnership with the trade involved in these two important segments. The Business Tourism Section facilitates the trade through the following activities:

- Participation at overseas promotions.
- Production of promotional material.
- Facilitating site inspections and familiarisation visits by overseas incentive houses and conference organisers.
- Support to representatives of various sectors in making bids for international association meetings.

A Business Tourism Forum has been established to drive the overall strategic direction of business tourism in full consultation with the main sectoral interests. The group consists of experts in the business tourism sector and its main functions are:

- Advising Fáilte Ireland on plans and initiatives.
- Assisting with the implementation of marketing plans.
- Monitoring and reviewing progress in the sector.
- Acting as a communication channel between industry and Fáilte Ireland.

Festival Marketing in Ireland

This fund is primarily intended to assist festivals/cultural events with marketing activities, e.g. angling and walking festivals seeking marketing support. However, other elements of expenditure by festivals/events will be considered if they are to be of long-term benefit and/or raise the profile of the festival/event considerably, e.g. audience research, feasibility studies, certain programming and operational costs. The aim is to encourage a spread of visitors throughout the country.

Sports Tourism

The International Sports Tourism Initiative was introduced by the government in January 2000 to attract major international sporting events to Ireland with tourism potential, i.e. events that deliver significant overseas visitor numbers, significant global media coverage, appeal to our target markets and showcase the physical landscape and/or special-interest product.

The initiative is co-ordinated by Fáilte Ireland and support is given in the form of sponsorship towards events that meet the criteria of the initiative and deliver substantial tourism benefits to Ireland. The promotion of Ireland as a premier sports tourism destination has been an important part of Fáilte Ireland's tourism marketing strategy in recent years. By using event sponsorship as a marketing tool, the initiative provides Fáilte Ireland with an invaluable opportunity to communicate the general/activity holiday message through the global media coverage that major international events command.

E-Business

Fáilte Ireland offers a number of e-business services to the Irish Tourism Industry. Advice is given on business planning, marketing, revenue generation, new media and technology. An online marketing guide has also been produced, which gives advice and tips on how best to market products on the web.

Research is continuously carried out on current online trends and Fáilte Ireland interfaces with its partners in the European Travel Commission (ETC – www.etc-corporate.org) and the European Union (EU) to evaluate new developments on the Internet and in the new media field in general. Fáilte Ireland is also a member of the International Federation of IT in Tourism (IFITT).

Fáilte Ireland has a comprehensive online presence with approximately twenty websites. The corporate website (www.failteireland.ie) gives detailed information on all the activities of the organisation. The consumer website (www.ireland.ie) is a comprehensive website with information on all approved accommodation and the range of tourism products available throughout Ireland and it also gives a comprehensive list of special offers for home holidays. The organisation has also developed specific websites for all major products: golf, walking, language learning, etc.

Recent Tourism Ireland Publications

- Tourism Ireland Updates, March 2006, August 2005, January 2005
- New & Developing Markets Update, April 2006
- Tourism Ireland US Market Update
- Contact, February 2006
- Contact, November 2005 Edition
- Tourism Ireland Annual Reports, 2006, 2005, 2004

Fáilte Ireland Publications

- Domestic Tourism
- Agenda 2006 Reference Guide
- Developing Regional Tourism, 2006
- Special Interest Tourism Plans, 2005
- Tourism Facts, 2004
- Visitor Attractions
- Hotel Review Summary, 2005
- Visitor Attitudes Survey, 2004
- Ireland Tourism Satellite Account First Steps Project
- Tourism Research Scheme
- Tourism Facts, 2003
- Summary of Activities, 2003
- Regional Tourism Marketing Plans, 2003
- Tourism Product Marketing Plans

- Summary of Activities, 2004
- Product Marketing Plans, 2004
- Regional Tourism Marketing Plans, 2004

ITIC Publications

- How Tourism to Ireland is Changing – Regional Distribution, June 2005
- Investment in Overseas Marketing by the Irish Tourist Industry Confederation, September 2004

Irish Hotels Federation Publications

- IHF Marketing Plan, 2005/2006

Table 4.10 Irish tourism websites

Tourism Ireland	www.tourismireland.com
Fáilte Ireland	www.failteireland.ie
Regions of Ireland	
South East Regional Tourism	www.southeastireland.com This is the tourism site of the South East Regional Tourism Authority, which takes care of tourism development and marketing for the South East Region. This site includes special offers.
East Coast and Midlands Regional Tourism Authority	www.eastcoastmidlands.ie This is the tourism site of the East Coast and Midlands Regional Tourism Authority, which takes care of tourism development and marketing for the Midlands and East Coast. This site includes special offers.
North West Regional Tourism Authority	www.irelandnorthwest.ie This is the tourism site of North West Regional Tourism Authority, which takes care of tourism development and marketing for the North West Region. This site includes special offers.
Shannon Development	www.shannonregiontourism.ie This is the tourism site of Shannon Development, which takes care of tourism development and marketing for the Shannon Region.

Dublin Tourism	www.visitdublin.com This is the tourism site of Dublin Tourism, which takes care of tourism development and marketing for Dublin City. This site includes special offers.
Ireland West Regional Tourism Authority	www.irelandwest.ie This is the tourism site of Ireland West Regional Tourism Authority, which takes care of tourism development and marketing for the West of Ireland. This site includes special offers.
Northern Ireland Tourist Board	www.discovernorthernireland.com This is the official site of the Northern Ireland Tourist Board.
HERITAGE AND CULTURE	www.heritageireland.ie www.heritagetowns.com www.art.ie (Arts Council Events Information) www.museum.ie (National Museum) www.nch.ie (National Concert Hall)
SPORT	www.sportireland.ie www.gaa.ie (Gaelic Athletic Association – hurling and football) www.fai.ie (Football Association of Ireland) www.irfu.ie (Irish Rugby Football Union) www.iha.ie (Irish Horseracing Association) www.iwai.ie (Inland Waterways Association of Ireland)
OTHER SITES	
Golf in Ireland	www.golf.ireland.ie
Walking in Ireland	www.walking.ireland.ie
Angling in Ireland	www.angling.ireland.ie
Cycling in Ireland	www.cycling.ireland.ie
Water Based Activities in Ireland	www.waterbased.ireland.ie
Equestrian in Ireland	www.equestrian.ireland.ie
Heritage in Ireland	www.heritage.ireland.ie
Genealogy in Ireland	www.genealogy.ireland.ie
Festivals and Events in Ireland	www.festivals.ireland.ie
Learning English in Ireland	www.learnenglish.ireland.ie

Source: Colin Gilligan, Lecturer in Hospitality Operations, GMIT, 2007.

The Industrial Development Agency, Ireland (IDA) (www.idaireland.com)

The Industrial Development Agency was established by the Irish government to provide industrial development by attracting foreign investment into the country. The objective of the IDA is to continue to create the welcoming business environment, that has attracted over 1,050 overseas companies to set up in Ireland.

The agency has a network of thirteen international and ten regional centres in Ireland and promotes itself as a one-stop-shop for all aspects of Foreign Direct Investment (FDI) into Ireland. The IDA operates an extensive support and assistance programme to potential investors and primarily focuses on the technological, pharmaceutical, engineering and international traded services sectors.

Information provided by the IDA includes the following:

- Annual Reports — give detailed information on recent activities, regional performance, organisational resources, IDA accounts, output and exports, R & D, employment.
- Listing of manufacturing companies and financial services in each county — breakdown by county of manufacturing companies in the region (names, addresses, types of business, numbers employed, etc.).
- Listing of manufacturing companies classified by sector — as above but by industry.
- Overseas companies in Ireland — a listing of the grant-aided overseas firms in production in the Republic of Ireland.

Údarás na Gaeltachta (www.udaras.ie)

Údarás na Gaeltachta is a regional development agency which addresses the specific language, social and economic needs of the Gaeltacht and its community. It places a lot of emphasis on companies improving research and development capacity and strengthening their technical and management capabilities. The Gaeltacht comprises large parts of counties Donegal, Mayo, Galway and Kerry, all on the western seaboard, as well as smaller areas of counties Cork, Waterford and Meath.

An important aspect of An tÚdarás activities is the provision of support and assistance to Gaeltacht businesses in developing new markets, new technologies, new products and strategic relationships to increase profitability and enhance viability.

Shannon Development (www.shannon-dev.ie)

Set up in 1959 to promote Shannon International Airport in the post-jet era, Shannon Development is Ireland's only dedicated regional development company. The company's brief is to generate industry, tourism and regional development in the wider Shannon area, known as the Shannon Region. This covers an area of some 10,000 square kilometres spanning counties Clare, Limerick, North Tipperary, South Offaly and North Kerry, which collectively have a population of over 407,000 people. Shannon Development-assisted companies (Shannon Free Zone and indigenous enterprises throughout the Shannon Region) also made a substantial contribution to the region's economy – with employment at 19,739; sales of *c.* €4.4 billion; exports of *c.* €3.1 billion and economic expenditure of just under €2 billion.

The mission of Shannon Development is 'Pioneering Regional Development for the Knowledge Age', and over the past forty-five years the company has worked, singly and with many different partners from the statutory, community and private sectors, to develop the region to its full potential. Shannon Development's primary focus is to identify the critical needs or obstacles to development in the region, and to lead and encourage the identification and development of solutions. The company strongly communicates its position and plays a leadership role in relation to important regional development issues such as airport access, transport infrastructure and broadband connectivity. Key activities include:

- Developing and strengthening the indigenous industry sector in the Shannon Region, and building up a knowledge-age business culture through targeted supports for enterprise.
- Continuing to develop and manage the Shannon Free Zone as a world-class location for international investment in manufacturing and internationally traded services.
- Developing the Shannon Development Knowledge Network – a network of leading-edge technology business locations with direct linkages to third-level educational institutions. The network includes the National Technology Park in Limerick, Kerry Technology Park in Tralee, Tipperary Technology Park in Thurles, Birr Technology Centre in Offaly and Information Age Park Ennis in Clare.
- Developing new tourism marketing programmes and new tourism products in the Shannon Region, in conjunction with the industry, to proactively respond to the many challenges facing Irish tourism.
- Managing commercial tourism businesses, e.g. castle banquets and day-visitor attractions, through a wholly owned subsidiary company – Shannon Castle Banquets & Heritage.
- Leading and encouraging regional development at urban and rural levels to ensure economic inclusion and balanced spatial development.

Forfás (www.forfas.ie)

Forfás is the national board responsible for providing policy advice to government on enterprise, trade, science, technology and innovation in Ireland. Legal responsibility for the promotion and development of these sectors is vested by the State, through the department of Enterprise, Trade and Employment, in Forfás. Among Forfás's functions are:

- Research, analysis and policy advice on competitiveness and economic development, through the National Competitiveness Council and the Expert Group on Future Skills Needs.
- The promotion of scientific research and innovation in close association with Science Foundation Ireland and the Advisory Council for Science, Technology and Innovation (ACSTI). ACSTI has taken over responsibilities of the former Irish Council for Science, Technology and Innovation (ICSTI).
- Industrial policy development and coordination for state bodies such as IDA Ireland and Enterprise Ireland.

Forfás publishes a number of reports on issues such as international trade and investment reporting, data analysis of employment education and training in Ireland, benchmarking Ireland's broadband performance, and many more. Reports can be downloaded from their website at www.forfas.ie.

3. DIRECTORIES

Commercial directories provide profile data on companies, industries, manufacturers, organisations or individuals. They are always a good starting point in unfamiliar situations. They can be used to generate a list of company names, addresses and telephone numbers for promotional or research purposes; identify company personnel such as the finance or marketing director; to profile all manufacturers of a specific product; identify competitors; to locate companies, new outlets or new partners in a particular area.

Kompass Ireland

Kompass Ireland[6] is one of the most comprehensive sources of hard commercial information about 50,000 plus companies and industrial products in Ireland. It provides:

- Lists of manufacturers, distributors, finance companies and other commercial organisations.
- Detailed information about a great range of products, and where they can be sourced.
- Product information to source both potential customers and suppliers.

Kompass uses an internationally recognised classification and cross-referencing system designed for detailed searches using well-defined headings. You can search companies on:

- Company name.
- Geographical areas.
- Type of business (manufacturer, exporter, etc.).

- Employee number.
- Executive role/department.
- Industry sector.
- Product sector.
- Year company founded.
- Executive name.
- Top 1,000/2,000 companies.

Similar criteria are used to locate industrial products, from process engineering equipment to computer printers. Kompass also supplies a wide range of related services for sales, marketing and product sourcing.

It is compiled in association with the Irish Business and Employers Confederation (IBEC), and the Northern Ireland Chamber of Industry and Commerce. The aim of bodies such as IBEC is to promote the development of business in Ireland and to ensure a favourable economic and administrative environment, which will encourage investment and enterprise — economic growth — in Ireland. The Northern Ireland Chamber of Industry and Commerce has a similar function. These industrial bodies believe that a key factor that will help businesses become competitive is readily available access to information. It does this by providing the user with:

1. An alphabetical index of products and services.
2. An alphabetical index of companies.
3. Trade names, principles and agencies.

These profiles of Irish industry are derived from firms who supply:

1. Detailed company information, including company names, addresses, telephone and fax numbers, corporate logo, email and website, executives, banks, office hours, share capital, date of establishment, complete product range and number of employees for 18,600 of the top Irish companies.
2. Products and services information covering 54,000 products and services and 750,000 trade names. Kompass also publishes sectoral directories on Irish industry, acts as Irish representative for other national Kompass publications and provides online access to European Kompass databases.

Kompass is a worldwide network of companies specialising in business-to-business information databases of products and services. This lets the user quickly pinpoint a product company from the wealth of raw data available. Users can locate precisely the suppliers of the product or component needed. It is also possible to search for companies by name or geographical location. There are Kompass directories for 70 other countries worldwide. These range from directories covering important trading countries such as Japan, to EC countries such as Belgium, France and Germany. Such a global directory is important in the Europe of a single market.

Kompass data is published as a printed book and on CD-Rom. The electronic products can be used to print out mailing lists or transfer data to the user's computer. Kompass on Disk comprises 115,000-plus top Irish companies in a Windows database. Users can search for companies, suppliers and products using eight criteria (e.g. location, company size, product type, industry, executive title), build mailing lists and export data to their own databases.

Kompass also publishes directories of specific industrial sectors (food, construction, engineering, electronics, computers, chemicals and pharmaceuticals, etc.). Other directories include details of the top 1,000 and 2,000 firms, top finance and manufacturing firms. Products may be custom-designed for specific projects. Kompass will also help companies create their own computerised database using its information. Also available is a wide range of information on foreign countries and markets, compiled by the international Kompass network including 1.9 million companies in 70 countries, referenced by 54,000 products and services, keywords, 750,000 trade names and 3.5 million executive names.

Data is also accessible via the Internet. It can be searched by geographical area, by company size (number of employees), type of product and company classification (manufacturer/distributor). It is possible to generate customised mailing lists. A specialised database containing details of financial services companies is also available, as is a database containing data on the geographical location of businesses. Some information is available free of charge on their website (www.kompass.ie); other data can be obtained by purchasing a subscription.

IPA Administration Yearbook and Diary

The Institute of Public Administration (IPA) is the Irish national centre for development of best practice in public administration and public management. The IPA Yearbook & Diary was introduced over forty years ago to serve Irish businesses (40% public service and 60% private sector). It has become indispensable to people working in every facet of Irish life. Published in December each year, it contains data on the following areas:

- Legislature, executive and judiciary;
- Diplomatic representation and the civil service;
- North/South island of Ireland bodies;
- Defence forces;
- Local administration;
- Health organisations;
- Financial institutions;
- Major companies and co-operatives;
- Management consultants;
- Media & communications;
- Education;
- International Affairs;

- Social Administration;
- State-sponsored bodies;
- Trade and professional organisations;
- Social, cultural and political organisations.

The directory in this publication contains the official name, address, logo, telephone, fax numbers, email and web-site addresses of each organisation listed, as well as the following: a description of the organisation's activities; key personnel; senior to middle management levels; chairperson and chief executive's photographs.

Because this publication is so all-embracing, it is worthwhile spending some time looking through the contents pages, the different chapters and the index to get an idea of its scope.

Examples of sections likely to be of direct use to marketing people are those on communications — containing listings of all newspapers (both national and provincial), advertising agencies, market research companies, etc. — and statistics, which contains figures for agriculture, trade, industry, etc.

Examples of some, perhaps less obvious, uses of the directory are the ways it can be used to access sectoral data which leads us to the role of other types of yearbooks.

Other well-known directories useful to the marketing researcher are summarised below. Remember, many directories traditionally published in hardback form are available now as databases, and are being classified as databases. You can expect this trend to continue as the Internet deepens its impact upon secondary sources of data and desk research.

Table 4.11 Useful directories for the researcher

Directory	Description
Thom's Commercial Directory	This lists businesses in 157 towns in Ireland. Separate classified listings are available for businesses in Dublin, Cork, Limerick and Galway.
Macmillan Dictionary of Marketing and Advertising	This dictionary provides concise but informative definitions for people who are exposed to marketing 'jargon' and need a clear explanation of their meaning.
Kelly's Business Directory	This is a comprehensive guide to British Industry. It contains information on industrial, commercial and professional organisations in the UK. It can be used for checking names, addresses and telecommunication details and also for market research purposes.

Directory	Description
Directory of European Industrial and Trade Associations	The directory is designed to provide information on national industrial and trade associations (and, where appropriate, regional associations of significance); it covers all the countries of Europe except Great Britain and the Irish Republic, which are covered fully by the Directory of British Associations.
MAPS	MAPS are the official Media and Services directory of the Association of Advertisers in Ireland. The MAPS directory contains thousands of contacts in the media and Irish communication industry.

4. TRADE ASSOCIATIONS AND PROFESSIONAL BODIES

Bodies that are organised to represent interests of their members on a trade and professional basis are another important source of information. Such associations publish or hold detailed information on industry sales, growth patterns, trade members and the like. Special studies relevant to the trade are conducted.

Generally speaking, trade professionals and associations publish an annual report, a regular trade journal and/or *ad hoc* research reports. These can provide the researcher with useful statistical and industry data. Some of the more relevant associations used by marketing researchers are presented below to illustrate their use in desk research. For example, in the tourism area, professional bodies include the Irish Hotel Federation, the Irish Hotel and Catering Industry (IHCI), the Irish Country Holidays, the Restaurant Association, the Hotel Sales and Marketing Association (HSMA) and the Vintners Association, to name a few.

Chamber of Commerce

The Chamber of Commerce came into effect on 16 November 1791, 'for the purpose of acquiring and disseminating useful information on the important subjects of agriculture, commerce, science and other sectors'. The Chamber of Commerce and Industry, in its 215-year history, has always fostered and promoted business growth and development in the interest of economic progress for the city and the region. It is Ireland's biggest business network, with over 60 local chambers and 13,000 members.

Most people join the Chamber in order to make contact with other business people in the city and to actively participate in the life of the business community. Members see the Chamber as a means of promoting business-to-business trade within the area and together to promote the city as a location for business — whether it be tourism, manufacturing, services, retailing, education, or culture. Services provided to members and of possible use to the researcher, encompass the following:

- In becoming part of this strong, active, local community group, businesses achieve a certain credibility and recognition.
- The Chamber represents its members in matters such as rates and taxation through lobbying elected representatives and officials of the local authorities, state agencies and government or to the appropriate organisation on such matters.
- The Chamber is involved in the provision of information to individuals and groups through conferences and seminars, circulars to members, the European business centre, a trade reference library.
- The Chamber provides secretarial, fax and telex bureau services to both members and non-members.
- The Chamber is involved in promoting the source of goods and services locally.
- The Chamber establishes national and international links to keep towns in tune with developments and opportunities locally and worldwide.

The Marketing Institute of Ireland (www.mii.ie)

The Marketing Institute is the representative body for the marketing profession in Ireland. The Institute represents over 3,500 marketing professionals in Ireland and abroad. It is a national organisation with regional councils in Athlone, Cork, Dundalk, Galway, Limerick, Sligo, Tralee and Waterford, and a national secretariat based in Leopardstown, Co. Dublin. The Institute is non-profit making and all income generated is spent on developing member services and the Institute's education programme.

Publications include *MII News; The Marketing Review; Programme of Events; Yearbook and Diary*, occasional publications. Marketing Institute Business Services provides a Consultants Register; Code of Practice; international affiliation with ESOMAR; European Marketing Confederation; information service; professional development in marketing — seminars and courses; in-company training.

The most effective way to keep abreast of marketing change is by attending the specialist MII seminars of the Professional Development in Marketing programme. Presented by top-calibre national and international practitioners and academics, these seminars are designed for busy professionals who need to keep abreast of developments in both theory and practice. Other services include in-company training, certification and FÁS funding.

Checkout *Magazine (www.checkout.ie)*

Checkout Magazine provides information on the food trade in Ireland and is issued to food and associated manufacturers, suppliers and distributors, multiple outlets, wholesalers, cash and carrys, group and independent grocery stores.

The publishers of this magazine produce an annual *Checkout — Yearbook and Buyer's Guide.* Typical material from this is a comprehensive analysis of Ireland's major food and drink categories, critical forces shaping the future of European retailing, and detailed data on individual companies, listing such things as main products, brand names and relevant management contacts.

In addition to the monthly magazine *Checkout Ireland,* which has been in continuous publication for more than 40 years, Checkout also publish *The Checkout Ireland Yearbook and Buyer's Guide,* and *The 100 Top Brands in Ireland.* See www.checkout.ie.

The Marketing Society of Ireland (www.marketingsociety.ie)

The Marketing Society, based in Bray, Co. Wicklow, provides a forum to keep over 300 marketing professionals up to date with the latest and most innovative developments in marketing and market research. The society issues and defends guidelines for marketing research practitioners. It publishes a list of Irish research firms and also represents the interests of members to state and international authorities.

5. THE INTERNET AND DATABASES

The Internet has become a very important source of external secondary information for the marketing researcher, having significantly increased the quantity and accessibility of secondary data. The Internet provides volumes of useful and timely information, much of it free. Being a global phenomenon makes the Internet even more valuable as a source of secondary data as the researcher can access data from around the world about the home market or international markets. Burke notes that, in many cases, information about distant markets is easier to get online than by any other means.[7]

The primary advantage of Internet data is the speed at which the data is available. Data is readily accessible 24 hours a day, 7 days a week. However, data on the web is only of quality if it comes from original sources and is current.[8] A key benefit of conducting secondary research on the Internet is that much of the online information has been indexed and is searchable. Another advantage of the Internet is its ability to combine nearly all data sources into one information source.

The Internet, like all other sources of information, has its limitations. Even the best search engines catalogue only a fraction of available information. Online research can generate volumes of irrelevant information, especially if the user chooses the wrong search engine for a particular purpose, or does not use efficient search techniques. Another danger of using online secondary research is that the ease of information retrieval may distract users from focusing on the quality of the information. Anyone can publish on the Internet and users must be sceptical about the validity of online information unless it comes from a known or trusted source.[9]

Secondary data available can be broken down into two main areas: (1) material for which a subscription is required, and (2) material that is accessible free of charge. In relation to the former, a number of research organisations provide very comprehensive reports and analyses that can be downloaded on the Internet. It is also possible to access online databases. Databases are computer-stored issues of journal articles, newspapers, conference proceedings, trade statistics and other official publications on a wide range of topics. Databases can be online or offline. Most of the major databases are now accessible on the Internet, and it is possible to access up-to-date references and, in many cases, full text versions of articles and resources via the Internet. All libraries in third-level institutions in Ireland have access to these resources. Some of the more widely used databases are given in the table below.

Table 4.12 Databases useful to the marketing researcher

Database	Description	URL
ABI Inform	This database provides access to accounting, advertising, finance, economics, human resources, management and marketing information.	www.proquest.com
Blackwell Synergy	This is a multidisciplinary database covering areas such as agriculture, business, computer science,engineering, science, medicine and social science. Access to 850 of Blackwell Publishing's journals.	www.blackwell-synergy.com
Mintel	Publishes global market intelligence reports covering market sectors such as consumer goods, the clothing, finance and food retail industries and the technology sector.	www.mintel.com
Datamonitor	Datamonitor Market Research contains the full text of reports covering the UK, France, Italy, Germany, Spain, Europe, the US and the world. The material is written by a specialised team of industry experts who rely on data drawn from exclusively	www.datamonitor.com

Database	Description	URL
	commissioned Gallup surveys, consumer panels and in-depth trade interviews. Reports typically discuss products, the competitive environment, pricing, market share and other key issues affecting industries. Most records have tables containing valuable facts and figures on companies and products.	
Euromonitor	International Statistical Information and market analysis. Access information by country, company, consumer market/ lifestyle, etc.	www.euromonitor.com
Emerald	Emerald full text offers access to marketing, management, finance and industrial relations journals.	www.emeraldinsight. com
Dialog Data-Star	Dialog and Data-Star Service provides access to over 350 databases with worldwide coverage. The service provides an extremely comprehensive collection of business information, including news, industry analysis and market research.	www.datastarweb.com
Business Source Premier	Covering management, accounting, marketing, HR and finance. Business Source Premier contains 7,400 full-text articles, encompassing peer-reviewed journals, trade magazines and other business information sources, including EIU country reports.	www.epnet.com

Database	Description	URL
Fact Finder	Fact Finder is a database of Irish business information. It contains the full text of Irish Business Journals as well as abstracts of articles from the business pages of *The Irish Times, Irish Independent, Irish Examiner* and *The Sunday Business Post.*	www.factfinder.ie
Lexis Nexis Professional	A business, legal and news database covering international jurisdictions, the US, Europe, UK and Ireland. Business coverage includes industry news, company profiles, and country reports.	www.lexisnexis.com
Major Companies of Europe	This established seven box set provides essential data on 5,800 of Europe's largest companies, with 36,500 of Europe's named senior executives.	www.biz-lib.com
Market line	A business information database containing company, industry and country profiles. Data available includes key corporate information; SWOT analysis; business history and company, industry and country rankings.	http://dbic.data monitor.com/home/
Comtrade	The Comtrade database of the United Nations Statistics Division (UNSD) is by far the most comprehensive source of trade statistics as it covers over 110 reporting countries.	http://comtrade. un.org/

In addition to specialist research organisations, leading newspapers and journals also provide access to their archived material. Access to some material requires payment of a subscription fee, but others allow access to their archives free of charge.

Table 4.13 Newspapers (www.irishnewspaperarchives.com)

Name	URL
The Irish Times	www.ireland.com
The Economist	www.economist.com
The Wall Street Journal	www.wsjeurope.com
The Sunday Business Post	www.sbpost.ie
Irish Independent	www.unison.ie
Irish Examiner	www.examiner.ie

Other non-government organisation (NGO) sites that researchers might find useful are given in the table below.

Table 4.14 Useful marketing research websites

Name	URL
Business and Finance	www.businessandfinance.ie
FinFacts	www.finfacts.ie
Amarach	www.amarach.ie
Nua	www.nuasoft.ie
Media Live	www.medialive.ie
Brint	www.brint.com
Accenture	www.accenture.com
PricewaterhouseCoopers	www.pwcglobal.com

Search Engines

It is important to remember that each search engine gathers and collates resources according to the way in which the engines have been designed, and each system is different. This means that for each Internet search engine, the same query typed into the system may produce different results. Search engines are a great place to start your research. To maximize the value of a search engine, make your keywords as specific as possible or enter a phrase in quotes. Here are a few of the more popular engines.

Table 4.15 Popular search engines

Search Engine	Description	URL
Alta Vista	One of the most powerful search engines; particularly useful for complicated searches. Also offers a free translation service, a full-text index of newsgroup archives and a business and residential telephone directory.	www.altavista.com
Dogpile	Meta search engine searches using a number of search engines at the same time.	www.dogpile.com
Google	Google is the most popular search engine, indexing a huge number of web pages. It will bring you directly to the most popular websites.	www.google.com
Search Engine	**Description**	**URL**
Google Scholar	A new service aimed at the academic community. It searches publisher's websites for journal articles as well as providing links to library catalogues and other sites of academic interest.	www.scholar.google.com
Met Crawler	One of the best meta search engines, this one allows searching for an exact phrase and offers a single interface for nine search engines, including FAST, Ask Jeeves, Looksmart, Lycos and Overture.	www.metacrawler.com
Yahoo!	One of the largest and most popular Internet directories.	www.yahoo.com

Source: adapted from www.enterprise-ireland.com and *Guide to Literature Searching*, James Hardiman Library, NUI Galway 2006.

Searching the Internet for Secondary Sources of Information

Having decided to search your topic on the Internet, the next step is to associate your problem or topic through *keywords, key authors* or *key organisations*. Ask yourself the following questions:

— What keywords may be used to describe or associate with your topic?
— Who are the key authors writing in this field?
— What are the key organisations related to the topic?
— Which geographical regions are most important to your topic?

That is, consider what are likely to be the main words used to describe your problem. You must remember that the Internet is a multicultural environment, so there may be many ways of expressing your problem. Think of synonyms for your keywords and variations in spelling. Try to identify key authorities like research centres or authors writing in this field. Searching names of authors and organisations on the Internet can sometimes yield more valuable sources than keywords.

The next step in searching the Internet is to combine keywords and names of authors or authorities into a search strategy. You can combine search terms with the words 'and', 'or' or 'not'. If you think of it as a mathematical equation, the 'or' is like the plus sign, the 'not' is like a minus sign, and the 'and' is like the items when two sets are combined and you have results that are common to both sets.

Source: 'Reflective Internet Searching: An Action Research Model', Sylvia Lauretta Edwards and Christine Bruce, *The Learning Organisation*, Vol 9, No. 4, 2002.

Looking forward, the Internet, databases and search engines will continue to grow in importance to the researcher. *Beware,* however, as the Internet and databases can tend to return more *data* than *information* and there is a lot of useful data not published on the web.

6. EU AND EUROPEAN

Eurostat

Eurostat is the statistical office of the European Communities. It publishes official harmonised statistics on the European Union and the euro zone and offers a comparable, reliable and objective portrayal of a changing Europe. A vast range of data broken down by region and country of the enlarged European Union is available. Figures are published under the following headings:

- General statistics
- Economy and finance
- Population and social conditions
- Industry, trade and services
- Agriculture and fisheries
- External trade
- Transport
- Environment and energy
- Science and technology.

These figures are available for free on the Eurostat website, www.europa.eu.int/comm/eurostat/

(*Source:* Eurostat Mini Guide, 2006).

Eurostat Yearbook

In order to focus on the major questions concerning the development of the European Union, Eurostat provides a practical statistical guide — *Europe in Figures – Eurostat Yearbook*, containing essential, accurate and recent information on the current situation in Europe. This yearbook, which presents Europe in figures, offers an outline of the data provided by the statistical office of European Communities. The content of the yearbook includes:

- Statistics showing changes in society, the growth of the economy, the environmental and ecological picture, business activity and the development of individual sectors.
- Comparable data on the twenty-five member states, the euro zone, the candidate countries, major trade partners and a number of economic or geographic associations or areas.

It covers:

- Chapter 1: Statisticians for Europe
- Chapter 2: People in Europe
- Chapter 3: The economy
- Chapter 4: The environment
- Chapter 5: Science and technology
- Chapter 6: Sectors and enterprises
- Chapter 7: Agriculture, forestry and fisheries

Some examples of other publications by Eurostat include:

Eurostat — Basic Statistics of the European Union

This booklet compares the major aspects of all EU member states, other European countries, the USA, Canada, Japan and the CIS. The thirty-third edition contains, for the first time, data from Cestat, Central Europe Co-operation in Statistics, covering the Czech Republic, Slovakia, Poland and Hungary. Topics include: general statistics; economy and finance; population and social conditions; energy and industry, agriculture, forestry and fisheries; foreign trade; services and transport and the environment.

Eurostat — Data for Short-term Economic Analysis

This publication is designed to monitor the evolution of economic activity in the European Union, euro zone and member states. It presents monthly and quarterly macroeconomic data, followed by an economic classification of the indicators such as output, demand, prices, labour market, external transactions and monetary and financial markets.

Statistics on Science and Technology in Europe

This publication presents key data and indicators describing science and technology developments in Europe, and also compared with the rest of the world. It contains chapters on government appropriations or outlays for R&D expenditure, personnel, patents, high-tech trade, human resources in science and technology and on other indicators related to high-tech and knowledge-intensive sectors.

European Information Centres (EICs)

There are six European Information Centres (EICs) in Ireland. They were set up both in Ireland and throughout the European Union to improve the information flow to business sectors. They are based in and run by existing business organisations (mainly the Chamber of Commerce). There is a network of 270 centres in the Community. Access to information is freely available. Information at the centres comes under the following headings:

EU Legislation

Information is provided on directives, regulations, decisions, parliament reports, preparatory documents and opinions of EU committees.

EU Policy

This covers issues such as employment policy, social policy, competition policy, consumer policy, environment policy and tourism policy.

EU Programmes and Funding

The EIC can help with information on structural funds, community initiatives, R & D, exchange programmes, joint venture initiatives. (There is a system in place whereby Irish companies can search for joint venture partners through the network of EIC centres.)

National Information

A selection of documents is held in the EICs such as government publications, *CSO Statistics, Statutory Instruments* and *Irish Business Procedures*. Publications such as *PESP* and the *Culliton Report* are also available.

Europa

Europa (http://europa.eu.int) is the portal site of the European Union and provides up-to-date coverage of European Union affairs and essential information on European integration. Users can also consult all legislation currently in force or under discussion, access the web-sites of each of the EU institutions and find out about the policies administered by the European Union.

The information on Europa comes under six main headings:

- 'News' is aimed principally at journalists and other people professionally involved in the information industry. It is divided into two sections: Latest press releases, which are updated regularly, and an agenda of upcoming events.
- 'Activities' brings together information and links from all of the EU institutions and agencies to provide 'mini-portals' for thirty-two policy areas of the EU. Key sites from the European Parliament, Council of the EU and the European Commission are listed, along with links to other relevant EU institutions and agencies. Links are also provided to clear summaries of EU legislation.
- 'Institutions' provides a general introduction to each of the institutions and to European decision-making procedures. It also contains links to the institutions' home pages.
- 'The EU at a glance' is aimed at the general public and sets out to provide clear answers to key questions concerning such things as the objectives of the European Union, European citizens' rights, the history of the EU and travelling in Europe. It also contains maps of the EU member states and applicant countries.
- 'EU Documents' provides access to the conclusions of European Councils, the General Report on the activities of the European Union and the Bulletin of the European Union. Other documents, such as the Official Journal, the Treaties and documents on current legislation and legislation under preparation, may be obtained via EUR-Lex.
- 'Information sources' is a gateway to various databases, information services and official publications about the European Union. It also provides access to the latest statistics, the list of information relays in the European Union and practical information about recruitment opportunities and traineeships, as well as access maps to the European institutions.

Eurobarometer, Public Opinion in the EU

Eurobarometer public opinion surveys have been conducted on behalf of the Directorate-General for information, communication, culture and audio-visual of the European commission each spring and autumn since 1985. The Eurobarometer report includes:

- How Europeans felt about public life at the end of the millennium.
- People's expectations of the near future.
- Level of perceived knowledge about the EU.
- Level of awareness of current EU affairs.
- Public assessment of media coverage of EU offices.
- Support for the EU and its policies.
- Single currency, the euro and employment.
- Attitudes to enlargement and CAP.
- Attitudes towards the European Parliament.
- Attitudes towards people from outside the EU.
- Holiday destinations.

Organisation for Economic Co-operation and Development

OECD compiles data relating to Ireland, together with comparable figures for other countries. For example, 'Monthly Statistics of Foreign Trade', 'Energy Prices' and 'Financial Market Trade'. Irish firms exporting to other countries generally use this type of data.

7. SYNDICATED SERVICES

Some data is collected on a regular basis and sold by specialised firms on a subscription basis to manufacturers. Such data is known as syndicated data and is produced for the needs of a number of users. For example, confectionery manufacturers in Ireland buy industry data about product size, weight, price and promotions on a monthly basis to monitor competitive actions. Data supplied on a syndicated basis is generally about:

1. Product flows through wholesalers, known as wholesalers' audits.
2. Product flows through retailers, referred to as retail audits.
3. The effect of the marketing mix on the consumer, called panel data.
4. The number of people reading, listening or watching different media sources, labelled media data.

It is worth noting at this point that most researchers do not classify syndicated services as secondary data — however, given the small size of syndicated services in Ireland, relative to other European countries such as the UK, Germany, France and the USA, we present syndicated services under the heading of secondary data. There are many examples of syndicated sources. Four, of interest to the Irish marketing researcher, are as follows:

Euromonitor International (www.euromonitor.com)

Euromonitor International is a provider of global market intelligence, tracking international trends in both consumer and industrial markets. Following a standardised format for easy cross-country comparison, these studies provide an in-depth understanding of market structures, supply and demand trends, competition, levels of development and future potential. Euromonitor produces numerous reports on the Irish market. Examples include reports on household cleaning products, pet food, cosmetics and toiletries, alcoholic drinks and packaged food. They also produce European and international marketing forecasts, which predict market growth (over the period 2006–2016) and value data for over 330 consumer products, and track over 100 socio-economic and lifestyle indicators in countries across Europe (including Ireland).

Mintel

Mintel publishes over forty-five reports each month, covering a wide range of sectors and focusing on topical marketing issues. Divided between UK–specific, European and USA reports, Mintel reports analyse market sizes and trends, market segmentation, consumer attitudes and purchasing habits, as well as assessing the future of the market. By providing a comprehensive picture of the consumer, Mintel's reports provide thorough analyses of specialist sectors, breaking down often complex issues into easy-to-understand sections.

AC Nielsen

AC Nielsen Retail Measurement Services capture point-of-sale and causal information from all retail channels, highlighting incremental changes in market dynamics. Utilising both in-store scanning of universal product codes (UPCs) and store visits by professional auditors, AC Nielsen offers a complete portfolio of sample- and census-based information services[10].

AC Nielsen tracks measures including descriptive characteristics (e.g. flavour and size), sales volume, selling price, and observed promotion and merchandising execution, encompassing an organisation's own brands as well as competitive brands. This helps management gauge penetration among retailers, overall product performance, promotion effectiveness and more, supporting long-term strategic planning as well as tactical decision-making.

Maintaining a large-household consumer panel, AC Nielsen provides insights into consumer purchase behaviour across every outlet — from warehouse clubs to convenience stores, supermarkets to independent chemists and mass merchandisers to bookshops. Such consumer panel information helps organisations identify target audiences and quantify the impact of advertising and other promotional initiatives.

With panellists carefully selected and geographically dispersed, the AC Nielsen consumer panel is a demographically balanced representation of Ireland's population. Readable at national, regional, local-market and account levels, AC Nielsen represents an excellent source for understanding the link between product purchase/shopping behaviour and the varied consumer segments across the population. AC Nielsen covers the following industries: food; personal and household products; durables; services and commercial/industrial.

AC Nielsen also provide a virtual store on the Internet that provides a graphical means of locating relevant information. By clicking on departments and then categories, information can be accessed for millions of products. The web-site is located at http://acnielsen.com. Some sections of the virtual store include: dry grocery, alcoholic beverages, frozen foods, and health and beauty aids.

Joint National Readership Survey (JNRS)

This research is conducted and published by Lansdowne Market Research, twice a year. JNRS publications provide information on who reads what and also contain a 'Special Interest Group' section. They also provide some very relevant lifestyle questions. Topics covered in JNRS include: books; business decision involvement; central heating; clothing; confectionery; department/major store; drinks; farming; finance; food items; grocery shopping; holiday/short breaks; home improvements; home purchases; household items and products; leisure activities; lifestyle; motoring; pet ownership; property; sports and activities; sports wear and equipment; telecommunications; tobacco; toiletries; and transport. Media measured includes Irish national newspapers, magazines and cinema attendance.

The survey is undertaken on behalf of a consortium of Irish publishers, the Association of Advertising Agencies (IAPI) and Advertisers (AAI). It is the authoritative industry basis for buying and selling advertising space in Irish newspapers and magazines. Some of these topics include:

- *Expenditure*: This includes questions covering expenditure on products and services. The survey covers some 80 items purchased recently for the home and establishes how much people have spent on their purchases for the home in the past three years.
- *Leisure activities*: The JNRS questionnaire asks about a large number of leisure activities, covering everything from eating in fast-food restaurants to visiting ploughing championships. It identifies different levels of involvement, detailing weekly, monthly, three-monthly and less often for each activity. This section on leisure also includes book purchasing and reading. It also deals with involvement in sports, covering 38 different sports/activities, and collects information on the following levels of participation:
  - Play or do.
  - Watch on TV.

- Read in a newspaper.
- Play or watch as a spectator.

Purchasing of sportswear and sports equipment in the past year is also included in this section.

- *Motoring*: This section contains information on the makes of car motorists have bought in the past three years and the price ranges in which they buy their new or second-hand cars. The survey also provides information on car ownership — annual mileage, membership of motoring organisations and insurance coverage, the type of car people own (two- or four-door saloon, hatchback, etc.), as well as the engine size. The survey continues to look forward to identifying the types of car people plan to buy in the near future.
- *Wine*: This section monitors trends in the consumption of wine.

Other syndicated media data sources range from the Joint National Listenership Research (JNLR, undertaken by TNS/mrbi), to Joint National Outdoor Research. See www.medialive.ie for more examples in press, cinema, radio, TV and the Internet.

Marketing Research Uses

Syndicated data such as that outlined above provides the researcher with the ability to: track sales performance; monitor price changes; manage distribution; analyse promotion execution and impact; and evaluate new item success. It pinpoints opportunities and trends, enabling researchers and managers to identify and capture new markets and product niches. Such valuable data assists the researcher in determining *who* buys *what*, *how much* they buy and *where* they shop. Additionally, advanced analytical and forecasting tools, based upon the data, can allow the researcher to provide insights into marketplace activities. In summary, syndicated data is well suited to both qualitative and quantitative research.

8. GREY MATERIAL

There is a virtually endless array of books, leaflets, dissertations, newspapers and magazines that contain information relevant to marketing decisions. Grey material can be defined as 'that which is produced on all levels of government, academics, business and industry in print and electronic formats, but which is not controlled by commercial publishers'.[11] It is literature that is somewhere between black and white — material not (yet) formally published but already in discussion. A formal publication may follow later, but in many cases the research may not be made public at all. Nevertheless, when it is publicly available, grey material may contain comprehensive, concrete and up-to-date information that can be of use to the researcher.

The Golden Pages is the classic example of grey (or not so grey!) material. Other examples include papers or reports written to inform funding bodies about the results of research projects, to support grant applications, to inform rapidly a specific scientific community, or to present preliminary results at conferences or as dissertations. Such material is disseminated quickly, often to a limited number of people, and is often given descriptions such as research reports, technical reports, preprints, committee reports or working papers.

While the Internet can be a huge source of grey material, marketing researchers should not overlook material that may be available (only) in hard copy format. Grey material is to be found in all libraries, including of course the Central Library in the ILAC shopping centre in Dublin. This library has a specialised Business Information Centre, which provides a range of company and market information. The centre holds books, international records, journals, databases, newspaper cuttings, and has a collection of Irish company reports. For further information on this service see www.iol.ie/dublincitylibrary/business.htm.

Remember that there are numerous more sources of potential use to a researcher, so be prepared to develop your own list and update it on a regular basis.

SUMMARY

Data collection begins with secondary data. Secondary data is data collected by another person for another reason. It is the opposite of primary data. Secondary data tends to be inexpensive, easy to access but may not be accurate or timely.

The two major types of secondary data are internal and external. Internal data is already in existence within the firm. It is typified by accounts, customer profiles or sales reports. It may come in a form that lends itself to immediate use or it may need modification.

External data is data already in existence outside the firm. It encompasses government statistics (CSO), government information from the various departments, public and state bodies, trade associations and professional organisations, commercial directories, syndicated retail and media data, databases, the Internet, EU and miscellaneous sources.

The most important development in recent years has been the computerisation of information, via online databases and the Internet. The advent of the Internet has had a major impact on the area of external secondary data collection. A lot of valuable data can be collected free of charge. Many marketing research organisations and providers of business data and intelligence have made their resources available to subscribers on the web. Secondary data available on the web can be broken down into two areas: material for which a subscription is required, and material that is accessible free of charge.

Regardless of the source or type of secondary data pursued, the most important aspect of desk research is to be thorough, exhaustive and diligent. Remember, secondary data should always be completed before engaging in any primary research.

QUESTIONS

1. What is desk research?
2. What is the difference between primary and secondary data?
3. Secondary data has been called the 'first line of attack' for marketing researchers. Discuss this description.
4. What role do secondary sources of data play in the research process?
5. What criteria can be employed to judge the accuracy of secondary data?
6. What are some of the advantages and disadvantages of secondary data relative to primary data for a marketing research study?
7. Differentiate between internal and external secondary data. Which should be analysed first, and why?
8. How might internal data be helpful to the researcher?
9. What is meant by the term 'Online Database'? Describe six online databases that are of interest to the marketing researcher in Ireland.
10. How can the Internet be used to assist in the process of collecting secondary data?
11. What are the main secondary information sources available in the Republic of Ireland? Outline the different types and give examples of each.
12. What is meant by a 'syndicated source'?
13. What types of data are available from syndicated data sources?
14. What is a computerised database? What use has it regarding secondary data?
15. Why is it desirable to use multiple sources of secondary data?
16. Describe three different methods research suppliers can use to collect syndicated data. Which do you consider to be most reliable?
17. Explain what is meant by the term grey material, giving examples to illustrate your answer.

PROBLEMS AND ASSIGNMENTS

1. List some major sources of information for the following situations:
    (a) The marketing research manager of a national food chain has to prepare a comprehensive report on the fast-food industry.
    (b) Mr Murphy has several ideas for instant soda bread mixes and is considering entering this industry. He needs to find the necessary background information to assess its potential.
    (c) The current market size and profile for the Irish Alginate Market.
2. Select a company of interest to you and develop a competitive profile for that firm, indicating the source for each piece of data used.
3. Select an industry of your choice. Using secondary sources, obtain industry sales and the sales for the major firms in that industry for the past year. Estimate the

market shares for each major firm. From another source, obtain information on the market shares for these same firms. Do the two estimates agree?

4. List the various sources of published secondary data in Ireland released by the CSO within the past year. Use a library and the Internet to identify this information.

5. What secondary sources in Ireland might be sourced to find information on the following:
   (a) Information on tourist numbers for Waterford county for last year.
   (b) Information on the importation of a certain product to Ireland from Spain.
   (c) Information on a certain company in your county.
   (d) Information on demographic profiles of the Irish population.
   (e) The amount of expenditure on a certain product/service in the past year.

6. Obtain data on beer consumption in your county for the latest available year. Calculate the *per capita* consumption for this area and compare to that for the country as a whole. What accounts for the difference?

7. What would be the best source for the following data:
   (a) Birth rates in your county.
   (b) Attendance figures for Lansdowne Road Stadium last year.
   (c) Annual sales in the top three fast-food chains in Ireland.
   (d) Median weekly earnings of full-time, salaried workers for the last three years.
   (e) Trends in automobile ownership.
   (f) Brands of laptop computers recently introduced to the Irish market.

8. You are opening a new retail store that will sell personal computers and software. What secondary data are available in your area to aid you in deciding where to locate the store? Would the same data be relevant to someone opening a convenience copying centre?

9. Use the Internet to see if you can find information to answer the following questions:
   (a) What is today's weather like in New York?
   (b) Is there information about China and the demographics of its population?

10. Suppose you are doing a project for Aer Lingus. Identify, from secondary sources, the attributes of factors passengers consider when selecting an airline.

Case Study
Thornton Readymix*

John Thornton was the owner and Managing Director of Thornton Readymix, which, as its name implies, was a supplier of readymix concrete within a radius of about twenty miles from his base in the west of Ireland. He was the only supplier of readymix in the area and was largely shielded from competition by the rugged nature of the terrain, except at the fringes of his area where he faced some competition from suppliers in neighbouring districts.

Readymix concrete cannot be transported more than twenty miles economically, as the value of a load at €250/€350 could not sustain the cost of transport to and from the customer's site.

For some time, John had been contemplating entering the market for concrete blocks. He had good knowledge of the economics of block production and distribution, but was totally unsure of the size of the market. Clearly, he needed some estimate of the volumes he could expect to sell if he was to enter that market.

The Market for Concrete Products

Readymix concrete consisted of sand, aggregate (stone chips), cement and water. The ingredients, in defined quantities, depending on the strength of concrete required, were loaded from silos into a truck-mounted mixer. They were constantly mixed *en route* to their destination to ensure a uniform standard of product and to prevent premature setting of the concrete. Readymix was normally delivered and invoiced to the customer in cubic metres.

Concrete blocks could be seen as complementary products for several reasons. They used the same ingredients, albeit with different configurations. Customers for concrete were also likely to be customers for blocks. Concrete was used for foundations, floors and driveways, blocks for wall construction. While different types of blocks were available, the standard block used in construction in Thornton's local area was a solid block 18 inches by 9 inches by 4 inches. These were normally laid to create a double skin with a layer of insulation between the two sets of blocks.

There were several ways of producing blocks, which varied in accordance with the volume produced. Thornton knew that he would be at the lower end of the scale of quantity produced. This would mean using his existing silos and loading the ingredients into a block-making plant. He had purchased such a plant relatively cheaply and had laid out a large concrete flat surface area. Blocks were produced in the plant and laid out on the flat surface in rows to dry. When dry, they were stacked ready for delivery.

Thornton had done his sums on the proposed new project. He knew the price of blocks from phone calls to the nearest suppliers, both of whom were more than twenty miles away. The price for blocks, delivered to site, was €300 per thousand, excluding VAT. Thornton estimated that the new project needed a turnover of about €300,000 per annum to generate a reasonable return. At €250,000 turnover per annum, the project would break even.

The Problem

'The very man' said Thornton, as he spotted Dave McCarthy striding purposefully towards the bar in his local pub one evening. 'I saw your photo in the local paper recently, something to do with marketing, and I need an expert in marketing to solve a problem for me.'

'Yes,' replied McCarthy, 'for my sins, I am the new Regional Chairman of the Marketing Institute and we launched our new programme last week.'

'Right,' continued Thornton, 'my problem is simple. I have been looking at expanding into concrete blocks. I would need to sell about 750,000 blocks per year to break even and one million blocks to make a reasonable profit, but I have no idea of the size of the market for blocks in this area.'

McCarthy thought for a few moments. 'How much readymix do you sell in a year and is there any correlation between sales of readymix and blocks?'

'It varies,' said Thornton. In a normal year I would sell 5,000 cubic metres. However, if there is a large project such as the new pier in the harbour, the runway extension or the big new factory up on the industrial estate, sales can go as high as 10,000 cubic metres in a very good year. And no, there is no correlation, as far as I can see, between the sale of readymix and blocks. For example, we lay a lot of driveways where no blocks are involved and if we have to lay a heavy-duty factory floor, the volume of blocks would be small.'

'OK, so that is one theory shot down. Let us approach it from a different angle. What is the main use of blocks in this area?'

'That's easy,' replied Thornton. 'House construction would account for the bulk of the business.'

'How many blocks are used to build the typical house?' asked McCarthy.

'Around 4,000 is standard,' replied Thornton.

'And what about other uses?'

'House extensions, retail outlets, factories and other commercial premises would use most of the rest, and they are not major users. For example, that new factory extension which you built last year was about 10,000 sq. ft. wasn't it?'

'Yes,' said McCarthy, 'it is about 50 feet wide by 200 feet in length with a double skin of blocks 10 feet high. From 10 feet up it is metal cladded.'

'So that leaves you with two walls 200 feet by 10 feet and two walls 50 feet by 10 feet, both multiplied by two for the double skin. I am ignoring openings and internal walls which probably cancel each other out. Given that a block is 18 inches by 9 inches or 1.125 square feet, that suggests a total of about 9,000 blocks.'

'OK,' replied McCarthy. 'That seems reasonable. So, based on your experience, what proportion of blocks might be accounted for by house construction and what proportion by other uses?'

'I would say that the proportion is 3:1 in favour of house construction,' said Thornton, after a brief pause.

'OK, leave it with me and I will contact you in the morning. Now how about a pint, market research is thirsty work.'

The Answer?

The following morning Thornton received the following fax.

John — A phone call to the Central Statistics Office (CSO) produced the information that 1,047 houses were built in this county last year. That figure is 5% up on the previous year, having been steady at about 1,000 units built for the past several years. Your catchment area accounts for almost exactly 33% of the county's population, assuming you cannot sell blocks outside a twenty-mile radius. This is also based on CSO district population figures.

It seems to me reasonable to assume that the level of house building in this part of the country is, at least, as high as in the rest of the county. While you have no competitor manufacturing blocks in your catchment area, blocks are coming in mostly, I assume, from O'Reilly to the north and Greeley to the south, both about 30 miles away. I hope this information is of some help in reaching a decision.

Regards, Dave

Questions

1. Estimate the total market for blocks in Thornton's area.
2. What other factors should he take into account in deciding whether or not to enter the block manufacturing business?
3. What, in your view, is Thornton's best course of action?

*This case was written by Gerry Mortimer, Dublin Institute of Technology. It is intended to be used as a basis for class discussion rather than to illustrate either effective or ineffective handling of an administrative situation. The case is based on a real situation, though certain information has been disguised. © Gerry Mortimer, Dublin Institute of Technology.

Case Study
Kylemore Abbey*

Introduction

Kylemore Abbey is the only Irish abbey for the nuns of the Order of St. Benedict. Regarded as one of Ireland's most romantic buildings, Kylemore Abbey is nestled at the base of Duchruach Mountain (1,736 ft) on the northern shore of Lough Pollacappul, in the heart of the Connemara mountains. The Benedictine nuns purchased Kylemore Abbey in 1920. A classic mansion in an area of unsurpassed beauty, Kylemore Castle was built in 1868 by Mr Mitchell Henry, surgeon, politician and financier, as a gift for his wife, Margaret Vaughan. The castle's neo-gothic architecture displays all of the decorative features of a building of that period.

Today the abbey is the home of the Irish Benedictine nuns who devote themselves to the monastic life of prayer and work. The nuns have graciously opened the estate to the education and enjoyment of all who visit, developing excellent facilities as well as conserving the many historical features. They regard it as their pride and duty to preserve and cultivate the heritage entrusted to them, for all who visit, and for future generations.

Marketing an Abbey

Among her many other duties, Mother Abbess Magdalena FitzGibbon, OSB oversees Kylemore Abbey's marketing strategy. However, marketing an abbey and its associated enterprises is not an easy task and it needs to be managed with great care and consideration. The main purpose of the marketing strategy is to promote the trading or commercial aspects of the nuns' initiatives. However, Mother Abbess is mindful that the marketing strategy must also reflect the non-trading or spiritual aspects of the nuns' communal life. Mother Abbess's main objective is to find a way to manage successfully the marketing and branding for a diverse product portfolio, which includes the following:

- *Abbey Tour* – The Visitor Centre shows a video on the past and present life of Kylemore. Visitors are invited to tour the grounds, view the exhibitions in the abbey reception rooms, and visit the recently restored Gothic Church, which is a beautiful miniature cathedral. Entrance fee for the tour, which also includes the Walled Victorian Garden, is €11 per adult and €7 per person for pensioners, students and tour groups with more than ten people. The entrance fee for the Abbey Tour and the Walled Victorian Garden contributes substantially to sales turnover, accounting for 55% of the trading sector's turnover.
- *Walled Victorian Garden* – Mitchell Henry's six-acre walled garden was restored and opened to the public in 2000. The advent of the Great Gardens of Ireland Restoration Scheme, which availed of EU funds, made it feasible to restore the gardens to their original splendour. Kylemore Abbey's Victorian garden is one of the largest walled gardens in the country and the nuns are making it a botanical centre of excellence.
- *Craft/Gift Shops* – The main craft shop is located near the Abbey and the Visitor Centre. A smaller gift shop has recently opened on the grounds of the Walled Victorian Garden. Mother Abbess Magdalena and her team of buyers for the craft shops strive to offer a select range of unique, high-quality, handcrafted products as well as the Abbey's own range of pottery and home-made food products such as jams, jellies, chutney, garnishes, cakes, and puddings. The craft/gift shops account for 35% of the turnover for the trading sector.
- *Restaurant and Tearooms* – All the catering facilities within Kylemore Abbey serve home-cooked food and some of the produce comes from the Abbey's farm and garden. The nuns of Kylemore are known for their culinary expertise and take great care in preparing their meals and repast. They believe, according to the Rule of St. Benedict, that good food is God's gift to us, and the sharing of food creates community. The restaurant and tearooms' contribution to the trading sales turnover is 5%.
- *Pottery* – The pottery offers a unique opportunity for visitors to purchase a distinctive range of ceramic products in the studio. Kylemore pottery, crafted

on-site at the Abbey, is sold exclusively through the Abbey gift shops. The pottery accounts for 3% of the trading turnover.

- *Fishery* – Kylemore Abbey Fishery consists of the Kylemore, Middle and Castle Lakes, with five-and-a-half miles of the Dawros River that enters the sea at Ballynakill Bay. Some of the greatest assets of the fishery are the open panorama of the lakes, the variety of fishing, the spawning streams, and the stunning scenery. Fishing permits can be bought at the Visitor Centre. The fishery accounts for 2% of the trading turnover.

- *Nineteenth-Century Model Farm* – The nuns intend to recreate Mitchell Henry's farm and offer visitors a unique opportunity to experience a fully functioning nineteenth-century farm, demonstrating farming techniques typical of the period. The nuns will also restore the more unusual features that Mitchell Henry, a man of progressive Victorian ideas, employed in his agricultural and horticultural experiments. One such development was a multifunctional turbine, powered by water from Lough Tougher, which provided energy for an automated sawmill, a mechanical washer for vegetables and a mechanical grinder for meal and wheat. It is anticipated that restoration of the farm will be finished by 2010.

The main objectives for Kylemore Abbey's future growth are to:

- Expand market share of the existing product markets (e.g. Abbey Tour, Restaurants, Retail Craft Shops, Victorian Gardens, etc.)
- Explore innovations for specialised market niches (e.g. corporate incentive market, educational and demonstration holidays, spiritual retreats/renewal programmes, etc.)
- Develop new markets for new products (e.g. fully functioning nineteenth-century farm; book publications, cards, calendars, etc.)
- Capitalise further on a strong brand presence via a number of value-added products under the Kylemore Abbey brand (e.g. home-made salad dressings, sauces, breads, sweets, etc.)
- Broaden the customer base by developing the mail order and Internet business as a means to exploit potential markets in Europe and North America.

Heritage and Culture Tourism Sector

Kylemore Abbey has benefited from the spectacular natural amenities in which it is located. Indeed, Connemara and the Kylemore region have a long history of tourism, which was prompted by the natural beauty of the area. This tradition of tourism was a sound foundation on which the Benedictine nuns could build a successful enterprise.

Kylemore Abbey has evolved with the growth in tourism in Ireland (see Tables 4.16 and 4.17). In this respect, timing was excellent for ensuring growth for the estate. That is, as tourism increased in Ireland and in Connemara, it exploded in Kylemore Abbey. The Benedictine nuns, and in particular Mother Abbess Magdalena, have a strong vision for investing and reinvesting in the estate to facilitate the education and enjoyment of guests. In the achievement of this vision, their objectives were clear: to provide a high quality of service, produce, and presentation. Quality was identified as a priority and, in all aspects of the estate's activities, levels of quality were incrementally improved.

Kylemore Abbey receives about 190,000 visitors per annum (see Table 4.18). Nationally, Kylemore Abbey is ranked among the top twenty visitor attractions and is the number one fee-charging tourism attraction in the West of Ireland (see Table 4.22). Kylemore Abbey is considered to be a 'heritage' or a 'historical and cultural' tourism attraction. The Irish heritage tourism sector embraces a broad spectrum of tourism products, such as houses, castles, archaeological sites, museums, galleries, and intrepretive centres (see Tables 4.19 and 4.20). In addition to the environmental and scenic appeal of Ireland, Irish heritage and culture are important factors, which encourage people to visit. Ireland's heritage is a primary differentiating factor and an integral part of the country's overall appeal as a holiday destination. Heritage and culture are at the core of Irish tourism and have contributed significantly to its success. Indeed, 'heritage' serves as a main element in many of Fáilte Ireland's marketing communication messages.

The heritage segment is among the oldest and most mature segments within the tourism market. However, the tourism industry is increasingly competitive, as there has been a significant investment in adding to the number of heritage sites and improving facilities at existing sites. Currently, there are about 350 fee-charging tourist attractions open to the public, and many other notable sites (such as the National Gallery of Ireland) that do not levy charges, but are considered part of Ireland's 'heritage' product. Furthermore, there are new segments that are opening up within the tourism industry, such as 'health', 'aquatourism', and 'gardens'. With its Walled Victorian Garden, Kylemore Abbey also participates in the gardens sector. However, relative to the historical and cultural sector, the gardens sector is relatively small (see Table 4.21). Kylemore Abbey competes, not only with heritage and gardens attractions, but also with all other activities that visitors could pursue in their leisure time.

Kylemore Abbey's Customers

With respect to customers, it is believed visitors to Kylemore Abbey will plateau at around 200,000 visitors per annum. The nuns view this expected stabilisation in visitors as an opportunity to consolidate efforts and to ensure the high calibre of products and services is maintained. In this respect, the management team within Kylemore Abbey aim to invest further in staff training, customer service, quality and cultivating the 'right' customer by offering them the 'right' product.

Currently, 85% of Kylemore Abbey's visitors come from abroad. About half of these foreign visitors are from coaches touring the Connemara area and the other half are fly-drive customers from Shannon and Dublin airports who are driving around the West and Connemara. Typically, these are mature customers who seek a quality product and who appreciate Kylemore Abbey's beautiful natural environment, superb catering and shopping facilities. Essentially, these are customers who are seeking a 'unique experience'. Fáilte Ireland's *Visitor Attitudes Survey, 2004* noted that holiday makers identified the 'Irish people', 'scenery' and 'culture/history' as the top three factors distinguishing Ireland from other destinations. Holiday makers can readily experience these features when visiting Kylemore Abbey.

Marketing Kylemore Abbey

Mother Abbess Magdalena is aware that consumers are increasingly sophisticated and they want to know more about a product before they make a purchase or visit a tourism destination. Mother Abbess believes the main undertaking for Kylemore Abbey is to manage the marketing and branding for a diverse product portfolio. The qualities the Kylemore Abbey brand communicates most strongly are heritage, home-made, unique, high quality (i.e. ingredients and materials), Irish, traditional, reliable and thoughtful. The challenge is to develop this concept and communicate it to customers successfully, thereby enhancing the brand further, without diluting its value as an asset.

Questions

1. Given Kylemore Abbey's objectives, how may secondary sources be useful in developing a marketing and branding policy?
2. How may Fáilte Ireland's statistics on tourism be useful in understanding visitor trends to Ireland and to Kylemore Abbey?
3. Are there other secondary sources that should be sought in understanding Kylemore Abbey's customers and the heritage, culture and gardens tourism sectors?

* This case was prepared by Ann M. Torres, National University Ireland, Galway. It is intended to be used a basis for class discussion, rather than illustrating either effective or ineffective management practices. The case is based on a real situation, though some information has been disguised. The author wishes to thank Mother Abbess Magdalena FitzGibbon, OSB for her kind permission to use the material in this case.

Fáilte Ireland Tourism Facts & Figures

Table 4.16 Visitors to Ireland 1995–2004 ('000s)

Country	1995	1996	1997	1998	1999	2000	2001	2002	2003	2004
Britain	2,344	2,590	2,850	3,199	3,430	3,428	3,340	3,452	3,553	3,526
Mainland Europe	1,059	1,177	1,168	1,255	1,321	1,436	1,336	1,378	1,484	1,582
North America	660	729	777	858	950	1,056	903	844	892	956
Rest of World	168	187	213	221	243	261	261	245	249	319
Total Overseas Visitors	**4,231**	**4,682**	**5,007**	**5,534**	**5,943**	**6,181**	**5,840**	**5,919**	**6,178**	**6,384**
Northern Ireland	587	607	580	530	460	465	513	557	586	598
Out-of-State	**4,818**	**5,289**	**5,587**	**6,064**	**6,403**	**6,646**	**6,353**	**6,476**	**6,764**	**6,982**
Domestic Tourism	6,924	6,170	6,850	6,934	7,285	5,478	6,307	6,452	6,657	7,001

Source: Bord Fáilte, Facts 2000: Tourism Facts (July 2001); Bord Fáilte Statistics Dept. (May 2002) and Fáilte Ireland: Tourism Facts 2004.

Table 4.17 Visitors to the West Region 1995–2004 ('000s)

Country	1995	1996	1997	1998	1999	2000	2001	2002	2003	2004
Britain	310	347	378	358	427	427	437	442	372	409
Mainland Europe	353	411	386	353	382	431	381	394	380	393
North America	235	288	293	299	339	366	338	292	348	353
Rest of World	54	52	77	61	74	86	64	62	59	95
Total Overseas Visitors	**952**	**1,098**	**1,134**	**1,071**	**1,222**	**1,310**	**1,220**	**1,190**	**1,159**	**1,250**
Domestic Tourism	1,331	1,090	1,073	1,323	1,257	944	1,171	1,144	1,249	1,251
Northern Ireland	84	87	87	73	77	44	70	61	82	43
Total Tourists	**2,367**	**2,275**	**2,294**	**2,467**	**2,556**	**2,298**	**2,461**	**2,395**	**2,490**	**2,544**

Source: Bord Fáilte, Facts 2000: Tourism Facts (July 2001) and Bord Fáilte Statistics Dept. (May 2002) and Ireland West Tourism: Tourism Facts 2004.

Table 4.18 Total Visitors to Kylemore Abbey 1995–2004

1995	1996	1997	1998	1999	2000	2001	2002	2003	2004
155,672	189,716	165,873	185,834	194,671	190,542	186,452	188,777	189,050	190,000

Source: Bord Fáilte, Facts 2000: Tourism Facts (July 2001), Kylemore Abbey 2002 and Fáilte Ireland: Tourism Facts 2004 and Kylemore Abbey 2005.

Table 4.19 Visitors to Irish Historical & Cultural Tourism Products 1995–2004 ('000s)

Country	1995	1996	1997	1998	1999	2000	2001	2002	2003	2004
Britain	530	549	566	595	558	886	788	684	709	805
Mainland Europe	604	619	568	568	586	647	583	546	591	733
North America	409	464	465	505	540	576	587	456	522	658
Other Areas	113	106	112	122	118	118	149	102	110	171
Total Heritage & Culture Enthusiasts	**1,656**	**1,738**	**1,711**	**1,790**	**1,802**	**2,227**	**2,107**	**1,788**	**1,932**	**2,367**

Source: Bord Fáilte, Facts 2000: Tourism Facts (July 2001) and Fáilte Ireland: Tourism Facts 2004.

Table 4.20 Visitors to Irish Historical & Cultural Tourism Products by Type of Tourism Attraction for 2004 ('000s)

Country	Houses & Castles	Monuments	Museums & Art Galleries	Heritage & Interpretive Centres
Britain	438	315	329	303
Mainland Europe	537	439	381	246
North America	582	483	299	336
Other Areas	130	109	105	85
Total Heritage & Culture Enthusiasts	**1,687**	**1,346**	**1,114**	**970**

Source: Bord Fáilte, Facts 2000: Tourism Facts (July 2001) and Fáilte Ireland: Tourism Facts 2004.

Table 4.21 Visitors to Gardens Tourism Products 1995–2004 ('000s)

Country	1995	1996	1997	1998	1999	2000	2001	2002	2003	2004
Britain	187	183	158	186	168	227	149	120	101	121
Mainland Europe	243	281	210	236	247	251	155	150	160	199
North America	133	174	133	162	176	147	132	77	98	139
Other Areas	42	39	46	50	47	32	32	29	24	42
Total Gardens Enthusiasts	**605**	**677**	**547**	**634**	**638**	**657**	**468**	**376**	**383**	**501**

Source: Bord Fáilte, Facts 2000: Tourism Facts (July 2001) and Fáilte Ireland: Tourism Facts 2004.

Table 4.22 Top Attractions with Over 150,000 Visitors for 2003

Rank and Name	Region	No. in 2003
1. Knock Shrine Pilgrimage Centre*	Ireland West	1,500,000
2. Dublin Zoo	Dublin	772,332
3. Guinness Storehouse	Dublin	738,000
4. The National Gallery of Ireland*	Dublin	706,000
5. Cliffs of Moher Visitor Centre*	Shannon	650,000
6. Book of Kells	Dublin	467,513
7. Irish Museum of Modern Art*	Dublin	309,000
8. Bunratty Castle & Folk Park	Shannon	307,145
9. Waterford Crystal Visitor Centre	South East	303,000
10. Fota Wildlife Park	South West	301,313
11. St. Patrick's Cathedral	Dublin	275,922
12. Blarney Castle	South West	228,552
13. National Museum of Archaeology and History*	Dublin	260,000
14. Rock of Cashel	South East	245,316
15. Brú na Boinne Visitor Centre	Midlands East	216,957
16. Powerscourt Gardens	Midlands East	209,904
17. Aillwee Cave	Shannon	200,000
18. Muckross House, Gardens and Traditional Farms	South West	195,882
19. Dublin Castle	Dublin	190,000
20. Kylemore Abbey Ireland	West	189,050
21. Kilkenny Castle	South East	184,904
22. Clonmacnoise	Mid West	161,830
23. Kilmainham Gaol	Dublin	153,883

*not fee-charging

NOTE: Kylemore Abbey is ranked as No. 20 among visitor attractions and No. 15 among fee-charging visitor attractions in Ireland.

Source: Fáilte Ireland: Tourism Facts 2003, Fáilte Ireland Statistics Dept. 2004 and Kylemore Abbey 2004.

Case Study
The Kenny Gallery*

Introduction

Tom Kenny recognises that, among the many legacies his parents instilled, the phrase 'to associate with excellence' has a special resonance. In 'All Things Irish' (*Biblio,* July 1998), P. Dininny notes that the Kenny family firmly believe 'the work of Irish writers and painters are as [excellent] as can be found anywhere.' The Kenny family are entrepreneurial, curious and keen to take a risk on fresh ideas. Kenny's is a successful enterprise, experiencing cumulative but substantial growth over its sixty-six years.

The Kenny Gallery is the longest-running gallery under the same name and management. In addition to its permanent exhibition, the gallery organises over fifteen solo exhibitions a year, and hence Kenny's is frequently mentioned in the Irish media. Kenny's pursues its own path and Tom Kenny, Art Gallery Director, has sought to develop a different kind of gallery, thereby allowing people to have a relaxed, enjoyable gallery experience, rather than the stuffy, staid experience typically expected of galleries and museums.

Company Background

Maureen and Desmond Kenny opened their one-room bookshop, Kenny's, in 1940. Since then, Kenny's has evolved into more than a bookshop, encompassing the:

- *Online Bookshop* – which specialises in new and second-hand books of Irish interest, but also offers a wide selection of antiquarian books, maps and prints. Kenny's also works with libraries, booksellers, and collectors in Ireland, Europe, North America and Asia. In January 2006, Kenny's closed its bricks-and-mortar store in favour of its online operations.
- *Book Club* – a service offered to Kenny's 1,500 book club members in over forty-four countries. Every three or four months, Des Kenny and his nephew Tomás Kenny handpick a selection of books suited to each member's interests and budget. Books are sent to a member's address on approval and may be returned if not required.
- *Book Bindery* – according to *The Art of Leather Bookbinding* (Kenny's Press Pack), The Kenny Book Bindery has the specialised expertise required to 're-cover an old volume, fine bind special editions, or prepare a presentation book.' 'Gerry [Kenny] continues the craft of leather binding books by hand, in tandem with using modern methods for binding paperbacks, thesis and ring binders.'
- *Art Gallery* — established in 1968 in the living room of the Kenny family home in Salthill, Galway. The Kenny Gallery was the first architect-built commercial gallery in the West of Ireland. Kenny's aim was to promote Irish artists by showcasing and exhibiting their work in Ireland and abroad. The Kenny Gallery

has recently expanded its operations into the spaces once occupied by the retail bookshop. Consequently, the gallery has over 7,000 sq ft for its exhibition space and is now the largest commercial gallery in Ireland.

Strategic Vision and Kenny's Brand

Although Kenny's has evolved over the years, their core values remain relatively constant, namely, to be associated with excellence; pursue great, unique and fresh products; explore new ideas, even madcap ones, before dismissing them; and continuously create an audience, even if it is on a one-to-one basis. The strategic vision for The Kenny Gallery should be considered in the context of Kenny's core business, which concentrates on the sale and promotion of books with an Irish interest and art produced primarily by Irish artists.

The main objectives for The Kenny Gallery are to:

- Expand the customer base within Ireland and abroad.
- Explore innovations (e.g. Internet, direct marketing) for pre-selling and promoting to individual and corporate clients.
- Develop further the tailored services (e.g. consultancy, collection management, valuation, finance) offered to individual and corporate clients.
- Capitalise further on the strong presence afforded by the Kenny's brand.

Any strategies implemented on behalf of The Kenny Gallery must take into consideration the Kenny's brand. The qualities the Kenny's brand communicates most strongly are Irish, personal, unique, traditional, high quality, excellence, reliable, progressive, and thoughtful. The corporate identity for Kenny's is being redesigned and the new identity aims to reinforce these existing brand values.

Ireland's Cultural Industry

In an article in the *Irish Banking Review* ('Economic Contribution of the Cultural Sector: Some Policy Issues, Summer 2001), J. O'Hagan notes that the cultural sector in Ireland has experienced extraordinary success over the last decade. The notion of 'cultural industries' was introduced in the 1980s, after a number of studies were conducted in the US and the UK on the economic impact of arts activity. Cultural industries include five sectors:

- *Performing Arts:* theatre, opera, dance, live and recorded music;
- *Media:* film, television, video, animation, radio production and broadcasting, literature and book publishing;
- *Combined Arts:* arts festivals and art centres;
- *Visual Arts and Design:* visual arts, illustration, photography, art galleries, applied design, and craft;
- *Heritage and Libraries:* museums, heritage centres, and libraries.

In 1993 the EU realised the increasing economic importance of cultural industries and funded a pan-European pilot study to collate employment data within the sector. In 1994 a follow-on study from the EU pilot was commissioned by Temple Bar Properties and overseen by various State bodies, including the Arts Council and the then Department of Arts, Culture and the Gaeltacht. Coopers & Lybrand, now known as PricewaterhouseCoopers, conducted the study with the aim of exploring the employment and economic significance of the cultural industries in Ireland (*The Employment and Economic Significance of the Cultural Industries in Ireland*, Coopers & Lybrand Corporate Finance, 1994). Although this empirical study was the first of its kind in Ireland, J. O'Hagan notes that 'it remains the most up-to-date, reliable source of data on employment in the sector.' The study's key findings with respect to art galleries are as follows:

- Ireland's cultural industries had a gross aggregate value of €560 million (£441 million) and a minimum export value of €151 million (£119 million). Art galleries accounted for 2% of the aggregate value (The Arts Council (1994), *The Arts Plan 1995–1997*).
- The total level of employment within the cultural industries was estimated at 21,500 (i.e. in terms of full-time equivalents) and accounted for 1.9% of total employment in Ireland. Of the 21,500 employed in the cultural industries, 1% were employed in art galleries (J. Durkan, *The Economics of the Arts in Ireland* (1994)).

Another study conducted by the Policy Studies Institute in the UK in 2000 (S. Selwood (ed), *The Cultural Sector in the UK: Profile and Policy Issues* (2001) has important implications for Ireland 'since the level of employment in the sector, relative to aggregate employment, and the structure and nature of employment are very similar in Ireland and Britain.' Of particular interest was that 2.4% of total employment in Britain was either in a cultural industry and/or cultural occupation. 'This [level of employment] came to a total of 647,000 jobs in Britain and on a pro-rata basis to 40,000 jobs in Ireland.' (J. O'Hagan, *Irish Banking Review* (2001)) By assuming that the relationship between employment levels and gross revenue remained the same as in 1994, this implies that Ireland's cultural industries grew to achieve a gross value of just over €1 billion in 2000.

In 2005 the total art sales in Ireland were conservatively estimated in 'The Irish Art Market in 2006' (*The Investor*, vol 4, no. 2, March 2006) at €50 million. 'Although the breakdown of dealer versus auction sales in Ireland is not known, as dealers do not publicise their sales data, the international breakdown has been estimated at 50:50.' The Irish art market did exceptionally well in 2005. Adam's, DeVere's, and Whyte's, the three largest Irish auction houses, sold over 3,000 works of art. The average price for art bought at auction was €7,150, with a top price of €820,000. The current strength of the Irish art market is partly attributed to the recent interest displayed by 'pure investors – who are cost-conscious, savvy and forward thinking.'

Marketing the Arts

Although art, in its broadest sense, may be considered a product, it poses distinctive challenges in the realm of marketing. Art possesses intangible, unique qualities that are difficult to emulate or replicate. Moreover, a piece of art is inextricably linked to the creator, and, in this sense, the artist's name becomes the product brand. Thus, the personality of the artist as well as the qualities of the medium (e.g. sculpture, oil, watercolour, ceramics), form the basis on which brand values may be developed. Some believe the marketing of artists and their creations is built on the emotional and/or spiritual relationship forged between an artist and a client, which is often facilitated by an intermediary, such as a gallery.

Even though the principles of marketing may still apply to art, the implementation of the marketing process requires heightened awareness of how art differs from traditional products. Art and commerce are not always easy companions. For example, it is not always suitable to market only popular products, or what the market demands now. Many who work in the arts believe an important feature of the arts is introducing and persuading the market to what it may want in the future. Another consideration relates to the extent to which it is appropriate to exploit art for commercial purposes. Some believe that in the drive to popularise art, something of the original experience, as intended by the artist, is lost. Finally, there is the issue of balancing the pursuit for new audiences with cultivating existing ones.

Marketing at Kenny's

The Kenny Gallery showcases contemporary Irish art and has pieces from over 280 artists, ranging in price from €50 to €500,000. In an interview with Tom Kenny, Art Gallery Director of Kenny's, in April 2003, he said, 'The works of Jack Yeats, Paul Henry, Sean Keating, George Campbell, Louis Le Brocquy, Andy Warhol and many others have gone through the doors of Kenny's.'

The principal avenues The Kenny Gallery uses to promote are colour brochures, magazine spreads, colour posters, web site (www.kennys.ie), direct marketing, exhibitions, personal selling, word-of-mouth and publicity. With respect to publicity, Kenny's has a long tradition of using public relations to promote their business. Press releases about current and forthcoming exhibitions are sent to newspapers and radio stations in Galway, and also to those located in the artist's hometown and/or current residence. Hence, the publicity generated from press releases has a wider, more national scope.

The Kenny Gallery organises over 15 one-person exhibitions each year, including retrospectives of established artists. For example, Kenneth Webb has held numerous exhibitions at Kenny's and, in 2003, he celebrated the fiftieth anniversary of his collaboration with The Kenny Gallery. In August of 2006, The Kenny Gallery celebrated Kenneth Webb's eightieth birthday with a special exhibition. Kenneth Webb believes that, in addition to providing a forum to sell his work, Tom Kenny and his staff have been invaluable in offering the emotional support and enthusiasm vital to building an artist's confidence and reputation. However, Tom believes with 'a great product [i.e. an artist and their work], genuine enthusiasm flows naturally, and essentially, that kind of sincerity can't be faked.' He also believes that 'exhibitions are not hard-sell occasions; they're a social event, a party, to celebrate an artist.'

Tom Kenny strongly advocates variety in exhibitions as being essential to drawing customers into the gallery on a continual basis. Hence, the discovery of new artists for exhibitions is pursued earnestly. On occasion, there are group exhibitions on selected themes, such as: *Hung, Drawn and Quoted – An Exhibition of Literary Cartoons, Cleití Agus Clúmh – Images of Irish Birds, Women Artists of Ireland* and *The Art of Hurling*. With respect to *The Art of Hurling*, Tom secured sponsorship for the exhibition's colour catalogue and posters from Guinness, who, coincidently, are also sponsors of the GAA's All-Ireland Hurling Championship. The catalogues and posters were a success not only for Kenny's, but also for Guinness, and a number of posters were given to their sales representatives to distribute to publican clients. Consequently, *The Art of Hurling* exhibition poster is hung in numerous 'hurling pubs' throughout the country and abroad. Tom views exhibition catalogues and posters as additional exposure for The Kenny Gallery, and more importantly, they offer exposure with a long life. For Tom, marketing 'is about creating an audience all the time, and not just through the media.'

Exhibitions are a significant opportunity for sales (38% of sales), and consequently, many of the gallery's marketing efforts, such as press releases, catalogues and posters, revolve around them. In addition to exhibitions, other avenues for sales are the shop (50%), the Internet (7%) and corporate clients (5%). Overall, personal selling is an important component to the gallery's promotional mix. Tom characterises The Kenny Gallery's selling style as low-key, unobtrusive, relaxed, friendly, personal, knowledgeable, helpful and honest. It is definitely not a hard-sell approach. People are encouraged to wander around at their own pace, and are never rushed. Consciously, the gallery staff members do not impose their tastes on customers, and encourage indecisive clients to take pieces on a three-week approval. According to Karen Golden, Art Gallery Manager, their philosophy is that 'people need to see how a piece will look in their home or office, and whether they'll love living with it for a long time.'

Gallery Customers

The majority of the gallery's sales are to individuals (95% of sales). Approximately 60% of the sales are to customers who reside in the West of Ireland, an additional

10% from Irish customers who reside outside the West of Ireland, and the remaining 30% are to international customers. Therefore, the typical gallery customer is an individual who resides in the West of Ireland, has a high level of disposable income, and is between 35 and 60 years of age.

Tom and his staff have noticed the profile of gallery customers is changing. Karen Golden notes the increase in the number of younger people who are buying art and paying for it over a period of time. 'Apparently, it's becoming more hip to buy art.' In this respect, the peak age groups for buying art are 25 to 35 and 45 to 60 years of age. Tom and his staff believe that the ten years between these age groups are when many people are busy with children and families and other purchases take precedence over art. Interestingly, gender is not a significant characteristic in profiling customer groups. While there is a slightly higher representation of women purchasing art, men are progressively more interested in acquiring art products. Although a sizeable proportion of sales have always been attributed to tourists, foreign customers are on the rise, primarily due to Kenny's Internet presence.

Many of Kenny's corporate clients (5% of gallery sales), avail of consultation services for advice on creating an artistic layout to suit their business environment. A member of Kenny's consultation team goes to the client's building, photographs it, and develops a theme to match the client's vision and budget. Moreover, Kenny's advise on lighting and arrangement to display the client's collection to its best advantage. Finally, as part of the package, Kenny's hangs the artwork. Kenny's advice and proposals are offered to both corporate and individual clients free of charge. As Karen Golden notes, 'This kind of personalised service always pays dividends.'

Gallery Competitors

If one were to consult the *Golden Pages*, there are over 150 art galleries listed in the Republic of Ireland alone. However, some of these galleries are museums (about 10%) and a sizeable proportion (more than 25%) comprises craft shops selling pieces of art as part of their retail stock. The Arts Council produced a guide listing exhibition space in over 250 venues, including art centres, arts festivals, art schools, libraries, colleges, and universities, many of which do not sell the art they exhibit. Additionally, there are hundreds of hotels, restaurants, pubs and businesses that display and sometimes sell the work of local artists.

Kenny's most direct competitors are those commercial galleries that operate on a professional, full-time basis, and develop exhibition programmes over the course of the year. These direct competitors are twenty to forty in number and are scattered throughout the country, in the main cities (e.g. Dublin, Belfast, and Cork) and larger towns (e.g. Sligo, Dingle, Castlebar and Macroom). However, galleries, like people, have distinct personalities, which are largely influenced by their location, the gallery managers, and the type (i.e. medium – oil, ceramics, textiles) and style (e.g. modern, traditional) of art they sell. Kenny's has always pursued its own path and The Kenny Gallery is no different. Kenny's is aware of competition and works especially hard to distinguish itself from competitors, by exploiting Kenny's assets (e.g. brand and reputation) and competencies (e.g. its knowledge, service, variety, and stable of artists).

Web Innovation

Although Kenny's has accumulated a lot of experience over sixty-six years, the opportunity to exploit new avenues for business are proactively sought. The Internet is one avenue Kenny's has implemented to their advantage. Kenny's has received numerous awards for its innovative use of web technology. In 1998, the European Commission selected their web site as the best example of innovative use of multimedia and the Internet by an SME. In 2001, Irish DHL awarded Kenny's the *Exporter of the Year*, largely due to its use of e-commerce. In 2004, Kenny's won the Marketing Institute West Region Award for Marketing Excellence.

'Kenny's established a web presence [www.kennys.ie] in October 1994 and, according to web folklore, was the second bookshop in the world to go online; the first was a Californian based sci-fi bookshop,' which has gone out of business (W. Golden, *Kenny's Bookshop and Art Galleries, Ireland* (2002), Working Paper, Dept of Accountancy and Finance, NUIG). Hence, Kenny's is the bookstore with the longest established Internet presence. Ireland on Line (IoL), an Internet service provider, offered to develop a web site for Kenny's as a pilot project. From IoL's perspective, Kenny's well-established international reputation, and its exciting database of 30,000 catalogued books, lent itself to serve as a model to demonstrate the Internet's commercial potential to other firms. From the beginning, the web site attracted visitors, generated enquiries, and consequently prompted Kenny's to invest further in the web site. From 1998, all art exhibitions were showcased and catalogued on the web site. As Tom Kenny, Art Gallery Director, noted:

> We knew we had made progress on this objective when, in early 2001, a lady rang from the west coast of the United States and opened her conversation with, "I have just spent two days getting lost in your web pages", and followed this up with an order for two pieces of original Irish art that were displayed on the website. (W. Golden, *Kenny's Bookshop and Art Galleries, Ireland* (2002), Working Paper, Dept of Accountancy and Finance, NUIG)

The web site has provided the art gallery with an additional avenue through which to promote new exhibitions and Kenny's existing inventory of visual art. 'Initially, the pages generated little in terms of direct sales. However, over time, as existing customers became more aware of the web pages and the presence of the exhibitions in virtual format, sales began to materialise.' For example, 'People who were unable to physically attend the opening night of the exhibition began to reserve paintings, having only looked at them virtually.' The gallery has found the web site, along with a digital camera and e-mail facilities, to be invaluable sales tools. One staff member related how:

> *A potential customer, having looked at our web site, found an artist whose work she really liked. The problem for her was that all of the items shown in the exhibition had been sold. She e-mailed and asked had we any new paintings by this particular artist? I took the digital camera, photographed the four new paintings we had in stock by this artist, and e-mailed the images to her. The next day, I had an e-mail order for one of the pictures. The picture was priced at €700.* (W. Golden, *Kenny's Bookshop and Art Galleries, Ireland* (2002), Working Paper, Dept of Accountancy and Finance, NUIG)

The gallery sends direct e-mail marketing campaigns to customers who have previously provided their details to the gallery and who have requested information of interest to be sent to them. Kenny's e-mail campaigns allow the gallery to send digital images of paintings by particular artists to customers who have expressed an interest in that artist. The success of these campaigns is such that when six images are sent to nine potential customers, it typically results in the sale of four pieces of art, with an average value of €1,050 per piece. (W. Golden, *Kenny's Bookshop and Art Galleries, Ireland* (2002), Working Paper, Dept of Accountancy and Finance, NUIG)

The Kenny Gallery views the web as a pre and post-selling tool. Web use among gallery customers has increased substantially; the staff believe that up to a third of gallery customers use the web to research artists and their work prior to purchase. Customers are able to view exhibition pieces ten days prior to the exhibition opening and may reserve or buy an art piece online. Many customers use the web site, after buying a piece of art, to reassure themselves of their purchase. Other customers use the web to monitor the progress of a favourite artist. To facilitate customers' research efforts, The Kenny Gallery has been developing online profiles for their stable of artists (as examples, see the micro sites profiling Pádraic Reaney, Kieran Tobin and Gerald Davis). These micro sites have the potential to become a considerable resource not only to customers, but also to art students, art historians and individuals who have an interest in Irish art. The gallery's enterprise resource planning (ERP) system, which went live in August 2003, has not been fully optimised as a sales analysis tool. In particular, Tom Kenny and his staff are considering how the ERP system may be used to gain insights as to how customers use the web. Indeed, the ERP as an internal information system may provide other insights into customer behaviour.

What Next?

Although The Kenny Gallery is a successful venture, Tom Kenny wants to ensure the gallery's future profitability and has a number of issues to consider in developing a long-term strategy to achieve his vision. Among these considerations is how technology may be used to understand and communicate with customers as a means to facilitate growth. Understanding customers is essential, as Tom aims to keep pace with the gallery's changing customer profile and preferences. Competition is always a relevant issue, and Tom recognises new, as well as well-established, galleries may affect The Kenny Gallery's positioning strategy. Moreover, Tom wonders whether using technology wisely can provide The Kenny Gallery with a competitive edge.

Questions

1. How may technology facilitate The Kenny Gallery's communication with its customers to promote the gallery and its art products?
2. How may The Kenny Gallery use data gleaned from online interactions to gain insight into customer behaviour?
3. If The Kenny Gallery were to employ a data warehousing and data-mining initiative, what kind of information should the gallery seek?

*This case was written by Ann M. Torres, National University Ireland, Galway. It is intended to be used a basis for class discussion, rather than illustrating either effective or ineffective management practices. The case is based on a real situation, though some information has been disguised. The author wishes to thank Tom Kenny and Karen Golden for their kind permission to use the material in this case, 2006.

CHAPTER 5

FOCUS GROUPS, IN-DEPTH INTERVIEWS AND PROJECTIVE TECHNIQUES

CHAPTER OVERVIEW

▶ Introduction ▶ Focus Groups ▶ Types of Focus Groups ▶ Planning and Conducting Focus Groups ▶ Selecting the Moderator ▶ Moderator Discussion Guide ▶ Advantages and Disadvantages of Focus Groups ▶ Online Focus Groups ▶ In-depth Interviews ▶ Projective Techniques ▶ Types of Projective Techniques ▶ Advantages and Disadvantages of Projective Techniques ▶ Summary

INTRODUCTION

In Chapter 3, the distinction was made between exploratory research and other research designs. It was pointed out that exploratory research was one way of generating qualitative data. While it is fair to say that exploratory research is carried out to collect information in order to provide insights into the management problem and to identify courses of action, it is also true to say that exploratory research is, on its own, capable of answering the research problem. Remember, the concept 'qualitative' refers to data collection methods that generate soft or attitudinal type data. Qualitative data collection methods can be used for either exploratory or descriptive research purposes as detailed in Chapter 3. In practice, most researchers use the term 'qualitative research' to denote qualitative data collection methods.

Qualitative research can be defined as the collection of data which is open to interpretation, for instance on attitudes and opinions, and which might not be validated statistically.[1] It produces what is frequently referred to as 'soft data'. Qualitative research does not provide statistical answers. The purpose is to assess the minds of consumers to discover their impressions, expectations and prejudices. Qualitative research is predominantly a diagnostic tool to find out what the issues are and what respondents feel about them. You cannot do qualitative research and then try to pour quantitative results out of it.[2]

Extensive qualitative research convinced Murphy Brewery in Cork that the brand's traditional burgundy coloured livery and counter mounts were too conservative, and did not appeal to drinkers in the important 18 to 25 age category. Murphy has now adopted a cream and black livery for all of its stout products.[3]

Qualitative research conducted by Green Isle, who produce Goodfella's pizzas, showed emotional aspects of fun, freedom, social and a cosmopolitan outlook associated with pizzas.[4]

Qualitative research is generally applied in customer satisfaction research, service quality research, and customer complaint analysis. Irish Distillers spent three years and £500,000 on researching their new Polo drink. Part of the research included qualitative product test studies. Among the nuggets of information the research threw up was that young adults didn't want a long bottle, they were fussy on price and they believed they were already being bombarded by too many other products.[5] The principal factor which has led to the growth in qualitative research in Ireland is probably recognition of increased consumer sophistication, leading to a much greater concentration on finding out *why* people do things (or don't) as distinct from *what* they do.[6]

In summary, applications of qualitative research include:

- generating ideas on new product development, packaging, design, strategy, branding or image;
- examination of advertising strategy, execution and pre-testing;
- exploring the purchasing decision-making process;
- as an exploratory study before quantitative research;
- after a quantitative study to add depth to issues.

Phelim O'Leary, a specialist in this area, has documented the development of qualitative research, and points out that qualitative research has developed from a fringe area of marketing to a widely used and sophisticated set of procedures.[7] He goes on to say:

> Throughout the past decade there has been a consistent growth in the volume of qualitative market research conducted in Europe. At home this has been driven by Irish companies which have a consumer marketing focus and more recently has been added to by a widening range of organisations and institutions somewhat outside the classical marketing field; this would include government agencies, voluntary charitable groups, schools, political parties and the churches . . . A renewed, and welcome, emphasis is the more frequent collaboration of qualitative research with quantitative methods in the pursuit of solutions and valuable market intelligence.

In this chapter we examine three qualitative research methods, namely focus groups, in-depth interviews and projective techniques. By the end of the chapter, you will be able to:

1. describe qualitative research;
2. examine the main qualitative research tools;
3. discuss the growing role of focus groups;
4. outline in-depth interviews; and
5. explain projective techniques.

FOCUS GROUPS

Focus groups had their beginnings in group therapy used by psychiatrists. A focus group consists of eight to twelve participants who are led by a moderator in an in-depth discussion on a particular topic or concept. The main purpose of the focus group is to gain insights by listening to a group of people from the appropriate target market. The group is generally selected so as to include people who have common backgrounds or experience regarding the topic at hand, e.g. householders who burn solid fuel or recent purchasers of life insurance. The objective of focus group research is to learn and understand what people have to say and why. Focus group sessions are used to explore and define the attributes and issues in customer terms.[8] The emphasis is on getting people to talk at length and in detail about the topic in question and provide discussion and debate, and hence new ideas.

Focus groups are useful in exploratory research where the goal is to develop ideas and insights before proceeding toward further investigation into the topic of interest. Before you even start working on a survey, it may be advisable to organise some customer focus groups to identify what are the key issues for customers.[9] But this group interviewing approach can also be of more immediate value — for example, in identifying problems associated with existing products, in evaluating the attractiveness of new alternative products and their features, in probing the effectiveness of advertising and in determining customer attitudes, perceptions and behavioural patterns. Focus groups are widely used to consider the potential of alternative brand names.[10] One company carried out consumer focus groups to check reaction to the brand name but not to construct the name itself.[11] Green Isle Food Group used focus group research to monitor consumer response to its Goodfella's pizza TV advert depicting an Italian wedding scene.[12] Irish retailer Superquinn has made extensive use of focus groups to monitor customer perceptions of product and service quality levels at Superquinn. Bord Fáilte conducted seventeen focus groups around the world, which showed a low recognition factor of the shamrock.[13] Guardian Direct use focus groups with employees to help with decision-making.[14] Prior to launching its 'Big Pint' strategy, Guinness conducted 60 focus groups using skilled consumer psychologists. From this and other research, it became apparent that Guinness needed to be lowered from a pedestal upon which many drinkers placed it and it had to be given a more accessible image.[15] Recently, focus groups have become popular in industrial organisations, government and even academia. Colleges now use focus groups to help them develop marketing plans.[16]

The value of the technique lies in the unexpected findings often obtained from a free-flowing group discussion.

In summary the main objectives of focus groups are:

1. to generate ideas;
2. to better understand customer language;

3. to uncover customer needs, attitudes, perceptions and motives;
4. to generate information helpful in structuring customer questionnaires;
5. to interpret quantitative data findings.

Growing Popularity of Focus Groups

Marketers are using numerous variations of the focus group and other qualitative techniques to gain an even better understanding of what motivates consumers and why they make certain purchase decisions. Focus groups are probably the most important qualitative research procedure. Few qualitative interview methods in marketing have received as much positive press as focus group interviews.[17] They are so popular that many market research practitioners consider this technique synonymous with qualitative research.[18] However, focus groups are but one aspect of qualitative research. Yet the growing popularity of the focus group technique has virtually overshadowed other qualitative tools. Focus groups tend to be used more extensively by consumer goods companies than industrial goods companies. This can partly be explained by the fact that it is probably much easier to assemble a group of ten consumers of a domestic household product than to assemble a group of ten organisational buyers.

Box 5.1 Examples of how banks in Ireland use focus group research

Focus Groups at Bank of Ireland

Visit any Bank of Ireland branch today and you will find literature supplied in Mandarin, Polish and Russian as well as in English. It has also moved to recruit native speakers in some of its key branches. 'We conducted a number of migrant focus groups to get a better understanding of their needs and attitudes towards financial services. The key issue they had was accessibility with the language barriers. We found the product needs weren't any different from anybody else, so our first move was to translate all the key products and brochure literature.'

Focus Groups at AIB

Focus group research at AIB indicated that people do not expect or want to be loved by their banks — they have family and friends for that. Customers just want three fairly simple things: outstanding service, to feel valued, and continuous improvement. The bank took the hint and developed a series of advertisements that focused on people's lives, rather than banking services. 'AIB's message was "we do ordinary things, people do extraordinary things". Our job is to enable people to do whatever they want.'

Focus Groups at Ulster Bank

Focus groups conducted by Ulster Bank showed that students were interested in what the bank had to offer rather than freebies, and that students were becoming far more financially savvy. To reflect this, last year Ulster Bank launched a 'no gimmicks' campaign to recruit student customers. The bank's message was, 'Some banks would do anything to attract students, we simply believe in better banking.'

Focus Groups at First Active plc

Good marketing research was behind the recent launch of the 100% mortgage by First Active plc. 'We used (focus group) qualitative research to gain consumer insight and give direction to the development of a new financial product. Our research showed that there was a massive pent-up frustration on the part of young people who wanted to get on the property ladder. They were caught in a trap, paying sometimes €1,000 in rent but unable to get a deposit together to break out of the rental market. The irony of it is that they could afford a mortgage.'

Source: 'Customer Loyalty as Elusive as Ever', *Irish Marketing Journal*, 31 March 2004; 'Going After the Poles and the Chinese', *Business and Finance Magazine*, 20 October 2005; 'Carry on Campus', *Irish Medical Journal*, 1 August 2005; 'Market Research in Search of Killer Insight', *Irish Marketing Journal*, 1 September 2005.

TYPES OF FOCUS GROUPS

Focus groups can be classified into three major areas: exploratory, clinical and experiencing.[19] But in practice marketing research practitioners rarely make these distinctions.

Exploratory Focus Groups

Used at the exploratory phase of the market research process to help in problem definition, generating hypotheses, explaining ideas and preparing for quantitative research.[20] For example, a focus group may be used to decide the content of a future questionnaire. A research director once commented: 'We use focus groups for fishing.'

Clinical Focus Groups

This is qualitative research in its purest form, and is based on the premise that a person's true motivations and feelings are subconscious in nature, and that what consumers say cannot be taken at face value. But this requires employing moderators skilled in clinical psychology, and with an ability to entice participants into revealing inner feelings and thoughts. Validating findings from clinical focus groups can also be a problem.

Experiencing Focus Groups

This approach is an opportunity for the market researcher to experience a 'flesh and blood' consumer of the product or service. It allows the researcher to relive the consumer's experiences when buying, using, reusing and disposing of the product. When conducting research, Japanese firms prefer to talk to people who have actually experienced the product or service.

Calder adopts a similar classification. He suggests that focus groups can be used for three different types of purposes:[21]

1. *Clinical* — to uncover consumers' underlying feelings, attitudes, beliefs, opinions, and the subconscious causes of their behaviour.
2. *Exploratory* — to generate, develop and screen ideas or concepts.
3. *Phenomenological* — to discover consumers' everyday life experiences, such as their thoughts, feelings and behaviour.

PLANNING AND CONDUCTING FOCUS GROUPS

The first step to planning a focus group is to establish the objectives of the marketing research project. This begins with a general statement of the management problem. What does management want to achieve? Following that, the objectives of the qualitative research should be clearly specified. These objectives can be set by asking the question, 'What information is needed to meet the needs of management?' The research objectives will guide what questions to ask during the focus group. Research objectives have been discussed in Chapter 2. NTL's cable customers in Dublin, Galway, and Waterford received the Discovery Channel following focus group customer research carried out in Ireland by MRBI, which revealed a strong preference for the Discovery Channel over National Geographic Channel.[22]

Recruiting Participants (and Group Composition)

Researchers normally establish a screening profile for the group participants. A focus group should be reasonably homogenous in terms of demographic and socio-economic characteristics. Participants feel more at ease once they realise they share similarities such as age, job situation, leisure pursuits, family composition, etc. Commonality among group members prevents interactions and conflicts about side issues among group members.[23] The session therefore does not become rife with too many arguments and different viewpoints stemming from diverse backgrounds. *e.g. similar demographic characteristics.* The participants should also have adequate experience with the object or issue being discussed. Initially prospective participants may be contacted by telephone in order to qualify them and then to solicit their co-operation in the focus group. For this, inducements and rewards such as monetary compensation, free products or gift certificates may be used. To overcome the problem of 'no shows', the researcher may need to over-recruit or have replacement standbys.

The researcher should strive to avoid repeat or 'professional' respondents in focus groups. These are people who have already participated in numerous focus groups. It is highly unlikely that they are representative of the target market in question. Most participate simply to get the respondent fee.[24] Another issue in respondent selection relates to allowing people to participate in a group that contains a relative, friend or neighbour. Participants with these pre-established relationships may tend to talk to each other and not to the whole group.

Number of Participants

A typical group will consist of eight to twelve people, but there is no ideal number of participants. However, groups of fewer than eight are unlikely to generate the energy, momentum and group dynamics ('snowballing') necessary for a successful session. Having a higher number of respondents participate in the group gives rise to a broad spectrum of responses and encourages the 'domino' or 'snowball' effect — what one respondent says sparks off comments from others. Snowballing and inter-stimulation within focus groups may lead participants to feel more excited so that they cannot hide or relax their responses.[25] Likewise, groups of more than twelve may be too crowded and may not be conducive to a cohesive and natural discussion.[26] Focus groups normally run for an average of one and a half to two hours, with a maximum of two hours. This period of time is needed to establish rapport with the respondents and to explore in depth their beliefs, feelings, ideas and insights regarding the discussion topic. But, the more participants, the less time available for each to speak and air their opinions. Researchers who wish to collect information from different categories of people should conduct several focus groups; for example, one focus group may consist only of men and another only of women. Most focus group experts believe that six focus group sessions can satisfy the needs of exploratory research.[27]

The Setting

The physical setting for the focus group is also important. A relaxed, informal atmosphere encourages spontaneous comments. Light refreshments should be served before the session and made available during the session. Purpose-built focus group facilities are available in Ireland — The Grafton Suite (www.graftonsuite.ie), Focus Suites (www.focusireland.com/) and iReach (www.ireach.ie/iview) are examples of these facilities. Videoconferences can broadcast sessions to a remote facility where a number of people can observe the proceedings live over a television monitor whereby the clients observing from afar can move the camera to look at individuals in the group, the moderator, or the entire group. They can also communicate with the moderator through email. Focus groups using videoconference technology may become more popular in the coming years.[28]

In reality, most Irish focus group settings consist of booking a conference room in a hotel, arranging seating, and installing a tape recorder and possibly a video camcorder. A circular seating arrangement enables all participants to see each other.

Videotaping the session allows for recording facial expressions and body movements. Some researchers may choose to use a living-room setting as an alternative to conference-room setting, believing that the informality of the living room will make the participants more at ease, as in a typical home-like setting.

SELECTING THE MODERATOR

The key figure in the focus group interview is the interviewer, in this case referred to as the moderator. The moderator is a critical factor influencing the effectiveness and usefulness of the focus group.[29] He or she must be sensitive to the feelings and comments of group members, but also possess the firmness necessary to successfully direct the group along the intended path of discussion by the ability to maintain a high degree of interaction among group members. Unskilled moderators may end up conducting individual interviews with each of the participants rather than working the group's dynamics. One or more of the group participants may tend to be domineering. The moderator must reduce their effect by calling for the opinions of others. Qualifications required of the moderator depend on the type of groups being conducted. For a clinical focus group, it is advisable to have a trained psychologist. Disagreement exists among researchers as to the educational requirements for moderators of exploratory and experiencing focus groups. But at minimum, moderators need to have good interpersonal and communication skills and a knowledge of the discussion topic at hand.

MODERATOR DISCUSSION GUIDE

A discussion guide is an outline of the topics to be covered during the session. See page 164 for an example of a focus group discussion guide. The discussion agenda is based on the research objectives and client information needs. It serves as a checklist and provides a detailed outline of the issues to be addressed during the discussion, including the approach, the types of questions to be raised, the sequence of issues, and any stimuli (e.g. alternative sample packaging) to be introduced. But inflexible formats and highly structured question sequences should be avoided, especially when attempting to find out the unexpected and new. The moderator's guide usually flows through three stages. Firstly, rapport is established between the moderator and the participants. Individual participants may be asked to introduce themselves. This acts as an 'icebreaker', particularly for more timid participants. Also, at this stage the rules of group interaction are explained by the moderator and the objectives of the research are outlined (unless the purpose of the research and the name of the sponsoring organisation is deliberately being hidden from the group). The second stage of the session consists of the moderator attempting to provoke intensive discussion in the relevant areas. The final stage is used to summarise the group's response to determine the extent of agreement.

Box 5.2 Ten traits of a good focus group moderator

1. Be experienced in focus group research.
2. Provide sufficient help in conceptualising the focus group research design, rather than simply executing the groups exactly as the client specifies.
3. Prepare a detailed moderator guide well in advance of the focus group.
4. Engage in advance preparation to improve overall knowledge of the area being discussed.
5. Provide some 'added value' or 'insights' to the project beyond simply doing an effective job of conducting the session.
6. Maintain control of the group without leading or influencing the participants.
7. Be open to modern techniques such as visual stimulation, conceptual mapping, attitude scaling, role-playing, projective techniques or collages, which can be used to delve deeper into the minds of participants.
8. Take personal responsibility for the amount of time allowed for the recruitment, screening and selection of participants.
9. Share in the feeling of urgency to complete the focus group while desiring to achieve an excellent total research project.
10. Demonstrate the enthusiasm and exhibit the energy necessary to keep the group interested even when the hour is running late.

Source: Thomas L. Greenbaum, 'Do you have the right moderator for your focus groups? Here are 10 questions to ask yourself', *Bank Marketing*, Vol. 23 No.1 (1991), 43.

Example of Focus Group Discussion Guide
An Evening Business Studies Degree

Introduction

This is a focus group session to explore your motivations and feelings about an Evening Business Studies Degree. We want to find out your principal reasons for undertaking the course and your reactions and suggestions to what you've experienced.

Most of you may already know the guidelines for focus groups. I'm a facilitator, not a judge. My role is to encourage members of the group to give their views and discuss and exchange ideas on the issues raised. To facilitate this, I have a semi-structured questionnaire here to lead us through issues important in planning a course such as this.

There's one golden rule. Everyone is free to raise what they feel about each issue without criticism. Each of your views is as important as the next person's. The discussion should last about two hours. There will be a break for refreshments. Recording is for transcription purposes only. I hope nobody has any objections to this.

Here's another suggestion

Focus groups should be constructive. Therefore this one follows the structure of the questionnaire. It's easy to complete. But please do so in relation to the points raised and in a constructive way. At the very end, there will be an opportunity to raise any issues close to your heart.

Focus group checklist

Original decision

Let's go back to the beginning when you decided to take this course.

What made/encouraged you to undertake the evening Business Studies Degree?
Probe: Spontaneous?
            Influences of friends?
            Change in lifestyle?
            Change in job?
            Encouragement at work?
            Other?
What other courses, colleges, if any, did you consider?
Probe: Accountancy?
            Marketing?
            Other degrees?
            Institute of Technology?
            Open University?

What was the clinching factor(s) for this university?

How important is the title Business Studies Degree?
Probe: Enterprise and Management?

How would you feel if it had been called a BA?
Probe: Or BBS?

Had you considered an evening BA?

How significant was the Diploma being awarded after two years?
Probe: Reasons.

Expectations

What, if any, were your expectations about how the course would be conducted?

Probe: Had you a chance to attend university lectures before?

Compared to school/training events?

How much of the content did you expect to be covered in the lectures?

What were your expectations about home study?

Delivery

In the university, course delivery means the way the course is provided, e.g. duration, number of nights per week, form of examination or assessment, class content and structure, etc.

Let's get your feelings. What about setting off on a four-year programme? How did you feel?

Probe: Try it?

Diploma?

Knew others who did it?

There's a lot of material to cover, so how else could the course be structured to cover the material in that or a shorter period?

Probe: Was there too much, or just about right amount of time in lectures?

Distance learning format?

How significant is being with the class? Support?

More at-home assignments/readings supported by less frequent tutorial-type lectures? Form? Frequency? For what subjects?

What about using IT for course delivery?

What subjects not suited to distance format?

Grading

In terms of grading, what's your reaction to the grading systems used in the course?

Probe: Individual assignments versus group ones?

Amount of continuous assessment versus final examination?

During the course

Take your mind back to during the course.

Tell us your impressions, feelings and mood as you went through the course.

What are your thoughts/reactions to the subjects you were doing each year?

What subjects should have been included/dropped?

What skills were covered or could have been covered?

End

Given all you've told us, has the course lived up to what you'd expected and hoped for?

If you had known what you know now, would you do it again?

What changes would you make, if any?

Finally — have we left anything out you feel is significant and that you'd like to talk about?

Thank you for your time.

Analysing the Results and Preparing the Report

While the purpose of focus groups can vary, the primary purpose is to build a foundation for the conclusive research phase of the project. Focus groups provide a wealth of insight into how and why buyers purchase products. This may, for example, be used later to formulate question content and sequence in questionnaire design. Often managers believe they can use qualitative research as a substitute for quantitative research. This is not necessarily so and may prove later to be an incorrect assumption. Because the number of participants is small, frequencies and percentages are not usually reported in a focus group's summary. Instead, reports typically include expressions like 'Most participants thought that . . .', 'Some members felt that . . .', 'Many agreed that . . .'.

Before sitting down to write the report, the researcher attempts to pull together common themes or trends in response patterns by viewing and listening to the audio-visual recordings and referring to any notes taken during the session. With a well-planned discussion guide which has been properly adhered to, the analysis of focus group findings should be straightforward. The last step is to write the actual report. A liberal sprinkling of respondents' actual remarks (verbatim) can be used in the report to enforce or dramatise findings.[30]

Developments and Variations on Focus Groups

1. *Mini-groups* — typically four to five participants.
2. *Two-way focus groups* — consisting of two groups. The second group listens in on the first group, then holds its own discussion.
3. *Conflict focus groups* – two groups, each of whom hold different views.
4. *Dual-moderator group* — two moderators share the responsibility of moderating the group.
5. *Client-participant group* — clients sit in on the focus group and are identified to the participants. They may also take part in the discussion and answer queries.

A more recent development is where specialist firms (www.itracks.com) provide focus groups on the Internet. Net users can enter *chat rooms* where selected topics are identified. There they can submit their comments in a public forum. Online focus groups are covered later in the chapter.

ADVANTAGES OF FOCUS GROUPS

In comparison with other forms of research, focus groups offer the following specific advantages. These can be summarised as the ten S's.[31]

1. *Synergism*: Putting a group of people together will produce a wider range of information, insight and ideas than will individual responses secured privately.
2. *Snowballing*: A 'bandwagon' effect often operates in a group interview, in that one person's comment triggers a chain reaction from the other participants. (It should be noted that in practice, the snowball effect can also be a disadvantage. It can result in a 'follow-the-leader' approach, where one strong-minded individual may raise a point and persuade others to his or her line of thinking.)
3. *Stimulation*: Usually after a brief introductory period, the respondents want to express their ideas and expose their feelings as the general level of excitement over the topic increases in the group.
4. *Security*: Because the participants' feelings are similar to those of other group members, they feel comfortable and are therefore willing to express their ideas and feelings.
5. *Spontaneity*: Since participants are not required to answer specific questions, their responses can be spontaneous and unconventional and should therefore provide an accurate account of their views.
6. *Serendipity*: Ideas are more likely to arise out of the blue in the group than in an individual interview.
7. *Specialisation*: Because a number of participants are involved simultaneously, use of a highly trained, but expensive, interviewer is justified.
8. *Scientific scrutiny*: The group interview allows close scrutiny of the data collection process, in that observers can witness the session and it can be recorded for later analysis.
9. *Structure*: The group interview allows for flexibility in the topics covered and the depth with which they are treated.
10. *Speed*: Since a number of individuals are being interviewed at the same time, data collection and analysis proceed relatively quickly.

DISADVANTAGES OF FOCUS GROUPS

Disadvantages include the possibility that people who submit to the interview process may not be typical of the population they are presumed to represent. This presents a problem when attempting to generalise upon the results of the session, which is why focus groups are frequently used as an exploratory technique or when statistical extrapolation to the larger population is not of critical importance. It can, of course, be said that if the focus group members are not typical of the population, then that is the fault of the sampling procedure, not of the credibility of the focus group methodology. A related problem is the inevitable small sample size when compared with the more statistically powerful survey research approaches. According to Bank of Ireland, 'focus groups can be quite good if you have a specific topic, you know the target market you're after and the target market is sitting in the room with you. But for broad brush issues, the focus groups are not great. You can get very conflicting views.'[32]

The quality of the research results depends heavily on the skills of the moderator. Another problem with the focus group interviews is the inherent subjectivity of the results. Results can be more easily misjudged than the results of other data-collection methods. Different researchers may reach dissimilar conclusions based on the same set of interview data. Also, the unstructured nature of the responses makes coding, analysis and interpretation difficult. Finally, there is the danger that the decision-makers may consider the findings as conclusive evidence rather than exploratory information.

ONLINE FOCUS GROUPS

The use of the Internet in qualitative marketing research is becoming more commonplace, particularly the use of online focus groups. Respondents, who have been pre-recruited, are asked to log on at a web-site at a certain time to participate in the study. Once in the virtual 'room,' the respondent's screen typically is divided into two parts: one side has the flowing text of the discussion, and the other can be used by the moderator to show images for the respondent to comment on.[33] On-line focus groups are ideal for locating and researching markets that are hard to recruit, have irregular demand patterns, touch on sensitive topics, are online based and are geographically dispersed.[34] Furthermore, they are 'user-friendly' in that they enable connections between individuals in an environment of their own choosing.[35]

There is evidence to suggest that the level of anonymity enjoyed by online focus group participants can lead to more free-flowing, uninhibited expression by virtual focus group participants — particularly when presenting ideas orally in the 'real world' might inhibit group members.[36]

Online focus groups tend to last around 90 minutes and will address 40–45 pre-prepared questions.[37] The moderator should have access to an electronic version of the discussion guide so that questions can be put to the group quickly. Indeed, it is important that the moderator possesses fast keyboard skills. Online focus groups can also make use of specific conferencing software, which has provisions for 'public' and 'private' communications in both 'real-time' (synchronous) and non-synchronous modes.[38] One such software provider is Greenfield Online (www.greenfield.com) who produce a product called 'FocusChat'.

An online moderator must have specific online skills to be able to facilitate an online focus group. For example, he or she must be aware of emerging online 'vocabularies' and special symbols called 'emoticons' which are used to indicate physical expressive functions (e.g. ☺ for a smile), and where online convention dictates that typing in capital letters represents shouting.[39]

The depth of transcripts that can be derived from just an hour of discussion is powerful: potentially dozens of pages of verbatim responses available instantly. The main advantages of online focus groups lie in the speed of recruitment, elimination of travel costs and time required to set up the physical location for the focus group. While they might not always be able to replace in-person interviews, these benefits can make them a very effective tool, especially when used in conjunction with offline methods. For example, companies can use this methodology to enhance findings discovered in face-to-face groups.[40]

Online Focus groups do, however, have limitations. They do not allow for touch/feel experiences or the ability to capture the facial expressions (consternation, excitement, interest) of respondents as they are exposed to ideas and concepts.[41] Also, there may limitations in their ability to explore, in detail, highly emotional issues or subject matters.[42]

IN-DEPTH INTERVIEWS

Also known as individual extended interviews, in-depth interviews are another way of obtaining qualitative data. Like focus groups, they are also an unstructured and direct way of obtaining information, and are used primarily for exploratory research. But unlike focus groups, in-depth interviews are conducted on a one-on-one basis. They are particularly appropriate when:[43]

1. intensively probing needs behaviour or attitudes, e.g. car purchase;
2. examining potentially embarrassing subject matters, e.g. sexual habits;
3. eliciting confidential personal data, e.g. use of off-shore banking accounts;
4. detailing socially acceptable norms, e.g. family planning or breast feeding;
5. understanding complicated decision-making patterns, e.g. mortgage purchase;
6. interviewing professional people, e.g. purchasing managers who cannot be gathered together as a group;
7. interviewing competitors who are unlikely to reveal information in a group setting, e.g. local hotel-owners.

The technique uses extensive probing in the context of a personal interview to get a single respondent to reveal motivations, beliefs, attitudes and feelings on a topic.[44] The purpose of the technique is to descend beneath the superficial answers that are often provided by respondents and to disclose the more fundamental reasons underlying the respondent's attitudes and behaviour.[45] A survey of corporate purchasing and materials management was carried out by KMPG Stokes Kennedy Crowely on behalf on the Marketing Institute and the Irish Institute of Purchasing and Materials

Management (IIPMM). The survey examined the constraints and barriers to developing better business-to-business relationships between purchasers and suppliers. One of the ways it did this was by asking those responsible for purchasing for their views on the marketing and selling capabilities of indigenous Irish companies. Qualitative research involving in-depth interviews was conducted with key purchasing managers in twenty organisations.[46]

The following are some key phrases that the interviewer may use to this end: 'What do you mean by that?' 'Would you elaborate on that?' 'Can you give me an example?' 'Can you be more specific?' 'What else?' Essentially, the direction of the interview is determined by the respondent's initial reply.[47] In addition, the interviewer's mannerisms (such as nodding the head, smiling or other non-verbal expressions of approval), repeating the answer as a question ('So you thought the hotel staff were friendly?'), or interviewer silence can also be used to elicit more in-depth responses from the participant. While the interviewer may attempt to follow a rough outline, the actual wording of the questions and the order in which they are asked is determined by the subject's responses. Unlike focus group interviews, which often disguise the purpose of asking certain questions, in-depth interviews generally employ undisguised techniques, so that the purpose of the interview is clear to the subject. (See page 174 for an example of a in-depth interview guide.)

The interviewer must gain the confidence of the person being interviewed so that an honest, open discussion will take place. The success of the interview depends very much on the interviewer. He or she must develop a rapport with the interviewee, without passing judgment on what the respondent says. The interviewer must avoid the appearance of superiority and remain objective. Above all, the interviewer must probe into attitudes, beliefs and feelings and not accept brief 'Yes' and 'No' answers. In-depth interviews may last for half an hour, an hour or up to two hours.

Normally the interviewer will take brief notes during the session, and it is advisable (with the permission of the interviewee) to tape record the discussion. This allows the interviewer greater flexibility when conducting the interview and also ensures that all important issues are recorded and available as transcripts.

Application of In-depth Interviews

As with focus groups, the primary use of in-depth interviews is for exploratory research. But for several reasons, which we will look at later, in-depth interviews are probably used less frequently than focus group research. The disadvantages of the technique contribute to its limited use.[48] However, in-depth interviews may be used to address special problem situations such as those outlined earlier. A project undertaken for a leading firm of chartered accountants involved up to 50 interviews with their existing and prospective clients, as well as influential bankers, solicitors, senior management from state agencies and financial journalists. The principal objective was to investigate how these various well-informed business or professional people regarded the client firm *vis-à-vis* competition. Clients were questioned in great detail about the nature and perceived quality of the service they got from their accountants. They were probed about attributes they considered important in an accountancy firm. Was, for example, the concept of an accountancy firm providing a complete range of financial, legal, and business services (the so-called 'One-stop shop') appealing or not?[49]

Advantages and Disadvantages

In-depth interviews are versatile, but they require careful planning, training and preparation.[50] The main strength of the in-depth interview is in its ability to uncover more complete answers to questions than might be answered at a more superficial level during survey research. The one-to-one in-depth interview also has the advantage of respondents revealing attitudes or motives that they may be reluctant to discuss in a group setting.

In-depth interviews have a number of weaknesses. Firstly, because of the one-to-one nature of the research, sample sizes are small and statistical extrapolation of research findings becomes a problem. In-depth interviews are much more expensive and are more physically exhausting for the interviewer to conduct than focus groups. Typically, an interviewer may conduct four or five one-hour interviews in a day, whereas one focus group lasting one and a half hours can cover up to twelve respondents. Interpretation of the in-depth interview is subjective and dependent on the interviewer's view of what was said. Another problem is the difficulty of editing, coding and analysing the qualitative results.

The disadvantages of the technique contribute to its limited use.[51] Therefore, unless a situation demands a very high level of rapport on a one-to-one basis between interviewer and respondent, the focus group interview is generally capable of providing the same information at a lower cost.

Killarney All-Weather Centre. Local Tourism Experts' Survey.

In-Depth Interview Guide

A. Introduction
Introduction
Purpose of the research

B. Tourism in Killarney
What are the principal reasons for visitors to visit Killarney?
What are the major attractions of Killarney town to the visitor (not including the Lakes)?

What do you think are the major weaknesses of Killarney town as a tourism centre?
Do you feel the town is weak in its ability to attract/keep visitors? Why?
What do you estimate the average length of stay of visitors to Killarney to be?

If accommodation is provided, could you estimate what percentage of your business are one-night stays:

- Under 30%.
- Between 30% and 50%.
- Between 50% and 75%.
- Over 75%.

Do tourists, in your experience, complain about the lack of things to do in Killarney? Are there sufficient activities for tourists in Killarney?

How do you rate existing tourism attractions in the region?

Is there a need for a large weather-independent visitor attraction in Killarney town? Why/Why not?

C. Reaction to the proposed attraction
Show proposed centre and explain . . .

What is your reaction to the proposed centre?
What central themes should it include?
What would you see as the key success factors of the proposed attraction?
Are there any successful attractions which the centre should/should not be modelled on?
Any other product/marketing suggestions (theme, facilities, etc.)?
Would you be willing to recommend this new attraction to your guests?

D. Impact on tourism in the town
Would such an attraction make it easier for you to attract more visitors to Killarney/aid the performance of your business?

Would the centre be beneficial to the long-term development of tourism in the greater Kerry area/region? How?

Would such an attraction:

- make Killarney a more attractive place to visit?
- increase tourist numbers?
- increase tourism spend?
- affect length of stay of visitors to Killarney?

How and to what extent?

How do you feel a new attraction would fare as regards visitor numbers?

E. Other details
Is there an opportunity for tourist operators in the region to work more closely in selling their products?

Do you carry brochures/posters from various day attractions in the area?

Do you operate on a commission basis with any day attraction operators in the region?

F. Close
Thank you/any concluding comments.
Consent to follow-up, if necessary.
Agreement for use of the information gained from the discussion/confidentiality.

PROJECTIVE TECHNIQUES

These techniques are often used in conjunction with individual in-depth interviews. Projective techniques are derived from the field of clinical psychology.[52] The objective of projective techniques is to delve below surface responses to obtain true feelings, unlock attitudes or subconscious motivations. Both focus groups and in-depth interviews are direct subconscious approaches in which the true purpose of the research is disclosed to the respondents or is otherwise obvious to them. Projective techniques are different in that they attempt to disguise the purpose of the research. A projective technique is an unstructured, indirect form of questioning that encourages respondents to project their underlying beliefs, motivations and attitudes or feelings regarding the issues of concern.[53] People are often reluctant or cannot reveal their deepest feelings, or they may be unaware of those feelings because of psychological defence mechanisms. Projective techniques rely on stimulus ambiguity to obtain a more free and open response. Because the stimulus is ambiguous and has no true meaning, the respondent has to project himself or herself into the task, i.e. the respondents are provided with an opportunity to 'indirectly' express their feelings through a third party or by interpreting the behaviour of others.

As Oscar Wilde once said, 'A man is least himself when he talks in his own person; when he is given a mask he will tell the truth.'

TYPES OF PROJECTIVE TECHNIQUES

The most common forms of projective technique used in marketing research tests are:

- word association;
- sentence completion;
- story completion;
- cartoon tests;
- picture response;
- role-playing;
- personification;
- third person;
- psychodrawing;
- time travel.

These techniques can be classified under four main headings[54] which are: association, completion, construction and expressive techniques.

Association Tests

A respondent is presented with a stimulus and asked to respond with the first thing that comes to mind. The most popular is that of word association. The respondent is presented with a list of words, one at a time, and asked to respond with the first word that comes to mind. The test words related to the subject of the research are dispersed throughout the list and are intermixed with some 'neutral' words so as to hide the purpose of the study. The words are read to the respondent in rapid sequence and the subject responds with the first word that comes to mind. Rapidity of response is crucial to the technique so as to avoid time for defence mechanisms to come into play. 'First-thought' responses are more likely to reveal the respondent's strongest feelings towards the stimulus. If a respondent does not respond to a stimulus word within a reasonable period of time (e.g. five seconds) the eventual response should be either disregarded or discounted. Hesitation in responding (sometimes referred to as 'response latency') may indicate that the respondent is emotionally involved with the word and is possibly seeking an acceptable response. As an example of word association technique, consider the following (note: test words are identified by an asterisk):

Stimulus	Word
Bicycle	_____
Shop	_____
Canteen*	_____
Library	_____
Food*	_____
Smoking	_____
Seating*	_____
Staff*	_____

Word association tests are used to evaluate brand names, pre-test words for questionnaires, and to obtain top-of-mind reaction to companies, products, retail outlets and concepts. When United Beverages launched the highly successful Finches brand and was deciding on a name for the product, initial brainstorming sessions produced a list of 75 possibilities. From this, United Beverages initiated a screening process which narrowed the list to just six names. Those names were Simmons, Appian, Chase, Manns, Morgans, and Finches. Word association tests were then used to explore the perceived image of each of the brand names.[55]

A variation of the word association test is where respondents are asked to give the first two or more words that come to mind, rather than just the first word.

Completion Tests

The subject is required to complete an incomplete stimulus situation. Completion tests are also based on the principle of free association and can be used in conjunction with word association tests. The most commonly used in marketing research are sentence completion and story completion. The objective is for the interviewee to project themselves into the scenario presented.

Sentence Completion

An extension of the word association concept; but will probably produce larger responses than single-word answers, though one-word answers are acceptable. Again, it is important that respondents do not devote excessive time to the formulation of answers. With sentence completion, the interviewee is presented with a more direct stimulus than is the case with word association. However, it is important that the purpose of the study remains disguised. For example:

As I was walking into Aldi I noticed . . .

Story Completion

An extension of sentence completion, story completion provides the respondent with the beginning of a story, then asks him/her to complete it. Story completion provides a more structured and detailed scenario for the respondent. The respondent is given enough time to direct attention to the particular topic of interest, but the ending is left open. The interviewee projects himself/herself into an imaginary scenario. For example:

'It was a Saturday afternoon in November. Rachel parked her car in the car park opposite the shopping centre. It was raining and she had forgotten to bring an umbrella with her. Never mind, she thought. All I need to do is to collect my evening dress from the dry cleaners and then I can go home, light a fire and relax. As she approached the counter, she handed the ticket to the attendant and waited. The attendant returned with the dress. Rachel noticed that the red wine stain was still visible on the dress. She . . .'

The story completion technique, because of its nature, tends to provide data which is even more qualitative than that resulting from word association or sentence completion.

Construction Techniques

While related to completion techniques, construction techniques require the respondent to construct a response in the form of a story, dialogue or description. Less initial structure is provided to the respondent than with a completion test. The most commonly used construction techniques are cartoon tests and picture response.

Cartoon Tests

Cartoon techniques present cartoon-type drawings (similar to those seen in comic books) of one or more people in a particular situation. A typical cartoon test consists of two characters, one with a sentence in bubble form above its head, the other with a blank bubble above its head. The figures presented are vague and without expression so as to not suggest a response. The respondent is asked to fill in the blank bubble. The individual is allowed to project any subconscious or socially unacceptable feelings into the cartoon character. The settings can be used for discussions about products, services, packaging, store personnel, promotional activity, etc.

Picture Response

Picture response (or interpretation as it is sometimes referred to) has its origins in clinical psychology where it is known as a 'thematic apperception test' (TAT). With picture response, respondents are asked to react to a picture or series of pictures in which consumers and products are the centre of attention. These pictures are usually relatively vague, so that the respondent must use his or her imagination to describe what is occurring and what might happen next. Hence, themes (thematic) are elicited on the basis of the perceptual interpretative (apperception) use of picture.

The TAT is probably the most ambiguous of commonly used projective research techniques, but is also probably the most flexible, since pictures can be constructed to depict nearly any type of marketing situation. However, interpretation should ideally be carried out by trained individuals.

An imaginative application of the picture response technique is where the researcher collects a wide variety and number of picture postcards. These can range from the abstract to the relatively straightforward. The postcards are spread on a flat surface such as the floor or a table. Respondents are asked to pick, for example, three postcards that best describe their thoughts, feelings, attitudes, etc. towards the object in question and to explain why. The whole procedure can be extremely insightful and revealing. It is particularly useful in focus group settings, for not only does it provide a means for respondents to 'project' their feelings but it also serves as a very useful exercise to relax the group. After all, the sight of grown adults on their knees on the floor selecting postcards is enough to make any group feel at ease!

Expressive Techniques

The respondents are presented with a verbal or visual situation and asked to project the attitudes and feelings of *other* people onto the situation. There are two variations of this: role-playing and third-person technique.

Role-playing

In role-playing, the consumer is asked to assume the role of another person or an object. The researcher assumes that the respondent will project their own feelings into the role. The 'acting out' of brands, stereotypes, fantasies, etc. may be an individual or group activity.[56] For example, the consumer may assume the role of a car salesperson. The role-playing consumer can then be asked to sell a given car to a number of different 'consumers' who raise varying objections. The means by which the role-player attempts to overcome these objections can reveal a great deal about his or her attitudes. Role-playing can be especially useful in exploring issues of gender. For instance, gender reversal can be employed to examine brands which are predominantly male or female, e.g. a group of men 'become' women buying bath oil.[57]

Third-person Technique

By asking the respondent how friends, neighbours or the average person would think or react in a given situation, the researcher can observe the respondent projecting his or her own attitudes onto this third person, rather than directly expressing personal beliefs and attitudes. By enabling the interviewee to respond in the third person, it reduces the social pressure to give an acceptable answer.

A frequently cited example of this indirect projective technique is a study which was conducted in 1950, when Nescafé Instant Coffee was new to the US market. Two shopping lists, identical except for the brand of coffee, were given to two groups of women:

> A pound and a half of hamburger.
> Two loaves of Wonder Bread.
> Bunch of carrots.
> One can of Rumford's Baking Powder.
> (Nescafé Instant Coffee) (Maxwell House Coffee, drip grind).
> Two cans Del Monte peaches.
> Five pounds potatoes.

Respondents were given the following instructions: 'Read the shopping list. Try to project yourself into the situation as far as possible until you can more or less characterise the women who bought the groceries. Then write a brief description of her personality and character. Whenever possible, indicate what factors influenced your judgment.'

48% of the housewives given the list which included Nescafé described the Nescafé user as lazy and a poor planner. Other responses implied that the instant coffee user was not a good wife and spent money carelessly. The Maxwell House user, on the other hand, was thought to be practical, frugal, and a good cook.[58]

Personification can be looked at as a variation of the third person technique. It involves the respondent attributing human characteristics to inanimate objects. In focus group research on cars, for example, the moderator may ask 'If a Toyota Avensis was a person, what sort person would it be?' Or, 'If this package were a person, what would it be like in terms of age, gender, likes and dislikes, and lifestyle?' A similar approach is to ask the respondent to write an obituary for example, for a brand that has just 'died'. Respondents are asked to write an obituary giving reasons for death as well as for what the brand will be remembered for.

Two other projective techniques[59] include:

Psychodrawing

Respondents produce abstract paintings of their feelings about the subject, e.g. a brand or a company service. The painting is titled and personally signed. An art gallery is constructed, with each 'artist' explaining the emotions and meanings of his or her painting for the others in a small group.

Time Travel

The respondent enters an imaginary time capsule and can move back or forward in time to defined years. 'It is 1937, we are in the bathroom of a suburban house in Dublin . . . picture this in detail . . .'

Time travel is useful for establishing historical contexts and future projections.

ADVANTAGES AND DISADVANTAGES OF PROJECTIVE TECHNIQUES

The primary value of projective techniques is that they enable the researcher to get information that probably would not be available through direct questioning or by other means, e.g. observation. The types of data that these techniques generate are particularly important at the exploratory phase of a research project, especially when insights and ideas are important. The results of projective techniques can also be used directly for decision-making and may even eliminate the need for further study of the research problem.

On the negative side, projective techniques generally require trained interviewers, and responses need to be interpreted by qualified analysts. This can make them expensive to use. Also, reliance on small sample sizes (and usually non-probability selection procedures) makes it difficult to project the findings to a larger population. Non-response may also be a problem. Respondents may be required to engage in behaviour that may well seem strange to them (e.g. role-playing). Therefore, those who participate are likely to be different to those who do not. Despite these limitations, projective techniques are a very useful research tool and particularly suitable to exploratory type research.

Box 5.3 Qualitative research in marketing

In reviewing the marketing literature, it is evident that less attention has been paid to qualitative marketing research, perhaps due to the propensity to apply quantitative approaches, and consequently there is mystique, scepticism and ignorance about qualitative research. It has been regarded as being synonymous with 'motivation research' and 'hidden persuaders', both of which were considered as being within the province of strange people called psychologists. Coupled with the relative youth of the discipline of marketing and its attempts to establish credibility, the emphasis in marketing research was more on the quantitative approaches. This reflects the path of economics and social sciences, which also sought the level of 'respectability' of the natural sciences through quantification. This has led some to express concerns that, in following this route, academic marketing has tended to shift away from the creativity, spontaneity and individual insight that often characterise successful marketing practices.

As well as this, there have been a number of other perceived constraints to qualitative research in marketing. These include the volume of the data, the complexity of the analysis, the detail of the classification record and the velocity and flexibility of analysis. However, a range of software packages has helped to overcome these constraints and permitted marketing researchers to broaden their research horizons. This has generated widespread agreement of the advantages of harnessing computer-processing power in qualitative research.

Qualitative techniques are highly appropriate for marketing research in the services industry, given the dynamic nature of the service delivery, and they mostly occur through human interaction. The examination of complex and dynamic service situations can be more effectively achieved with qualitative research techniques since they offer an open, flexible and experiential approach.

It is interesting to note that the combination of both qualitative and quantitative approaches can add even more value: neither qualitative nor quantitative methods have universal applicability, but qualitative methods can be used to determine the plausibility of quantitative research.

Source: Adapted from Millikin, J. (2001) *Qualitative Research and Marketing Management, Management Decision*, Volume 39 Number 1, pp. 71–78.

SUMMARY

Qualitative research has developed from a fringe area of marketing to a widely used and sophisticated instrument. This chapter examined three qualitative research methods, namely focus groups, in-depth interviews and projective techniques.

Focus groups are probably the most important qualitative research procedure. They can be classified into three major groups: exploratory, clinical and experiencing. The main purpose of the focus group is to gain insights by listening to a group of people from the appropriate target market. A typical group will consist of eight to twelve people. A focus group should be reasonably homogenous in terms of demographic and socio-economic characteristics. The key figure in the focus group interview is the moderator. A discussion guide is used to outline the topics to be covered during the session. Often Irish focus group settings consist of booking a conference room in a hotel, arranging seating, and installing a tape recorder and possibly a video camcorder. The value of the technique lies in the unexpected findings often obtained from a free-flowing group's discussion. Whilst online focus groups can deliver many advantages in terms of speed, cost and access to respondents, they may in certain circumstances be limited, both in terms of subject matter that can be discussed and in terms of the quality and depth of output.

In-depth interviews are another way of obtaining qualitative data. But, unlike focus groups, in-depth interviews are conducted on a one-to-one basis. The technique uses extensive probing and aims to disclose the more fundamental reasons underlying the respondent's attitudes and behaviour. While the interviewer may attempt to follow a rough outline, the actual wording of the questions and the order in which they are asked is determined by the subject's responses. Above all, the interviewer must probe and not accept brief 'Yes' and 'No' answers. The main strength of the in-depth interview is in its ability to uncover more complete answers to questions than might be answered at a more superficial level during survey research. In-depth interviews may last for an hour, an hour and a half, or up to two hours.

Projective techniques are derived from the field of clinical psychology. A projective technique is an unstructured, indirect form of questioning that encourages respondents to project their underlying beliefs, motivations and attitudes or feelings regarding the issues of concern. Projective techniques rely on stimulus ambiguity to obtain a more free and open response. These techniques can be classified under four main headings which are: association, completion, construction and expressive techniques. Examples of individual projective techniques include: word association, sentence completion, cartoon tests, role-playing and personification. Although they have limitations, projective techniques are a very useful research tool and particularly suitable to exploratory-type research.

QUESTIONS

1. Differentiate between qualitative and quantitative research techniques.
2. What are the basic uses for exploratory research?
3. Why would an organisation consider conducting a focus group? Why are focus groups becoming more popular?
4. What are the three types of focus groups and how do they differ?
5 How are the participants of focus groups recruited? What are some of the pitfalls that should be avoided during the recruitment process?
6. What are some of the difficulties that may be encountered during a focus group interview and what strategies can the moderator employ to avoid them or minimise their effect?
7. What key qualities should a moderator possess?
8. Why should one safeguard against professional respondents?
9. Should the members of a focus group be similar or dissimilar? Why?
10. What physical facilities and equipment are required to conduct a focus group?
11. Discuss the purposes of a focus group interview and describe how such an interview would be carried out. What are the advantages and disadvantages of this technique compared to the in-depth interview?
12. Under what circumstances would you suggest that a in-depth interview be conducted rather than a focus group?
13. Describe how the Internet is used to conduct online focus groups. What are they strengths and weaknesses of using the Internet to conduct focus group research?
14. What is the purpose of projective techniques? Under what circumstances would projective techniques be preferred over focus group and/or in-depth interviews?
15. Describe and illustrate the major types of projective interviewing techniques and when they should be applied.
16. Describe the word association technique. Give an example of a situation in which this technique is especially useful.
17. How do third-person techniques differ from sentence completion techniques?
18. What is meant by role-playing?

PROBLEMS AND ASSIGNMENTS

1. How might exploratory research be used to screen various ideas for advertising copy in television commercials?
2. Develop a projective technique to determine students' attitudes towards cheating in exams. Would mini-groups or individual in-depth interviews provide better data on college students' attitudes towards cheating?
3. Following the methods outlined in the text, develop a plan for conducting a focus group to determine consumers' attitudes towards and preferences for imported

automobiles. Specify the objectives of the focus group, write a screening questionnaire, and develop a moderator's outline.

4. If a researcher wanted to conduct a focus group with teenagers, what special considerations might be necessary?

5. What projective techniques would you use to help develop a campaign to reduce drinking and driving by college students? Why would you choose these methods?

6. Toothpaste manufacturers have found consistently that if they ask for detailed information on the frequency that people brush their teeth, and then make minimal assumptions as to the quantity of toothpaste used on each occasion as well as spillage and failure to squeeze the tube empty, the result is a serious over-statement of toothpaste consumption. How would you explain this phenomenon? Would it be possible to design a study to overcome these problems and obtain more accurate estimates of consumption? Describe how such a study would be conducted.

7. Most projective techniques attempt to assess a respondent's true feelings by asking indirect questions rather than using direct questions that could give a respondent a better idea as to the researcher's motives. Is this deception?

8. Discuss the issues involved in determining when and where a car tyre manufacturer should conduct focus groups to get feedback from customers on its line of wet-driving winter tyres. Give a brief description of customers who would be good candidates for this type of focus group.

9. Using the Internet, connect with a special interest bulletin board such as one for college students. Conduct an online focus group exploring what factors are used as criteria to choose destinations for the summer holidays.

Case Study
VIVAS Health: developing a strong brand in a regulated health insurance environment*

Introduction
Deirdre Ashe, the Marketing Director for VIVAS Health, sat in her office contemplating the company's recent marketing performance. The company is the fastest growing health insurer in Europe. Founded in 2004, it quickly gained 2% of the market, confounding analysts who predicted that the duopoly of VHI and BUPA would in no way be challenged by the latest entrant. VIVAS Health was formed after Oliver Tattan, Chief Executive, spotted a gap in the market. He formed the view that the market for private healthcare and private health insurance was in its infancy in Ireland, and that there was room in the Irish market for a third player. Product differentiation, aligned with price-follower tactics, were key elements in the market entry strategy.

Changing Consumer Behaviour

Private health insurers generally cover elective care (planned surgeries and treatments that are generally treated in the public healthcare system, e.g. hip replacements, scans, heart by-pass operations, appendix removal, childbirth, etc.) and hospitalisation expenses (upgraded accommodation and hospital treatment). The proportion of the Irish population covered by voluntary health insurance is among the highest in the EU, reflecting a lack of confidence in the public health system. According to a study undertaken by Insight Statistical Consulting, an estimated 52% of the population buy private health insurance, mainly because it provides faster access to care and increased choice over providers (*The Private Health Insurance Market in Ireland*, HIA (2005)). A survey undertaken by Amarach Consulting in 2003 and published by the Health Insurance Authority (HIA) prior to company launch showed that consumer behaviour was highly conservative, with only a fraction of customers switching between insurers, despite the fact that such a move could save them money. Brand loyalty was another entry barrier. VHI Healthcare was seen as one of Ireland's most recognised and trusted household brands — people accepted the motto 'VHI cares' and trusted that their insurer would pay claims when the need arose. A key question facing VIVAS Health was whether a market characterised by inertia would be interested in its brand proposition.

Brand Proposition

Building brand-name awareness among stakeholders was the first marketing task, all the more important given that VIVAS decided to sell its plans through intermediaries, mostly life-insurance brokers and bank branches. Financial advisers were paid by commission to offer advice and sell the most relevant and best-value health insurance plan to their clients. Stakeholders included the government, the media, health-care providers, hospital administrators, corporate business, human-resource directors and the consumer. As a new, unknown company, it had to provide answers to the following questions: Who are you? How are you different? According to the Marketing Director, VIVAS Health is a 'challenger brand': in a market dominated by one player, it was positioned as an Irish entrepreneurial company who represented innovation, choice and value for money. VIVAS Health prides itself on being the first to provide:

(a) access to private A&E in the Galway Clinic.
(b) home help after major operations and the birth of a baby.
(c) prescriptions.
(d) GP referred MRI scans.
(e) overseas cover for procedures not available in Ireland.
(f) cover for laser eye surgery.
(g) cover for tooth whitening treatments.

(h) cover for primary care (GP, dentist) and alternative medicine such as reflexology, massage therapy, homeopathy, etc.

VIVAS Health's strategy was to offer customised plans as opposed to what the CEO called the 'one size fits all' mentality of other insurers. VIVAS Health was the first Irish insurer to offer health-insurance plans tailored to suit the specific needs of the consumer. For instance, a plan was developed to suit teachers and nurses following research. The latter plan included benefits such as counselling, stress management and access to alternative practitioners to help protect a person's back – a common concern in the nursing profession.

Analysis of competitors' plans revealed that health cover automatically included maternity benefits — even if the subscriber was a single man. Thus VIVAS Health developed the 'me plan', giving the customer the flexibility to opt out of cover they felt was unnecessary. All plans have tiered pricing, ranging from a basic no-frills plan which strips down the insurance plan to the core minimum benefits required by law (level 1), to a premium-priced plan (level 5) aimed at older consumers who want comprehensive cover.

The company's mantra is 'choice' – choice in terms of insurer and choice in terms of insurance benefits – and this forms a strong theme in its communications strategy. Advertising is described as 'anti-category'. The 'man in the newsagent' advertisement depicts a man picking up different sections of various newspapers; he then proceeds to the counter and scans and pays for the customised newspaper himself – to the amazement of onlookers. The advertisement helps convey the message that the consumer is empowered, capable of making an informed decision about the type of cover required.

VIVAS Health's goal was to create a fresh and exciting brand proposition that would capture the imagination of the consumer. The name VIVAS caught the Marketing Director's attention because of its connotations of living life to the full. Considerable thought has gone into the design of the logo, the web site and promotional materials, which differentiate the brand. People buy health insurance because it represents protection against the costs of major illness. Thus the brand logo symbolises nurturing, peace of mind, support at a time when one needs it most. Vibrant colours – red and green – are used, and visual material is interwoven with text on the web site (www.vivashealth.ie) to convey a feeling of energy and activity.

Research and Market Segmentation: Meeting Customers' Needs

In the insurance market, the ideal customer is one who is unlikely to claim against the insurance policy. Yet VIVAS Health actively encourages their customers to make a claim. Younger customers in particular want to pay for what they are most likely to use, such as laser eye surgery. According to the Marketing Director, offering customers extra benefits, the 'added-value insurance plans', has helped the company create a 'bonded customer'. Churn is not a problem for the company. Creating an emotional bond with a consumer can be difficult in a product category that is viewed with disinterest by many consumers. Research conducted by the Health Insurance Authority (2003) found that many consumers never read the information sent to them by their insurer. However, VIVAS Health appeals to a distinct type of customer. Focus group research shows that their customers are very loyal and, once they are satisfied with their initial encounter with the company, they spread positive word-of-mouth advertising. According to the Marketing Director, the company attracts the 'early adopters, individuals who are well informed, savvy, empowered, they are people who tend to be early adopters in a number of categories such as telephone, mortgage, health'.

The market was segmented on the basis of the following:

- Demographics (age, gender, occupation, income, family, life-cycle stage).
- Behavioural (benefits sought, attitudes towards health, predisposition to switch).
- Psychographics (lifestyle, personality).

Age and gender are important segmentation variables. For instance, younger customers are less likely to claim for catastrophic illness. Anecdotal evidence suggests that females are more health-conscious than males, and male consumers do not need cover for maternity benefits. Thus the 'me plan' was designed for a lifestyle without the responsibilities of parenthood. The names of the plans were carefully chosen to suggest benefits, e.g. the 'we plan' is aimed at families and parents-to-be, and the plan includes benefits such as three days' postnatal home help, child counselling and speech therapy.

Predisposition to switch is an important segmentation variable. Most of VIVAS Health's customers come direct to the company from either VHI or BUPA, with the majority of subscribers coming from VHI. According to the Marketing Director, consumer behaviour has evolved considerably, which surprised her, given that the HIA 2003 survey found that only 6% of consumers surveyed had switched. This survey highlighted the need to educate consumers and make them aware that they can transfer between insurers without being subject to additional waiting periods. Switching behaviour can be attributed to the new entrant, the rise of the price-sensitive customer, and growing consumer awareness of how easy it is to transfer insurance. Sales promotion has helped the company attract switchers. Analysis of competitors' plans showed that students over the age of 18 were charged an adult rate, and VIVAS decided to increase the age to 23, thus families moving from VHI to VIVAS Health could make significant savings. Analysis of market trends revealed that students live at home and stay in higher education for longer periods, and many do not enter full-time employment until they are past the age of 21. Focus group research revealed that the age 18 as a cut-off point was contentious. Special promotional offers, such as the 50%

discount for children and for students up to the age of 23, sent a strong message to the market that the brand represented value for money.

The Future

Company strategy is to grow aggressively in the future, and marketing plans need to be reviewed in the light of a changing marketplace.

A key marketing task is the attraction and retention of customers in a more competitive market place. Both VHI and BUPA Ireland are innovating to keep rivals at bay. VHI's LifeStages Plan, launched shortly after VIVAS Health entered the market, illustrates the trend towards tailoring products for consumers. The plan is designed for individuals who do not envisage a need for cover in high-tech hospitals where cardiac procedures are performed, but who want cover for day-to-day expenses, including maternity care, visits to dentists, doctors and alternative practitioners, and so on. VIVAS Health considers, however, that its innovative approach towards business will keep it one step ahead of the competition. Having a small share of the market enables it to offer special promotions that are not easily matched by its counterparts, as it is not always cost effective for a large organisation to offer discounts to a large volume of subscribers.

Although innovation is a feature of the insurance sector, it can be difficult to decide which areas to invest in and which to ignore. Should more cosmetic surgeries and treatments, dental care, GP cover and outpatient cover be offered? Should greater protection be provided from out-of-pocket expenditure associated with major illness? Should a 'whole-life' or 'preventative' approach to health be encouraged? Irish insurers are looking with interest at developments in other markets, where plans have been developed to reward subscribers for leading healthy lifestyles, e.g. undergoing regular screening, joining a gym. However, the Irish health insurance market is a highly regulated one and insurers are precluded from adopting price discrimination tactics. Insurers are required by regulation to apply community-rated premiums, i.e. no discrimination in premium calculations on the basis of age, health status, claims history or other factors. Other important features are open enrolment (insurers are compelled to accept all individuals who demand private health-insurance coverage), minimum benefit (insurers cannot provide health insurance below a minimum level) and lifetime cover (as individuals get older their health may deteriorate, but insurers cannot deny individuals the right to renew cover from one year to the next). As a small company, VIVAS Health has a limited marketing budget, and, like every insurer, it has to balance tensions between attracting customers and attracting a high frequency of claims.

Customer satisfaction lies at heart of marketing. Research suggests that subscribers are not knowledgeable about health insurance. The HIA survey (2003) revealed that people didn't know what plan they were on, the benefits of the plan, or what they were paying. Many insurance plans require the subscriber to contribute a certain amount towards their medical expenses, known as the excess. However, many consumers only educate themselves about the cover they have taken out when they need to make a claim. The latest study by the HIA (2005) found that 10% of claimants were dissatisfied with the way in which their claim was handled, with the main reason cited relating to expectations not being met and treatments not being covered. Thus, bringing clarity to insurance plans, fulfilling promises and offering a high level of customer care are seen as the keys to long-term business prosperity.

VIVAS Health has its own direct sales force responsible for dealing with corporate business. Some research suggests that this segment treats health insurance plans as commodities and cost savings are the motivating factor for many switchers. A key issue for the Marketing Director is the development of a marketing strategy that will result in further market penetration of the corporate sector.

The Marketing Department has decided to undertake focus group research. Focus groups would be a good medium for exploring the reaction of different segments to the company's marketing strategies. It would give the company the opportunity to explore people's motivations for taking out health insurance, test their reactions to new insurance benefits and advertising concepts, and help them deal with adverse comments. The research objectives are as follows:

- to identify key market segments and develop customer profiles;
- to explore people's motives for buying health insurance;
- to test customers' reactions to new advertising and product concepts;
- to obtain information on how best to promote new insurance benefits; and
- to explore people's perceptions of the VIVAS Health brand.

Questions

1. Evaluate the company's market entry strategy.
2. What are the strengths and weaknesses of focus group marketing research?
3. Develop a list of issues that the focus group interviewer could use as a basis for group discussion and identify different types of participants.
4. This company chose to commission a programme of focus group research. Given the aims of the company, what other research tools might the company have used? Explain your selection.
5. Recommend a marketing mix strategy for a new insurance plan to be launched by VIVAS Health in the future.

*This case was written by Dr Breda McCarthy, Department of Management and Marketing, University College Cork, and is based on interviews conducted with Deirdre Ashe, Marketing Director, and Oliver Tattan, CEO, VIVAS Health. The case study is intended to be used as a basis for class discussion rather than to illustrate either effective or ineffective handling of an administrative situation (2006).

Case Study
The Ethnic Mobile Phone Market*

Background

The five years spanning 2001 to 2006, and 2005 to 2006 in particular, have witnessed a dramatic growth in the number of non-nationals entering Ireland to live and work. The *FÁS Quarterly Labour Market Review* (March & Oct 2005), a *Sunday Times* article dated 15 May 2005 and the CSO *Labour Market Review* dated 7 February 2006, suggest that:

- 140,000 citizens of new EU countries obtained an Irish PPS number between April 2004 and Sept 2005. This represents 7% of the national workforce in Ireland.
- The influx of citizens from new EU nations is strongly driven by Polish immigration, and those with Polish citizenship accounted for 53% of new PPS allocations in 2005.
- 33,000 non-EU work permits were issued in 2005 — approximately half of these were new permits and half were renewals.
- Notwithstanding immigration from new EU countries, Chinese migrants account for a significant proportion of the Irish population. Although accurate statistics are difficult to pinpoint, it is estimated that Ireland is home to approximately 60,000 Chinese nationals.
- Of new immigrants to Ireland, 60% are between the ages of 18 and 30, and 28% are between the ages of 30 and 45.

The rise in the number of non-nationals now living in Ireland is continuing to generate a niche market opportunity for those operating in the telecommunication sector in general, and the mobile phone industry more specifically.

As a consequence of immigration, and the expansion and increased specialisation of outbound calling destinations, a national mobile telecommunications service provider wished to explore the potential of customised tariffs/packages aimed at Polish and Chinese immigrants in particular. More specifically, the company wished to target pre-paid mobile-phone users – those who pay for their calls in advance through the use of top up cards.

In order to inform the development of firm pre-paid propositions aimed at the Chinese and Polish communities in Ireland, the telecommunications company wished to:

- explore the motivation of these community members when it came to selecting a pre-pay network;
- determine the key evaluative criteria they considered when doing so; and
- elicit their reaction to some preliminary ideas about tariff structures and communications of pre-paid tariff propositions for calls to China and Poland.

Research Objectives

As a result, the following broad objectives were identified:

1. To explore the frequency with which, and means by which, Chinese and Polish immigrants communicate with friends/relatives 'at home'.
2. To identify the evaluative criteria that drive the selection of an Irish pre-pay mobile service provider.
3. To gauge perceptions of telecommunications companies in the context of international calls and texts.
4. To determine what would need to happen/change in order for a mobile network provider to be more appealing to Chinese/Polish immigrants.
5. To identify the role of communications in driving consideration of a mobile-phone network operator and determine the most effective communications methods for each ethnic group.
6. To examine the appeal of some potential international calling rate propositions under development.
7. To determine the likely success of the service being offered and to elicit suggestions for how this service might need to change in order to be of maximum appeal to current and potential customers.

Research Methodology and Target

Given the potential difficulty of locating and recruiting a sufficient number of Chinese and Polish immigrants because of underdeveloped/unavailable databases, it was reckoned that acquiring sufficient base sizes to accommodate the samples needed for quantitative research was impossible. For this reason, the most effective and informative research approach was deemed to be qualitative research (i.e. a series of focus groups would be required to fulfil research objectives). The key target for this focus group research should be Polish and Chinese immigrants working and living in Ireland. All participants must have owned a mobile phone for at least six months, and must also be pre-pay customers.

Questions

Equipped with this research brief, the reader is asked to:
1. Develop a focus group moderator discussion guide that addresses the research objectives identified by the mobile telecommunications service provider.
2. Identify any research implementation challenges likely to arise as a result of the particular nature of the research brief and suggest approaches to deal with these challenges.
3. Discuss how the research findings would aid the development of a communications and advertising programme.
4. What cultural insights might the research identify, which, if overlooked, could result in inappropriate or unappealing target audience communications?

* This case was written by Orla Murphy, Market Research Manager, Vodafone. It is intended to be used as a basis for class discussion rather than to illustrate either effective or ineffective handling of an administrative situation (2006).

Case Study
Altobridge*

Altobridge began in 2002, after Mike Fitzgerald, CEO, noticed a gap in the market for developing a product that would allow global communications anytime, anywhere. The Altobridge management team has an impressive proven track record in the development and launching of leading-edge wireless solutions such as transportable emergency wireless networks and the world's first mass-market wireless service on cruise ships.

Altobridge's management team experienced first-hand the dramatic drive for Micro Cellular and Pico Cellular technology throughout the period of 1995 to 2002. During this time, the team played a leading role in identifying, designing and successfully deploying innovative and differentiating value-added wireless applications across the globe, including: In-Building Coverage Solutions, Wireless Office Solutions, Rural Wireless Solutions, Emergency Network Solutions, Underground Solutions and Wireless on Board Ships. It is interesting to note that all members of the management team come from a technological background with one member having worked in the aeronautical, land and maritime industries.

The Products

Currently Altobridge cannot bring some of their product to market because of restrictions set by the aeronautical industry and regulators who set the RF (Radio Frequency) levels. These restrictions include the banning of in-flight communications due to the possibility of interference with the airplane's systems. The regulations regarding the level of RF that are allowable on aircrafts are not a problem with the product developed by Altobridge because it eliminates the possibility of interference by dictating very low power levels. 'Certainly, operating at maximum power outputs of 2W, handsets could present an interference problem. Because our solution is based on GSM technology, however, we are able to set the power at a much lower and safe level,' says Mike Fitzgerald, CEO of Altobridge. He continues to say, 'Whilst we welcome this latest UK CAA report and the efforts made by the Authority, together with BAE Systems and Vodafone, it remains imperative in this era of continuing acceleration in the use of personal wireless devices that industry and regulators work together to address the goal of developing devices and systems which will generate no adverse effect on avionics equipment.'

Other barriers include safety concerns regarding true personal in-flight wireless and telephony via individual handsets. Altobridge has developed a number of options for potential customers in how to deliver the in-flight communications to passengers. 'At a time when airlines need a shot in the arm to boost revenues, the Altobridge SIM solution can deliver a much-needed revenue stream through the provision of a personal communications and m-commerce service,' explained Fitzgerald. 'The utilisation of SIM-card technology to bring standard communications devices into the mobile telephony world is not new, but what is unique about the Altobridge architecture is the ability to do so within the bandwidth restrictive environs of the aircraft.'

Altobridge has developed a number of products for particular markets. The Altobridge AM Gateway Platform™ supports voice calls and text messaging (SMS) in exactly the same way as a land-based GSM network. Subscribers roam onto the airborne network in the same way that subscribers roam from one country to another. The network architecture that would enable this technology is currently patent pending by Altobridge.

This product can be also used within the maritime market. Post 9/11, it became apparent that container shipment security had to be tightened up because of the potential risk ports posed with regard to terrorist attacks. Prior to 9/11, there was no product that tracked ships, so containers were unable to be tracked while in transit. Altobridge developed a system that will track containers while in motion, thus eliminating the risk factor. Within the maritime market, they will also be targeting superyachts, cruise and ferry passengers, and crew calling.

There appears to be a conundrum for Altobridge with regard to putting their energies into R&D or bringing a product to market and making some sales. For a relatively small company, they have been focusing on product development rather than market development. They need to address these issues and make decisions for their future.

The Target Market

Despite significant developments in the global wireless applications industry, two major markets have been ignored — the wireless communications at sea and wireless communications on aircraft. Altobridge has identified a unique solution that can overcome the technological and regulatory barriers of entry associated with these particular market sectors. The company has provided a solution that monitors and manages the RF. Their products will provide an easy to install price-insensitive wireless communication for the airline industry and a real-time container communication system for the sea sector. Altobridge can provide significant added value to this sector by minimising supply chain disruptions through a scheduled technological tracking reporting mechanism. Mike Fitzgerald says ships and aircraft represent 'the final frontier of GSM coverage' and says Altobridge is 'early in the GSM solution'. The new technologies that are patent pending could open up a potential market of one billion users globally. Fitzgerald states that 'revenue from shipping, which is the company's smallest projected business unit, is enough to make Altobridge profitable'. He goes on to claim that 'research has shown that the demand for wireless applications in the aviation industry alone is worth several billion dollars a year in recurring revenue through roaming charges'.

Currently the management is unsure as to whether or not it should target both markets individually or simultaneously. Fitzgerald believes that the latter is the preferred option. However, some of his team members believe that they should roll out their products separately in the two different markets. In fact, Fitzgerald believes that the company should pass on the responsibility of the 'roll out' to another company by formulating a license agreement and moving on to the next innovative requirements of the wireless industry. Prepared to listen to his team members, Fitzgerald has requested proposals on how best to target the identified markets.

Exercise:

Set out a qualitative research proposal that would facilitate Altobridge in effectively targeting the wireless communications at sea and wireless communications on aircraft markets. In your proposal detail:
1. What qualitative research technique(s) should be used and why?
2. Who should the technique(s) be aimed at?
3. Outline and prepare the relevant supporting guides and/or supporting materials required.

* This case was written by Breda O'Dwyer and Ann Sears, Institute of Technology, Tralee. It is intended to be used as a basis for class discussion rather than to illustrate either effective or ineffective handling of an administrative situation. 2006.

CHAPTER 6

SURVEYS, OBSERVATION AND PANELS

CHAPTER OVERVIEW

▶ Introduction   ▶ Survey Methods of Data Collection   ▶ The Personal Interview   ▶ The Telephone Interview   ▶ CATI   ▶ The Postal Interview ▶ Reducing Non-Response in Postal Questionnaires   ▶ Methods of Estimating the Degree of Non-Response Error   ▶ Online surveys   ▶ Combining Survey Techniques   ▶ Observation Methods   ▶ Advantages and Disadvantages ▶ Summary

INTRODUCTION

In the previous chapter we discussed qualitative research and examined three qualitative data collection methods, namely focus groups, in-depth interviews and projective techniques. We now move on to look at *quantitative* research by describing surveys, observation and panels in this chapter. These techniques are descriptive by nature. In the next chapter we will examine experimentation, which is associated with causal research.

The reader, upon completion of this chapter, will be able to:

1. discuss survey research;
2. outline the three main survey methods;
3. examine personal interviews;
4. examine telephone interviews;
5. examine postal questionnaires;
6. describe observation research; and
7. understand panels and omnibus surveys.

SURVEY METHODS OF DATA COLLECTION

The survey process by which respondents are questioned may appear deceptively simple. The reality, however, is probably best summed up by the following quote: 'Questioning people is more like trying to catch a particularly elusive fish, by hopefully casting different kinds of bait at different depths, without knowing what is going on beneath the surface.'[1] When evaluating the quality of information obtained from survey results, one must make some determination as to the accuracy of these results. This requires a careful examination of the research methodology used and an eye for the various forms of survey error that might occur. Primarily, in order to obtain meaningful results from the interview process, the following conditions must apply:

1. A correctly defined population.
2. Representative sample of the population.
3. Selected respondents are available and co-operative.
4. Respondents understand the questions asked of them.
5. Respondents have the knowledge, facts, attitudes or opinions to contribute.
6. Respondents are willing and able to respond.
7. The interviewer understands and correctly records the response.

There are two basic methods we can use to obtain information from individuals. We can ask them or we can observe them. Collectively, they are known as descriptive research. Descriptive research has already been introduced in Chapter 2.

The first of these alternatives, an approach that is sometimes mistakenly equated with market research itself, is survey research. A survey methodically gathers information from respondents by communicating with them. A survey can be conducted in person, by telephone, or by post. It is probably fair to say that surveys are the most widely used method of data collection in marketing research. However, there is no best method of data collection. Each research problem must be examined to determine the best way to collect the data.[2]

The most common marketing research surveys are 'cross-sectional', that is to say surveys of cross-sections of populations. One frequently hears the words 'survey' and 'questionnaire' being mentioned in the one sentence. Survey research relies on a questionnaire (or measuring instrument) of some sort to record responses. It should be stressed that the use of questionnaires is not intrinsic to surveys. One can have surveys based on observation where no questions are asked of any respondents. Questionnaires will be discussed later in the text.

Survey research is the systematic collection of data from a sample of respondents, usually involving the measurement of a large number of variables such as:

1. depth and extent of knowledge;
2. attitudes, interests and opinions;
3. behaviour — past, present or intended;
4. classification variables, demographic and socio-economic variables.

Survey research is usually conducted when the market researcher has already developed an understanding of the area to be researched. Therefore, other marketing research methods, such as observational research (discussed later in this chapter) and secondary data analysis, are more likely to be used to improve or supplement the survey method rather than to take its place. The popularity of survey research is due in part to its versatility.

Sources of Error in Survey Research

Broadly speaking, there are three sources of error that impinge upon survey work:

Sampling Error

Error of this type occurs when selecting samples that are not representative of the population. In other words, it is the difference between the sample value and the true value of the population mean. Some degree of sample error will be present whenever we select a sample. Because sampling error is the result of chance, it is subject to the laws of probability. Sampling error is covered in more depth in Chapter 10.

Response Error

Response error occurs when respondents, for whatever reason, give an incorrect answer. Respondents can answer questions in a certain direction that consciously or unconsciously misrepresents the truth. Interviewer error can also give rise to response error. Response error is covered in Chapter 8.

Non-Response Error

Error of this type occurs when respondents refuse to be interviewed or cannot be contacted. Non-response is a problem because those who respond are likely to differ from those who do not respond. Item non-response (where respondents choose not to answer certain questions) is also a form of non-response. Non-response error is a particular problem in postal surveys. When attempting to manage non-response error, researchers can employ two strategies:

1. Pre-survey approach to non-response. This is dealt with later in the chapter, under the heading 'Reducing non-response in postal questionnaires'.
2. Post-survey approach to non-response. Five methods to deal with the effect of non-response error are also detailed later in this chapter.

Survey research can be classified based on the modes of communication and administration. There are three major traditional survey methods:

1. Personal interviews.
2. Telephone interviews.
3. Postal interviews.

Each method has its own advantages and limitations. Variations of each method also exist, e.g. rather than posting the questionnaire to the respondent, it may instead be distributed within the body of a magazine or newspaper, or attached to a product sample. It is also possible to 'mix' these survey methods in order to take advantage of their individual strengths and compensate for their respective weaknesses. For example, a combination of telephone interviews and personal interviews may be used to communicate with respondents. We will now look at each survey method in turn.

THE PERSONAL INTERVIEW

Personal interviews are direct, face-to-face communications between the interviewer and a respondent. Personal interviews may take place in a variety of different locations, including the home of the respondent, on a street corner or in a shopping centre. They are sometimes referred to as face-to-face interviews.

The Procedure

The personal interview begins with the interviewer approaching the respondent. The first concern is to ensure the full co-operation of the interviewee. This is followed by a brief explanation of the study and how the respondent can help. Respondents must be made to feel that both the study and his or her responses are important. Having gained the respondent's co-operation, attention now turns to the data collection instrument. This helps standardise the data collection procedure. The researcher asks the required questions in the proper sequence, using the exact wording. The interviewer may encourage the respondent (e.g. by asking for clarification, repeating the question, pausing, nodding, etc.) to provide additional information if an initial response is vague or overly brief. The interview ends with the interviewer thanking the respondent for his or her co-operation.

Advantages of the Personal Interview Method

Because there is greater interaction between interviewer and respondent, the personal interview has great flexibility. The interviewer can explain and clarify complex questions, probe for additional information, administer complex questionnaires, utilise unstructured techniques and present visual cues such as advertisements and product concepts to the respondent, all as part of the questioning process.

The personal interview tends to have less non-response error than other survey methods. Refusal rates tend to range from about 10% to 30% on average. Interviewers rely primarily on their sales ability to convince individuals to co-operate. Most provide an introductory statement designed to secure co-operation: 'Good afternoon, I am conducting Marketing Research for . . .'. It is more difficult for the respondent to say 'No' in a face-to-face situation. Also, respondents typically are required to do no reading or writing — all they have to do is talk. Another strength of this method is its ability to obtain more information. Once on board, respondents are generally reluctant to cut short a face-to-face interview by saying 'That's enough'. It is easier for respondents to hang up the telephone or return an incomplete postal questionnaire. The personal interview offers the best degree of sample control. The interviewer has greater control over who is interviewed (unlike telephone and mail). Sampling procedures that do not require a list of the sampling units rely heavily upon the personal interviewer in the process of selecting the sample.

Limitations

Personal interviews are often impractical to conduct over wide geographical regions for reasons related to time and cost — the need to travel between interviews, set up appointments and schedule return visits to contact 'not at home' non-respondents, for example. Only one-third (30% to 40%) of the interviewer's time on the job is devoted to interviewing itself.[3] There is also the high cost of using trained interviewers in the field.

A second difficulty is the potential for interviewer bias. The rephrasing of questions, the interviewer's tone of voice or physical appearance may influence the response. Interviewers may unknowingly inject bias into the respondent's answers. Cheating can also be a problem. Interviewers may deviate from standardised procedures, cut corners to save time, falsify answers to sensitive or embarrassing questions, or fake all or parts of a questionnaire. Therefore, interviewer ability and integrity are important to reducing response error. Interviewers should be properly trained, and procedures to discourage cheating established. One such technique involves contacting (or threatening to contact) a small number of the respondents to determine either the existence or quality of interviews conducted. A final difficulty with the personal interview is that the respondent is not anonymous and may therefore be unwilling to provide confidential information or answers to sensitive questions on a one-to-one basis.

Shopping Centre Intercepts

Increasingly, personal interviews are being conducted in large, high-traffic centres. Shoppers are intercepted in the public area of the shopping centre, or asked to come to a 'permanent' interviewing facility (room) in the centre. However, some shopping centres may not permit market research interviewing as they view it as an unnecessary nuisance to shoppers. The advantage of this method is that it is more efficient for the respondent to come to the interviewer than *vice versa*,[4] and thus many interviews can be conducted quickly.

It also allows the interviewer to show respondents (in the test facility) large, heavy or immobile products such as durable goods and have their reaction recorded. A major problem with shopping centre interviewing is that refusal rates tend to be high. People are usually in a hurry to shop. Also, some people shop at malls more frequently than others and therefore have a greater chance of being interviewed.[5] Furthermore, shopping centres tend to attract a certain type of person, based on the shops they contain, and may produce an unrepresentative sample of the larger population (unless they are the population of interest).

THE TELEPHONE INTERVIEW

Telephone interviews involve phoning a sample (unless it's a census) of respondents and asking them a series of questions. Telephone interviews are becoming increasingly popular and are probably one of the most efficient methods for collecting data quickly.[6] If proper sampling (including using computer-generated random numbers to account for those persons who may be ex-directory) and call-back procedures are employed, the telephone approach probably produces a better sample than any other survey procedure.[7] While telephone interviewing is also two-way conversation between interviewer and respondent, the fact that it is voice-to-voice and not face-to-face communication means that it has its own unique problems, strengths and limitations.

The Procedure

While the telephone interview has many characteristics similar to that of the personal interview, i.e. respondent co-operation must be sought, questions can be clarified, respondents can be probed, etc., it does not lend itself as much to the collection of lengthy and detailed information. The use of complex measurement scales is also restricted. Telephone interviews are more suited to concise and straightforward data collection.

Telephone interviewing depends on a representative sampling frame — a list of population units with their telephone numbers.[8] The telephone directory is the normal sampling frame used, but telephone directories are limited in that:

1. not everyone has a telephone;
2. there are many unlisted numbers;
3. new or recently connected telephones are not included.

There are two main approaches to overcoming the problem of unlisted or new numbers. One technique is the use of random digit dialling, in which the last four numbers of the telephone number used are selected randomly, using a random numbers table or a computer-based random-number generator. The second approach is called plus-one dialling in which a number is selected from the directory by means of systematic sampling. However, rather than dialling the number listed and selected, 'plus-one' is added to the final digit (e.g. 509492 becomes 509493). The revised number is then dialled. While these two techniques help overcome the problem of unlisted and new numbers, they do not distinguish between household and business telephone numbers. Secondly, there may be a higher refusal rate than when surveying listed telephone numbers.[9]

Finally, as with personal interviews, it is recommended to use carefully selected and well-trained interviewers, and to validate their interviews by calling a small sample of numbers they claim to have called.

Advantages of the Telephone Interview Method

As the cost of personal interviews may be prohibitively high, the cost of telephone interviews is somewhat less. Travel time and cost of travel are eliminated. This is especially important when respondents are geographically dispersed or when call-backs are required. A second advantage is the speed of data collection. Of the three survey methods, it is the fastest way to obtain data. With a short questionnaire, an interviewer can complete up to ten interviews per hour. Because the interviews are being carried out from a central location, it is easier for the researcher to monitor and control the quality of the interviewing. Because of the absence of face-to-face contact, there is less opportunity for interviewer bias — that is not to say that interviewer bias is completely eliminated. The interviewer can still vary the tone of his or her voice, ask leading questions or misrepresent respondents' answers.

Limitations of Telephone Interviewing

Telephone interviewing has some limitations. Firstly, only a limited amount and detail of information can be collected. A good rule-of-thumb is to keep the interviews approximately fifteen to twenty minutes long; respondents are unlikely to stay on the phone for a longer period unless they are highly interested in the survey subject. In general, refusal to co-operate is directly related to interview length. It is easier for the respondent to terminate the interview by simply hanging up. Therefore, telephone interviews must be relatively short, simple and interesting. As already mentioned, the telephone book as a sampling frame may not be representative of the population of interest. Random digit and plus-one dialling helps reduce this problem. It does not, however, compensate for households that do not have a telephone. This can be particularly so in rural and lower-income areas. A related problem is when a single telephone serves an entire block of apartments or flats.

Because visual aids cannot be used in telephone interviews, certain types of research such as packaging, print advertising, or some concept tests cannot be conducted on the phone. This limitation can be overcome by sending the respondent the required visual material in advance. Because of the more impersonal nature of telephone interviewing, response error or interviewer bias, while still present, is probably less than in the personal interview method. Finally, ownership of telephone answering machines (and call-answering services) is making access to consumers increasingly more difficult. However, if enough call-backs are made at different times and on different days, most respondents are contactable.

COMPUTER ASSISTED TELEPHONE INTERVIEWING (CATI)

The use of computers to guide and manage the telephone interview process has become popular. Telephone interviewers, wearing headsets, are seated at computer terminals. The computer may or may not dial the number to be called. Monitors display the questions, one at a time. As the interviewer asks the question, he or she records the response directly into the computer, and it is automatically stored in memory. Therefore, the time-consuming steps of coding, editing and entering data are eliminated. Because the responses are entered directly into the computer, interim and update reports, or data analysis or results can be provided almost instantaneously. This type of computer assisted interviewing works best when answers to the questionnaire are highly structured, i.e. pre-coded possible responses to the questions, with unacceptable answers being rejected by the computer. This may also help increase the accuracy of the data being collected. It is expected that voice recognition technology will be a standard feature of CATI in the future.

A variation of the above is the Completely Automated Telephone Survey (CATS). A computer dials a phone number. A recording is used to introduce the survey and ask the questions. The respondent uses the push buttons on the telephone to respond and interact with the computer.

Box 6.1 The growing dominance of computer and telephone

The image of market research as an industry whose main protagonists are people with clip-boards collecting information from passers-by in streets or from people at home is one that is changing rapidly. Pencil and paper have been the main tools of the industry for many years, ticking boxes and completing questionnaires. But as the information needs of industry become more complex, questionnaires are becoming longer and more complicated, putting severe strains on this method of data collection.

The telephone and the computer are also increasingly important as tools of the industry, but the real revolution has now begun as their capabilities have been combined to produce the interview method used to an ever greater extent today — computer assisted telephone interviewing. In fact there are two revolutions underlying this change. The computer is changing the way market research is undertaken, with new standards of accuracy being achieved and, alongside this, new skills required for scripting of questionnaires for off-screen delivery.

But perhaps more important has been the revolution in how we communicate. The telephone is now accepted as a standard tool of market research, with the resulting data standing alongside that collected face-to-face. This change in attitude to telecommunications is exemplified by our use of the fax. We no longer feel the need to ring to ensure that our fax message has been received. The medium has achieved a level of trust that would have been unheard of ten years ago and is now commonplace.

The advantages of computer and telephone interviewing are as follows:

- Increased speed of project turnaround.
- Greater quality control of interviews and interviewers.
- The ability to use more complex questionnaires.
- Reduced interview time.
- Automatic and clean data entry — elimination of error.
- No key punching.
- Reduction in costs.

Basically, the programme takes care that data entry is correct, that rotations of questions are accommodated automatically, and that routings through quest-ionnaires are followed. And, because data is being entered directly to the computer, there is no need for checking and editing questionnaires or for key punching. The computer leads the interviewer though the interview and does not allow the wrong data to be entered. With interview times on the telephone set to be less than 25 minutes, interviewee fatigue is not a factor. The saving in time is substantial. What may take six to seven weeks by pen and paper can be achieved in seven to eight days. The set of questions agreed on Friday can produce results a week later with 1,000 or more interviews completed. Such timings as these are becoming standard in the UK. One company is now promising results at 9.30 in the evening from a questionnaire going into the field at 3.30 the previous afternoon.

It is becoming a positively utopian state of affairs for marketing management. Reliable, usable information available very swiftly and at short notice. And has this wonderful state of affairs reached these shores? It has, because since January of this year, the market research agency MRC has been operating its Telephone Research Centre in the north of Dublin, using the latest software available in Europe.

Built using state-of-the-art telecentre design and computer technology, the Centre has twenty workstations and can provide a research facility of up to twelve hours a day, seven days a week. The panel of interviewers now consists of around 100 individuals, fully trained to MRC's standards. As partners in the Euro-quest group of market research agencies, these standards are international. The question of language, or of regional accents if this arises, is not a problem because the panel has been recruited to provide this facility.

Sample management is a critical aspect of any telephone research unit. The computer system in MRC's Telephone Research Centre has been designed to accept samples from clients in a variety of formats. For random sampling, the Centre is equipped to use the Irish telephone directory as the core universe, with a statistically valid methodology for 'capturing' non-listed numbers. 'Who gave you my number?' is a question that management at the Centre gets asked fairly often. The answer, entirely truthfully, is that no one did. It was arrived at on a totally random basis, increasing the statistical validity of the method. Another bugbear of the industry is the fear of refusals; in point of fact, the rate of refusals for telephone interviews, at around 10%, runs lower than for face-to-face.

In face-to-face interviewing, a similar revolution is going on as laptops have begun to take over from pen and paper. CAPI (Computer Assisted Personal Interviewing) provides even more advantages for clients, but cost is not, yet, one of them. With a mission to be at the forefront of technological advance in the industry and raise quality standards, MRC are also providing this service to their clients with a 'fleet' of laptops now in constant use north and south of the border.

The atmosphere of innovation and technology at MRC, pushing at the boundaries of the possible, in this exciting development for the market research business in Ireland, has almost to be seen to be believed. It's far removed from pencil, paper and clipboard on Grafton Street.

Source: from *IMJ*, 'Computers and the telephone take over from pencil and paper', pp. 12–13, November 1996.

THE POSTAL INTERVIEW

The postal survey is a self-administered questionnaire sent to respondents through the post. It is very much a paper and pen method of collecting data.

There is no interviewer available to:

1. ask the questions;
2. probe for more information;
3. induce co-operation;
4. record answers;
5. clarify questions for the respondent;
6. guide the interview.

The questionnaire is administered to the respondent by the respondent, and the respondent completes and returns the questionnaire.

The Procedure

As mentioned previously, as there is no interviewer present to clarify issues or to encourage the respondent's co-operation, the construction of the questionnaire and related materials is crucial to the success of this survey method. The researcher must make decisions about the various elements of the postal interview package. It is composed of:

- the out-going envelope;
- the cover letter;
- the questionnaire itself;

- the return envelope;
- the incentives used.

Unless the curiosity and co-operation of the respondent are quickly aroused, it is likely that the respondent will 'shelve' the questionnaire. The cover letter that accompanies the questionnaire is an important means of inducing the reader to complete and return the questionnaire. The cover letter should at least:

1. Explain the purpose and importance of the study.
2. Say how and why the respondent was chosen for participation.
3. State who is sponsoring the study.
4. Indicate why the respondent's co-operation is important.
5. Detail what the respondent is being asked to do.
6. State how the information provided will be used.
7. Indicate whether the respondent will remain anonymous.
8. State what degree of confidentiality applies.

The cover letter, while not too long, may also indicate the amount of effort and time required from the respondent, mention a token incentive and refer the reader to a pre-paid reply envelope.

Advantages of Postal Interview Method

Postal surveys are particularly versatile in reaching all types of people (i.e. consumer or business) in all geographic areas, rural and urban areas, and at the same low cost. The postal survey method generally will have a cost advantage over other survey methods, though it is not cheap. It may necessitate follow-up mailings which require additional postage and printing costs.

The interviewer–respondent interaction is absent in the postal survey. Therefore this dimension of response error is eliminated. (However, as we will see in Chapter 8, response error can still occur in postal surveys.) Also, interviewer bias in the selection of sample members is eliminated.

Another advantage of postal surveys is that the respondent has more time to formulate and record his or her answers. The questionnaire can be filled in at a time and pace convenient to the respondent. In some situations, for example business-to-business marketing research, postal surveys allow respondents to collect facts, such as sales or inventory figures, that they may not know off-hand. In consumer research, the respondent may be able to give a more valid and accurate answer by having the time and flexibility to check in the fridge or consult other family members.

Postal questionnaires have been shown to be superior when collecting data on sensitive or embarrassing topics.[10] This can be attributed to the anonymity of the respondent. Anonymity can also reduce the possibility of respondents giving socially acceptable answers, i.e. reduce social desirability bias.

Limitations of Postal Surveys

The primary limitation of this method is that of non-response error. Surveys that are boring, confusing or too complex get thrown in the bin. Response rate refers to the number or percentage of respondents that return the questionnaire. Mail surveys are usually plagued by low rates of return, typically 10%, and often drag over many weeks. Often the questionnaires received are either poorly filled out or incomplete, further adding to analysis problems.[11] However, although exceptional, it is not unknown for a properly planned and well-designed postal survey to achieve response rates of up to 70%. Much depends on the length of the questionnaire, content, group surveyed, incentives employed and other factors.[12]

A fairly high response rate can be achieved if certain techniques are used by the researcher to increase participation.[13] These techniques will be discussed later. However, non-response is only a problem if the respondents are different to those who do not respond. Certain types of people — people with more education, higher-level occupations, women, students and others have been shown to have a greater probability of not responding.[14] People who have a particular interest (e.g. a hobby) in the topic of the research have a greater probability of responding. As a general rule-of-thumb, the questionnaire should not exceed six pages in length. An over-lengthy questionnaire will most likely be discarded by the respondent.

Sequence bias is also a threat in postal surveys — respondents can change their answers after seeing later questions, and there is no control over the order in which questions are answered. There may also be problems with open-ended questions in postal surveys, whereby responses from less articulate and less literate participants may be very brief or non-existent. Postal questionnaires are therefore often highly standardised with structured questions and clear-cut instructions. Another problem with the postal survey is the turnaround time required. A time lag of two to three weeks is common for receiving the majority of responses. The researcher needs to factor in time for follow-up mailings, leading to a total turnaround time of up to five weeks.

This makes postal surveys unsuitable for measuring certain characteristics, e.g. changes in political opinion leading up to an election. It also makes the responses vulnerable to external events taking place during the study.

There is no guarantee that the intended respondent, i.e. the person's name on the envelope, will be the actual person who fills out the questionnaire. This is a particular problem with business-to-business research. A busy director or financial controller may request a subordinate to fill in and return the questionnaire.

Postal surveys also require suitable mailing lists. In Ireland, An Post offer a range of direct mail services through their dm.works division (see www.dmworks.ie for more details.) Firms such as Precision Marketing Information Ltd (PMI) (see www.pmi.ie) can provide tailored consumer databases that can be used for survey purposes. Researchers can specify the exact kind of customer they want to mail –

based on, say, their lifestyle preferences or their geographical location – and PMI will provide a database complete with phone numbers and further information if needed. PMI Lifestyle is a database containing detailed lifestyle information on over 400,000 individuals. PMI also provide access to their 'Irish Consumer Marketing Database', which is one of the largest and most sophisticated consumer databases for the Irish market, containing information on over 3.6 million Irish households.

Kompass Ireland (www.kompass.ie) are leading suppliers of sales and marketing directories and databases in print, CD and on the Internet. Their database currently contains details on over 100,000 Irish businesses and 170,000 executives. Marketers access the database by selecting on the basis of region, county, postcode, size, executive type, activity, industry sector or top 1,000 or 2,000 companies. The database (or individual lists from it) is available as a printed list, on label, on CD, via email or can be downloaded from the web.

Finally, like telephone interviewing, it is not possible for the market researcher to make concurrent observations (e.g. physical appearance and non-verbal cues) as is the case with the personal interview.

With all these limitations, one might easily wonder why postal questionnaires are ever used. Bank of Ireland phased out paper questionnaires in favour of the telephone and the Internet to survey its customers.[15] They are, nonetheless, a frequent and popular choice among market researchers.

REDUCING NON-RESPONSE IN POSTAL QUESTIONNAIRES

As we have already mentioned, non-response is always a potential hazard when conducting postal survey research. In fact, whatever the survey mode used, those who respond may be different to those who choose not to. Those who respond may be more involved with the product, they may have more education, or they might be more satisfied with the service provider than the target population of interest.[16] Researchers have developed a number of techniques to influence the response rate of postal respondents. These are dealt with in summary form in Box 6.2 and Box 6.3. It should be noted that some of these techniques could also be applied to other survey methods. There is evidence that with the main types of survey methods, the inclusion of some monetary incentive or product promotion will increase response rates.[17] To encourage people to fill in and return postal questionnaires, Bank of Ireland promises a donation to a group of charities for every response it gets back.[18]

Improving Returns

There are many examples in the research literature of studies which examine the difficulties of improving postal survey returns. A number of helpful ideas on improving response rates are available.[19]

Box 6.2 Methods used to increase postal survey response

Inducement	*Examples*
Preliminary notification	Advance letter or postcard, telephone pre-notification.
Foot-in-the-door	Use of small initial incentive and then a larger subsequent incentive to those who comply with the small incentive.
Personalisation	Hand-addressed envelope, personal signature, individually typed/addressed cover letter.
Anonymity	Assurance of anonymity, use/non-use of ID number.
Response deadline	Different due dates following receipt of questionnaire.
Appeals	Social utility, help the sponsor, egoistic.
Sponsorship	Company, trade association, university researcher.
Incentives	Non-monetary (for example, ballpoint pens, summary of findings), monetary (for example, given to sample member, donated to charity).
Questionnaire length	Printing on both sides of sheet, white space related to perceived length.
Questionnaire size, reproduction and colour	Standard A-sizes, printed, mimeographed, various colours.
Type of postage (out-going)	Commemorative stamp, metered postage, first class, third class.
Type of postage (return envelopes)	Business reply permit, regular stamps, metered postage.
Follow-ups	Different intervals, postcard, letter, replacement questionnaire

Source: Jeffery Connant, Denise Smart and Bruce Walker, 'Mail survey facilitation techniques: an assessment and proposal regarding reporting practices', *Journal of the Marketing Research Society*, Vol. 32 No. 4 (1990), pp. 569–80.

Follow-ups

Follow-ups, or reminders, are very sucessful in increasing response rates. Since each successive follow-up results in added returns, the very persistent researcher can potentially achieve an extremely high total response rate. However, the value of additional information thus obtained must be weighed against the costs required for successive contacts.

Preliminary Notification

There is evidence that advance notification, particularly by telephone, is effective in increasing response rates; it also serves to accelerate the rate of return. However, follow-ups are a better investment than preliminary notification.

Concurrent Techniques

1. *Questionnaire length.* Although common sense suggests that short question-naires should obtain higher response rates than longer questionnaires, research evidence does not support this view.

2. *Survey sponsorship.* There is little experimental evidence concerning the influence of survey sponsorship on response rates; however, the sparse evidence that does exist suggests that official or 'respected' sponsorship increases response rates.

3. *Return envelopes.* A study that tested the hypothesis that return envelopes increase reponse rates suggests that the inclusion of a stamped, return envelope does encourage response because it simplifies questionnaire return.

4. *Postage.* Many tests regarding postage are reported in the literature, but few studies have tested the same variables. The existing evidence shows that special delivery is very effective in increasing response rates. Findings do not show a significant advantage for first class over third class, for commemorative stamps over ordinary postage, for stamped mail over metered mail, or for multiple, small-domination stamps over single, larger-dominational stamps.

5. *Personalisation.* Empirical evidence suggests that personalisation of the mailing has no clear-cut advantage in terms of improved response rates. Neither personal inside addresses nor individually signed cover letters significantly increased response rates; personally typed cover letters proved to be somewhat effective in most but not all cases cited. The one study that tested the use of titled signature versus one without a title did show a significant advantage in favour of the title.

6. *Cover letters.* The influence of the cover letter on response rates has received almost no experimental attention, although the cover letter is an integral part of the mail survey. It is the most logical vehicle for persuading individuals to respond, yet the few studies that are reported offer no insights as to its formulation.

7. *Anonymity.* Experimental evidence shows that the promise of anonymity to respondent — either explicit or implied — has no significant effect on response rates.

8. *Size, reproduction and colour.* The few studies that examined the effects of questionnaire size, method of reproduction and colour found no significant difference in response rates.

9. *Money incentives.* A monetary incentive sent with the questionnaire is very effective in increasing response rates. Larger sums bring in added response, but at a cost that may exceed the value of the added information.

10. *Deadline dates.* The few studies that tested the impact of deadline dates found that they did not increase the response rate; however, they did serve to accelerate the rate of questionnaire return.

Box 6.3 Types of appeals used in survey research

Appeal	*Wording of appeals*
Social utility	'Your assistance is needed!! Your attitudes and opinions can provide information that contributes to understanding how consumers can be better served by local retail shopping facilities . . . Your co-operation is truly appreciated.'
Help-the-sponsor	'We need your assistance!! Your attitudes and opinions are very important to our successful completion of this study . . . We truly appreciate your co-operation.'
Egoistic	'Your opinions are important!! It's important for you to express your opinion so Madison's retailers will know the types of products and shopping facilities you would like to have available . . . Thanks for expressing your opinions.'
Combined appeal	'Your opinions are important and useful!! Your attitudes and opinions are important for three reasons: (1) they can provide information that leads to an understanding of how consumers can be better served by local retail shopping facilities; (2) they will enable Madison's retailers to know the types of products and shopping facilities you would like to have available; and (3) they will help us successfully complete this study . . . thank you for your co-operation.'

Source: Michael J. Houston and John R. Nevin, 'The effects of source and appeal on mail survey response patterns', *Journal of Marketing Research*, August 1977, pp. 347–87, published by the American Marketing Association.

METHODS OF ESTIMATING THE DEGREE OF NON-RESPONSE ERROR

Despite all efforts, it is next to impossible to totally eliminate non-response in survey research, be it postal, telephone or personal interview. Five methods to deal with the effect of non-response error are briefly presented below:

1. Sensitivity analysis

This approach requires the researcher to determine how different each successive call-back group is from the previous respondent group. If the research decision is insensitive to this difference, no further call-backs are necessary. The central question here is how different the non-respondents would have to be in order for this difference to have an effect on our decision.

2. Trend projection

If, from successive call-backs, a trend emerges on the variables under study, this trend can be utilised to estimate the characteristics of the non-respondent group.

3. Sub-sampling of non-respondents

A separate study is conducted with a sample of the non-respondents. This data is then used to make generalisations about *all* of the non-respondents.

4. Subjective estimate

The researcher uses judgment and past experience to estimate the proportionate effect of non-response.

5. The 'ostrich' approach

Here the researcher merely assumes that non-respondents are the same as respondents, i.e. there is non-response but no non-response bias. This is obviously a risky approach to deal with non-response in survey research.

ONLINE SURVEYS

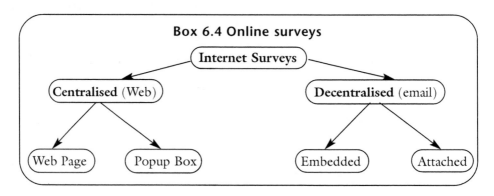

Box 6.4 Online surveys

Online surveys are increasing in popularity. One reason is the cost: in most cases costs are less than for phone and mail surveys or personal interviews, three of the most common type of survey. Also, the online survey is not as inconvenient as the phone call in the middle of dinner or one's favourite TV programme. The online survey can be completed in one's own time and place. Quick response time and ability to target specific populations are also advantages worth noting. As Internet usage becomes more widespread, the disadvantages of this method in terms of sampling limitations and representativeness is substantially reduced. There is evidence that online surveys have fewer missing responses and they can be coded/presented in a more flexible manner. Contingent coding can be used, whereby different respondents receive different questions/question patterns based on their response to previous questions. Also, the survey turnaround (response) time can be shorter relative to a paper survey, and the time required for data entry and cleansing can also be greatly reduced as the data is collected at source in an electronic format.[20]

To save money and expedite market research surveys, Procter & Gamble is conducting more of its consumer marketing research online. Using the Internet, P&G can build and manage detailed proprietary panels of consumers who register for future surveys at their web-site in return for a coupon or other monetary incentive. As respondents are asked to register their personal details online, reports can be customised according to specific demographic data such as age, salary, area of residence, and number of children.[21]

Online surveys can be centralised (completed by the respondent on the web) or decentralised (sent out to potential respondents via email) (see box 6.4 above). Decentralised surveys will be discussed later in this section.

With the centralised approach, there are generally two options. The survey can be presented as part of a web-site, on one or more web pages. Alternatively, the survey can be presented to potential respondents who visit the web-site via a 'pop-up box' (which appears automatically as an additional minimised browser window). If the survey is part of a web-site, the researcher has two options. One option is to make the survey accessible to everyone who visits the web-site, by having a link to the survey appear on the web-site's home page. In this case, the survey participants are, of course, self-selecting (this issue is discussed in more detail in Chapter 10). The second option is to invite a sample (or indeed an entire population) via an email message to visit a specific URL and participate in the survey. By using this method, the researcher has complete control over the sample, provided the particular URL is not available from publicly accessible web pages or any other source.

The ability to present the survey in an attractive format (e.g. making appropriate use of graphics and colours) and to make the survey easy and quick to complete, using devices such as drop-down boxes (containing predefined responses), are also significant advantages of the web survey over email,[22] and a likely reason why completion rates for web surveys is higher than for email surveys.[23] However, respondents must have access to the web to complete the survey.

When designing web-based surveys, researchers should bear certain design factors in mind. Scrolling is an issue, especially for Web survey pages with many items or many item alternatives. Depending on their web browser software and their screen resolution and settings, some respondents may be able to view survey pages in their entirety, while others are forced to use scrollbars. Scrolling, viewing additional pages, and using extra key clicks to move safely from one page to the next can make survey tasks longer and more tedious.[24] Recognising difficulties associated with scrolling, developers of survey tools suggest the use of short survey pages. Some online survey tools require respondents to click on a 'continue' button at the end of each page before moving to the next page.

When respondents are completing a web survey, it is not always practicable to stop half way through, and return and complete the survey later: both of these are possible when a paper survey or an email survey is being carried out.[25]

Web surveys also offer the possibility to include graphic images, sound and video clips to create surveys that are 'interesting and involving'.[26] Web surveys do, however, require much more time and money to construct than email surveys. Bandwidth (bandwidth refers to the maximum amount of data that can pass through a connection over a given time, usually measured in bps (bits-per-second)) limitations may also be a constraint on the use of multimedia web surveys. As bandwidth increases, it becomes feasible to incorporate multimedia features such as video and audio clips as part of a web survey.

Tools such as Survey Monkey (www.surveymonkey.com) allow researchers to create their own survey using an online survey editor, selecting from over a dozen types of questions and using options such custom skip logic and question randomisation to help eliminate bias. Researchers can also use a pop-up invitation generator to maximise response rates and an automated email notification and list management tool to track respondents. Results can be viewed as they are collected in realtime and the application allows ease of production for graphs and charts as well as downloading the raw data into Excel or SPSS.

Looking ahead, the use of Internet Telephony (Voice Over Internet Protocol or VoIP) and Web Cameras (Web Cams) may well mean that the personal survey, telephone survey and Internet survey will merge to result in a rich multimedia experience for the respondent.[27] VoIP allows researchers and consumers to communicate telephone-to-telephone, computer-to-telephone or computer-to-computer, with the Internet carrying the voice traffic. Companies offering these facilities include Net2phone (www.net2phone.com) and Dialpad (www.dialpad.com). Indeed, it is very possible that the telephone and online survey methods will merge. For example, software provided by itracks (www.itracks.com) can seamlessly integrate online and telephone interviewing.

Decentralised surveys, where email is used to distribute the questionnaire directly to the chosen sample, are the fastest and simplest of the two options, offering the widest reach and requiring the least set-up time.[28] When compared to traditional mail surveys, there are no costs for paper, printing, envelopes, stamps and related administrative work.[29] Decentralised surveys can generally be distributed in one of two ways: embedded in the text of the email, or as a file (most often a Microsoft word document) attached to an email.

In the case of an embedded email survey, the text in the email can either be in Plain text or HyperText Markup Language (HTML) format. Plain text format – also called American Standard Code for Information Interchange (ASCII) format – is the most portable format (meaning it can be used on the greatest number of computers) because it is supported by nearly every software application on every type of computer. It is quite limited, however, because it cannot contain any formatting commands: hence, survey layout can often be a problem. HTML emails allow for greater control of formatting. However, some types of email software cannot read HTML emails, and this can cause a problem. Where plain text emails are used, researchers should stick to short questions with very simple formatting. Open response questions are preferable as they make the least demands on formatting.

When an attached questionnaire is used, the respondent detaches the file from the email message and saves it to his or her PC hard drive. The file is then opened, the survey completed and re-saved. It is then necessary for the respondent to email the researcher and attach the completed survey to the email. Hence, using an attached questionnaire is more complex for the respondent, and may raise issues of compatible software.[30] It also raises issues in terms of the technical ability of the respondent – some respondents may be unable to manipulate the attachment.[31] So, in order to complete an attached email survey, the respondent has to be technologically capable of downloading, completing and re-saving the file and attaching it to an email to return it to the researcher.

Respondents who download an attached survey also leave themselves open to the risk of catching a computer virus. Respondents completing surveys on the web run less of a risk of being infected by viruses. Therefore, researchers using attached surveys should ensure that the files they send are virus-free. Given the greater level of technical competence, greater commitment of time and the greater risks of virus infection that result from using email surveys, it has been suggested that attached surveys are most useful in business-to-business surveys or internal employee surveys.[32]

Regardless of which type of email survey is used, it is important to include an email subject line that captures the respondent's interest and clearly indicates the topic. The researcher should tell the respondent exactly how their email address was obtained, why they have been contacted and the identity of the organisation that is conducting the research.

Response rates for attached surveys can be much lower than for embedded surveys. Despite the fact the attachment offers more opportunity to replicate a printed questionnaire, it presents more obstacles for the respondent. So it is best to only use attached surveys where the respondent is likely to have:

- A strong interest in responding.
- Time available to download, re-save and re-attach the survey.
- Knowledge of how to carry out these operations.
- The software to enable the attachments to be easily accessed (which may depend on whether the respondent uses a Microsoft or Apple operating system).
- Low fear of acquiring a PC virus.

- No issue downloading the attachments through security firewalls (firewalls are almost always used as part of computer networks and can sometimes prevent the delivery of email attachments on security grounds).

The main advantages of using email for survey administration are:[33]

- Instant delivery.
- Instant return of undelivered surveys.
- Quicker response time.
- Lower cost.
- Emails are usually only read by the addressee.
- Greater convenience for respondent.

The main disadvantages stem from the lower level of security of email compared to traditional mail and that it is impossible to guarantee respondent anonymity.[34] However, advances in email security minimise this issue.

Web surveys are, without doubt, a more powerful tool than email surveys. Email survey questionnaires cannot typically include skip pattern logic, and randomisation. Their real-time nature also offers the opportunity to validate data as responses are made (i.e. by requiring valid responses), which simplifies and speeds up the data-cleaning process and enables sophisticated analysis to be performed in real time rather than after the study has been taken out of field.[35] It is also possible to write a piece of software to interpret responses and transfer them directly to a database.[36]

Internet surveys (both web and email) are, like traditional mail surveys, self-administered. This can have drawbacks. Respondents can resize and reposition windows or choose tiled or cascaded windows, which can affect the way the survey is viewed by the respondent. They also can run concurrent applications, split their attention between surveys and other tasks, walk away from a survey, or ask others to respond to a survey on their behalf.[37]

Although they have numerous advantages over paper-based surveys, electronic surveys can have lower response rates than for offline surveys.[38]A number of factors have been suggested to explain why this may be so.[39]

- Lack of anonymity.
- Lack of tangible image and cosmetic features.
- Difficulty in offering particular incentives online.

The tendency for some respondents to want to read through a hard copy (printed version) of the survey means that they have to consider the time and cost to print it out: an effort that would not be necessary if the survey was posted to them in hard copy format. It could be said that printed surveys involve less pre-investment of time and resources for the researcher to develop: the need to de-bug the survey software and make it simple and transparent for the respondent to use cannot be underestimated. It has been suggested that printed surveys are much easier because what you see is what you get: there are fewer hidden intricacies.[40] However, this must be offset against the automation of data entry, which results in time, money and accuracy gains. When choosing one survey method over another, while cost is an important issue it should not be the driving factor. The relative quality of the data collected should be the key driver of methodological considerations in this regard.

It is recommended that a reasonable length for an online survey will be similar to telephone surveys – about twenty minutes.[41] It does, however, vary according to the type of population concerned, the topic and the incentive(s) offered.

Advantages & Disadvantages of Online Surveys

There is an emerging consensus that online research will become a major way of gathering data quickly and accurately in the future. According to Gerard O'Neill of Amárach Consulting, 'The main challenge in Internet research is get a good sample and to police the management and usage of the database so that it complies with data protection legislation.' Luke Reaper of TNS mrbi agrees. 'We believe online research will surge in the future. Even now we are conducting more and more quantitative surveys online with ordinary consumers as opposed to the business sector. The advantages and potential disadvantages are summarised in Figure 6.1:

Figure 6.1 The strengths and potential weaknesses of online surveys

Major Strengths

- Global reach
- B-to-B and B-to-C appeal
- Flexibility
- Speed and timeliness
- Technological innovations
- Convenience
- Ease of data entry and analysis
- Question diversity
- Low administration cost
- Ease of follow-up
- Controlled sampling
- Large sample easy to obtain
- Control of answer order
- Required completion of answers
- Go to capabilities
- Knowledge of respondent vs non-respondent characteristics

Major Potential Weaknesses

- Perception as junk mail
- Skewed attributes of Internet population: upscale, male, etc.
- Questions about sample selection and implementation
- Respondent lack of online experience/expertise
- Technological variations
- Unclear answering instructions
- Impersonal
- Privacy issues
- Low response rate

Source: Joel R. Evans and Anil Mathur, 'The Value of Online Surveys', *Internet Research*, Vol. 15, No. 2, pp. 195–219, Emerald Group Publishing Ltd, 2005.

COMBINING SURVEY TECHNIQUES

Since each of the methods of data collection has its own strengths and limitations, it may be necessary to combine two or more approaches to survey research. For example, in a tourism research study, personal interviews may be carried out with tourists visiting the area, telephone interviews conducted with regional tourism information offices and postal questionnaires sent to tour operators.

Alternative Means of Administration

The preceding discussion covered the traditional and primary methods of collecting survey data. However, there are also variations of the above and emerging survey approaches.

- Restaurants, hotels and service providers frequently have short questionnaires available for guests and customers to fill out after they have experienced the service, e.g. Mother Hubbards, Bewleys, Statoil, etc. However, it is interesting to note that only 1% of most hotel guests complete their questionnaires.[42]
- Self-administered questionnaires are left on a table/counter with instructions, pens and deposit box at the exit point of, for example, a tourism attraction or bookshop seeking customer feedback. UCI introduced a 'viewpoint' box in the cinema for people to air their views. It also provides a freepost facility for those who want to take the questionnaire home.[43]
- Using the drop-off method, questionnaires are hand-delivered to the respondent's home or place of business and are collected at a later date (e.g. census of population research). A variation is where the respondent returns the completed questionnaire by post.
- Questionnaires are distributed via print media such as magazines and newspapers. Completed questionnaires are returned to a 'freepost' address.
- Fax surveys an alternative means of collecting information from business markets.

- Use of an automated interviewing line can eliminate some of the problems associated with postal and telephone interviewing. It can work as follows: an appropriate mailing list and sample are developed and a package is mailed in the typical way. The package contains a unique ID number, stimulus materials, and instructions to call a 1800- number. The 1800- number is available 24 hours a day, seven days a week. Respondents call at their convenience. Participants key in their responses using their telephone key pads.
- Computer interactive surveys and interactive kiosks (see Box 6.5) are becoming popular at trade shows, exhibitions and conferences. The respondent interacts directly with an on-site computer. The questions appear on a computer screen and the respondent replies using the keyboard or touch screen. It is probably best to use only dichotomous or multiple-choice type questions.
- Laptops have begun to take over from pen, paper and clipboard for personal interviews — CAPI (Computer Assisted Personal Interviewing). CAPI is provided through specialised software. Examples of packages in use at present are Blaise (www.westat.com/blaise), Quancept (www.spss.com/quancept_cati/) and Microtab (www.microtab.com), each of which has its merits according to the type of survey being carried out.[44]

Box 6.5 Using interactive kiosks for research

Traditionally, researchers have used phone and exit interviews, shop intercepts and postal surveys to study retail shopping experiences. Although these methods have their strengths, there is an alternative, and that is kiosk-based research. Kiosks are multimedia touch-screen computers contained in free-standing cabinets. They can be programmed to perform complicated surveys, show full colour scanned images (store layouts, products), play high-quality stereo sound clips and show video segments. With little need for instruction, most people enjoy these interviews and 'play' them with little reservation. Kiosks can also be used at trade shows and exhibitions. Kiosks, like exit interviews, score high in terms of capturing recent experiences and are useful for interviewing low-incidence respondents because they are on site. At the same time, kiosk-based research tends to be less expensive than exit interviews, allowing a higher number of stores to be included in the survey. A bonus is that people tend to give more honest answers to a computer than to another human being. Kiosks have several other advantages. Internal control, for example, is much higher with kiosks than with other methods. Because the survey is preprogrammed, the researcher doesn't have to worry about whether the correct visual stimuli were shown or whether the right skip pattern was followed. Although kiosk-based research does not replace the more traditional ways to capture the shopping experience, it should be considered a less expensive, easily implemented alternative, especially when evaluating hard-to-reach populations.

Source: Adapted from *Marketing News*, 2 January 1995, Vol. 39 No. 1, 'Using interactive kiosks for retail research', Beth Schneider.

Box 6.6
Virtual reality shopping and market research are still in their early stages, but the implications are far-reaching and will affect many companies

'A shelf full of washing powder stares you in the face. Every conceivable brand is there, row upon row. They are brightly coloured and neatly stacked. They could be yours. Just press a button. This is not a dream. This is virtual reality shopping with a vengeance. Neat pictures of supermarket shelves are depicted on the screen. Each shelf displays a different sort of product. You move from one to another with ease and choose what you would like to buy.

Visionary Shopping is a system developed by Harvard academics and is providing what is described as 'a virtual-reality computer simulation of a supermarket'. Its main use currently is as an alternative market research tool. In Britain, two companies have tried it out — one a snacks manufacturer and one a producer of soft drinks.

Virtual reality techniques have significant potential in new product development (NPD) research. Virtual shopping can reduce the NPD timescale and assist consumers in examining new concepts.

It is 10% to 20% cheaper than conventional market research and it takes two weeks rather than six months. If respondents are interested in something, they simply touch it and it emerges from the shelf. Closer inspection can be achieved by touching a magnifying glass at the side of the screen. If it looks worth buying, simply touch the article again and it drops into a screen trolley.

'We have three basic types of market research — price of goods, promotions of goods and package testing. These work particularly effectively because consumers can actually look at a shelf on the screen to make their purchasing decisions rather than read options from a list,' says Dr Stephen Needel, President of VS.

One of the most obvious ways in which companies can benefit from virtual reality is in the area of packaging. 'The new design does not even need to be made up. We can put it in the system just using the artwork and test it out. This can save manufacturers hundreds of thousands of dollars,' explains Needel.

4D shopper puts consumers in a virtual store, asking them to shop as they would normally shop. This system is used to test the sales impact of:
– Category management
– Pricing
– Promotions
– Packaging
– New products
– Substitution behaviour
– Choice behaviour

A criticism of VR-based techniques is that they generate an unusually high level of interest in shopping due to their novelty. More research is needed to assess how these techniques affect consumer behaviour.'

Source: www.4dshopper.com (2006)

Source: Adapted from: *The Evening Standard*, 'Couch potatoes in the supermarket', MCC95, February 02 (765) by Joanne Hart; 'VR techniques in NPD research', *JMRS*, October 1995, Vol. 37 No. 4, p. 345 (11), Philip Rosenberg and Leslie Chernatony; and www.4dshopper.com(2006).

Table 6.1 Strengths and weaknesses of principal survey methods

	Mail	Telephone	Personal	Internet
1. Flexibility	Poor	Good	Excellent	Fair
2. Quantity of data that can be collected	Good	Fair	Excellent	Good
3. Control of interviewer effects	Excellent	Fair	Poor	Excellent
4. Control of sample	Fair	Excellent	Fair	Fair
5. Speed of data collection	Poor	Excellent	Good	Excellent
6. Response rate	Poor	Good	Good	Poor
7. Cost	Good	Fair	Poor	Excellent
8. Sample frame	Good	Excellent	Fair	Poor

(*Source*: *Principles of Marketing*, Chapter 8, p. 328, European edition 1999, Philip Kotler *et al.*)

Panel Research

A panel or longitudinal survey is a form of sample survey from which comparative data from the sampling units are taken on more than one occasion. It is a form of continuous research reporting on the behaviour of the same respondents over time. Panels can be made up of individuals, households, firms or retail outlets and are a convenient method of obtaining continuous information over a period of time.[45] A longitudinal study that gathers data from the same sample of individuals over time is called a consumer panel. Households are commonly selected on the basis of random sampling.

Most panels use some form of 'diary' which members fill in with details of purchases or product usage. Diary data that is recorded regularly over a period of time allows the researcher to track repeat-purchasing behaviour and changes in purchasing habits. Completed diaries are posted back to the researcher or collected at regular intervals.

Panels are by nature longitudinal. This makes them different to regular surveys which are typically cross-sectional, i.e data is collected at a single point. Continuous research can be equated to a motion picture, whereas one-off survey research is akin to a snapshot.

The advantage of panel research over one-off surveys is the ability to measure changes in the behaviour of individuals. A continuous panel is one way of conducting quasi-experiments, that is to say that the effect of changes in price, advertising and packaging, etc. can be monitored through panel research. Experimentation is dealt with in the next chapter. Because there is an ongoing relationship between the panel members and the research company, there is also more opportunity to collect attitudinal and classification information to help better understand the observed changes in behaviour.[46]

A major drawback with panels is the problem of mortality. For one reason or another, panel members may choose not to continue and drop out. Incentives are offered to encourage continuing participation. There is always the possibility that those who drop out will differ from those who remain on the panel. Replacements should be as representative as possible. There is a tendency for newly recruited panel members to initially change their behaviour because of the novelty of the reporting responsibility. It may therefore be advisable to exclude the results from these households until the novelty has worn off and their behaviour has returned to normal. This may take a week or two.

There can also be the problem of selection bias. Many individuals or households may refuse to participate, thereby raising the question of how representative are panels of the population of interest.

A.C. Nielsen (www.acnielsen.com and www.acnielsen.ie) operates a retail audit service. It monitors the performance of Fast Moving Consumer Goods (FMCGs) by collecting data in a sample of retail outlets spread throughout the country. The sample outlet data is grossed up to the total number of outlets in the country to give estimates on volume of sales, market share, average retail selling price, distribution and out of stocks. A number of different services, or Indices, is provided. For example, food, off-licences, chemists, and confectionery are all separate services.

Overall, panels are not as commonly used in Ireland as in the UK, Europe and USA. Abroad they are frequently called syndicated services. This is dealt with in Chapter 4.

ONLINE PANEL RESEARCH: BULLETIN BOARDS

Bulletin boards are asynchronous, that is to say they keep discussions active for an extended period of time – typically a week – and respondents can logon at times convenient to them, and have time to offer a considered response or, where necessary, do background research before responding.[47] They also keep messages for participants until they are ready to read and reply to them, making it very flexible and convenient for participants.[48] While online focus groups are typically limited to between six and eight participants, online bulletin board discussions can involve up to twenty participants and last for five days or more.[49]

The use of bulletin boards in conjunction with other online tools is also worthy of note. Research has shown that survey respondents who were invited to complete the survey from an invitation and a link on a bulletin board gave more complete responses and higher quality responses than respondents who received the survey as an email attachment.[50]

Box 6.7 Procter and Gamble bring research home

Procter and Gamble (P&G) is launching an ethnographic research venture designed to find out how consumers behave in their own homes. Set up in conjunction with British research firm EveryDay Lives, the research will initially be carried out in the UK, Italy, Germany and China. Twenty families in each country are being filmed in their homes, with the aim of creating an archive of videos showing how people interact with products. P&G researchers developing new products worldwide will then study their behaviour. P&G spokesperson Martha Depenbrock comments: 'The idea is to be able to see what people do in their natural environment, rather than in a focus group.'

Source: Adapted from *Marketing News – The Magazine of the Marketing Institute*, 2000, Vol. 13, No. 6, p.2.

Omnibus Surveys

Omnibus surveys are shared surveys. Like panels, they are a form of continuous research. This means that measurement is conducted on an ongoing basis and is designed to monitor and track changes in the marketplace. Omnibus surveys are good at tracking consumer purchasing, awareness and attitude trends. Omnibus surveys are run by research companies. Clients buy space in the questionnaire by adding questions to meet their requirements.[51] For the client company, it can be a quick and cheap method of collecting information at short notice. Such surveys consist of several sections, each dealing with a different topic and conducted confidentially for an individual client. Individual client companies share the costs but not the results. Questions can be directed to all adults or to particular groups — such as housewives, young people, car owners, alcohol drinkers, or simply to people who use the company's product.[52]

Interviewing and other administrative costs of each survey are shared collectively by the participating clients. Omnibus surveys can therefore provide a very economical facility for obtaining national and regional survey data on products or services.[53] Questions can cover many areas of interest to individual clients, e.g. brand awareness, price awareness, frequency of purchase, place of purchase, media exposure etc.[54]

In Ireland, Millward Brown IMS (www.imsl.ie) and Lansdowne Market Research (www.lmr.ie) are two companies which offer an Omnibus service. The following are some of the marketing issues recently covered by Lansdowne Omnibus surveys:[55]

- Measure trial and consumer acceptance, following the launch of a new snack food.
- Monitor brand switching activity in the beer market to identify recruitment and defection levels for individual brands.
- Track homemakers' shopping patterns and customer satisfaction with multiple and symbol group stores.
- Annually monitor the corporate image of major public companies.
- Identify emerging niche sectors within the alcoholic drinks market.
- Evaluate performance of advertising for a wide selection of branded products before, during and after advertising campaigns.
- Measure attitudes to editorial content of newspaper, radio and TV programmes.
- Determine awareness, comprehension and reactions to new services in the financial sector.
- Measure public opinion on a wide range of social and political issues.
- Track penetration of emerging technology

In May 2001, Lansdowne Market Research launched a new telephone omnibus survey called 'Telebus', designed to compliment their face-to-face Omnibus survey, which consists of a nationally representative survey of 1,000 adults aged over fifteen with a land-based telephone. Telebus is conducted every month from a purpose-built CATI Centre in Dublin City. The total survey has a maximum length of twenty minutes and results are presented with a full demographic (by sex, age, social class, etc) analysis. Clients pay for this service on a 'per question' basis.[56] A telephone omnibus survey facility is also provided by TNS mrbi PhoneBus (www.tnsmrbi.ie/).

OBSERVATION METHODS

We have already looked at surveys as a methodology for conducting descriptive research. Observation research is the second way to conduct descriptive research. There is a long tradition of observational research in the social sciences, especially amongst those researchers influenced by social anthropology. The term observation is usually used to refer to methods of generating data which involve the researcher immersing himself in a research setting, and systematically observing dimensions of that setting, interactions, relationships, actions, events, and so on.[57] In this section we restrict ourselves to observation of ongoing and current behaviour. Observation involves systematically recording the behavioural patterns of people, objects and occurrences without questioning or communicating with them. Information may be recorded as events occur or may be completed from records of past events. It can be a source of low-cost research information. Yet it is probably one of the most under-utilised approaches to collecting marketing research data. However, it is rare for a research design to rely entirely on observational research. In practice, observational research is used with other data collection methods. Some retailers use a mixture of survey and observational research. Retailers use a data collection technique called 'super walks', where a researcher walks with a shopper through the store recording the shopper's comments while observing their buying behaviour and decision-making.

Mystery shopping is a technique that is becoming increasingly popular. This is where the researcher poses as a customer to find out what happens in the normal interaction between the customer and salesperson. Mystery shopping has changed from a hiring-and-firing technique used predominantly in restaurants (and mainly in the US) to a 'nurturing' learning tool. Researchers are now beginning to use it more as a means of evaluating the shopping/buying process. Traditionally it was confined to banks and fast-food outlets and petrol stations, but now it is used almost everywhere that a service is delivered.[58]

Box 6.8 What makes an effective mystery shopping programme?

- Defining clear objectives is essential. These objectives should take into account existing training and operational procedures and desired standards of customer service and sales performance.
- Questionnaires should be designed to record objective observational feedback. There should be a mixture of closed and open questions and plenty of opportunity for assessor comments and suggestions for improvement.
- Some issues of front-line performance are more important than others. To reflect this, individual questions, and questionnaire categories, should be weighted. Appropriate weighting is critical to the overall framing of the evaluation.
- Assessors should receive comprehensive training and clear written instuctions. All evaluations should be completed over a similar period of time, with assessors provided with specific scenarios and instructions to ask for the same or similar products/services.
- Completed questionnaires should be quality checked for validity, accuracy, consistency and objectivity.
- Reporting on timely basis. Turnaround time should be kept to a maximum of 30 days.
- If possible, reports should be location-specific and also provide summary information. Questionnaire category statistical results should be outlined in depth, backed up with adequate qualitative information. This qualitative

information is important as it improves the actionability of the findings by providing the reasons behind the various category scores.

- Mystery shopping should not be used as a once-off audit. Ongoing programmes are more effective and objective and also allow companies to make real positive changes to front-line performance.

Source: 'Taking the mystery out of mystery shopping', *Marketing Institute News*, July/August 1998. Aidrian Bushnell.

The same scientific approach should be used when carrying out observational research, as is applied to other types of research. If proper hypotheses, objectives and sampling procedures are followed, the results may be generalised to a larger population. Observational research is frequently used as an exploratory research tool. In some instances, observation may be the only way to obtain the desired information, e.g. toy manufacturers may provide young children with a prototype or a competitor's toys and observe how they play with them. After all, very young children cannot easily communicate verbal responses.

Box 6.9 Look and learn!

'We often ask too many questions when all we really need is to observe what people are doing. I don't think that the Japanese car companies asked people in this country if they wanted a cup holder in their car. I believe that they observed people getting into their cars first thing in the morning holding a cup of coffee and looking for a flat surface on which to put the cup.'

Source: 'Changing demands', *Journal of Advertising Research*, January/February 1996, Vol. 36 No. 1, p. 31(4), by Watts Wacker.

Observational techniques fall into five different classifications as follows (most observational research will possess two or more degrees of these classifications).

1. Natural versus Contrived Observation

Natural observation involves observing behaviour as it takes place naturally in the environment, for example, as people are shopping in a supermarket or availing themselves of bank services. A cereal company may conduct observational research in the cereal aisle of a supermarket. They may wish to know how the in-store purchase decision appears to be made for adult versus children's cereal. Contrived observation, on the other hand, involves creating an artificial environment and observing behaviour patterns. An artificial environment may include a simulated supermarket aisle or a test kitchen. Contrived observation allows the researcher to control extraneous variables and is often more efficient than waiting for the same situation to occur of its own accord. However, behaviour that is observed in an artificial environment may be different to what would occur in a real-world situation.

2. *Open versus Disguised Observation*

In observation research, the respondent may or may not be aware that he or she is being observed. Disguised observational research enables respondents to behave naturally, since people tend to behave differently when they know they are being observed. Research can be disguised by using hidden cameras, one-way mirrors, or researchers dressed as sales staff or posing as shoppers.

There are two schools of thought as to how much the presence of the observer will affect people's behaviour patterns. One viewpoint is that the observer effect is small, the other is that the observer can seriously bias the behaviour patterns.

3. *Structured versus Unstructured Observation*

Observation can be structured or unstructured in much the same way as surveys. For structured observation, the researcher specifies in detail what is to be observed and how the measurements are to be recorded. Structured observation requires using a structured questionnaire-like data collection instrument. Structured observation is appropriate when the decision problem has been clearly defined, the information needed has been specified, and the behaviour patterns to be observed are not overly ambiguous. Structured observation reduces the potential for interviewer bias, increases the reliability of the data, and is most suited to conclusive research. In unstructured observation, the researcher is free to note whatever he or she deems relevant. It is most suited to exploratory research, when flexibility is required to identify key components of the problem and to generate hypotheses.

4. *Direct versus Indirect Observation*

In direct observation, researchers directly observe current behaviour. Much of the observation done in marketing research is of this type. Behaviour is observed as it actually occurs. Indirect observation refers to observing some record of past behaviour, i.e. the effects of the behaviour are observed rather than the behaviour itself. Sherlock Holmes could be considered as an expert in indirect observation. Likewise with archaeologists and forensic scientists. One approach to indirect observation is called the analysis of physical traces. Two examples come to mind. One is where the researcher (with permission) studies the refuse of households in an attempt to determine buyer or usage behaviour. Alternatively, the researcher may conduct a pantry audit. The observer inspects the respondent's cupboards or fridge for the pre-determined products or brands.

Other innovative applications of trace analysis include:

1. Erosion of floor tiles around an exhibit or painting in a museum or art gallery as an indicator of relative popularity.

2. The position of car radio dials in cars brought in for service to determine which national or local radio station is best for the garage to advertise in.
3. An analysis of the cars in the parking area of the Point Depot as an indicator of the target audience for a Murray Raphael Seminar.
4. Brand preference studies and relative store emphasis on different brands is noted by observing the size of the inventory displayed, i.e. number of facings.

Analysis of secondary data and other published sources is another application of indirect observation. Content analysis is an observational technique used to analyse written material (usually advertising copy). Content analysis can be used to measure the change in the content of advertising over a time period. The frequency of appearances of African Americans and other minorities in USA mass media has been a topic of content analysis.

5. *Human versus Mechanical Observation*

In mechanical observation, mechanical devices rather than human observers record the behaviour being observed. Compared to human observation, such devices may offer increased accuracy, lower costs, and the ability to tackle special measurement requirements and the recording of ongoing behaviour for later analysis. The major mechanical devices used in observation include:

(a) Traffic counters used to measure vehicle or people flow over a stretch of roadway or street. At its simplest, it may consist of the observer pressing a button on the counter every time an object passes, e.g. street people-counts used to determine a suitable retail shop location. A more sophisticated application, which reduces or eliminates the necessity for the observer to be present, is the use of laser or electronic-based traffic counters.

(b) Video cameras are used to record shopping behaviour in supermarkets, car showrooms, banks, etc. Video cameras can be used to assess traffic flow patterns, in-store promotional material, package designs and floor displays, etc. The primary advantage of this approach is repeat viewing and the ability for a number of analysts to view the behaviour sequences at the one time.

(c) The audiometer, which was developed by AC Nielsen, is used to record television viewing and radio listening behaviour. This technology is used to measure TAM ratings of a representative sample of the population.

(d) Eye tracking equipment such as oculometers and eye cameras are used to record gaze movements of the eye. It can be used to assess the effectiveness of TV and print advertising, promotional material and packaging design by determining how long the respondent looks at various parts of the stimulus. To determine the relative strengths in colour in advertising, an eye movement recorder was used to study how people actually read. The study was used to ascertain how advertisements are read in the context of the total newspaper, and a separate study looked specifically at the reading of advertisements themselves.[59]

(e) A Pupilometer measures changes in the diameter of the pupils of the respondent's eye as it is exposed to marketing stimuli. The assumption is that increased pupil size reflects positive cognitive activity.

(f) A Psycholovometer measures changes in perspiration rate. The respondent is shown stimuli such as brand names, advertisements, packages and slogans. The device measures the person's emotional reaction to these stimuli. The general principle involved is not unlike the lie detector. It is assumed that involuntary physiological changes such as increased perspiration accompany emotional reactions.

(g) Voice pitch analysis measures emotional response by monitoring normal voice frequency. Changes in the respondent's voice can be used to interpret response to marketing stimuli.

Note: Items (d) to (g) measure physiological reactions to stimuli. Yet there is no strong evidence to support the argument that a physiological change is a valid measure of future sales, attitude change or emotional response.

(h) Electronic scanning is an observational method whereby laser scanners at supermarket checkouts 'read' the UPC codes on products, and the store's central computer can produce instantaneous information on sales. With a better knowledge of what to stock, how to display it and how to price and promote the brand, retailers can improve profit margins and depend less on price-cutting promotions. Among the information contained in the code are such descriptors as brand, size or weight and flavour. Store inventory data is automatically reduced to reflect the purchase. Analysis of the purchases may reveal brand share and other relevant marketing information, such as tracking sales with advertising and promotions. In Ireland, EPOS systems are provided by companies such as CBE (www.cbe.ie), Merit Solutions (www.meritsolutions.ie), Retail Solutions (www.retailsolutions.ie), Retail Systems Technology (www.rstepos.com) and Data Pac (www.datapac.com).

OBSERVATION & THE INTERNET

Marketing researchers have unrivalled opportunities to observe online consumers due to the fact that the Internet allows an incredible amount of data to be collected for analysis. As consumers move through a web-site, every step or 'click' can be followed and recorded in detail.

When data on the type of web pages visited, the order in which they are visited and the amount of time spent on particular pages is combined with information such as the user's identity and demographic profile, a comprehensive picture of the user can result, which may enable to marketer to get close to the ultimate goal of 'one-to-one marketing'.[60]

Due to the fact that data is generated automatically as part of a web-site's 'log files', data collection and processing can be largely automatic as well. As a result, consumer profiles can be produced at virtually no extra cost and effort. Proprietary software packages such as Webtrends (www.webtrends.com) and CustomerCentric Solutions (www.customercentricsolutions.com) can analyse this data and make them available in a format suited to marketing decision-making.

The term 'netnography' has been coined to describe the application of ethnography to the Internet.[61] Netnography is concerned with the study of the cultures and communities that are emerging on the Internet. As a marketing research technique, netnography uses the information that is publicly available in online forums such as bulletin boards, chat rooms and web-sites to identify and understand the needs and decision influences of online consumer groups.

In comparison to traditional and market-oriented ethnography, netnography is far less time-consuming and obtrusive. Compared with focus groups and personal interviews, netnography is also much less obtrusive, because it is conducted using observations of consumers in a context that is not fabricated by the marketing researcher. The limitations of netnography stem from its narrow focus on online communities, which leads to difficulty generalising results to groups outside the online community sample, the need for the researcher to have specialised interpretive skills and the potential for anonymous self-promotion by manufacturers and retailers.[62]

Box 6.10 Applying NASA technology to shopper psychology

People can only describe about 20% of their behaviour through the traditional interview: most shopping activity is subconscious. Retail research and design company, ID Magasi, overcomes the limitations of purely qualitative research by filming and interviewing shoppers to uncover conscious and subconscious behaviour patterns, as well as qualitative data on penetration and conversion rates. One of the latest techniques used by ID Magasin is the Eye Mark Recorder, which was used by NASA in the design of the space shuttle cockpit. It reveals the visual cues shoppers use – and the much higher amount they ignore. This enables understanding of the search and selection process and establishes the draw of the various elements of the store or display. The data is then meticulously scrutinised to see why the customer behaves in a particular manner, which is central to analysis and enables researchers to provide objective and precise briefs to the creative team. The resulting design work is grounded in reality rather than perceived wisdom and conjecture, ensuring visual and psychologically compelling output. Such research has been improving profits for both retailers and manufacturers and has eliminated the guesswork from design.

Source: Adapted from *Irish Marketing and Advertising Journal*, 2002, Vol. 28, No. 2, p.2.

Box 6.11 Londis and Shoe Rack use EPOS

Londis are a household name in convenience retailing. Being a very competitive market sector, the need for fast stock turnover and accurate stock profiling is paramount. Having assessed a variety of EPOS systems, Londis piloted Retail Manager Plus, available from Retail Solutions, in two of its busier stores. Utilising industry standard hardware and supported by Retail Solutions, Retail Manager Plus has now been installed in all Londis stores in Ireland.

Modular point of sale (POS) terminals with weighing scales and bench laser scanners attached are the standard in-store configuration. All terminals are linked via a standard network hub to a central computer system. Multi-save and mix-and-match promotions are handled automatically at POS Londis head office price bulletins and product file updates are downloaded each night and are automatically reflected on the in-store system. This reduces file maintenance duties by the individual branch owner.

Decision-making information such as the slowest and fastest moving line is readily available and allows local competitive pricing measures to be implemented. Store sales are transmitted to head office via the Internet for analysis of overall spend patterns.

Shoe Rack is the largest multiple independent retailer in Ireland. The company carries 60,000 stock items (pairs of shoes) including all sizes and variants, so stock control used to be extremely difficult and time-consuming. Shoe Rack now has point-of-sale tills in all of its shops, combined with a back-office system that allows it to control all the information needed to streamline the business. The system generates a barcode in Dublin for each stock item and sends it to the factories where the products are barcoded and sent directly to the shops. All the required information is instantly accessible. At the touch of a button, management can access how the company is performing, how a particular shop is performing, find out the stocking levels in seconds, what the top selling lines are, pinpoint the performance of a single line, how well a particular pair of shoes is selling and which is the best-selling colour.

Source: 'Information at your Fingertips', 31 May 2004, *Futura Magazine* and http://www.retailsolutions.ie/aboutus/londiscasestudy.html, 2006.

Box 6.12 Loyalty cards — 'High stakes in the big card game'

Loyalty cards are about much more than enticing customers to stick to a particular retailer. They give an opportunity to learn about shoppers' wants and needs. But the key test will be if the company can exploit its database detailing customers' behaviour more successfully than its rivals.

The objective is to identify a store's most profitable customers and maximise their spending. Every time the customer goes to the checkouts, their cards are swiped and information about the contents of their trolleys is transmitted to a computer database. The retailer can then pinpoint customers who spend heavily on highly profitable items, as well as those who go for cut-price offers. Making use of this information can take a number of different forms. The profitable customers can be sent special offers and news of store improvements. Spending habits can be analysed in order to revise the products on offer or alter the store layout.

As one retailer explains, 'A loyalty scheme is purely a means of identifying the customer when they come into the store and in exchange for that information, you have to give them something back, which is usually points they can spend. A retailer without such information is like an army fighting with bows and arrows against laser guns and night vision goggles.'

Source: Adapted from 'High stakes in the big card game', *The Observer*, 12 May 1996, p. 5, Alexander Garrett; *Checkout*, 1 September 2004, on fact finder.

Box 6.13 Nectar hopes to keep customers sweet

The founder of the Air Miles scheme is to come to the aid of four famous high street names, through what is claimed will be the UK's largest ever loyalty card programme. J. Sainsbury, Debenhams, BP and Barclaycard are to transfer their in-company loyalty schemes to a joint programme called Nectar. The Nectar card will be useable at 1,800 stores run by the four firms, with further retailers expected to join the programme in the future. Points will be exchangeable for 'rewards' such as consumer goods, flights, holidays, meals and cinema tickets.

The move represents a u-turn for the UK retail sector, as in recent years there has been a move away from loyalty cards following concerns that they fail to attract new business. Supermarket giant Safeway famously scrapped its loyalty card programme in 2000, claiming customers preferred immediate discounts to points. 'People have lost interest in loyalty card points and don't think they give value,' Safeway chief executive Carlos Criado-Perez said at the time. However, the value of a successful loyalty card scheme has since become apparent, when Sainsbury's reported slower than expected growth in sales for the three months to 22 June 2002. Sainsbury chief executive Sir Peter Davis blamed slowing market conditions in the UK, and cited a 'short-term impact' from the company's decision to suspend its Air Miles customer loyalty scheme.

Nectar is designed to allow shoppers to rack up points more quickly, thereby encouraging consumer participation, as well as helping the four retailers cut the cost of administrating their stand-alone schemes. 'In the new scheme, our customers will be able to earn points faster from a larger number of retailers, accessing a greater value of rewards,' BP retail chief Graham Sims said. Nectar will be run by the UK arm of Mr Mills' Loyalty Management International firm, which is reported to be preparing to spend £50 million launching Nectar.

Source: adapted from BBC News Online, 5 June 2002, at http://news.bbc.co.uk/ 1/hi/programmes/working_lunch/2026592.stm ; BBC News Online, 24th July 2002 at http://news.bbc.co.uk/1/hi/business/2148405.stm

ADVANTAGES AND DISADVANTAGES OF OBSERVATIONAL RESEARCH

Observational research permits the measurement of actual behaviour, rather than reports of preferred or intended behaviour. Certain types of data can only be collected by observation. These include behaviour patterns which the respondent is unaware of or unable to communicate. For example, observation is a very effective form of research when the subjects are children or animals. Observation allows the researcher to obtain information on attitudes or behaviour that people may be unwilling to provide.

The potential bias caused by the interviewer and interviewing process is reduced or eliminated. Observation may be combined with other data collection methods at relatively low cost, for example, using a traffic counter to measure street or store traffic. The primary limitation of observational research is that while behaviour can be observed, no information is obtained concerning the factors which motivate that behaviour. Underlying beliefs, feelings, attitudes and preferences cannot be observed. A particular brand selected in a supermarket may not be the respondent's preferred choice. Perhaps the preferred brand was not in stock or the item was being purchased for another member of the family or as a gift. Observational research requires drawing inferences that may not necessarily be true.

Observing the purchase of a product in a supermarket tells very little about how the product is actually used or consumed. It is also difficult to observe certain behaviours such as personal hygiene (e.g. using a deodorant) that occurs within the home. Also, most observation requires some degree of subjective judgment on the part of the observer. Observation may be time-consuming and expensive if the behaviour to be observed is not reasonably predictable or occurs infrequently.

Finally, observation raises ethical issues. It is inappropriate for researchers to collect information on individuals without their permission as this directly conflicts with the ethical responsibility that a professional researcher adheres too.

SUMMARY

Survey research is the systematic collection of data from a sample of respondents.

A survey methodically gathers information from respondents by communicating with them. It can be conducted in person, by telephone, or by post. Survey research is usually conducted when the market researcher has already developed an understanding of the area to be researched. It is probably fair to say that surveys are the most widely used method of data collection in marketing research. Survey research usually relies on a questionnaire (or measuring instrument) of some sort to record responses.

Survey research can be classified based on the mode used to administer the questionnaire. There are three major survey methods: personal interviews, telephone interviews and postal interviews. Each method has its own advantages and limitations. Variations of each method also exist.

Personal interviews are direct, face-to-face communications between the interviewer and a respondent. Personal interviews may take place in a variety of different locations, including the home of the respondent, a street corner or a shopping centre. The researcher asks the required questions in the proper sequence and using the exact wording. The interviewer can explain and clarify complex questions, probe for additional information, administer complex questionnaires, utilise unstructured techniques and present visual cues such as advertisements and product concepts to the respondent, all as part of the questioning process. The personal interview tends to have less non-response error than other survey methods. However, personal interviews are often impractical to conduct over wide geographical regions. There is also potential for interviewer bias to occur. Increasingly, personal interviews are being conducted in large high-traffic shopping centres.

Telephone interviewing involves phoning respondents and asking them a series of questions. Telephone interviews are becoming increasingly popular and are probably one of the most efficient methods for collecting data quickly. As the cost of personal interviews may be prohibitively high, telephone interviews are relatively inexpensive. Because of the absence of face-to-face contact, there is less opportunity for interviewer bias. It does not, however, lend itself as much to the collection of lengthy and detailed information. The use of complex measurement scales is also restricted. Telephone interviews are more suited to concise and straightforward data collection. Telephone interviewing depends on a representative sampling frame. Because visual aids cannot be used in telephone interviews, certain types of research such as packaging, print advertising, or some concept tests, cannot be conducted on the phone. This limitation can be overcome by sending the respondent the required visual material in advance. Another option is to conduct surveys on the Internet, either by sending a survey as a file attached to an email message or by hosting the survey on a web-site.

The postal survey is a self-administered questionnaire sent to respondents through the post. It is very much a paper and pen method of collecting data. The questionnaire is administered to the respondent by the respondent and the respondent completes and returns the questionnaire. The construction of the questionnaire and related materials is crucial to the success of this survey method. Postal surveys are particularly versatile in reaching all types of people (i.e. consumer or business), in all geographic areas, rural and urban areas, and at the same low cost. The postal survey method generally will have a cost advantage over other survey methods, though they are not cheap. The respondent has more time to formulate and record his or her answers. The questionnaire can be filled in at a time and pace convenient to the respondent. The primary limitation of this method is that of non-response error. A fairly high response rate can be achieved if certain techniques are used by the researcher to increase partcipation. Despite all efforts, it is next to impossible to totally eliminate non-response in postal surveys. Five methods to deal with the effect of non-response error were briefly presented.

Observation research is another way of conducting descriptive research. Observation involves systematically recording the behavioural patterns of people, objects and occurrences without questioning or communicating with them. It can be a source of low-cost research information. Yet it is probably one of the most under-utilised approaches to collecting marketing research data. Observational techniques fall into five different classifications. Observational research permits the measurement of actual behaviour, rather than reports of preferred or intended behaviour. Certain types of data can only be collected by observation. These include behaviour patterns which the respondent is unaware of or unable to communicate. The primary limitation of observational research is that while behaviour can be observed, no information is obtained concerning the factors which motivate that behaviour.

QUESTIONS

1. What conditions must apply in order to obtain meaningful results from the interview process?
2. Distinguish between sampling error, response error and non-response error.
3. Outline the type of variables survey research can be used to measure.
4. What is the purpose of survey research? What type of variables does this type of descriptive data collection method measure?
5. What factors should you consider when choosing among mail, telephone, personal and shopping centre-intercept interviews and what are their limitations?
6. What is meant by random digit dialling?
7. Which of the four interview methods mentioned in Question 5 is the most common, and why?

8. How has computer assisted telephone interviewing (CATI) revolutionised the way in which market research is undertaken?
9. What should be included in the cover letter that accompanies a postal questionnaire?
10. What techniques are available to the researcher to reduce non-response in postal questionnaires?
11. Outline the four methods for dealing with non-response error.
12. Differentiate between response error and non-response error in a survey. How can these difficulties be minimised when conducting survey research?
13. Why is it sometimes necessary to combine two or more data collection methods?
14. Discuss the various ways that the Internet can be used to administer a survey.
15. What are the trends in questionnaire administration? What methods are becoming increasingly popular?
16. Name the types of mechanical observation and explain how they work.
17. Describe how observation can be conducted on the Internet.
18. When are observational techniques used and what are the relative advantages and disadvantages of using this technique?
19. Name and outline the five classifications of observational techniques.
20. Why is it sometimes advantageous to conduct observational research by means of exerting control over the observational setting (i.e. contriving to ensure that the situation you would like to study does, in fact, occur) instead of relying on natural situations to occur on their own?
21. What is the difference between direct and indirect observation? How could one employ indirect observation in identifying the relative popularity of various cigarette brands among spectators at a college football game?
22. What is trace analysis and what are some innovative applications of this observational technique?
23. What are some of the major mechanical devices used in observation?

PROBLEMS AND ASSIGNMENTS

1. How would you decide if a shopping centre-intercept interview approach is appropriate for a particular research project?
2. Which survey method is best for the following situations:
   (a) Administration of a complex attitude scale to measure the impact of a major new product launch by a competitor?
   (b) Administration of a questionnaire on the viewing of 'X-rated' movies on DVDs?
   (c) Administration of a questionnaire to determine the number of people that read a feature article in a Sunday paper?
   (d) Administration of a questionnaire by a university to determine students' attitudes towards a proposed change in the core curriculum?

3. Describe a marketing research problem in which both survey and observation methods could be used for obtaining the information needed.

4. How might one go about setting up an observational study to determine the incidence of car-pooling among faculty versus commuter students at your college or university?

5. What are some of the commonly used mechanical and/or electronic observational devices and what advantages and disadvantages do they have compared to human observation? Discuss.

6. What biases, if any, might be introduced by offering to give respondents €10 upon receipt of the questionnaire? The purpose of the payment is to ensure a high response rate. Will it work?

7. Even with the use of expensive gifts and call-backs, all three interview methods can sometimes produce low response rates — under 30%. What are some ways to increase these response rates?

8. How would you overcome some of the problems you might anticipate in designing a survey to establish the kind of paint used by the 'do-it-yourself' market when members of this sample group last redecorated a room?

9. You decide to take a telephone survey of 40 families in the 021- exchange area. You want an excellent representation of all subscribers in the exchange area. Explain how you would carry out this survey.

Case Study
Recreation in the Irish uplands*

Anyway, go up to the hills, as sages and saints have done since the beginning of the world...and catch some inarticulate vision of the strange equation in which you stand on the one side and the universe on the other.

Robert Lloyd Praeger

Generations of Irish schoolchildren have been told that Ireland is shaped like a saucer, with mountains forming the rim and the bog of Allen forming the hollow in the middle. In Ireland and elsewhere, some mountain-tops have been regarded as spiritual and special, attracting people to make gruelling pilgrimages to their summits. As Ireland becomes more urbanised, increasing numbers of people have been turning to the countryside for their recreation. Among environmentalists, there has always been an awareness of the importance of mountain ecosystems. There has been a growth in hillwalking and mountaineering activities, manifested by the proliferation of clubs and the development of climbing walls around Ireland. The increase in car ownership in Ireland has supported recreation in the uplands and has allowed people to travel further.

Outdoor activities, such as hillwalking, cycling, trekking and water-based leisure pursuits, have the potential to deliver significant returns both to local service providers and to the economy generally. A report by Bord Fáilte (2003) revealed that hiking or hillwalking was the most common activity engaged in by tourists during their visit to Ireland, followed by golf, angling, cycling, language study, equestrian and cruising. Under the National Development Plan, policies will be designed to develop 'special-interest tourism' products, with the aim of assisting rural communities, reducing congestion in the more popular holiday locations, and lengthening the tourist season.

The Mountaineering Council of Ireland (MCI) is the national representative body for climbing and hillwalking in Ireland (including Northern Ireland) and it represents the interests of its members. Its aims are as follows:

1. To represent and encourage mountaineering, hillwalking and rambling in Ireland.
2. To provide and coordinate appropriate services to members.
3. To promote the conservation and responsible use of the upland environment.

At present, the MCI has a membership of over 5,000, which includes 100 clubs along with individual members. Unlike most national representative bodies (i.e. GAA, IRFU), participants in the recreational activity do not have to be members of a club to engage in the activity. Previous research commissioned by the MCI revealed that approximately 10% of all visitors to the Irish uplands are members of the MCI. A key challenge for the MCI in the future is to attract non-members. At present, it offers many services to its members and provides information through its website (www.mountaineering.ie) and the *Irish Mountain Log*, a quarterly journal. The council:

- develops codes of good practice;
- protects the wilderness of mountains and cliffs and recognises their environmental value and fragility. The council believes that human impositions on the landscape (i.e. masts and antennae), over-grazing, road construction, litter, etc. have an impact on the visual appeal of the uplands and the quality of the recreational experience;
- maintains standards in mountain training and safety;
- runs an insurance scheme for members;
- publishes guidebooks;
- frequently arranges lectures on the exploits of renowned mountaineers;
- is involved with assisting members interested in Alpine, Himalayan and other expeditions;

As a national body, the MCI receives grant aid from the Department of Tourism, Sport and Recreation. The MCI recognises that walking and climbing are valuable and worthwhile activities with many health, social, educational and economic benefits. For instance, climbers and hillwalkers require motor fuel, maps, guidebooks and specialist items of clothing such as rucksacks, boots and rain-gear. They tend to visit pubs and cafés near the upland area and often stay in guesthouses, hostels and camping sites or use other forms of accommodation.

The MCI has decided to carry out market research in order to obtain information on visitors to the Irish uplands. The MCI hopes that this survey will help it accomplish its objectives which are as follows:

- gain an estimate of the number of visitors to the uplands;
- develop a demographic profile of visitors to the uplands;
- assess the attitudes and habits of visitors to the uplands;
- evaluate the economic and environmental impact of recreation in Irish uplands; and
- increase membership rates of the MCI.

The MCI believes that a quantitative research technique such as surveys will yield the information they require. The MCI has asked lecturers in the Waterford Institute of Technology to design a questionnaire and examine the various issues that are relevant to the study.

Assignment

1. How should the survey be administered?
2. What groups should the MCI include in its sample?
3. What sample size do you recommend?
4. What variables, or aspects of the recreational experience, should the questionnaire measure?
5. What incentives should be used to increase the response rate?
6. Design a questionnaire to suit the information needs of the Mountaineering Council of Ireland.

*This case was written by Dr Breda McCarthy, Lecturer in Marketing at University College Cork, and Jack Bergin, Lecturer in Sports and Recreation at Waterford Institute of Technology. It is intended to be used as a basis for class discussion rather than to illustrate either effective or ineffective handling of an administrative situation. The case is based on a real situation, and the authors wish to thank the MCI for their permission to use the material in this case (2006).

Case Study
Carroll Meats*

Seamus Carroll founded Carroll Meats in 1979 and he quickly built up a reputation as a supplier of high-quality sliced meats. Since then, the founder has attempted to grow the company by adding value to traditional products, introducing new products and entering new markets.

In the late 1990s, Carroll decided to enter the chilled ready-meals segment. At the time, he felt that there was a gap in the market as there was no other Irish producer of a branded ready-meal product. As a supplier of cooked meats, he knew the retail trade well and the major supermarket buyers in Ireland were willing to stock a branded product that had a good profit margin. Today the current product range is limited, and Carroll is considering the introduction of an innovative product, new product line or product variant to the market.

The market for chilled ready meals in Ireland

The chilled ready-meals (vegetable, meat or fish-based meals) market is a well-developed sector in Ireland. The sector tends to be dominated by private-label sales by multiple retailers, such as Tesco and Marks and Spencer. In contrast to the frozen ready-meal sector where branding is the norm, there is very little branding of chilled ready meals. Large manufacturers have been deterred from entering the market on account of several other factors:

Problems of short shelf life

- Potential for growth of food-borne bacteria (particularly salmonella and listeria) if temperature abuse occurs.
- High wastage levels.
- Handling of these products during transportation and in the retail shops is complicated.
- The high level of own-label penetration, which reflects the close co-ordination required between retailer and supplier to ensure product quality and safety.
- Barriers to international trade due to the need for efficient hygiene and temperature control.

The factors that have contributed to the growth of ready meals in the EU are numerous and varied:

- an increase in the number of single-person households;
- increasing household penetration of microwave ovens;
- a move towards lighter meals, together with greater health/weight consciousness;
- consumer interest in ethnic foods;
- a move away from family meal occasions;
- increase in female participation rates in the labour force, which is linked to increasing demand for convenience products;
- the increasing sophistication of the 'chill-chain';
- changes in technology and packaging (i.e. foil containers have been replaced by PET containers that can go straight into the fridge, freezer, microwave or conventional oven).

Chilled ready meals tend to be perceived as high-priced luxury goods; hence their consumer base is relatively affluent. The product appeals to the buyer who does not always have the willingness, or ability, to prepare meals. The market is mainly comprised of professional people with busy lifestyles, who are well travelled and eat alone – even if they live as families. Consumers also purchase ready meals when faced with time pressures or to get out of the rut of daily meal preparation. It is expected that the consumer profile will change as the products become more widely diffused through the population.

Marketing strategy

The product range consisted of Italian, Chinese and Indian dishes, such as lasagna, curry and stir-fry, which were sold with an accompaniment such as rice. Carroll decided to base the products on mainstream international dishes in order to appeal to the perceived conservative nature of the Irish customer. The whole product range was available pre-packed and sold as a microwave product. The product lines, chilled ready meals and processed meats were sold under the company brand. The following choice criteria were important to consumers:

- freshness is one of the main selling points of chilled foods;
- high quality;
- nutritional value;
- convenience;
- taste;
- novelty.

Carroll has to make a decision concerning pricing: should he adopt a premium pricing strategy for the new product or should he emphasise value for money? The former pricing strategy would support a high-quality positioning strategy, but would increase the cost of packaging and ingredients. With regard to distribution, existing channels will be used: multiples, city-centre convenience stores and garage forecourts.

Market Trends

Chilled, branded products are in the growth stage of the product life cycle, and there is strong competition from the retail chains that distribute private-label products nationally. Competition from multinational corporations is limited; they produce frozen products for the international marketplace. The competitive situation has allowed the company to enter the market with little or no advertising. Brand names of competitors in the chilled foods segment are not well known, and own-label brands do not use national TV advertising.

Carroll monitors market trends and believes that he has a general feel for the type of issues that are of concern to consumers in relation to their food consumption.

The owner is in regular contact with salespeople, he reads the trade press and talks to owners of similar companies at trade fairs. In this sector of the food market, consumers generally tire of eating the same products on a regular basis, and Carroll is aware that a broad product range and/or high rate of product turnover is required to maintain consumer interest. Carroll is worried that food scares (e.g. bird flu) will affect sales of traditional meat-based dishes. He believes that the Irish market could mirror trends in the UK market. The per capita consumption rate of ready meals is higher in the UK than Ireland. However, the UK market shows signs of approaching maturity, due to competition from alternatives (take-away in particular) and the expectation that microwave ownership will plateau. In the UK, private label sales of chilled foods are the norm, and there has been growth in the number of 'budget brands' which are positioned very closely in price terms to cheaper frozen products.

According to Carroll, chilled foods are sometimes bought on impulse. Therefore factors such as the attractiveness of the product, the impression of freshness and the range of products, all help stimulate impulse purchasing. The convenient nature of the product means that independent outlets such as city centre convenience stores (e.g. SPAR) and garage forecourts are important in generating impulse purchases. Some of these smaller retailers are not in a position to sell own-label products since private-label manufacturers are not interested in supplying small retailers. Small independent retailers are restricted by space to the number of lines they can carry. They do not have sufficient turnover or highly sophisticated distribution systems to overcome problems related to short shelf life and temperature control which, together, can result in high wastage levels.

Packaging plays an important role in keeping food products fresh. In the EU, the trend towards 'green' products has seen the growing use of recyclable board trays rather than plastic. Modified atmosphere packaging provides a shelf life of around six days, vacuum packaging somewhat longer, but is generally not appropriate to ready meals. Technology such as pasteurisation or irradiation is effective in lengthening the shelf life of products, but the former is felt to compromise texture and eating quality and the latter is not used because retailers and manufacturers fear adverse consumer reaction.

Marketing Research Activity

The company's marketing activity to date has been intuitive and *ad hoc* in nature. The owner-manager acknowledges that his lack of marketing expertise may hamper the future growth of the company. To date, he has undertaken little or no marketing research. He knows very little about the attitudes and perceptions of his customers to his products. Also he would like to expand the product range in order to retain existing customers and attract new ones. He would like to undertake a formal marketing research project in order to assess how customers view his products and to explore areas for improvement.

Questions

1. Which survey approach would you recommend and what variables should the survey measure?
2. What question response format should be used? Why?
3. Design a questionnaire to suit Seamus Carroll's needs.

*This case is based on secondary data, and was written by Dr Breda McCarthy, Lecturer in Marketing at UCC. It is intended to be used as a basis for class discussion rather than to illustrate either effective or ineffective handling of an administrative situation. The case is based on a real situation, and the author wishes to thank Carroll Meats for their kind permission to use the material in this case (2006).

Case Study
Sligo Town Retail Forum – Mystery shopping in Sligo Town*

In September 2006, Sligo Town Retail Forum embarked on a campaign to improve the service levels offered by retailers in Sligo Town Centre. This was the culmination of many months of discussion, during which retail owners in the town centre expressed concern as to what they perceived as low levels of customer service experienced by shoppers to the town. Many problems were identified, such as: no opening times on display; poor layout and display of merchandise in certain shops; slow acknowledgement of the customer by staff; little enthusiasm by staff to be customer-friendly; and, in certain cases, the upkeep of the premises needed more attention. Obviously, these issues did not apply to all shops to the same degree and the forum were reluctant to embark on any campaign purely on comments made at meetings.

Consultations with local marketing and development organisations took place and this resulted in a four-phase action plan being put in place as follows:

- Phase one – January 2007: Mystery shopping of selected retail outlets including; jewellers, ladies boutiques, mobile phone outlets, sports shops, gift shops, pharmacies, florists, shoe shops, bookstores and men's clothing outlets.
- Phase two – April 2007: Survey research of management, staff and customers of each of the outlets that was mystery shopped.
- Phase three – September 2007: Implementation of training programs for staff of retail outlets to improve levels of customer service in each premises that was surveyed and mystery shopped.
- Phase four – January 2008: Follow up mystery shopping to ensure that customer service programs are being implemented in the selected outlets.

Prior to any mystery shopping being undertaken, a number of decisions needed to be made. It was agreed at a forum meeting in November 2006 that 30 premises would be mystery shopped. Six 'mystery shoppers' were recruited with the help of the Institute of Technology, Sligo. Each was responsible for a particular store type and had to undergo one full day of training on how to conduct and report on the research. All mystery shopping was to be carried out during one week in January and retailers were not be told when it would take place. Final reports were due in mid-February.

It was hoped that the mystery shopping would highlight issues for retailers under four headings:

1. First Impressions.
2. Staff.
3. Organisation and layout of the store.
4. Customer Service.

The following is the generic research instrument that all mystery shoppers were to use in the various retail outlets:

SLIGO TOWN RETAIL FORUM: MYSTERY SHOPPING OBSERVATION INSTRUMENT

Name & Address of Premises _____

Date visited _____

Mystery Shopper _____

Time at which premises was entered _____

Time at which mystery shop was completed _____

Total time spent in premises _____

Overall marks awarded _____

1. What was your initial impression of the shop?

   a. Attractive, welcoming, neat and tidy   ☐ 10

   b. Attractive but untidy   ☐ 5

   c. Unwelcoming   ☐ 0

Comment

2. Was the window display eye-catching?

   a. Yes   ☐ 10

   b. No   ☐ 0

Comment

3. Were the opening and closing times easy to identify on entering the premises?

    a. Yes   ☐ 10

    b. No   ☐ 0

Comment

4. Please allocate marks on the following aspects of the exterior appearance with 10 being excellent, 5 being good and 0 being poor.

    The building (good state of repair)   ___ out of 10

    Colour scheme   ___ out of 10

    Consistent with other premises on the street   ___ out of 10

    Signage   ___ out of 10

  Comment

5. Was there any refurbishment being carried out during your visit to this shop?

    a. Yes   ☐

    b. No   ☐

Not a coded question.

Comment

6. Was the service environment entrance and interior wheelchair and pram accessible? (i.e. Was there enough space to get in and move around comfortably?)

    a. Yes   ☐ 10

    b. No   ☐ 0

Comment

7. When you entered were you welcomed by a member of staff?

    a. Yes   ☐ 10

    b. No   ☐ 0

7.1 If Yes, what form did this acknowledgement come in?
      (please tick the following)

Eye contact ☐

A smile ☐

A nod ☐

Verbal greeting ☐

Not a coded question.

Comment

8. Was a member of staff immediately available to you?

a. Yes ☐ 10

b. No ☐ 0

8.1 If no, how long did it take for a member of staff to come to your assistance?

Within 1 minute ☐ 10

Within 5 minutes ☐ 5

Over 5 minutes ☐ 0

You had to ask ☐ 0

8.2 If there was a delay in serving you did you receive an apology?
a. Yes ☐ 10

b. No ☐ 0

Comment

9. Were the staff...

	Yes	No
a. Wearing uniforms	☐ 10	☐ 0
b. Wearing name badges	☐ 10	☐ 0
c. Easily identifiable	☐ 10	☐ 0
d. Well groomed	☐ 10	☐ 0

Comment

10. How did the assistant handle your enquiry?
    Please tick the appropriate box

    a. Had excellent knowledge of product, showed great interest
        and explained everything clearly.   ☐ 10

    b. Had good knowledge, but explanation was rushed,
        employee had little interest.   ☐ 5

    c. Had little to no knowledge, didn't bother to explain
        and had no interest?   ☐ 0

Comment

11. Did the sales assistant go through the sales process efficiently and ensure this
    product/service was the correct one to suit your needs?

    a. Yes   ☐ 10

    b. No   ☐ 0

Comment

12. Were staff sales-minded enough to encourage you to buy more or buy something
    more expensive?

    a. Yes   ☐ 10

    b. No   ☐ 0

Comment

13. Were dual prices clearly displayed?

    a. Yes   ☐ 10

    b. No   ☐ 0

    Comment

14. In relation to layout and organisation of the store, please tick yes or no to the
    following statements

                                                       Yes   No

    a. Did you feel comfortable in the service
        environment?   ☐ 10   ☐ 0

    b. Was there enough space between display
        units to allow you to browse comfortably?   ☐ 10   ☐ 0

c. Were products located in clearly differentiated
sections?   ☐ 10   ☐ 0

d. Did the in-store lighting compliment the products
on display?   ☐ 10   ☐ 0

e. The store was not over-stocked.   ☐ 10   ☐ 0

f. The colour scheme was complimentary
to the store.   ☐ 10   ☐ 0

g. The store was clean.   ☐ 10   ☐ 0

h. There was appropriate music playing in the
service setting.   ☐ 10   ☐ 0

i. The temperature of the store was just right.   ☐ 10   ☐ 0

j. Brochures/sales literature were easily available
to you.   ☐ 10   ☐ 0

Comment

15. Did the assistant close the sale effectively?
(Did the assistant ensure you were fully satisfied with the product, inform you on
return procedure and thank you for your custom?)

a. Yes   ☐ 10

b. No   ☐ 0

Comment

Questions

1. In what way can this research instrument be improved?
2. What training would you expect the mystery shoppers to receive prior to
conducting this research?
3. Should the staff of the retail outlets be made aware of details of the research?
4. Will this research help the Sligo Retail Forum make a decision regarding
observations and training to be undertaken in the future?
5. Advise the forum on whether or not they should use a generic research
instrument for all the retail outlets being mystery shopped.

*There is no organisation entitled 'Sligo Town Retail Forum', but there are committees
operating within the Chamber of Commerce that fulfil the role of a retail forum. The forum
mentioned in the case is hypothetical, but the research instrument used is real. This case study
was written by Emer Ward, Lecturer in Marketing, Institute of Technology, Sligo (2006).

CHAPTER 7

EXPERIMENTATION

CHAPTER OVERVIEW

▸ Introduction   ▸ Experimental Terminology   ▸ Causality and Causal Explanations   ▸ Validity and Experimentation   ▸ Experimental Designs; Pre-Experimental Designs; True Experimental Designs; Quasi-Experimental Designs and Advanced Experiments   ▸ Selection of an Experimental Design   ▸ Test Marketing   ▸ Simulated Test Marketing   ▸ Summary

INTRODUCTION

So far, the data collection methods discussed generate either exploratory or descriptive data. In this chapter, we turn our attention to causal research and the associated data collection method, experimentation.

Experiments measure cause-and-effect relationships. To do this, experiments create an 'artificial' situation to allow the researcher to test the effect of one or more variables, such as advertising or a price decrease on another variable, say, the level of sales. This artificiality is the very essence of experimentation and causal research. It explicitly permits the researcher to control factors that may confuse the relationship between the variables. It enables the researcher to proactively participate in the testing process. These two reasons make experiments a very powerful data collection method. However, as we will see later, issues such as costs, security, and ethics mean that, in practice, experimentation has not been as popular in marketing as one would expect. This is changing though, with tools such as simulated test marketing and web sites bringing about a significant growth in this area over recent years.

Against this background, our discussion begins in this chapter with the terminology of experiments. We then consider the basic principles of causality and their role in experimentation. This leads us to the concept of validity and to the question of field versus laboratory experiments. The various experimental designs are then detailed. We conclude our discussion by examining test marketing and simulated test markets. Upon completion of this chapter, the reader will:

1. understand the nature of experiments as a data collection method;
2. learn about the concept of causality and causal research;

3. examine the role of validity in experimentation;
4. be able to detail potential threats to internal and external validity;
5. be able to select and conduct experiments;
6. gain an insight into test marketing; and
7. appreciate simulated test marketing.

The discussion presented in the chapter surrounding causality and the advanced experimental designs is, by nature, abstract and theoretical. To this end, readers may wish to confine themselves to the sections on validity and true experiments for a general, broad insight into experiments.

EXPERIMENTAL TERMINOLOGY

To fully understand experimentation and causality within the data collection phase of any research project, an appreciation of the standard experimental terminology is needed, together with a knowledge of the accepted symbols used. Some of the more important terms[1] include:

(a) Experiment

This is a data-collection tool, method or technique where the researcher consciously and explicitly controls and manipulates one or more independent variable(s) to determine the effect(s) it has on a dependent variable, under controlled circumstances. It asks the question 'Did X cause Y?' An experiment has three elements:

1. the factor being acted upon, namely the dependent variable;
2. the factor causing the imposed change, the independent variable;
3. the results or outcome of the change.

(b) Independent Variable

This term refers to a variable causing the effect. The independent variable is manipulated by the researcher. It can also be referred to as the experimental or treatment variable (these terms are used in the text to acquaint the reader with them). It is denoted as X. If there is more than one independent variable, these are shown as X_1, X_2, X_3, and so on. Examples of independent variables include price changes, satisfaction levels, new brand names, packaging changes, product variations and alternative advertising themes. Different levels of an independent variable can be tested; for example, the effect of income levels on the purchase of shares. The different income levels are represented as X_1, X_2, X_3, and are referred to as treatment levels of an independent, variable income. The term 'treatment levels' is generally reserved for discussion of advanced or statistical experiments.

(c) Dependent Variable

The dependent variable is the factor being influenced or affected by the independent variables. Sales levels, market share, brand preferences and awareness levels are traditional dependent variables. A measurement of the dependent variable is taken — this is referred to as an observation or measurement. It is represented as O. More than one measurement of the dependent variable is shown as O_1, O_2, O_3. Measurement of the dependent variable can occur either before or after the application of the independent variable. This is traditionally labelled as either a pre- or post-measurement observation. It is denoted by:

$$O_1 \quad X \quad O_2$$

and reads, a pre-measurement of sales at time period 1, followed by, X, the application of an independent variable, e.g. a 5% price increase and O_2, a post-measurement of sales at time period 2. The physical measurement or observation of the dependent variable can take several forms, e.g. observational techniques, surveys, use of scaling techniques such as the Likert scale, and physiological measures. (These are described and detailed in the forthcoming chapters.)

(d) Extraneous Variables

Extraneous variables are any other variables other than the independent or dependent variable(s). They can be controllable (e.g. price) or uncontrollable variables (e.g. competitors' price) and are external to the experiment. They are factors outside the researcher's control or knowledge that may alter the value of the dependent variable, e.g. competitors' price changes or pack alterations. Extraneous variables therefore confuse and confound the results of an experiment. Much of the researcher's energy is exercised through minimising or, better still, eliminating extraneous factors. Such variables can seriously hinder a researcher in answering 'Did X cause Y?'

(e) Test Units

These are individuals, groups of people, objects, shops or items which participate in the experiment. These test units are also known as experimental subjects — showing that they (products, people, stores) are participating in an experiment. Measurements are taken from the test units to describe the effects, if any, of the independent variable on the dependent variable. If there is more than one test group, we classify these as either an experimental or control group.

The experimental group consists of test units or members who receive the independent or treatment variable, i.e. they are the group of subjects exposed to the independent variable. EG can be used to denote the term experimental group.

The control group is a group of test units who do not receive the independent variable. They reflect the normal environment before, during and after the treatment.

The control group has to be similar in composition and nature to the experimental group so as to enable us to measure the true effect of X, the independent variable. CG is sometimes used as an abbreviation to represent the notion of a control group.

When test units do not know if they are receiving the independent variable (i.e. they do not know if they are in the experimental or control group), we say they are blind. When the test units and researchers do not know which group is the control or experiment group, we refer to this as a double-blind test. These terms are commonly used in the medical profession and pharmaceutical industry when conducting experiments.

(f) Randomisation

Randomisation, R, is the random assignment of test units to either the control or experimental group. It eliminates any subjective bias on the researcher's part with regard to the selection of experimental subjects. The purpose of random assignment is not to ensure identical groups as one might expect, but rather to disperse differences between test units randomly between the groups.

Additional Comments

The time occurrence of events in experimentation is always written and read from left to right. That is, symbols to the left represent activities that occurred first. Hence:

$$O_1 \quad X \quad O_2$$

reads pre-measurement (or pre-test) of dependent variable, then application or manipulation of the independent variable and post-measurement (post-test) of the dependent variable. From a practical perspective, the pre-measurement, O_1, could be a questionnaire measuring a person's attitude towards a product, say a beer. X could be the showing of a new TV advertisement about the product and O_2 could be the same questionnaire measuring the person's attitude towards the product.

X's and O's vertical to each other demonstrate stimulus and measurement are taking place simultaneously.

$$O_1 \quad X_1 \quad O_2$$
$$X_2 \quad O_3$$

The presence of parallel rows indicates that randomisation has been used to equalise the groups, such as that shown above. Alternatively, some researchers will use the notation of (R) to denote the use of randomisation. A dashed line is used by some researchers to denote the absence of randomisation.

$$O_1 \quad X_1 \quad O_2$$
$$-----------$$
$$X_2 \quad O_3$$

CAUSALITY AND CAUSAL EXPLANATIONS

To understand experimentation as a data-collection method, we must first explain the concept of causality. Our approach here is from the scientific perspective as opposed to the everyday common sense stance. From the scientist's view, causal statements are tentative by nature as all causal explanations are more or less probable. Causality states that a change in one variable causes a predictable change in another variable. Such inferences are difficult in marketing and the social sciences as, generally speaking, a variety of variables explain a probable outcome. It is difficult to predict the outcome due to the complexity of factors and units involved. As a result, many marketing explanations are descriptive in nature. They take the form 'X and Y occur together in a pattern'. In the scientific sense, to say 'X causes Y' implies each of four types of evidence have to be demonstrated by the researcher. These are:

1. concomitant variation;
2. temporal sequence;
3. theoretical support;
4. non-spurious association.[2]

1. Concomitant Variation

Sometimes referred to as associative variation, concomitant variation demonstrates a correlation between X and Y, i.e. the presence of X is associated with the presence of Y, or technically speaking, the independent variable X is associated with the dependent variable Y. This suggests that a rise in X will give rise to a predictable rise or decrease in Y. The relationship between X and Y can be positive or negative, i.e. a positive relationship means that the two variables move in the same direction, so an increase in X will give rise to an increase in Y, or a decrease in X will equate with a decrease in Y. Alternatively, a negative relationship means that a change in one direction in the independent variable gives rise to an opposite change of direction in the dependent variable. So, a price increase results in a drop in sales.

Therefore, concomitant variation, implying a consistent pattern, is one type of scientific evidence needed to demonstrate a causal relationship. However, while concomitant variation is necessary, it is not sufficient.

2. Temporal Sequence

Time precedence is concerned with the time order of occurrence of events or the sequential occurrence of variables. It refers to the fact that a researcher has to be able to show that X occurred in time before Y. This enables the researcher to measure a change in Y due to a change in X. If changes in X occurred after changes in Y, then we do not have sequential variables or a necessary condition for causality. For example, to demonstrate that a change in advertising had an effect on awareness levels, you have to be able to show that the change in advertising happened before changes in awareness levels.

3. Theoretical Support

The third type of evidence required for causal explanations is theoretical support, i.e. the claim that X causes Y is expected to fit with the body of knowledge already in existence or into a known conceptual model. However, caution is advised in rigidly applying this rule, as the story of Galileo classically illustrates.

4. Non-Spurious Association

To infer a causal relationship between X and Y, a researcher must be able to account for, or eliminate, all other possible explanations. That is, that observed changes in Y were not caused by factor(s) other than X. To take the preceding example, a change in awareness levels can happen because a competitor launches a new media campaign; a government report draws attention to the product or consumers actively pursue an information search. Essentially, this type of evidence focuses the researcher's attention on possible explanations other than the one being investigated, so as to rule them out.

In conclusion, the nature of causality requires that to determine that X causes Y, four criteria be fulfilled: concomitant variation, temporal sequence, theoretical support, and non-spurious association. Given this scientific stance, a causal explanation between X and Y is always inferred from the presenting evidence. Causality cannot be only one of a number of factors giving rise to a change in Y. In other words, causality and causal explanations demand, more than any other data collection method, an absence or elimination of error or sources of error. We now turn our attention to such a discussion.

VALIDITY AND EXPERIMENTATION

Recall that validity is about measuring what we really wanted to measure. With respect to causality and experiments, this means measuring changes that the independent variable, and only the independent variable, brings about in the dependent variable, i.e. did X really cause Y? To answer such a question, there are two main types of validity to be considered in any causal study or experiment. These are internal validity and external validity.

Internal Validity

Internal validity asks 'Did X really cause the difference in Y?' It is concerned with establishing that X was the sole cause of changes in Y and not outside factors, Z, A or B. So, internal validity rules out alternative explanations and aims to control for errors which may detract from establishing and measuring a causal relationship. There are seven threats to internal validity that concern a researcher. These are: history; maturation; testing (a) the main effect and (b) the interactive effect; statistical regression; instrumentation; mortality; and selection bias.

History

History errors occur due to specific events external to the experiment that happen between the pre- and post-measurement (O_1 and O_2), which affect the dependent variable, thus confounding the estimation of the treatment variable. Typical examples include competitive changes in pricing or promotional spend; government; media story; food scare; new competitive products — all of which are outside the control of the researcher. In marketing, the longer the time span or duration of the experiment, the greater the threat to internal validity from history. Note, the term 'history', as used here, does not relate to historical events or past events prior to the running of the experiment.

Maturation

Maturation denotes changes within the test units that occur over time between O_1 and O_2, i.e. the pre- and post-measurement times. These changes are not due to the independent variable, but due to the passage of time itself. For example, when the test units are people — hunger, tiredness or degree of concentration can alter with the time of day or even year and so alter the pre- or post-measurement. Organisations that are test units can also change. Stores can increase in size, shop traffic can fluctuate and shops can be renovated. A further corollary to this arises — the greater the time period between O_1 and O_2, the more likely an experiment will suffer from maturation error.

The Testing Effect

This threat to internal validity focuses upon the possible effects of a measurement taken before the experiment, which can alter the experimental results. An alternative way to think about the testing effect is to think about the effect that running an experiment has on subjects. There are two such effects: the main testing effect, and the interactive testing effect.

The *main testing effect* is said to have occurred when a measurement influences following measurements, e.g. respondents are asked as part of an experiment if they have seen an Oscar-winning film, *Titanic*. 10% say they have. As a direct result of the questions in O_1, the pre-measurement phase, many respondents decide to go to the film. Upon the next measurement two weeks later, 70% say they have seen the movie. The dramatic attendance increase between O_1 on O_2 could be a direct result of being asked the question about the film in the first place. This is the effect of O_1 on O_2 and is the main testing effect.

The *interactive testing effect* happens when the pre-measurement, O_1, influences the test unit reactions to the independent variable, X. For example, in asking consumers about genetically modified foods, consumers may be more sensitive to GMF news afterwards or even actively look for information. A further measurement, O_2, could result in greater changes in attitudes and knowledge, beyond that expected.

This elevated result reflects the treatment variable plus the interactive effect of O_1. The use of a control group can counteract the testing effect.

Instrumentation

Instrumentation error takes place when there are changes in the measuring instrument or measuring process between the pre- and post-measurement time, i.e. O_1 and O_2. For example, a hand-made chocolate firm is considering introducing a new line of white chocolates. Consumers are approached before the launch of the chocolates and are asked if they love white chocolates. After the launch, consumers are asked if they like white chocolate. The alteration of the question from loving chocolates in O_1 to liking chocolate in O_2 will result in instrumentation error. O_1 is not comparable or compatible with O_2. So any change to the wording, layout or scales within the measuring instruments can pose a threat to internal validity. Hence, it is recommended to keep the measurement instrument as constant as possible, to avoid instrumentation error.

Mortality

When respondents leave or drop out of an experiment, 'mortality' has occurred, i.e. those subjects lost to the experiment may be different to those who remained. Suppose, in an experiment to test a new vitamin, those leaving the experimental group were people who do not believe in vitamins. Thus, the results may be a reflection of the group composition and their attitudes to vitamins, rather than the independent variable itself. Careful selection and screening of respondents can counteract possible mortality threats.

Statistical Regression

When respondents are chosen to participate in an experiment due to an extreme score or position on a variable, there is the possibility of their further scores gravitating to the population mean. If this threat materialises, statistical regression is said to have occurred. Consider the following hypothetical situation.

A researcher specifically chooses ten drivers who failed their driving test first time round.

O_1: Drivers fail driving test for the first time.
X: Each driver receives a complimentary course of driving lessons.
O_2: All drivers pass the test on the second sitting.

The results show dramatic improvement for all experimental participants. However, it is possible that the participants failed their driving test first time for some reasons other than their lack of driving skills. Perhaps they had to use a new car for the driving test, one which they were not used to. Perhaps some of them were sick before the first test, or extremely nervous, or just having a bad day. Hence, it is possible that the failure to pass the test obtained in the pre-measurement phase was due to other random factors rather than the participants being really poor at driving! Given such a result, when a group is purposely chosen because of its extreme score on a variable, statistical regression may affect the experiment.

Selection Bias

The final threat to the internal validity of an experiment is selection bias. It happens when participants are assigned to the experimental or control group by means other than randomisation. That is, a bias is introduced because respondents have a different propensity to react to the independent variable. Suppose the respondents are members of a political group opposed to hare coursing. Some participants may purposely choose the control group to avoid seeing hurtful or unsettling pictures, while others may select the experimental group to strongly voice their opposition to hare coursing. In both situations, the participants are reacting differently to the independent variable. This can arise as the respondents were not equivalent in their attitudes towards hare coursing.

The best methods for preventing selection bias is the use of both *matching* and *randomisation* of respondents. Matching refers to the procedure which ensures that groups of respondents are comparable on the dependent variable, i.e. like is compared with like. For example, in an experiment to test the effectiveness of a new flea spray for domestic animals, the animals could be matched according to type, i.e. all cats are grouped together, while dogs constitute another group and budgies the third group. Randomisation refers to respondents being randomly assigned to the control and experimental matched groups, so as to distribute or scatter the effect of extraneous factors among all groups. As previously noted, random assignment eliminates any subjective selection bias on behalf of the researcher.

External Validity

Having established that X really did cause Y (and not some outside factor) we now pose the question 'So what, can we generalise the results?' We are querying the external validity of the experiment, given that we are satisfied with the internal validity. External validity is required if the results of an experiment are to be applied to the whole population in the real world. Much of the difficulty in generalising to the real world can be attributed to the artificial nature of the experiment, i.e. to the control which a researcher actively pursues. Thus, the threats to external validity often become an issue in deciding whether to use a laboratory or field setting for the experiment.[3]

In a laboratory experiment, the test units are placed in artificial surroundings so as to increase the researcher's control over extraneous variables and ensure a high internal validity content to the experiment. However, the use of a laboratory approach can induce reactive error. The 'Hawthorne Effect'[4] is a classic example. In a 1920s experiment to study the effect of different working conditions on workers' productivity, the results showed that regardless of the combination of working conditions used (rest periods, lighting and length of shifts), productivity continuously increased. It transpired that the productivity increase was due, not to the working conditions, but to the presence of the researchers and the experiment itself. Workers were aware they were part of an experiment, which of itself induced a higher level of morale, regardless of the working conditions. The artificial nature of the experiment resulted in a threat to the external validity of the experiment.

In a field experiment, the test units remain in their natural setting, perhaps their home, in supermarkets, in their office or a factory. In this life-like or market setting, test units are less likely to react to the experiment (the opposite holds true for laboratory settings) but they are more open to errors from outside events. Competitors are well known for their ability to 'scuttle' an experiment — they purposively increase their advertising rate in the experimental area or decrease their price, so as to confuse the results of the experiment. If not anticipated or managed, such actions can threaten the external validity of most experiments.

So, generally speaking, external validity requires the researcher to control for respondents reacting to the experiment, the experimental setting, and the independent variable. This reactive error and surrogate threat to external validity demands a balance between the advantages and disadvantages associated with field and laboratory experiments, as presented in Table 7.1 below. These advantages are relative and not absolute, as the controls for one type of validity (internal or external) often conflict with the other. At this point we'll note that there are two main types of field experiment, test marketing and simulated test marketing. Our discussion of these is left to the end of the chapter as these are best understood when you have an appreciation of experimental designs.

Table 7.1 A comparison of field and laboratory experiments

	Field experiment	*Laboratory experiment*
Internal validity	Weaker	Stronger
External validity	Stronger	Weaker
Cost	More	Less
Time	More	Less
Place	Shop/store/home	Research centre/office

Box 7.1 summarises the different types of validity threats to experimentation.

Box 7.1 Summary of validity threats to experiments

Internal validity threats

1. History

The effect of outside events that occur between O_1 and O_2.

2. Maturation

The effect of changes within the test units between O_1 and O_2.

3. Testing

The main testing effect is the effect of O_1 on O_2. The interactive testing effect is the effect of interaction between O_1 and test units reactions to experimental treatment, X.

4. Statistical regression

The tendency for groups initially chosen because of their extremely high or low scores on a variable to gravitate toward the mean.

5. Instrumentation

Changes in the measuring instrument or process between O_1 and O_2.

6. Mortality

The effect of test units dropping out of the experiment and changing the composition of the experimental and control groups.

7. Selection bias

Assignment of subjects to experimental and control groups such that test units are initially different on the dependent variable being measured, or differ in terms of their responsiveness to the experimental treatment, X.

External validity threats

A question of field versus laboratory setting. Often referred to as reactive error and surrogate error.

So far, we have examined the issues of experimental terminology, causality, internal and external validity and the question of field or laboratory experiments. We are now ready to turn our attention to the various types of experimental designs and the different methods to deal with threats to the validity of experiments.

EXPERIMENTAL DESIGNS

The term 'experimental design' refers to the testing procedure where the researcher manipulates an independent variable to specifically measure the effect on a dependent variable. To this end, four conditions have to be met. There has to be:

1. An independent variable to be manipulated.
2. Test subjects to experience the independent variable.
3. A dependent variable that is measurable.
4. A method for controlling extraneous factors.

If these conditions are met, there are four main categories that experimental designs can fall into. These are:

1. Pre-experiments.
2. True experiments.
3. Quasi-experiments.
4. Advanced (statistical) experiments.

This categorisation of experimental designs reflects the degree of control they afford the researcher over threats to both internal and external validity. Pre-experimental designs, by definition, provide little protection against validity problems, whereas true and statistical designs explicitly control for such errors. We will now examine each category of experimental designs, starting with the weakest category of experiments and progressing to the strongest.

Pre-experimental Designs

These are not real experiments insofar as they offer minimal control to the researcher over the experimental situation. Internal and external validity are not managed. However, they present an oversimplified insight into the more complex experimental designs and therein lies their value. The first of these pre-experimental designs is the 'after only' design.

The 'After-Only' Design

This is the most basic of all experimental designs. As suggested by its name, this design involves a measurement or observation of the dependent variable after test units have experienced the independent or treatment variable. This is represented as:

X   O

A typical case is the use of a new promotional tool by a south-east food manufacturer. In an effort to increase sales, a special offer is advertised in all local supermarkets and shops — a free loaf of bread with every home-making marmalade kit. The conclusion drawn is that the loaf of bread caused the sales of marmalade-making kits. While logic would suggest we agree with this conclusion, any good marketing manager would ask a number of questions. What were the level of sales before the promotional offer? What were competitors doing? What was happening in the market? Any of these issues could also explain the sales of the marmalade kits.

Thus, serious threats to validity abound with this design, so much so that the 'after-only' design is best thought of as an exploratory case study method or a useful technique for establishing a hypothesis for further testing.

The 'Before-After' Design

In this design, the dependent variable is measured before and after the independent variable is administered to the experimental subjects. This design was used to evaluate a large fee increase for doctors, by using multiple observation points before and after the fee increase.[5] It was also used by 'O & M who had the unenviable task of disassociating Impulse from the 1980s concept of romance, men flapping bunches of petunias at women, to the 1990s view of the romance interlude.'[6] Research showed the key shift was to make the heroine dynamic, self-confident and independent, reflected in the 'Art School' campaign, where the interaction between the female student and a male model raised many eyebrows as well as other bits of the anatomy! Sales increased by 20% and claimed usage among 11–16-year-olds grew by 24%. The following notation represents the before and after experimental design:

$$O_1 \quad X \quad O_2$$

The difference between this and the previous design is the use of the pre- or before measurement of the dependent variable. Returning to the design above, an example illustrates. All students of a college in north-west Ireland are asked to express their first choice of daily national newspaper. A week later, a competition is held in the college by one daily paper offering students a free return air ticket to anywhere in the world. After the end of the competition, the same college students are again asked to express their first preference in daily national newspapers. The results read as follows:

O_1 The before measurement   = 10% gave *The National* as their first preference.

X Fly Anywhere Competition

O_2 The after measurement   = 80% gave *The National* as their first preference.

The effect or result of X, the Fly Anywhere Competition, is O_2 minus O_1. In this case, 80%–10% = 70% increase in first preference.

The results, O_2–O_1, can be attributed to the independent variable. But it is still evident that other uncontrollable variables, such as price increases of competitors, out-of-stock alternative newspapers or lecturers' recommendation of *The National* paper could have interfered with or influenced the experiment, thus rendering the results questionable. To this end, the 'before-after' design is threatened by internal validity errors; history, maturation, instrumentation and the testing effect. These threats suggest the need for an alternative experimental design.

True Experimental Designs

True experimental designs empower the researcher with control over the experimental situation, thus eliminating or minimising serious internal and external validity threats. Control is achieved through the use of control groups and random assignment of test units to either the experimental or control group(s). It is these two factors which differentiate the pre-experimental designs from true designs, as the major deficiency of equivalent groups is overcome. Furthermore, statistical analysis is enhanced by the use of random assignment (in conjunction with probability sampling as discussed in Chapter 10).

The 'Before-After with Control Groups' Design

Known as the classic experimental design, the 'before-after with control group' is depicted as follows:

(R) O_1 X O_2
(R) O_3 O_4

The effect of independent variable, X, is

$$E = (O_2 - O_1) - (O_4 - O_3)$$

This has all the elements of the 'before-after' design, plus two significant and critical additions. Firstly, there is the use of a control group — a group of test units, similar in nature and profile to those who experience the experimental treatment, except for the fact that the control group are not exposed to the independent variable. This enables the researcher to assume that both groups (experimental and control) are equally affected by extraneous factors, such as history, maturation, testing and instrumentation. Secondly, the test units are randomly assigned to the various groups, thus selection bias is managed.

Take the area of sales promotions. Sales promotions are a popular promotional element of the marketing mix of Irish breweries. High levels of competition within this market call on the breweries to come into direct contact with their consumers and communicate with them at the point of sale, in the pub. To this end, the 'before and after with control group' design has been used to good effect in the Irish breweries industry[7] to test the effects of Guinness in-pub sales promotion. The design consisted of two pre- and post-measurements.

(R) O_1 O_2 X O_3 O_4
(R) O_5 O_6

Two pre-tests were conducted with the experimental group before the in-pub promotion, to measure consumers' perceptions of the brand image of Guinness. The pre-tests used a questionnaire specifically constructed to measure the different components of brand image. One further pre-test was completed by consumers, using the same brand image questionnaire, who were part of a control group and therefore would not be exposed to the in-pub promotion. All participants were matched and randomised prior to any pre-measurements. The in-pub promotion was run over a week-long period. Two post-measurements (consumer's brand image) were taken of the experimental group; one post-measurement was taken from the control group. The results were positive — the in-pub promotion led consumers' evaluation of the brand image of Guinness to increase, though only to a small extent.

However, in practice, such experimental designs can suffer from validity threats, e.g. if participants dropped out, the design would suffer from a mortality error. On external validity, the design does not perform so well — it is open to reactive error emanating from the experimental setting, the experiment itself or the selection of respondents from the population. So, while several major threats to internal validity are dealt with by this design, replication of the experiment several times may be needed to deliver external validity. This poses huge cost and time constraints.

In addressing the need to provide marketing education and training to the owner/manager of the small firm, FÁS (then AnCO)[8] tested an open-learning programme in marketing by using a variation of the 'before-after' design. It incorporated two phases: a pre-measurement and post-measurement, to control for the interaction effect — a particular threat to this study.

(R)   CG O_1
(R)   EG   X O_2

The pre-measurement phase consisted of a survey of all small firms in Ireland, to establish a baseline of their marketing knowledge. Then, a survey was conducted among those small firms who completed the course, to test their marketing knowledge. The results of two surveys were compared, with the improvement in marketing knowledge being attributed to the open-learning package.

However, the problems of history and statistical regression still remain with this design. Take the situation where the government or a state agency was to launch a marketing grant to assist small firms with their marketing. Such an outside event, if occurring at the same time as the experiment, could leave managers more interested in marketing, more willing to learn about marketing and thus more receptive to a marketing learning package. To specifically control for these threats, an alternative experiment is required.

The 'After-Only with Control Group' Design

This true experimental design, the 'after-only with control group', is the same as the 'before-after with control group', without any pre-measurement. It is depicted as follows:

(R)   X O_1
(R) O_2

The effect of the independent variable is calculated as:

$$E = O_2 - O_1$$

In our college newspaper example, we would randomly assign two similar colleges to the groups, and measure sales in both colleges after the competition was run. The effect of the competition would be: the sales of the newspaper in the experimental college minus the sales of the newspaper in the control college, as shown by the equation above.

Internal validity threats from history, maturation, selection and statistical regression are controlled for by the random assignment. The big advantage of this design is its ability to control for the interactive effect (as there is no pre-measurement, there can be no interaction between the pre- and post-measurement), as well as controlling for other threats to internal validity such as history and maturation. The assumption is that the 'before' measurement is the same in both cases. In practice, this assumption should be confirmed by using secondary data. Since the subjects are only measured once, the threat of testing effect is also managed. However, different mortality rates between the experimental and control groups could pose a threat to the design, as can external validity threats.

The simplicity of the 'after-only with control group' design lends itself well to many marketing mix situations. For example, price changes, new packaging and promotional tools, plus new advertising campaigns, can be assessed and analysed.

The Solomon-Four Group

The Solomon-Four Group is a true experimental design that combines the best of the two preceding designs ('after-only with control' plus the 'before-after with control') and for this reason can be regarded as the Rolls Royce[9] of classic designs available to a researcher. It is symbolised as follows:

(R)EG	1	O_1	X	O_2
(R)CG	1	O_3		O_4
(R)EG	2		X	O_5
(R)CG	2			O_6

Several measures of the independent variable are possible, e.g. $(O_5 - \frac{1}{2}(O_1 + O_3)) - (O_6 - \frac{1}{2}(O_1 + O_3))$.[10] The advantage of this design is that it caters for the isolation, quantification and control of specific internal validity threats, and is the least susceptible to sources of error. For example, it enables the investigators to capture the effect of the before measurement on the experimental and control group. Since all groups are pre-selected to be equivalent, the pre-measurement should be the same for all except for random factors. Despite the Solomon-Four Group being the ideal design, it is, nevertheless, rarely used in marketing research practice, due to its complexity and the extreme costs associated with conducting such an experiment.

Quasi-Experimental Designs

Quasi-experimental designs are classic designs adapted for ease of use. These involve periodic measurements (pre- and post-) and adopt the term 'Quasi' because there is no randomisation, i.e. subjects are not pre-assigned to either an experimental or control group. In reality, it is not always possible or practical to implement a true experimental design. Given this, quasi-experiments appear to be like true designs. To some extent this is correct as they can control for some extraneous factors, e.g. maturation, testing and instrumentation. However, the absence of randomisation limits their ability to deal with threats such as history, the interactive effect and, specifically, selection bias. Nevertheless, they offer a practical alternative to true experimental designs. Some of the more popular quasi-designs are the times-series design and multiple time-series.

The Time-Series Design

This is an extended before-after design, with multiple observations taken before and after the experimental treatment. It is depicted as:

$$O_1 \quad O_2 \quad O_3 \quad O_4 \qquad X \qquad O_5 \quad O_6 \quad O_7 \quad O_8$$

It is often used when introducing a price change, a package alteration or new advertising theme. The multiple pre- and post-measurements reflect the reality in the marketplace where marketing mix changes could take six to eight weeks. The effect of X is calculated by taking the mean of the post-measurements minus the mean of the pre-measurements. Say, for example, you are a biscuit manufacturer. You are planning to include the 'Made in Ireland' logo on all your biscuit lines next July. To measure the effect of this pack change on sales, you decide to monitor sales of all your brands for the year, let's say on the last day of every month.

Figure 7.1 Measuring the effect of a pack change

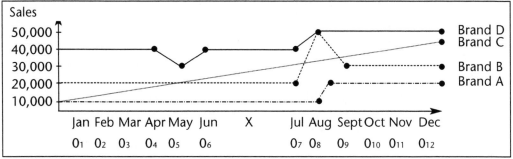

The effect of the pack change is the result of the mean sales, O_7–O_{12}, per brand, minus the mean sales, O_1–O_6, per brand.

The pre- and post-measurements can all come from the same sample (test units) over time, (secondary source – syndicated services data). This is often referred to as panel data (refer to Chapter 4). The alternative is for the pre- and post-measurements to come from separate population samples and is often the case for firms who monitor sales. This time-series quasi-experiment is useful when records are naturally kept at set time periods in the natural environment, as is the case in the retail trade. It is also a useful adaptation when reactive error is unlikely in the natural environment.

The Multiple Time-Series Design

This is the same as the time-series design, with the addition of a control group. It is symbolically represented as:

$$O_1 \quad O_2 \quad O_3 \quad O_4 \qquad X \qquad O_5 \quad O_6 \quad O_7 \quad O_8$$
$$O_9 \quad O_{10} \quad O_{11} \quad O_{12} \qquad\qquad O_{13} \quad O_{14} \quad O_{15} \quad O_{16}$$

Under the auspices of this design, we use a control city, town or store where sales are monitored over time, but there is no treatment variable introduced as there is in the experimental city, town or store. This approach gives the researcher more control, minimising the effect of errors, e.g. history.

However, the groups are not randomly assigned. The groups are assumed to be comparable. To this end, the researcher must carefully select the control group to be equivalent to the experimental group. It is also advisable that a log or journal be kept of external happenings to afford some control over history. Another threat can arise from the interaction testing effect, but this is minimised if frequent record-keeping is a natural part of the environment. So, in practice, this design is well suited to marketing mix changes, as opposed to attitudinal or behavioural changes in the consumer.

Advanced (Statistical) Experimental Designs

So far, the discussion of experimental designs is based on two assumptions. Firstly, that both the control and experimental groups are similar with respect to the variables of interest; and secondly, we are testing the effect of one, and only one, independent variable. Of course, many occasions arise in marketing when these conditions are not met. We often want to control for the effect of one or two extraneous variables, such as a competitor's price or store size. It is reasonable for a manager to want to test different levels of an independent variable, e.g. a price increase of 5%, 7% or 10%, or four different advertising campaigns. In such circumstances, the researcher will opt for a statistical or advanced experimental design.

In essence, these designs (four in total) are an extension of the true experimental designs previously examined. These designs can measure different experimental stimuli simultaneously, i.e. different treatment levels can be measured within the one experiment, such as different price increases or different advertising themes.

Furthermore, these advanced designs can cater for the test units being classified according to a known factor. This is referred to as a blocking factor. So, these statistical designs provide a framework for testing the impact of different treatment levels and other factors. The statistical designs in question that exhibit these characteristics are: the Completely Randomised design; the Randomised Blocks design; the Latin Square design; and the Factorial design.

1. The Completely Randomised Design

Consider a situation where a shampoo manufacturer wishes to increase the price of his product. He is unsure whether to increase the price by 1%, 3% or 5%. To test the effect of the various price increases on sales he could utilise the completely randomised design. Such a design allows for the measurement of different levels of the independent (or treatment) variable, in this case, price. Test units are randomly assigned to different experimental treatments at the same time (X_1 equals one price increase, while X_2 equals another level of the price increase, and so on). The assumption behind this design is that extraneous factors will not unduly affect one group of test units more than another, as the test units are similar.

Table 7.2 Completely Randomised design

Different levels of the independent variable price increase			
		X_1 1% increase	X_2 3% increase	X_3 5% increase
	(R)	sales a	sales e	sales b
9 shops (a – i)	(R)	sales d	sales g	sales f
	(R)	sales c	sales h	sales i
		Average sales	Average sales	Average sales
		X_1	X_2	X_3

As Table 7.2 shows, the test units are randomly assigned to different levels of the independent variable, over an agreed time period. The average sales levels for each level of the independent variable are analysed, using a statistical technique known as analysis of variance. (Analysis of variance is dealt with in Chapter 13.) Given that it is used to analyse all four of the statistical designs, it is worth noting that analysis of variance measures the variance occurring between treatments, known as the treatment effect. It compares the average result (say sales) for the treatment groups to determine the probability that the observed differences (in sales) occurred by chance. If the differences in sales did not occur by chance, then the treatments brought about the differences, and the results, are said to be significant. In our case, it enables the manager to calculate the effect of the different price increases on sales. From the results of this analysis, the shampoo manufacturer can infer which price increase to use.

Of all the four advanced designs, the completely randomised design is the least expensive. It is also the easiest to administer. It is used when the test units are known to be identical or very similar to each other, and thus randomisation of the stores to the different treatment levels assumes the groups of stores are equivalent. Of course, the main problem is this matching of groups or test units. In reality, test units are rarely identical. A further problem arises, especially if this design were used in a field experiment, i.e. the real world. Extraneous factors, such as store type or size, might play a role in the level of sales. If these problems cannot be satisfactorily solved, then an alternative design must be chosen.

2. The Randomised Block Design

This design is well suited when the researcher wishes to isolate the influence of one extraneous factor. It takes the notion of stratification and applies it to experiments. It 'blocks' the effect that an important extraneous variable may have on a dependent variable; hence the name 'randomised block design'. Common extraneous variables that marketing managers may wish to block include age, store size, store type, educational level or competitive price. This 'blocking effect' essentially means that test units are grouped into similar clusters or blocks, before random assignment of the independent variable. As an example, consider the previous example of a shampoo manufacturer who wishes to determine the effect of price increases on sales. He may be worried about the various distribution channels and their reaction to the price increases. In such circumstances, he will want to control for any variance that channel types may have on sales. This gives the researcher a precise picture of the treatment's impact on the dependent variable. It does so by isolating one key extraneous variable. That is to say, the advantage of the randomised block design lies in its ability to measure the effect of the treatment variable at different levels of the blocking variable.

Table 7.3 shows the randomised block design in operation. The extraneous variable has to be identified prior to the experiment. This, and the different levels of the treatment variable, are all measured at the same time during the experiment. Analysis of variance is used to determine the treatment effects.

Table 7.3 Randomised Block design

Different levels of the independent variable price increase			
	X_1 1% increase	X_2 3% increase	X_3 5% increase
Blocking factor Store type			
National chains (R)	sales	sales	sales
Corner shops (R)	sales	sales	sales
Health food shops (R)	sales	sales	sales
	Average sales X_1	Average sales X_2	Average sales X_3

3. The Latin Square Design

To control or block for the effect of two or more extraneous variables, e.g. the type of outlet and store size, the Latin square design is used. The name is derived from the two extraneous variables being used as blocking factors to form the rows and columns of a square table. Treatment effects are then randomly assigned to the cells within the square. This requirement is central to the Latin square and, because of it, there must be equal numbers of rows and columns, i.e., 2 X 2 or 3 X 3 or 4 X 4. The Latin square is therefore a natural extension of the previous design.

An example best illustrates; let's return to our shampoo manufacturer. As well as being concerned about the types of distribution outlets having different reactions to the proposed price increases, the manager is seriously concerned about the store size. He knows from past experience and historical sales records that sales are influenced by the size of the store. So, to determine the best price increase, 1%, 3% or 5%, he also needs to control for, or block the influence of, store type and size.

Table 7.4 Latin Square design

		Blocking factors — store types and size		
		National	Corner stores	Health shops
Small	(R)	X_1	X_2	X_3
Medium	(R)	X_2	X_3	X_1
Large	(R)	X_3	X_1	X_2
		Average sales	Average sales	Average sales

As with previous designs in this section, over an agreed time period, treatments (recall, these are the different price increases, where 1% increase = X_1, 3% increase = X_2 and 5% increase = X_3) are randomly assigned, subject to the restriction of each treatment appearing once and once only in each row and column. (This restriction rule does not apply to the randomised block design.) So, each treatment is tested in each store type and store size. The sales results are noted and the average treatment effect (average sales in this case) is calculated, using analysis of variance. From this, we can determine the main effect of the different price increases for the various store types and sizes.

What we cannot do with this design is measure the interaction between the two extraneous factors. Thus, the Latin square design suffers from one notable limitation — the assumption that there is no interaction between the treatments and the blocking factors. Hence, we are unable to calculate the inter-relationship between the store types, store sizes, price level increases and sales. Coupled with this is the 2 X 2 or 3 X 3 requirement, making this an expensive and complex design in practice.

4. The Factorial Design

If our shampoo manufacturer wants to know about the simultaneous effects of two or more independent variables, then a factorial design must be utilised. A factorial design measures the effect of interacting variables on a dependent variable. So, it moves away from the blocking approach of the previous designs, and focuses upon a number of independent variables.

To continue with the shampoo example, any changes in sales could be attributed to both the store type and size and the price increases. With such a design, the manufacturer can estimate the main effects of the two independent variables and the interaction between them. He can measure the *main effects* of each independent variable and the *interaction effects*, when their combined effect does not equal the sum of their individual effects.

The design looks like the figure below. The three variables and their treatment levels are as follows:

X_1 =   Price increases
level 1 = 1%
level 2 = 3%
level 3 = 5%

X_2 =   Store type
level 1 = national chains
level 2 = corner shops
level 3 = health food shops

X_3 =   Store size
level 1 = small, under 5,000 sq. feet
level 2 = medium, 5,001 to 10,000 sq. feet
level 3 = large, over 10,001 sq. feet.

Figure 7.2 Factorial design

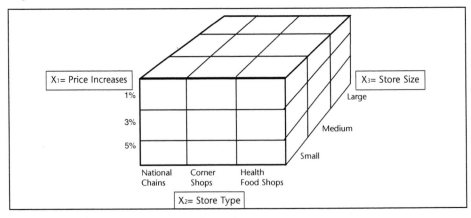

This is a 3 x 3 x 3 factorial design. In the case of store type, we might want to consider national chains versus all other outlets. This would result in a 3 x 2 x 3 design, with 18 cells, as the first independent variable has three treatment levels, the second variable has two treatment levels and the last independent variable has three treatment levels. Thus, in the factorial design, a cell is required for each possible combination of independent variables. A full factorial design, consisting of 32 product combinations or cells (4 brands x 4 prices x 2 bundling features) was effective in estimating the unit demand for a new product in a relatively new product category. It enabled management to explore a range of product, pricing and promotional support alternatives to develop a realistic guide for the marketing strategy.[11]

Crayola, a section of Binney & Smith and Hallmark, launched a creative arts and activities portal, known as Crayola.com. Parents and teachers are the site's target market, with the site providing arts and crafts project ideas and lesson plans, while also selling art supplies. To attract people to the site and convert browsers to buyers, Crayola used experimentation and, specifically, the factorial design. Based upon their internal secondary data and experience, they identified a set of stimuli that could be varied to drive traffic to Crayola.com. One of the stimuli was an email to parents and teachers that included five key attributes and related levels affecting the consumer response rate. The email was sent out with:

- Two subject lines: 'Crayola.com Survey' and 'Help Us Help You'.
- Three salutations: 'Hi user name : -)', 'Greetings!' and 'user name'.
- Two calls to action: 'As Crayola.com grows, we'd like to get your thoughts about the arts and how you use art materials' and 'Because you as an educator have a special understanding of the arts and how art materials are used, we invite you to help build Crayola.com'.
- Three promotions: a chance to participate in a monthly draw to win €100 worth of Crayola products: a monthly draw for one of €1 Amazon.com gift certificates: and no promotion.
- Two closings: 'Crayola.com'; and 'EducationEditor@Crayola.com'.

This resulted in a total of 72 possible versions of the e-mail (2 x 3 x 2 x 3 x 2 = 72). While Crayola were able to test all 72 variations, that experiment would have been expensive and cumbersome. So, instead, Crayola created a subset of sixteen emails to represent the 72 possible combinations. Over a fortnight, they sent the sixteen types of emails to randomly selected samples of customers, tracking and analysing their responses.

The 'best' email of the 72 options yielded a positive response rate of 34%. It was three times as effective at attracting parents as the 'worst' email. The experimentation also yielded surprising results. A price reduction on a product line generated sufficient volume to create higher revenues while maintaining the site's profitability. Conventional wisdom suggests that price increases would have been more effective.[12]

In conclusion, factorial design is undoubtedly the best experimental design. With advances in technology, web-sites, the Internet and software, the measurement of effects of independent stimuli on behavioural responses, in the form of experimentation, is becoming more precise and cost effective than traditional market testing.

SELECTION OF AN EXPERIMENTAL DESIGN

An important question for any researcher at this point is the selection of the best design for a study. In choosing the most appropriate experimental design, the researcher balances two issues, the potential threat to internal validity against the pragmatics of the project, e.g. cost, test units and the time dimension. By way of summary, the various experimental designs are presented in Table 7.5 together with the potential validity threats or errors, as one method to select the most appropriate experimental design for any given project.

Table 7.5 Experimental designs and their ability to combat validity threats

Experimental designs	Validity threats						
	History	Maturation	Testing Effect	Instrument-ation	Mortality	S/Regression	S/Bias
Pre-experimental designs							
After-only	No	No	Yes	Yes	No	No	No
Before-after	No	No	No	No	Maybe	No	Maybe
True experimental designs							
Before-after with control	Yes	Yes	Maybe	Yes	No	Yes	Yes
After-only with control	Yes	Yes	Maybe	Yes	No	No	No
Solomon-Four	Yes	Yes	Maybe	Yes	Yes	Yes	Yes
Quasi-experimental designs							
Time-series	No	Yes	No	No	Maybe	No	No
Multiple time-series	Maybe	Yes	No	No	Maybe	No	No

As can be seen from Table 7.5, a general rule of thumb is that the more formal and statistical the design, the more control the researcher has over validity threats. Against that, the more complex the design, the more costly and time-consuming the experiment.

Another way to select the most appropriate design is to consider the independent and dependent variables, coupled with the desired levels of control, as depicted in Figure 7.3.[13]

Figure 7.3 Which experimental design can be utilised?

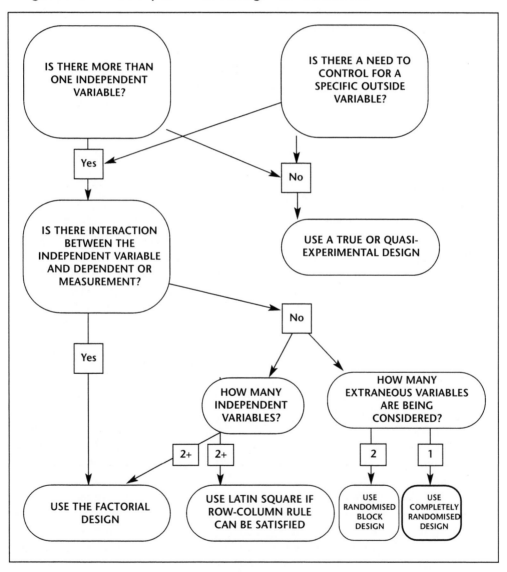

Essentially, the researcher uses the number of independent variables (one, two or more), the number of levels of the independent variable(s) (treatments, one or two or three or more) and the degree of main and interaction effect to select the best design.

From all of the preceding discussion, it is evident that experiments are a very powerful method for collecting data. Yet, the survey approach is generally regarded as the most popular tool for marketing researchers. This apparent anomaly arises because of the expensive nature of experiments, the complex nature of the marketplace and difficulties with implementing experiments, e.g. competitors becoming aware of marketing plans before full product launch.

Experiments cost significant time and money when compared with other data collection methods, but, more importantly, managers may perceive the cost of running an experiment as outweighing the benefits of the supplied information. Consider, for example, the cost of testing three different advertising campaigns in three different countries. The ads, with three different languages, have to be produced and aired in three different countries, possibly on three different TV channels. Meanwhile, sales have to be measured before, during and after the advertising campaigns. A host of factors, varying from country to country, have to be controlled for, before one can consider the analysis stage.

In the preceding example, another problem is the advance knowledge competitors can glean about a marketing plan or some key factor within, as a result of running an experiment. The advantage of being the first mover can be lost as competitors are given time to react and respond. It has been known for concepts to be stolen in this manner and militates often against the use of experiments.

Finally, it may be administratively impossible to implement the conditions necessary to run an experiment. For example, retailers may not be willing to co-operate, a control group may not be feasible and there are moral and ethical concerns when the test units are humans.

This use, or non-use, of experiments leads us to the final topic before finishing our investigation of experimentation — that of test marketing and the development of simulated test marketing.

TEST MARKETING

Traditionally the most popular form of field experiment, test marketing involves the use of representative areas, e.g. towns or television regions, some as test areas, others as control areas, to derive a sales estimate of the effect of an independent variable, like a new product or advertising campaign. Within these test areas, all other factors are kept constant and the independent variable is introduced with changes in the dependent variable monitored. In this manner, a company can gain experience and knowledge of what is likely to happen at a national launch. Test marketing allows the researcher to use experiments as a 'toe in the water'.

In Ireland, Guinness test-marketed a new range of premium taste beers in twenty Dublin pubs, aimed predominantly at male lager and ale drinkers, aged 28 to 40.[14] Mars Ireland test marketed their Celebrations chocolates and achieved 40% of the test market; moreover, 97% of the research respondents said they would purchase the product again — resulting in a successful national launch.[15] Stella Artois, from the Guinness Ireland Group, was test marketing in the Temple Bar and Grafton Street areas of Dublin[16], while McDonald's asked people if they would like to 'McOrder' while waiting at the petrol pumps as part of their on-the-go eater test market.[17] Beamish Red Irish Ale was launched on a test market basis in a number of Dublin and Cork outlets.[18] Baileys with a hint of mint chocolate and Baileys with a hint of crème caramel were test marketed at seven UK airports[19] and C&C Wholesale test marketed new bottles of 220 ml of club tonic, club white and club ginger in key Dublin outlets and Cork Crimson Gin, a premium gin, used test marketing in the 20–40 year age group before launching the product onto the market.[20, 21]

Having successfully completed extensive test marketing pilot initiative in pubs throughout Dublin, ambient advertising medium View Station was set for its official launch nationwide. The system uses digital video technology in high-traffic/high-profile, affluent pub environments. While only three inches thick, its LCD display screens offer superior-to-TV visual clarity and ads are repeated 50 times a day or over 800 times in a two-week cycle.[22] Finally, Baileys The Whiskey was test marketed in Dublin, offering consumers the opportunity to experience the character of Baileys in the form of a premium whiskey.[23]

To conduct a test market, a number of steps have to be undertaken. Firstly, the objectives of the test market need to be articulated. These generally include determining sales levels and volume, frequency of purchase, repeat purchase rates, awareness levels, and effect on other sales of related products. Once completed, the next decision is to choose between a field or controlled (laboratory) test market. Then, an appropriate experimental design is selected, based upon the desired control over validity threats, cost and time constraints. The question as to how long a test market should last is important, as it has to be long enough for consumers to become aware of the product and buy it again. Next, the issue of the actual test markets, cities or regions is confronted. The selected areas must be representative of the whole population. In practice, it can be hard to achieve this in a miniature sample. That done, the treatment variables are applied, all the necessary observations are made and the results are analysed. Management is then in a position to make decisions about the national launch and marketing strategies to employ, should they wish to proceed.

The procedure, as described above for test marketing, can take the form of either a *standard test market* or a *controlled test market*. A standard test market is where the firm selects a number of cities, TV areas or other test units to market the product (and marketing mix) as it would do in a national launch. Sales forecasts are based upon audits of retailers, stores, distribution paths and consumers. This enables the company to evaluate the optimum marketing mix and make any necessary changes. The advantage of such a test market is the high degree of external validity given to the results. Using the 'real world', in every sense of the word, truly allows the firm to gauge the market reaction to the new product launch. Against this, the chosen locations have to be fully representative of the population at large. Coupled with this, sufficient time has to be allowed for the market and customers to respond to the new product, whilst guarding against competitors interfering with the launch.

On the other hand, controlled test marketing is where the company chooses the outlets through which to release the product, uses its own sales force and tests different marketing strategies (the firm is not confined to testing one particular strategy in all outlets in one area). This approach is cheaper and easier to implement than the standard test marketing procedure, but it is not as realistic.

Standard test marketing and control test marketing, two forms of test marketing, have historically been confined to the larger or multinational firms, due to cost and time demands, and the noted problems of experimentation highlighted above, such as competitive reaction, or inability to match towns or areas. In more recent years, one of the most interesting experimental developments (and an answer to many of the historical difficulties of test marketing mentioned above) has been simulated test marketing.[24, 25]

SIMULATED TEST MARKETING

Simulated test marketing is the third type of test marketing available to a researcher. In general, this test marketing experimental method generates probability data about awareness levels, purchase levels and consumption likelihood. 'Mock' computer situations (simulated test marketing in laboratory or virtual experiments, as opposed to standard or controlled which are in the field) are created to determine 'consumer reaction to marketing initiatives prior to their market entry'.[26] These reactions are combined with marketing plan information to predict the likelihood of usage, sales volume and probability of repeat purchase.[27,28,29,30] Lyons successfully used STM to identify round teabags as a differentiating factor to arrest a decline in their market share for Tetley tea.[31]

Simulated test marketing is made possible as consumers are exposed to a new product or marketing programme in a simulated shopping environment. In this way, the manufacturer's products can be shown alongside competitive offerings in a photograph or slide presentation. The alternative is to allow consumers to purchase from shelves stocked with the products in question. Those consumers who choose the test product are asked to use a free sample at home and provide feedback. In this way, the new product with its price and the competitive products with prices can be shown in a photograph, slide presentation, computer simulation or video presentation. The type of consumer exposure is chosen to represent the dominant marketing vehicle which will be used in the product launch. In some cases, no consumer advertising is used with the launch of a new product, the consumers are exposed to a picture of the shelf set or an actual shelf set with prices. After exposure to the new product, most simulated test market designs use an attitudinal question concerning the probability of purchase, such as that in Box 7.2, to identify consumers who are likely to purchase the new product. Those consumers who are likely to purchase the test product are given the test product in its actual size to use at home and provide feedback.

Box 7.2 Sample attitudinal measurement often used in STM

Certainly will purchase	90% chance
Almost certainly will purchase	80% chance
Very probable will purchase	70% chance
Good possibility will purchase	60% chance
Fairly good possibility will purchase	50% chance
Fair possibility will purchase	40% chance
Some possibility will purchase	30% chance
Slight possibility will purchase	20% chance
Very slight possibility will purchase	10% chance
No chance will purchase	0% chance

Behavioural measures of purchase interest are also used in simulated test market designs; however, they are used less frequently than attitudinal measures due to the cost of conducting the research. Behavioural measures are obtained by allowing respondents to actually purchase the test and/or competitive products in the study. Respondents are exposed to the new product and competitive advertising. Next, consumers are exposed to actual shelves in the test product category. This methodology allows consumers to purchase from actual shelves stocked with the products in question. Consumers use their own money to purchase the test product in some cases, in other cases they use coupons provided by the research company. The consumers are called for feedback concerning the new product after they have used it at home.

These trial, retrial, and purchase and repeat rates (probabilities) are transcribed into advanced analytic software packages, to predict sales levels and market share. Variables, such as estimated advertising spend, shelf space, pricing and other promotional expenses, are also included.

The accuracy of the simulated test marketing forecasts are tracked by the research companies generating the forecasts. All products actually launched into the marketplace are investigated after the launch year. The sales forecast and actual year-one sales are compared. The success of each forecast is included in the accuracy record for the particular simulated test market model. Since simulated test marketing models have been successful in forecasting the sales of the new products, the methodology has grown in use over time.

There are many advantages to be had from utilising simulated test marketing.

- One key advantage is the realism offered by STM over and above other data collection methods and traditional test marketing. It sets products in a competitive context, positioning the test product against other valid options.
- Consumer purchase behaviours and reactions are measured, linking the consumer's attitudes to actual behaviour. This is difficult in actual test marketing.
- STM allows a company to test their proposed marketing plan or mix before committing themselves to a full launch, in a cheaper and quicker manner than test marketing.
- STM provides accurate quantitative estimates of possible sales levels, market share and product cannibalisation. The noise and clutter of actual stores are recreated. Management and researchers have a large degree of control and flexibility over the independent and dependent variables, and different price levels can be easily tested. As a result, most consumer packaged goods companies are using STM to screen their ideas early in the development process, so they can identify the better ideas and allocate more effort and resources to them.
- STM can be conducted in twelve weeks or less.
- The information from STM is confidential and not available to competitors.
- Finally, for experimentation, STMs are also relatively inexpensive — simulated test markets can cost 10%–12% of the standard test market.

SUMMARY

Causal research establishes that a change in an independent variable causes a predictable change in a dependent variable. To demonstrate such an effect, the experiment is used as the data collection method for causal research. Experiments are defined as studies to manipulate an independent variable to measure the effects on a dependent variable. Four factors are required: concomitant, temporal sequence, theoretical support, and non-spurious association.

Experiments pay particular attention to internal and external validity. Threats to internal validity include history, maturation, the testing effect (main and interactive), instrumentation, mortality, statistical regression and selection bias. External validity translates into a question of field versus laboratory experimental setting.

Experimental designs can be classified as pre-experiments; true experiments; quasi-experiments or advanced statistical experiments. This categorisation of experimental designs reflects the degree of control they afford the researcher over threats to both internal and external validity.

Test marketing is the experimental testing of a new marketing development, e.g. a new product, new promotional theme or a new marketing mix. It can be a standard, controlled or simulated test market to provide estimates to likely sales levels, consumers' reactions, and potential problems with proposed marketing mix strategies. As technological advances continue in both hardware and software applications, it is inevitable that experimentation, in the form of simulated test marketing, becomes more widely used.

KEY TERMS

Causal research	Statistical regression
Experiment	Mortality
Independent variable	Matching
Dependent variable	External validity
Test units	Reactive error
Control group	Field experiments
Experimental group	Laboratory experiments
Randomisation	Pre-experimental designs
Internal validity	True experiments
History	Quasi-experiments
Maturation	Statistical experiments
Testing	Test marketing
Main effect	Standard test marketing
Interaction effect	Control test marketing
Instrumentation	Simulated test marketing
Selection bias	

QUESTIONS

1. How do the scientific notions and common-sense notions of causality differ?
2. Describe some independent and dependent variables that could be used in consumer goods experiments.
3. What is the purpose of randomisation and matching in experimental design?
4. Indicate the kind of evidence needed to demonstrate the existence of a causal relationship.
5. Describe, and give an example of, each of the following error types:
   (a) testing effect;
   (b) interaction error;
   (c) maturation;
   (d) history;
   (e) selection bias;
   (f) mortality;
   (g) instrumentation;

(h) main effect.

6. How can the statistical regression effect exert an influence on the results of an experiment? Provide a real or hypothetical example of a situation in which this effect is likely to be present.

7. Is it possible for a marketing experiment to have high internal validity, but very low external validity? If so, provide an example of a situation in which this would be likely to occur.

8. Experiments may be conducted in a variety of settings that are usually classified as laboratory or field.
    (a) What differences distinguish laboratory from field settings?
    (b) What concerns should the experimenter be particularly aware of in each setting?

9. What are the distinctions between pre-experimental, true experimental and quasi-experimental designs?

10. Explain how various measurements of the experimental effect in a Solomon-Four group design can provide estimates of the effects of certain extraneous variables?

11. What is the key characteristic that distinguishes true experimental designs from pre-experimental designs?

12. What is a time-series experiment? When is it used?

13. Suggest at least three specific situations in marketing, in which you think an experiment would be an appropriate research design. Which of the various designs would you recommend for each of the situations? What specific internal and/or external validity threats would you face with your suggested designs?

14. What ethical problems do you see in conducting experiments with human subjects? In your answer, refer to a 'Code of Conduct' from a recognised body at either national or international level.

15. Explain:
    (a) controlled test marketing;
    (b) simulated test marketing.
    How are they different from traditional test marketing?

16. Which of the following products or marketing strategies are likely to be test marketed? Why, or why not?
    (a) a computerised robot lawn mower;
    (b) a line of eight-ounce servings of vegetarian dishes for senior citizens;
    (c) a forklift truck;
    (d) a new brand of eye-drops especially for brown-eyed people;
    (e) a new, heavy-duty kitchen mixer;
    (f) an advertising campaign to drink a cola drink in the morning.

PROBLEMS AND ASSIGNMENTS

1. A leading manufacturer of frozen food products decided to test the effectiveness of an in-store display. Eight large supermarkets, near the company's head office, were selected for the experiment. The display was set up in four of the stores, and sales were monitored for a period of two weeks. The sales of the other four stores were also recorded, but no displays were used. Sales volume for the frozen food products increased by 1% in the stores that used in-store displays compared to the stores that did not.
   (a) What type of design was being used? Justify your answer.
   (b) Diagrammatically represent the design.
   (c) Discuss the threats to internal and external validity for the design.

2. The product development team at Bord na Móna has been working on several modifications of their highly successful fireplace log. The most promising development is a new log that comes prepacked and burns an hour longer. At a recent strategy meeting, the marketing director suggested a test market before a national launch of the new log. He pointed out that a test market would be a good way to evaluate the effectiveness of two alternative advertising and promotional campaigns that have been proposed by Bord na Móna's advertising agency. He felt that effectiveness should be evaluated in terms of the trial and repeat purchasing behaviour. He also wanted to assess Bord na Móna's current distributor's acceptance of the new product. The Bord na Móna CEO is not very enthusiastic about the idea of test marketing. He is concerned that Bord na Móna's competitors could easily duplicate the new log; and that the seasonal nature of log sales makes it imperative to reach a decision on the new log by early April, only four months away.
   (a) What information should be obtained from the test market in order to satisfy the marketing director?
   (b) What constraints must the test-marketing operate to satisfy the CEO?
   (c) What test market approach should be pursued? Why?

3. A manufacturer of gas cookers has designed an improved model that will reduce gas usage and decrease cooking times. However, this new model will increase the product's price by 15% because of new components and design changes. The company wants to assess to what extent the new model will affect sales of its existing gas ovens. Suggest an experimental design, justifying your choice, that will enable management to make a decision as to whether to launch the new cooker.

4. The student union at your university or college is considering three alternative brands of burgers to be offered in the student restaurant. Design an experiment to determine which brand of burgers students would prefer.

5. Bord Bia, in conjunction with Bord Iascaigh Mhara and a group of mussel farmers, has developed a new frozen mussel dinner — one heats it and serves it

in the tray. The group overseeing the development are not considering test marketing the product. They are planning to go with a national launch. What are the advantages of doing so, given that the group already had five successful food launches in the Irish market over the past three years? What are the disadvantages of not test marketing?

6. What experimental designs would you advocate in the following circumstances? How would you recruit the test subjects? What treatment would you apply to the subjects? How would you measure results?
   (a) The acceptability of a prepackaged custard.
   (b) The response to an addition to a confectionery counter-line popular with primary schoolchildren.
   (c) The response of the Irish public to a new Irish drama on RTÉ One;
   (d) The awareness of males, 18–35, to a new line of shoes by Dubarry.

8. 'Drimavoughane' is a goat's cheese sold locally in the south-east of Ireland, where it is popular with restaurants. The firm feel that Drimavoughane is losing market share among restaurants to the national brands. However, no exact measures of the restaurant's attitudes or consumption patterns exist. Management is considering placing an advertisement in the local newspapers and/or local radios. However, they are not sure how effective this would be. Design a study to test the effectiveness of the advertisements.

9. State the type of experiment being conducted in the following situations. In each case, identify the potential threat to internal and external validity.
   (a) A major distributor of telecommunications equipment is considering a new sales pitch for its salespeople. The sales territory with the largest sales figures for the past year is selected, the new sales strategy is implemented, and the effect on sales is measured.
   (b) Procter & Gamble wants to determine if a new package design for Fairy washing-up liquid is more effective than the current pack. Ten supermarkets are randomly selected throughout Ireland. In five of them, randomly selected, Fairy is sold in the new packaging. In the remaining shops, the old package is used. Sales are recorded for both groups of supermarkets for three months.

10. The Marketing Society of Ireland has asked you to design an experiment to measure the effect of compensation on response rates when conducting Internet surveys among Irish businesses. This involves 600 firms who will be assigned to one of the following conditions: no compensation; €1 compensation; and €3 compensation. Describe how your design would work if it were:
    (a) a Completely Randomised design;
    (b) a Randomised Block design;
    (c) a Latin Square; or
    (d) a Factorial design (suggest another independent variable to use).
    Which is the most appropriate design? Why?

11. Connor McWilliams, the newly appointed marketing manager of a highly popular and successful pottery shop in Temple Bar, has requested a larger budget for shop-window displays. McWilliams thinks that continuous changes in the shop window display, to reflect local events such as St Valentine's Day and St Patrick's Day, will attract customers. Specifically, he expects customers to come into the shop more often, increase their purchase amount and develop a more positive image of the shop and products. The owner is not convinced and has asked McWilliams for proof to justify the increased expenditure on displays. Identify the independent variable(s), the dependent variable(s) and the likely extraneous variables to impact on the dependent variable.

12. A manufacturer has developed a new food product to test marketing stage. Previous experience suggests the appeal of this type of product to customers may vary both across regions of the country (Dublin, other urban and rural) and in the type of outlet (small local shops, Centra/Spar-type co-ops, and large supermarkets). So, in addition to attempting to estimate the overall sales of the new product, the manufacturer wishes to determine whether sales vary across region, across type of store and also whether there is some interaction between store type and region. Describe briefly how an experiment could be designed to answer the manufacturer's question. (Adapted from a Marketing Institute of Ireland examination paper, 1996.)

Case Study
Introduction of Nutritionally Enhanced Eggs, A New Product*

Background

The Rynn Egg Company, REC, of Greaghnafarna, Country Leitrim, produces fresh eggs for distribution in grocery stores throughout Ireland. The use of nutritional supplements has increased among consumers in Ireland. Most of the supplements are consumed through tablets. Management at Rynn Egg Company wants to take advantage of consumers' interest in nutritional supplements and enhance the nutritional value of their eggs with the nutrients consumers are purchasing in tablet form. Nutritionally enhanced eggs, designer eggs, are eggs that have been altered nutritionally in some way or specially raised. The eggs are commanding a premium price and it appears that consumers are willing to pay extra for an egg enhanced with omega-3 fatty acids, lycopene, lutein, or vitamin E. Rynn Egg Company hired an animal nutritionist to help them produce designer eggs enhanced with lycopene and omega-3 fatty acids.

Long-chain omega-3 fatty acids have been proven to reduce the risk of cardiovascular disease by lowering the serum triglyceride levels and raising the HDL (good) cholesterol levels. Lycopene is an antioxidant that can be boosted in eggs. This carotenoid imparts a red colouring to food, and is found most abundantly in tomatoes. There are also high concentrations found naturally in pink grapefruit, papaya and watermelon. As with other antioxidants, lycopene fights free radicals and helps inhibit DNA oxidation to prevent many types of cancer by preventing and repairing damaged cells. It is easily absorbed and is deposited in the liver, lungs, prostate, colon and skin. Preliminary research has shown that lycopene may reduce the risk of macular degeneration. It is also associated with lowering the risk of lung, bladder, breast, cervical and skin cancer.

Since REC has never sold designer eggs in Ireland, the management team does not know which nutrient would generate a higher level of purchase interest among consumers. Nancy Rynn, President of REC, wants to insure the success of the new product introduction. Therefore, REC commissioned the Galway Market Research Institute to conduct simulated test marketing research to evaluate consumer purchase interest in nutritionally enhanced eggs. She used simulated test marketing methodology rather than a traditional test market because a simulated test market:

- provides a sales forecast that can be projected nationally;
- allows the testing of multiple prices and positionings;
- provides confidentiality;
- is less expensive than a test market; and
- is an empirically validated methodology.

Simulated Test Market Results for Designer Eggs

The simulated test marketing research used the laboratory experiment component of simulated test marketing in a three-cell study design. One cell examined the purchase interest of 150 egg consumers in lycopene enhanced eggs at €4.29 for a dozen, an 87% premium over the regular eggs sold by REC. The second cell examined the purchase interest of 150 egg consumers in eggs enhanced with DHA Omega 3, also priced at €4.29 for a dozen. Cell three examined the purchase interest of 150 consumers in eggs nutritionally enhanced with both lycopene and DHA Omega 3, priced at a 96% premium, €4.49 for a dozen. A competitive board was used to remind respondents of competitive eggs in stores at their market prices. The respondents were past-year purchasers of eggs that were geographically dispersed to reflect national demographics for each cell.

Using one-way analysis of variance with the Tukey post-hoc test of the ratio purchase interest data shows significant differences between cells. The purchase interest rates for each cell were forecasted based on the use of a proprietary model and an eleven-point purchase interest scale. The results show that the new product is a niche product and attractive to a small proportion of egg consumers, 10.4% to 13.5%. Tables 7.6 and 7.7 show a similar purchase interest for the eggs nutritionally enhanced with a single supplement and a significantly higher purchase interest for the eggs enhanced with both DHA Omega 3 and lycopene.

The nutritional enhancement of eggs with two nutrients, coupled with an increase in price to €4.49, generated an increase in likely purchasers over the lower-priced eggs enhanced with one nutrient.

Table 7.6 Mean likelihood to purchase nutritionally enhanced eggs in the next year

	DHA Omega-3 Eggs Price €4.29 (N=150)	Lycopene Price €4.29 (N=150)	DHA Omega-3 and Lycopene Price €4.49 (N=150)	F Statistic
Mean Purchase Likelihood	10.40%	11.50%	13.5%	12.208**

** Significance at the .05 level

Table 7.7 Mean likelihood to purchase nutritionally enhanced eggs in the next year
Tukey Post Hoc

N=450		Mean Difference
DHA Omega-3 Eggs €4.29	Lycopene Eggs €4.29	1.10
	DHA Omega-3 Eggs and Lycopene Eggs €4.49	2.99 **
Lycopene Eggs €4.29	DHA Omega-3 Eggs €4.29	1.10
	DHA Omega-3 Eggs and Lycopene Eggs €4.49	1.89**
DHA Omega-3 Eggs and Lycopene Eggs €4.49	DHA Omega-3 Eggs €4.29	2.99**
	Lycopene Eggs €4.29	1.89**

** Significant difference at the .05 level Tukey Post Hoc

Impact of Price on Purchase Interest

In order to examine the impact of price on the purchase interest, respondents were asked if they thought the price was just right, too high, or too low. Table 7.8 shows that respondents indicated that the €4.29 price for eggs nutritionally enhanced with one nutrient and the €4.49 price for a dozen eggs enhanced with two nutrients are considered too high for most egg consumers.

Table 7.8 Price of nutritionally enhanced eggs

	DHA Omega-3 Eggs Price €4.29 (N=150)	Lycopene Price €4.29 (N=150)	DHA Omega-3 and Lycopene Price €4.49 (N=150)	Chi-Square
Just right	27.1%	29.2%	23.1%	1.15
Too high	69.8%	70.8%	75.2%	
Too low	3.1%	0.0%	1.7%	

** Significance at the .05 level

Table 7.9 shows that price is a limiting factor in attracting consumers to the nutritionally enhanced eggs produced by REC. Over three-fourths of consumers who are not likely to buy the nutritionally enhanced eggs indicate that the price is too high. Further, more than a third to a half of consumers that are likely to buy one of the nutritionally-enhanced egg concepts indicate that the price is too high.

Table 7.9 Price of nutritionally enhanced eggs: likely buyers and likely non-buyers

	Likely Buyers	Non Likely Buyers	Chi-Square
DHA Omega-3 Eggs Price €4.29 (N=150)			
Just right	47.8%	22.6%	27.76**
Too high	34.8%	77.4%	
Too low	17.4%	0%	
Lycopene Price €4.29 (N=150)			
Just right	50.0%	18.67%	11.98**
Too high	50.0%	81.33%	
Too low	0.0%	0.0%	
DHA Omega-3 and Lycopene Price €4.49(N=150)			
Just right	49.2%	21.0%	32.62**
Too high	44.3%	79.0%	
Too low	6.5%	0%	

**Significance at the .05 level

Questions

1. What is the dependent variable in this experiment?
2. What is/are the independent variable(s) in this experiment?
3. After reviewing the results of the simulated test market, would you recommend that REC introduce nutritionally enhanced eggs to the Irish market? If you would, what product would you introduce and at what price?
4. Design an experiment that would test the type of packaging that should be used for the new product introduction: cardboard or clear plastic. Describe the sample that would be used in that experiment.
5. Evaluate the validity of the experimental design for the problem described here and for your new experiment.
6. Are the main effects in the experiment described here? Explain your answer.
7. Are the interaction effects in the experiment described here? How would you determine the presence of such effects? Explain your answer.

*This case was written by Professor Marianne McGarry Wolf, Agribusiness Department, California Polytechnic State University, San Luis Obispo, California. Research assistance was provided by Cherylin Hyle, Research Assistant, Agribusiness Department, California Polytechnic State University, San Luis Obispo, California. It is intended to be used as a basis for class discussion rather than to illustrate the effective or ineffective handling of an administrative situation. The case is based upon a real situation, though certain information has been disguised. © Marianne McGarry Wolf, 2006.

PART 3

DATA COLLECTION AND ACQUISITION

CHAPTER 8

QUESTIONNAIRE DESIGN AND FIELD WORK

CHAPTER OVERVIEW

▸ Introduction ▸ Guidelines for Questionnaire Development ▸ Preliminary Considerations ▸ Question Content ▸ Decide on Response Format ▸ Question Wording ▸ Question Sequence ▸ Physical Characteristics ▸ Pre-test ▸ Field Work ▸ Selection of Field Workers ▸ Training of Field Workers ▸ Supervision of Field Workers ▸ Validation of Field Workers ▸ Evaluation of Field Workers ▸ Summary

INTRODUCTION

The two main methods of collecting primary data are asking questions and observing. Survey research (in whatever form — personal interview, telephone, postal or online) relies on the use of a questionnaire. The heart of a survey is the questionnaire,[1] which is a formalised means of collecting data from respondents. The primary purpose of a questionnaire is measurement. There are a number of ways to apply survey questionnaires: personal interview, telephone, postal or self-administered. Questionnaires can be used to measure customers' behaviour, their attitudes, awareness and characteristics. By using a questionnaire, the researcher provides standardisation and uniformity in the data-gathering process. If researchers go out and ask people somewhat different questions, they will get answers that are not directly comparable. A questionnaire standardises the wording and sequencing of the questions and allows the field workers to achieve speed and accuracy in recording the data. Because the data are collected in common form, a questionnaire enables the recorded information to be edited and summarised more quickly and with less error.

A questionnaire has three objectives.[2] Firstly, it must translate the information needed into questions that the respondent can and will answer. Secondly, a questionnaire must uplift, motivate and encourage the respondent to co-operate and complete the interview. Thirdly, a questionnaire should minimise response error.

Given this, at the end of this chapter the reader will be able to:

1. discuss questionnaire design;
2. describe the seven steps of questionnaire design; and
3. explain fieldwork issues.

GUIDELINES FOR QUESTIONNAIRE DEVELOPMENT

Questionnaire design is a major source of non-sampling error. Questionnaire design is more of an art than a scientific undertaking and is beset with potential pitfalls. It is a skill that the researcher learns through experience. The design of an appropriate questionnaire involves no firm set of foolproof procedures. There are, however, a number of rules or guidelines that can be followed. These rules have emerged from the accumulated experience of researchers. While these rules are useful in preventing serious errors, the fine-tuning of a questionnaire requires the creativity of a skilled researcher. Ultimately, a sound questionnaire requires the application of guidelines, common sense, concern for the respondent, a clear understanding of the information needed, and extensive pre-testing. But the best data collection instrument is not necessarily the one that is perfect. Rather than attempting to develop the 'ideal' questionnaire, the practicality of conducting marketing research may require developing a questionnaire that is both workable and adequate for the task at hand. After all, out-of-date information collected through use of a perfect questionnaire is of little use.

Questionnaires can be classified according to their degree of structure and directness. The type of questionnaire used is, to an extent, dependent on the method of survey. Highly structured questionnaires consist of a series of structured formal questions which limit the responses of the respondent, whereas unstructured questionnaires are made up of more open, investigative-type questions. Structured questionnaires tend to incorporate more multiple-choice, dichotomous and scale-type questions. Unstructured questionnaries lend themselves more towards open-ended-type questions as in an in-depth discussion guide. In practice, most questionnaires are a mix of both the structured and unstructured type. Directness, on the other hand, refers to the degree to which the respondent is aware of the purpose of the study. While any combination of structure and directness is possible, the use of unstructured indirect questionnaires is more akin to applying projective techniques.

The discussion of questionnaire design will be presented as a series of seven steps. While the steps are presented sequentially, they are, in fact, interrelated. Not only do decisions made during the early stages influence choices later in the sequence, but decisions made during the final stages may compel the reconsideration of earlier choices. For example, decisions on question sequence will often influence the wording of the questions involved. The seven steps can be summarised as shown in Figure 8.1.

Figure 8.1

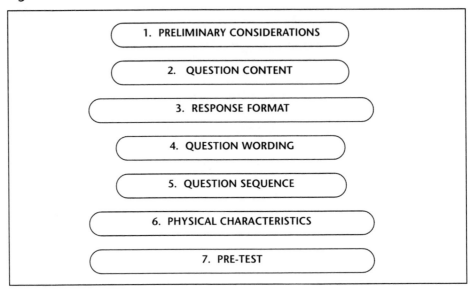

The major part of this chapter will be devoted to the problems encountered in constructing good questionnaires. Some of this will also be pertinent to observation forms.

PRELIMINARY CONSIDERATIONS

The researcher must make decisions regarding:

1. What information is required?
2. Who are target respondents?
3. What method of communication will be used to reach these respondents?
4. How will the resulting data be processed and analysed?

1. What information is required?

Decisions made during the early stages of the research process will influence the questionnaire design. The preceding chapters stressed the need to have good problem definition and clear objectives for the study to deal with the management problem at hand. Research objectives (listing of information needs) should be spelled out as clearly and precisely as possible. The questionnaire is the link between the information needed and the data to be collected. The questions from the questionnaire should flow logically from the list of information needs. It is helpful to write each question number opposite the objective that the particular question will help accomplish. A questionnaire is relevant if no unnecessary information is collected and only the information needed to solve the marketing problems is obtained. The collection of data that is not required increases the cost of the project — more about this later.

2. Who are the target respondents?

The characteristics of the respondent groups have a great influence on questionnaire design. Questions that are appropriate for a group of college graduates may not be appropriate for respondents with a second-level education. If, for example, CERT wished to conduct a survey with summer workers in the hospitality industry, it may choose to design one questionnaire for third-level students and have another designed specifically for sixth-year secondary students. Likewise, a questionnaire designed for use on children would require much simpler language than that designed for use on adults. A questionnaire must 'speak' to respondents in an understandable language and at the appropriate intellectual level. The more heterogeneous the groups, the more difficult it is to construct a single questionnaire that is appropriate to everyone. Marketing jargon and business terminology should be avoided where possible (unless that is your respondent group). It is best to use simple, everyday language, as long as the result is not insulting or demeaning to the respondent.

3. What method of communication will be used?

The method of administering a questionnaire (personal interview, telephone, postal etc.) will also have a bearing on its structure and content. In personal interviews, respondents see the questionnaire and interact with the interviewer. More difficult and complex questions can be asked of the respondent. In telephone interviews, the respondent does not see the questionnaire, whereas postal questionnaires are self-completing. This poses its own problems for the type and style of questions that may be asked of the respondent. In general, a more conversational style of writing is appropriate for personal and telephone interviews. These factors and others were discussed in Chapter 6, where we examined the characteristics of different approaches to collecting marketing research data. In all such cases, the decision as to which survey method is used will affect the types of questions to be asked and the general nature of the questionnaire design.

4. How will the data be processed and analysed?

Consideration must also be given to the latter stages of the research process. Decisions regarding editing, coding, processing and statistical analysis of the data need to be factored in to the design of the questionnaire; for example, where statistical analysis is to be employed, highly structured questionnaires are needed.

QUESTION CONTENT

When evaluating possible questions for inclusion in the data collection instrument, the following issues must be considered:

1. Is the question really necessary?

Although it seems obvious that no question should be included in a questionnaire unless it is necessary, there may be a tendency to include interesting questions that have no particular contribution to the research objectives. The answers to these questions may be 'nice to know' but convey no managerially useful information. If there is no satisfactory answer to the question 'How am I going to use the data generated by this question?' that question should be eliminated. Unnecessary questions add to the expense of the survey and increase the demands made on the respondents, thereby possibly decreasing the chances of their co-operation. In certain situations, a 'dummy' question is included at the beginning of, or strategically throughout, a questionnaire in order to obtain respondent involvement and rapport prior to asking more sensitive or controversial questions; or questions may be asked in order to disguise the true purpose or sponsorship of the study. For example, questions may be asked about competing brands merely to hide the identity of the brand under study.

2. Does the respondent have the information requested?

Once we are sure that our question is necessary and addresses the information needs, we must consider the respondent's ability to provide an accurate answer. Certain factors limit the respondent's ability to provide the desired information. The respondent may not know the answer, may know the answer but have forgotten it, or may be unable or unwilling (due to confidentiality) to articulate the answer.

3. The respondent may not know the answer

Respondents are often asked questions on topics that may not fall within a given respondent's experience. They are 'uninformed' in the sense that they have never known the answer to the question. Asking a respondent about a brand or store that they have never encountered is an example of this problem. Respondents will often be more than willing to answer questions they do not know the answer to. Although uninformed, they may be reluctant to admit a lack of knowledge on a topic. This is especially so when a question is worded in such a manner that implies that a respondent should know the answer. Uninformed respondents are a source of measurement error.

Respondents who falsely report awareness of marketing stimuli such as brand names, logos, product promotions, advertisements, etc. are guilty of 'bogus recall' or 'spurious awareness'. The researcher should be wary of continuous 'yea-saying' respondents. Where there is doubt, filter questions should be used to determine familiarity and past experience with a product category. Filter questions are asked before questions about the topic itself. They are essentially screening questions that are used to filter out respondents who are not sufficiently informed. Filter questions can be indirect ('What brands of deodorant are you familiar with?') or direct ('Have you ever used Fiacla toothpaste in the past year?').

4. Can the respondent remember the information?

Not only should the individual have the information sought, but he or she should remember it. However, in many situations respondents cannot recall the answer to a question. Can *you* answer the following questions?

- What products were advertised before the nine o'clock news last Sunday?
- What did you have for lunch five days ago?
- What brand of petrol, if any, did you purchase two weeks ago?

We may have known the answers to these questions once, but do not remember when questioned specifically. Our ability to remember various events is influenced by the event itself, its importance, the length of time since the event, and the amount of recall stimuli provided to jog our memory. Three aspects of forgetting are of concern to the researcher:

- *Omission*, which is the inability to recall an event that actually took place.
- *Telescoping*, which occurs when a respondent remembers an event as occurring more recently than it actually occurred.
- *Creation*, which occurs when an individual 'remembers' an event that did not actually occur.

Researchers cannot easily change the ability of an individual to remember things. They can, however, try to ask the person most apt to remember, e.g. recent purchasers. If the event could be considered relatively unimportant to the respondents, they can limit their questions to events that have happened recently. In fact, when memory is involved, researchers must be cautious not to overestimate the accuracy with which respondents will remember the information they want.

Consumers are particularly poor at remembering quantities of products. Classification of users into heavy users and light users of a product on the basis of reported use has been found to misclassify up to 75% of respondents in some product categories.[3] Another factor which affects our ability to remember is the stimulus we are given. An unaided recall approach does not provide the respondent with cues. Questions like 'What brand of coffee do you remember being advertised on TV last night?' rely on unaided recall. The aided recall approach attempts to stimulate the respondent's memory by providing cues; for example, 'From the following list of coffee brand names, which one do you remember being advertised on TV last night?' Aided recall is an attempt to overcome the memory problem.

5. Ability of the respondent to articulate

When respondents are unable to articulate their responses on an issue, they are likely to ignore that question and/or refuse to co-operate with the remainder of the survey. This may be particularly so for open-ended questions — 'Why do you use this dry cleaning service?', where respondents may have difficulty in verbalising the issue.

Closed-ended questions, lists of alternatives to choose from, and pictures, etc. may help respondents to better articulate their response. Projective techniques is another method researchers use to help respondents to verbalise answers.

6. Willingness to respond accurately

Assuming that the respondent can answer the question, he or she may be unwilling to do so. Unwillingness to respond accurately can be manifested in:

- a refusal to answer a specific question(s), i.e. item non-response error;
- deliberately providing an incorrect answer. This distortion results in measurement error.

Non-response or distorted answers can result from any of the following reasons:
- The situation or context may not seem appropriate for disclosure. For example, it may be inappropriate for a family planning clinic to carry out on-street personal interviews to determine the public's family planning activities. Such questions are perhaps better asked by a nurse or GP.
- The information requested may be considered personal or embarrassing to the respondent. Questions on topics such as sexual behaviour and orientation, purchase of personal hygiene products, consumption of alcohol, theft and car accidents, readership of certain magazines, etc. may result in refusals or distortions.
- Requests for 'prestige' or 'normative' information. Questions that have a bearing on prestige or adherence to social norms include education level obtained, income earned, amount of time spent reading quality newspapers or watching educational TV, purchase of high-prestige magazines, etc. These questions typically produce answers with an upward response bias. Likewise, ownership or usage of low prestige or less socially acceptable products or services is typically understated by respondents.

How to deal with respondents who are unwilling to respond accurately

Intuitively, it would seem that anonymity would increase the likelihood of respondents providing accurate answers to sensitive questions. However, in many instances, assurances of anonymity are not sufficient to encourage unwilling respondents. A number of techniques have been developed to seek out potentially embarrassing or sensitive information.

1. Placing of sensitive topics at the end of the questionnaire. By then rapport has been created, any initial mistrust has been weakened and the legitimacy of the survey established.
2. Counter biasing statement. Begin with a statement that suggests the behaviour in question is relatively common. For example, if we anticipate that responses will

tend to be distorted in the 'Yes' direction we can preface the question with a statement that makes the 'No' response more acceptable for the respondent, i.e. the question is intentionally biased in the opposite direction. For example, 'For various reasons people delay in paying their TV licence on time. Have you ever delayed from paying for your TV licence on time?' Ideally, the prefacing statement should contain an amount of counter bias, equal to the response bias resulting from the question itself. There is a danger that too much or too little counter bias will be introduced. Some respondents may admit to behaviour they did not engage in because it may suddenly seem embarrassing to have not engaged in the behaviour in question. Also, unethical researchers who use counter biasing statements could arrive at findings that are purposely distorted to suit their own agenda.

3. Use an indirect statement.
4. Phrase the sensitive question so that it refers to 'other people' and allow respondents to reveal their attitudes by expressing them indirectly through a third party. As an example:
    'Q9. For one reason or another most people find it difficult to attend Mass every week on at least one occasion. Do you think this is acceptable?'
5. Another approach is to hide the potentially sensitive questions within a group of other more innocent questions. The entire list of questions can then be asked quickly. Respondents may be more likely to respond than might be the case if the question was asked in a vacuum.
6. Provide response categories rather than asking for specific figures. For example, 'What is your age?': a. 20–29   b. 30–39   c. 40–49   d. 50–59   e. 60+.
    Using age categories, e.g. 45–54 has an advantage in that people can get over the psychological barrier of being, for example, in their fifties.

If the sensitive information is being sought by means of personal interview, the interviewer can provide the respondent with a card containing labelled response categories such as:

(a) under €25,000
(b) €25,001–€30,000
(c) €30,001–€40,000
(d) over €40,000

and ask them to respond with the appropriate letter, e.g. (c).

Another approach to overcoming non-response and measurement error caused by sensitive questions is the 'randomised response technique'. The respondent is presented with two questions, one sensitive or potentially embarrassing, the other a neutral question with a known probability of 'Yes' response, e.g. 'Were you born in February?' The respondent, depending on the outcome of a random procedure (e.g.

flip of a coin) is asked to answer the question that is associated with the random outcome, which he alone observes. As a result, the researcher receives only a 'Yes' or 'No' response, but does not know what question the respondent has answered. The proportion of respondents who answer 'Yes' to the neutral question is determined through secondary sources (e.g. Census of Population) or through another research survey. The proportion of respondents who answered 'Yes' to the sensitive question can then be determined by means of a formula. For example:

- Sensitive question: 'Have you ever used drugs?'
- Neutral question: 'Were you born in February?'
- P ('Yes' to sensitive question)

$$= \frac{P(yes) - P(\text{neutral question}) \, P(\text{yes to neutral question})}{P(\text{sensitive question})}$$

If the proportion of respondents who answered 'Yes' is .20, the proportion born in February (obtained from census data) is .10 and the probability of answering each question is .5, the estimate of the proportion of respondents who answered 'Yes' to the sensitive question is as follows:

P(yes to sensitive question)

$$= \frac{.20 - (.5)(.10)}{(.5)} \qquad = 0.3$$

The result of our finding is that 30% of respondents have used drugs.

However, the researcher cannot determine which respondents have answered 'Yes' to the sensitive question. This would preclude any opportunity to determine, for example, if drug-taking behaviour was associated with any particular demographic characteristic.

DECIDE ON RESPONSE FORMAT

Once the content of an individual question has been determined, the researcher needs to decide what type of question to use. In the development of a questionnaire, three basic types of questions may be utilised:

1. Open-ended.
2. Multiple-choice (multichotomous).
3. Dichotomous.

Each poses a different degree of structure on the person's responses, and has its own particular uses, advantages and disadvantages. In terms of the amount of structure involved, open-ended questions have the least, and dichotomous questions the most, structure.

1. Open-ended Questions

Open-ended questions are those in which the respondent can reply in his or her own words. The researcher does not limit the response choices. In postal or self-completing questionnaires, space is provided in which the respondent can write the answer. In the personal or telephone interview, the respondent verbally reports the answer to the interviewer, who records it on the questionnaire. Open-ended questions are useful in the following circumstances:

- At the beginning of a questionnaire or as a lead-in to a section or topic to establish rapport and gain the respondent's co-operation.
- When there are too many possible responses to be listed, or the researcher is not sufficiently aware of all possible responses.
- When verbatim responses are required to give a flavour of people's answers or to cite as examples in the report. This 'real-world' terminology (as different from laboratory or marketing jargon) can be useful later for designing promotional and advertising material.

Examples of open-ended questions include:

'Why do you shop here?'
'What do you think of Irish vegetables?'
'How do you eat yours?'

Open-ended questions are easy to formulate and elicit a wide variety of responses. Because there is no fixed set of response alternatives from which to choose, respondents are less likely to be swayed toward a response that does not reflect their true opinion regarding the subject of the question. This makes them particularly suitable for exploratory research or problem identification research. Open-ended questions are also often used to probe for additional information.

Certain weaknesses limit the usefulness of open-ended questions. A principal weakness is the large amount of interviewer bias they permit. Interviewers rarely record respondents' answers verbatim, or summarise them accurately. Much depends on the speed and skill of the interviewer. The result is a mixture of interviewer and respondent rather than respondent alone. Tape recorders should be used if verbatim reporting is important. Secondly, the depth of responses to open-ended questions depends, to a great extent, on how articulate the respondent is in an interview or the willingness to compose a written answer to a postal survey. Another problem with unstructured questions is the time and cost associated with coding responses.[4] Classifications must be established to summarise the response, and each answer assigned to one or more categories. As each answer is, to an extent, unique, this involves subjective judgments that are prone to error, and the danger of forcing data into a category. Pre-coding can overcome some of the disadvantages of open-ended questions. Essentially, a multiple-choice question is presented to the respondent as open-ended. The response alternatives are not read to the respondent. Instead, the interviewer selects the appropriate response category based on the respondent's reply to the open-ended question. It does, however, require sufficient familiarity with subject areas to anticipate respondents' answers.

2. Multiple-choice Questions

Also known as multichotomous questions. The multiple-choice format typically presents the respondent with a question and a set of alternatives that will be mutually exclusive (no overlap occurs and only one alternative can be selected) and collectively exhaustive (the alternatives include all possible responses). From the list of possible answers provided, the respondent must select the one that expresses his opinion. The checklist is a variant of the multiple-choice approach and asks the respondent to select all alternatives that apply to him.

For example:

'How would you rate the quality of this product'?

Very good ☐   Good ☐   Average ☐   Poor ☐   Very poor ☐

'Which of the following factors do you consider important when choosing a restaurant? Please tick as many as apply.'

Location ☐
Good food ☐
Friendly staff ☐
Decor ☐
Reputation ☐
Prices ☐
Signage ☐
Atmosphere ☐

Several of the issues discussed in Chapter 8 with respect to itemised rating scales also apply to multiple-choice answers. Multiple-choice questions overcome many of the disadvantages associated with open-ended questions. They are generally easier for both the interviewer and the respondent. They ensure greater ease of data recording and tabulation, thus eliminating interviewer bias and editing subjectivity. Multiple-choice questions are easier for the respondent to answer in both an interview and a postal survey. Indeed, they are almost essential for securing adequate co-operation in self-administered surveys. Likewise, respondents who are more articulate are less likely to be over-represented. However, there are limitations to the multiple-choice question format. Firstly, good multiple-choice questions require time and effort. Exploratory research may be necessary to ensure that all potentially important response categories are included. If important response alternatives are not included, significant bias can be introduced to the findings. Also, showing the respondent a list of response categories can cause distortion in the resulting data. The researcher may be providing answers that the respondent might not have considered. The respondent may end up choosing a 'responsible' alternative. Similarly, if the respondent does not agree with any of the response categories, he may select one anyway. This problem can be somewhat overcome by providing an alternative such as 'Other — please specify', 'None', 'No opinion', or 'Don't know'. Even so, there may still be a strong tendency for the respondent to choose from the alternatives. For example:

Which of the following reasons is most important in your choice of fridge-freezer?

Price ☐
In-store service ☐
Brand name ☐
Guarantee ☐

Other (please specify) _____

A further problem with multiple-choice questions is the respondent's tendency to select an alternative purely because of order or position bias. We will look at this next.

Position Bias

Multiple-choice questions tend to bias results by the order in which the alternatives are presented. When statements or ideas are involved, there is a bias towards the first or last item on the list, particularly the first.[5] This position bias can be minimised by using a split-ballot technique, i.e. alternating the order in which the alternatives are presented. This will require multiple versions of the questionnaire to be prepared, unless the alternatives are being presented on separate cards as outlined earlier. In that instance, it is only necessary to have differing forms of the card that is shown to the interviewee. When the alternative response categories are numbers (e.g. prices or quantities), there is a bias towards the central position of the numbers array. Central positions are chosen more than either extreme. Unfortunately, it is not easy to rotate most numbers since logically they should appear as a sequence; for example, increasing or decreasing order. Even if the numbers are presented out of order, the respondent will tend to mentally sort them into a sequence before making a choice.

How Many Response Categories?

Ideally, the response categories should be mutually exclusive and collectively exhaustive. However, it is frequently impractical to include all possible alternatives. As a general rule of thumb, the range of opinion on most issues can be captured best with five to seven categories. A list of brands might include twenty or more names. Rather than listing all twenty names, perhaps only the top five to seven names are listed, with the remainder confined to an 'Other, please specify' category. As well as the number of alternatives presented, consideration must be given to the range of the alternatives. This was previously discussed when we considered the issue of balanced and unbalanced attitude scales. An unethical researcher could intentionally bias the survey results to his favour, for example:

'Compared to Brand X, how do you rate our company's product?'

Excellent ☐   Very good ☐   Good ☐   Poor ☐

'Do you think that protection of the ozone layer is important?'

Extremely important ☐ Very important ☐ Important ☐ Not important ☐

Unless there is a specific reason to do otherwise, e.g. evidence that the vast majority of candidates will report on one side of the issue, a balanced set of alternatives should be presented.

Dealing with Uncertainty and Ignorance

When drafting multiple-choice questions, it is necessary to consider respondents who genuinely do not know the answer, have forgotten the answer or have no opinion on the issue. A neutral response category such as 'Don't know, no opinion', 'Neither like nor dislike', 'None', etc. should be provided to cater for the above. If there is a likelihood of both ambivalence and ignorance, then both a neutral category and a 'Don't know' category are appropriate.

3. Dichotomous Questions

The dichotomous question is an extreme form of the multiple-choice question, and allows for only two response categories, e.g. 'Yes' and 'No', male or female, agree or disagree. In practice, however, the two alternatives of interest are often supplemented by a neutral alternative, such as 'Don't know', 'No opinion', 'Both' or 'Neither'. While this may allow respondents to avoid taking a position on the issue, not to do so would force respondents to choose one of the dichotomous alternatives. As a rule, it is best to include a neutral category, if a substantial proportion of respondents can be expected to be neutral. However, a source of bias can occur when respondents who are not neutral select the neutral category for reasons of convenience or embarrassment. Because both multiple-choice and dichotomous questions represent closed-ended questions, much of our discussion on the advantages and limitations of multiple-choice questions also apply to dichotomous questions and will not be repeated here. For example, dichotomous questions also suffer from position bias. In fact, dichotomous questions can often be framed as multichotomous questions and *vice versa*. Consider the following:

'Do you intend to go abroad for Christmas?'

Yes	☐
No	☐
Probably will	☐
Probably will not	☐
Definitely will not	☐
Undecided	☐

Dichotomous questions are best suited for determining points of fact, e.g. 'Did you go on a foreign holiday last year?', and other clear-cut issues on which the respondent has a well-developed viewpoint.

Concluding Words on Question Format

Most questionnaires mix open-ended, multiple-choice and dichotomous question formats. As the expense of editing open questions militates against their use, if it is at all possible, avoid them. Answers to open-ended questions can help to interpret closed-end questions. In addition, a change of pace can eliminate respondent boredom and fatigue.

QUESTION WORDING

Once the marketing researcher has decided on the desired question content and structure, the next task is the actual writing of the questions. It is critical that researcher and respondent assign the same meaning to the questions asked, otherwise the results will be seriously biased.[6] Poor phrasing of a question can cause respondents to refuse to answer it or to answer it incorrectly, either on purpose or because of misunderstanding. The first condition, known as item non-response, can increase the complexity of data analysis.[7] The second condition produces measurement error, in that it does not reflect the respondent's true score on the issue. Even small changes in wording can shift respondent answers. While there are no clear 'right' or 'wrong' ways of asking questions, it is important for the researcher to be sensitive to the effect of question wording and the answers obtained.

Box 8.1 Asking the right question is crucial!

A stranger arrived in a small town and he wanted to get to know the locals. So he went over to the village square where an old-timer was standing with 'a kind of mean-looking German shepherd'. Looking at the dog fairly tentatively, the stranger asked 'Does your dog bite?' The old-timer replied 'Nope'. So the stranger reached down to pet the dog. The dog lunged at him, nearly taking his arm off. The shocked stranger turned to the old-timer and said: 'I thought you said your dog doesn't bite.' He replied 'Ain't my dog.'

The moral: it's important to ask the *right* question.

Source: Buffett: *The Making of an American Capitalist*, by Roger Lowenstein.

How do we ensure that the words we select are likely to be clear to our respondents? A good first step is to consult an up-to-date dictionary and thesaurus and ask the following six questions of each word.[8]

1. Does it mean what we intend?
2. Does it have any other meanings?
3. If so, does the context make the intended meaning clear?
4. Does the word have more than one pronunciation?
5. Is there any word of similar pronunciation with which it might be confused?
6. Is a simpler word or phrase suggested?

While it is sometimes hard to develop good phrasings of questions, the following guidelines should be considered in designing the wording of a question.

1. Define the issue

A question should clearly define the issue being addressed. Junior newspaper reporters are trained to define the issue in terms of who, what, when, where, why and which (i.e. how) — the six W's.[9] These can also serve as a guide to the researcher preparing a questionnaire. Each question should be checked against those points to be sure that the issue is clear. Who, what, where and when are particularly important. The why and how may be applicable in some questions.

Consider the following example: 'Which brand of coffee do you use?' By subjecting the above question to a who, what, where, when analysis the meaning of the question becomes less clear. Does the 'who' refer to the respondent alone, or does it also refer to other members of the respondent's household? 'What' is the brand of coffee. But perhaps more than one brand of coffee is being used. Does the 'what' refer to the brand used most recently, the brand used most frequently or the preferred brand? 'When' is also not clear. Does the interviewer mean last month, last week or the last time? Does 'where' refer to at home or at work? A better wording for the question is: 'Which brand, or brands, of coffee did you personally consume at home during the last week?'

2. Use simple, clear and unambiguous words

The challenge is to choose words that can be understood by all respondents, regardless of education level, but do not sound patronising. If in doubt, it is best to err on the side of simplicity. There is always great potential for respondents to misunderstand what they are being asked, even when simple words are used. The most common pitfall is to use jargon or specialised terms.

Consequently, the questionnaire must use terminology native to the target respondent group. Questionnaires designed for children must use a simpler vocabulary than those designed for third-level students.

Use clear and unambiguous words and questions. Not only should the words used be simple, but they also should be unambiguous. The same is true for questions; for example, care must be taken to avoid words which have different meanings across socio-economic groups. A TD once referred to his supporters as 'people who eat their dinner in the middle of the day'. Other socio-economic groups refer to a meal at this time of day as lunch, and have dinner (or supper) in the evening. A better solution might be to use 'midday meal' and 'evening meal'. But even those may be subject to misinterpretation. The words used in a questionnaire should have a single meaning which is known to the respondents.[10] Researchers have found that words such as 'usually', 'regularly', 'normally', 'frequently', 'kind', 'about', 'always', 'ever', 'often', 'occasionally', 'sometimes', 'many', 'good', 'fair', and 'poor', lack an appropriate time reference, so respondents choose their own, with the result that answers are not comparable.

For example, try to avoid asking the following:

'In a typical fortnight, how often do you listen to local radio?'

1. Never.   ☐
2. Occasionally. ☐
3. Sometimes.   ☐
4. Often.   ☐
5. Regularly.   ☐

These words have different meanings to different respondents. Response bias is inevitable, e.g. does 'regularly' mean always, almost always, more than any other, or what? Thus, while the question would get answers, it would generate little real understanding as to the frequency of listenership. A much better approach would be to provide concrete alternatives and to ask about the most recent instance of the behaviour. For example:

'In the last two weeks, how often have you listened to local radio?'

1. Not at all/never. ☐
2. One or two times. ☐
3. Three or four times. ☐
4. More than four times. ☐

This provides respondents with a consistent frame of reference. Respondents are no longer free to superimpose their own interpretations on the response categories.

Problem words in questionnaire design

All, always, any, anybody, bad, best, could, daily, ever, every, everybody, everything, fair, few, just, know, like, might, more, most, much, never, none, now, own, quite, see, should, today, where, you.

Box 8.2 A Questionable Question

'"Most people are willing to pay a small entrance fee to a museum." To what extent do you agree with this statement?'

There are three flaws in this:

*   The phrase 'most people' makes it difficult for respondents to do anything other than agree — who knows what the rest of the population thinks?
*   What is meant by 'a small entrance fee'? Small is a relative term which different people will interpret in different ways.
*   The question itself asks the extent to which the respondent agrees — it doesn't suggest that people might disagree.

Source: *Creative Arts Marketing*, Elizabeth Hill, Catherine O'Sullivan and Terry O'Sullivan, 1997, p. 87, Butterworth-Heinemann.

---

3. Avoid Leading Questions

Leading questions suggest or imply certain answers, or indicate the researcher's own point of view. A leading question causes a constant measurement error in the research findings. Consider the following question: 'Do you own a Whirlpool dishwasher?' This question will result in more reports of ownership of Whirlpool dishwashers than will the question: 'What, if any, brand of dishwasher do you own?' Another example of a leading question: 'Do you think that men's shoes priced at €200 are over-priced?' An unbiased statement can be easily biased by prefacing it with 'Don't you think' or 'Don't you agree'. Bias may also occur when respondents are given cues about the sponsor of the project. With the use of a brand or company name in a question, there is a tendency for respondents to respond favourably towards the sponsor, e.g. 'Is Dawn your favourite brand of orange juice?' produces more measurement error than 'What is your preferred brand of orange juice?'

4. Avoid Loaded Questions

Loaded questions suggest social desirability or are emotionally charged. A loaded question introduces a more subtle bias than a leading question, and suggests a feeling of approval or disapproval. Examples of loaded questions include:

- 'How do you generally spend your free time — watching TV, or what?'
- 'Should the government increase income taxes in the next budget in order to improve our children's education system, or should they keep income tax unchanged?'
- 'Last year, a greater number of people than ever were injured at work. Do you think the government is doing enough?'

Yes ☐
No ☐
No opinion ☐

Also, the suggestion that an attitude or position is endorsed by a prestigious organisation, group or individual, can bias the response, e.g.:

'The Irish Medical Organisation has suggested that Irish people do not include enough fibre in their diet. Do you agree?'

Yes ☐   No ☐   No opinion ☐

'In your opinion, should the Alzheimer Society of Ireland have more than one national fundraising tea day per annum?'

Yes ☐   No ☐   No opinion ☐

5. Avoid Double-barrelled Questions

A double-barrelled question is one in which the wording calls for two responses. Making the mistake of asking two questions instead of one is easy, for example, 'Do you like the taste and aroma of the coffee?' When multiple questions are asked in one question, the result may be exceedingly difficult to interpret. A respondent may feel torn between a 'Yes' to one part of the question and a 'No' to the other. As a rule, when the question includes 'and' review it to see whether two responses are required. If yes, split the initial question to two separate questions. According to Payne — 'since question marks are not rationed, there is little excuse for the needless confusion that results [from] the double-barrelled question'.[11]

6. Avoid Generalisations and Estimates

Questions should always be asked in specific rather than in general terms. Questions dealing with estimates of volumes of product used or frequency of store visits should be designed in such a way that the respondent does not have to answer by giving an estimate or making a generalisation. Consider the following question: 'How many litres of milk do you purchase in a year?' To provide the answer requires that the respondent compute how many litres per day and multiply that by 365 (or by 4 and 52). This burden should not be placed on the respondent. The results would be more accurate if the question asked 'How many litres of milk did you purchase in the last week?' with the researcher doing the calculations later to estimate annual consumption. A related problem is asking burdensome questions that may tax the respondent's memory. Questions relating to prior behaviour should be kept relatively recent.

7. Avoid Implicit Alternatives

An implicit alternative is one that is not expressed in the options. As a rule it is best to state clearly all relevant alternatives to a question, unless there is a special reason for not doing so. Further, as the order in which explicit alternatives are presented can affect the response, the split-ballot technique should be used to rotate the order in which the alternatives appear.

8. Avoid Implicit Assumptions

Questions should be worded so that the answer is not dependent upon implicit assumptions about what will happen as a consequence. Implicit assumptions are assumptions that are not stated in the question — for example:

Q1.   'Do you favour legislation requiring all new cars to be fitted with an air-bag?'
Q2.   'Do you favour legislation requiring all new cars to be fitted with an air-bag, even though it will require a small increase in the retail price of the car?'

Q2 Is a better way to word this question. Q1 fails to make its assumptions explicit and may result in an inflated estimate of respondent support for mandatory car air-bags.

9. Consider Using Both Positive or Negative Statements

Questions designed to measure attitudes and lifestyle are frequently worded as statements to which the respondents indicate their degree of agreement or disagreement. However, the response obtained can be influenced by the directionality of the statements; whether they are stated positively or negatively. If this problem is anticipated, it is better to use dual statements, some positive, others negative. Two different questions, incorporating the alternative statement, could be used. For example:

'Do you think TV advertising should be increased during Christmas?'
'Do you think TV advertising should be decreased during Christmas?'

Another approach would have been to state both alternatives, the positive and the negative:

'Do you think TV advertising should be increased or decreased during Christmas?'

A Final Word on Questionnaire Wording

When all is said and done, there is, however, no one correct wording for a question. It is possible that different wording may get different answers, yet no one can say one wording is right and the others wrong. One way to resolve this is by using the 'split-ballot' technique. Whenever there are two wordings from which to choose, and if there is no basis on which to pick one over the other, one of the words can be used on half of the questionnaires and the other on the other half. Comparison of the two halves of the questionnaire will permit a better interpretation of the results than would be possible where only one wording is used.[12] A word on question length — short questions are not always best, but if at all possible the number of words per question should not exceed twenty.

QUESTION SEQUENCE (QUESTIONNAIRE FLOW AND LAYOUT)

While there are no rules cast in stone regarding the optimum sequence in which questions should be asked, there are some general guidelines. Mostly it is common sense. To an extent, the flow of questions will be somewhat influenced by the research objectives set earlier.

After a brief initial explanation regarding the nature and purpose of the survey, what is required of the respondent, and perhaps offering assurances regarding confidentiality, the first few questions are normally screening (sometimes called filter) questions. These are used to determine whether the respondent fits the predetermined selection criteria and qualifies to participate in the survey.[13] Examples of screening questions include:

'Are you visiting Killarney on holidays?'
'Have you stayed at this hotel before?'
'Do you own a car?'

The next questions should be simple and interesting. They are referred to as warm-up questions and are designed to put the respondent at ease and to encourage co-operation. These questions may not be of primary concern to the researcher and may or may not relate to the research objectives. Within the main body of the questionnaire the researcher should:

- Use transition statements to inform the respondent of what is ahead, particularly with regard to moving on to a new topic or section, e.g. 'Next I will ask you questions regarding your leisure activities'. This helps respondents switch their train of thought.
- Group related questions (topics) together, e.g. Section A, Section B and so on.
- Within a section, move from the general to the specific. This is known as the funnel approach.
- Ask questions about present behaviour before examining past behaviour.
- Record behaviour before asking attitude questions, as this helps focus the respondent's mind on the topic in hand before expressing an opinion.
- If possible, try to place together questions that are similar in format. Yet attempt to avoid boring sequences in the questionnaire, e.g. too many rating scales or too many multiple-choice questions one after the other.
- Use 'skip' questions (also called 'branching' questions) where appropriate; e.g. 'If NO please go to Q7'. The researcher may also choose to incorporate directional lines and arrows to guide the respondent through the questionnaire.
- Complicated and difficult-to-answer questions are best placed deep in the questionnaire. Sensitive questions are best placed near the end of the questionnaire.
- Place questions of a classificatory nature, e.g. demographic information such as age, income, occupation, gender, education level, etc. in a final section at the end of the questionnaire.
- Thank the respondent for their co-operation.

PHYSICAL APPEARANCE OF QUESTIONNAIRE

The final matter to be dealt with in designing the questionnaire, before submitting it for pre-testing, relates to its physical appearance and layout. While certain changes may have to be made following the pre-test, the researcher should test the questionnaire in as close to final form as possible. The format, spacing and positioning of questions can have a significant effect on the results.[14] The appearance and layout of a questionnaire is a major determinant of the response rate. The physical appearance of the questionnaire is especially important in postal or self-administrated questionnaires. That is not to say that it is not important to have a good layout in questionnaires designed for personal interviews and telephone interviews. Much of the discussion which follows in this section, while particularly important for postal and self-administrating questionnaires, is also relevant to other survey methods. The objective of good questionnaire appearance and layout is to ensure that the tasks of the interviewer and respondent are as clear, logical and simple as possible. Several key considerations of layout and design follow:

1. Questionnaires should be designed to appear as short as possible. If it is more than three pages, it may be advisable to use a booklet form of questionnaire rather than stapling a large number of pages together. Booklets are easier to use, look professional, allow the use of double-page format, and minimise the problem of lost pages.
2. The questionnaire should be as professional-looking as possible. It should be printed on high-quality paper, and have a 'typeset' appearance.
3. While it is advisable to have the questionnaire 'appear' short, the researcher should avoid the temptation to crowd questions together to make the questionnaire look shorter.
4. The questionnaire should allow for plenty of open space. A crowded questionnaire appears complex, difficult and can lead to errors in data collection. Ultimately, it is better to allow the questionnaire to be one or one and a half pages extra rather than using a crowded one.
5. Each question should be reproduced on a single page. Split questions and response categories can mislead the interviewer and respondent into thinking that the question has ended at the end of a page. Rows and columns of answers should spread far enough apart, so that the interviewer or respondent can easily pick the proper row or column. Decent margins and white space should be used to separate questions. Columns of multiple boxes should be kept to a minimum. Multiple-question formats, if used properly, can make the questionnaire look interesting and inviting. If possible, response categories for a question should be listed in a single column rather than multiple columns. It is easier for the respondent to read downwards than sideways.
6. Directions and instructions for individual questions should be placed as close to questions as possible. Instructions for questions should be distinguished from the question itself, by using a different type (or capital letters). It is a good idea to divide the questionnaire into different sections with heading or subtitles for groups of questions. This helps the respondent follow the nature and logic of the questionnaire. Numbering is especially important if branching questions are used. Numbering of questions is also required if responses are to be coded. Clear instructions will be helpful to both respondent and interviewer, especially

directional advice and 'skip question' instructions which will ensure that the questionnaire is used properly.

7. Each questionnaire should be numbered sequentially. This makes the field control of questionnaires, coding and analysis easier. However, numbering of postal questionnaires may make the respondent suspicious of loss of anonymity.

8. Consideration must be given to the amount of space required for open-ended questions. Researchers have found that the more lines or space left for recording the response to open-ended questions, the more extensive the reply. Likewise, it has been found that giving respondents more detailed information, through the use of larger questions, improves reporting behaviour.[15] However, this has implications for questionnaire size. As a rule, three to five lines is probably sufficient for open-ended replies. Researcher judgment is required. In some instances it may be necessary to colour-code the questionnaire by printing on different colours of paper. For example, if panel research is being conducted which requires respondents to complete three separate questionnaires (contained in a folder) over a three-day period, it is a good idea to colour-code questionnaires to be completed over the period of time.

9. It is a good idea to spend some time phrasing the title of the questionnaire. A well-worded title can arouse interest among respondents, indicate the importance of the study, e.g. 'Awareness Study for Croí', gain their co-operation, or even appeal to their ego — for example 'Study of Top Executives'. A decision will have to be made whether or not to include the name of the sponsoring organisation. Realising that this can bias respondents' answers, it may be necessary to use a fictitious name for the sponsoring organisation.

10. As mentioned earlier, reproduction of the questionnaire should be neat and make use of good quality paper. Otherwise the respondent will perceive the study as of little importance and not deserving of their time and effort.

Computer-aided design has replaced word processing packages in the preparation of questionnaires. Professional researchers, in particular, are now using specialised computer software, e.g. SNAP (www.mercator.co.uk), to help simplify the process of questionnaire layout. Apart from creating a questionnaire complete with response categories, it can also code the questions, perform data analysis and graphically present the results. Software programmes like this are also capable of linking to other software packages. Tabulated results can, for example, be exported to other packages such as SPSS for further analysis. An important feature of packages like SNAP is their ability to deal with sequence bias. It is possible to randomise question order in a scale, giving each respondent a unique question order. Response categories can also be randomised, which prevents question format effects (e.g. recency effects).[16] Other software packages include Keypoint (www.camsp.com), The Survey System (www.surveysystem.com) and Sphinx (www.lesphinxdeveloppement.fr/index.php?langue=en). The reader is encouraged to visit one or more of these sites and compare the range and capabilities of the various software available to researchers. Onsite demonstrations are available.

Pre-coding of questionnaires

Pre-coding of questionnaires, in order to speed up the process, is common given that most surveys are now tabulated by computer. The objective of pre-coding is to associate each possible response with a unique number. Codes that will be entered in the computer are printed on the questionnaire. Usually the code identifies the column number(s) in which a particular response will be entered. Pre-codes are placed alongside each response and in parenthesis.

While it is recognised that coding is very much an issue which needs careful consideration at the questionnaire design stage of the research project, we have decided to delay our discussion of coding until Chapter 12.

PRE-TESTING THE QUESTIONNAIRE

After a first draft of a questionnaire has been finalised, it should then be pre-tested. No survey should be taken without a pre-test. The pre-test, which is a trial run of the questionnaire, should simulate as closely as possible the actual research conditions under which it will be administered. Pre-test respondents should be similar in aspects to those respondents who will form the actual survey, i.e. pre-test respondents must be taken from the 'population of interest'. All aspects of the questionnaire should be tested. Misinterpretations, lack of continuity, poor skip patterns, question content, wording, sequence, instructions, sufficient response categories, etc. are all open to scrutiny in the pre-test.

While it is a good idea to administer the pre-test questionnaire in person, a pre-test should also be conducted using the same survey mode as the actual survey. Pre-testing of postal questionnaires places additional demands on the timing of the survey. Such pre-tests help reveal problems peculiar to the chosen survey method. The pre-test provides the *real* test of the questionnaire and the mode of administration.

There is no set answer as to the number of respondents that should be involved in the pre-test; it is very much dependent on the final number and variety of target respondents, the complexity of the questionnaire and the time available. One author suggests five to ten respondents as being sufficient for a pre-test.[17] If the pre-test resulted in extensive design and question alterations, a second subsequent pre-test with a different sample of respondents is necessary. While pre-testing is very important, excessive pre-testing in order to develop the 'perfect' questionnaire is a temptation to avoid. One pre-test is the bare minimum, and is probably as much as most questionnaires get. If a pre-test suggests only minor changes, once these changes have been made, the questionnaire is ready to go to final draft and distribution to field operators.

Finally, the researcher should consider coding and tabulating the pre-test research findings. Tabulating the results of a pre-test helps determine whether the questionnaire will meet the objectives of the research. Simple cross tabulations and other statistical analysis should be carried out where possible. Analyses of pre-test data helps to ensure that all data collected will be put to use and that all necessary data will be obtained.[18]

Considerable time and effort must be devoted to the end stage of questionnaire development to ensure that the questionnaire, or interview guide, is free from errors. It is too late once the survey is in the field to find out that a word is spelt incorrectly or that a response category has been omitted. Typing, spacing, numbering and pre-coding must be given rigorous proof-reading.

FIELDWORK

This section of the chapter focuses on field operations. This phase of the research project refers to what type of contact is made with respondents, how the data collection instrument is administered, and how the data is recorded and returned for processing. The market research project is no better than the data collected in the field.

The success of field operations requires investment in the selection, training, supervision and evaluation of field workers. Field personnel must clearly understand what is expected of them and how this performance will be measured. Marketing research data is not always collected by the person who designed the research. It is frequently collected by a field force that has little training in marketing research. The nature of fieldwork varies with the mode of data collection. A distinction can be made between field-based data collection (e.g. personal interviews and observation) and office-based data collection (e.g. telephone interviews and postal surveys). This section focuses on the interviewing process conducted by personal interviewers. However, many of the issues apply to all field workers when translated into their specific settings. The field-work data collection process will be presented under five headings:

1. Selection of field workers.
2. Training of field workers.
3. Supervision of field workers.
4. Validation of fieldwork.
5. Evaluation of field workers.

1. Selection of Field Workers

One frequently sees job advertisements in national and local newspapers for market researchers. While every research firm will have their own selection criteria, it is probably fair to say that at least some or all of the following criteria will be considered to be desirable when selecting field workers:

- Pleasant appearance.
- Outgoing personality.
- Good communication and listening skills.
- Accuracy and attention to detail.
- Patience and tact.
- Integrity and honesty.
- Resilience and energy (stamina).
- Well organised.
- Efficiency and reliability.
- Reasonable standard of education.
- Previous interviewing experience an asset but not essential.

Applicants may be asked to carry out a dummy interview to assess their ability. Interviewers who are similar to respondents tend to work well, that is to say, interviewer age, social background and education level should fit, as much as is practical and feasible with that of the respondent. In some instances, specifically male or female interviewers may be the preferred choice of respondents; for example, interviewing of female respondents regarding personal hygiene products.

2. Training of Field Workers

Training of interviewers is required at two levels. On one level, interviewers need to be trained in the art of interviewing, i.e. approaching the respondent, gaining the respondent's co-operation, handling objections and refusals, asking questions, probing, recording the data, and terminating the interview. On another level, interviewers need to be trained and briefed on the particular study at hand. Interviewers are not provided with too much information about the purpose of the study, thus ensuring they will not transmit any preconceived notions. Interviewers may not, for example, be provided with the name of the client firm.

Asking the questions and probing

Training in the art of asking questions is an important aspect of the above.
   Interviewers should:

1. Ask the questions using the exact wording.
2. Read the question slowly.
3. Ask the questions in the order they appear in the questionnaire.
4. Ask every question contained in the questionnaire.
5. Repeat questions that are misunderstood.
6. Carefully follow all instructions and skip patterns.

Question probing is commonly used when respondents' answers are overly brief. Probing encourages respondents to enlarge, clarify or explain their answers. Probing also helps respondents to focus more clearly on the content of the interview. It is not uncommon for individual questions to have written abbreviated probing instructions to guide the interviewer. Frequently-used probing techniques include nodding, repeating the question, pausing or silence, repeating the respondent's answer, asking for clarification or additional information. Regardless of which probing technique is used, care should be taken so as not to bias the respondent's answers.

Field workers also need to be trained on how best to record responses. Some practical advice here is to:

- Write legibly.
- Record responses during the interview.
- Use the respondent's own words.
- Avoid summarising or paraphrasing respondents' answers.
- If a question is not answered note why.
- Complete all interviewer identification data, e.g. time, date, ID number, etc.
- Carry out field editing as soon as is possible (see Chapter 12).

Terminating the Interview

Having acquired all the necessary information, the interviewer is ready to close the interview. Before signing off, it may be necessary to answer any final questions the respondent may have and to record any end-of-interview spontaneous comments and remarks. The interviewer should then thank the respondent for their time and effort. Ideally the respondent should exit the interview with positive feelings about what has occurred.

3. Supervision of Field Workers

A certain amount of supervision of field workers is advisable, especially when interviewing is widely dispersed. The purpose of supervision is to ensure that field workers are following the correct procedures. Elements of field supervision include quality control and editing, sampling control, and control of cheating. Misbehaviour by survey interviewers includes actions forbidden either explicitly or implicitly in codes of ethics, interviewer training, or interviewing instructions. As examples of misbehaviour, interviewers can reword questions, answer questions when interviewees refuse to respond, or fabricate answers to entire questionnaires.[19] Quality control refers to checking to see that field procedures are being followed. Field workers may require additional training or clarification. It can be helpful if the supervisor also does some interviewing. This helps the supervisor better understand or appreciate problems that field workers may be having. The field supervisor is also responsible for collecting completed questionnaires from the field workers at the end of each day. The supervisor should edit completed questionnaires to ensure that all relevant questions have been filled in, that there are no obvious omissions, that quotas are reached, and that the writing is legible.

Sampling control is also an important aspect of supervision. Sampling control ensures that the sampling plan is being adhered to and that the correct sampling units (e.g. male, over 30 years with college education) are being selected for interview. Quota samples are often seen as time-consuming and the interviewer may stretch the requirements to obtain seemingly qualified respondents.

4. Validation of Fieldwork

Validation of field work is carried out by the supervisor to ensure that interviewers are submitting authentic interviews. The most glaring example of cheating is when the interviewer fills out questionnaires without carrying out interviews. Frequently, cheating is confined to falsification of certain data within the questionnaire. This type of cheating is more difficult to detect. Study-design and implementation influence the predisposition to cheat. If respondents are difficult to locate and interview, cheating increases. Other 'motives' for interviewer cheating are unreasonable deadlines and difficult-to-complete questionnaires. Interviewers may also fake answers to questions they find embarrassing to ask because of sensitive subjects. Or an interviewer might be tempted to go to the household next door for an interview rather than recording that the sampling unit was not at home, which would require a call-back. Careful recording of the number of completed interviews will help ensure that the sampling procedure is being properly conducted. Cheating can be minimised through proper training, supervision and validation of field work.

In order to validate field work, the supervisor calls a percentage of all respondents (e.g. 10%). Anything over this would be more rigorous but time-consuming. In most instances this will require the supervisor to call upon a subsample of the sample to determine whether the interview actually took place and to verify the respondent's answers, including demographic details recorded. As an alternative to repeating the whole interview, the supervisor may instead re-ask the respondent a portion of the questionnaire. This, however, is not a foolproof recheck. Responses and demographic details are cross-checked against the data recorded on the questionnaire by the interviewer. Field workers should be made aware of supervisory verification call-backs. This forces interviewers to be more conscientious about their work.

5. Evaluation of Field Workers

Field interviewers' performance can be evaluated across a number of criteria. More specifically:

- the quality of interviewing;
- the quality of data obtained;
- response rates;
- cost and time per completed interview.

SUMMARY

A questionnaire is a formalised means of collecting data from respondents. The primary purpose of a questionnaire is measurement. Survey research (in whatever form — personal interview, telephone, postal or online) relies on the use of a questionnaire. Using a questionnaire provides standardisation and uniformity in the data-gathering process. Questionnaire design is a major source of non-sampling error. The design of an appropriate questionnaire involves no firm set of foolproof procedures. There are, however, a number of rules or guidelines that can be followed. The discussion of questionnaire design was presented as a series of seven steps, namely: preliminary considerations, question content, response format, question wording, question sequence, physical characteristics, and pre-test.

The researcher must make decisions regarding:

1. what information is required;
2. who are target respondents;
3. what method of communication will be used to reach these respondents;
4. how the resulting data will be processed and analysed.

When evaluating possible questions for inclusion in the data collection instrument, the following issues must be considered: Is the question really necessary? Does the respondent have the information requested? The respondent may not know the answer, or the respondent may not remember the information. Assuming that the respondent can answer the question, he or she may be unwilling to do so. A number of techniques have been developed to seek out potentially embarrassing or sensitive information from respondents who are unwilling to respond accurately. Once the content of an individual question has been determined, the researcher needs to decide what type of question to use. Three basic types of questions may be utilised. These are open-ended, multiple-choice, and dichotomous. Each of these poses a different degree of structure on the person's responses, and has its own particular uses, advantages and disadvantages. In terms of the amount of structure involved, open-ended questions have the least and dichotomous questions the most, structure.

Having decided on the desired question content and structure, the next task is the actual writing of the questions. Poor phrasing of a question can cause respondents to refuse to answer it, or to answer it incorrectly. A question should clearly define the issue being addressed. The challenge is to choose words that can be understood by all respondents. Not only should these words used be simple, but they should be unambiguous. The same is true for questions. A loaded question introduces a more subtle bias than a leading question, and suggests a feeling of approval or disapproval. Double-barrelled questions and questions involving generalisations or estimates should be avoided. Questions should be worded so that the answer is not dependent upon implicit assumptions about what will happen as a consequence.

While there are no rules cast in stone regarding the optimum sequence in which questions should be asked, there are some general guidelines. Mostly it is common sense. To an extent the flow of questions will be somewhat influenced by the research objectives set earlier. The final matter to be dealt with in designing the questionnaire, before submitting it for pre-testing, relates to its physical appearance and layout. The objective of good questionnaire appearance and layout is to ensure that the tasks of the interviewer and respondent are as clear, logical and simple as possible. The pre-test, which is a trial run of the questionnaire, should simulate as closely as possible the actual research conditions under which it will be administered.

The success of field operations requires investing in the selection, training, supervision and evaluation of field workers.

QUESTIONS

1. What is a 'questionnaire'? What is its purpose?
2. Outline the seven stages to questionnaire development.
3. The preliminary considerations of questionnaire design require the reader to make four decisions. What are they?
4. Discuss the issues to be considered when evaluating possible questions for inclusion in the data collection instrument.
5. How does the respondent affect the phrasing of the questions?
6. What are the reasons why respondents may be (a) unable to answer the question asked, and (b) unwilling to answer the question?
7. Describe some techniques which might be used to extract embarrassing or sensitive information from respondents.
8. What is the randomised response technique? How does it work?
9. What is telescoping error? What does it suggest about the period to be used when asking respondents to recall past events?
10. What is a multichotomous question? A dichotomous question? What are some of the key things researchers must be careful about in framing multichotomous and dichotomous questions?
11. Under what circumstances would dichotomous questions be inappropriate?
12. Do open-ended questions have any weaknesses?
13. What are the advantages and disadvantages of multiple-choice questions?
14. What is an ambiguous question? A leading question? A question with implicit alternatives? A question with implied assumptions? A double-barrelled question?
15. What are the key considerations regarding layout and physical appearance of a questionnaire?
16. How can the physical features of a questionnaire affect its acceptance by respondents and its handling and control by the researcher?
17. Why is it so important to pre-test the questionnaire? Discuss the issues involved.

18. What criteria might the researcher use when selecting field workers?
19. Discuss supervision and validation of field work.

PROBLEMS AND ASSIGNMENTS

1. Construct a set of five structured, indirect questions to measure what might be 'communicated' by males wearing jewellery, such as neck chains, rings and bracelets.
2. Provide an example of a multiple-choice question:
   (a) In which the alternatives are unbalanced.
   (b) In which the possible responses are not mutually exclusive.
3. List ten ambiguous words that should not be used in framing questions.
4. Design a questionnaire suitable for assessing the market for home insulation products among householders.
5. Do the following questions define the issue? In each case explain why or why not:
   (a) What is your favourite lager?
   (b) How often do you go out drinking?
   (c) Do you consume vodka?
      1. Yes   2. No
6. Provide an example of a survey question that would have an upward bias — that is, people would be likely to give a 'Yes' response.
   (a) Rephrase the question so that there would be a downward bias — that is, people would be likely to give a 'No' response.
   (b) Rephrase your original question so that respondents would be likely to provide a truthful response.
7. Develop a series of questions for determining the proportion of households where one parent of the family abuses alcohol. Use the randomised response technique.
8. Design a short questionnaire to measure your classmates' knowledge of, and attitudes to, laptop computers.
9. Based on the following list of research questions, determine the research objective(s) of this questionnaire: are any of the questions unnecessary and, if so, why?
   (a) How many hours per week do you work on average?
   (b) What type of magazines do you read?
   (c) Do you feel you have enough 'free time' away from work?
   (d) What kind of hobbies do you have?
   (e) Would you describe yourself as a well-rounded person?
10. Evaluate the following questions and suggest improvements:
   (a) When you eat dinner out, do you sometimes eat at the same place?
      Yes?   No?
   (b) Is the current level of government regulation on environmental protection adequate or inadequate?
      Adequate?   Inadequate?

(c) Where do you buy most of your clothes?

(d) Please indicate how much of an average issue of *Woman's Own* magazine you usually read:

1. Less than one-third?

2. One-third to half?

3. Over half?

(e) Do you often attend the theatre?

(f) What kind of hobbies do you have?

(g) Everybody knows that teenagers and their parents have lots of arguments. What are some of the things you and your parents have argued about lately?

11. Use the randomised response model to estimate the percentage of respondents who indicated they did not report all their income to the tax authorities in a survey in which a total of 16% answered 'Yes', and given 10% of the sample were estimated to have their birthdays in June (and so would have answered 'Yes' to the innocuous question) and a coin toss was used to choose which of the two questions to answer.

Case Study
Ovelle Pharmaceuticals*

Introduction

Sitting in her office on the Coes Road, Dundalk, Joanna Gardiner, Ovelle's newly appointed Managing Director, is brimming with enthusiasm for the pharmaceutical business which her grandparents had established some seventy years previously. She has just signed off on a series of quirky radio ads using the 'Save your Skin' slogan, designed to boost brand awareness on a national level. She has, by all accounts, already turned what was a small, family-run – and, according to some, floundering – company into a highly competitive, growth-oriented venture, widely respected within the skincare market.

Joanna is now gearing up to lead Ovelle through a major expansion phase which will extend their export sales to the global market – a market controlled by just a handful of multinational companies. From a marketing perspective, the time is right. The general toiletries market, within which the skincare market is categorised, is forecast to grow by some 16% over the next five years. But competing at the global level and taking on the big players will inevitably mean more changes within the company – significant further investment, a new recruitment drive and an international marketing campaign.

Company Background

Founded in 1934, Ovelle Pharmaceuticals is a privately owned family business based in Dundalk, Co. Louth, Ireland. The company have always been viewed as a small, owner-managed business, manufacturing old-fashioned, unbranded traditional creams and lotions, such as Calamine Lotion, Silcock's Base and emulsifying ointments. Such products were typically sold over the counter by pharmacists all over the country and were highly regarded by GPs.

Joanna only became involved in the business in 2000, when the company was, for the most part, seen as small and static, content to continue servicing its existing markets without deliberate expansion. Joanna's role at that point had been mainly marketing and promotion, a role she envisaged retaining for the foreseeable future. However, shortly after Joanna joined the company, Ovelle underwent a major restructuring. Staffing levels were reduced and a strategy was developed to refocus the business as a sales-led organisation. To fund the planned restructuring, two local private investors were secured, in addition to funding from Enterprise Ireland (the State agency responsible for supporting indigenous enterprise in the manufacturing or internationally traded services sector). This resulted in the company moving from a family-owned business run by her father, Sean Gardiner, to a company with significant external shareholding. Joanna played a major role in the restructuring process and, in 2002, she was appointed Managing Director.

Under Joanna's direction, Ovelle's new challenges would include growing the export business and introducing a branded skincare product line. With an increase in skin complaints such as eczema, psoriasis and dry skin, Joanna saw an opportunity to produce irritant-free pharmaceutical products that were not damaging to the skin. The resulting Elave® brand would be more consumer-friendly, taking less time and effort to administer, yet it would deliver the same benefits as the company's existing product line. Another key challenge would involve bringing the company from a turnover of around €2m with a loss of €0.3m, to a profitable, growth-oriented operation.

Ovelle's Product Range

Ovelle's core competency is the formulation, development and production of dermatological, pharmaceutical and healthcare products. Fully licensed by the Irish Medicines Board (IMB) to manufacture multidose liquid, semi-solid and solid pharmaceuticals, Ovelle's manufacturing permit is recognised in all EU countries and by the World Health Organisation. Their product range includes emollients, antiseptics, muscle and skin treatments, coal tar preparation and sun blocks for the domestic and export market, which they supply to pharmaceutical wholesalers, pharmacy chains and independents.

Ovelle operate the Quality Assurance Standards (QAS) and Good Manufacturing Practice (GMP) in their production processes – internationally recognised standards for the pharmaceutical industry. Their manufacturing licence requires quality assurance of the highest standards, typically in excess of ISO9000 and the Q Mark. As a result, Ovelle are in the envious position of being registered suppliers for the

United Nations and the United Nations Children's Fund, and carry out contract manufacturing on behalf of aid agencies worldwide.

The company's key brand – Elave – is a range of irritant-free body washes, shampoos, lotions, oils, facial cleansers and intensive creams. These products contain no alcohol, soap, colouring dye, perfume, parabens or formaldehyde. Sales of the Elave range have grown dramatically over the past three years, making it the number one brand in the Irish skincare market for dermatology products, ahead of its key competitor, E45. Highly recommended by pharmacists, dermatologists and GPs for the treatment of a wide range of skin conditions, Elave products are now sold nationwide in selected multiples, including Boots, McCabe's and MacCauley's retail pharmacy chains, as well as in some of the Dunnes Stores, Tesco and Superquinn outlets.

Within a relatively short space of time, Ovelle have significantly refined their product range. In 2000, they had just two products under the Elave range. By 2005, they had fifteen Elave products. They have also developed their export business, which now accounts for around 33% of their turnover.

The Competition and Industry Trends

Ovelle's biggest competitor product is E45, a range which consists of products specially formulated for people with dry skin. All E45 products are perfume-free and their washing products contain no soaps or detergents. Like the Elave range, E45 products have been dermatologically tested and endorsed by healthcare professionals (www.E45.com). However, the exact make-up of the competition depends very much on your particular perspective, i.e. what market is Ovelle actually in? In the strictest sense, Ovelle is firmly grounded in the skincare market, more specifically within the dry-skin and dermatological market. But these days, the lines between dermatological and cosmetic skincare products are more than just slightly blurred.

Since the mid 1990s, individuals worldwide have been spending more per capita on skincare than ever before. The trend towards better skincare is set to continue, with European and Japanese consumers showing even greater awareness of the retail skincare market than in the United States (Feedback.com, March 2004). Today, the consumer skincare market includes a vast array of anti-aging products, anti-fungals, moisturisers, medicated shampoos, body washes, lotions, oils, facial cleansers, intensive anti-irritant creams and sun-care products.

However, accurate data for the skincare market is difficult to come by, with not all over-the-counter sales being tracked, and marketing reports typically categorising skincare products within the more general *toiletries* industry, which tends to overlap with the *cosmetics* industry. In the USA, for example, the skincare market witnessed a compound annual growth rate of 14.5% between 1995 and 2000. In the UK, the toiletries industry, which is led by multinationals Unilever and

Procter & Gamble, grew by 3.3% in 1999 to around £3.42b. Current forecasts indicate that the sector will continue to grow by more than 16% between 2005 and 2009 (*Toiletries Market Report Plus*, 2000; 2005, www.researchandmarkets.com).

The reasons for the phenomenal growth of the skincare market can be explained in part by the industry's improved access to research and technology on a global scale, better scientific testing facilities, greater consumer awareness of skincare (including being better educated about the potential skin damage caused by the sun and other environmental effects, as well as being able to recognise potentially harmful chemical ingredients) and an increase in Internet shopping. Furthermore, the industry has been quick to note that skincare consumers are loyal customers who tend to stick with their chosen brand – something that is not typically seen in cosmetics – its sister industry.

According to *The New York Times*, today's skincare companies are adopting the scientific approach to gain commercial advantage, with consumers witnessing as much as a 100% price increase on some of the traditional leading brands, such as Olay or Neutrogena.

> The plethora of *molecules du jour* was probably inevitable. More than a decade ago, companies began putting alpha-hydroxy acids, retinols and retinoids, vitamins C and E, and all kinds of other scientific ingredients into what used to be mundane creams. Their sales shot up. (Claudia H. Deutsch, 'Scientific Solution to Save Your Skin', *The New York Times*, 13 July 2003).

However, visually attractive packages that carry labels with complex formulae and high-tech sounding ingredients promising to *reduce*, *diminish* and *protect* are not without their critics:

> ...they talk about some high-tech sounding protein that slows the aging process...but very few ingredients do the things they say they do, and I'm not sure all of them are safe. (Dr Leslie Baumann, University of Miami School of Medicine, quoted in *The New York Times*, 13 July 2003).

In contrast to the scientific approach, there is also evidence of an underlying trend towards natural ingredients, with an interest in herbal derivatives and an increased awareness of potentially harmful chemical ingredients. Indeed, in recent years, critics of the skincare industry have been quick to alert consumers to the staggering proliferation of toxic chemicals appearing in everyday personal care products and the long-term safety of continued exposure to chemicals such as Propylene glycol (PG), used in toothpastes and aftershaves; Polyethylene glycol (PEG), found in most skin cleansers; Isopropyl and Alcohol, found in body rubs and hand lotions; Sodium lauryl sulphate (SLS), a foaming ingredient found in toothpastes and bubble baths; and Formaldehyde, used in moisturisers and shampoos. It is claimed that such harmful and toxic chemicals not only contribute to the development of skin complaints such as asthma and eczema, but that they can also cause much more serious conditions such as Crohn's disease, IBS, ME, MS or cancer (*Toxic Chemicals in Toiletries*, 2006, www.health-report.co.uk/toxic_toiletries.html).

Back at Ovelle, Joanna Gardiner is all too aware of the resulting confusion in the market place, but sees a clear opportunity for her product range:

> These days consumers are more educated about good skincare, and are not just buying to treat skin complaints such as eczema, psoriasis or dry skin; rather they are buying to *protect* their skin. They are much more conscious of the dangers of long-term exposure to chemical-based ingredients that appear in so many everyday skin products. The time has come to cater for the '*worried well*', not just those with actual skin complaints.

Moving Forward – The Decision to Compete in the Export Market

It has taken Joanna five years to turn Ovelle around from a floundering business to one with the potential to be a real player in the global market place. 'We have a great team of people here now,' says Joanna proudly, 'and there's a great atmosphere.'

Ovelle are now gearing up for the expansion phase, which will obviously mean new markets as well as a new export strategy. For example, the scale of the UK market is completely different to Ireland, and securing a major retail chain like Boots could add millions to Ovelle's turnover within the space of a few months. Joanna is planning to double the company's turnover within the next three years and, if she is serious about that, then she needs to get really serious about the export business.

With the 'Save your Skin' slogan established alongside the Elave brand, Ovelle will be the first Irish company to market a product range that is completely SLS-free, as Joanna comments:

> I think we are ready now to move from managing a 'dry-skin problem' to focusing on the 'worried well'. When it comes to skincare, people are going back to basics, though so-called 'organic' skincare products are still a long way off. There are common chemical additives that can trigger adverse skin reactions, so we have simply removed them from our product range.

There is no doubt that Ovelle's 'Save your Skin' and SLS-free principles have played a critical role in the company's marketing strategy to date. However, the big challenge is how to weave them into the new export strategy to take on the global competitors. From a marketing perspective, the time is right. One third of children nowadays get eczema – a figure that used to be one in twenty – the increase being largely due to chemicals in washes and harsh perfumes used in soaps. In many ways, concerns about skincare would appear to be developing in the same way as concerns about food – people are starting to check product labels for potentially harmful additives. Concerns over the safety of certain chemicals in skincare products are becoming more common (See, for example, UK 1st edition feature – 'How Safe are your Toiletries', *Express* newspapers, 14 December 2004). However, taking on the global players will inevitably mean more changes within the company – significant further investment, a new recruitment drive and an international marketing campaign. But is Ovelle ready for another major shake-up? Is Joanna? Regardless of what the future holds, it looks like Joanna is going to be around for a while.

'I really believe in what we are doing now,' says Joanna. 'We are doing something with a lot of integrity – we are the first chemical-safe skincare range on the market and I am very committed to that. Sometimes, I don't know if I could ever leave this.'

Questions

1. Using relevant secondary data sources, identify and assess the domestic market in which Ovelle operates.
2. What market research would be necessary to confirm the view that 'people are going back to basics when it comes to skincare'? The Managing Director asks you to prepare a research brief to address this question.
3. Working in teams, prepare a questionnaire that will identify current consumer attitudes towards available skincare products.

*This case was prepared by Dr Colette Henry as the basis for class discussion rather than to illustrate either effective or ineffective handling of a business or marketing situation. Colette Henry is Head of Department of Business Studies and Director of the Centre for Entrepreneurship Research, Dundalk Institute of Technology. The accompanying case questions and teaching note were written by Maeve McArdle and John Sisk at Dundalk Institute of Technology. Maeve McArdle lectures in Business Strategy and Marketing, and John Sisk lectures in Applied Marketing, International Marketing and Market Research. The authors are extremely grateful to Joanna Gardiner for her time and her inspiration in helping to prepare this case. © Colette Henry, 2006.

Case Study
An Online Business Administration Degree Course

Background

In the summer of 2006, a well-known university launched an online Business Administration Degree course. Targeted at potential students from Eastern Europe and the Middle East, the programme was publicised by means of visits to universities in the target countries, and advertising in magazines such as *The Economist*.

The programme promised:

- A degree from a widely acknowledged and well-respected university with an excellent reputation both in Ireland and internationally.
  - That graduates' degrees would achieve the same academic standard as campus-based students.
  - Access to the same academics that teach and assess campus-based students. Access, in some cases, included tutorial support.
  - Access to a 'learning group' of students studying the same course across the world.
  - Participation in online seminar discussions and in some course units, team tasks that a learning group would undertake together.

- Ease of access to learning materials:
  - All essential materials would be available online through the university and through the dispatch of additional core textbooks.
  - Access to an online library was also available.

- Access to the course from any standard Internet browser.
  - The entire course of study was designed so that the lessons, activities and assignments could all be delivered directly via computer.

In order to graduate, candidates would undertake a combination of units and half units that added up to the equivalent of twelve whole units. In terms of study hours, this translated to 150 hours for each half unit and 300 hours for each whole unit. In addition:

- Students would be permitted to complete the degree in a minimum of four years and a maximum of eight.
- Each full unit would be assessed by one three-hour unseen written examination and each half unit by one two-hour unseen written examination.
- Students would also be required to submit a 10,000-word dissertation. To obtain the degree, students would need to complete examinations for twelve units and pass in a minimum of nine. A maximum of four units could be completed in a given year.

While similar online courses were available at the time of launch, the assumed key benefit of this particular course relative to others was the fact that it would rely solely on online interaction and would not involve face-to-face interaction of any kind, thereby allowing potential students from around the globe access to a standard of education, internationally recognised qualification, and flexibility of study that may not have been available to them locally.

Although no concrete market research was conducted prior to the launch of the distance-learning programme, in light of the high esteem in which the university and its qualifications were held, the prospective ease with which the course could be accessed and the ability of the course to be completed at a distance, it was assumed that the programme would appeal widely to English-speaking prospects from around the world.

Despite high initial interest levels when the course first launched (i.e. approximately 700 online inquiries), only thirty-two actual applications resulted from these inquiries, and only nine potential students were ultimately eligible for the course – in all, a disappointing result for the university and little understanding of why the programme did not prove more successful.

Given the high development cost of the online programme, rather than disbanding the initiative the university considered exploring and targeting other potential markets – the US/North America and Western Europe in particular.

Research Proposal

In order to explore the potential of the online programme, research to determine the reasons why the programme did not achieve a higher uptake level in the Eastern European and Middle Eastern market was proposed.

Despite the fact that the programme had not succeeded as hoped in the market, it was determined that access to the database of those originally interested in the programme would be key to valuable information about the barriers to uptake.

It was agreed that the first phase of research would directly target the 700 individuals who originally made enquiries about the programme. The research objectives were as follows:

- To determine whether marketing lines of communication for the programme were functioning as planned by establishing:
  — Where individuals heard or learned about the course.
  — How easy or difficult it was to find out about the university, the Business Administration course, and other similar courses.

- To identify the competitive set in the market.

- To investigate what, if any, other courses did individuals consider when investigating further education online.
  — What, if any, course did individuals actually apply for?
  — What, if any, course did individuals actually commence?
  — What benefits did these courses offer over the university course?

- To establish the initial perceived benefits of the university's Business Administration Degree course:
  — Cost.
  — Entry-level requirement.
  — Flexibility in participation.
  — Other?

- To identify the key barriers to application for or uptake of Business Administration courses, e.g.
  — Cost.
  — Reputation of course/organisation.
  — Access to the Internet.
  — Levels of face-to-face interaction with tutors/educators as part of the course.
  — Entry-level requirements.
  — Lack of or restricted access to the Internet.
  — Other?

While impossible to anticipate the possible response rate to the survey, it was determined that a minimum of 100 responses would be required in order to achieve an overall sense of the barriers to uptake. A response of this level would not, however, allow for analysis of respondents by key demographics such as gender, age and education level. For this reason, in order to encourage as high a response rate as possible, it was agreed to restrict the length of the online survey to ten minutes and to offer an incentive in the form of entry into a draw for €300 – tactics which have proven to both maximise interest in and response to online surveys.

Questions/Exercises

1. Design an online questionnaire to address and examine the barriers to further consideration of the course by prospective applicants. In doing so, bear in mind that there is limited capacity for open-ended questions. Given that respondents may have a limited level of fluency in the English language, the questionnaire must be written in plain English.
2. In light of the fact that respondents might have enquired online from company-based computers with company based e-mail addresses, what are the likely implications, if any, for dispatching the survey?
3. Considering the length of time it will take to complete the survey and analysis, should reminder e-mails be dispatched? At what point should they be sent?

* This case was written by Orla Murphy, Market Research Manager, Vodafone. It is intended to be used as a basis for class discussion rather than to illustrate either effective or ineffective handling of an administrative situation (2006).

Case Study
Brenda Morgan's Evolution into the World of Business*

Introduction

Brenda Morgan, founder of the Morgan Institute, finished up the radio interview with Kerry Radio, and was now pondering the change in direction the company had taken since February 2005. Over the past year, the Morgan Institute received positive publicity from airing time on the Sunday business show on Today FM and Kerry Radio. New markets have emerged for the company as a direct result of those interviews. Now Brenda had plans and strategies to formulate for the future of the business. Growth decisions needed to be made, of that she was sure, but which markets to target had yet to be decided.

Idea Development

Brenda trained as a teacher, obtained her Higher Diploma in Education (HDip) and taught in second-level education for ten years before starting her own business in the summer of 2003. After years of teaching in a non-permanent position, she realised her job would remain non-permanent and began to consider other possibilities for her future. At the same time, Brenda had become disillusioned with her teacher training. She said, 'I realised that, despite all of my teacher training, none of my training equipped me to teach students how to study and how to learn'.

From this realisation, Brenda recognised a gap in the market – students in second level did not really know how to study and how to learn. She wished to change that phenomenon; she called it her 'student mission'. Brenda decided that she would 'up skill' to get the necessary training that would enable her to help her students. However, none existed in Ireland. In April 2003, she trained as a 'PhotoReading Instructor' which is considered the pinnacle of Accelerated and Advanced Learning. This training would become the basis of her business idea.

The Start-up Phase

In the first year of business, Brenda developed a full-time evening-support programme for fifth- and sixth-year students. This programme was launched in September 2003 and made available in two locations: Tralee and Killarney. Brenda's selection of these locations was based solely on convenience. At the time, she was teaching fulltime in Killarney and living in Tralee. 'I began with seventeen students in Killarney and five in Tralee. I was advised by family and friends not to run with Tralee, but I was stubborn and knew that it would take off. I had done a lot of ground work in Killarney and not in Tralee,' stated Brenda.

At that time, Brenda had no business training or business experience. Marketing efforts were almost non-existent, promotional efforts were based on word-of-mouth, there was no pricing strategy in place, and competitors were unknown. Since Brenda was unaware of competition, she was unable to use these as a benchmark or a positioning tool. Her financial advisor was worried by this fact and suggested the need for a competitive analysis, but there was no time to conduct this analysis. The academic year was about to start and it became necessary to identify a price sooner rather than later. It was decided to charge €2.50 per hour and the course began in September 2003. Much time was spent on developing and designing the product from the customer's perspective. This process was not a problem to Brenda – after all she had solid knowledge and experience of the educational sector. The Study Manager programme was developed to include the following:

1. A small, supportive, positive study group.
2. Active supervision (teacher willing and able to help with homework).
3. Study plans designed for the students in each of their subjects.
4. Study deadlines – students had to produce work monthly.
5. Regular progress reports for parents.
6. Training in how to approach study in a brain-friendly way.
7. It was a thirty-two week programme, Monday to Thursday, 5.00 p.m. – 9:00 p.m.

Source: Morgan Institute

The business idea was accepted by the target market and the two locations achieved full capacity. The idea was a success, and a business was born.

The Growth Phase

The second year of the business started without any external funding. By now Brenda had dedicated herself full time to the development of her business idea. She expanded the customer base to include second- and third-year students, branding it as the Junior Programme. However, the product was not modified to suit the particular needs of this type of student. Essentially, the same programme was being offered to two different customer segments. It was quickly recognised that the needs of the Junior Programme students were vastly different to those in the original programme (now known as the Senior Programme) and adjustments were made to the product offering accordingly.

As the third year of the business started, Brenda, together with her mentor and financial advisor, decided to roll-out the Study Manager Programme in Cork and Dublin. They had also decided to rebrand the product, calling it 'The Advanced Study Programme'. 'All was great,' said Brenda. The company was expanding with little or no investment. Notwithstanding this success, Brenda was certain that action was still needed. Her learning curve was propelled into 'top gear' as she had to learn quickly about marketing and finance and how to apply these concepts to keep her company in business. Money was tight. How would she 'spread the word' within the school sector? Brenda had come to recognise that schools were able to make a significant profit from evening study, and consequently they perceived her as a direct form of competition. This, she believed, was the root of the lack of proactive cooperation from the schools.

Although she did not realise it, she decided to adopt a 'pull-strategy'. She contacted the schools in early October/November 2005 with regards to providing the students with information on the 'Advanced Learning Programme'. The response was amazing. Schools were calling her from all over the country, asking her to present the talk to their students. They were delighted with the opportunity of an alternative to their existing supplier – Student Enrichment Services. Teachers wanted to know more about the product offering and were particularly interested in acquiring training for their own benefit. The positive effect of 'word-of-mouth' had been realised for The Morgan Institute, and better yet it was it was cost-free! Brenda was getting better at promotional efforts. She would go to a school and spend a day training students in groups comprising thirty to fifty students, for an individual fee of €25.00 per student. But more importantly, each student was asked to fill in a form with their name and address. Brenda had initiated and generated her first database of students, which could now be used for direct marketing and other research purposes. The school market had opened the floodgates – again.

The Future of the Business

As Brenda got into her car after the Radio Kerry interview, she felt optimistic for the future and confident with her self-acquired business skills. Brenda had a number of options; it was simply a matter of selecting the most effective strategy for the long-term success of the business. But what would be the right way to go and why? Maybe she did not fully know the answer to this yet, but Brenda knew one thing for sure – she was determined to make it work! Brenda wishes to survey existing student users in order to establish current levels of satisfaction with her own and competitor offerings, as well as identifying areas for product improvement.

Questions

1. Design an appropriate questionnaire for students that utilises alternative question types and response formats. Write an introduction to the student questionnaire.
2. Should a separate questionnaire be designed for non-user students? If so, how might the question content differ from the questionnaire aimed at the user group students?
3. Draft a questionnaire cover letter aimed at teachers that explains the research and encourages their cooperation in the distribution and collection of the questionnaire.

* This case was written by Breda O'Dwyer and Ann Sears, Institute of Technology, Tralee. It is intended to be used as a basis for class discussion rather than to illustrate either effective or ineffective handling of an administrative situation (2006).

CHAPTER 9

MEASUREMENT CONCEPTS AND ATTITUDE SCALES

CHAPTER OVERVIEW

‣ Introduction   ‣ Attitude Components   ‣ Attitudes and Behaviour
‣ Measurement and Scaling   ‣ Scales of Measurement   ‣ Validity and
Reliability Concept   ‣ Measurement of Attitudes   ‣ Attitude Rating Scales
‣ Attitude Scaling Techniques   ‣ Summary

INTRODUCTION

The most frequently used definition of attitudes was formulated by Gordon Allport over 50 years ago. He wrote, 'attitudes are learned predispositions to respond to an object, or class of object, in a consistently favourable or unfavourable way'.[1] Such a definition assumes that attitudes are learned, that they are a forerunner to behaviour and that they are stable. Attitudes towards brands are consumers' learned tendencies to evaluate brands in a consistently favourable or unfavourable way; that is a consumer's evaluation of a particular brand on an overall basis from poor to excellent. Attitudes have both strength and direction, i.e. attitudes can be strongly or weakly held and they can be both positive or negative. Against such a background, by the end of this chapter the reader will be able to:

1. define attitudes;
2. describe the components of an attitude;
3. discuss measurement scales;
4. outline validity and reliability; and
5. explain rating scales and scaling techniques.

ATTITUDE COMPONENTS

Attitudes are generally viewed to have three main components. The following statement illustrates these components: 'Jim *believes* Glenlo Abbey Golf Course is conveniently located, has excellent fairways and commands panoramic views of the Corrib river. Jim *likes* playing golf at Glenlo Abbey. He *intends* to play golf there every Saturday'. This short statement has identified the three components of an attitude which are:

1. the cognitive component;
2. the affective component;
3. the behavioural (or conative) component.

Cognitive   ⟶   Beliefs
Affective   ⟶   Liking
Behavioural ⟶   Intention

The link between these three components illustrates what is known as the high involvement hierarchy of effects, i.e. the buyer passes through the stages of: awareness, knowledge, liking, preference, intention to buy, and purchase (see Figure 9.1). However, these stages can occur in different sequences, depending on the degree of buyer involvement with the purchase and the degree of differentiation among the alternatives.

Figure 9.1

Attitude components	*Hierarchy of effects model*
Cognitive	Awareness Knowledge
Affective	Liking Preference
Behavioural	Intention to buy Purchase

We will briefly look at each of these components in turn.

Cognitive: 'I think or I know . . .'

The cognitive component refers to the respondent's awareness of and knowledge about an object. A researcher may conduct an attitude measurement study to determine, for example:

*   Whether consumers view an Irish-made cereal being of equal quality to Kellogg's.
*   If customers are aware that a particular brand of soft drink is now available in lemon and lime flavour.

Affective: 'I like or I dislike . . .'

The affective component refers to the respondent's positive or negative feelings with regard to an object. It is sometimes referred to as the 'feelings component'. Under this component, an attitude measurement study may attempt to analyse the following:

- A local environmental group may wish to determine how many residents are not in favour of a new sewage treatment plant in a particular location.
- A local radio station wishes to find out if listeners are satisfied with a new breakfast show format.

Behavioural: 'I intend to . . .', 'I purchased . . .'

The behavioural component refers to buying intentions and actual purchase behaviour. It reflects a predisposition to action. The 'evoked set' is that set of brands from which we are predisposed to purchase. Examples of behavioural attitude measurement include:

- A financial services company may wish to know how many of its existing customers intend to use its new pension planning service.
- A cable TV operator wishes to determine what percentage of its subscribers have rented a movie video in the past week.

ATTITUDES AND BEHAVIOUR

Reinforcing, changing or modifying attitudes is often an important part of marketing strategy. Most marketing research studies contain questions designed to measure a respondent's attitudes. It is generally assumed that there is a link between attitudes and behaviour. Attitudes are assumed to be an important predictor of behaviour, i.e. having a positive attitude towards a product, service or retail outlet means we are more likely to purchase or use it. However, the student should note that attitudes alone are not an absolute guarantee that behaviour will occur, nor does intended behaviour, because of situational influences, always translate into actual behaviour.

MEASUREMENT AND SCALING

Before addressing the subject of attitude measurement, it is necessary to define measurement and to discuss the types of scales that can be used in measurement. We also need to examine marketing variables and concepts.

Marketing Variables

When we speak of measuring marketing variables, we are attempting to measure one or more of the following:

(a) *State-of-mind variables.* These refer to variables such as attitudes, personality and brand awareness which are internal to the individual and are therefore difficult to measure.
(b) *State-of-being variables.* Examples of variables of this kind include age, income, gender, marital status, number of children and product ownership. These are external to the respondent and are easier to measure than state-of-mind variables.
(c) *Behavioural variables.* Behavioural variables are concerned with past, present or future courses of action. Measurement of product purchase, usage and intention to buy fall into this category.

Measurement and Concepts

Before we can examine *how* to measure something, we must first consider *what* it is we want to measure; that is to say we must first identify and define the relevant *concept* involved. A concept (or 'construct' — the terms concept and construct have similar meanings and are frequently used interchangeably) can be defined as a symbol that we attach to some aspect of reality. Thus the concept 'lawnmower' refers to the generalisation of the characteristics that all lawnmowers have in common. In marketing research we are required to address concepts such as attitude, brand loyalty, personality, channel power, low-involvement purchasing, market segmentation and product positioning. Many of these concepts are not directly observable and exist in the minds of individuals. Some concepts are easier to define than others. For example, the concept 'chair' is perhaps easier to define than 'brand loyalty'. The concept 'chair' is closely related to a physical reality and there will be little disagreement as to what is meant by the term. 'Brand loyalty', on the other hand, is a more abstract concept and more difficult to define in a physical sense. It is therefore more difficult to measure. In a marketing research study, concepts must be precisely defined and measured; otherwise the usefulness of the information collected is questionable. In fact the researcher should define the relevant concepts in such a way that allows for practical measurement and ensures consistency by avoiding disagreement over its meaning. There are two approaches to defining a concept: a conceptual definition and an operational definition.

A conceptual definition defines an object in terms of other concepts. This approach is similar to that used in a dictionary where words are used to define other words. A good conceptual definition attempts to delineate the main characteristics of the concept as it differs or compares to other concepts; for example, brand loyalty versus habitual purchasing behaviour.

An operational definition, on the other hand, specifies how a concept is to be measured. It describes the meaning of a concept by outlining the procedures necessary to measure it. The operational definition translates the concept into one or more observable events. Thus a conceptual definition logically precedes and directs the development of an operational definition. It is possible to have several operational definitions of the same concept. The researcher must choose the operational definition that fits best with the objectives of the research. However, while operational definitions of a particular concept may vary across different research studies, the definition should be consistent within any given research study.

Box 9.1

Examples of concepts and possible operational definitions

Concept	Possible operational definition
Customer	Based on company warranty card records, any individual or group that has purchased one or more of our company's products within the past twelve months.
Small sailboat	Sailboats manufactured in Ireland that are less than 13 feet 7 inches in length and have a manufacturer's suggested retail price of €5,000 or less.
Exposure to point-of-sale display	Stopped and visually examined display for five seconds or more as determined by hidden observer with stopwatch.
Brand loyalty	Based on consumer panel data, number of consecutive months in which a reporting household purchased our brand one or more times.
Product awareness	When asked to mention five brands of beer, subject mentions our brand in a personal interview situation.
Product attitude	When asked to mention five brands of beer that taste good, subject mentions our brand in a personal interview situation.

Source: Adapted from *Marketing Research*, Ronald M. Weiers, Prentice-Hall, 1988.

Measurement can be defined as a standardised process of assigning numbers or other symbols to certain characteristics of the objects of interest, according to some predetermined rules. Note that we measure the attributes of objects, and not the objects themselves. We do not measure a person, for example, but we may choose to measure the attributes of a person, i.e. income, social class, education, height, weight, attitudes, etc. In marketing research, numbers are usually assigned because mathematical and statistical analyses can be performed only on numbers and they can be communicated throughout the world in the same form without any translation problems. An important aspect of measurement is the specification of rules for assigning numbers to the characteristics. This assignment process must be isomorphic, that is to say, there should be one-to-one correspondence between the symbol and the characteristic in the object that is being measured; and the rules for assigning numbers should be standardised and applied uniformly. They must not change over objects or time.

Scaling, which can be considered an extension of measurement, is the process of creating a continuum on which objects are located according to the amount of the measured characteristic they possess. An example of a scale that is often used in research is the dichotomous scale for gender. The object with male/female characteristics is assigned a number 1 and the object with the opposite characteristic is assigned the number 0. This scale meets the previous two requirements of the measurement process, i.e. that it is isomorphic. Measurement and scaling are basic tools used in the scientific method and are used in almost every marketing research situation. Scaling is commonly used in the process of measuring attitudes. There is no clear point from which to start measuring an attitude. Attitudes are something akin to temperature in this respect. Zero has been arbitrarily assigned on the thermometer (at different places for Fahrenheit and Centigrade), but this leads to difficulties such as the one defined in the conundrum: 'How cold is twice as cold as zero?' There is no agreed 'zero' at which to start measuring attitudes. The most common procedure is to measure in two directions from some neutral point. Attitude scaling is the process by which respondents are classified as having an unfavourable, neutral or positive attitude.

SCALES OF MEASUREMENT

As previously stated, measurement in marketing research frequently deals with numbers. There are four characteristics of the natural (counting) number system 0, 1, 2, 3, 4, 5, 6, 7, 8 and 9. Firstly, each number in the series is unique. Secondly, the ordering of the numbers is given by convention; for example, $2 > 1$ and $1 > 0$. Thirdly, we can define equal differences, for example, $4 - 3 = 2 - 1$, $9 - 7 = 5 - 3$. Fourthly, we can define equal ratios; for example, $8/4 = 6/3$. The manipulation of numbers using mathematics or statistics involves one or more of these four characteristics of the numbering system. It is traditional to classify scales of measurement on the basis of the mathematical comparisons that are allowable with them. There are four basic levels of measurement, which are nominal, ordinal, interval and ratio. Each represents a different kind of number assignment rule, or 'scale' of measurement. As we proceed from the weakest (nominal) to the strongest (ratio), two things happen. Firstly, the numerical requirements for scale membership become more stringent. Secondly, the permissible modes of data expression and analysis become more liberal, that is to say more types of statistical operations are permissible. Also, because the higher levels of measurement contain all the properties of lower levels, we can convert higher-level scales into lower-level ones (i.e. ratio to interval or ordinal or nominal; or interval to ordinal or nominal; or ordinal to nominal). Therefore, it is very important to understand the different types of scales, and to be able to identify them in practice, for their properties put significant restrictions on the interpretation and use of the resulting measurements.

Nominal Scale

Nominal scales are very common in marketing research. It is the simplest type of scale. A nominal scale partitions data into categories that are mutually exclusive (every individual or object must belong to one of the categories), and collectively exhaustive (the categories don't overlap). The numbers assigned to objects or phenomena serve as labels for identification or classification. The numbers themselves have no mathematical value. They cannot be ordered, added or divided. Examples of nominal scale numbers include Personal Public Service PPS numbers, student identification numbers or numbers on football jerseys. Application of the nominal scale to marketing measurement is generally for the purpose of coding questionnaire responses in which the data collected place the respondent into a particular category. Numbers assigned to represent the categories (1 for male, 2 for female) cannot meaningfully be added, subtracted, multiplied or divided. The only permissible operation on the numbers in a nominal scale is counting. Only a limited number of statistics (all of which are based on frequency counts) are permissible. These include frequency, percentages, mode and chi-square statistical test, plus some other non-parametric tests.

Please indicate your gender.   Male ☐   Female ☐

Have you visited *this branch* in the
last six months?   Yes ☐   No ☐

Please indicate below which Irish terrestrial TV stations you watched yesterday? – it doesn't matter for how long or how short a period you watched.

RTÉ One   _____
RTÉ Two   _____
TV3   _____
TG4   _____

Ordinal Scale

The ordinal scale goes beyond the simple identification capabilities of the nominal scale, and allows the possibility of 'greater than' and 'less than' as additional descriptors of marketing phenomena. However, the scale does not provide information on how much more or less of the characteristic various objects possess. Ordinal numbers are used strictly to indicate rank order. The object ranked 1 has more of the characteristic in question compared to the object ranked 2, and the object ranked 3 has less of the characteristic than 2 or 1. Ordinal scales indicate relative position and not the magnitude of the difference between the objects. We cannot say that the difference between 1 and 2 is the same as that between 2 and 3. Likewise, we cannot say that the difference between 1 and 3 is twice that of the difference between 1 and 2. A typical ordinal scale in marketing asks respondents to rate brands.

'Please rate the following five brands in terms of value for money, in order of preference, 1 being the most preferred and 5 being the least preferred.'

Brand name	Bill — Respondent No. 1	Jane — Respondent No. 2
A	2	1
B	1	3
C	5	5
D	4	4
E	3	2

In the above example, we cannot say that Bill preferred Brand B twice as much as Brand A. Nor can we say that both respondents preferred Brand D over Brand C by the same amount. For Bill, it may have been a close call between C and D. Jane may have preferred D over C much more. A scale such as excellent, good, fair, poor is also ordinal by nature. Excellent is higher than good but again we do not know by how much. Because we do not know the amount of difference between the objects, the permissible arithmetic operations are limited to statistics such as the median or mode (but not the mean) and rank-order correlation.

Example of Ordinal-scaled Questions

'Please rank the following Irish Sunday papers according to preference. 1 for your first choice, 2 for your second choice, and so on.'

_____ *Sunday Independent*

_____ *Sunday Tribune*

_____ *The Sunday Business Post*

_____ *Ireland on Sunday*

_____ *Sunday World*

Interval Scale

Interval scales possess all the requirements of an ordinal scale, plus the 'equality of difference' characteristic of the number system. They make use of a constant unit of measurement or equal interval between scale value. The difference between 1 and 2 is the same as between 2 and 3, but is only half the difference between 2 and 4.

However, this unit of measurement is arbitrary. Interval scale has no fixed or absolute zero point where none of the characteristics being measured is present, i.e. zero does not denote absence of the attribute. The most common examples of interval scales are the Fahrenheit and Celsius scales used to measure temperature. The freezing point of water is assigned a different numerical value on each scale, 32 on Fahrenheit and 0 on Celsius. Both scales use constant units of measurement, but the degrees on the Fahrenheit scale are 5/9 as large as those on the Celsius scale. Equal differences in temperature are measured by equal-volume expansion in the mercury used in the thermometer. The arbitrary zero point of interval scales restricts the statements that a researcher can make about the scale points. Multiples may not be expressed as if they refer to absolute values; one cannot say that 60°F is 'twice as hot' as 30°F. We can, however, say that 60°F is hotter than 30°F or that 65°F is 5°F cooler than 70°F; or that the difference between 60°F and 50°F is equal to the difference between 50°F and 60°F. The use of interval scales in marketing research is common. Attitudinal, opinion and willingness to buy are often treated as interval data. As an example, consider the following.

Toyota cars are:

	Strongly disagree			Neutral		Strongly agree	
	−3	−2	−1	0	1	2	3
Stylish	☐	☐	☐	☐	☐	☐	☐
Reliable	☐	☐	☐	☐	☐	☐	☐
Well engineered	☐	☐	☐	☐	☐	☐	☐
Economical	☐	☐	☐	☐	☐	☐	☐
Safe to drive	☐	☐	☐	☐	☐	☐	☐
Sporty	☐	☐	☐	☐	☐	☐	☐
Value for money	☐	☐	☐	☐	☐	☐	☐

As the possible responses are physically located at equal intervals on the questionnaire, they are assumed to represent equal intervals in terms of the measurement process. Most researchers treat the data from such scales as if they were equal interval in nature, since the results of most standard statistical techniques are not affected greatly by small deviations from the interval requirement.[2] The use or assumption of interval scale data means that interval scales are amenable to computation of an arithmetic mean, standard deviation, and correlation co-efficient. However, ratios calculated on interval data are not meaningful. A ratio, e.g. three times as much, 10% more than, etc. requires a ratio measurement scale.

Ratio Scale

A ratio scale has all the properties of an interval scale plus a meaningful absolute zero point and equal intervals of measurement. At the zero point, none of the characteristics being measured is present. Unlike the Fahrenheit and Celsius scale, the ratio measurement of temperature is known as the Kelvin scale. The Kelvin scale has an absolute zero point and represents the absence of heat ($-273.15°C$). Because there is universal agreement as to the location of the zero point, comparisons among the magnitudes of ratio-scaled values are acceptable. All arithmetic operations are possible, including multiplication and division. Not only is the difference between 3 and 6 the same as the difference between 12 and 15, but also 12 is four times as large as 3 in an absolute sense. A great many important marketing phenomena possess the properties of a ratio scale. These include sales, market share, costs, ages, usage, income, number of purchases, etc. The entire range of statistical techniques can be applied to the analysis of ratio-scaled data. However, this produces only a minimal gain in analytic technique beyond those available for interval data. While the ratio scale is the 'ultimate' scale of measurement, ultimately, quite a lot of marketing research information will be in nominal, ordinal or interval (sometimes by assumption) form.

Examples of Ratio Scales

Please allocate 100 points among the following five brands of mineral water according to your degree of preference for each:

_____ Galway

_____ Perrier

_____ Tipperary

_____ Evian

_____ Kerry

On average, how many times a week do you listen to a local radio station?

0 ☐   1 ☐   2 ☐   3 ☐   4 or more ☐

Table 9.1 Summary of the four primary levels of measurement

Level	Description	Number system	Marketing examples	Typical methods for describing	Analysing
Nominal	Uses numerals to identify objects, individuals, events, or groups	Unique definition of numerals (0, 1, 2, . . . 9)	Brand numbers, store types, sex classification	Frequency Percentage Mode Cross-tabulation	Chi-square test
Ordinal	In addition to identification, the numerals provide information about the relative amount of some characteristic posed by an event, object, etc.	Order of numerals (0<1<2 . . . <9 . . .)	Preference rankings, market position, social class	Median Mode Percentile	Rank order Sign test Non-metric multi-dimensional scaling
Interval	Possesses all the properties of nominal and ordinal scales plus the intervals between consecutive points are equal	Equality of differences (2 −1 = 6 − 5) Equality of ratios (1/4 =2/8)	Attitudes, opinions, index numbers	Range Mean Standard deviation	Correlation analysis Discriminant analysis Analysis of variance Metric multi-dimensional scaling
Ratio	Incorporates all the properties of nominal, ordinal, and interval scales plus it includes an absolute zero point		Age, income, costs, sales, market share	Geometric mean Harmonic mean	Coefficient of variation

Source: Adapted from S. S. Stevens, 'On the Theory of Scales of Measurement', *Science* 103, 7 June 1946), pp. 677–680.

VALIDITY AND RELIABILITY CONCEPT

To have confidence in the results of a marketing research study, the researcher must be concerned about two characteristics of the measures being used to collect information. These two concepts are called *validity* and *reliability*. They can be defined as follows.

Validity: a measuring instrument is valid when it measures what it is supposed to measure. The instrument is valid to the extent that its measurements are free from systematic error (bias).

Reliability: a measuring instrument is reliable when the results it delivers are consistent. The instrument is reliable to the extent that its measurements are free from non-systematic (random) error.

The researcher, therefore, must be concerned with whether we are measuring what we wish to measure and whether our measurement is accurate. Ideally, it is desirable that the marketing information we collect have both validity and reliability. A necessary precondition for validity is that the measuring instrument is reliable[3]. But a reliable instrument may not be a valid one. A bent ruler will provide consistent results, but it is not a valid measure. Or if you forget to put your watch forward one hour in summer time it will still be a reliable measure (it will say seven every twelve hours) but it will not be valid (incorrect time). Of the two, validity is probably the more important than reliability. This is especially so for a once-off study. However, if the research instrument is to be used repeatedly (e.g. consumer diary research), the role of reliability in the research findings becomes more important. A measuring instrument that could be considered low in validity was that which was used to research the market for 'New Coke'. It failed to measure customer loyalty to traditional coke.

Most practising marketing researchers probably do not spend a great deal of time measuring the validity and reliability of a research instrument. Often the issue of validity and reliability is left to those conducting academic research projects. Nonetheless, they are important concepts and deserve attention.

Validity

Validity can be examined from a number of different perspectives. The major approaches to the assessment of validity are as follows.

Content Validity

Content validity (also called face validity) is the weakest form of validity. It concerns the extent to which the measurement instrument 'appears to be measuring' what it is intended to measure. Content validity involves a subjective judgment by the researcher, or by asking another expert professional whether in his or her opinion the instrument is measuring what it purports to measure. The emphasis is on the expert's critical eye. For example, a questionnaire designed to measure a retail outlet's level of customer service that does not contain references to friendliness of staff, car parking facilities, opening hours and delivery service, cannot be considered to have content validity. After all, these are important aspects of customer service that are not being measured. Some writers distinguish between face validity and content validity as follows. Does, say, a scale measuring attitudes to something, seem to the person taking the scale to be as they would expect such a test to be? Content validity is taken to refer to the extent to which the test items cover the entire range, or domain, of what the test is supposed to measure.

Predictive Validity

Predictive validity refers to the ability of our measuring instrument to predict some future event. Predictive validity is most often associated with 'intent-to-purchase' measurements. A measure of buying intentions is valid if it can be shown through sales records to predict future sales. If the predicted results are highly correlated with the actual results, then the measurement is deemed to have predictive validity. The GMAT is used to predict how well a student with a particular score on the test will do in an accredited MBA programme. The wide use of this test by colleges attests to its predictive validity. Measurement instruments that are low in predictive validity are either not measuring intent to purchase, or there is a weak relationship between intent to purchase and actual future purchasing behaviour.

Concurrent Validity

Concurrent validity involves correlating two different measurements of the same marketing phenomena which have been administered at the same, or about the same point in time. The findings of a new measurement technique may be compared against the findings of an established measurement technique. Until recently, engineers relied on tape measures to measure the physical distance between objects. Suparule is a Shannon-based company which markets an alternative measuring technique that uses laser technology. The traditional and new technology methods of measuring distance both produce similar results. It can be said that there is concurrent validity between the new method and the established measurement technique. Likewise, a new measurement technique for measuring service quality levels could be compared against the well-established SERVQUAL method. If the new technique produces similar findings, it is assumed that concurrent validity exists.

Construct Validity

Construct validity is present when a logical argument can be advanced to defend a particular measure. Establishing construct validity occurs during the statistical analysis of the data. The empirical evidence should be consistent with the theoretical logic behind the concepts. A measure has construct validity if it behaves according to the underlying theory. It is present whenever our measure of a particular concept is related to measures of other relevant concepts in a theoretically expected way. For example, a measure of brand loyalty may be considered valid if consumers, who are loyal to a particular brand, also record very favourable attitudes towards that brand. The difficulty of this kind of validation is in the unobservable nature of many of the constructs (e.g. personality, attitudes, involvement, lifestyles) which we use to try to explain marketing behaviour (e.g. purchase behaviour) related to these constructs, in that we cannot observe the constructs themselves. Construct validity is the most difficult type of validity to establish.[4] If the construct exists, it is also true that it should be measurable by several different methods. If, for example, the following question was asked of the population by means of the three main survey methods: 'Are you in favour of extending pub opening hours?', a common measurement value, e.g. postal 42% in favour, telephone 44%, and personal interview 47%, may be evident. It is of course recognised that each of these survey methods has its own strengths and limitations.

Convergent Validity

The use of two or more independent measuring techniques should produce a common (but not necessarily equal) measurement value. Convergent validity exists if, for example, the following questions were asked of the population by means of the one survey method: 'What time should pubs close at?' Or 'What time should pubs stay open until?' Both questions, though worded differently, should, all other factors being equal, generate similar responses, e.g. Closing time 11.30 p.m.; Open until 11.30 p.m.

Discriminant Validity

While construct validity is the degree of correlation among different measures that purport to measure the same construct, discriminant validity is the lack of or low correlation among constructs that are supposed to be different. It involves demonstrating a lack of correlation among differing constructs. In other words, questions that measure different objects should yield different results. Supposing, in a survey of school principals regarding school security, a seven-point scale was used: 1 denoting 'Not concerned' and 7 denoting 'Very concerned'. When analysed, the average for the question dealing with fire safety was 6.2, whereas the average for a question dealing with theft of school equipment was 3.8. Therefore, school principals were found to be more concerned with fire safety than theft. This seems reasonable. In the above example, two different constructs were being measured. The difference between the averages demonstrates discriminant validity.

Reliability Assessment

Reliability refers to the extent to which a scale produces consistent results, if repeated measurements are made.[5] If you step on and off a bathroom scales repeatedly over a two-minute interval, it should show the same measurement value. If not, it is unreliable. In marketing research, a reliable measurement scale should be relatively free from the interference of transient or situational influences. If we measure the same marketing phenomenon over and over again with the same measurement instrument, we should get the same or highly similar results. Therefore, reliability is the degree to which measures are free from random error. Even if a study is undertaken just once, it is important that the measurement is free from random error. Otherwise, how can we be confident that the findings resemble the actual value? There are several approaches to the assessment of reliability.

Test-retest Reliability

Test-retest (also known as stability) estimates are obtained by repeating the measurement using the same instrument at two different times, and under as nearly equivalent conditions as possible between the two measurements. Assuming that the objects or individuals have not changed in the interim, the two measurement scores should correlate. The higher the correlation coefficient, the higher the reliability. There are several problems associated with the test-retest assessment of reliability. Firstly, it may be difficult to locate and gain the co-operation of respondents for a second testing, or the research question may require the person's initial reaction to a new product. Secondly, the first measure may sensitise the respondent's response to the second or subsequent measurements. Equally, respondents may attempt to remember answers they gave the first time. Thirdly, the likelihood of a true change in attitude (versus a random fluctuation) or other form of maturation of the subject, is increased further if the time interval between the test and the re-test is too long. Environmental and personal factors may change, causing the second measurement to change. Therefore, a very short time interval will bias the reliability estimate upwards, whereas longer periods have the opposite effect. Thus, if a particular measuring instrument does not show a high degree of consistency between observations recorded during the first and second measurements, we are not certain whether the instrument is unreliable or whether the changes are due to some of the above-mentioned factors. An alternative means of reliability assessment may be required to overcome the problems of the test-retest method.

Split-half Reliability

The split-half approach to reliability assessment is concerned with the internal consistency of the measuring instrument rather that its stability over time. It involves two measurements taken at the same point in time. The theory of internal consistency is based on the idea of equivalence. Equivalence relates to the amount of error that may be introduced by different samples of items used to measure a phenomenon. At its simplest, split-half reliability works as follows, e.g. a list of twenty items are on a summated scale (a summated scale is where a number of items are summed to form a total score). Each item on the scale measures some aspect of the construct measured by the entire scale, and the items should be consistent in what they indicate about the characteristic. If, for example, hotel image was believed to consist of fourteen independent items, and we wished to measure hotel image on a single favourable or unfavourable image dimension, each item is assumed to measure this composite single dimension independently. The split-half approach randomly divides the fourteen items into two groups of seven. The research takes the results obtained from one half of the scale items and checks them against the results from the other half. High correlation between the halves indicates high internal consistency, which means that the items can be split into halves randomly or based on odd-and-even numbered items. A problem with the split-half reliability assessment approach is that the results will depend on how the scale items are split. To overcome this, an average split-half measure of similarity — coefficient alpha — can be obtained from a procedure that has the effect of comparing every item to every other item.

Equivalent Forms Reliability

The equivalent forms method is used when two alternative measuring instruments are designed to be equivalent but not identical. For example, two equivalent questionnaires can be constructed to measure store loyalty. Although the questions used to measure store loyalty are different in each questionnaire, the number of questions used to measure store loyalty should be approximately equal. The two equivalent forms are administered to the same groups of subjects, at two different times, usually two to three weeks apart, although in some cases they are given one after the other. The results are compared to determine the degree of discrepancy, as in the test-retest approach. A high correlation between the two forms would suggest that the scale is reliable. A low correlation reflects either low reliability or non-equivalent forms. There are two problems with this approach. Firstly, the difficulty of designing forms that are truly equivalent. Secondly, the expense and time delay. Even if equivalence is established, it may not have been worth the effort.

A final word on reliability. Reliability is a necessary condition for validity. However, a reliable instrument may not be valid. A reliable but invalid measurement will yield consistently inaccurate results.

MEASUREMENT OF ATTITUDES

A variety of techniques have been developed to measure attitudes. The measurement techniques in this chapter tend to be of the self-administered variety, i.e. self-reporting, in which the consumer responds to questions posed. Self-administered techniques are by far the most widely used techniques for measuring attitudes, and are the most appropriate for conclusive research studies. Other means of measuring attitudes include observation and projective techniques (see Chapters 5 and 6). These methods are more appropriate for measuring attitude in exploratory research situations.

Measurement of attitude is much more difficult and uses less precise scales than these found in the physical sciences. Attitude is not observable, nor is it defined by any single, agreed-upon definition. It is a construct (i.e. not directly observable, but measurable through indirect measures) that exists in the mind of the consumer. Often, attitudes are measured at the nominal or ordinal level. There are, however, more sophisticated scaling procedures that enable the researcher to measure attitudes at the interval level. Conclusions obtained from attitude scale measurements are strictly limited by the properties of the scale that is used. It is not possible to attribute the more powerful properties of the interval scale to the lower level nominal or ordinal scales. Failure to recognise these limits can lead to serious misinterpretations; for example, assuming a ratio scale, where there was in fact only an interval scale.

The attitude measurement techniques discussed in this book can be grouped under two headings:

1. Attitude rating techniques.
2. Attitude scaling techniques.

We will look at each in turn.

ATTITUDE RATING TECHNIQUES

Rating scales are widely used to measure consumer attitudes, and many types of rating scales exist. The more popular rating scales will be discussed here.

Graphic Rating Scales

The respondent is asked to indicate the position on a continuum that corresponds to his or her attitude. The continuum runs from one extreme of the attitude in question to the other. A theoretically infinite number of responses are possible and the respondent indicates his or her attitude toward a concept by placing a mark at a point on the continuum. At its simplest, the graphic rating scale would look like this:

Unreliable   _____ X _____   Reliable

Inconvenient   _____ X _____   Convenient

Variations of the above might include providing hatch marks, with or without accompanying numbers. As well as at the extremes, verbal descriptions may be included along the continuum. The scales can be arranged horizontally or vertically.

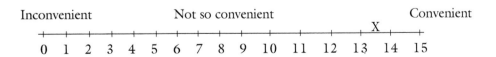

Inconvenient   Not so convenient   Convenient

0   1   2   3   4   5   6   7   8   9   10   11   12   13   14   15

If the scale does not contain numeric intervals, analysis can be carried out by using a ruler, or superimposing a marked template on the scale. When designing the scale, it is better not to make the ends of the continuum too extreme, nor to have too many hatch marks or numeric intervals. If the anchors are too extreme, it tends to force the respondent into the centre of the scale. Instead of hatch marks and/or numbers, the researcher may use any one of several graphic techniques to record the responses. These graphic techniques are particularly helpful for recording the response of children or if a language barrier exists. Examples include using happy/sad face scales and thermometer scales.

Non-Comparative or Comparative

Graphic rating scales can be either non-comparative or comparative. The preceding examples were all of the non-comparative type, whereby the respondent is free to choose his or her own frame of reference. At this point, it is important to point out that some authors choose to discuss the measurement of attitude under the broad heading of comparative and non-comparative scales. In this book, we use this heading as it applies to the individual measurement scales; preferring instead to detail attitudes under the heading of Attitude Rating Techniques and Attitude Scaling Techniques. An example of a comparative graphic rating scale could be:

Compared to *The Irish Times*, the *Irish Independent* is:

Easy to read   Not easy to read

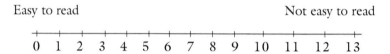

Graphic rating scales are easy to construct and simple to use. Numerical data obtained from the scales is usually treated as interval data. However, while graphic rating scales are used in marketing research, they are generally not considered as reliable as itemised rating scales.[6]

Itemised Rating Scales

The itemised rating scale is similar to the graphic rating scale except that the respondent is asked to choose from a limited number of identified categories, rather than placing a check mark on a continuous scale. Many of the more widely used scales in attitude measurement fall into the category of itemised scales. Itemised scales are easy to construct and administer, but do not allow for the fine distinctions that can be achieved in a graphics rating scale. This limitation is compensated for by the fact that the definitive categories of itemised rating scales probably produce more reliable ratings. Examples of itemised rating scales include:

Drying ability of a Whirlpool dryer is:

Very good   Good   Neither   Poor   Very poor

1 ☐   2 ☐   3 ☐   4 ☐   5 ☐

Shopping at Dunnes Stores is:

Very boring   Neither   Very enjoyable

-3 ☐   -2 ☐   -1 ☐   0 ☐   +1 ☐   +2 ☐   +3 ☐

The Cork Jazz Festival is well organised:

Strongly agree   Agree   Neutral   Disagree   Strongly disagree

☐   ☐   ☐   ☐   ☐

When developing itemised scales, the following issues must be considered:

1. Whether to have an odd or even number of categories.

Some researchers may believe that respondents should not be provided with a neutral category. Their reasoning is that everybody has some degree of an attitude and that by not providing a neutral category it forces the respondent to come down off the fence. Other researchers argue that respondents may be genuinely ambivalent or have a neutral attitude on the subject in question, and should therefore be provided with a neutral category. This can be achieved by having an odd number of categories with the central position neutral.

As well as providing a central neutral position, it may be advisable to have another category for the 'Don't know' or 'No opinion'. After all, it is possible that a certain percentage of respondents may never have heard of or used the object in question. Uninformed responses like this should not be 'forced' into a neutral category. By not doing so, they are not included in the calculation of measures of central tendency, i.e. by providing a 'No opinion' response category you get a more accurate measure of the average response to the item.

2. Whether to use balanced or unbalanced scales.

In a balanced scale, the number of favourable response categories equals the number of unfavourable responses. An unbalanced scale will have more positive or negative categories. However, there may be instances when an unbalanced scale is the way to go. For example, it would be reasonable to assume that responses to a statement like 'Protection of the ozone layer is important for future generations' would be skewed to the positive or favourable response categories:

Disagree	Neutral	Agree	Strongly agree	Very strongly agree
☐	☐	☐	☐	☐
−1	0	1	2	3

3. How many categories should the scale have?

As a rule of thumb, a five- or seven-scale category is probably sufficient. More than that is likely to be confusing to the respondent; however, the greater the number of response categories, the greater the precision of the scale. In some instances, a two- or three-category scale will be sufficient, i.e. 'Agree, Neutral, Disagree'. There is no correct answer to the number of categories to use. The researcher must use judgment.[7]

4. To what extent should responses be labelled and identified?

When providing guidance to respondents, the researcher may choose to provide: numbers versus no numbers; label only the end points of the scale; or provide verbal descriptions for all categories. The labelling of responses is an important issue as the presence of labels can affect responses.[8] Also, a combination of equally spaced categories and ordered numerical designations increases the possibility of assuming that the data obtained is by nature interval. It is common practice to treat rating scales as interval scales and to compute mean and standard deviations. The researcher should exercise caution in making such an assumption, as potential for measurement error exists.

It should also be noted that the verbal descriptions provided throughout the scale may not concur with the respondent's. By providing only extreme verbal descriptions, the respondent may feel that he or she is being forced less into a particular category on the scale.

Rank-Order Rating Scales

These scales require the respondent to arrange a number of objects with regard to some common criterion, e.g. product features in terms of importance, advertisements in terms of awareness or services with regard to liking. Ranking is widely used in surveys. The rank-order method is comparative in nature and the result is a purely ordinal scale that describes the objects from most favoured to least favoured. The respondent assigns a rank of 1 to the most preferred brand, 2 to the second most preferred and so on. Nothing is said about the distance between the objects. For example, the distance between 1 and 2 is not necessarily the same as the distance between objects 3 and 4. Also, perhaps none of the items on the list is the respondent's preferred first choice. The respondent may actually dislike, in an absolute sense, the brand ranked 1. The ranking technique may force respondents to make choices they might not otherwise make. In practice, respondents should not be expected to rank more than six items, otherwise it becomes arduous. Despite its limitations, the rank-order scale is a popular choice for researchers; mostly because it resembles the shopping environment where the consumer is required to make direct comparisons among competing alternatives. An example follows.

'Please rank the following brands of washing powder according to whiteness. No. 1 should be the most preferred brand, no. 6 the least preferred. No two brands should receive the same rank number.'

Daz   ☐

Bold   ☐

Persil   ☐

Tide   ☐

Omo   ☐

Radion   ☐

Surf   ☐

Paired-comparison Rating Scales

The previous technique required the respondent to consider all objects simultaneously. When using paired comparisons, the objects to be ranked are presented two at a time, and the respondent has to choose between them according to some criterion.[9] The data obtained is ordinal by nature. Paired-comparison overcomes the problem, as in rank-order, of ranking a large number of objects: it is easier for the respondent. Before a ranking of all objects can be obtained, all possible combinations of pairs have to be presented. This means that for n objects, $(n(n-1)/2)$, paired comparisons include all possible pairings of objects.[10] For example, if there are six objects to be evaluated, n = $(6(6-1)/2)$ or fifteen paired comparisons. For five objects, the number of comparisons is ten. But the more objects, the more comparisons required. With ten brands, for example, there are 45 paired comparisons. This geometric expansion means the number of objects to be evaluated should be confined to a relatively small number. It should be noted that the comparison of two objects at a time is seldom the way choices are made in a retail situation. Thus, an item may do very well in a paired comparison test, but not perform as well in an actual market situation.[11] Also, respondents may prefer one object over another, but they may not like it in an absolute sense.

Example of paired comparison rating (Fanta, Coke, Lilt, 7-Up, Club Orange)

Please evaluate the following brands of soft drink according to taste:

_____ Fanta	versus	_____	Coke
_____ Fanta	versus	_____	Lilt
_____ Fanta	versus	_____	7-Up
_____ Fanta	versus	_____	Club Orange
_____ Coke	versus	_____	Lilt
_____ Coke	versus	_____	7-Up
_____ Coke	versus	_____	Club Orange
_____ Lilt	versus	_____	7-Up
_____ Lilt	versus	_____	Club Orange
_____ 7-Up	versus	_____	Club Orange

Constant-sum Rating Scale

The constant-sum rating scale requires respondents to allocate a fixed number of rating units (usually 100) among several objects, to reflect the relative preference for each object or attribute. The units used can be points, pennies, chips, etc. If an object is considered unimportant, the respondent allocates it zero points. If an object is twice as important as some other object on the list, it receives twice as many points. The data obtained is considered closer to interval scale. The technique is best used for relatively small numbers of objects, otherwise respondents may misapply points such that the total is more than, or less than 100. For example, a respondent may allocate 106 or 94 points. This can be adjusted for by dividing each point allocation by the actual total and multiplying the result by 100.

'Please divide 100 points among the following soft drinks according to your degree of preference for each.'

Coke _____

Fanta_____

7-Up _____

Pepsi _____

Lilt _____

Fractionation-rating Scale

This rating scale can be considered a variation of the previous scale. Respondents are required to rate an object by comparing it with a reference object. As an example:

If the Institute of Technology Tralee (ITT) scored 100 points in terms of being a 'fun' college, how would you compare each of the following colleges to ITT?

ITT	100
GMIT	_____
LIT	_____
AIT	_____
CIT	_____
WIT	_____

With a scale of this nature, there is always the danger that a respondent will assign an outrageously high number of points to an object, that in no way reflects his or her preference or perceived value of the object. A solution would be to put a ceiling on the number of points the respondent can assign to any one given object. The constant-sum approach provides much the same information, but avoids the problem of extreme ratings. The researcher may therefore choose not to use the fractionation scale.

ATTITUDE SCALING TECHNIQUES

The rating scales methods outlined earlier require the respondent to react to a stimulus that typically consists of a single statement or question. However, attitudes toward complex objects such as health insurance, financial institutions, cars, educational establishments and pension funds have many facets. Thus it is often unrealistic to attempt to capture the full picture with one overall attitude scale question. The techniques in this section involve a battery of questions or statements in order to provide a more complete view of the respondent's overall attitude. These techniques measure a sample of beliefs towards the attitude objects (such as agreement or disagreement with a number of statements about the attitude object) and combine the sets of answers into some form of average score. The more popular scaling techniques employed in marketing research are Thurstone, Likert, semantic-differential and Stapel scales. Since these are versions of the itemised rating scale, we must keep in mind the various issues and problems associated with itemised rating scales, as discussed earlier in the chapter.

Thurstone's Scale

In the late 1920s, Louis Thurstone developed the concept that attitudes vary along continua and should be measured accordingly. The construction of this Thurstone scale is a complex process that requires two stages. The first stage is a ranking operation performed by judges who assign scale values to attitudinal statements. The second stage consists of asking subjects to respond to the attitudinal statements. Thurstone scales can be adapted to measure attitudes towards any type of object using the following procedure:

1. A large number (75 to 100) of statements or adjectives (favourable and unfavourable) relating to the attitude object(s) are collected by the researcher.

2. Then, a group of judges (15 to 20) classify these statements into eleven groups of approximately the same size. This eleven-category bipolar scale represents the judgments of the panel members as to which statements are most favourable, and which are least favourable, about the subject. The sixth or middle pile is the neutral position.

3. Mean scores for each of the original 75 to 100 statements are determined on the basis of the piles in which they were placed by the judges.

4. The 20 to 25 statements with the smallest variance are chosen to be included in the survey.

5. The selected items are incorporated into the questionnaire in random order and the respondent is asked to select all the items with which he agrees, and his score is calculated as the average of the values (medians) of the items selected.

For example:

Attitudes towards a restaurant are being assessed using a Thurstone scale. A respondent indicates three statements with which they agree.

Statement	Value assigned by judges
1. The restaurant has a homely atmosphere	2.8
2. The restaurant provides a good selection of wines	1.7
3. The restaurant has consistently good quality food	2.4
Average	2.3

Because of the two-stage procedure, a Thurstone scale is both time-consuming and expensive to construct; however, the scale itself is easy to administer and requires a minimum of instructions. Some critics question whether the judges are representative of the ultimate respondents. The attitudes of those who judge the original collection of statements may bias the selection of those used in the test. It would be unwise to deliberately include judges with extreme views about the matter under survey.

Likert Scale

Rensis Likert published 'A Technique for the Measurement of Attitudes'[12] in 1932, in which he described a new method of attitude scaling known as Likert scales. Sometimes referred to as the summated rating scale, the Likert scale is one of the most widely used attitude scaling techniques. It is simple to administer and overcomes some of the criticism associated with the Thurstone scale. This makes the technique particularly useful for mail surveys and personal interviews with children.[13] The Likert scale usually consists of two parts, the item part and the evaluative part. The item part is essentially a statement about a certain product, service, attitude or event. The evaluative part is a set of response categories ranging from 'Strongly agree' to 'Strongly disagree'. Likert scales differ from Thurstone's scales in that respondents are presented with a series of statements and asked to indicate their degree of agreement or disagreement by selecting a point on a 3, 5, 7 or 9 point scale. Typically, each scale item has five response categories ranging from 'Strongly agree' to 'Strongly disagree'.

In reality, the number of response alternatives may range from three to nine.[14] Consider the following example from a study of food shopping behaviour.[15]

'When buying food for my family, price is no object.'

Disagree	Neutral	Agree	Strongly agree	Very strongly agree
☐	☐	☐	☐	☐
−1	0	1	2	3

Note: Some researchers use 'Neither agree or disagree' as the midpoint.

The various degrees of agreement are assigned scale values, although the particular values differ from researcher to researcher. Thus, for example, for a five-point scale, a statement can be assigned a numerical score ranging from −2 to +2 or 5 to 1, or 1 to 5. The weights assigned are not printed on the actual questionnaire. The data collected by using Likert scales, may be presented on an item-by-item basis (profile analysis), or a total (summated) score can be calculated for each respondent, as a measure of the respondent's overall attitude towards the object of the survey. If a summated approach is used, the scoring system for each item statement must be consistent across high and low scores. This is known as directional consistency (see below). While a summated score has its advantages as a summary statistic, its main disadvantage is that it loses the richness and detail which are obtained if one analyses the responses individually. Because each statement is a rating scale in its own right, such analysis is possible with Likert scales but not with Thurstone scales.

In constructing Likert scales it is important to use items which invite the respondents to express a clear opinion, i.e. to avoid neutral statements and to vary the presentation between positive and negative statements in order to avoid the respondents getting into a mind-set and automatically ticking the same box. The procedure for developing summated Likert scales is now described.

Constructing Likert Scales

Likert scales are developed in a manner similar to that used for Thurstone scales. The following section summarises the major steps, as proposed by Rensis Likert, in the development and administration of the Likert scale instrument.

1. The researcher identifies the concept to be scaled.
2. The researcher collects a large number of statements relevant to the attitude in question, that can be clearly identified as either favourable or unfavourable. The number of statements at this stage will be relatively large — perhaps 50 statements or more. The key is to develop *attitude revealing* statements and to avoid universally accepted statements of fact.

3. The next step is to administer the collected statements to a group of people reasonably representative of eventual respondents. At this stage, the purpose is to eliminate statements that contribute very little to the eventual attitude score a respondent receives. In the pre-test, the respondent indicates agreement or disagreement with each statement by checking one of the following direction-intensity descriptors (assuming a five-point scale).

Strongly agree	(+2)
Agree	(+1)
Neutral	(0)
Disagree	(−1)
Strongly disagree	(−2)

The numbers in brackets are for scoring purposes and need not be shown to the respondents.

4. Next, compute each respondent's score by summing the scores of responses to each question. In the scoring process, weights are assigned so that the direction of attitude — favourable to unfavourable — is consistent over items. This directional consistency can be achieved by either multiplying each individual's responses to unfavourable statements by −1, or by reversing the rating of the responses for unfavourable statements.

	Strongly agree	Agree	Neutral	Disagree	Strongly disagree
Positive +	5	4	3	2	1
Negative −	1	2	3	4	5

5. Following the pre-test, it is necessary to eliminate those statements that do not discriminate between high and low scores on the total test. Selecting respondents with extreme scores (high or low) according to total score can do this. Then, determine the average score on each statement among those in the high quantity and similarly among those in the low quantity. Those statements on which these averages differ by the largest amount are the most discriminating.

6. Administer the refined test with the population or sample of interest. Each item response is algebraically added to provide a total attitude score for that respondent. Alternatively, individual statements can be profiled across respondents by computing the mean or median value for each item statement for the total group, or for each group that one wishes to compare with each other or with some 'ideal' profile.

It is possible that two individual respondents could have the same summated score but yet have rated various statements differently, i.e. specific attitudes towards components of their overall attitude could differ markedly.

Marketing research practitioners rarely follow the exact textbook-like process prescribed by Likert. The scales are often created by the client and researcher or following the completion of a focus group. As mentioned earlier, the main advantage of Likert scales is the ease of construction and administration. It does, however, take longer for the respondent to complete than other itemised rating scales. While output of the Likert is of the ordinal type, practitioners frequently treat the Likert total attitude score as an interval-scale result.

Figure 9.2

Profile analysis of two restaurants

Profile analysis of two restaurants

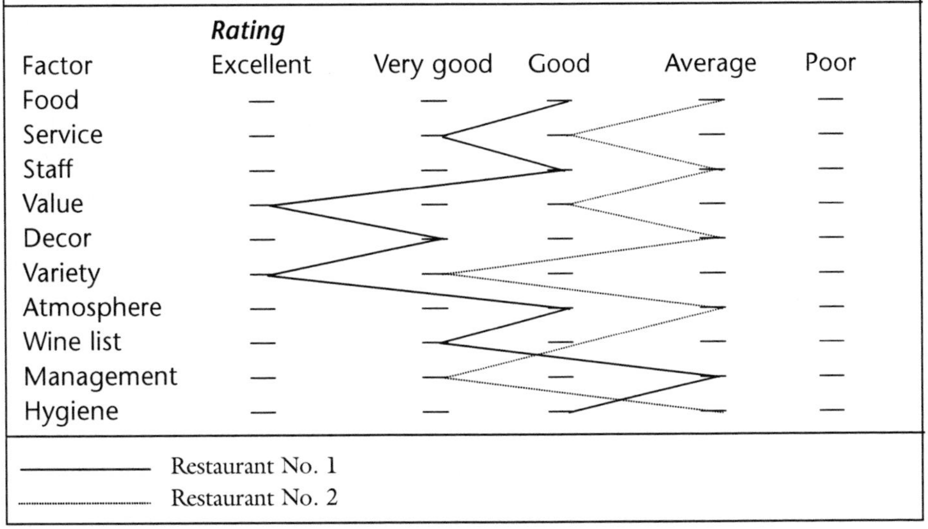

———————— Restaurant No. 1
···················· Restaurant No. 2

Semantic Differential

A special type of rating scale borrowed from another area of research (semantics), this scaling technique was originated by Osgood, Suci and Tannerbaum[16] who discovered that the perceived meaning of a variety of words and concepts could be stated in terms of three components:

1. Potency, e.g. strong-weak.
2. Activity, e.g. fast-slow.
3. Evaluation, e.g. good-bad.

In marketing research, the semantic differential is widely used to describe the set of beliefs that comprise a person's image of an organisation or brand. It is also a revealing procedure for comparing the images of competing brands, stores, or services.[17] In general, only the evaluative, e.g. good/bad component, of the attitude is measured. In this technique, the respondent is asked to express his or her feelings on an object by selecting a position along a five- or seven-point rating scale bounded by bipolar adjectives or phrases that have semantic meaning. In the original work of Osgood *et al.*, only single-word bipolar adjectives, not phrases, were used. However, common practice in marketing research applications is the adjectival phrases (e.g. a bank study might use the phrase 'low interest on savings' and 'favourable interest on savings'. These phrases are not bipolar opposites). Some researchers prefer unipolar scales, while others use bipolar scales. However, the midpoint of the scale has two different meanings. With unipolar scales, the midpoint is simply a step on the scale from 'warm' to 'cold', whereas on a bipolar scale it is a neutral point. The scoring of the semantic differential can be illustrated by using a seven-point scale bounded by the anchors 'fast' and 'slow'.

Fast — — ✓ — — — — — — — — Slow

Respondents are asked to mark the blank that best indicates how best one or the other term describes the attitude object. Each position on the scale is assigned a numerical value, e.g. −3 to +3 or 1 to 7. The words (adjectives, phrases) should be carefully selected. Exploratory research generally is required to ensure that important attributes are represented and described in words that are familiar to respondents.[18] Semantic differential scaling may include as many as ten or fifteen different adjective pairs. Some adjective pairs will be quite concrete, others may be adjective pairs that are more abstract yet quite revealing (similar to projective techniques). For example:

Budweiser beer is:

sweet	—	—	—	—	—	—	—	bitter
weak	—	—	—	—	—	—	—	strong
colourless	—	—	—	—	—	—	—	colourful
angular	—	—	—	—	—	—	—	rounded
beautiful	—	—	—	—	—	—	—	ugly
masculine	—	—	—	—	—	—	—	feminine
old fashioned	—	—	—	—	—	—	—	modern
tasteful	—	—	—	—	—	—	—	tasteless
elegant	—	—	—	—	—	—	—	plain
undependable	—	—	—	—	—	—	—	dependable

In the past, supermarkets have been surveyed using semantic differential scales. These were designed to give profiles of them as seen by consumers. The following bipolar scales were considered to be most relevant in one study.[19]

Example of a five-point semantic differential scale which was used to measure attitude towards supermarkets:

good	—	—	—	—	—	bad
friendly	—	—	—	—	—	unfriendly
modern	—	—	—	—	—	old fashioned
pleasing	—	—	—	—	—	annoying
convenient	—	—	—	—	—	inconvenient
clean	—	—	—	—	—	dirty
neat	—	—	—	—	—	disorderly
large	—	—	—	—	—	small
sincere	—	—	—	—	—	insincere
reliable	—	—	—	—	—	unreliable
active	—	—	—	—	—	passive
low prices	—	—	—	—	—	high prices
roomy	—	—	—	—	—	crowded

The bipolar adjectives in a semantic differential scale should ideally be randomised in order to avoid positive bias. The phrases are randomly flipped to avoid having all the good ones/positive ones on one side. Randomly assigning favourable and negative ends of the descriptors in a semantic differential scale minimises what is sometimes referred to as the 'halo effect'.[20] Halo effects refer to distortions of consumer perceptions of attribute-specific properties, which can render the interpretation of attribute-specific satisfaction data meaningless.[21] Also if respondents are likely to be ambivalent to the survey topic, it is better to use a balanced set of negatively and positively worded questions.[22] Before the researcher can begin to assign codes and summing occurs, he must reverse the individual scale items where necessary so that each attitude continuum ranges from unfavourable to favourable or *vice versa*.

Earlier we said that semantic differential can be used to compare images of competing brands, stores and services. Competing brands can be subjected to the same test and their profiles compared. In the supermarket example, respondents could be asked to rate two or more supermarkets on the same scale and profile presented for each (as in the restaurant example cited earlier).

Semantic differential data are typically analysed using the profile analysis approach. Profile analysis involves computing the arithmetic mean or median value for each set of bipolar adjectives, or verbal phrases for each object evaluated. The values calculated are compared by plotting or statistical analysis. It is possible that two or more brands compared would have similar aggregate scores yet their profiles be quite different. While the mean is most often used as the summary statistic, there is controversy as to whether the measurements can be treated as interval data. Critics argue that the data obtained will have only ordinal properties because the weights are arbitrary. Depending on whether the data are assumed to be interval or ordinal, the mean or median will be used to compare the profile of competing brands. An alternative to profile analysis is aggregate analysis. It requires that the scales across all adjective pairs be summed for each individual. Each individual is assigned a summated score. Individual scores can then be compared as the basis of total scores. However, profile analysis is the more preferred approach for marketing decision-making.

Figure 9.3

```
+5
+4
+3                    +3
+2                    +2
+1                    +1
Fast service         Friendly staff
-1                   -1
-2                   -2
-3                   -3
-4
-5


Alternative presentation
```

	Jurys	Fitzpatricks	Travelodge	Best Western
	+5	+5	+5	+5
	+4	+4	+4	+4
	+3	+3	+3	+3
	+2	+2	+2	+2
	+1	+1	+1	+1
Expensive				
	−1	−1	−1	−1
	−2	−2	−2	−2
	−3	−3	−3	−3
	−4	−4	−4	−4
	−5	−5	−5	−5

Stapel Scale

A derivative of the semantic differential scale is the Stapel scale. It was originally developed in the 1950s by Jan Stapel to measure the direction and intensity of attitudes simultaneously. The adjective pair of the semantic differential is replaced by a single adjective or phrase, i.e. unipolar. This is particularly helpful when it is difficult to create pairs of bipolar adjectives. Points on the scale are numerically identified with typically ten categories numbered from −5 to +5, without a neutral point (zero). In reality, any even number of numerical values can be used, e.g. −3 to +3. The scale is usually presented vertically. Respondents are asked to evaluate how accurately the adjective or phrase describes the object to be evaluated. In the second example below, +5 is very expensive; −5 is very inexpensive. The higher the numerical response category, the more the term describes the concept.

An example(s) of the Stapel scale is shown in Figure 9.3.

Results can be analysed the same way that semantic differential data are treated. Figure 9.4 presents Stapel scale comparative profiles of two hypothetical fast-food restaurants.

Figure 9.4 Stapel scale comparative profiles

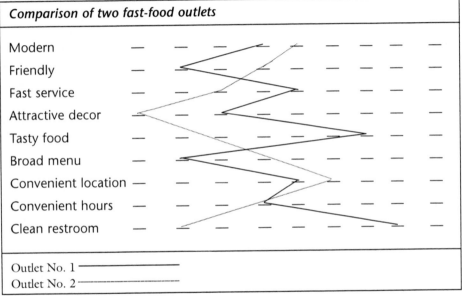

Comparison of two fast-food outlets
Modern
Friendly
Fast service
Attractive decor
Tasty food
Broad menu
Convenient location
Convenient hours
Clean restroom

Outlet No. 1 ——————
Outlet No. 2 ·······················

The Stapel scale produces results similar to the semantic differential.[23] It is particularly suitable for administration over the telephone.[24] Neither is there any need to pre-test bipolar adjectives or phrases to ensure true bipolarity. Despite this, the Stapel scale is little used in commercial research. Semantic differential and Likert scales remain more popular. A problem with the Stapel scale is that descriptor adjectives can be phrased in a positive, negative or neutral way. The choice of phrasing could be said to affect the scale results.

SUMMARY

Attitudes towards brands are consumers' learned tendencies to evaluate brands in a consistently favourable, or unfavourable way. Attitudes are generally viewed to have three main components, which are the cognitive component, the affective component and the behavioural component. The cognitive component refers to the respondent's awareness of and knowledge about an object. The affective component refers to the respondent's positive or negative feelings with regard to an object. The behavioural component refers to buying intentions and actual purchase behaviour. Most marketing research studies contain questions designed to measure a respondent's attitudes. It is generally assumed that there is a link between attitudes and behaviour. Attitudes are assumed to be an important predictor of behaviour.

There are four basic levels of measurement, which are nominal, ordinal, interval and ratio. Each represents a different kind of number assignment rule, or 'scale' of measurement. As we proceed from the weakest (nominal) to the strongest (ratio), two things happen. Firstly, the numerical requirements for scale membership become more stringent. Secondly, the permissible modes of data expression and analysis become more liberal, that is to say more types of statistical operations are permissible.

To have confidence in the results of a marketing research study, the researcher must be concerned about two characteristics of the measures being used to collect information. These two concepts are called validity and reliability. The researcher, therefore, must be concerned with whether we are measuring what we wish to measure and whether our measurement is accurate. Validity can be examined from a number of different perspectives. There are six major approaches to the assessment of validity. Reliability refers to the extent to which a scale produces consistent results if repeated measurements are made. There are three approaches to the assessment of reliability, test-retest reliability, split-half reliability and equivalent forms reliability.

A variety of techniques have been developed to measure attitudes. Self-administered techniques are by far the most widely used techniques for measuring attitudes. The attitude measurement techniques discussed in this book can be grouped under two headings: attitude rating scales and attitude scaling techniques. Rating scales are widely used to measure consumer attitudes, and many types of rating scales exist. The rating scales methods require the respondent to react to a stimulus that typically consists of a single statement or question. Attitude scaling techniques, on the other hand, use a battery of questions or statements in order to provide a more complete view of the respondent's overall attitude. The more popular scaling techniques employed in marketing research are Thurstone, Likert, semantic-differential and Stapel scales.

QUESTIONS

1. Define 'attitude'. What are the components of an attitude?
2. Distinguish between the cognitive component and behavioural component of an attitude.
3. What is meant by measurement, and why is this process important to marketing research?

4. What are the primary scales of measurement?
5. Differentiate between a nominal and an ordinal scale.
6. Why is a ratio scale more advantageous than an interval scale?
7. Distinguish between the validity and the reliability of a measure.
8. Discuss the major ways in which the validity of measurement is assessed.
9. What are the three methods of assessing reliability?
10. Outline the main attitude rating scales.
11. Give an example of the following rating scales: (a) graphic; (b) rank order; (c) constant sum.
12. What are the important decisions involved in constructing an itemised rating scale? How many scale categories should be used in an itemised rating scale? Should an even or odd number of categories be used?
13. What is the difference between balanced and unbalanced scales?
14. Distinguish between attitude scaling techniques and attitude rating scales.
15. How does one construct a Likert scale?
16. What is a semantic differential scale and how is a person's overall attitude assessed with this type of scale?
17. How does a Stapel scale differ from a semantic differential scale? Which is more commonly used?

PROBLEMS AND ASSIGNMENTS

1. Mary says she'd be willing to pay €5,000 more for a used '03 Opel than for a used '01 Fiat. This comparison between the two cars represents what scale of measurement?
2. Identify the type of scale (nominal, ordinal, interval, or ratio) being used in each of the following:
   (a) I think there are too many stray cats in my neighbourhood.

   Disagree   **Agree**

     1   2   3   4   5

   (b) How many brothers do you have?
   (c) Please rank the following activities in terms of your preferences by assigning ranks 1 to 5.

i.	Going to the gym	_____
ii.	Eating out	_____
iii.	Going to the movies	_____
iv.	Shopping	_____
v.	Watching DVDs	_____

(d) What is your bank account number? _____

(e) On an average weekend, how many cups of tea do you consume?

    i.   Less than 1 cup   _____

    ii.   2 to 4 cups   _____

    iii.   5 to 7 cups   _____

    iv.   8 to 10 cups   _____

    v.   More than 10 cups   _____

3. Having read Chapter 8, design a questionnaire that includes a Stapel, Likert and a semantic differential scale for measuring the loyalty of a brand of your choice.

4. Develop a battery of attitude scales to predict whether or not people who currently smoke will try to quit smoking within the next year.

5. How would you select a set of phrases or adjectives for use in a semantic-differential scale to evaluate the image of banks and other consumer financial institutions? Would the procedure differ if you were going to use a Likert scale?

6. Advertising is an expenditure that ultimately must be justified in terms of an effect on sales and profits, yet most evaluations of advertising are in terms of the effects on attitudes. How do you account for this apparent mismatch?

7. You receive the results of a paired-comparison preference test of four soft drinks from a sample of 200 persons. The results are as follows:

	Coke	Fanta	7-Up	Lilt
Coke	X	50*	115	35
Fanta	150	X	160	70
7-up	85	40	X	45
Lilt	165	130	155	X

* Read as 50 persons preferred Fanta over coke.

(a) How do these brands rank in overall preference in this sample?

(b) Develop an interval scale for these four brands.

8. Below is a Likert type scale that might be used to evaluate your opinion of the educational programme you are in. There are five response categories: 'Strongly agree' through 'Neither agree nor disagree', to 'Strongly disagree'. If 5 represents the most positive attitude, how would the different items be valued?

(a) This programme is not very challenging.

    SA   A   N   D   SD

(b) The general level of teaching is good.

    SA   A   N   D   SD

(c) I really think I am learning a lot from this programme.

    SA   A   N   D   SD

  (d) Students' suggestions are given little attention here.

      SA   A   N   D   SD

  (e) This programme is below my expectations.

      SA   A   N   D   SD

9. One of the problems in developing rating scales is the choice of response terms to use. Below are samples of some widely used scaling codes. Do you see any problems with them?

  (a) Yes ___   Depends ___   No ___

  (b) Excellent ___   Good ___   Fair ___   Poor ___

  (c) Excellent ___   Good___   Average ___   Fair ___   Poor ___

  (d) Strongly Approve ___   Disapprove ___   Strongly Disapprove ___

10. A researcher thinks many respondents will answer 'Don't know' or 'Can't say' if these options are printed along with agreement categories on the attitude scale. The researcher does not print either 'Don't know' or 'Can't say' on the questionnaire because the resulting data will be less complicated to analyse and report. Is this appropriate?

Case Study
Competing for Your Euros – The HELPOUT Charity*

The Irish are among the most generous people per capita when it comes to charitable donations. As a result, competition for the donor pound is fierce. According to the Revenue Commissioners, there are more than 5,800 organisations with charitable exemption status. Of these, 280 are qualified to receive corporate donations. Many Irish charities are now well-established 'brand names', e.g. Trócaire, Goal, Concern, St Vincent de Paul, Alzheimer Society of Ireland, Irish Cancer Society. All of these names are probably well known to you and most likely you will have been asked to make a donation or buy a daffodil or some other token by a fundraiser for at least one of these. But there are also all the schools, social and sporting clubs, local causes and committees, who are often only known in their own local community, asking donors to dig deep into their pockets. So what stops people from giving?

Potential donors may be put off by a number of reasons, among them:

- the sheer number of charities in the State;
- the lack of a registry and legislation on accountability;
- suggestions of financial impropriety by one well-known organisation in the sector and allegations against others in recent years;
- donor fatigue – just too many charities asking too often;
- inappropriate methods of asking – the 'hard sell' , or lottery-based products.

Despite such difficulties, charities have found donors are still giving, but perhaps more hesitantly than before. But how do they convince people that they are the charity most deserving? What are the issues of most concern to you when you are asked to give money to charity? Research carried out by the National College of Ireland looked at some of these points.

More than 50% of respondents perceived charities as honest, while another 35% were not sure. Almost one-third were concerned about the accountability of such organisations. The research revealed that 'respondents feel that 20c in the euro is an acceptable level of administration costs, but they believe that in the case of home-based organisations only 50c of each euro donated goes to the cause, while in the case of overseas organisations it is believed that only 40c gets to the cause.'

Irish donors have very little knowledge of where their donations actually go unless the charity voluntarily provides the information. Irish legislation does little to provide donors with a framework, rating, or benchmark by which to judge individual charities. Despite the recommendation of a special government advisory group in 1996, which examined the charity/fundraising sector, there is no register of charities in the Republic. For several years, charities have been pushing for a register of charities similar to the structure developed in Britain. In the absence of a register, many charities self-regulate in the belief that public accountability and professionalism are key to the survival of the sector. The Law Society has recommended a raft of changes to the way charities are regulated in a new report entitled 'Charity Law: The Case For Reform' published in July 2002.

The report calls for strict controls on public fundraising and recommends the establishment of a national database showing the calendar of collection permits granted throughout the State. Also included in the recommendations is a stipulation that charitable organisations register with a new independent State-funded watchdog, the Charities Office. Only small charities with a turnover under €2,000 would be exempted from registration. However, they would still have to file annual accounts, which would be publicly available on the Internet. The Charities Office would be empowered to investigate cases of suspected fraud or misconduct. The report says new legislation is needed to regulate street trading by charities, such as the collection of promises for money, standing orders, and the sale of tokens such as happy hearts or daffodil pins.

Like many in the sector, Third World charity Trócaire feels strongly that it has an obligation to provide donors with information and assurances as to how their money is spent. As a trust the charity has no legal obligation to publish its accounts, yet it does so each year in its annual report for the purpose of public accountability.

In July 2002 the charity published a donor's charter that promises, among other things, that Trócaire will continue to maximise donations by seeking matching funds and hold administration costs to acceptable levels. 'If people want to make a donation, they're entitled to know what they're donating to and entitled to have their questions answered,' says Mr Owen Keenan, chief executive of Barnado's.

Administration or fundraising costs vary in different areas because some charities are more administration-orientated than others. Because of this, it is difficult, if not impossible, to benchmark charities against each other purely on the basis of the amount of money spent on such expenses. However, it is obviously a source of concern for donors.

The issues raised in this brief discussion on the Irish charity sector highlight a number of areas needing to be researched. You have been appointed by the newly formed charity HELPOUT to carry out some specific research on donor attitudes towards Irish charities. In particular you have two objectives. The first is to report on donor attitudes towards charities and the second on attitudes towards giving money to charity.

Assignment

Design a questionnaire which uses the following;

1. A five point semantic differential scale to measure donor attitudes towards charities, in particular the issues raised in the article.
2. A set of questions on attitudes towards different fundraising approaches, e.g. buying a token, going to a charity event, giving money to a street collection, sponsoring a participant in a mini marathon, etc. These questions should use a Likert Scale.
3. Discuss whether it would be (a) desirable and (b) feasible to use Thurstone's Scale in your research.

Web addresses that may be useful to the student for this case include:

> www.cafonline.org
> www.barnardos.ie
> www.concern.ie
> www.trocaire.ie
> www.alzheimer.ie
> www.irishcancer.ie

*This case was written by Declan Doyle, Head of Wexford Campus, Institute of Technology, Carlow. The HELPOUT charity is a totally fictitious charity and should not be associated with any actual organisation.

Case Study
Measuring Service Quality at the Bridge House Restaurant*

The Bridge House, award-winning restaurant and bar 'in the heart of Dublin', welcomes its guests to an elegant decor and offers an intimate and friendly atmosphere. The background music will charm the customers and complements the ambiance and the quality and freshness of food.

The restaurant is a well-established and up-market establishment which has been operating in Dublin for the last twenty years. It began by offering simple, straightforward cuisine to the regular patrons consisting of mostly local business people in winter and attracting additional tourists in summer. It is open from Monday to Saturday from 11 a.m. to 3 p.m. for lunch and 6.30 p.m. until 11 p.m. for dinner. From June to September, the restaurant also opens every Sunday for dinner.

The Bridge House held the reputation as the 'best restaurant in Dublin' for a decade. It focuses on delivering good quality food in a relaxed atmosphere with efficient and friendly service. The restaurant offers a variety of food, with dinner costing approximately €32.50, and provides a four-course meal with dishes such as local seafood. The Early Bird menu costs €19.95 and is available from 6.30 p.m. to 7.30 p.m. The à la carte menu ranges in price from €15.95 to €24.95 and contains mouth-watering dishes and a wide selection of seafood.

The owners, Theresa and Barry O'Leary, feel that their mission is to deliver quality food and service in a friendly atmosphere. However, this is getting increasingly difficult. Several new restaurants have opened in Dublin in the last year, offering new 'cuisines', trendy atmospheres, sleek decor, and attracting a trendy clientele. The restaurants are spending heavily on promotional activities including grand openings and thus receiving much publicity. However, their staff are mainly students and have received no official training and receive minimum wages.

Theresa has not noticed a reduction in sales as a result of this competition and their restaurant appears to be holding on to market share and sells 400 lunches a week and 250 dinners; Theresa feels that their core competence is service. Comment cards have revealed that the food still scores high, but service has dropped from 'very good' to 'good'. Theresa knows that providing good quality service on a consistent basis will mean that customers will be continually satisfied, will want to return and use the service again and they will want to recommend the service to those around them. It costs five times more to get a new customer than to keep an old one. By retaining existing customers and gaining new customers through positive word of mouth, Theresa feels that the restaurant's customer base will continually grow without the need for expensive and unpredictable advertising. A growing customer base, in line with increased sales turnover, will enable the restaurant to become more efficient in its activities and avail itself of economies of scale. This in turn will enable the restaurant to increase its profits and offer attractive pricing structure to its customers, especially in the quieter 'shoulder' and winter months.

Theresa has decided to carry out a more extensive survey on patrons to identify their deeper perceptions of the quality of the service. She feels that the best approach is the comparison of expectations to perceptions regarding the actual service encounter. The problem is to identify what research method to use and what aspects of the service to research, e.g. is friendliness more important than speed? Theresa decided to carry out some focus-group interviews which consisted of informal discussions with eight to ten customers. The participants expressed their views with regard to the aspects of the service that *they considered important to them*. From this initial exploratory research, Theresa learns that some of the most important aspects are:

- Dependability and accurate service performance.
- Promptness and helpfulness.
- Competence, courtesy, credibility and security.
- Good communications and good customer understanding.
- Atmosphere and ambiance, appearance of physical elements of service.

Theresa now wishes to set up an informal service-quality information system that will provide relevant data on an ongoing basis which can be used for decision-making purposes. She wants to use a quantitative method that can be administered on a regular basis and comparisons made. Luckily she has all her regular clients (250) on a database that she uses for direct mail and from them she chooses a random sample of 25. The main problem she feels is how to measure the important attributes of service as identified from the focus groups – perhaps some type of attitude scales could help? Theresa ponders these problems as she shuts the restaurant door late Sunday evening. Tomorrow (she hopes) will reveal the best approach to solving the service-quality measurement task.

Assignment

1. Describe the non-comparative scaling techniques that Theresa could use to measure service quality in the restaurant (include Likert and Semantic differential scales in your answer).
2. Draw up a questionnaire that includes rating scales to measure service-quality using the attributes identified in the case study.
3. Discuss the criteria used for scale evaluation and explain how to assess reliability, validity and generalizability.

* This case was written by Monica Nielsen, Galway-Mayo Institute of Technology. It is intended to be used as a basis for class discussion rather than to illustrate either effective or ineffective handling of an administrative situation. The case is based on a real situation, though certain information has been disguised. © Monica Nielsen, Galway-Mayo Institute of Technolgy (2006).

CHAPTER 10

THE SAMPLING PROCESS

CHAPTER OVERVIEW

▸ Introduction   ▸ Sampling Terminology, Basic Sampling Concepts
▸ A Census or a Sample?   ▸ The Sampling Process   ▸ Defining the
Population ▸ Choosing a Sampling Frame   ▸ Choosing a Sampling Method
▸ Selecting a Sample Type   ▸ Sample Size Determination   ▸ Selection and
Validation of a Sample   ▸ Online Sampling   ▸ Summary

INTRODUCTION

Sampling is about taking a small portion of the larger part and drawing conclusions about the larger part from our experience of the smaller part. Put simply, sampling is finding out a lot from a little, in a scientific way. Sampling enables us to study some cases instead of all the cases, while still enabling us to draw conclusions about all the cases. Some examples of sampling in action include:

- A telecommunications company wanting to estimate the bad debt provision from a population of several hundred thousand accounts.

- The government wishing to estimate the average expenditure per household in Ireland.

- A political party seeking to gauge the extent of their popularity in the public domain.

- An established food company wanting to estimate its potential market share for a new fast food product.

- A local hotel needing to estimate customer membership levels for an extension to its leisure centre.

- A health farm wishing to estimate the demand level for therapeutic facilities in order to apply for capital grants.[1]

From a practical marketing application, sampling asks the questions: who do we want to talk to? Who has the needed information? The aim of sampling is to make inferences about a population within acceptable margins of error. Finding the right person (object, item, shop, product or entity) to talk to is one of the signs of good market research.

The instinctive reaction for some people is to react negatively to the very words 'sampling' and 'statistics'; that is, to have a mental block or switch off (a sort of statistical seizure).[2] If you can add, subtract, multiply, divide, and calculate a square root, then there is no logical, rational reason for such an emotional reaction. As a researcher you can certainly grasp the concepts of sampling and statistics, with a small amount of effort. Researchers don't have to be statisticians to use sampling and basic statistical principles. The aim is to be comfortable with the general use, interpretation and analysis of data. Essentially, an investigator should be competent and able to collect data from a small group or set of items, persons or objects and use this group to reflect upon the larger group or population, make recommendations and therefore assist management with decision-making.

This chapter presents the principles of sampling and the related statistics. The reader is assumed to have a limited knowledge of mathematics. For further, more in-depth analysis of the topic, please refer to Churchill.[3] Upon completion of this chapter, you will be able to:

1. define basic sampling terminology;
2. outline the general principles of sampling;
3. detail the steps necessary to conduct sampling;
4. define a population;
5. discuss the practical use of sampling frames in Ireland;
6. differentiate between the different types of sampling and sampling methods; and
7. design a sampling procedure for a marketing problem.

SAMPLING TERMINOLOGY, BASIC SAMPLING CONCEPTS

Sampling is one of the few areas in marketing research that at first glance appears to have a vocabulary of its own. The terminology of sampling is that of the statistician and mathematician. It provides an appropriate starting point to an understanding of the concepts and ideas behind the marketing use of sampling. The more detailed statistical terminology, closely affiliated with sample size determination and derivation, is dealt with in the next chapter. The basic concepts which appear frequently in this chapter are as follows.

• *Population*

The population is the total set of people, shops, items, members and/or objects of interest. The term 'population' refers to each and every member from whom information is needed. It can also be referred to as the universe. A population member or element is one individual case from the total. A population has to be defined, according to designated specifications. Examples of possible populations or universes could be:

1. all those working in the home in Ireland in 2007;
2. all third-level, full-time students in Dublin city, as of October 2006;
3. all registered charities in Europe, as of January 2008;
4. all multinational corporations operating in Munster during the financial year 2007/2008;
5. all five-star hotels in Ireland as of August 2007.

Thus, the concept of population can be applied to people, firms, retailers, accountants, teenagers, students, doctors, stores and products alike. The symbol, N, denotes the size of a population. The population is what we make inferences about, based upon information from a sample.

Sample

This term denotes a smaller group of items, members or objects, taken from a particular population, that we measure or observe. It is a subset of the population or universe. A sample should be the miniature or mirror of the population under examination. The symbol, n, refers to the number of elements in a sample. The aim of a sample is to enable the researcher to draw inferences or conclusions from the sample about the population.

Census

A census is where all members or cases of a given population are observed/measured. Talking with every working urologist in the Republic of Ireland would qualify as a census, if the population of interest were defined as qualified, practising urologists in the 26 counties in 2007 (note, this excludes retired urologists).

Parameter

A parameter is a numerical dimension, measure, value or characteristic of the population we are interested in. It is better referred to as a population parameter. Sampling is used to estimate a population parameter. Parameters tend to be unknown at the time of conducting the study and actual information is needed about their value. Examples of parameters include the average amount spent on shoes by men; the number of female smokers in Ireland, or the number of married couples owning their own home.

Estimate

An estimate is a sample statistic. It is paired with the population parameter and taken as a measure of the population parameter. A common estimate is the sample mean, the average of the sample, e.g. the average length of time (days) a patient spends in hospital or the average amount spent per car (€s) in 2007.

Probability Laws

Mathematical laws governing the likelihood of a certain event occurring. As used in sampling, probability theory says that sample units have a known chance of selection, and so estimates can be made to determine how close the sample mirrors or reflects the population. Thus, a correctly selected sample will be, within measurable limits, representative of the population of interest.[4]

Sampling Error

Sampling error is the probable measurement of difference between the actual population parameter and the observed sample estimate of it. Sampling error is a result of taking a sample rather than a census. Sampling error is inherent in the sampling process.

A CENSUS OR A SAMPLE?

In wishing to learn about a particular population and describe its characteristics, one of the first issues to arise is the question of whether the researcher should be concerned with *all* members or *some* members; that is whether one should conduct a census or a sample. A census is a complete canvass of all population members, a sample is a selection of a smaller number of members from the population — for example, the Census of Population, 2006. Taken on the night of Sunday, 23 April 2006, 'the census figures relate to the *de facto* population, i.e. the population recorded for each area represents the total of all persons present within its boundaries on the night of Sunday, 23 April 2006, together with all persons who arrived in that area on the morning of Monday, 24 April 2006, not having been enumerated elsewhere'.[5]

Since every project has its own unique features and merits, a census or sample is thus dependent upon the particular features of the study and the compromise possible. Like many other issues in marketing research, the answer lies in balancing the different constraints of the project in hand. These constraints have a tendency to cluster around the following.

Time Requirements

Marketing problems are under severe time pressures. As a general rule, samples take less time than a census, the one exception being where there is a very small, finite, contained and accessible population. It is less time-consuming to research 1,000 people than the entire 4.2 million Irish population. However, if there are only five manufacturers of urology products in Ireland, a census is a sensible approach.

The Financial Cost

In most circumstances, a sample will physically consist of smaller numbers than a census and is therefore cheaper to pursue. However, the exception to this general rule-of-thumb is the small contained finite population, in which case a census is a practical alternative to a sample, as in the case of the urology manufacturers above.

Required Information, Related Decision

The management decision and required information has to be reviewed at this point, as more efficient use of money and time can be made by undertaking a sample. A sample can allow the researcher to control other dimensions of the project. For example, money could possibly be better spent on training interviewers and so minimising interviewer error, than talking with an additional 100 people. If properly conducted, a sample can be nearly as accurate as a census.

Pragmatic Reasons

Practical considerations often dictate the use of samples in place of a census, e.g. the destructive nature of measurement and investigation — if, as part of a quality drive, you eat all the produced Easter eggs, you would have none left to sell! Clearly, common sense calls for a sample.

A census would further be avoided if gathering information from people were a difficulty. It can happen that by talking with people, they are sensitised to the topic and so the results of the data collection process are not representative of the population's true opinion on the topic. Weiers[6] concisely expresses this when he writes 'it is desired to measure changes in the population rather than to induce changes by means of the measurement process itself'.

One development relating to the issues of census or sample is the shift from audit sampling in the retail sector to census data, based upon scanner-based tracking, giving rise to data drilling or data mining to monitor sales.

Accuracy and Confidence

The final issue to be considered in choosing between a sample or census is the needed accuracy, confidence and objectivity in the results. If little or minimum error can be tolerated in the results, the tendency is towards sampling because:

1. sampling error can be calculated and so is subject to statistical estimation, thus the accuracy of the results can be defined;
2. a census is more prone to non-sampling error, e.g. interviewer bias, analysis error;
3. sampling error can be reduced by increasing the sample size.

The accuracy and confidence required in the results is a measure of the preceding three variables. In choosing a sample or census, accuracy and confidence are the single best barometers.

A final comment on the question of a sample or census. It would appear from the above that samples are the preferred choice of most researchers and this is true in practice. Samples are generally more convenient, easier and more economical than a census.

THE SAMPLING PROCESS

Once the decision has been made to undertake a sample, the researcher engages in the sampling process. It can be thought of as consisting of seven stages, as shown in Figure 10.1. These stages are essentially sequential decisions and form the discussion for the remainder of this chapter.

Figure 10.1 The sampling plan

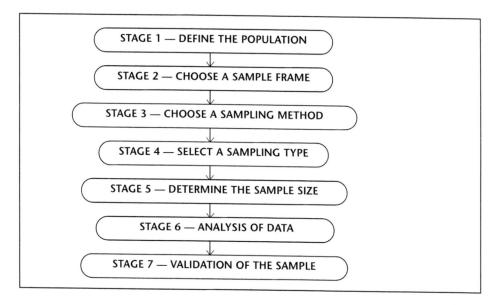

STAGE 1 — DEFINE THE POPULATION

STAGE 2 — CHOOSE A SAMPLE FRAME

STAGE 3 — CHOOSE A SAMPLING METHOD

STAGE 4 — SELECT A SAMPLING TYPE

STAGE 5 — DETERMINE THE SAMPLE SIZE

STAGE 6 — ANALYSIS OF DATA

STAGE 7 — VALIDATION OF THE SAMPLE

1. Defining the Target Population and Its Parameters

In deciding who to seek data from, the first step in sampling is about defining the population of interest. A population is defined as the total and entire group of persons, items/objects that the researcher wants to know, study and describe. A population is the totality of cases. Like problem definition, population determination has to be explicit and it can be equally difficult — there are many examples in marketing where people, objects and items do not lend themselves to easy and convenient classification. For example, consider a population that is to include all those people in Ireland who are against property taxes.

This aside, the objectives of the study are the sole determinants used to identify the target population. The defined population must contain all of the members of interest, otherwise it is not a population. To assist in achieving this completeness, and provide a manageable basis for defining a population, a population should have:

1. an *element*; this is the person we want to gather data from, or an entity which has the desired information. It can on occasions be the same as the unit. For example, we could be studying the smoking habits of all young teenagers to assist with government policy guidelines. Given this, the element we might wish to seek information from are 13–15-year-old-teenagers, male and female (the 13–15-year-olds are the elements of interest). In identifying the element of analysis, we often have to identify the population parameters we are also interested in. For example, we could be interested in 13–15-year-old teenagers who have smoked or are smoking (this excludes those teenagers who have not smoked). Careful planning and attention to detail are important at this point, to ensure an efficient sampling process. A fish manufacturer wanted to find out about the perceptions and expectation of retailers with respect to new added value fish products for the Irish market. At first glance, it seemed like a good idea to talk with retail store managers. However, secondary data from Bord Iascaigh Mhara quickly highlighted that the fish counter managers had more responsibility, experience and knowledge about specific developments in the fish trade and therefore were the real element of analysis for the study.

2. a *unit* — the unit contains or houses the unit of interest. Thus, the unit is often the access point to the element of analysis. In our illustration above, to talk with and so access 13–15-year-olds, we would approach households where the majority of such people reside. Alternatively, we could approach schools, or other such places where teenagers are most likely to be found. A recent and welcome development to note here are the different sampling units that the Internet brings to marketing. Internet units of analysis can be in the form of; (a) web pages, (b) web-sites or (c) Internet users.[7]

3. a *time* dimension — for example, during the year 2007. This provides a temporal boundary for the population. Continuing our example, we would also specify the time, e.g. a year or month, 2008 or December 2008.

4. a *geographic* boundary — this defines the extent of the population. In most Irish circumstances, this is either Ireland; a province(s); a county(s); a city(s) or a town(s). Completing our example, the geographic extent could be the island of Ireland, as we wish to generalise about all teenagers.

In practice, population definition can be easier for the consumer market than for the industrial market. This is attributable in part to the fact that there are more documented secondary data sources available for the consumer market. Secondly, population or universe definition is increasing in difficulty due to the collapsing boundaries between industries and organisations — a trend being fuelled by the 'global village' syndrome. Thirdly, as the number of variables used to define the population increases, say age and income plus social class, occupation and education, the cost of population definition increases. One method of dealing with these difficulties is to conduct exploratory research to determine the population.

2. Choosing the Appropriate Sampling Frame/List

A sampling frame is a list of all of the units (and elements) of the defined population, where no member is excluded and all members are mentioned once, and once only. If observable or documented, the frame is referred to as a direct list. Secondary sources of data can be of immense help in compiling such a list. Directories such as Kompass and Thoms are regularly used to this effect. The Register of Electors is commonly used as well, as are association/professional memberships, e.g. surgeons, dentists, lawyers. These are examples of sample frames — where every member is included and written down.

On occasions, it may be possible to generate a required list, but impractical to do so. Given such a situation, the researcher can work under the assumption that they have such a list. For example, in wishing to study the general public, a researcher would need a list of every individual who resides in Ireland at a given point in time. It is theoretically possible to compile such a sample frame, but unrealistic: it would absorb too much time and money. To this end, the researcher would assume that the list is readily available, in the form of households, and continue with the sampling process. This is an example of an indirect sample frame. Commonly used sample frames in Ireland are presented in Table 10.1.

Table 10.1 Sample frame list examples in Ireland

Consumer/households	Manufacturing firms	All firms	Miscellaneous
1. Register of Electors	1. IDA	1. Chambers of Commerce	1. Fáilte Ireland
2. Postal Districts	2. Enterprise Ireland	2. Golden Pages	2. Business & Finance Top 1,000
3. AC Nielsen	3. Kompass	3. Kompass	3. Financial Times

Sampling frames can be a difficult area for researchers in Ireland. Depending upon the population definition, it can be hard to generate or access lists easily. Industrial markets, services and small businesses are a few illustrations where generating a sample frame can be difficult. In such circumstances, creativity is called for — the researcher may need to collate a number of different and existing sources to generate their list. Other sampling frames, e.g. persons with the HIV virus, may not be available for confidentiality reasons.

A further problem associated with frames is sampling frame error. Frame error is said to have occurred when a list of the population is incomplete or inaccurate, due to missing, duplicated or incorrect elements. That is, there is a discrepancy between the defined population and the actual list or sample frame of that population. The effect of sampling frame error may be to introduce a bias in the results of the research. A classic frame error illustration in most countries is the telephone directory. At first glance, the telephone directory would seem to provide a listing of all residents. But it excludes those who do not have a phone, those who are ex-directory, those who have recently moved residence, those who have a mobile phone, but no fixed phone, those with only e-mail addresses and those who are nomadic, such as Travellers and the homeless.[8] Another example is the Register of Electors — a list of the names and addresses of all people over the age of 18. It is updated and published every year, but suffers from missing elements, persons who have not registered, duplication, students who have moved address and are registered twice or three times, and incorrect elements, persons returned from abroad or persons who have died.[9]

A special word of warning about sampling frames and the Internet – the Internet is continuously expanding, with new sites being set up every day. Consequentially, any Internet-based sampling frame (and for that matter, the Internet sampling population) is constantly changing. While no sampling frame is perfect, an Internet sampling frame is less stable because of the inherent change built into it. Thus, any results generated from a survey or experimentation based upon an Internet sampling frame can be difficult to generalise to a larger or general population. One way to overcome this difficulty is to conduct a survey or experiment over several time points.[10]

In conclusion, the perfect and ideal sample list is rarely available, implying that many researchers experience frame error. Nevertheless, potential sources of such error are best recognised in advance and minimised whenever possible.

3. Choosing a Sampling Method

Once we have a satisfactory population list, our next step in the sampling process is to choose between conducting a probability (random) or non-probability sample.

Probability is a type of sampling where each unit has a known chance of being selected. Inclusion and exclusion in the sample is determined by pure chance and the likelihood of this is known. This process can be likened to a number from 1–100 being picked out of a hat. Being based upon the notion of random selection, randomness in this context has a precise meaning — every member has a known (and under some circumstances discussed further on, an equal) chance of selection. Thus, probability sampling allows for generalisations to be made about the many from the few, i.e. the sample is used to make inferences about the whole population. The results generated by the sample, broadly speaking, equal those that would have been generated by a census if sampling had been correctly undertaken. Probability sampling also enables the calculation of the sampling error. Remember, a sample statistic estimates the true population value, so sampling error tells us how different our sample statistic is from the unknown population value. Another way to think about sampling error is to reflect on how accurate the sample results are — how closely do they mirror the real population and its parameters or values? All of these issues — error, accuracy, random selection, and generalisations — can be managed through the use of probability sampling.

So, by definition, probability sampling excludes the researcher from choosing the sample members and so eliminates selection bias on behalf of the interviewer as well as subjective selection. This, as well as the sampling error estimation, is the great advantage of probability sampling. For these reasons, probability sampling is normally, but not exclusively, used for descriptive research and for causal research. Examples of marketing applications of probability sampling include advertising and promotional studies, pricing studies, sales, market forecasts and brand preferences.[11]

In practice, two things need to be known:

1. each element in the population (hence a sampling frame); and
2. the total number in the population.

In Ireland, some of the larger Irish surveys employ probability sampling on a regular basis, such as the JNRS, as described in Chapter 4.

Non-Probability Sampling

By contrast, non-probability sampling is not based upon any probability principles or laws. The probability of selection is unknown. It is inherently subjective, and not objective, as the sample members are chosen consciously by the researcher. The representativeness of the observed sample is unknown for non-probability sampling. Drawing inferences about the entire population is not possible, as the amount of sampling error cannot be determined. So, non-probability sampling relies solely on the researcher's skills and experience and not on predetermined selection rules.

The main advantages of non-probability sampling are that it:

1. is cheaper, in terms of costs and the time demanded of the investigator;
2. is sometimes easier to conduct;
3. is more convenient than the probability method of sampling; and
4. can be used in the absence of a sampling frame.

Talking with the first ten people who pass by in a shopping centre is the classic example of non-probability sampling. Alternatively, a researcher may have been instructed to talk with 25 UK visitors, 35 US and 15 Japanese tourists, to reflect the breakdown in visitors to Ireland in general, according to Fáilte Ireland statistics.

In the past, non-probability sampling has been closely associated with qualitative data and exploratory research. However, recent times have seen a trend towards the use of probability sampling when conducting exploratory research. With more sophisticated computer models becoming ever available, non-probability sampling is becoming more sophisticated. Quota sampling, one form of non-probability sampling, is discussed later on in this chapter.

The choice between probability and non-probability sampling becomes a question of the advantages and disadvantages of both sampling types, as applied to the particular project. As is evident from the above discussion, probability sampling is statistically superior to non-probability sampling, as probability sampling allows for the calculation of sampling error. Remember, sampling error is defined as the measurement of difference between the actual population parameter and the observed sample estimate of it. In reality, this means that the chosen sample, for whatever reasons, doesn't necessarily mirror the population. Thus, from a marketing researcher's perspective, sampling error can be managed by either increasing the sample size, which decreases the amount of error, or using probability sampling, which calculates the amount of error present. (This statistical dimension to the sampling process is considered in more detail in the next chapter, as we turn our attention to sample size determination.) However, this theoretical advantage of probability sampling can be outweighed by practical considerations; for example, the choice of sampling type is inextricably linked to the availability of a suitable sampling frame. Thus, the choice between probability and non-probability sampling is a question of balancing the purpose of the study with likely error, time and costs. A basic checklist to assist with the decision-making between probability and non-probability sampling is provided in Box 10.1.

Box 10.1 Probability or non-probability checklist

1.	Is there a lot of existing knowledge about the problem?	Yes	No
2.	Do you require very specific information?	Yes	No
3.	Is the research data quantitative?	Yes	No
4.	Is a high level of accuracy called for?	Yes	No
5.	Do you want to generalise the results from your sample to the population?	Yes	No
6.	Do you have an accurate sampling frame?	Yes	No
7.	Is a defined level of confidence required about the results?	Yes	No
8.	Do you want to be able to estimate the amount of sampling error present?	Yes	No
9.	Is there a large budget?	Yes	No
10.	Is serious investment being made?	Yes	No

More 'Yes' answers than 'No' suggest that probability is the preferred sampling mode. More 'No' answers point in the direction of non-probability sampling.

4. Selecting a Sampling Type

Once the decision has been made to pursue either probability or non-probability sampling, the researcher must then turn their attention to the selection of a specific sampling type. Under the auspice of probability sampling, one can choose from simple random sampling, systematic random sampling, stratified random sampling, cluster sampling, area sampling or multi-stage sampling. Non-probability encompasses convenience, purposive, judgment and quota sampling.

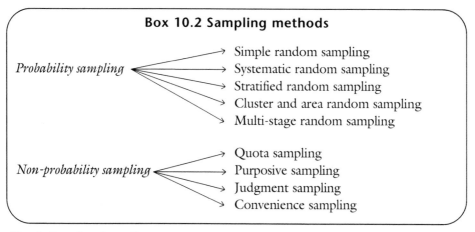

Box 10.2 Sampling methods

Probability sampling
→ Simple random sampling
→ Systematic random sampling
→ Stratified random sampling
→ Cluster and area random sampling
→ Multi-stage random sampling

Non-probability sampling
→ Quota sampling
→ Purposive sampling
→ Judgment sampling
→ Convenience sampling

Simple Random Sampling

Simple random sampling (SRS), is the best-known method of probability sampling. It underpins other probability methods and, for these reasons, it serves as a useful point to begin our discussion.[12]

In simple random sampling, sample members are selected randomly from a population list that contains every member. Each member has a known and an equal chance of being selected. The 'equal' chance of a sample member being selected is a unique feature of simple random sampling. SRS can be with or without replacement. With replacement, SRS means that a member, when picked, is put back into the hat, so to speak, and can be picked again. Without replacement, the more common form of SRS, means that once a member is selected, it is not returned to the list, and so the sample member cannot be chosen again.

The single biggest strength of simple random sampling is its simplicity. Computer-generated random numbers make the administration of simple random sampling very easy and effortless. This is particularly true for a relatively small population. One of the biggest disadvantages of SRS is its dependency upon a complete and accurate sampling frame. Without such a listing, SRS is not possible. Another problem for SRS is its inability to control for sample variation. If the population is heterogeneous, and the sample selected is small, it could potentially be non-representative of the population — you can technically draw all those who are similar and miss some members who are different. An illustration is presented by manufacturing firms in

Ireland. Suppose you generate an accurate and complete list of all firms, large, medium and small, who are manufacturing products at present. It is conceivable, though highly unlikely, that a SRS could result in 90% of the drawn sample being small firms, or 99% being large firms — to the exclusion of the other firms. This would result in an overestimation or underestimation of the sample statistics, e.g. the mean. Such a situation is likely when dealing with a small sample size. A further drawback of SRS is the possible wide geographical spread of the selected sample and therefore the increased costs of travel and data collection. This problem becomes more accentuated when researching and sampling in and across Europe.

Therefore, there are two practical requirements to be fulfilled for a researcher to evoke simple random sampling. These are:

1. an accurate, complete sample frame; and
2. a random selection procedure, e.g. computer-generated random numbers or traditional random tables.

In practice, the generalised procedure for simple random sampling is as follows:

1. Define the population, i.e. unit, element, time, geographic boundary and population parameters of interest.
2. Obtain or generate an accurate, up-to-date, valid and reliable list of defined population.
3. Number the population members or items from 1 to N.
4. Use a random selection procedure (a computer can generate a list of random numbers or alternatively pick a random starting point and select numbers from tables of random numbers).
5. Continue selecting sample members/items until sample size is reached (sample size is predetermined using the relevant formula in the next chapter).
6. Numbers selected constitute the sample members.

Suppose we want to mail our new Christmas hamper catalogue to a sample of managing directors in Ireland. We obtain a relevant and accurate listing from a commercial organisation. We can assign a number to each member and either use computer-generated random numbers or use random tables to select the sample, as illustrated in Box 10.3.

• If there are 10 items in the population, number items from 1–10 and take 2 digits at a time in the random tables.
• If there are 100 items in the population, number items from 1–100 and take 3 digits at a time in the random tables.
• If there are 1,000 items in the population, number items from 1–1,000 and take 4 digits at a time in the random tables.

Box 10.3 Hypothetical listing of managing directors in Ireland

Numbers assigned to population members	*Managing directors*
1	Ruth Kelly
2	Judy Casburn
3	Niall Daveron
4	Denis Nielson
5	Robert Nielson
6	Richard Dunne
7	Kevin Long
8	Catherine O'Connor
9	Michael Keady
10	James Kelly
11	Rory Concannon
12	Catherine Bane
13	David Clancy
14	Siobhan Taxter
15	Bernard Kenny

Based upon the tables in Appendix 1, taking the right-hand column, the following numbers and associated directors were selected: 2, 4, 5, 7, 10 and 11.

Systematic Random Sampling

Systematic random sampling is a variation on simple random sampling.[13] Every n^{th} member of the population is chosen from the sample frame, having started from a random starting point. For example, you have a population of 400 and want a sample of 40. 400 divided by 40 = 10, so n^{th} = every tenth member on the list — hence the name systematic. 1/10 is the sampling fraction. A random starting point is chosen between 1 and 10 (from computer-generated random numbers or random tables) for the first sample member selected and from then on, every following 10th.

The main benefit of systematic random sampling is its ability to deal with a sampling list where ordering is involved, i.e. the population is arranged according to some criteria. For example, if companies are listed according to size or turnover, a systematic sample will produce a selection of elements with varying turnover or size that may be more representative of the population than a simple random sample might be. Another reason for using systematic sampling is its ease of administration. It is not necessary to number every item/member, but just to have a list of the population. Furthermore, we work on the assumption that the population being studied is homogenous — all population members are similar, so systematic sampling is useful as in the case of some commercial directories and professional/trade bodies.

As with simple random sampling, systematic sampling may not satisfactorily deal with periodic population heterogeneity. For example, a highly dispersed population living in different European countries will increase the cost of the research, because it is possible, in drawing a systematic sample, to have most of the sample from one country — which does not fully represent the actual population. Thus, variations that occur in parts of the population (and not all of the population) can result in systematic random sampling producing a less representative sample. Given this, a researcher should consider such 'periodicity' when considering systematic random sampling.

The generalised procedure for systematic sampling is:

1. Define the population, unit, element, time, geographic boundary and population parameters of interest.
2. Obtain or generate an accurate, up-to-date, valid and reliable list of defined population.
3. Calculate the sampling interval.
4. Pick a random starting point, using computer-generated random numbers or random tables between 1 and N/n.
5. Take every n^{th} member/item, until sample size is reached.

Let's say we have a population of 200 students who went parachuting during their summer holidays. Using the formulae in Chapter 11, suppose we require a sample size of 50 students from our population. According to the procedure for systematic sampling, the sampling interval is $200/50 = 4$. We select a random starting point, between 1 and 4, say 2, using random tables in Appendix 1 or computer-generated random numbers. We then return to our population list and select the sample. We start with the second population member, and take every following fourth. So, our systematic sample consists of sample members 2, 6, 10, 14 and 18 and so on. We then collect the needed information from the corresponding respondent.

Stratified Random Sampling

Suppose in our previous example we knew that our parachuting student population was broken down into 100 females and 50 males. We might want to use this information to give us more detailed knowledge about our population (we know from secondary data that female students are more likely to take up parachuting than male students and want to investigate why). In such circumstances, we could use stratified random sampling, a form of probability sampling that allows the researcher to account for variations within the total population. Thus, the concept of segmentation, well known to marketing people, is reflected in stratified random sampling. An entire and whole population is taken and divided into mutually exclusive and collectively exhaustive smaller parts or strata. Members within an individual stratum are similar, while the strata are heterogeneous and vary with respect to the parameter of interest. Within each stratum, simple or systematic random sampling, or another form of probability sampling, is applied. Thus, stratified sampling involves sampling of sub-populations or strata as if they were a separate population, e.g. younger people who text vs. older people who talk. The advantage to such an approach lies in the ability of stratified random sampling to facilitate a researcher in examining the relationship between the selected strata and the parameter(s) of interest which can result in a better estimate of the parameter(s) of interest than either simple or systematic random sampling could produce. This superiority of stratified random sampling is related to the degree of variability across strata and within strata. The higher the similarity within strata and the greater the difference between strata, the more effective the stratified random sampling.

Numbers and Dimensions of Bases of Strata

Once the decision to use stratified sampling has been taken (i.e. there is high variation between population groups and low variation within groups) the researcher has to choose the numbers of strata relevant to the project, along with the differentiating factors, or bases for strata. A decision also has to be made regarding the use of proportionate or disproportionate stratified random sampling.

Generally speaking, it is recommended that there are no more than five or seven strata within the sample (this also assumes a relatively large population). Any more groupings within the sample and the researcher can experience administration and cost difficulties that outweigh the usefulness of stratification. Diminishing returns arise as one increases the number of strata.

The dimensions or bases for selecting the strata are dependent upon the parameters of interest and generally follow usual segmentation principles in marketing — these can be based upon demographic factors, such as age, income, social class, occupation and/or education, psychographic variables, i.e. lifestyle and personality or behavioural variables, heavy or light consumer, brand loyal or usage pattern. Such sub-population detail demands that the researcher has prior knowledge to stratify the population. This knowledge, secured from secondary sources and/or previous research, is used in advance of the sample selection. It is normally recommended to have strata in which the members are as similar as possible while being as different as possible from other members of other strata.

A further issue for the researcher to consider is the question of stratified random sampling being either proportional or disproportional. Proportional stratified sampling signifies that all group strata are proportionally represented in the sample, as in the population. So, if you have 10% of small firms in the population, then the sample contains 10% of small firms. Disproportionate stratified sampling signals that one stratum is weighted as more important than another in the population with respect to the parameter of interest, and therefore should be sampled more extensively. Thus, some strata have more or less variability than others. A commonly used rule in disproportionate sampling is the 80/20 rule or the Pareto principle. For example, 80% of food sales are accounted for by 20% of the grocery outlets, the major multiples. So, 80% of the sample is drawn from the major multiples and the remaining

20% of the sample is taken from the other grocery sellers, such as corner shops, petrol forecourt shops and tobacco outlets.

The generalised procedure for stratified random sampling is:

1. Define the population, unit, element, time, geographic boundary and parameters of interest.
2. Obtain or generate an accurate, up-to-date, valid and reliable list of defined population.
3. Obtain reliable secondary sources of data to stratify population, or alternatively, conduct exploratory research to establish key variables.
4. Choose number and bases of strata.
5. Stratify population list into sub-population lists.
6. Using the relevant formula, determine the sample size.
7. Determine whether to use proportionate or disproportionate sampling.
8. Pick a random starting point, between 1 and N/n, using computer-generated random numbers or random tables.
9. Take every nth member/item, until sample size is reached within stratum one and proceed to stratum two.
10. Repeat steps 6 and 7, until sample is selected.

As is evident from the above discussion, the strength of stratified sampling lies in its ability to combat the issue of population heterogeneity, which can plague simple and systematic random sampling, especially in marketing. This lends more reality to the study. Another advantage of stratified sampling is where the 'strata' vary in size, some being very small and some being large — stratification provides a more accurate picture of the population. In effect, stratified sampling also allows the researcher to treat each stratum as a separate sample, thus allowing for detailed analysis within and across strata (as described in Chapters 13 and 14). Thus, stratified sampling decreases and controls for sampling error. It is less likely to over- or under-estimate the sample statistics, e.g. the mean. This ability to deal with population heterogeneity is very useful from a marketing perspective, as two or more groups can be compared. For example, most branded products compare the attitudes of heavy consumers to light consumers to assist with decisions about product positioning or new advertising campaigns.

From a practical perspective, good secondary data is needed to stratify the population. This may be a potential pitfall, if such information is not readily available. Linked to this potential drawback is the inherent rise in costs associated with the relative complexity of administering stratified random sampling.

The Household Budget Survey 2004–2005 conducted by the CSO[14] (as detailed in Chapter 4), makes use of stratified sampling, where 'an overall random national sample of approximately 16,000 private households (i.e. 8,000 originals and 8,000 substitutes) was initially selected so that each private household in the State had an equal chance of being selected'.

Box 10.4 Stratification of the 2004–2005 Household Budget Survey

As in previous Household Budget Surveys, the sample was stratified for operational and economy reasons to distinguish between two different types of survey areas, namely:
(a) town survey areas located in towns with 1,000 inhabitants or more
(b) country survey areas covering towns with less than 1,000 inhabitants and all rural areas.

A two-stage sample design was used. This comprised a first stage sample of 2,600 blocks (or survey areas) randomly selected at county level to proportionately represent the following eight strata relating to population density:

1. County Borough
2. Suburbs of County Boroughs
3. Environs of County Boroughs
4. Towns 10,000+
5. Towns 5,001–10,000
6. Towns 1,000–5,000
7. Mixed Urban/Rural Areas
8. Rural Areas

Each block was selected to contain, on average, 75 households. In the rural areas, each block was further divided into four sub-blocks, each containing approximately eighteen households. The rural survey areas were randomly selected from within these sub-blocks.

The second sampling stage involved the random selection of two independent samples of four original households and four substitute households for each survey area. The number of original sample households constituted the quota of co-operating households to be realised in each survey area and the interviewer systematically approached as many substitute households as was necessary to realise this quota. In this fashion, variations in response by region and town size were controlled.

The actual number of households for which satisfactorily completed returns were obtained in particular areas was sometimes less than the required quota. This was either because the number of substitute households was not sufficient when the response was low or some of those who initially promised to co-operate dropped out of the survey during the fourteen-day diary/record-keeping and substitutes could not be introduced before the interviewer left the area.

Source: www.cso.ie, 2006.

Cluster Sampling

Under this form of probability sampling, the population is sub-divided into manageable clusters or groups, as opposed to individuals, and simple random sampling is conducted to select the clusters or groups. So, cluster sampling selects groups rather than individuals and involves sampling from a sample of the population. Unlike stratified sampling, a list of the population members is not required, the idea being that groups naturally form or cluster together. As the old adage goes, 'birds of a feather flock together', i.e. social classes tend to live in the same areas, people of like professions or interests congregate together in clubs. To use cluster sampling:

1. Define the population of interest, i.e. element, unit, time, geographic boundary and parameters of interest.
2. Classify the population according to predetermined cluster information drawn from secondary sources of data or previous research.
3. Randomly select a sample of clusters or groups for further sampling.
4. Collect data from members within the selected cluster, by conducting either a sample or census.

For cluster sampling to work, the clusters have to be mutually exclusive and collectively exhaustive. Advantage-wise, cluster sampling saves time and money, as well as providing an estimate of the sampling error. Against this, cluster sampling can suffer from too tightly defined clusters and so hinder the administration of the study.

From first appearances, cluster sampling is identical to stratified sampling, and there are obvious similarities. Both forms of sampling divide the population into sub-groupings. Both use criteria to break down the total group into smaller groups (the same criteria can be used in either forms). However, there is one fundamental difference. In stratified sampling, we have a complete population list which is then stratified according to predetermined variables. This implies that each population member (regardless of stratum) has a known chance of inclusion in the sample. The sample is selected from each sub-group. By contrast, in cluster sampling, there is no physical population listing (though the researcher works on the assumption that one could be developed, given time and cost constraints), and the clusters are chosen first; and from within each chosen cluster, sample members are selected. So, in cluster sampling, one chooses a sample of sub-groups and thus utilises probability sampling twice.

Area Sampling

Area sampling is a variation upon cluster sampling. When a population is concentrated in certain areas, it is normal to use area sampling. A simple random sample is taken of groups or areas instead of a simple random sample of individuals. In this manner, area sampling is a form of cluster sampling based upon geography.

Suppose you are establishing a pizza and fast-food restaurant chain in Leinster. You break the population down into mutually exclusive and collectively exhaustive groups. In this case, we might use the CSO classification of country or county borough for our area sampling.

Figure 10.2 Area sampling in operation

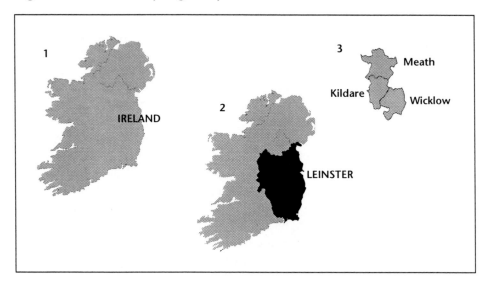

Area sampling is a practical method for conducting a probability sample when no sample listing is available, but it is theoretically possible to generate a list. The geographic restriction tends to decrease costs and time constraints while still enabling sample error calculations. Compared to simple random sampling, area sampling can suffer from the fact that people with similar demographic and psychographic profiles tend to live in similar areas — potentially leading to a reduced statistical efficiency for this approach.

Multi-stage Sampling

Multi-stage sampling (as opposed to single stage, such as cluster sampling described above) is where probability selection methods are pursued at a number of different stages within a sampling procedure. The effect of this is a probability sample where every member has a known chance of being included in the final sample. For example, in proceeding from province to county to urban and rural districts to particular households, we are using a four-stage sampling approach. In this manner, multi-stage sampling combines the advantages of cluster and area sampling for practical application, and cost and labour savings. It allows researchers to use probability sampling at a macro level, where there is no relevant sampling frame or list.

Multi-stage sampling is different from stratified sampling, in that multi-stage sampling divides the population into groups or clusters, from which a few clusters or areas are sampled. Remember, in stratified sampling, the population is also divided into groups, or strata, and all strata are sampled.

Non-Probability Sampling

There are occasions in marketing research when probability sampling is not required or feasible. For example, as is often the case with exploratory research, becoming more familiar with the population and their views is more important than having a representative sample. In such circumstances, non-probability samples, which are not statistically derived, provide no estimate of sampling error and do not enable one to generalise from the sample to the population, are valid. They are, however, very popular when there is no sample frame, and ease of use, cost and time are a concern.

Consider the situation where a small kitchen-units manufacturing firm for the Dublin market wants to look at potential ways of expanding the business. With three employees and very limited marketing resources, the firm just wants initial ideas to consider. Surveying and probability sampling are neither required nor possible for this company at this time. Instead they may be better served to talk with ten important customers and ask them what other furniture needs they have or have had in the recent past. Such customers might be in the office at an appropriate time, or the firm might have such discussions when fitting the kitchen. Either way, the results would not be used to generalise about other customers or the market, but would be of great value in suggesting further avenues of investigation.

As already identified, there are four types of non-probability sampling, convenience, purposive, judgment and quota sampling. Quota sampling is the most popular of all the non-probability methods, because of the ready availability of demographic data which assists with the administration of quota sampling. In recent years, hybrid sampling is occurring with increasing regularity. This is where probability and non-probability are combined to improve the overall results. For example, area sampling is first chosen and then followed by judgment sampling. The broad types of non-probability sampling are now discussed.

Convenience Sampling

Here, the units or members for sampling easily present themselves to the investigator for selection — customers walk into your shop, people in the street or shopping centre. Respondents are chosen 'because they are there', or by accident, because they are walking down the street, hence the name, convenience. Radio chat-shows, such as Joe Duffy's *Liveline,* are an example. This sample is the easiest to access, relatively cheap compared with probability sampling, and not time-bound. It has the advantage of facilitating large numbers of questionnaires to be completed, quickly and economically. Against these advantages, convenience sampling may be seriously non-representative. Take people walking down a street — it excludes those working, those in shops at that time, and those elsewhere, so the results generated pertain to the sample and the sample only. As with all non-probability sampling, inferences and generalisations about the population are not possible. For these reasons, convenience sampling is acceptable for exploratory research, where it may assist in developing further hypotheses. It is not generally recommended for descriptive or causal work.

Purposive Sampling

Purposive non-probability sampling is where the sample members or units are chosen specifically because they are *not* representative of the population. They are chosen according to some predetermined important factor(s) or their extreme position(s) with respect to the product, service, company or attitude they hold. The assumption here is that representativeness is explicitly rejected as the marketing problem calls for the abnormal data, instead of the normal data. A drinks manufacturer might purposively pick respondents who either hate or love the new flavoured carbonated drink to establish the range of opinion. A car manufacturer may select professionally qualified drivers because of their ability to handle difficult driving conditions, or a fast-food restaurant may choose to talk with strict lifelong vegetarians when introducing new vegetarian product alternatives. So, sample members are selected in light of important, predetermined criteria, that are not necessarily representative of the population, but relevant to the success of the project on hand, as laid down by the researcher.

Judgment Sampling

This form of non-probability sampling uses the expertise of the researcher to hand-pick the sample units, in an attempt to bring representativeness to the sampling approach. The units are judged by the researcher to be representative or typical of the population. For example, the Consumer Price Index from the CSO is based upon a judgment sample of market basket items.

Alternatively, the researcher can use 'experts' to identify the sample. If dealing with a small finite population, such as those Irish companies hand-making customised carpets, judgment sampling can be effective. It is cheap, easy and time-saving. It is dependent on the researcher having an excellent knowledge of the population. It is based on the premise that the researcher *thinks* the sample is representative of the general population, rather than actually being so.

Snowball sampling is another term often associated with judgment sampling. It is where the researcher asks the respondent to name other potential participants who are experts or conform to the population definition. For example, in examining the effect of the Internet on marketing practice in Ireland, snowball sampling was effectively used to identify Internet experts who may not have been nationally known, but possessed in-depth knowledge and/or experience of the topic.[15] While a cost-effective method for a small population or emerging area, it can suffer from 'friends recommending friends' and so detract from the results, i.e. respondents from a similar background will tend to hold similar attitudes, opinions, views and expectations.

Furthermore, it cannot be guaranteed that the judgment or snowball sample is representative of the population (as is the case with all non-probability samples).

Quota Sampling

The most popular of all the non-probability sampling methods is quota sampling. It is the one non-probability method that *attempts* to replicate the population *without* using random selection. Predetermined controls, such as age, sex and social class, are used to select sample units. These controls are proportionate to the population. If the population has 20% female members, then 20% of the observed sample is also female. The assumption is that the sample is representative from a practical dimension (if conducted correctly) but, theoretically speaking, there is no calculation of sampling error. Quota sampling thus attempts to select a sample that resembles the population, but there is no mechanism to confirm or falsify this.

To illustrate, take the following hypothetical situation. You are marketing manager for an organic yogurt product, and are considering introducing a new variety and wish to test the market. You don't have a complete listing of all yogurt purchasers, so you segment the market by age and social class, using Census of Population and Household Budget Survey figures from the government publications by the CSO. It results in the matrix shown in Figure 10.2.

Figure 10.3 Hypothetical yogurt consumption, 2007

35% = ABC1	65% = C2DE
55% = 15–35	45% = 36+

You now deliberately select elements for your sample that reflect the population statistics, so that the aggregate picture from your research reflects the total population. Accordingly, since 35% of the population are ABC1, you require 35% of your sample to be ABC1; and since 45% of the population are 36+, you require your sample to have 45% of respondents 36+. On this basis, fieldworkers select respondents that conform to the predetermined criteria for the quota sampling. Interviewing of respondents continues, until the desired number of respondents is fulfilled. In Ireland, quota variables are readily available from the CSO at a district electoral division (DED).

Controls can be one-dimensional, such as age; two-dimensional such as age and social class; or more, such as age, social class, occupation and income. Regardless of the number of controls selected, they have to be easy to use, current, available, accessible and relevant. As a result, good secondary sources are critical to quota sampling, and used extensively in the administration of quotas. An added benefit to quota sampling is that a sampling frame is not needed. Furthermore, the researcher does not have to call back to a particular respondent if they are not at home. They can proceed to another respondent who meets the quota criteria and is at home, thus saving money and time for the researcher. For example, the first election day survey in Ireland was conducted among a representative quota sample of 1,239 electors who had voted or actually intended to vote in the 1997 election. The sample extended across 200 locations covering all 41 constituencies in the Republic.[16] While a sample of 1,000 votes gives a margin of about +/-3%, there are serious concerns that even this minimum sample of 1,000 electors is too small to measure support for parties under Ireland's proportional representation system.[17] Quota sampling is therefore commonly used in the consumer markets, but less so in the services and industrial markets. Nevertheless, quota sampling, like all other non-probability sampling methods, may not be representative of the population, despite the researcher's efforts.

One of the biggest hurdles to employing quota sampling can be the interviewer bias that is naturally present in selecting units. This can be counteracted by employing trained, experienced interviewers and stringent field controls. Another disadvantage of quota sampling concerns those who refuse to be interviewed. Their very refusal could mean they are different in some way from those who positively respond. This inherent selection bias, in effect self-selection, results in us having no estimate of sampling error or knowing how representative the sample is of the population.

Of all of the non-probability sampling methods, quota sampling is the most extensively used method in Ireland for survey work by professional research organisations.[18] The quota predetermined criteria are drawn from CSO Census of Population data, normally at district electoral division. This offers all firms a practical, cost-effective and speedy alternative to probability sampling.

5. Sample Size Determination

Sample size is the next issue for the researcher to confront in the sampling process — this is given special attention in the next chapter.

6. Selection and Validation of Sampling

This step in sampling overlaps with fieldwork, normally considered under the data collection heading. Suffice it to say that actual selection and validation of the sample occurs during the fieldwork stage of the marketing research project. This administration of the sampling procedure should aim to maximise the collection of information and minimise the amount of error. The validation of the sample is a simple checking that the actual sample units or members are who they are meant to be, i.e. they are part of the defined population.

ONLINE SAMPLING

As with most of the technological developments in marketing research, sampling on the Internet raises a number of issues not encountered in the offline environment.[19, 20, 21, 22, 23, 24, 25] For instance, coverage is a particular problem for consumer surveys because the level of Internet usage in Ireland remains relatively low. The penetration of the Internet has not as yet developed to the extent that it represents the population as a whole. H. Taylor describes the Internet population as being younger and possessing a higher standard of education than the public at large.[26]

Furthermore, there is no central listing of email addresses and no online analogue of the telephone book or random-digit dialling.[27] The marketing researcher cannot, in general, buy a good sampling list, such as can be obtained for the telephone. Added to this, is the complication that people change their email addresses far more often that their telephone numbers or their place of residence.[28] It is worth bearing in mind the need for attention to detail. The exact email address must be captured since there is no room for error. The postal service might be able to deliver a letter with typographical errors in the address printed on the envelope or an address that is less than precise, but this is not tolerated on the web.[29]

Another issue of primary concern to the marketing researcher is 'spamming'. Spam email is unsolicited, unwanted email. Given that the cost of sending an email is practically zero, there is the constant danger that organisations, not understanding how to use the Internet for communication purposes, adopt a 'mass communication' approach and send a standard message to as many recipients as possible and unintentionally create spam research emails. Disagreement remains as to whether participation in mass emails should be restricted to those who explicitly agree to receive such messages, or whether an 'opt-out' only approach should prevail.[30] ESOMAR guidelines state that researchers should not send unsolicited email messages to respondents who have indicated that they do not wish to receive such messages. However, it is much safer to adopt the principle of 'informed consent' and obtain the permission of a potential respondent before sending a survey.[31] Permission can be obtained during a web-site registration process or via an offline method such as a telephone interview or print media advertisement. Such an online/offline hybrid design that recruits respondents offline through the telephone or in-person interviewing can be very effective.[32]

Based on the foregoing, it is clear that marketing researchers should be extremely wary of opportunities to purchase lists of email addresses that have been collected from the Internet using 'spiders' and other web crawling devices. Owners of these email addresses will not be aware that their addresses have been captured and will certainly not have provided their prior informed consent to be approached in connection with the research project in hand. Furthermore, such email addresses are often captured from very specific interest sites or from very heavy users of the Internet who may not be representative of the population. Sample units can also be recruited through placing advertisements in relevant online newsletters (also called 'ezines') or by placing banner or button advertisements on relevant web-sites.

Many online researchers have found it necessary to use a double opt-in procedure for recruiting participants for their surveys, obtaining, then verifying, permission to send questionnaires via e-mail before doing so. The firms communicate with prospective respondents by e-mail or via a web-site.[33]

One way to ensure precise online samples is to construct a sampling frame from those persons who visit a particular web-site. As the researcher has control over which visitors are approached to be part of the sample, it is possible to accurately construct an online quota sample. A good example of this is the case of an online survey, where web-site visitors are offered a chance to complete a survey via a 'pop-up box' (a minimised browser window). The researcher has complete control over the visitors who can see the pop-up box, and can control for one or more predetermined 'trigger' such as a specific domain (such as .ie, .co.uk or .com), time of the day, visitor number, or access to a specific web page. The term 'cookie' refers to information files that are downloaded onto a user's hard drive when a user visits a web-site. Their purpose is to enable a user's preferences or unique traits to be remembered on future requests, and to authenticate users when they return to a web-site so they don't have to log in every time. They are commonly used for online shopping and on personalised portals or web gateways. Privacy advocates have raised concerns over the role of cookies – they fear that companies could piece together information that could be used against individuals, especially if offline information is merged with online information, and the issue has attracted the attention of the European Commission.[34]

The Internet has a number of advantages in terms of sampling, than in the offline environment. The richness and granularity of information is higher online; it becomes easier to achieve more accurate samples; the cycle time for processing information decreases and the cost per respondent decreases. In software, computers, networking, technical publishing, semiconductors and graduate education, it is rapidly becoming feasible to use the Internet for sampling respondents for quantitative research, such as surveys.[35] The main drawback of targeting survey respondents via the Internet is the anonymity of respondents. Some users, mainly in chat rooms, are known to create alternate personae. Multiple submissions can also be a problem as they invalidate data, and on the Internet they may be easier to create.

Online marketing researchers should be wary that the possible ease of achieving very large sample sizes (particularly relative to those available offline) raises the risk of burning out respondents and reducing their willingness to co-operate with another project in the future. Hence, sample sizes should only be as large as is required.[36]

SUMMARY

Sampling is central to the success of a marketing research study and is one of the most powerful tools a researcher has. Sampling allows us to study some of the cases of interest, at the same time drawing useful conclusions for all.

Throughout this chapter, we have examined the basic concepts of sampling — the population, the sample, population parameters, sample estimate and sampling error, along with the sampling process itself.

The first consideration is whether to conduct a census or a sample. If a sample is chosen, the researcher proceeds with defining the population, generating a sampling frame, selecting a sampling type and form, determining a sample size and selecting the actual sample.

The researcher can choose between probability and non-probability sampling, depending on the nature of information sought, population of interest, error tolerance, time and cost constraints. The probability sampling methods include simple random sampling; systematic random sampling; stratified random sampling; cluster sampling; area sampling and multistage sampling. Non-probability embraces convenience sampling; judgment sampling; purposive sampling and quota sampling. Each form of sampling has its own advantages and disadvantages which need to be considered for the project on hand.

KEY TERMS

Sampling	Census
Population	Sample
Sample estimate	Population parameter
Probability	Non-probability
Sampling process	Element
Unit	Sampling error
Sampling proportion	Selection bias
With replacement	Without replacement
Simple random sampling	Systematic random sampling
Stratified random sampling	Strata
Cluster random sampling	Area random sampling
Multistage random sampling	Convenience sampling
Judgment sampling	Purposive sampling
Quota sampling	Hybrid sampling
Sample size	Validation

QUESTIONS

1. Why is sampling used so often in marketing research?
2. Distinguish between a census and a sample.
3. Identify the steps involved in the sampling process.
4. What is meant by the term 'population'?
5. What is meant by a 'sampling frame'?
6. Give an example of a perfect sample frame. Justify your choice.

7. Why is a telephone directory often not an acceptable sample frame of a particular city or area?
8. What distinguishes a probability sample from a non-probability sample?
9. How should a simple random sample be selected? Describe the procedure.
10. Which sampling method typically produces more precise estimates of a population mean — simple random sampling or stratified sampling? Why?
11. What is a convenience sample?
12. Distinguish, using examples, between the different types of non-probability sampling procedures.
13. What are the benefits of stratified sampling?
14. Simple random samples are rarely used for door-to-door interviewing. Why do you think this is true?
15. Compare and contrast stratified random sampling with quota sampling.
16. Detail the advantages and disadvantages of online sampling.

PROBLEMS AND ASSIGNMENTS

1. XYZ Q-Stacker supplies computer chips to the car and consumer electronics industries. XYZ Q-Stacker sells to different-sized companies in each of these industries and to companies in all regions of the world. Historically, XYZ Q-Stacker management has noted sales differences by industry type, size, and geographic region. XYZ Q-Stacker desires to select a quota sample to predict the sales level of a new product offering.
   (a) What control characteristics should be used for this quota sample?
   (b) What would one need to know about these control characteristics for them to be useful in this study?
   (c) State how many respondents would be specified for each cell.
   (d) What inferences could be drawn about XYZ Q-Stacker's entire customer base from such a sample?
2. You are asked to make recommendations as to the type of sample to be used, the method of selecting the sample, and the sample size, in each of the following situations:
   (a) The manager of the appliance department of a local department store chain is planning a major one-day non-price promotion of food processors, supported by heavy advertising in the two local newspapers. The manager asks you to recommend a method of sampling customers coming into the department. The purpose is to assess the extent to which customers were drawn by the special advertisement, and the extent to which the advertisement influenced their intentions to buy. A pre-test of the questionnaire indicates that it will take about three minutes to administer. The manager is especially interested in learning whether there are significant

differences in the response to the questionnaire among (a) males versus females, (b) gift buyers versus other buyers, and (c) age groups.

(b) A major airline wants to run a preliminary study on the attitudes of university students towards air travel. The company's research director already has submitted an interview plan and has estimated that, on average, each interview will require between an hour and an hour-and-a-half to administer. It is estimated that the cost of interviewing and interpreting the interview will be roughly €75 per respondent.

(c) A sample of homeowners in the Dublin South area is desired for a major segmentation study conducted by a large financial institution. A lengthy personal interview lasting over one hour will be conducted with each respondent. A sample size of 3,000 is targeted.

3. The host of a phone-in programme on a local radio station suggests that listeners call in to record their 'votes' concerning whether or not the city council should permit free parking on parking meters in the city centre area on Saturdays. Of 230 telephone calls recorded during the three-hour programme, 84% of callers felt that parking should be free on Saturdays. What is your opinion of this sampling technique? If you were the county council or mayor, how would you respond?

4. 'The Big Shirt Company', a manufacturer of clothing for large-sized consumers, was in the process of evaluating its product and advertising strategy. Initial efforts consisted of a number of focus-group interviews. Each focus group consisted of ten to twelve large men and women of different demographic characteristics who were selected by the company's research department using on-the-street observations of physical characteristics.
(a) What type of sampling method was used?
(b) Critically evaluate the method used.

5. A leading film-processing company wishes to investigate the market potential for a new line of digital processing equipment. Because this is a completely new technology, it is felt that industry leaders might offer insights into the desires of customers and consumers. However, a list of industry leaders does not exist. Discuss possible methods of generating a sampling frame for the influential people in the digital processing industry.

6. A mobile telephone company wants to investigate the needs of its customers. Propose a stratification scheme for the sample and discuss the benefits of your scheme.

7. John Murphy, the owner of a local hotel, is interested in assessing customer satisfaction with his hotel. John's hotel does not accept reservations. Because all of his customers are walk-ins, John has no way of knowing how many people will stay in his hotel on any given night. All of the hotel guests must check in with the front-desk receptionist; due to the small size of the hotel, there is only one check-in desk. John has decided to distribute a survey to every tenth room that checks in:

   (a) What type of sampling is to be used?

   (b) Critically evaluate this method.

8. Name some possible sampling frames for the following:

   (a) Patrons of a wine bar.

   (b) Owners of hamsters.

   (c) Tennis players.

   (d) Fishing rod owners.

   (e) Retailers of *Home and Garden Magazine*.

   (f) Emigrants to the US of less than two years.

   (g) Women wearing size 10 dresses.

9. Identify the following sample designs:

   (a) The names of 20 patrons of a bingo hall are drawn out of a hat and a questionnaire is administered to them.

   (b) A radio talk-show host invites listeners to call in and vote 'Yes' or 'No' on banning nuclear weapons.

   (c) A dog-food manufacturer wants to test a new cat food. It decides to select 100 cat owners who feed their cats canned food, and 100 who feed their cats dry food.

10. A financial services company wants a survey of Internet users to see if they are interested in using the company's financial planning Internet services. Previous studies have shown that Internet usage differs greatly by age, education and gender. The total sample size will be 1,000. Using actual information about Internet usage, or supplying reasonable assumptions, indicate how stratified simple random sampling should be applied for each of the following stratification situations:

   (a) Age ranges of 18–25, 26–50, and 51–65.

   (b) Education levels of second-level, some third-level, third-level qualification and postgraduate qualification.

   (c) Gender: males versus females.

11. A 'Lotto' player is curious about the randomness of winning lottery numbers. He has kept track of the winning numbers in the past five weeks and finds that most numbers were selected 25% of the time, but the number 6 was one of the winning numbers 50% of the time. Will he be more or less likely to win if he picks a 6 in this week's lottery, or will it not make any difference in his chances? Relate your answer to simple random sampling.

12. A local retailer has asked you to select a sample of 50 'fashion leaders'. These leaders will be paid €20 each to 'evaluate' the shop's layout and merchandise selection. The shop carries men's and women's clothing. Describe the sampling process you would use.

13. For each situation below, critique the method used and suggest alternatives you consider better where appropriate:

(a) To study attitudes toward a fast-food chain, interviewers were stationed in the car parks of the chain, and questioned all those willing to answer.

(b) In studying the results of a screening method for credit card applications for a department store, folders of applicants were selected at a fixed interval beginning at the front for each file drawer.

(c) To develop information on the purchasers of its new video game, the manufacturer made the activation of the product warranty conditional upon the receipt of the warranty card, which also contained a short questionnaire.

14. Define the appropriate target population and the sampling frame in each of the following situations:

(a) The manufacturer of a new cereal brand wants to conduct in-home product usage tests in Dublin.

(b) A national chain store wants to determine the shopping behaviour of customers who have its store charge card.

(c) An Irish TV station wants to determine households' viewing habits and programming preferences.

(d) The regional branch of the Marketing Institute wants to test the effectiveness of its new-member drive in Waterford.

Case Study
Assessing the Quality of Life in Waterford City*

A key objective of modern public policy is: 'How to maintain, improve, and measure quality of life' (Jones, A. and Riceborough, M., *Comparing Quality of Life Research – International Lessons.* University of Birmingham, http://www.curs.bham.ac.uk/whatsnew/publications.htm, 2002). The criticality of this objective is reflected in the efforts of researchers in the United Kingdom, Australia, Canada and New Zealand to measure the quality of life (QOL) of each country's citizens so that researchers can track the future development of each of their respective countries. The European Union has also placed QOL issues and the measurement of QOL at the top of their social policy agenda (European Foundation, 2006).

In the Irish context, the Irish government recognises that QOL issues are paramount to the formation of its own public policy (National Spatial Strategy, 2002–2020). At a local government level, City Development Boards (CDBs) were created by the Taskforce on Local Government and Local Development in March 2002. A major goal set for each CDB was to implement a ten-year strategy for the economic, social and cultural development of each CDB's respective city. A significant component of the board's strategic framework involves the measurement of their citizens' quality of life (QOL). A major issue facing the CDB's goal of improving the QOL of their citizens is the identification of dimensions which positively and negatively impact QOL. This knowledge would enable the CDB to target problem areas with intervention strategies. The success of the intervention strategies would then be assessed over time by periodically measuring QOL. However, in order to implement the foregoing, the board needs a base index, thereby providing a benchmark for QOL longitudinal studies. To measure QOL, researchers must first identify its dimensions – called 'domains' and then identify 'indicators' to measure each domain.

In this case study on Waterford City, a task force of CDB members was formed in order to manage the QOL project. The overall aim of the group was to benchmark how the citizens of Waterford rate their quality of life.

The task force then decided to outsource their research problem to a local research group. Researchers soon determined, from discussions with their client and from their own 'desk' research, that:

- The goal of their client required the collection of 'hard' data.
- Due to resource issues, a survey of the entire city's population would not be viable; therefore it would be imperative that their sampling strategy ensured that survey respondents would be representative of the population of interest.
- Conceptualising quality of life would be problematic; their qualitative research indicated that a generally accepted definition of QOL doesn't exist – either nationally or internationally.
- Because there isn't a general consensus on what QOL is, this meant that the measurement of QOL would also be problematic; there were many differing measurement scales available to them.

Questions

1. Define the population of interest and develop a profile of the population.
2. Based on your description, prepare a sampling strategy that results in a sample that is representative of the population of interest. Discuss and rationalise the decisions you have made.
3. Compare and contrast the advantages/disadvantages of probability sampling and non-probability sampling.

References

European Foundation, 2006, Quality of Life. Available from http://www.eurofound.eu.int/areas/qualityoflife/index.htm [Accessed 10 March 2006].

Department fo the Environment and Local Government, 2002. National Spatial Strategy, 2002–2020. Available from: http://www.irishspatialstrategy.ie/publications.shtml [Accessed 11 March 2006].

*This case was written by Dr Mary Holden, Waterford Institute of Technology. It is intended to be used as a basis for class discussion rather than to illustrate the effective or ineffective handling of an administrative situation. The case is based upon a real situation, though certain information has been disguised.

Case Study
Galway Bay Health Farm*

Introduction

Agritourism seeks to target those segments of the market that want environmentally satisfying holidays, away from congested visitor centres. Margaret and Gerry McNulty, who operate a health farm as well as a deer farm in Oranmore, County Galway, are an example of the innovative opportunities that exist for agritourism development.

The McNultys, like many other owner/managers, find it is a challenge to maintain excellence in their operations, while meeting their customers' changing demands. As the McNultys are expanding the health farm's physical facilities and services, they are relying on their efforts in marketing communications to augment client numbers. Moreover, increasing competition from other health farms, spas and relaxation centres means the McNultys must identify the appropriate market segments to target and the most effective means of communicating with these markets.

Health Tourism and Factors Affecting Demand

The idea of taking leisure/recuperative holidays is not new. Since the days of the ancient Greek and Roman baths, people have been taking health breaks to escape the stresses of everyday urban life while improving their general health. Recently, this activity has rapidly increased in popularity. A shift in the age profile of the population of the industrialised world towards the 40 plus age group, increased leisure time, higher disposable income and a greater awareness of the importance of preventative medicine, are all factors contributing to the increased interest in health farms, spas and relaxation centres.

In Continental Europe, spas are considered an important complement to modern medicine as well as being popular holiday destinations. The traditional spa is now a modern resort offering a wide range of facilities. The improvement to facilities and the enhanced range of services offered within these Continental spas are in recognition of the need to attract the health-conscious visitor.

Health farms are a British spin-off from the demise of the traditional spas, from a level of 80 centres early in the previous century to a current level of single-figure locations. Over the last two decades, they have changed radically with the development of a wide range of treatments, a greater emphasis on exercise, pampering and relaxation, as well as a vast improvement in the quality of food and accommodation. The line is now narrowing between health farms and hotels that have special health and leisure facilities. The target market is similar, with the 35 to 65 age group identified as the predominant market segment, although the younger, fitter user (i.e. under 35 years), who typical takes a day or weekend break, is becoming an increasingly important segment.

There is a lack of market information on health farms, spas and relaxation centres, largely because different countries define the product differently. Approximately 16 million Europeans visit health resorts or spas each year. In Europe, Germany is by far the biggest user of spas, followed by Italy, Austria, France and Switzerland. Within the USA, 15 million Americans visit health resorts or spas each year, with 'Baby Boomers' (i.e. those born between 1945 and 1965) representing 60% of the market.

The growth in health farms, spas and relaxation centres worldwide is being driven by a number of broad societal changes that are greatly influencing the market place:

- The 35 to 65 age group has the disposable income to escape the escalating stress of everyday life. In addition, people within this demographic segment are typified as having an increased desire to achieve a higher state of wellness and longevity as they age.
- The 35 to 65 age group has the propensity and the ability to purchase upscale travel products. Moreover, they have been shown to spend ever-increasing amounts of money on health, fitness and beauty aids.
- By the year 2020, half of the world's population will be over the age of 40. The growth in this demographic segment can be attributed to both increased life expectancy and the sheer volume of the people moving through the life cycle.
- People over 65 years of age spend three times what those under 65 do on health-care products and services. This expenditure includes traditional and alternative medical practices.

Galway Bay Health Farm's Competitors

There are a number of small health farms and centres in Ireland, including Ireland's first accredited thalassotherapy centre at Inchydoney in Co. Cork; the only centre of this kind outside of Continental Europe. There are nine health farms and centres approved by Fáilte Ireland, one of which is the Galway Bay Health Farm. These health farms are also members of the Health Farms of Ireland Association, the consortium representing health farms and recommended by Tourism Ireland Ltd. A full list of Fáilte Ireland-approved health farms is given in Table 10.2.

A number of other resorts and centres operate and market themselves as health spas and health tourism products throughout the country. However, these resorts have not been approved by Fáilte Ireland as health farms and are listed in Table 10.3. Health spas are priced on a per person basis, either by pamper, one-day non-residential programmes, weekends, or two- to six-day residential programmes. Typically, prices are inclusive of treatments, meals, use of facilities, exercise classes, lectures and a medical and/or nutritional consultation. Prices at health farms in Ireland range from €75 for a one-day non-residential programme to €2,500 for a seven-night stay. Typical treatments include massage, aromatherapy and reflexology, as well as a wide range of beauty treatments.

Table 10.2 Members of the Health Farms of Ireland Association

Name	Location
Claureen Health Farm	Lahinch Rd., Ennis, Co. Clare
Cloona Health Centre	Westport, Co. Mayo
Delphi Mountain Resort & Spa	Leenane, Co. Galway
Galway Bay Health Farm	Oranmore, Co. Galway
Powerscourt Springs Health Farm	Coolakay, Enniskerry, Co. Wicklow
Rosmoney Spa & Seaweed Baths	Westport, Co. Mayo
Temple Country House & Spa	Horseleap, Moate, Co. Westmeath
The Sanctuary (An Tearmann Beag)	Mooresfort, Kilross, Co. Tipperary
Walton Court Country House Retreat & Spa	Oyster Haven, Co. Cork

Source: Health Farms of Ireland Centres, Retreats and Spas, 2006.

Table 10.3 Supply of other health tourism products in Ireland

Name	Location
Annaghdown Seaweed Baths	Corrundulla, Co. Galway
Anvil House Therapeutic Centre	Fouksmill, Co. Wexford
Ard Nahoo Health Farm	Mullagh, Dromahaire, Co. Leitrim
Ballycoursey Lodge Health Spa	Enniscorthy, Co. Wexford
Bridíns Health & Beauty at Clarence House	Wexford City
Buttercups at The Grand Hotel	Malahide, Co. Dublin
Centre for Holistic Health	Cork City
Celtic Seaweed Baths	Strandhill, Sligo
Coolbawn Quay Lakeshore Spa	Lough Derg, Co. Tipperary
Dolphin Day Spa	Batterstown, Co. Meath
Dunboyne Castle Hotel & Spa	Dunboyne, Co. Meath
Eskine House of Silence	Tahilla, Co. Kerry
Grove House Longevity & Health Centre	Mallow, Co. Cork
Hagal Healing Farm	Coomleigh, Bantry, Co. Cork
Hot Seaweed Baths	Enniscrone, Co. Sligo

Name	Location
Imperial Hotel & Escape Salon & Spa	South Mall, Cork City
Johnstown House and Spa	Enfield, Co. Meath
Kilkee Thalassotherapy Centre	Kilkee, Co. Clare
Kachina Natural Spa	Moneen, Castlebar, Co. Mayo
Lakelands House	Annyalla, Castleblaney, Co. Monaghan
Lilac Lodge Spa	Hotel Kilkenny, College Rd., Kilkenny
Lios Dána Holistic Centre	Inch Beach, Annascaul, Co. Kerry
Little House of Avalon	Ballinasloe, Co. Galway
Minehill Health Studio	Kilternan, Co. Dublin
Monart Destination Spa	The Still, Enniscorthy, Co. Wexford
Mulvarra House	Graiguenamanagh, Co. Kilkenny
Olde Rectory Manor Country House & Health Spa	Duncormick, Co. Wexford
Pauline's Beauty Salon	Deehan House, Tullamore, Co. Offaly
Pine Lodge Health Retreat & Spa	Tullamore, Co. Offaly
Plush Day Spa	Castletroy, Co. Limerick
Radisson SAS Hotel & Spa Cork	Ditchley House, Little Island, Cork
Re Fresh	Leopardstown, Dublin
Sakura Spa	Roganstown, Swords, Co. Dublin
Samhin So, Lochan Beag	Inverin, Co. Galway
Sligo Natural Health Centre	Drumcliff, Co. Sligo
Spirit One Spa	Radisson Hotel, Galway City
Tinarana House Rejuvenation Centre	Killaloe, Co. Clare
Thalassotherapy Centre, Inchydoney	Inchydoney, Co. Cork
Thalassotherapy Centre, Rochestown Park Hotel	Rochestown, Co. Cork
The Buff Day Spa	King St., Dublin City
The K Club	Straffan, Co. Kildare
The Laurkur Clinic	Blackrock, Co. Dublin

Source: Golden Pages, 2006

Product Development

Margaret McNulty relies quite heavily on customer feedback and suggestions to give her an indication of how the health farm should evolve. In addition, Margaret travels to Australia, the US and the Continent, where the health industry is more progressive, to gather ideas for her own premises. As a result of these efforts, Margaret will be expanding her premises to incorporate a yoga room, a relaxation room, a dining room for fifty people, ten treatment rooms, a jacuzzi and a counter-stream swimming pool. Plans for the expansion are drawn and approved and Margaret has received a grant from the Tourism Product Development Scheme (National Development Plan, 2000–2006) towards 30% to 50% of the building costs. Margaret aims to have the extension completed in 2006.

In addition to the physical product attributes, Margaret continuously monitors and updates the services she offers her clients. She aims to run select residential programmes and shorter pamper days with greater intensity. Margaret acknowledges that her own training in aerobics, nutrition and marketing have greatly facilitated product development, as she is able to identify and employ the most suitable people to provide product services. Margaret believes it is the quality of customer care that people remember most from their stay at Galway Bay Health Farm.

Analysing Customers

People who come to Galway Bay Health Farm are predominantly women (80%) between the ages of 24 to 54. They come from a variety of occupations, such as housewives, teachers, nurses, medical personnel, professionals, pensioners, and self-employed. Those who come for a day are often younger women and students who want to have a day to pamper and indulge themselves. Many professionals who come for two to three days are looking to take some time off from their normal routine and have a short holiday. Those who come for the longer residential programmes are often:

- brides who want to take a week of health and beauty;
- single women who want to have a holiday on their own;
- people who want to lose weight and start a new regime; and
- those who need a respite from the stresses in their lives.

In addition, Margaret caters to local companies that seek a customised product, either to entertain customers or to reward staff. These firms usually buy packages of pamper days that can be tailored to suit the needs of customers and staff. To gauge the interest of corporate clients in health farms, the Galway Bay Health Farm undertook a small-scale survey of ten multinational companies within Galway city.[37] The findings indicated the majority of the firms had not used a health farm, spa or relaxation centre in the past. However, all companies indicated they organise health- and activity-based programmes for the employees of clients. The preferred times of year are spring and summer for programmes which generally last either half a day or one full day. Little or no interest was expressed in beauty treatments or alternative therapies. The types of programmes in which the corporate market was most interested were: stress management, relaxation, team-building, keep fit, gym and aerobics. The majority of companies surveyed were prepared to pay between €75 and €150 per person per day. Moreover, the majority of companies indicated they were likely, or somewhat likely, to arrange for employees or clients to visit a health farm within the next twelve months. All firms requested more information about Galway Bay Health Farm and offered further contacts either in their own companies or outside that may require the services of Galway Bay Health Farm.

Another development in the corporate sector is the recent deal agreed with Boots Chemists in the UK and Ireland. Boots has bought a number of gift certificates for pamper days that will be incorporated in their gift hampers for Christmas, Valentine's Day, Mother's Day, etc. Each hamper includes a number of cosmetic and beauty products as well as a 'surprise gift', which is usually a gift certificate for a health/beauty service that 'fits' with the character of the hamper. Galway Bay Health Farm is the only Irish health farm to be included among the possible 'surprise services'. Margaret believes this access to a wider audience will translate into favourable word-of-mouth publicity at a far greater return on investment than other forms of advertising she might have undertaken.

Approximately one-third of the people who come to Galway Bay Health Farm are repeat clients. Of those who come to the health farm for the first time, about half will come as result of word-of-mouth recommendation and/or through the receipt of a gift certificate. About one-third of the health farm's annual turnover can be attributed to gift certificates. Margaret sells about 500 gift certificates a year with a minimum value of €100. Margaret's efforts to maintain contact with clients are principally conducted through direct marketing efforts such as direct mail and e-mail. The database of over 2,000 clients is a useful tool for segmenting, targeting and positioning purposes and is instrumental in guiding her marketing efforts for Galway Bay Health Farm.

Customer Numbers

The number of customers who have come each year is outlined in Table 10.4 and indicates that client numbers have steadily increased. In 1999 the Galway Bay Health Farm began offering single-day and weekend programmes to clients. Much of the growth experienced since then is attributed to the wider range of programmes offered. With respect to seasonality, there are no dramatic peaks and troughs in client numbers. Currently an average of seventy-five clients come to Galway Bay Health Farm each month. The breakdown of clients according to country of origin is given in Table 10.5 and shows the majority are from Ireland.

Table 10.4 Breakdown of customers by year, 1994–2009 (projected)

Year	No. of Clients	Year	No. of Clients
1994	25	2002	607
1995	111	2003	652
1996	231	2004	833
1997	173	2005	898
1998	287	2006 (est.)	950
1999	368	2007 (est.)	1,000
2000	552	2008 (est.)	1,025
2001	563	2009 (est.)	1,050

Source: Galway Bay Health Farm, 2006.

Table 10.5 Breakdown of customers by country of origin

Country of Origin	% Total Clients
Ireland	80%
Northern Ireland	5%
England/Scotland/Wales	3%
America/Sweden/Germany	12%
Total	100%

Source: Galway Bay Health Farm, 2006.

Marketing Communications

The tools Margaret finds most useful in promoting her business are word-of-mouth, publicity, the Internet, sponsorship, direct mail, advertising in the *Golden Pages*, and attending trade shows. Figure 10.4 gives the relative breakdown of funds spent in 2005 and budgeted for in 2006 on marketing communications.

With the expansion to the health farm's physical facilities in 2006, Margaret expects she will be investing significantly more in the marketing and promotion of her enterprise. She wants to ensure she is using the appropriate marketing communications tools to reach her customers. Hence Margaret is thinking of doing some kind of survey. Although Margaret is confident about her product, she is concerned about acquiring the 'right' information she needs to make informed decisions about her marketing communications plan. How would you advise her?

Figure 10.4 Marketing communications methods breakdown for 2005 and 2006

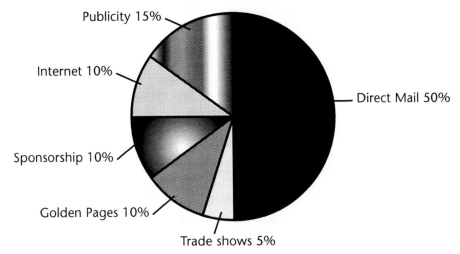

Source: Galway Bay Health Farm, 2006.

Questions

1. With respect to Margaret McNulty's customer base, how would you define the population?
2. What sources of information could she use to develop a sample frame?
3. Do you believe she should engage in probability or non-probability sampling, or perhaps both?
4. Given your answers to the above questions, what suggestions would you make to Margaret McNulty in designing a survey to address her informational needs?

*This case was written by Ann Torres, Marketing Department, NUI, Galway. It is intended to be used as a basis for class discussion rather than to illustrate the effective or ineffective handling of an administrative situation. The case is based upon a real situation, though certain information has been disguised. © Ann Torres.

CHAPTER 11

SAMPLE SIZE DETERMINATION

CHAPTER OVERVIEW

▸ Introduction ▸ Non-Probability Sample Size Determination ▸ The Normal Distribution Curve ▸ The Sampling Distribution for the Mean ▸ The Sampling Distribution for the Proportion ▸ Confidence Intervals ▸ Sample Size Formulae ▸ Sample Size Determination, Finite Populations ▸ Summary

INTRODUCTION

We have seen from the last chapter that there are five key questions every researcher needs to ask about sampling.[1]

1. How has the population been defined?
2. What sampling method was used?
3. What level of accuracy was chosen?
4. How big was the sample?
5. What degree of confidence can be placed in the findings?

So far, we have answered these with the one exception of 'How big a sample to select?' This issue, sample size determination, is the focus of this chapter.

In choosing an appropriate sample size, we are deciding upon the accuracy we want our sample to have and the amount of error we can or cannot tolerate. That is to say, sample size is about how similar we want our sample to be, compared to the population from which it is drawn. At this point, it would seem as if sample size is all about statistics. While this is true of probability sampling, it is important to know that there are a number of alternative methods available to marketing researchers in determining the sample size for non-probability samples. This aside, statistical theory continues to play an important part in sample size determination.

As with the previous discussion about sampling theory, statistical sample size determination has its own terminology. At this point, it is useful for the reader to review some of the basic concepts in statistics, such as measures of central tendency and dispersion, as these and others impact upon sample size. Chapter 12 presents some of these together with worked examples. That done, we examine the normal distribution, standard deviation, mean and confidence intervals, to understand how accuracy, confidence, error and sample size are related. As one would expect, this discussion can get complex, so we confine ourselves and our discussion of statistical principles to simple random sampling. Formulae for stratified random sampling and cluster sampling[2] are beyond the scope of this book. Thus, by the end of this chapter, the reader will become knowledgeable about the:

1. characteristics and properties of a normal distribution curve;
2. standardised value Z;
3. confidence interval estimates;
4. computing of sample size formulates for large and small samples; and
5. non-statistical considerations for non-probability sample size determination.

NON-PROBABILITY SAMPLE SIZE DETERMINATION

When we are using a non-probability sampling procedure, such as convenience or quota sampling, we do not need statistical formulae for non-probability sampling. Instead, we can employ less objective strategies to determine the best-suited sample size for our sample. Suppose you are conducting exploratory research to gauge if there is an opening for a complementary school of alternative medicine and healing in Ireland. Time and money are severely limited. You have already chosen non-probability sampling. How do you decide on the number of people to include in your sample? Faced with such a situation, you can choose from the following options:

1. Intuition, Convenience

You pick a particular number for no other reason other than it is what suits you, the time and budget constraints and it is a figure you are psychologically comfortable with. For example, you choose 1,000 people as a nice, round, even number. This is very much the 'thumbs in the air' approach.

2. Cost Limitations, Affordability

This translates into how large a sample we can afford — what our budget constraints are at the sampling phase, but also at other stages, such as fieldwork, photocopying, etc.

3. Industry Standards, Comparability

This is where you try to emulate what other similar projects or industry standards have done in an effort to be comparable with them, e.g. other healing schools have been set up in France and Switerzland, and have interviewed 5% of the total adult population, so you take 5% of the Irish population as your sample size. This assumes that the previous projects had chosen suitable sample sizes.

Remember, in choosing a sample size for non-probability samples, statistical generalisation is not required; therefore, we can be more flexible in selecting the exact number of respondents to gather information from, as each of the above approaches demonstrate. Now, we are ready to consider statistical sample size approaches used for probability samples. To this end, we begin by examining the normal distribution curve.

THE NORMAL DISTRIBUTION CURVE

Suppose that the marketing researcher collects a large set of data, say 10,000 values from a sample, relating to the daily sales figures for a retail outlet. If these sales figures were listed individually, the sheer volume of numbers would obscure any information contained in the sample figures. Hence the maxim, 'a picture is worth a thousand words'. A histogram can provide a pictorial or graphical view of how such data is distributed. Even more useful, it is possible to express the distribution (of a histogram) in a neat and compact form by a mathematical formula. Hence, in the interest of extracting information from a sample, we can go from raw data to a histogram to a mathematical formula for the distribution of the data.

One of the more useful and popular probability distributions is the normal distribution, also known as the normal curve, as shown in Figure 11.1.

Figure 11.1 The normal distribution curve

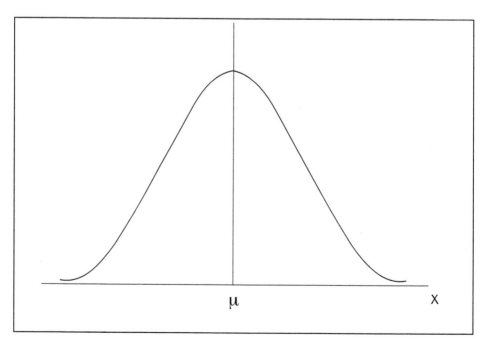

The appropriate mathematical formula for this normal curve is X~N(μ,σ). This formula tells us that:

1. X is just a symbol and represents the random variable of interest, e.g. shop sales, the height of students, the number of shoes purchased, etc. X is not a fixed quantity; it is random, i.e. shop sales are not fixed, but randomly change from day to day and hour to hour.
2. '~' reads 'distributed as'.
3. N stands for normal.
4. μ is the expected value of X, or the long-term average of X.
5. σ^2 refers to the variance of X and is a measure of the spread or dispersion of the data in a sample about its own sample mean.

The properties, among others, of this N (μ,σ^2) curve are:

1. The curve is symmetric about its mean.
2. It is a bell-shaped curve, the highest point being the mean. The curve falls away relatively slowly at first either side of the mean, μ. In other words, there is a high probability of the data values occurring just a little above or below the mean. The further one moves away from the mean, in either direction, the smaller the probability of a data value occurring.
3. Prob (a < X < b) = area under the curve between a and b. Don't get lost in the symbols. X is the random variable of interest and a and b are simply specified values of X. For example, say X represents the daily sales figures of newspapers in Ireland and we want to find the probability that the daily sales figures on any given day will exist between 140,000 and 210,000 papers. We simply write this as Prob(140,000< X <210,000) or P(140,000< X <210,000).
4. X~N(0,1) reads that the curve has a mean = 0 and standard deviation = 1.

This characteristic X~N(0,1) is often referred to as the *standard normal distribution*, where we denote the random variable X, by the special symbol, Z where Z~N(0,1). In other words, the standard normal distribution is very valuable to us, as it enables us to transform any ordinary variable X, e.g. X~N(5,1) or X~N(2,12) into a standardised value, Z, using the equation:

$$Z = \frac{X - \mu}{\sigma}$$

which reads as the value to be transformed minus the mean, divided by the standard deviation[3]. Suppose that the auditing times for companies in Cork city are well described by a normal distribution with a mean of 7 hours and a standard deviation of 3 hours. What is the probability that an accountant will spend more than 10 hours auditing any particular company in Cork city? Well, using the terminology above, let X = auditing time of a Cork city company. Then, X ~N (7, 3). We require P (X > 10). Using the transformation $Z = \frac{X-\mu}{\sigma}$, we obtain

$$P(X>10) = P\left(\frac{X-\mu}{\sigma} > \frac{10-7}{3}\right) = P(Z>1) = 0.3413.$$

Therefore, there is a 34.13% probability that an accountant will spend more than 10 hours auditing any particular company in Cork city. The advantages of applying this transformation lie in probabilities of the resultant variable Z being found in Appendix 2.

Thus, Z represents the standard deviations from the mean. Using a normal distribution table such as that in Appendix 2, we can say as shown in figure 11.2 that:

68% of observations will occur between Z = -1 and Z = +1; area = .682
95% of observations will occur between Z = -2 and Z = +2; area = .955
99% of observations will occur between Z = -3 and Z = +3; area = .977
(Note, these figures have been rounded up, e.g. 95% implies Z = −1.96 to Z = +1.96).

Figure 11.2 The normal distribution curve and Z values

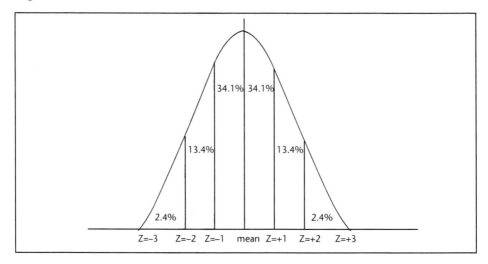

THE SAMPLING DISTRIBUTION FOR THE MEAN

Suppose that a clothing company wishes to estimate the average income of female shoppers in Ireland. To this end, a simple random sample of 120 females was selected and the average X noted. Now suppose we draw another 99 samples, each with a sample size of 120, to obtain a total of 100 samples. The variable X is subject to fluctuations, so the value of X changes from sample to sample. What is interesting is that the different means from the different samples from the same population can be arranged in a frequency distribution and that this sampling distribution (of the mean) will be approximately normally distributed[4]. So, the sampling distribution of the mean for large n (n ≥ 30) is normally distributed with

$$\overline{X} \sim N \quad \left(\mu, \frac{\sigma^2}{n} \right)$$

As the sample size increases, the more likely our sample mean is to cluster around the true population mean and so, the standard error of the mean decreases, as is intuitively expected. Furthermore, based upon the normal distribution, we can say that 95% of the sample means would be within ±1.96 standard error units of the population mean. The same logic applies to the sampling distribution for the proportion.

THE SAMPLING DISTRIBUTION FOR THE PROPORTION

The larger the samples taken, the more likely the sample proportions will be closer to the actual population proportion. Increasing the sample size will decrease the variability of the sampling distribution for the proportion. The sampling distribution for a proportion (P) for large samples, i.e. n ≥ 30, is also normally distributed with

$$P \sim N \left(\pi, \frac{\pi \left(1 - \pi \right)}{n} \right)$$

where   P = sample proportion
         π = population proportion
         n = sample size.

We can also say that –95% of the sample proportions would be within +/–1.96 standard error units of the population proportion.

Another issue for the researcher is to decide how much sampling error to tolerate; or, asked in another way, how confident does the researcher wish to be about the sample results? This introduces the concept of confidence intervals.

CONFIDENCE INTERVALS

In attempting to estimate a population value, the confidence interval is a statistical expression of how close we believe we have come to estimating it. It is a range of values that we are confident, but not certain, reflects the population parameter. It is based on the premise that $\mu = \overline{X} \pm$ sampling error. Consider the example where the gross earnings of a sample of 64 industrial workers in Dundalk is found to have a mean of €260 and a standard deviation of €32. The mean of €260 is a single estimate of the true average earnings of industrial workers in Dundalk. We know that if we took another sample of 64 workers, we would, more than likely, obtain a different value. To combat this shortfall, we use the confidence interval formula

$$\text{Confidence interval} = \overline{X} \pm Z \frac{\sigma}{\sqrt{n}}$$

where $\overline{X}$ = sample mean
   Z = Z value reflects the level of confidence we would like
   σ = standard deviation of the population
   n = sample size

So, in our example, there is a 95% chance that μ is contained between €252.16 and €267.84. In this manner, we often report the confidence interval for the unknown parameter in addition to the sample statistic. For 90% confidence, $Z = 1.65$; for 99% confidence, $Z = 2.58$. The 95% confidence interval is the most popular in marketing research. If we require any other confidence level, the normal distribution table (Appendix 2) is consulted to locate the Z that corresponds to the required level. For example, an 80% confidence, $Z = 1.28$.

Similar logic applies in calculating the confidence level for the mean, μ, when samples are small, i.e. samples with less than 30 respondents. The appropriate formula is:

$$\text{Confidence interval} = \overline{X} \pm t\,(n-1)\,\frac{s}{\sqrt{n}} \quad \text{where} \quad \frac{s}{\sqrt{n}} = \text{standard error of the mean}$$

The only difference between this formula and the previous one is that instead of referring to a normal distribution table (and therefore Z values), we now reference a t-table, as in Appendix 3, with n–1 degrees of freedom.

To estimate the confidence interval for the proportion P, we use:

$$P \pm Z \sqrt{\frac{P\,(1-P)}{n}}$$

where P = sample proportion
   Z = the Z value that equates with the level of confidence sought
   n = sample size.

As an example of the construction of a confidence interval for the population proportion, assume we have drawn a random sample of 50 shoppers from a shopping centre in Athlone. 75% of the shoppers have a credit card in their possession. We want to obtain a 90% confidence interval for the true population proportion of shoppers with a credit card, using the formula above for population proportion, $P = 0.75$,

Z = 1.65 and n = 50. Based on this, we could be 90% confident that the percentage of the shoppers with a credit card is between 65.9% and 85.1%.

SAMPLE SIZE FORMULAE

We are now in a position to use the concept of the confidence interval, the sample mean and standard deviation, along with the normal distribution curve to determine, in advance, the degree of confidence we seek. Thus, when estimating the population mean, the sample size formula is:

$$n = \frac{Z^2 \sigma^2}{E^2}$$

where n = unknown, to be determined, sample size

Z = number of standard error units reflecting the required confidence level (95% confidence ⇨ Z = 1.96)

σ = known or estimated standard deviation of the population

E = allowable error, the maximum difference we will tolerate between our sample mean and the population mean.

For example, a department store wishes to determine, within €150, the average credit card purchases for shoppers in Dublin. Based on past experience, the standard deviation of this population is estimated at €1,500. The manager in question wants to be 95% confident of the results and has asked you, the marketing assistant, what sample size is required. Using the formula above, where Z = 1.96; σ = 1500 and E = 150,

$$n = \frac{1.96^2 \ 1500^2}{150^2}$$

and the required sample size is 385.

Thus, by drawing a sample of 385 from this population, we are 95% certain that the sample mean (X) will not differ from the population mean, μ, by more than €150. If the manager reduced the allowable error from €150 to €50, in this scenario, Z = 1.96; σ = 1500 and E = 50. So, the required sample size would be:

$$n = \frac{1.96^2 \ 1500^2}{50^2} = 3457.44 = 3458 \text{ rounded up.}$$

That is to say, by drawing a sample of 3558 from this population, we are 95% certain that the sample mean, X will not differ from the population mean, μ, by more than €50. You'll note from these examples that, in order to achieve a more accurate estimate of μ, the sample size has increased. This result is to be expected, because in order to reduce error, we require more information from the sample, which is reflected by an increased sample size.

Turning our attention to the population proportion and sample size, the same logic applies. In this case, the formula is given by:

$$n= \frac{Z^2 (\pi)(1-\pi)}{E^2}$$

where n = required sample size

Z = Z value reflecting the associated level of confidence (for 95% confidence, Z = 1.96)

π = proportion of the population with the attribute of interest

E = allowable error or the maximum difference between the sample and population proportion that we are willing to tolerate.

For example, a financial body would like to determine, within 5 percentage points, the proportion of Irish women who have taken out a mortgage within the past month. Assuming a confidence level of 90% is satisfactory to you, the true proportion to be no more than 0.3, you wonder what sample size is required.

Employing the above formula for population proportion, where Z = 1.65; π = 0.3 and E = 0.05, n can be calculated as:

$$n = \frac{1.65^2\ 0.3\ (1 - 0.3)}{0.05^2} = 228.69 = \text{rounded up to 229.}$$

Thus, by drawing a sample of 229 from this population, we are 90% certain that the sample proportion (P) will not differ from the population proportion, π, by more than 5%.

If we do not know the value of π, which is frequently the case in marketing, the researcher still applies the above formula for population proportions. The question still remains, what value does the researcher assign to π? The only choice is where π = 0.5, implying that there is no reason to assume that the proportion of women who took out a mortgage in the past month is greater than those who did not, or vice versa, hence let π = 0.5. Applying the sample size formula, we obtain:

$$n = \frac{1.65^2\ 0.5\ (1-0.5)}{0.05^2} = 272.25, \text{ rounded up to 273.}$$

This says that by drawing a sample of 273 from this population, we are 90% certain that the sample proportion (p) will not differ from the population proportion, π, by more than 5%. This tells us that when we possess no information pertaining to the population proportion, π, we require more information from the sample (in the form of a larger sample size) to obtain the same error that is obtained when information about π is available.

Table 11.1 Sample sizes at a 95 per cent level of certainty

Population Size	5% margin of error	3% margin of error	2% margin of error	1% margin of error
50	44	48	49	50
150	108	132	141	148
250	151	203	226	244
400	196	291	434	384
750	254	440	571	696
1000	278	516	706	906
2000	322	696	1091	1655
5000	357	879	1622	3288
10,000	370	964	1936	4899
100,000	383	1056	2345	8762
1,000,000	384	1066	2395	9513

Source: Saunders, Mark, Lewis, Philip and Thornhill, Adrian, *Research Methods for Business Students*, 4th Edition, Prentice Hall, 2007.

One final comment, rather than opt to let $\pi = 0.5$ when it is unknown, in the interests of obtaining an estimate of the true proportion, π, we can undertake exploratory research or utilise secondary sources of data to identify π.

SAMPLE SIZE DETERMINATION, FINITE POPULATIONS

The discussion so far of sample size determination assumes that the sample is relatively small compared to the total population from which it is drawn. However, when the sample itself accounts for 5% or more of the population from which it is drawn, the sample size formulae derived earlier must be modified.

When estimating the mean of a finite population, the sample size formula is given by:

$$n = \frac{\sigma^2}{\dfrac{E^2}{Z^2} + \dfrac{\sigma^2}{N}}$$

where all the terms have been explained earlier, noting that N is the population size. Consider the previous example where the department store wishes to determine, within €150, the average credit card purchases for shoppers in Dublin where, based upon past experience, it is estimated that the standard deviation for this population is about €1,500. Assuming a confidence level of 95%, what sample size is required if we suppose the population consisted of 2,500 members? Employing the last formula, with N = 2500, we obtain:

$$n = \dfrac{1500^2}{\dfrac{150^2}{1.96^2} + \dfrac{1500^2}{2500}} = 332.99, \text{ rounded up to } 333.$$

If the population consisted of 1,000 members, then the sample size is given by:

$$n = \dfrac{1500^2}{\dfrac{150^2}{1.96^2} + \dfrac{1500^2}{1000}} = 277.54, \text{ rounded up to } 278.$$

From this, we note that the decrease in sample size depends on the population size.

When dealing with the sample size required when estimating the proportion of a finite population, the sample size formula is given by:

$$n = \dfrac{\pi\,(1-\pi)}{\dfrac{E^2}{Z^2} + \dfrac{\pi(1-\pi)}{N}}$$

where all the terms are as before and N = population size. Returning to our financial body who would like to determine, within 5 percentage points, the proportion of Irish women who have taken out a mortgage within the past month. If we assume that $\pi = 0.3$, the population = 2,500 members and we employ a confidence level of 90%, the required sample size is:

$$n = \dfrac{0.3\,(1-0.3)}{\dfrac{0.05^2}{1.65^2} + \dfrac{0.3(1-0.3)}{2500}} = 209.52, \text{ rounded up to } 210.$$

If the population consisted of no more than 1,000 members, then the sample size required is given by:

$$n = \dfrac{0.3\,(1-0.3)}{\dfrac{0.05^2}{1.65^2} + \dfrac{0.3(1-0.3)}{1000}} = 186.13, \text{ rounded up to } 187.$$

As was observed when determining the sample size for the mean of a finite population, decreases in sample size depend on the population size.

SUMMARY

In this chapter, we have been primarily concerned with the statistical methods used to determine sample size for probability simple random samples. Our examination began with the normal distribution curve, the distribution of the sample mean or proportion and the confidence interval giving the range of values likely to contain the population parameter. These assist in determining sample size formulae. The implementation of the formulae requires specification of the maximum desired error between the sample estimate and the population parameter and the selection of the level of confidence required. The larger the size of the sample drawn from the population, the closer the sample estimate will be to the value of the population parameter. An inverse relationship exists between sample size and the desired error, i.e. as sample size increases, error decreases and vice versa.

KEY TERMS

Mean	Standard deviation
Sample statistics	Population parameters
Frequency distribution	Normal distribution
Standardised normal distribution	Confidence interval
Parameter	Sample statistic
Sample mean	Sample proportion
Sampling distribution	Standard error

QUESTIONS

1. What methods can be used to determine the sample size for non-probability samples?
2. What is the mean and how can it be calculated?
3. What is the standard deviation and how can it be calculated?
4. Describe the properties of a normal distribution curve.
5. In a normal distribution, what value of Z is necessary for the area from $-Z$ to $+Z$ to be 0.75, 0.80, 0.85, and 0.97?
6. What is the sampling distribution of the mean?
6. What role does accuracy and levels of confidence play in sample size determination?
7. What is the most popular level of confidence in marketing research, and why?

8. Describe the appropriate sample size formula for:
   (a) dealing with a population mean
   (b) dealing with a population proportion
   (c) dealing with a finite population mean and
   (d) dealing with a finite population proportion?
9. When is the t-table employed in sample size determination?

PROBLEMS AND ASSIGNMENTS

1. Suppose that the average monthly food bill for residences in Cork city is €600, with a standard deviation of €200. What is the probability the resulting sample mean will be greater than €650, if a simple random sample of 100 homes is selected in the city?
2. Suppose it is known that 25% of Irish households are inadequately heated. What percentage of a simple random sample of 100 homes would have estimated the population proportion as 0.18 or more?
3. A sample of 64 items resulted in a sample mean of 160 and a standard deviation of 15.
   (a) compute the 90% confidence interval for the population mean;
   (b) compute the 95% confidence interval for the population mean;
   (c) assume the same sample mean and sample standard deviation were obtained from a sample of 120 items. Provide a 90% confidence interval for the population mean;
   (d) assume the same sample mean and sample standard deviation were obtained from a sample of 120 items. Provide a 95% confidence interval for the population mean;
   (e) what is the effect of a larger sample size on the interval estimate of a population mean?
4. In a simple random sample of 1,225 persons, the sample average annual consumer expenditure on leisure activities is found to be €900, with a standard deviation of €420. What is the 95% confidence interval for the population mean?
5. A random sample of industrial workers finds that 64% have one or more children. The survey is claimed to have an error of no more than 5 percentage points. Assuming the 95% confidence level, what sample size was used?
6. A simple random sample of 1,200 people includes 750 individuals who have a personal pension plan. What is the 90% confidence interval for the proportion of people in this population who have a personal pension plan?
7. A researcher would like to determine, within 6 percentage points, the proportion of the Irish population who have visited the cinema within the past week. Assuming a confidence interval of 90% is satisfactory:
   (a) without making any assumptions about the true value of the population proportion, what sample size is required?

(b) assuming the true proportion to be no more than 0.35, by how many individuals would it be possible to reduce the sample compared to the sample size above?

8. In Question 7, what would be the required sample size if the population of interest consisted of students at a college with an enrolment of 1,600?

9. A simple random sample of the general public found that 76% own a cat or dog. The results claim to have an error of no more than 5 percentage points. Assuming the 95% confidence level, what sample size was used?

10. A bank, in surveying 700 of its customers, has found the average savings account to have €550, with a standard deviation of €250. What is the 95% confidence interval for the population mean?

Case Study

The Examiner in association with Dairygold National Women's Survey*

A national women's survey was conducted by Rigney Dolphin Ltd, consultants, for *The Examiner* newspaper in association with Dairygold. 1,143 women were surveyed, in-home, during December (between the 9th and 19th), at 76 locations throughout the country. The margin of error in the results of the study is estimated at plus or minus 3%.

Women were interviewed about a range of attitudes and behaviours including crime, parenting, finance, working outside the home, working in the home, equality, feminism, media, home entertainment, sexuality, and eating habits. The questionnaire was developed to a stage where most questions were capable of being closed-ended. The inclusion of an 'other' category facilitated variability in response. The question format meant that data was collected in a standardised way, making computer coding and analysis easier, and minimising interviewer–interviewee interaction bias. A sample question is reproduced in Box 11.1.

Box 11.1 A sample question

Question 6   When you relax which of the following would you do?
(Tick all that are identified) *(Prompt 3)*

(a) Have your hair done	☐	(b) Have a social drink	☐
(c) Walk	☐	(d) Talk to a friend	☐
(e) Have a cup of tea	☐	(f) Aerobics	☐
(g) Gardening	☐	(h) Eat	☐
(i) Read	☐	(j) Listen to music	☐
(k)Sports	☐	(l) Other	☐

The Sampling Procedure

The sample was designed to represent Irish women. Multi-stage cluster sampling was deemed the most appropriate method. It was chosen as the method best able to capture the diversity of the members of the population both in terms of their opinions and geography. Multi-stage methods are often used where a heterogeneous group is being studied at the one time. The first stage of the sampling procedure involved a demographic breakdown of the research population. Women were demographically divided under the following headings:

A. Location: urban, rural-overall, rural (non-farming), farmers

B. Age: 15–24, 25–44, 45–64, 65+

C. Marital status: married, single, other

D. Parents/non parents

E. Working outside the home/working in the home

Following the demographic division of the sample, the second stage of the process was a locational split. Forty-four urban locations were selected in the towns and cities listed in Box 11.2, and a rural sample was selected from 32 locations throughout the country.

Box 11.2 Urban locations

Category 1	Category 2	Category 3	Category 4	Category 5
Dublin	Clonmel	Cavan	Gorey	Castlerea
Cork	Sligo	Portlaoise		
Limerick	Tralee			
Galway				
Waterford				

The Sample Frame

The sample frame was chosen to be representative of the population under study. Box 11.3 details the actual sample frame used in the study. As can be seen from the table, a sample size of 1,143 women was used. This was a large sample size which gave the authors of the study some confidence in the generalisability of their findings. Census and labour force survey data is provided in Box 11.4 for comparison purposes.

Box 11.3 Sample Frame

N = 1,143 women

Overall	100%
Urban	61%
Rural-overall	39%
Rural (Non-farming)	22%
Farmers	17%
Age 15–24	23%
Age 25–44	40%
Age 45–64	25%
Age 65+	12%
Married	52%
Single	31%
Martial status — Other	17%
Parents	60%
Non-parents	40%
Working outside home	40%
Working in-home	60%

Box 11.4 Census and labour force survey data

Total population*	3,523,900
Males	1,759,000
Females	1,765,000

Females in age categories:

0–14	459,600
15–24	300,300
25–44	463,300
45–64	310,800
65 or over	231,000
Total	1,765,000

Female marital status:

Single	453,500
Married	667,000
Separated/widowed	56,400

Female work status:

Outside home	377,000
In-home	640,600

* Figures may vary with rounding. Data in table is from similar time frame as the women's survey.

Source: Central Statistics Office — Population and Labour Force Surveys.

Questions

1. Discuss the appropriateness of the multi-stage cluster sampling procedure for this particular study.
2. Examine the reasons why such a methodology was chosen.
3. (a) What alternative methods of sampling would be available for the study? Consider factors such as representativeness in your answer.
   (b) If you were a marketer constrained by budget, what alternative sampling methods would you have considered in this case, and what trade-offs would this have involved?
4. In terms of the sample size used in the study, is it representative and why? How confident would you be in the results?
5. Determine the factors used to arrive at the sample size in this case.

* This case was written by Dr Tom O'Toole, IT, Waterford and Dr Frank Dolphin, Rigney Dolphin Research. It is intended to be used as a basis for class discussion rather than to illustrate either effective or ineffective handling of an administrative situation. The case is based on a real situation, though certain information has been disguised. The authors would like to thank *The Examiner*, Dairygold and Rigney Dolphin Research for their kind permission to use the material in this case.

PART 4

DATA ANALYSIS
AND PRESENTATION

CHAPTER 12

DATA PREPARATION AND PROCESSING

CHAPTER OVERVIEW

▸ Introduction   ▸ Data Analysis   ▸ Editing   ▸ Coding   ▸ Tabulating the Data   ▸ Statistical Summarisation   ▸ Tables and Graphs

INTRODUCTION

Most of the preceding chapters have dealt with the collection of data. This chapter is concerned with what we do after it has been collected, i.e. taking the raw data we have collected and converting it into a form that facilitates analysis and reporting. The end objective of most research is to provide information. There is a difference between raw data and information. Often a research survey will result in several hundred usable questionnaires of up to ten pages each. This represents a sizeable stack of paper. Data analysis helps transform this raw data into the 'list of needed information' which was established at the beginning of the marketing research process. That is to say, the raw data collected in the field must be transformed into information that will answer the marketing manager's questions.

CHAPTER OBJECTIVES

Having read Chapter 12 you will be able to:

1. Discuss what is meant by data analysis.
2. Describe the editing process.
3. Understand the coding process.
4. Explain simple and cross tabulation.
5. Discuss measures of central tendency and measures of dispersion.
6. Outline the main graphical methods of summarisation and presentation.

DATA ANALYIS

Data analysis can be defined as 'a set of methods and techniques that can be used to obtain information and insights from the data'.[1] Data analysis, while unique to each study, requires the research to perform the following tasks:

1. Editing.
2. Coding.
3. Tabulation.
4. Summarisation.

EDITING

After receiving all questionnaires from the field, a preliminary check is made before they are subjected to editing. This preliminary examination helps weed out unusable questionnaires. These may, perhaps, have missing pages, have sizeable portions or sections unanswered, have been completed by a demographically incorrect respondent or by a respondent that clearly did not take seriously (questionnaire dotted with 'funny' comments) or understand the task at hand, or the questionnaire was received after the pre-established cut-off date. Whatever the problem, this initial screening identifies returned questionnaires that are clearly unusable and unsuitable to more rigorous editing.

Editing is the process of reviewing questionnaires with the objective of increasing accuracy and precision. It requires checking for completeness, consistency and legibility of data and making the data ready for coding. Questionnaires are normally edited at least twice before being submitted for data entry. Fieldworkers and field supervisors are frequently responsible for conducting initial field editing on the same day as the interview. Less editing is required for Computer Assisted Personal Interviewing (CAPI) and Computer Aided Telephone Interviewing (CATI) interviews, since checks can be done during the interview.[2] After editing at field level, the questionnaires or interview forms are later subsequently edited in-house by the analyst. It is important that editing be done consistently. If possible, all (or sections) of the questionnaires should be edited by the same person. It is unwise to erase original data. Edited data should be inserted in a different coloured ink. Likewise, another colour should be used for coding. The editing function is time-consuming and tedious. It involves checking for a number of problems including:

1. *Ambiguity*. A response might be legible or it might be unclear, e.g. which of two boxes in a multiple choice question is ticked? Illegibility is more likely to occur when open-ended questions are used and when no interviewer is present.
2. *Inconsistent*. Many surveys use filter questions that direct the sequence of questions according to the respondents' answers. The editor must determine if the answers a respondent gave to one question are consistent with those for other, related questions. For example, a respondent who claims to have a third-level education may have later checked a box indicating that he has just completed the Leaving Certificate.
3. *Incomplete*. Respondents often fail to answer a single question, or a section of the

questionnaire, either deliberately or inadvertently. When an individual question is unanswered on an otherwise completed questionnaire, it is referred to as *item non-response*. If a questionnaire has too many missing answers, it may not be suitable for further data analysis.

4. *Inaccurate.* Unfortunately, most errors are not evident, but factual errors may be recognised.

5. *Interviewer error*, e.g. interviewers may not be giving respondents the correct instructions.

6. *Non-adherence to sampling instructions.* An inappropriate respondent may be included in the sample. For example, if the sampling is supposed to include homeowners, interviews with renters would not be acceptable.

7. *Responses too consistent.* If, for example, in a questionnaire containing a large number of multiple-choice questions the respondent has checked the first response category in each, it raises a doubt as to how seriously the respondent took his role as respondent.

When editing identifies one or more of these problems, there are several courses of action open to editors.[3]

1. Where practical, the questionnaire may be returned to the interviewer for his interpretation or for re-interview of the respondent.
2. The editor can attempt to interpret or infer what is recorded.
3. Throw out the particular questionnaire as non-usable.
4. Eliminate only the problem questions and retain the balance of questions.
5. Code illegible or missing answers into a category as 'Don't know' or 'No opinion'.

CODING

The primary purposes of editing and coding are to eliminate errors in the raw data and to process the data into categories so that tabulation can occur.[4] Editing eliminates errors or points of confusion in the raw data. Coding assigns the data into pertinent categories, to speed up tabulation. Careful editing makes the coding job easier. The design of the questionnaire should anticipate the editing and coding work, since the physical arrangement of the form must allow editing and coding space. Where possible, codes are assigned to the alternative answers, and included in the questionnaire format. This is referred to as pre-coding. Pre-coding is appropriate with dichotomous and multiple-choice questions, which have only limited selection of predetermined responses. When responses are of the open-ended type, it will be necessary to assign responses to categories that have been selected after the data have been collected. More about this later.

Coding Process

Coding is an important step in preparing survey documents for data entry. Coding means assigning a code, usually a number, to represent each specific response to each specific question.

There are two different methods of coding questionnaires, depending on the type of software being used to analyse the data. One method of inputting is to use American Standard Code for Information Interchange (ASCII) data which breaks down the data set into individual columns. The code will include the column position and the data field, e.g. if gender is a question, 1 could represent male and 2 female. Therefore, the question for gender would be assigned one column since both responses are not possible in that they are in fact mutually exclusive. This column is termed a 'field', which means a single item of data. All the combined fields, for instance, containing the demographic characteristics of the respondent, are then referred to as a record. Therefore, when the data is printed in a numerical format the columns represent the fields and the rows represent the records. Each record typically contains 80 columns and a number of records may be used for each respondent, depending on the size of the questionnaire.

Table 12.1

	Fields Columns 1–4	Columns 5–6	Column 7	Columns 8–9
Record 1	1247	27	1	12
Record 2	1248	32	2	14
Record 3	1249	45	2	11
Record 4	1250	58	1	09

In the above example, columns 1–4 represent the individual questionnaire, columns 5–6 represent the age of the respondent, column 7 represents the gender, and columns 8–9 represent the employment status of the respondent. Therefore, record one refers to questionniare number 1247 who is a male aged 27 with a job coded as 12. This example assumes that the oldest person to be interviewed will be aged 99 years. Therefore, should a respondent be aged 100 years or more either the age will be entered incorrectly as 99 years or the entire coding system will have to be changed. This is because 100 would obviously take up three columns, whereas the system has only allocated two columns for the age of the respondent.

This method of encoding is of benefit when the data input is being done independently of the analysis and the person inputting does not know which software package is being used.

The more usual method nowadays is to use statistical packages, e.g. SPSS, MINITAB or SAS, which use a spreadsheet or similar to assign a variable to each column and a row to every response.

Table 12.2

Respondent No.	Q.1	Q.2	Q.3a	Q.3b	Q.3c
1234	1	2	5	0	4

Using this format requires the researcher to take care in designing the questionnaire, particularly in relation to mutually exclusive and non-mutually exclusive responses. For example, if asking the respondent for their gender, as in a previous example, the answer will be male or female which, as before, will be assigned a single column for the variable 'gender'. But if the question asks the respondent to tick 'all which apply', then a column will need to be assigned to each possible response, as above (Q. 3a, Q. 3b, etc.). It is immaterial whether the columns are headed with the question number or the subject of the question once the person inputting the data is totally aware of the protocol being used. Once again, the questionnaire will contain the relevant codes for the responses beside each question and the responses are input as before, except in a spreadsheet format.

If a questionnaire contains only or mainly structured questions, it may be pre-coded, which means that the codes are assigned before the survey work is conducted and the codes printed on the questionnaire. If the questionnaire is unstructured and contains many open questions, the codes may be assigned after the field work is completed or by the interviewer from a codebook.

Categories

In a structured questionnaire containing many multiple-choice or dichotomous questions, the categories are established at the questionnaire design stage. It is important that all possible categories be included, so a response such as 'Other' may be required. It is just as important to assign a category for non-responses or missing data. The norm is to assign the number 9 or a multiple of 9 to missing data to overcome blanks in the questionnaire. This is because many software packages will read blanks as zero, which may be the value assigned to another response. Obviously the number 9 could not represent a legitimate response in this case.

Box 12.1

Please indicate *how many* of the following types of accounts or products you have in *your own name*. Please leave blank any boxes which do not apply to you. (For instance, if you have two current accounts with Bank of Ireland you should write '2' in the appropriate column)

	How many with BOI	*How many with other financial institutions*
Current account	☐	☐
Bank savings account	☐	☐
Other savings or investment account	☐	☐
Credit card	☐	☐
Life assurance	☐	☐
Mortgage	☐	☐
Other loans	☐	☐
Laser card	☐	☐
Other (please specify)	_____	

Box 12.2

Bank of Ireland	*Strongly agree*	*Agree*	*Neither agree nor disagree*	*Disagree*	*Strongly disagree*	
Strives to meet customer needs	5	4	3	2	1	12
Is honest in its advertising	5	4	3	2	1	15
Treats customers fairly	5	4	3	2	1	251
Gives value for money	5	4	3	2	1	16

Pre-coded Questionnaires

Many questionnaires, particularly if being completed over the telephone or independently by the respondent, will be pre-coded. In this type of questionnaire the record number, column number and response value are all printed on the questionnaire. Each questionnaire is assigned the same number of columns containing details of the questionnaire, such as week number, sampling point number as well as the responses to each question.

In this example from a Bank of Ireland customer survey, each response is numbered 1–5, representing the customer's attitude towards Bank of Ireland. At the right-hand side of the question the field number is shown. Therefore, the computer operator knows that the response to the first statement is to go in column number 12.

Post-coded Questionnaires

Coding is usually required for open-ended questions, where respondents write in their answers long-hand as opposed to choosing from existing answer categories listed on the questionnaire. Coding allows these qualitative answers to be further processed on a quantitative basis. The researcher will choose a number of questionnaires, e.g. 100. From these responses a categorisation of the responses to the open questions is designed and then applied to the entire survey. Again, it is important that the categories be mutually exclusive and exhaustive. This means that each response should fit into one, and only one category. It also means that every response must fit into a category even if it means adding an 'Other' or 'None of the above' category.

The coding process usually begins with a 'comment summary' (a list of paraphrased verbatim responses from a portion of completed surveys). From the comment summary, numeric codes are built for the most frequently occurring response categories. The advantage of postcoding is that the full range of responses is known in advance of data inputting. This allows for the elimination, or reduction, of the 'Other' category, resulting in more accurate findings.

Box 12.3

Please use the space below for any comments you would like to make about Bank of Ireland, the service we provide and your dealings with us.

_____

_____

_____

Post-coding is difficult to use as there is a danger of inconsistency between coders unless very specific instructions are issued beforehand. In practice, more than one coder may be used, each independently coding the completed questionnaires in an attempt to reduce the number of errors. Coding may be carried out before the completion of the questionnaire if the survey is based on work carried out previously. In this case, a code book is developed whereby the interviewer will transcribe the verbatim answer of the respondent and then assign a code from the code book to the response either on a separate code sheet or onto the actual questionnaire.

Development of a 'Code Book'

A code book provides explicit instructions as to coding and recording each variable. It may be used in the field to assist the interviewer or by the researcher to code the variables after the completion of the fieldwork. For example, if a respondent is asked a question such as 'What brand of beer did you last buy?', the interviewer will have a list of possible responses in a code book. This allows the interviewer to input a number rather than recording the response. On the other hand, the interviewer could simply write down the brand name and the coder would enter the relevant code prior to data entry.

It is important to emphasise that the person with responsibility for developing the code book should have input into the questionnaire design and meetings about the design involving the client. This helps to overcome problems which may not be apparent until the analysis stage and could prove to cause an expensive error. For example, a question may ask 'How many times in the past week did you read *The Irish Times*?' The code book could state '0–2 per week means an irregular reader', while '3–6 times equates with a regular reader'. However, the actual data might prove more beneficial than coded data in this case as the use of the code book serves only to limit the analysis to the prescribed categories. Alternatively, if the variable 'Other' proves to be a significant variable after data entry it could indicate that, at the precoding stage, an insufficient number of choices were given to the interviewee.

TABULATING THE DATA

Having assigned responses to categories, it is then necessary to count how many responses are in each category. This is called tabulation. Tabulation consists of three activities: sorting, counting and summarising. There are two types of tabulation — simple tabulation and cross tabulation. Tabulation can be done manually or by computer. When the tabulation is done by hand, it is referred to as 'tallying'. Otherwise, particularly for large amounts of data, a complete statistical package may be used (more about these later). Before tabulation can begin, the researcher should initially prepare a plan outlining which items of data are to be tabulated separately or in combination with other items. The type and number of tabulations should be determined early in the research process with research objectives and list of needed information stated.

Simple Tabulation

Simple tabulation (also called marginal or one-way tabulation) involves counting a single variable, i.e. on a question-by-question, or item-by-item basis. Tabulation for each variable is independent of the tabulation for the other variables. This leads to a frequency distribution (frequency table) of how many responses were in each of the categories. The relative occurrence, or frequency, of different values of the variable is expressed in percentages. The percentage is often easier to interpret than the actual numbers. A brief discussion on percentages will follow later.

Table 12.3 Example of frequency table for a simple tabulation

Type of PC	Number respondent	%
Dell	85	28
Fujitsu	92	31
IBM	90	30
Other	33	11
Total	300	100

Cross Tabulation

Cross tabulation (also known as bivariate cross tabulation) is an extension of simple tabulation. While a frequency distribution describes one variable at a time, cross tabulation describes two or more variables simultaneously. The premise is to look at the responses to one question in relation to responses to one or more other questions. A bivariate tabulation typically results in a table consisting of two or more rows, and two or more columns. Thus, the frequency distribution of one variable is subdivided according to the values or categories of the other variables. Cross tabulation tables are also called contingency tables. A series of cross tabulations may provide greater insights into a complex phenomenon than a single multivariate analysis.[5]

Table 12.4 Example of 2 x 2 matrix

Usage rate	Usage rate of store loyalty card			
	Males No.	%	Females No.	%
Regularly	50	17	80	27
Occasionally	100	33	120	40
Never	150	50	100	33
Total	300	100	300	100

Cross tabulation is one of the most popular ways of summarising marketing research data. Stopping with simple tabulation may not yield the full value of the research. While cross tabulation could be done manually, it is more common practice to do the analysis using a computer. A number of spreadsheet packages, such as Excel and nearly all statistical packages (e.g. SPSS, MINITAB, and SAS), can generate cross tabulations. Most cross tabulations are of the two-way variety. Yet little difficulty is presented when there are more than two variables being measured. What is required is to present the variables in a two-at-a-time fashion. If there are n-variables, there would be $[n(n-1)]/2$ different presentations. For example, for four different variables, there would be $[4(4-1)]/2$, or six two-way presentations required.

Perhaps the main issue in bivariate and multivariate tabulation is deciding which combination of questions should be tabulated. Surveys may contain dozens of questions. How many of these should be cross tabulated? It is easy to become swamped by the sheer volume of computer printouts if a careful tabulation plan is not developed. The number of cross tabs should be determined early when research objectives are stated. It is often tempting to add variables and develop different relationships among the variables because they might be of interest. However, any awareness of time, cost and spurious relationships should constrain the researcher from such an analysis. Through a preliminary investigation and a continuous contact with the situation, the researcher should be able to develop an intuitive feeling for what the key variables are. Common sense and experiences will go a long way in determining what relationships need to be analysed. To facilitate the comparison of data, one should show percentages rather than frequencies, for it will indicate more clearly the relative size of two or more values. The total number of respondents or observations may be used as a base for computing the percentage. The simplicity of calculating percentages has led to its wide applicability as a statistical tool in marketing research.

Box 12.4 Statistical packages on personal computers

PC-based statistical packages serve a useful purpose for the analysis of small-scale experiments or for teaching. There are a range of statistical analysis software available, each with its own strengths and certain weaknesses. The choice of analysis software is a matter for the individual researcher and any particular analysis requirements. Some packages lack the ability to read external files, e.g. Excel or other spreadsheets, requiring users to type in data. The available facilities and the size of the dataset, while restricted in some cases, are more than adequate for the needs of students and most researchers. The following is a brief description of three commonly used statistical packages, and associated web addresses. The reader is encouraged to visit these sites and to explore the capabilities of individual analysis packages.

MINITAB

MINITAB is a general-purpose data analysis system for organising, analysing, and reporting statistical data. It provides a wide range of basic and advanced functionality while maintaining a high ease of use. MINITAB excels at exploratory data analysis and includes full font, editing, and printing support. The program's import and export commands let you handle Excel, Lotus 1-2-3, Access, Filemaker, FoxPro and other database files.

MINITAB is designed especially for students and research workers with no previous experience of computers. MINITAB, which runs on Macs and Windows PCs, is easy to use thanks to a good interface with pull-down menus and dialogue boxes. As such, it is generally recommended as an entry-level package for new users. It will meet the requirements of most users, but some may need to use one of the more powerful packages.

MINITAB contains a wide range of statistical facilities, including descriptive statistics, data manipulation, T tests, analysis of variance, frequency tables, multiple regression, non-parametric statistics, matrix manipulation (including inversion and the calculation of eigenvalues and vectors) and exploratory data analysis.

URL: http://www.minitab.com

SPSS

SPSS stands for Statistical Package for Social Scientists, but is used by researchers from many other disciplines. SPSS is an integrated system for statistical data analysis. There is an SPSS Manager that helps you build commands and review output. The Manager includes a menu-based command generator, context-sensitive help, an online glossary, and extensive editing capabilities.

Its very powerful data manipulation facilities make it useful for analysing large quantities of data (both numeric and non-numeric, with limited facilities for free text). It has all the facilities available in MINITAB, except for matrix manipulation and exploratory data analysis, but also includes life tables, survival analysis, multivariate analysis and more advanced analysis of variance. SPSS is best suited for analysing medium to large data files or carrying out more advanced analysis than MINITAB can provide.

URL: http://www.spss.com

SAS (Statistical Analysis System)

SAS software provides statistical and graphical tools for analysing market research data. The SAS System also includes a point-and-click interface that provides easy access to commonly used techniques in market research analysis, including conjoint analysis, correspondence analysis, and discrete choice analysis.

SAS/STAT software provides extensive statistical capabilities. Ready-to-use procedures handle a wide range of statistical analyses, including analysis of variance, regression, categorical data analysis, multivariate analysis, survival analysis, psychometric analysis, cluster analysis, and nonparametric analysis.

URL: http://www.sas.com

STATISTICAL SUMMARISATION

There are two major kinds of summarising statistics.[6] The first provides measures of the midpoint of the distribution and is known as measures of central tendency. The second gives an indication of the amount of variation in the data comprising the distribution and is known as measures of dispersion.

Measures of Central Tendency

The three most common ways to describe the centrality of a set of data are the arithmetic mean, median and mode.

Mean

The arithmetic mean is properly computed from interval or ratio scale data. it is the most commonly used measure of centrality of a set of data and in non-statistical applications is frequently referred to as the 'average'. It is calculated by summing all the observations in a batch of data and then dividing the total by the number of items involved.

Thus, for a sample containing a batch of n observations $x_1, x_2 \ldots x_n$, the arithmetic mean (denoted by the symbol $\overline{X}$ — called 'X — bar') can be written

$$\overline{X} = \frac{(x_1, x_2 + \ldots + x_n)}{n}$$

For example, suppose that we have five scores: $x_1 = 10$, $x_2 = 12$, $x_3 = 15$, $x_4 = 18$, and $x_5 = 20$. Then the mean $(\overline{X})$ would be:

$$\overline{X} = \frac{10 + 12 + 15 + 18 + 20}{5}$$
$$= \frac{75}{5} = 15$$

Instead of writing the equation for the mean as above, we can shorten it to

$$X = \frac{\sum_{i=1}^{n} x_i}{n}$$

or simply:

$$\overline{X} = \frac{\sum x_i}{n}$$

where $\overline{X}$ = sample arithmetic mean

n = sample size

x_i = ith observation of the random variable X

$\sum_{i=1}^{n} x_i$ = summation of all x values in the sample.

An important characteristic of the mean is that we can calculate it without having to first arrange the data into a frequency distribution or to rank order the scores. Occasionally, however, arithmetic means must be calculated from absolute frequency distributions. In practice, the formula that we have already for the (arithmetic) means need extending, because real-life figures occur in groups, not individually. Suppose that we group the figures of our simple example (see Table 12.3). The xf column merely saves us the trouble of adding each x value separately. We would never add 12 equal heights of 5ft 10 inches separately, for example; instead we multiply to get the total contribution of 12 times 70 in. (i.e. 840 in.) from that height category. With grouped data, the midpoint of each category is multiplied by the number of observations in that category, the resultant values are summed, and this total is divided by the total number of observations. This process is represented in the following formula:

$$\overline{X} = \frac{\sum_{i=1}^{h} f_i x_i}{n}$$

where:

f_i = frequency of the ith class

x_i = midpoint of that class

h = number of classes

n = total number of observations

Table 12.5 Calculation of weighted arithmetic mean

x_i	f_i	$x_i f_i$
3	2	6
4	1	4
5	1	5
6	1	6
7	3	21
8	1	8
9	0	0
10	1	10
	10	60

$$\overline{X} = \frac{\sum x_i f_i}{\sum n} = \frac{60}{10} = 6$$

Averaging Means

Often we are given the means of two or more samples and we wish to find the mean of all the measures combined into one group. This is done by computing the weighted mean. Suppose that a test is given to three groups with the following results:

$$\overline{X}_1 = 60 \qquad n_1 = 10$$
$$\overline{X}_2 = 50 \qquad n_2 = 60$$
$$\overline{X}_3 = 40 \qquad n_3 = 30$$

where $\overline{X}_1$ and n_1 stand for the mean and the number of individuals in groups 1, etc. We wish to find the mean of the three groups combined, X_t.

Previously we learned that the mean is equal to the sum of the measures divided by the number of cases:

$$\overline{X} = \frac{\Sigma X_i}{n}$$

If we have the mean $(\overline{x})$ and the number of cases (n), we can obtain the sum of the measures by solving the equation:

$$\Sigma x = n\,\overline{x}$$

This is exactly the procedure followed in obtaining the mean for the total group. We get the sum of the observations for each group and add these, then divide this obtained sum by the total number of cases as follows:

X	n	$n\overline{x}$
60	10	600
50	60	3000
40	30	1200
	N = 100	Σnx = 4800

$$X_t = \frac{4800}{100} = 48$$

It should be noted that this mean cannot be obtained by averaging the three sample means. In this case, the average of the three means would be 50. Only when the number in each sample is identical can the means of the samples be averaged directly to obtain the mean of the total group.

The widespread use of the mean to describe the 'middle' of a set of data is not

accidental. Aside from the fact that it is a simple, familiar measure, the mean has the following desirable properties:
1. It can be calculated for any set of numerical data, so it always exists.
2. A set of numerical data has one and only one mean, so it is always unique.
3. It lends itself to further statistical treatment (for instance, the mean of several sets of data can be combined into the overall mean of all the data).

Probably the key weaknesses of the mean as a description of the centre of a set of data is its susceptibility to extreme values.

Median

If the data is of an interval nature, we may use the mean as a measure of central tendency. The median is the middle observation in data that have been arranged in ascending or descending numerical sequence. For example, the following data represents the number of times each of nine customers used ATM machines last month. (Note, the data has been arranged in numerical order).

$$2, 4, 5, 5, 7, 8, 10, 10, 13$$

When an array has an odd number of observations, the median is $(N + 1)/2$ observations from either end. Thus the median number of banking machine transactions for these nine customers is the fifth observation from either the top or bottom of the sequence (i.e. $(9 + 1)/2 = 5$). Therefore the median is 7. If the array has an even number of observations, the median is any point between the two middle values. Generally the median is taken to be the mean of the middle two values.

Say, on ten days, a bank has 18, 13, 15, 12, 8, 3, 7, 14, 16, and 3 foreign currency transactions. Arranging these figures according to size, we get:

$$3, 3, 7, 8, 12, 13, 14, 15, 16, 18.$$

The median is 12.5, the mean of 12 and 13.

The mean of the numbers in this example is 10.9 and it should not come as a surprise that it differs from the median, which is 12.5. Each of these averages describes the middle of the data in its own way. Like the mean, the median always exists and is unique for any set of data. It can also be used to define the middle of a number of objects, properties, or quantities which are not really quantitative in nature.

The median is most useful as a measure of central tendency, or central location, in situations where the data contains some extreme observations. Unlike the mean, the median is not easily affected by extreme values. If, in the previous ATM use example, the highest banking machine use rate for nine customers was 50 rather than 13, the median would still be 7. On the less desirable side, ordering large sets of data manually can be a very tedious job.

Mode

The mode can be computed for all types of data (nominal, ordinal, interval, and ratio). This is not true for the mean and median. The mode is the observation that occurs most frequently in a data set. In the following set of data the mode is 7.

> 4, 18, 11, 7, 10, 5, 33, 9, 12.
> 3, 11, 10, 6, 26, 37, 15, 7, 19, 10, 21.

The two main advantages of the mode are that it requires no calculations, only counting, and that it can be determined for qualitative as well as quantitative data.

A set of data may have two or more values that tie for most frequently occurring. When this happens, the distribution is bimodal or mulitmodal. Also a data set may have no mode if no one value occurs more frequently than another, e.g. there is no mode of the ages 18, 22, 28, 30, 25, 26. A weakness of the mode is that the most frequently recorded measurement may not really be very typical of the entire set of results obtained.

Measures of Dispersion

In the previous section, we saw that the mean, median and mode describe the central location of a distribution. However, the centrality of a set of data is only one characteristic of interest to decision-makers. It is also useful to determine the amount of dispersion (or spread) that exists among a set of measurements. Frequently used measures of how 'spread out' the data are include: the range, variance and standard deviation. The smaller these three values are, the more compact are the data.

The Range

The range is the difference between the largest and smallest observations in a batch of data. It is the simplest measure of spread.

> Range = X largest — X smallest

Using the following data (e.g. daily rates from a sample of eight Killarney hotels):

> €60, €52, €48, €58, €73, €69, €75, €64

> the range is €75 — €48 = €27

Although the range is the easiest measure of dispersion to calculate, it also conveys the least information. Since the range is determined by only the two extreme values, it provides no indication about the spread of the other values. It is unwise to use the range as a measure of dispersion when either one of its components are extreme observations. Of all the measures of variability, range is the most unstable. By this we mean that from sample to sample, the range varies more than any of the other measures. An illustration will show why this is so. Suppose that we have a distribution of scores, the lowest of which is 30 and the highest is 103. The next score below 103 happens to be 90. By the use of our formula, the range is found to be 74; but 13 of the points making up this range are the result of the high score of 103. The chances are good that the next sample will not contain this high deviate score, and hence the range will be much smaller. The range, like the mode, is a very unstable statistic, since it may vary considerably from sample to sample.

The Variance and Standard Deviation

The two most frequently used measures of spread are the variance and the standard deviation. Unlike the range, the variance and standard deviation consider all the data in their computation.

The variance and standard deviation provide numerical measures of how the data tend to vary around the mean. If the data are highly clustered around the mean, both the variance and standard deviation will be relatively small. If, however, the data are widely scattered around the mean, the variance and standard deviation will be relatively large.

Computing the Variance and Standard Deviation

The first step in computing the variance is to find the algebraic difference between each x_i value and the mean. As the sum of these differences for any set of raw data is zero, we must square each of the differences. The sum of the differences squared is then calculated. The final step in computing the variance of the population is to divide the sum of the squared differences by the population size, n. (When calculating the standard deviation for a sample, it is necessary for technical reasons to divide by n-1 instead of n).

i.e. $$\sigma_x^2 = \frac{\sum_{i=1}^{n} (x_i - \bar{x})^2}{n}$$

The notation for the population variance is σ_x^2

If we take the square root of the variance, we compute the standard deviation.

$$\sigma_x = \sqrt{\frac{\sum_{i=1}^{n} (x_i - \bar{x})^2}{n}}$$

For practical purposes, the most common measure of dispersion is probably the standard deviation. The steps to follow when calculating the standard deviation can be summarised as follows:

1. Find the arithmetic mean of the distribution.

2. Find the deviations of the value of all items from the arithmetic mean (AM).
3. Square each deviation.
4. Add the squared deviations.
5. Divide the total of squared deviations by the number of items (the result is the variance).
6. Find the square root of the variance. The result is the standard deviation.

A short example will make this explanation a little clearer.

Value of item		Deviations from AM	Square of deviations
5		−2	4
8		+1	1
12	AM $= \dfrac{35}{5} = 7$	+5	25
3		−4	16
7		0	0
35		0	46

$$\text{Variance} = \frac{46}{5} = 9.2$$

$$\text{Standard deviation} = \sqrt{9.2} = 3.03$$

In this example, ungrouped data have been used in a very short calculation. For grouped data (e.g. class intervals) the calculation of the standard deviation is a little more complex. For a more in-depth discussion on the calculation of standard deviation for grouped data, students should refer to a statistics textbook.

Finally, then, we can make the following generalisations regarding our measures of dispersion:

1. The more 'spread out' or dispersed the data, the larger our measures will be.
2. The more 'concentrated' or homogenous the data, the smaller our measures will be.
3. If the observations are all the same (i.e. no variation in the data), our measures will be zero.

A Word on Percentages

A percentage is just another summary measure, like the average or standard deviation. It simplifies and reduces data to a representative figure which is easier to grasp. In marketing research applications, a percentage is the proportion who answered a question in a certain way, multiplied by 100. The percentages are a popular way of summarising data and reporting research findings. Much statistical analysis depends on percentages. Whenever we want to compare different sizes or different shares or different rates of change, we call on percentages. Index numbers (e.g. cost of living, retail prices, wage rates, production, imports and exports), mark-ups, and discounts are all variants of the percentage. Where would we all be in ordinary conversation without the percentage? After all, it is easy to calculate and universally understood.

Unfortunately, misproper use of percentages can lead to distortion, misinterpretation and even deception.[7] Therefore, when one examines a percentage, two basic questions should be asked: in what direction should the percentage be computed, and how do you interpret the percentage of difference? When the objective of the research is to identify a relationship between the two questions (or variables), one of the questions is commonly chosen as a base for determining percentages. Conventionally, the rule to apply in determining which direction to use to compute percentages is to calculate percentages in the direction of the causal factor. The researcher needs to identify which variable is the independent variable and which is the dependent variable. The percentages should then be computed in the direction of the independent variable across the dependent variable.

Consider, for example, the question of the relationship, if any, between the number of cars that a family owns and family income. In this case, income is logically considered to be the cause, or independent variable, and multiple car ownership to be the effect, or dependent variable. The independent variable should be used as the base for computing the percentages.

The following are some caveats when using percentages:

- Distinguish between per cent and percentage point, e.g. an increase from 40–65% is an increase of 25 percentage points or 61.5%.
- Averaging of percentages is not possible, unless each percentage is based on the same number of items. A solution is to use a weighted average. This weights each percentage by its relative sample size.
- Percentages based on a very small number of items are misleading.
- Using percentages that are too large can be confusing to the reader, e.g. 'A 750% increase was observed'. It would be simpler to say a 'seven and a half times increase'.
- A percentage decrease can never exceed 100%. However, it is not uncommon to come across statements such as 'a 250% decrease'. This is not true and results from an incorrect figure being chosen as the base for analysis.

SUMMARISING DATA USING TABLES AND GRAPHS

Eventually the researcher must develop some conclusions from the data analysis and present the results. Data can be presented in tabular or graphic form.[8] Tables allow numerical presentation of data. Graphics present data in terms of visually interpreted sizes. Because tables and graphs are used to summarise and present data, this section is also relevant to Chapter 15 which describes the research report and the presentation of research findings.

The proper use of visuals within the marketing research report enhances the presentation of numerical data. It is often said that 'a picture is worth a thousand words'. Regardless of which type of visual is used, it should be uncluttered and self-explanatory. Visuals should be referred to by number and, needless to say, the key points of all visuals should be explained in the text preceding it. Each visual should be located on the same page or next page (unless it is placed in the appendix) to the text paragraph which refers to that same visual. Visuals should be referred to by number, e.g. 'as shown in Fig. 2.1'. Placing the visual within easy reach of the text which deals with it makes it easier on the readers. When reading a report, nobody wishes to have to sift through pages to find the relevant table or pie chart.

All the main spreadsheet programs such as Excel, Lotus 1-2-3, and Quattro Pro have graphics capabilities. There are also several specialised programs available to the researcher to create high-quality graphics. The most useful software program for this purpose is Microsoft Power Point, although tables and graphs can also be produced using SPSS or Microsoft Excel. Several data analysis packages such as SPSS, SAS and MINITAB are also capable of generating tables and graphics. With current computer graphics, virtually all charts can now be made three-dimensional. It should, however, be recognised that graphical presentation is not a substitute for statistical analysis.

Tables

Tables are extremely useful for summarising and presenting numerical data. Tables allow the reader to compare numerical data. They enable the researcher to present important information without getting bogged down in detail.

As a rule, the main section of the report should only contain relatively short summary tables. More detailed and comprehensive tables are best placed in the appendix.

Guidelines for Using Tables in Reports

Each table in the report should include the following:

1. A table number for reference purposes.
2. A title that illustrates the content of the table.
3. A sub-head containing the captions for the rows of the table.
4. A bannerhead that contains the captions for the columns.
5. A footnote, if required, to explain particular items in the table.
6. A source note to acknowledge a secondary information source.

Graphs and Charts

The most common graphical methods are as follows.

Line Graph

Line graphs are often used to show movements in a variable over time. Data values for each time period are joined to show trends in data at equal intervals. The dependent variable is generally shown on the vertical axis with the independent variable allocated to the horizontal axis. The x-axis is frequently used to depict time and, if so, we have what is known as a time series. A multiple line graph shows the relationship of more than one dependent variable to the independent variable.

Bar Chart

Bar charts are most suitable for categorical and discrete data, and are similar to a line chart. Discrete data are grouped into classes corresponding to a rectangle. The height of the bars represents the frequency of occurrence with the base of the column representing the class interval. Bar charts can be drawn horizontally or vertically, and can be plain, clustered, stacked, or multiple row. In the case of more complex bar charts, each bar should be clearly identified with a different colour or pattern.

Histograms are similar to bar charts except that no gaps are left between the bars and, unlike bar charts, histograms can be used for depicting either discrete or continuous data. The continuous nature of the data is emphasised by the absence of gaps between bars. In addition, the area of each column represents the frequency (rather than its height as is the case with bar charts). Therefore, if a class interval is twice as wide as the others in a histogram, the height of the column must be taken as half of the frequency for this larger class interval. Bar charts can be used to show trends between discrete time periods, and histograms used for continuous time periods.

Pie Chart

The pie chart is one of the simplest and perhaps most effective ways to show proportional relationships. Each segment of the pie represents its share of the total value. It can be difficult to interpret pie charts with more than eight to ten segments. A pie chart always shows only one data series and is useful when you want to emphasise a significant element. It is also possible to 'explode' or separate an important segment of the pie from the main part. In order to make smaller segments easier to see, a solution is to group them together as one collective 'other' category in the pie chart. You can then break down that category into a smaller pie or bar chart next to the main chart.

A problem with pie charts is that they do not allow you to show the passage of time, nor do they allow you to compare more than one group of data within a single chart. This can only be done by using multiple pie charts.

Other types of charts used for summarisation and presentation purposes include:[9]

- An *XY (scatter) chart* either shows the relationships among the numeric values in several data series or plots two groups of numbers as one series of XY co-ordinates.
- An *area chart* emphasises the magnitude of change over time. By displaying the sum of the plotted values, an area chart also shows the relationship of parts to a whole.
- Like a pie chart, a *doughnut chart* shows the relationship of parts to a whole, but it can contain more than one data series. Each ring of the doughnut chart represents a data series.
- In a *radar chart*, each category has its own value axis radiating from the centre point. Lines connect all the values in the same series. A radar chart compares the aggregate values of a number of data series.
- A *surface chart* is useful when you want to find optimum combinations between two sets of data. As in a topographic map, colours and patterns indicate areas that are in the same range of values.
- A *bubble chart* is a type of XY (scatter) chart. The size of the data marker indicates the value of a third variable.
- The *high-low-close chart* is often used to illustrate stock prices. This chart can also be used for scientific data; for example, to indicate temperature changes.
- *Pictogram.* A visual representation of categorical data in which pictures are used to summarise data, each picture being scaled in size or repeated a number of times to indicate relative magnitudes.

Guidelines for Using Charts in Reports

The guidelines for using charts are similar to those for tables, with some small exceptions. At a minimum charts should have:

1. A figure number, which is separate from that of any tables contained in the report.
2. A title which describes the content of the chart. However, unlike tables, where the number and title are placed above the table, the chart number and title are usually placed below the chart.
3. Explanatory legends to highlight the components of the chart.
4. Footnotes (less common with charts than tables) and a source note if necessary.

SUMMARY

Data analysis helps transform raw data into the 'list of needed information' which was established at the beginning of the marketing research process. Data analysis, while unique to each study, requires the research to perform the following tasks: editing, coding, tabulation and summarisation.

Editing is the process of reviewing questionnaires with the objective of increasing accuracy and precision. It requires checking for completeness, consistency and legibility of data and making the data ready for coding. After editing at field level, the questionnaires or interview forms are later subsequently edited in-house by the analyst. It is important that editing be done consistently.

Coding assigns the data into pertinent categories, so as to speed up tabulation. Careful editing makes the coding job easier. There are two different methods of coding questionnaires, depending on the type of software being used to analyse the data. One method of inputting is to use ASCII data which breaks down the data set into individual columns. This method of encoding is of benefit when the data input is being done independent of the analysis and the person inputting does not know which software package is being used.

The more usual method nowadays is to use statistical packages, e.g. SPSS, MINITAB or SAS, which use a spreadsheet or similar to assign a variable to each column and a row to every response. If a questionnaire contains only or mainly structured questions, it may be pre-coded, which means that the codes are assigned before the survey work is conducted and the codes printed on the questionnaire. If the questionnaire is unstructured and contains many open questions, the codes may be assigned after the field work is completed or by the interviewer from a code book.

Having assigned responses to categories, it is then necessary to count how many responses are in each category. This is called tabulation. Tabulation consists of three activities: sorting, counting and summarising. There are two types of tabulation: simple tabulation and cross tabulation. Tabulation can be done manually or by computer. Simple tabulation (also called marginal or one-way tabulation) involves counting a single variable, i.e. on a question-by-question, or item-by-item basis. Cross tabulation describes two or more variables simultaneously.

There are two major kinds of summarising statistics. The first provides measures of the midpoint of the distribution and is known as 'measures of central tendency'. The second gives an indication of the amount of variation in the data comprising the distribution and is known as measures of dispersion. The three most common ways to describe the centrality of a set of data are the arithmetic mean, median and mode. Frequently-used measures of how 'spread out' the data are include: the range, variance and standard deviation. The smaller these three values are, the more compact are the data.

Data can be presented in tabular or graphic form. Tables allow numerical presentation of data. Graphics present data in terms of visually interpreted sizes.

QUESTIONS

1. Describe the process of data preparation.
2. What is meant by editing a questionnaire?
3. Why is it necessary to edit survey questionnaires prior to analysing the data collected? What are some of the difficulties that can be uncovered and resolved at this stage of data collection and analysis?
4. Distinguish between the preliminary data analysis steps of editing, coding and tabulation.
5. What should an editor do with incomplete answers? Obviously wrong answers? Answers that reflect a lack of interest?
6. How do you identify data collection instruments that are unacceptable for data processing?
7. Differentiate between precoding and postcoding.
8. How does one go about developing a code book?
9. How should multiple responses be handled?
10. What are some potential problems that might arise when coding open-ended questions?
11. What is the difference between one-way tabulation and cross tabulation? Provide examples to illustrate this difference.
12. Give a brief description of two of the more commonly used PC-based statistical analysis packages.
13. Differentiate between measures of central tendency and measures of dispersion.
14. What generalisations can be made regarding measures of dispersion?
15. Detail some caveats associated with using percentages.
16. How does the use of visuals enhance the presentation of data?

PROBLEMS AND ASSIGNMENTS

1. Shown below is part of a questionnaire used to determine consumer preferences for cameras. Set up a coding scheme for the following three questions.

   Q.6 Please rate the following factors you would consider when shopping for a new camera:

		Not so important			Very important	
a.	DX film speed setting	1	2	3	4	5
b.	Auto film advance	1	2	3	4	5
c.	Autofocus	1	2	3	4	5
d.	Autoloading	1	2	3	4	5

Q.7 Where do you get most of your photo processing done? Please check only one option

a. _____ Pharmacy
b. _____ Corner shop
c. _____ Camera stores
d. _____ Department store
e. _____ Internet
f. _____ Self-service kiosk
g. _____ Other

Q.8 If you were to buy a new camera, which of the following outlets would you visit? Please check as many as apply.

a. _____ Pharmacy
b. _____ Camera shop
c. _____ Department Store
d. _____ Internet Website
e. _____ Other

2. You are president of a company that analyses and tabulates incoming data from mail surveys. One survey is causing you some trouble because a few of the questions deal with whether the respondent uses drugs on occasion. What could you do to ensure that a high percentage of respondents answer these sensitive questions truthfully? If you end up having received many surveys with these questions left unanswered, what might you recommend to your client company?

3. Establish response categories and codes for the following question that was asked to a sample of business executives. 'In your opinion, which types of companies have not been affected by the present economic climate?'

4. You have been assigned the task of preparing a coding manual for a study of personal computer users in 15 countries: Ireland, Canada, Mexico, Brazil, Japan, China, the UK, France, Italy, Germany, Spain, Austria, Hungary, Australia and New Zealand. Outline your approach.

5. Using data from a business magazine report, create the following types of graphs:
(a) Line chart   (b) Bar chart   (C) Pie chart

6. (a) Find the standard deviation of the numbers (a) 3, 6, 2, 1, 7, 5, (b) 3.2, 4.6, 2.8, 5.2, 4.4; (c) 0, 0, 0, 0, 0, 1, 1, 1.
(b) By adding 5 to each of the numbers in the set 3, 6, 2, 1, 7, 5, we obtain the set 8, 11, 7, 6, 12, 10. Show that the two sets have the same standard deviations but different means.

7. In a survey of 100 people, 15 respondents answer 'don't know' to a question that has 'yes' and 'no' as alternatives. The researcher uses 85 as a base for calculating the percentage of respondents who answer 'yes' or 'no'. Is this correct?

8. Suppose you were preparing two-way tables of percentages for the following pairs of variables. How would you run the percentages?
   (a) Age and consumption of alcohol.
   (b) Family income and eating out frequency.
   (c) Marital status and purchase of fashion clothing.
   (d) Crime rate and unemployment rate.
9. A researcher investigated attitudes toward her company and noticed that one individual answered all image questions at one end of a bipolar scale. Should she decline to use this questionnaire in the data analysis?
10. A researcher asks, 'What do you remember about advertising for Gillette Sensor Excel razors?' How should the code book for this question be structured?

CHAPTER 13

BASIC DATA ANALYSIS

CHAPTER OVERVIEW

INTRODUCTION

One of the primary concerns of a research design is to specify the types of data (qualitative and/or quantitative) that is to be collected and analysed. Aspects of qualitative data analysis would include locating individual words and phrases, creating alphabetic word lists, checking frequency of occurrence, attaching key words to segments of text, connecting words and exploring linkages between or among identified categories. As we have seen from the previous chapter, measures of central tendency, the mode, median and mean, together with measures of dispersion, the range, variance and standard deviation, make much sense of quantitative data. When used in conjunction with simple and cross tabulation, such data reduction and summarisation techniques assist the researcher in identifying, describing and displaying data.

While useful, there are many occasions in marketing when patterns emerge from the data, and describing such patterns is not enough. As well as observing patterns, we need to question their very existence. Perhaps the results occurred as a result of sampling error. Perhaps there is a pattern in the data, but it may not be significant. Or perhaps there is a pattern in the data, but it cannot be seen due to its complexity. In all of these circumstances, the researcher can perform statistical tests to measure the significance of differences between numbers, and to measure the relationships, associations and strength between variables. This takes the researcher into the domain of univariate and bivariate basic data analysis. Univariate analysis is data analysis concerned with one variable, while bivariate basic analysis focuses on two variables. When three or more variables are being simultaneously investigated, it is classified as multivariate analysis (this area is dealt with in Chapter 14).

While the terminology and mathematical formulae of data analysis can be overwhelming upon first reading, computer packages can readily perform the necessary calculations. Thus, the onus upon the researcher is to be knowledgeable of and understand the premise and purpose of the various analysis methods,[1] together with the appropriate circumstances in which to apply the techniques. Against this background, by the end of this chapter, the reader will be able to:

1. Understand qualitative data analysis;
2. Understand quantitative data analysis;
3. Discuss the steps for significance testing;
4. Conduct a hypothesis test for a population mean;
5. Conduct a hypothesis test for a population proportion;
6. Detail the chi-squared test;
7. Describe the basis of analysis of variance; and
8. Explain the concepts of regression and correlation.

QUALITATIVE DATA ANALYSIS

Qualitative analysis is the analysis of data that is, for the moment, devoid of numbers. Sources of qualitative data could include, for example, interview transcripts, consumer diaries, field notes and responses to open-ended questions. Trying to interpret what people have said in interviews, focus groups, etc., can leave the researcher with a feeling of being overwhelmed with data. For example, transcribing audio recordings can be a laborious and time-consuming task. Alternative approaches to transcribing audit recordings include: doing it yourself, paying somebody else to do it or transferring the recording to computer using voice recognition software. Each approach has its own potential difficulties. For example, by paying someone else to transcribe the audio-recording, the researcher may be missing subtle but pertinent nuances in the data. Problems can also be encountered training your voice and the voice of respondents to the voice recognition software. When transcribing audio recordings, the researcher also has to decide whether to transcribe the whole recording or just those sections pertaining to the research.

Decisions regarding data-analysis techniques should not therefore be confined to post fieldwork, but should be considered at the planning stage of the research project and at the initial decision to adapt a qualitative approach in the research design. This limits the potential problem of not knowing what to do with collected qualitative data at a later stage.

While there is no standard procedure of qualitative data analysis, typical steps in the analytical process would include:

1. Sorting, organising and filing the data into a more manageable form.
2. Becoming familiar with the data through examination and detecting patterns and themes emerging in the data which the researcher then develops into broad conceptual categories.
3. Re-examination and refining of identified categories.
4. Looking for links and relationships between categories.
5. Drawing together and interpreting the findings in a manner that addresses the research project objectives.

With qualitative data analysis, the researcher is looking for patterns, themes and relationships between elements in the data. There are no statistical tests for significance in qualitative research studies. Rather it is the responsibility of the researcher to determine and evaluate the relevance of what was observed. Tables and graphs are frequently used in quantitative data analysis and display, whereas qualitative data analysis is associated with diagrams, perceptual maps, matrix presentations or the use of tree taxonomy.

The analysis of qualitative data is aided by the availability of computer-aided qualitative data analysis software (represented by the acronym CAQDAS). Examples of this software are provided in Table 13.1. The reader may wish to consult some of these CAQDAS websites, download demonstration versions of the software and explore their respective features. Each CAQDAS programme has its own set of unique features and limitations, and consequently, deciding which programme to use in a particular research situation can be challenging. Dealing with the topic of which CAQDAS programme to choose is beyond the scope of this chapter.

Table 13.1

ATLAS.ti	(http://www.atlasti.de)
HyperResearch	(http://www.researchware.com/)
MAXqda	(http://www.maxqda.com/)
NVivo	(http://www.qsrinternational.com/)
QUALRUS	(http.www.ideaworks.com/qualrus)
The Ethnograph	(http://www.qualisresearch.com/)
Sonar	(http://www.thepowerexchange.com/ product_1449_detailed.html)

However, Lewins and Silver (2006) have an excellent discussion paper regarding this topic which is available on the Internet: http://caqdas.soc.

surrey.ac.uk/ChoosingLewins&SilverV5July06.pdf. Likewise, http://www.quarc. de/body_introduction.html and http://www.qualitativeresearch.uga.edu/ QualPage/ are other helpful sites that provide useful information on software for the analysis of qualitative data.

It is worth noting that, unlike statistical analysis packages, CAQDAS does not analyse data. It is best viewed as a tool that supports the process of qualitative data analysis. This is not to suggest that the researcher will always need or wish to use a CAQDAS approach to qualitative data analysis. There will be times when a manual non-technology approach or word-processing cut and paste will be sufficient. In fact, there is concern among some qualitative researchers that using CAQDAS software can distance the researcher from the data and may result in qualitative data being analysed in what is effectively a quantitative way.

TESTS OF SIGNIFICANCE

Quantitative data analysis is mathematical in nature, compared to qualitative analysis. One such basic quantitative analysis approach is captured by significance testing, also known as hypothesis testing and tests of significance. Hypothesis testing is one approach to making inferences about the population. Hypothesis testing is a statistical procedure that uses sample data to determine whether or not a statement about the value of a population parameter should be rejected. For example, we can construct hypothesis tests for situations involving one population mean and one population proportion[2], two sample means and two sample proportions.

Hypothesis testing involves two hypotheses. Recall from Chapter 3 that a hypothesis is a tentative statement about the expected outcome. Given this, we can now introduce the notion of a *null hypothesis* and *alternative hypothesis*, for the purposes of statistically testing the differences we observe in numbers generated by quantitative data methods such as surveys, observation or experiments.

A *null hypothesis* is a hypothesis that states that our results do not show any significant difference between the population and our sample(s) statistics, e.g. sample mean, sample proportion. The null hypothesis is symbolised by H_0. If it is proven to be true (by means of a statistical test), our findings show the differences in the observed numbers are due to chance and therefore are not significant.

An *alternative hypothesis* is a hypothesis that says our sample findings reflect a real difference between population groups. It is represented by H_1. If H_1 is accepted, on foot of the appropriate statistical test, then H_0 is rejected and the results are significant and worthy of the researcher's attention, as they did not occur by chance.

Essentially, a researcher proceeds on the assumption that any differences between sample and population measures are due to chance, unless proven otherwise, in which case the null hypothesis is rejected, the alternative hypothesis is accepted and the results are therefore significant. In this manner, it is the null hypothesis, and not the alternative hypothesis, that is subjected to hypothesis testing.

Hypothesis testing can be either non-directional or directional. The term 'non-directional' implies that the null hypothesis can be rejected if a sample finding is either very low or very high, i.e. there are two rejection regions. For this reason, non-directional testing is sometimes referred to as 'two-tail significance testing'. One-tail, or directional testing, is where there is one rejection region. It includes a > or < sign, while a two-tailed test includes a ≠ sign.

STEPS IN HYPOTHESIS TESTING

Suppose that you are in the process of buying a chain of restaurants from an existing owner who assures you that the average amount spent by patrons in such restaurants is at least €22. However, you may feel/believe/claim that this figure is too high. How do you test this? To test for significance in differences in numbers, we can follow a three-step procedure outlined below. (This basic procedure can then be adapted to different circumstances and different problems, as explained later on in the chapter.)

Step 1 — Formulate the Null and Alternative Hypothesis

In hypothesis testing we begin by making some assumption about a population parameter, e.g. in this example we make the assumption that μ (the true average amount spent by patrons in restaurants) $\geq$ €22. Thus we write

$$H_0: \mu \geq 22$$

We now define an alternative hypothesis which is the direct opposite of that stated in the null hypothesis, i.e. we define an alternative hypothesis which is a contradiction of the null hypothesis. Thus we write

$$H_1: < 22$$

The general approach adopted in hypothesis testing is to take a random sample from the population of interest. If this sample information is not inconsistent with the statement in the null hypothesis, then such a statement cannot be rejected. However, if the sample information is inconsistent with the null hypothesis, then it (H_0) can be rejected.

The null and alternative hypothesis are contradicting statements. Either the null or alternative hypothesis is true, but not both. The ideal hypothesis-testing procedure is one in which we reject H_0 when it is false and reject H_1 when it is false.

Step 2 — Determine the Observed Value of the Test Statistic

Here, we concern ourselves with the actual value of the statistic we wish to test. It could be either a sample mean or a sample proportion. In hypothesis tests pertaining to a population, we use

$$Z = \frac{\bar{X} - \mu}{\frac{\sigma}{\sqrt{n}}}$$

where $\bar{X}$ = sample mean
μ = population mean
σ = standard deviation
n = sample size

In our restaurant example, we conduct a survey of 64 patrons and find the average amount of money spent to be €20, with a variation of €5.50. Under such circumstances, the actual value of our observed test statistic becomes

$$Z = \frac{20-22}{\frac{5.5}{\sqrt{64}}} = -2.91$$

Step 3 — Choose the Appropriate Rejection Rule

Now we find the critical value, from appropriate statistical tables, of the test statistic. The critical region is that set of values of the test statistic for which we reject H_0. Thus the critical value defines the acceptance and rejection regions for H_0.

To determine the relevant critical value, we need to select a level of significance. The significance level is the probability of making a mistake; of rejecting a true null hypothesis. This is chosen by the researcher with 0.05 being the most popular level of significance in marketing practice. A 0.05 level of significance equates with $Z = +/-1.96$, as shown in figure 13.1 below; a 0.10 level of significance implies $Z = +/-1.65$, while 0.01 level of significance results in $Z = +/-2.58$.

Figure 13.1 Hypothesis testing and Z values

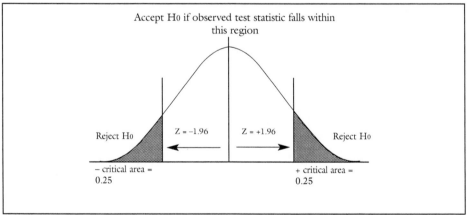

Note: Critical areas, – and +, when added equal the desired level of significance, 0.05.

Returning to our restaurant example, we select a 0.05 level of significant. This implies a critical value, $Z = +/-1.96$. Since our observed test statistic, $Z = -2.91$ is less than the critical value of Z, we reject H_0.

This procedure of hypothesis testing, a statistical method for measuring the probability of an observed difference between sample results being a real difference and not due to chance, can be applied to various different scenarios, such as the population mean, the population proportion, two sample means, large or small samples.[3] These different cases for hypothesis testing are now outlined.

TESTS CONCERNING A MEAN

Given a random sample X_1, X_2, X_3, . . . X_n from a population with unknown mean μ and variance σ^2, how do we test the null hypothesis

$$H_0: = \mu = \mu_0$$

against various alternative hypotheses? To answer this question, we follow the hypothesis-testing procedure outlined above, and adapt it to cater for the appropriate sample size.

Large Sample Case

If σ is not known, then it is sufficient to replace σ by:

$$S = \sqrt{\frac{\sum_{i=1}^{n} (X_i - \overline{X})^2}{n-1}}$$

Then the test statistics and critical region are given by test statistics:

$$Z = \frac{\overline{X} - \mu_0}{\frac{\sigma}{\sqrt{n}}}$$

Critical regions (at a specified level of significance α) are given in Table 13.2.

Table 13.2 Critical regions

H_1	Critical region
$\mu > \mu_0$	$Z > Z_\alpha$
$\mu < \mu_0$	$Z < -Z_\alpha$
$\mu \neq \mu_0$	$Z > Z_{\frac{\alpha}{2}}$ or $Z < -Z_{\frac{\alpha}{2}}$

where $Z \sim N(0,1)$.

We can also see that the form of the critical region, i.e. greater than, less than or use of both directional operators is determined by H_1. Tests in which the alternative hypothesis is of the form $H_1: \mu > \mu_0$ and $H_1: \mu < \mu_0$, i.e. tests in which a directional operator $(<, >)$ is used, are known as one-tailed tests, and a test of the form $H_1: \mu \neq \mu_0$ as a two-tailed test.

Consider the following three hypothesis tests:

(a) $H_0: \mu \geq 22$	(b) $H_0: \mu \leq 22$	(c) $H_0: \mu = 22$
(a) $H_1: \mu < 22$	(b) $H_1: \mu > 22$	(c) $H_1: \mu \neq 22$

The corresponding critical regions are given by, respectively,

(a) $Z < -Z\alpha$	(b) $Z > Z\alpha$	(c) $Z > Z$ or $Z < -Z$

or, adopting a pictorial representation, these corresponding critical regions are given by, respectively,

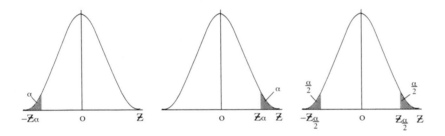

Recalling that $Z\alpha$ is the value such that Prob $(Z > Z\alpha) = \alpha$, e.g. Prob $(Z > 1.65) = 0.05$ Table 13.3 reports $Z\alpha$ and $Z_{\frac{\alpha}{2}}$ for some of the more commonly used levels of significance.

Table 13.3 Levels of significance

α	$Z\alpha$ (application to one-tail test)	$Z_{\frac{\alpha}{2}}$ (application to two-tail test)
0.01	2.33	2.58
0.05	1.65	1.96
0.1	1.28	1.65
0.2	0.84	1.28

For example, a retail credit association wants to test the hypothesis that for all shops in Tralee, Co. Kerry, the average charge account is €110.20. To be specific, it wants to test this hypothesis against the alternative hypothesis that the average is not

€110.20. Assuming a significance level of 0.1, what can they conclude if 110 accounts, selected at random, have a mean of €112 and a standard deviation of €8.5? There are three steps involved in the solution:

Step 1 — Specify the Null and Alternative Hypothesis

Let μ = true average of charge account. Thus we may write the null and alternative hypothesis as:

$$Ho: \mu = 110.20$$
$$H_1: \mu \neq 110.20$$

Step 2 — Determine the Value of the Test Statistic, Noting that S = 8.5 and σ = 110

$$\text{Test statistic} = Z = \frac{\overline{X} - \mu_o}{\frac{\sigma}{\sqrt{n}}} = \frac{112 - 110.20}{\frac{8.5}{\sqrt{110}}} = 2.11$$

Step 3 — Choose the Appropriate Rejection Rule

From examination of Table 13.2, we employ the rule *reject* Ho if $Z > Z_{\frac{\alpha}{2}}$ or $Z < -Z_{\frac{\alpha}{2}}$ where referring to Table 13.3 (application to two-tail test). Finally, since the value of the test statistic, 2.11, is greater than the critical value 1.65, we reject Ho.

Small Sample Case (n <30)

Under this scenario, the test statistics and critical region are given by

$$\text{Test statistic} \quad t = \frac{\overline{X} - \mu_o}{\frac{s}{\sqrt{n}}}$$

where $\overline{X}$ = sample mean

μ_o = population mean under Ho

$\frac{s}{\sqrt{n}}$ = estimated standard error of the mean

Critical regions (at a specified level of significance α)

Table 13.4 Critical regions

H₁	Critical region
$\mu > \mu_o$	$t > t_\alpha$
$\mu < \mu_o$	$t < -t_\alpha$
$\mu \neq \mu_o$	$t > t_{\frac{\alpha}{2}}$ or $t < -t_{\frac{\alpha}{2}}$

where t is described by t distribution with n–1 degrees of freedom. In each case the critical region is chosen so that Prob (test statistic is in the critical region/H₀ is true) = α.

For example, the manufacturer of a toy claims that it takes no longer than 13 seconds to assemble it. A suspicious parent believes that the true figure is greater and gives the toy to eleven children to put together. He obtained the following random sample of assembly times: 15.1, 12.7, 12.01, 13.5, 15.01, 16.9, 11.6, 13.4, 15.4, 17.9, and 14.4 seconds. Assuming a level of significance equal to 0.01, what can the suspicious parent conclude from this data? Following the hypothesis-testing procedure where:

Step 1 — Specify the Null and Alternative Hypothesis

Let μ = true average assembly time of toy, so we write the null and alternative hypothesis as:

$$H_0: \mu \leq 13$$
$$H_1: \mu > 13$$

Step 2 — Determine the Value of the Test Statistic

Noting the calculated values of s and X from the observed assembly times 15.1, 12.7 . . . 14.4 are given by s = 1.97 and X = 14.36.

$$\text{Test statistic} = \quad t = \frac{\bar{X} - \mu_o}{\dfrac{s}{\sqrt{n}}} = \frac{14.36 - 13}{\dfrac{1.97}{\sqrt{11}}} = 2.29$$

This test statistic is appropriate as the sample size n < 30, as given above.

Step 3 — Choose the Appropriate Rejection Rule

From examination of Table 13.4, we use the rule reject H₀ if t (n–1) >Tα (n–1) where, referring to Appendix 3, t₀.₀₁ (11–1) = 2.764. Finally, since the value of our test statistic, 2.29, is not greater than the critical value, 2.764, we do not reject H₀, rather we accept it.

P-VALUES

This provides an alternative approach in deciding whether or not to reject Ho. The p-value reports the probability of obtaining a sample result that is at least as unlikely as that observed when the null hypothesis is true. It is often called the observed level of significance. The p-value can be used in making a decision in a hypothesis test by noting that the value of the test statistic is in the critical region. Thus the decision in a hypothesis test will always be the same whether the p-value or test statistic approach is adopted. A small p-value indicates a sample result that is inconsistent, given the assumption that Ho is true. Small p-values lead to rejection of Ho, whereas large p-values indicate that the null hypothesis cannot be rejected. The decision rules based on these p-values are given in Table 13.5.

Table 13.5 P-Value decision rules

H_1	Reject Ho if
$\mu > \mu_o$	p-value $< \alpha$
$\mu < \mu_o$	p-value $> \alpha$
$\mu \neq \mu_o$	p-value $< \frac{\alpha}{2}$

We can apply the p-value method to the earlier example of a retail credit association wishing to test:

$$Ho: \mu = 110.20$$
$$H_1: \mu \neq 110.20$$

where the level of significance = 0.1. In our earlier solution, we rejected Ho as the observed value of the test statistic (2.11) was greater than the critical value (1.65). The p-value for this test is given by:

$$Prob (Z > 2.11) = 0.0174.$$

The appropriate rejection rule is given by the third row of Table 13.4 and thus we reject Ho if P-value $< \frac{\alpha}{2}$, i.e. in this case we reject Ho as $0.0174 < \frac{0.1}{2} = 0.05$.

TESTS CONCERNING A PROPORTION

In many areas of research the random variable of interest is the sample proportion. Frequently the researcher may wish to compare the sample proportion with a value that has hypothesised for the population. The procedure for conducting such tests is the same as that adopted for tests concerning a mean, considered earlier. We consider the case of large samples only, i.e. $n \geq 30$. The test statistic and critical region are given by:

Test statistic:

$$Z = \frac{P - \pi_o}{\sqrt{\frac{\pi_o (1-\pi_o)}{n}}}$$

where P is the sample proportion and

π_o is the hypothesised proportion, i.e. the value of π under H_0.

Critical regions: (at a specified level of significance α)

Table 13.6

H_1	Critical region
$\pi > \pi_o$	$Z > Z_\alpha$
$\pi < \pi_o$	$Z < -Z_\alpha$
$\pi \neq \pi_o$	$Z > Z_{\frac{\alpha}{2}}$ or $Z < -Z_{\frac{\alpha}{2}}$

where $Z \sim N(0,1)$. In each case the critical region is chosen so that Prob (test statistic is in the critical region/H_0 is true) = α.

To illustrate, a telesales company has observed that they have a 14% success rate in obtaining a personal meeting with customers contacted by telephone. A particular employee, Renee Scarry, has telephoned 290 individuals so far this year and has been able to meet 29 of them. In a non-directional test, at the 0.05 level of significance, is Renee's performance significantly different from the company's past performance?

Step 1 — Specify the Null and Alternative Hypothesis

Let π = company success rate in obtaining a meeting with clients. Thus we may write the null and alternative hypothesis as:

$$H_0: \pi = 0.14$$
$$H_1: \pi \neq 0.14$$

Note, we are assuming that Renee's performance is the same as the company's and we are looking for evidence to contradict this assumption.

Step 2 — Determine the Value of the Test Statistic

$$\text{Test statistic} = Z = \frac{P - \pi_o}{\sqrt{\frac{\pi_o (1-\pi_o)}{n}}}$$

where P = the sample proportion = 0.29

π_o = the value π of under H_0 = 0.14

n = sample size = 290.

Thus the observed value of the test statistic is 7.36.

Step 3 — Choose the Appropriate Rejection Rule

From examination of Table 13.6, we use the rule reject H$_0$ if $Z > Z_{\frac{\alpha}{2}}$ or $Z < -Z_{\frac{\alpha}{2}}$ where, $Z_{0.05} = 1.96$ and $-Z_{0.05} = -1.96$. Finally, since the value of the test statistic, 7.36, is greater than the critical value, 1.96, we reject H$_0$. Thus Renee's performance is significantly better than the company's performance.

Another example: an entrepreneur has developed, so he claims, a new ingredient which if added to stout will substantially improve its taste. The entrepreneur approaches a drinks company hoping to sell his new ingredient. The company, being somewhat sceptical, asked 90 people to test this new stout and a conventional stout. Of the 90, 50 reported an improvement in taste over the conventional stout. At the 0.05 level of significance, should the entrepreneur's assertion be accepted by the company?

Step 1 — Specify the Null and Alternative Hypothesis

Let π = the true proportion of people who think that the new ingredient improves taste. We would expect 50% of those trying both formulations of stout to choose the new formulation by chance alone if the ingredient fails to improve taste. Thus we obtain H$_0$, i.e.

$$H_0: \pi = 0.5$$

The entrepreneur claims that the new ingredient improves taste and thus we obtain H$_1$, i.e.:

$$H_1: \pi > 0.5$$

Step 2 — Determine the Value of the Test Statistic

$$\text{Test statistic:} \quad Z = \frac{P - \pi_0}{\sqrt{\frac{\pi_0(1-\pi_0)}{n}}}$$

where   P = the sample proportion = 0.556
         π = the value of π under H$_0$ = 0.5
         n = sample size, 90

Thus the observed value of the test statistic is 1.06.

Step 3 — Choose the Appropriate Rejection Rule

From examination of Table 13.6, we employ the rule reject H$_0$ if $Z > Z$ where, referring to Table 13.3, $Z_{0.05} = 1.65$. Finally, since the value of the test statistic, 1.06, is not greater than the critical value, 1.65, we do not reject H$_0$. Thus the company would be ill-advised to add this new ingredient to its existing stout.

THE CHI-SQUARE TEST FOR GOODNESS FIT

Often in marketing, we deal with frequency distribution data, i.e. data in the form of rows and columns. We use the chi-square test to test such data for significance, regardless of sample size. In fact, the chi-square test is one of the more popular statistical techniques used in marketing research.[4]

In chi-square testing, the fundamental approach is to compare an observed table of sample data with an expected table of sample data, this expected table of frequencies being derived under the assumption that the null hypothesis is true. If the two tables differ too greatly from one another, then this provides us with evidence to reject H_0. The steps involved in conducting the chi-squared test are the same as those involved in the earlier significance tests pertaining to the population parameters μ and π. The test statistic and critical values of the chi-square test are defined as follows:

$$\chi^2 = \frac{\Sigma (O_c - E_c)^2}{E_c}$$

where Σ = 'sum over all cells in the table'

O_c = observed frequency for each cell (the sub-script stands for 'cell')

E_c = expected frequency for each cell. The formula for E_c is given by $E_c = npc$ where n = sample size and pc is the calculated probability, under H_0 for each cell. Note that for this test to be valid, E_c must be at least 5. If this does not hold, adjacent categories should be amalgamated to ensure that this condition is satisfied.

We reject H_0 if $\chi^2 > \chi^2_\alpha (k-1)$ where k = the number of categories and k–1 are the associated degrees of freedom. The critical value $\chi^2_\alpha (k-1)$ is obtained from a χ^2 table, as in Appendix 4.

Traditionally, a magazine's new subscribers have had the following as their highest level of education: 15% less than secondary, 35% secondary school, 43% degree and 7% postgraduate degree. A recent sample of 200 new subscribers has, respectively, the following numbers of people from these four groups: 32, 86, 70, and 12. At the 0.10 level of significance, do the findings suggest that a change has occurred in the educational attainment of new subscribers? Applying the chi-square test:

Step 1 — Specify the Null and Alternative Hypothesis

H_0: A magazine's new subscribers have the following as their highest of education: 15% less than secondary, 35% secondary, 43% degree and 7% postgraduate degree.

H_1: The proportions specified in H are incorrect.

Step 2 — Determine the Value of the Test Statistic

Test statistic:

$$= \chi^2 = \frac{\Sigma (O_c - E_c)^2}{E_c}$$

The value of the test statistic = 7.074. Note that all the expected frequencies are greater than 5.

Step 3 — Choose the Appropriate Rejection Rule

Reject H_0 if $\chi^2 > \chi^2_{\alpha}(k - 1)$. Referring to Appendix 4, $\chi^2_{0.10}(4-1) = 6.25$. Finally, since the value of the test statistic, 7.074, is greater than the critical value, 6.25, we reject H_0. In this manner, in chi-square testing, a table of observed data is compared with one that assumes a certain hypothesis to be true.

OTHER SIGNIFICANCE TESTS

Some other tests to measure significance,[5] under specific circumstances, include:

1. the Mann-Whitney test; when data is from the ordinal scale, this test is used to compare two groups;
2. the Wilcoxom test; when data is non-metric, ordinal in nature and there are two matching samples, this test is employed;
3. the Kruskal-Wallis test; utilised when the data is non-metric and the researcher is drawing upon three or more independent samples.

ANALYSIS OF VARIANCE

Analysis of variance is used to specifically evaluate the results of experiments, i.e. to determine the influence of the independent variable on a dependent variable(s). It is based upon the premise that the total variance can be attributed to specific factors by means of mathematics formulae. Thus, this is a technique for simultaneously testing the equality of the means of several populations. This approach is known as the analysis of variance, or simply ANOVA. The method is best explained through the medium of an example.

A fast-food chain, Characters, expect mean gross sales of €800,000 per year per franchise. A random sample of outlets in Donegal, Cork and Dublin, over a period of four years, gave the following results in units of €100,000:

Donegal	8.7	7.4	8.0	7.5
Cork	8.7	9.2	9.1	8.3
Dublin	7.8	7.6	6.9	5.7

Assuming these to be independent random samples from normal populations with the same variance, is there evidence at the 5% level of significance of a difference in means gross sales among the three cities?

Let μ_1 = mean gross earnings for population 1 (Donegal franchise)
      μ_2 = mean gross earnings for population 2 (Cork franchise)
      μ_3 = mean gross earnings for population 3 (Dublin franchise).

The null and alternative hypothesis are stated as:

        H_0: $\mu_1 = \mu_2 = \mu_3$.
        H_1: Not all population means are equal.

In this example, the number of populations is three, but more generally we let k denote the number of populations. If the means of the three populations are statistically equal, then we expect the three means to be close together. The closer the sample means, the more evidence that the population means are equal. Conversely, the greater the distance between means, the greater the evidence that the population means are not equal. We may state these observations thus: if the variability between means is small it supports H_0, but if this variability is large it supports H_1. If the null hypothesis, H_0: $\mu_1 = \mu_2 = \mu_3$, is true (but not otherwise) then it can be shown that the variability among sample means can be used to estimate σ^2. In Table 13.7 we show some summary statistics for the three populations in question.

Table 13.7 Statistics for franchise outlets

Observations	Donegal	Cork	Dublin
1	8.7	8.7	7.8
2	7.4	9.2	7.6
3	8.0	9.1	6.9
4	7.5	8.3	5.7
Sample mean	7.9	8.83	7
Sample standard deviation	0.59	0.41	0.95

If the null hypothesis is true, then we may regard $\bar{X}_1 = 7.9$, $\bar{X}_2 = 8.83$ and $\bar{X}_3 = 7.0$ as three observations drawn from the same distribution.

Here, $\bar{X} \sim N(\mu, \frac{\sigma^2}{n})$. We require an estimate of the mean μ and variance σ^2. Intuitively an estimate of μ can be obtained from $\bar{X}_1$, $\bar{X}_2$, and $\bar{X}_3$, i.e., the mean of the sampling distribution of $\bar{X}$ is obtained by averaging the sample means $\bar{X}_1$, $\bar{X}_2$ and $\bar{X}_3$. Hence the overall sample mean is given by

$$\frac{7.9 + 8.83 + 7}{3} = 7.91$$

We compute the variance by calculating the sum of the squared deviations of the sample means from this overall mean, thus

$$s_{\bar{x}}^2 = \frac{(7.9-7.91) + (8.83-7.91)^2 + (7-7.91)^2}{3-1} = (0.915)^2 = 0.837$$

But since $\sigma_{\bar{x}}^2 = \frac{\sigma^2}{n}$ solving for σ^2 gives

$$\sigma^2 = n\,\sigma_{\bar{x}}^2 = 4\,(0.837) = 3.35$$

The result $n\frac{\sigma^2}{\bar{x}} = 3.35$ is referred to as the between samples estimate of σ^2 and is based on the assumption that the null hypothesis is true. A second estimate of σ^2 is now obtained. This estimate is based on the fact that when a simple random sample is drawn from each of the k populations, each of the sample variances pertaining to these populations provides an estimate of σ^2. These k estimators are pooled into a single estimator known as the within-samples estimate of σ^2. The within-samples estimate of σ^2 is not affected by the equality/inequality of population means because each of the k sample variances are calculated within each sample only, i.e. not between each sample. When the sample sizes are equal, the within-samples estimate of σ^2 can be computed by obtaining the mean of the individual sample variances, e.g. for the example in hand we obtain the within-sample estimate of σ^2 by:

$$\sigma^2 = \frac{0.59 + 0.41 + 0.95}{3} = 0.65$$

Thus, irrespective of whether the null hypothesis is true or not, a second estimate of σ^2 (the within-sample estimate of σ^2) is given by $\sigma^2 = 0.65$. Let us now compare the between-samples estimate of σ^2 and the within-samples of σ^2. The ratio of these two estimates is given by:

$$\frac{3.35}{0.65} = 5.15$$

As stated earlier, the between-samples estimate of σ^2 is only appropriate if the null hypothesis is true. If the null hypothesis if false, the between-samples estimates will be too large, i.e. it will overestimate. This remark provides us with the basis to conduct a hypothesis test — if the null hypothesis is true then the ratio

$$\frac{\text{between-sample variance}}{\text{within-sample variance}}$$

will be close to 1, but if the null hypothesis is false then the between-samples estimate will be larger than the within-sample estimate and thus the ratio above will be large.

The only question remaining is to define large, i.e. how large a value of the ratio is required to indicate that the null hypothesis is false. If we let

MSB denote between-samples variance and
MSW denote between-samples variance

then the quantity MSB/MSW is the test statistic used in testing hypothesis pertaining to the equality of k means. It is known to follow an F distribution (refer to Appendix 5) with k–1 and N–k degrees of freedom, where N is the total sample size drawn from the k populations. We reject Ho if

$$F = \frac{MSB}{MSW}$$

is large, i.e. if F is greater than the critical value F_α (k – 1, N – k), where Prob $(F > F_\alpha) = \alpha$.

In our example, the value of the test statistic is F = 5.85. From examination of the F-Tables in Appendix 5, we obtain $F_{.05}(2,9) = 4.26$. Since the test statistic, F = 5.85, is greater than the critical value $F_{.05}(2,9) = 4.26$, we reject Ho: $\mu_1 = \mu_2 = \mu_3$.

This concludes our discussion of significance testing. We now turn our attention to the significance of relationships between variables. The aim of these data analysis techniques is to examine the relationship, if any, between variables and assess the degree of association between variables. The former is called 'regression' and the latter is known as the correlation coefficient. The term 'correlation' reflects that variables are in some way related. While there is a huge array of such bivariate measures of association, we confine our discussion here to the more popular techniques.

THE SIGNIFICANCE OF RELATIONSHIPS AND ASSOCIATIONS, SIMPLE LINEAR REGRESSION AND CORRELATION

From the above discussion, simple regression and correlation are concerned with the significance of the relationship between pairs of observations, e.g. price and quantity, height and weight, etc. These quantities measure the extent of and the nature of the relationship between two interval or ratio-scale variables.[6]

With simple linear regression, we fit a straight line that provides the 'best fit' between the dependent variable, Y, and the independent variable, X, while correlation is used to measure the strength of this relationship between the two variables. A frequent implementation of simple linear regression is to provide a prediction of the value of Y given a value of X. Typical applications of both of these techniques in marketing research include describing the relationships between such dependent variables as sales, and independent variables such as price, advertising expenditure, quality of product, and other quantities under the control of the marketing manager.

For example, an environmental consulting firm is considering hiring its own statistician rather than continuing to use the services of a statistical consulting service. The firm wants to know how much to pay that statistician based on years of experience. A check on salaries provides the following information.

Annual salary (thousands of €)	24	20	32	34	35	47
Experience (years)	2	1	3	4	5	7

How can such data be of use to the researcher?

Let Y denote salary and X denote experience. More generally, Y is known as the dependent variable and X as the independent variable. This allows for a scatter plot, as presented in Figure 13.2.

Figure 13.2 Scatter plot

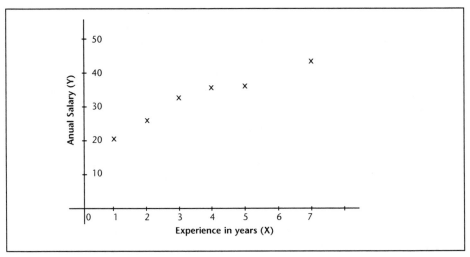

From a visual examination of the scatter plot, we observe that a straight line relationship seems to exist between Y = salary and X = experience. We would like to fit a straight line through this set of data. Although many straight lines could be drawn, we concentrate on a particular line know as the 'least squares regression line'. The formula for this line is given by $Y = \alpha + \beta X$

where $\alpha = \bar{y} - \beta \bar{x}$

and $\beta = \dfrac{n \Sigma xy - \Sigma x \, \Sigma y}{n \Sigma x^2 - (\Sigma x)^2}$

Note n   = Number of data points
      Σx = Sum of all the X values
      $Σx^2$ = Sum of the squared values of X
      Σy = Sum of all the Y values
      Σxy = Sum of the products of X times Y
      X   = Mean of the X values
      Y   = Mean of the Y values
      α   = Slope of the least squares equation
      β   = The constant term in the least squares equations, i.e. where the line
            intersects the Y axis.

In calculating a and b, it is helpful to lay out the calculation as follows:

X	Y	XY	X^2
2	24	48	4
1	20	20	1
3	32	96	9
4	34	136	16
5	36	180	25
7	47	329	49

Then

$$\beta = \frac{n\,\Sigma xy - \Sigma x\,\Sigma y}{n\Sigma\,x^2 - (\Sigma x)^2} = \frac{6(809) - 22(193)}{6(104) - (22)^2} = \frac{608}{140} = 4.34$$

and

$$\alpha = \overline{Y} - \beta X = 32.17 - 4.34\,(3.67) = 16.23$$

Finally, the least squares equation is given by Y = 16.23 + 4.34X. Using the equation to predict the salary as a statistician after six years of experience, i.e. find Y, when X = 6. Substituting for X = 6 we obtain Y = 16.23 + 4.34 (6) = 42.27.

The Pearson's product moment correlation coefficient, commonly known as the sample correlation coefficient, denoted by r, is given by

$$r = \frac{n\,(\Sigma\,x\,y) - (\Sigma\,x)\,(\Sigma\,y)}{\sqrt{(n(\Sigma x^2) - (\Sigma x)^2)\,(n(\Sigma Y^2) - (\Sigma Y)^2)}}$$

and is a numerical measure of the linear association between two variables that takes values between –1 and +1. Values near +1 indicate a strong positive linear relationship, values near –1 indicate a strong negative linear relationship, and values near zero indicate lack of a linear relationship. Figure 13.3 gives the values of the correlation coefficient for several scatter plots.

Figure 13.3 Correlation coefficients

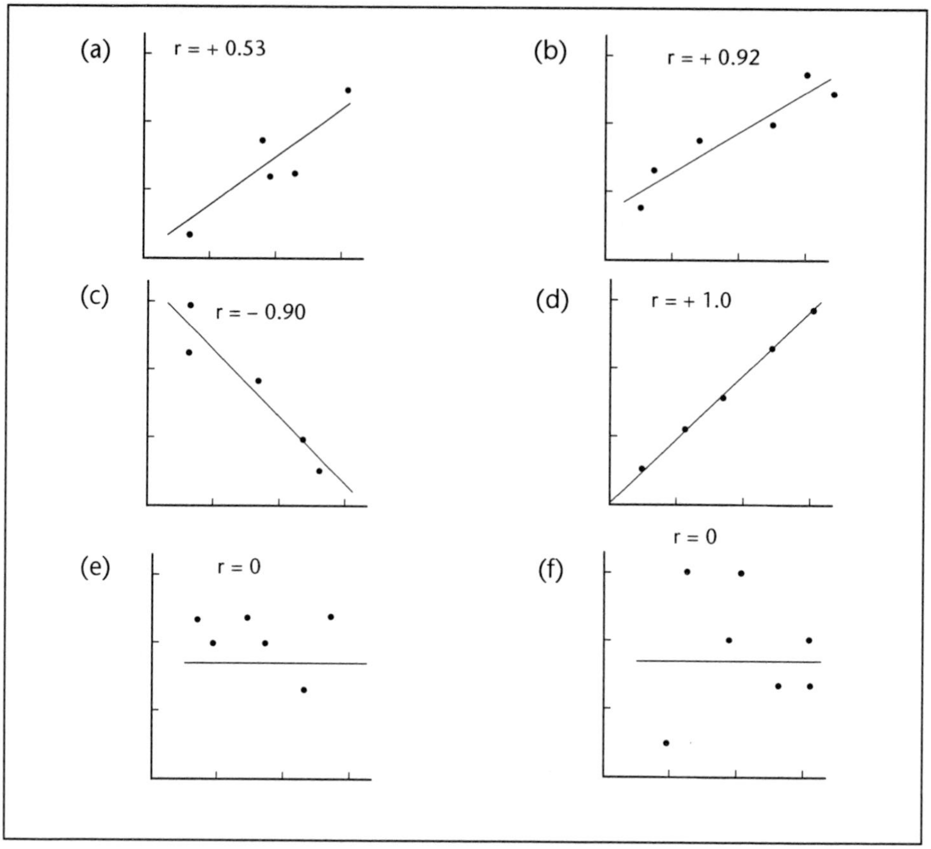

Thus, returning to our example, r = 0.986.

The sample correlation coefficient is almost equal to unity, so we say that a near perfect linear relationship exists between salary and experience.

The coefficient of determination is a measure of the goodness of fit of the estimated regression equation. It can be interpreted as the proportion of the variation in dependent variable Y that is explained by the estimated regression equation. This coefficient, denoted R^2, is given by

$R^2 = r^2$ i.e. the square of the sample correlation coefficient.

Thus $R^2 = (0.986)^2 = 0.972$, or 97.2% of the variation in Y is explained by the estimated regression equation.

The correlation coefficient is a measure of the linear association between two variables for which interval or ratio data are available. We now discuss a measure of the association between two variables when only *ordinal data* are available, i.e. the Spearman Rank-correlation Coefficient.

THE SPEARMAN RANK-CORRELATION COEFFICIENT

The Spearman Rank-correlation Coefficient is defined as

$$R_s = 1 - \frac{6 \sum_{i=1}^{n} d_i^2}{n(n^2 - 1)}$$

where
n = the number of items or individuals being ranked
x_i = the rank of item i with respect to one variable
y_i = the rank of item i with respect to a second variable and
d_i = $x_i - y_i$.

For example, the student union at the Institute of Technology, Sligo, surveyed both recent and current students to obtain information on the quality of lecturing at the Institute. An analysis of the responses provided the lecturing-ability rankings reported in Table 13.8 for ten lecturers.

Table 13.8 Responses concerning lecturer ability

Lecturer	Current students	Recent students (Graduates)
1	4	6
2	6	8
3	8	5
4	3	1
5	2	2
6	1	3
7	5	7
8	10	9
9	7	4
10	9	10

The computations for the required coefficient are given in Table 13.9.

Table 13.9 Spearman Rank-correlation Coefficient

Lecturer	x_i = Ranking by current student	y_i = ranking by recent student	$d_i =$ $x_i - y_i$	d_i^2
1	4	6	−2	4
2	6	8	−2	4
3	8	5	3	9
4	3	1	2	4

Table 13.9 *continued*

Lecturer	x_i = Ranking by current student	y_i = ranking by recent student	d_i = $x_i - y_i$	d_i^2
5	2	2	0	0
6	1	3	–2	4
7	5	7	–2	4
8	10	9	1	1
9	7	4	3	9
10	9	10	–1	1

From this, $R_s = \dfrac{1 - 6\,(40)}{10(100-1)} = 0.24$

The Spearman Rank-correlation Coefficient ranges from –1.0 to +1.0 and its interpretation is similar to that of the sample correlation coefficient in that positive values near 1.0 indicate a strong association between the rankings, i.e. as one rank increases, the other rank increases. Rank correlations near –1.0 indicate a strong negative association between the rankings, i.e. as one rank increases the other rank decreases. The value obtained in our example, $R_s = 0.24$, indicates a weak correlation between current and recent students. Lecturers ranked high by current students do not tend to rank high by recent students.

SUMMARY

Once data has been reduced and summarised, the researcher is then in a position to further analyse the data. One such analysis is qualitative, where the researcher looks for patterns or trends in words. Another is quantitative analysis, e.g. testing the data for significance of differences of numbers, i.e. hypothesis testing. Hypothesis testing is a statistical procedure that uses samples data to determine whether or not a statement about the value of a population parameter should be rejected. The hypothesis must be composed of two competing statements, a null hypothesis Ho and an alternative hypothesis H1. Hypothesis testing can be applied to a sample mean or proportion for either a large or small sample. If the data is in a frequency distribution form, the chi-square goodness of fit test is used. If dealing with experimental data, the analysis of variance is employed. Finally, regression and correlation measure relationships, that is the extent of and degree of association between variables.

KEY TERMS

Null hypothesis	Alternative hypothesis
Critical region	Critical value
Test statistic	Level of significance

One-tailed test

Analysis of variance

Chi-square test

ANOVA table

Dependent variable

Correlation

P-value

Spearman Rank-correlation coefficient

Dependent variable

Correlation coefficient

Independent variable

Simple linear regression

QUESTIONS

1. What is univariate and bivariate analysis?
2. Discuss the role and function of significance testing in marketing.
3. Discuss a hypothesis for (a) a population mean for large samples, and (b) a population proportion for small samples.
4. Detail the steps for undertaking hypothesis testing.
5. What is meant by the significance level of a test?
6. Explain why the chi-square test is popular in marketing.
7. What is analysis of variance?
8. Detail two techniques for measuring and testing the significance of relationships between two variables.
9. Define the Spearman Rank-correlation Coefficient.

PROBLEMS AND ASSIGNMENTS

1. The owner of a food manufacturing plant claims that 45% of Irish consumers purchase his product at least once a week. In a sample of 200 consumers, 80 purchased his product within the last week. For this situation:
   (a) Formulate the appropriate null and alternative hypothesis.
   (b) At the 0.10 level of significance, conduct a non-directional test of the null hypothesis.
2. The manager of a restaurant contends that patrons spend an average of 50 minutes in his establishment. In observing a sample of 80 customers, a market analyst finds their average stay to be 45 minutes, with a standard deviation of 15 minutes. In a non-direction test at the 0.10 level of significance, evaluate the manager's claim.
3. Using the data of question (2), repeat the test at the 0.01 level of significance.
4. In an experiment concerning the process of learning, the average time required by nine adults to comprehend a mathematical procedure was five minutes, with a standard deviation of 1.3 minutes. At a level of 0.05, does this support the claim that the average time required by a group of adults to comprehend such a mathematical procedure is not more than four minutes?
5. Consider the following hypothesis test, where p is the population proportion: a sample of 220 provided a sample proportion $P = 0.58$

(a) Compute the value of the test statistic, when $H_0 : \pi \leq 0.6$ and $H_1: \pi > 0.6$.

(b) What is your conclusion?

6. Eircom find that, at national level, 45% of phone bills are paid on time, 35% are paid two weeks in arrears and the remainder are paid a month in arrears. From a survey of 400 customers in the south of Ireland, the corresponding percentages were 65%; 30% and 5%.

(a) At the 0.05 level, is the payment period of the southern consumers significantly different from the rest of the country?

(b) At the 0.025 level, is there a significant difference?

7. A sample of 200 individuals was randomly selected from all candidates who recently took the examination of a certain professional body in Ireland. The examination results (pass/fail) and existing education qualifications of individuals in the sample were examined and were as follows

	Pass	Fail
Postgraduate	68	22
Graduate	17	9
Leaving Certificate	20	32
No qualifications	12	20

Analysis of these data produced a chi-square ($X_2 = 25.704$) with d.f. = 3,0 = .000019

(a) State the null hypothesis tested and indicate whether it would be accepted or rejected.

(b) Interpret the statistical information cited.

(c) Suggest at least one other statistical measure/index which might be used to further analyse these data.

(Adapted from a Marketing Institute of Ireland Examination question, 1996)

8. The attached table is extracted from the SPSS printout.

Cross tabulation of willingness to purchase from catalogue (V3) with whether respondent has purchased from it before (V4)

Count Row percent Column percent Total percent	Never ordered	Ordered before but not within past year	Ordered within past year	Row rotal
Unwilling	20 40.0 46.5 16.1	20 40.0 51.3 16.1	10 20.0 23.8 8.1	50 40.3
Somewhat willing	7 20.0 16.3 5.6	11 31.4 28.2 8.9	17 48.6 40.5 13.7	35 28.2

Very	16	8	15	39
willing	41.0	20.5	38.5	31.5
	37.2	20.5	35.7	
	12.9	6.5	12.1	
Column	43	39	42	124
Total	34.7	31.5	33.9	100.0

Raw chi square = 10.997 with 4 degrees of freedom
Significance = .027
Contingency coefficient = .285

(a) Interpret the table.
(b) Show clearly in your analysis which are the null and alternative hypotheses and illustrate the role of hypothesis testing in marketing research.
(c) Explain some of the dangers and pitfalls in the use of cross tabulations and their associated statistics.
(Adapted from a Marketing Institute of Ireland Examination question, 1993)

9. A group of 30 customers is randomly selected from those shopping in a large supermarket. They are asked, as they leave the store, to indicate on a ten-point equal interval scale, their assessment of value for money obtained in the store. A score of 1 indicate very poor value and a score of 10 represents excellent/ unbeatable value. They are also asked to state, to the nearest point, how much they have just spent in the store. In the situation outlined:
   (a) State a suitable null hypothesis which the researchers are likely to wish to test.
   (b) Identify an appropriate statistical test which would be used to test the null hypothesis and explain your choice.
   (c) How would you decide whether or not to accept the null hypothesis?
   (d) Can you suggest an alternative method of analysing these data?
   (Adapted from a Marketing Institute of Ireland Examination question, 1997)

10. An analysis of the sales performance and scores on a psychological test of 'salespersonship' of twelve sales executives produced the following data:

Table 13.10

Person	Number of units sold	Test score out of 100
A	59	75
B	37	45
C	45	16
D	32	72
E	16	34
F	11	16
G	23	40
H	16	32

Table 13.10 *contd*

Person	Number of units sold	Test score out of 100
I	43	25
J	21	32
K	25	45
L	17	35

Analysis of these data produced the following results:

	Mean	*Standard deviation*	*Est. standard error*
Units sold	28.75	14.60	4.21
Test score	38.91	18.71	5.40

The value of t is -1.9512. The corresponding probability value, with eleven degrees of freedom for a two-tailed test, is .074.

(a) State the null hypothesis tested and indicate, giving reasons, whether or not you would accept it.

(b) Interpret carefully the statistical results cited.

(c) Can you think of another way of analysing these data?

(Adapted from a Marketing Institute of Ireland Examination question, 1997)

11. A sample of 100 adults is randomly chosen from the population of an Irish city. An examination of the employment status and educational qualifications of individuals in the sample reveals the following pattern:

Education	*Employed*	*Unemployed*
No qualifications	10	12
Leaving Certificate	20	15
Higher education	30	13
	60	40

A chi-square (X_2) statistic and associated information is calculated and is as follows:

$X_2 = 3.768$ d.f. $= 2$ $p = .152$

A second random sample of 200 adults is drawn and it reveals a strikingly similar pattern.

Education	*Employed*	*Unemployed*
No qualifications	20	24
Leaving Certificate	40	30
Higher Education	60	26
	120	80

$X_2 = 7.535$ d.f. $= 2$ $p = .0231$

(Adapted from a Marketing Institute of Ireland Examination Question, 1992)

CHAPTER 14

MULTIVARIATE DATA ANALYSIS

CHAPTER OVERVIEW

▸ Introduction ▸ What is 'Multivariate' Analysis? ▸ Types of Multivariate Techniques ▸ Multiple Regression Analysis ▸ Conjoint Analysis ▸ Conjoint Analysis Five Steps ▸ Discriminant Analysis ▸ Discriminant Analysis Illustrated ▸ Factor Analysis ▸ Factor Analysis Illustrated ▸ Cluster Analysis ▸ Cluster Analysis Illustrated ▸ Multidimensional Scaling (MDS) ▸ MDS Considerations, Direct versus Derived ▸ MDS Illustrated ▸ Multivariate Techniques, Concluding Comments ▸ Summary

INTRODUCTION

In this last chapter concentrating on data analysis, we turn our attention to 'multivariate' analysis and away from univariate analysis (dealing with one variable, e.g. mean) and bivariate analysis (association between two variables, e.g. age and the right to vote). Our discussion here of multivariate techniques is rudimentary. The researcher is not obliged to have the degree of knowledge and understanding that a statistician would have of multivariate methods. However, as marketing researchers, we need to know what these techniques are, when to employ them, and their limitations, to enable effective and efficient management decision-making.

With this in mind, by the end of this chapter the reader will be able to:

1. explain the term 'multivariate' analysis;
2. distinguish between univariate, bivariate and multivariate techniques;
3. describe commonly used multivariate techniques; and
4. identify the appropriate marketing circumstance for their application, and specify their limitations.

WHAT IS 'MULTIVARIATE' ANALYSIS?

Multivariate analysis is data analysis dealing with several variables simultaneously — a distinguishing feature which differentiates multivariate techniques from other data analysis methods, i.e. univariate and bivariate analysis, as outlined above. More formally, multivariate techniques can be defined as 'all statistical methods that simultaneously analyse multiple measurements on each individual or object under investigation'.[1] Thus, multivariate techniques differ from univariate and bivariate, in that they *simultaneously* analyse multiple combinations of variables that are inter-related and thus cannot be separately interpreted.

In defining the term 'multivariate', the use of preprogrammed computer packages, for example, SPSS, MINITAB and SAS, is inescapable, as such computer applications are intrinsic to the processing and analysis of complex, large sets of data, utilising multivariate techniques. Recent technological advancements and the widespread availability of PC statistical packages are encouraging a significant growth in the use of multivariate applications — a trend which will no doubt continue to seriously impact upon marketing research.[2] Linked to this, is the development of new multivariate methods.[3, 4]

Multivariate techniques have the ability to deal with complex situations — reflected in the need to analyse several variables at any one point in time. This dimension to multivariate techniques is very valuable in marketing because it facilitates a more realistic analysis of markets, consumers, products and suppliers facing most firms (compared to univariate or bivariate techniques).[5] This said, any researcher planning to employ such techniques has to appreciate the assumptions, data collection requirements and limitations of such approaches. Be warned — failure to do so often results in a multivariate technique being applied in incorrect circumstances and thus giving rise to a potentially disastrous management decision. The old adage applies here — 'no information is better than wrong information'.

Therefore, multivariate techniques are appropriate for data analysis when:

1. the collected data pertains to multiple variables;
2. there are a large number of observations or respondents;
3. there may be interaction and/or interdependency between the variables;
4. there is a serious need by management to capture the realistic, complex and competitive marketplace, as is often the case in new product development, market segmentation studies, product positioning and media selection.

TYPES OF MULTIVARIATE TECHNIQUES

Multivariate techniques fall into two broad camps:

1. dependent techniques;
2. independent techniques.

The terminology here is reminiscent of that in experimentation. Dependent multivariate methods refer to the fact that the dependent variable is affected by the independent variable. For example, brand awareness is influenced by advertising; hence, brand awareness is the dependent variable and the advertising could be considered the independent variable. In this chapter, we confine ourselves to multivariate techniques that are based upon one dependent variable. There are multivariate dependent techniques that deal with two or more dependent variables, but these are beyond the scope of this chapter.[6,7] If there is no identified dependent variable, the researcher is then dealing with a host of variables (several or more) that are independent or interdependent upon each other. For example, age, social class, occasion, education, attitudes, lifestyle and personality all interact to influence the type and brand of coffee one drinks.

This classification of multivariate methods into either dependent or independent is used by researchers to choose the relevant and appropriate technique, given a particular situation, as shown in Figures 14.1 (a) and (b).

Figure 14.1 (a) Choosing the appropriate multivariate technique

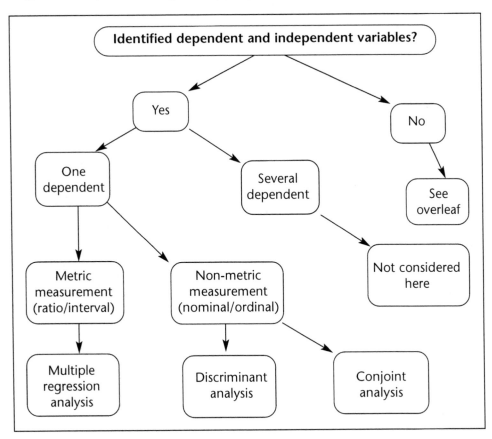

Figure 14.1 (b) Choosing the appropriate multivariate technique

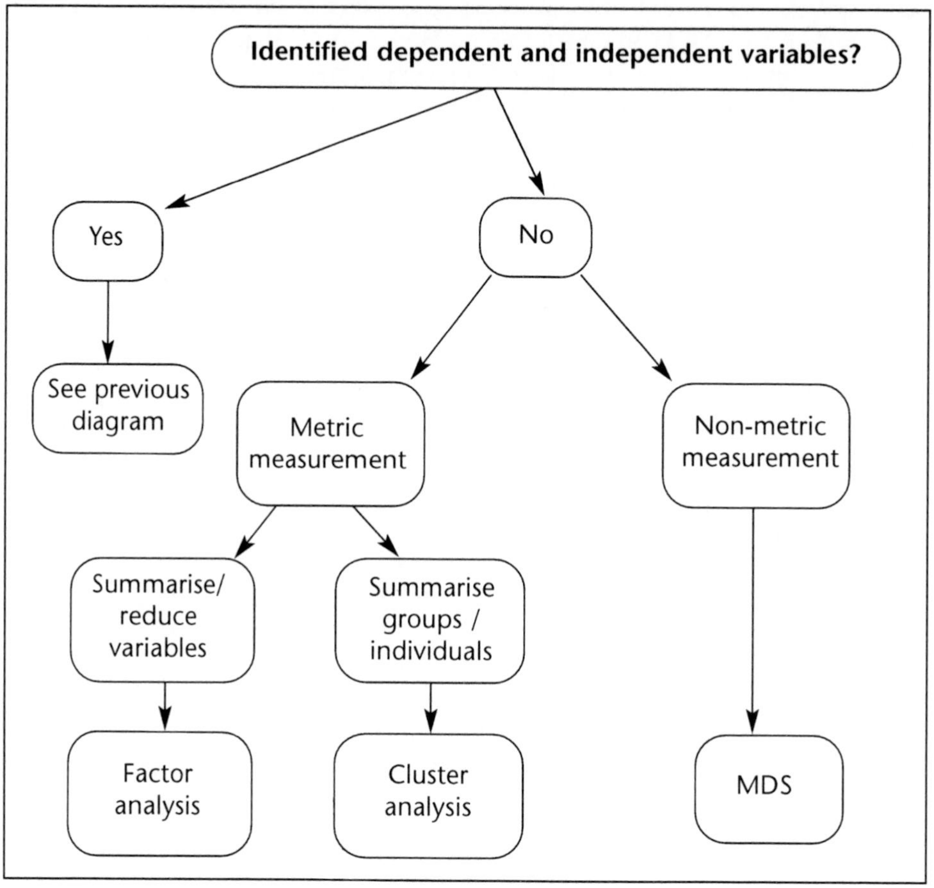

From the above figures, another dimension is brought to bear in deciding what technique to employ or how to classify multivariate methods — the issue of metric or non-metric data. Metric data is data based upon an interval or ratio scale of measurement and thus quantitative, while non-metric data is generated by either a nominal or ordinal scale and is qualitative in nature. It is also worth noting at this point that the metric/non-metric debate has to be factored into the design of a questionnaire or any other data collection instrument, to allow for the use of multivariate techniques at the data analysis stage, if so desired. As multivariate methods grow in popularity, the data collection process will increasingly reflect this.[8]

We now consider the more commonly used multivariate techniques in marketing, with the following questions in mind:

1. What does the technique do?
2. How does the technique work?
3. How is it used in reality?

MULTIPLE REGRESSION ANALYSIS

Multiple regression analysis is the study of how a dependent variable Y is related to two or more independent variables. Since many regression problems involve more than one independent variable, multiple regression is a valuable technique. Based upon an extension of regression analysis as presented in Chapter 13, the output and interpretation of multiple regression is similar.

Table 14.1 shows the monthly sales at a tourist attraction over a twelve-month period, together with the admission price and the mean number of hours of sunshine in each month. The number of visitors to the attraction per month is also given. Using a statistical package such as SPSS or Minitab, and the data provided in Table 14.1, consider the following questions:

1. How can we estimate the influence of the price, number of visitors and hours of sunshine on sales?
2. How can we use the results to predict sales when 28,000 visitors pay an admission of €5 during a month with a mean ten hours of sunshine?

Table 14.1 Regression printout

Month	Sales (€,000)	Price	Visitors (,000)	Sunshine (Mean daily hours)
Jan	33	3	10	3.0
Feb	42	3	11	3.5
Mar	45	3	14	4.5
Apr	68	3	16	5.5
May	75	3	17	6.5
Jun	180	5	25	10.5
Jul	195	5	30	11.0
Aug	210	5	35	11.0
Sep	78	3	18	6.0
Oct	42	3	12	3.5
Nov	32	3	10	2.5
Dec	26	3	8	2.0

The concepts of a regression equation and a regression model introduced in Chapter 13 can be applied here, i.e. the regression equation is:

$$E(Y) = \alpha + X_1 + X_2 + X_3.$$

In the context of the present example, if we let:

Y = Sales
α = slope of the least squares equation
X_1 = Price
X_2 = Visitors and
X_3 = (mean daily hours of) sunshine

then the regression equation is given by:

$$E(Y) = \alpha + \text{Price} + \text{Visitors} + \text{Sunshine}.$$

When the given data is submitted to a statistical computer package for analysis, the estimated multiple regression equation is given by:

$$E(Y) = -99.0 + 29.4 \,(\text{Price}) + 2.70 \,(\text{Visitors}) + 6.11 \,(\text{Sunshine}).$$

This tells us that, since the data relates to a tourist attraction, it is believed that peak season prices would be higher than off-peak prices due to price promotion being carried out to stimulate visitor interest. This belief is validated by the data, i.e. sales increase as prices increase (the coefficient of Price in the regression equation is positive). We further observe that there is a positive relationship between sales and the number of visitors and a positive relationship between sales and the mean daily hours of sunshine. Next, the units of measurement are used in interpreting the size of the coefficients:

- A one-unit increase in price will increase sales by 29.4 units or €29,400.
- A one-unit increase in visitor numbers means an extra 1,000 visitors and a sales increase of 2.70 units or €2,700.
- An extra hour of sunshine will account for 6.11 extra units of sales or €6,110.

To date, we have interpreted the regression coefficients. We now wish to test for a significant regression relation, i.e. in the multiple regression model, so we wish to test

$H_0: X_1 = X_2 = X_3 = 0$
$H_1:$ One or more of the parameters is not equal to zero.

If H_0 is rejected, we have sufficient statistical evidence to conclude that one or more of the parameters is not equal to zero and that the overall relationship between Sales and the set of independent variables Price, Visitors and Sunshine is significant. Alternatively, if H_0 cannot be rejected, we do not possess sufficient evidence to conclude that a significant relationship is present.

F-test

To conduct the required hypothesis test, we perform an F-test, i.e. adopt either one of the following decision rules.

1. Reject H₀ if $F > F\alpha (p, n - p - 1)$

where
F is the value of the test statistic and
$F(p, n - p - 1)$ is the critical value, which is obtained from an F distribution with p (number of independent variables) and $n - p - 1$ degrees of freedom (see Appendix 5).

2. Reject H₀ if the p-value associated with the test statistic is less than the level of significance α.

The calculation of this test statistic F is beyond the scope of this book; however, in practice such calculations are performed by statistical packages and thus the emphasis here will be placed on interpreting and utilising such output. In our example, the output is given in Table 14.2.

Table 14.2 Regression computer printout

The regression equation is
Sales =.−99.0 + 29.4 Price + 2.70 Visitors + 6.11 Sunshine

Predictor	Coef	Stdev	t-ratio	P
Constant	-98.995	7.022	−14.10	0.000
Price	29.353	3.243	9.05	0.000
Visitors	2.7019	0.5979	4.52	0.000
Sunshine	6.108	1.609	3.80	0.005

s = 3.930   R-sq = 99.8%   R-sq(adj) = 99.7%

Analysis of variance

Source	DF	SS	MS	F	P
Regression	3	51353	17118	1108.5	0.000
Error	8	124	15		
Total	11	51477			

Source	DF	SEQ SS
Price	1	47961
Visitors	1	3170
Sunshine	1	223

Unusual observations

Obs.	Price	Sales	Fit	Stdev.	Fit Residual	St. Resid
3	3.00	45.00	54.38	1.36	−9.38	−2.54R

In the analysis of variance part of the output, we obtain the value of the test statistic, i.e. F = 1108.50. With a level of significance α = 0.05 and referring to the F-tables in Appendix 5, the critical value is given by:

$$F\alpha \ (p, n - p - 1) = F0.05 \ (3.12 - 3 - 1) = F0.05 \ (3,8) = 4.07.$$

Since the test statistic is greater than the critical value (i.e. since 1108.50 is greater than 4.07), we reject Ho: $X_1 = X_2 = X_3 = 0$ and conclude that one or more of the parameters is not equal to zero and that the overall relationship between Sales and the set of independent variables, Price, Visitors and Sunshine, is significant. The p-value = 0.000 in the last column of the analysis of variance table also indicates that we can reject Ho as the p-value is less than α.

In our discussion of simple linear regression, we used the coefficient of determination to measure the goodness of fit for the estimated regression equation. The term 'multiple coefficient of determination' is applied when we are measuring the goodness of fit for the estimated multiple regression equation and again is denoted by R^2.

In this example, R^2 = 99.8%. Therefore, 99.8% of the variability in Sales is explained by the estimated multiple regression equation with Price, Visitors and Sunshine as the independent variables.

CONJOINT ANALYSIS

Conjoint analysis is a non-metric technique that tries to determine the relative importance that consumers attach to salient attributes, and the different levels of the important attributes. It starts with the consumer's overall or 'global' judgement about a set of complex alternatives. It then performs a decomposition of the original evaluations of the consumer into separate and compatible utility scales. Being able to separate the overall judgements into components provides a marketing manager with valuable information about the relative importance of the various attributes of their product, service or brand. Conjoint analysis also provides useful information about the value of various levels of a single attribute. So, four assumptions are central to conjoint analysis:

1. All products can be defined as a set of common attributes.
2. Alternative versions of the same product can be defined as a set of different attributes levels.
3. Consumers evaluate the utility of attribute level combinations when making a purchase decision.
4. Consumers trade off attribute level combinations when choosing between alternative products.[9]

CONJOINT ANALYSIS – FIVE STEPS

1. *Determination of the relevant attributes*

Product attributes are components or characteristics of the product. Consumers see products as having several attributes. The multiple attributes of a product generally fall into two classes, monotone attributes and non-monotone attributes. Monotone attributes are attributes like quality, where all consumers agree in their preference ranking of the various attribute levels, i.e. most people would prefer higher quality to less. Non-monotone attributes, in contrast, are attributes on which people have different preference orderings. For example, people disagree on their favourite colours for cars. Conjoint analysis starts with the determination of relevant product attributes that are believed to influence a consumer's preference. The attributes should include those most relevant to potential consumers and which can be influenced or manipulated by the producer.

2. *Relevant levels per product attribute*

The attribute levels are chosen so that each possible combination of attribute level results in a product that can exist in reality. It is necessary that for each combination of attribute level, the respondent can imagine a realistic product. By choosing attribute levels, the researcher should try to employ the full range of the attribute.

3. *Generation of the data*

Data collection procedures in conjoint analysis have largely involved variations on two basic methods: (1) the two-factor-at-a-time procedure and (2) the full-profile approach. The two-factor approach, also referred to as the trade-off procedure, considers factors (attributes) on a two-at-a-time basis. The respondent is asked to rank the various combinations of each pair of factor levels from most preferred to least preferred. The two-factor-at-a-time procedure is simple to apply and reduces information overload on the part of the respondent. It also lends itself easily to mail questionnaire form, since no special props are needed. In the full-profile approach, the respondents are asked to rank/rate the full product descriptions (full product profiles or combinations of levels of all the attributes) according to preference or likelihood of purchase.

4. *Estimation methods*

Each respondent provides a set of metric (or non-metric) scores for the combinations of attributes. Based on these scores, the conjoint analysis procedure calculates the contribution of each product characteristic (attribute level) to the buying intention. The contribution of the attribute level is termed its 'part-worth utility'. In conjoint analysis, an attribute is said to be important only to the degree that it makes a difference to the product choice, or that it differentiates between the various product offerings.

5. Analysis of the results

For each product profile, the total utility is calculated by summing the part-worth utilities of the levels of each of the attributes. Next to this, the relative importance of each attribute is estimated. The simplest way to measure this is to find the utility range for each attribute. The attribute with the widest range is considered as the most important.

DISCRIMINANT ANALYSIS

Discriminant analysis discriminates between respondents who fall into one group or category from those who fall into another group or category;[10] for example, jeep owners versus car owners. That is, discriminant analysis determines the characteristics of one group that differentiate it from the characteristics of another group. So, discriminant analysis classifies objects/subjects into groups and identifies those variables that best determine group membership. Thus, the objective in using discriminant analysis is to classify people/objects into one of two or more groups, based on the measurements of various independent variables, and predict which particular group or class an individual or entity belongs to.

On a technical level, discriminant analysis is a statistical technique which distinguishes one dependent variable with respect to a set of independent variables. The dependent variable is of the nominal/ordinal scale of measurement and represents a group measurement. So, for discriminant analysis it is important that the number and measurement level of the dependent variable is known in advance.

Discriminant analysis is utilised when:

1. there is an identified dependent variable;
2. there is only one dependent variable (other multivariate techniques can be used if there are two or more dependent variables;
3. the dependent variable is measured using non-metric scales;
4. there is a large set of observations or responses, i.e. large data set.

An important feature of discriminant analysis is the identification of those variables that best determine group membership. Here we examine members of known groups to identify those variables which best determine group membership. For example, if we are in the business of direct mail sales, we may wish to determine those variables that best discriminate between past interviewees who have purchased goods by direct mail, and past interviewees who have not purchased goods by direct mail. Such variables may include age, sex, marital status and proximity to shopping centres.

For the purpose of conveying the concepts in discriminant analysis we will suppose that for buyers and non-buyers of three types of car we have information pertaining to two independent variables — the age of each buyer/non-buyer and the number of children for each buyer/non-buyer. Scatter diagrams for each type of car are shown in Figure 14.2.

Figure 14.2 (a, b and c) Scatter diagram for discriminant analysis

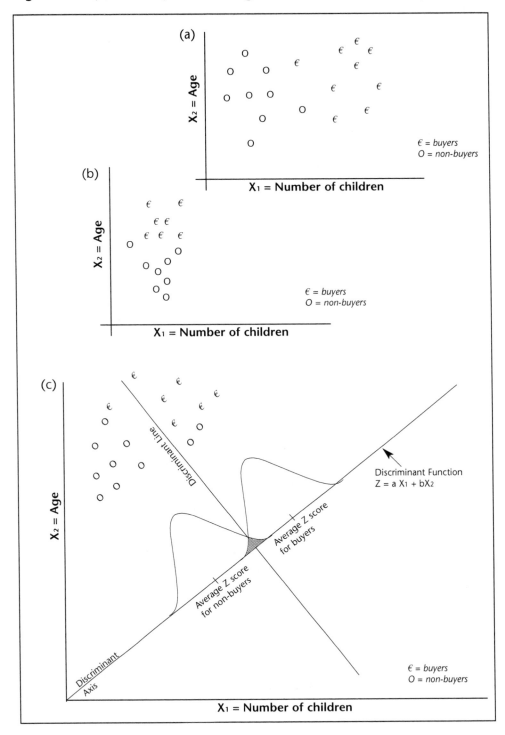

Car type 1:

Referring to part (a) in Figure 14.2, the ability of X_2 (age) to discriminate between buyers and non-buyers is very weak, particularly in comparison to variable X_1 (number of children) where the two groups are very distinct from each other along this dimension or variable. Thus the dimension X_1 is the only one that really separates the two groups.

Car type 2:

Referring to part (b) in Figure 14.2, the ability of X_2 to discriminate between buyers and non-buyers is very strong. This is in contrast to the discriminatory power of X_1. Thus the two groups are separated from each other only in the vertical direction.

Car type 3:

Referring to part (c) in Figure14.2, the groups are not separated by a single dimension as with car type 1 and 2 but with respect to both dimensions, indicating that both variables differentiate between the members of the two groups.

The discriminant axis is the line along which the groups are most separated. Discriminant analysis tries to find this straight line which discriminates one group from another, when imposed upon a scatter diagram, such as the one above. Statistically, it is the direction along which the ratio

$$\frac{\text{Variation between groups}}{\text{Variation within groups}}$$

is maximised. Maximisation of this ratio is intuitively appealing as we wish to distinguish between groups in such a manner that the variation within each group (or spread of data within each group) is small compared to the variation between each group (or spread of data within each group). If this ratio is large, then individuals in each group will be very close, or alike, to one another in contrast to the distance, or dissimilarity, of individuals between groups. The term 'centroid' can be taken to refer to the multidimensional mean.

DISCRIMINANT ANALYSIS ILLUSTRATED

To gain some insight into this technique of discriminant analysis, consider an example of a used-car salesman, Bernard Kenny. Bernard, in an attempt to identify genuine car buyers, has collected considerable survey data for three variables:

X_1: The customer's approximate age.

X_2: The number of minutes the customer spends examining the car in the forecourt before discussing a price with Bernard.

X_3: Whether or not the customer bought a car.

Figure 14.3 Scatter diagram pertaining to X₁ and X₂.

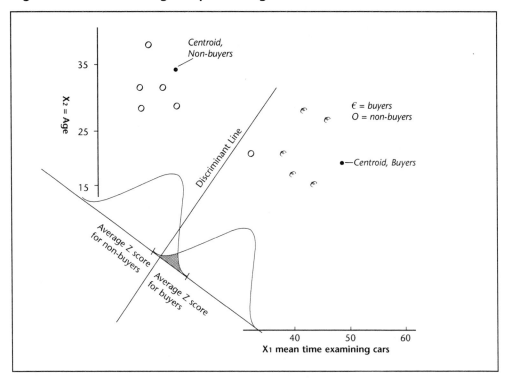

From observation alone, we note that both dimensions/variables X_1 and X_2 help to classify individuals into one of two groups. Buyers tend to be younger and spend greater time examining a car than non-buyers. The examination of centroids for both groups shows that the averages for buyers and non-buyers differ on both dimensions, i.e.

Table 14.3 Centroids for discriminant analysis

	Non-buyers	Buyers
X₁: Mean time spent examining cars	22.1	40.0
X₂: Mean age	37.0	27.3

In Table 14.3, the two groups have been classified by means of discriminant analysis. (The calculation of those entities pertaining to discriminant analysis has not been included here but, in practice, these calculations are performed by appropriate software, as previously noted.) The discriminant axis is neither horizontal or vertical but diagonal, indicating that both variables help to differentiate between individuals of the two groups. The discriminant line, i.e. our cut-off point for determining group membership, is located halfway between the centroids and is perpendicular to the discriminant axis.

With this information, Bernard can now classify future customers into one of two groups: potential buyers and potential non-buyers, and reflect this in his marketing strategy.

FACTOR ANALYSIS

Factor analysis is concerned with the identification of 'a few number of variables that are responsible for the correlation of a large number of variables',[11] i.e., factor analysis attempts to identify underlying common dimensions that explain the relationships in a complex set of large data. For this reason, it is sometimes referred to as a data reduction method. Essentially, the aim of this technique is to condense the larger data into a reduced data set or factors.[12]

A researcher frequently ends up with a large number of variables from a set of respondents drawn from a given population. However, it is frequently the case that many of these variables may be highly correlated and thus much of the information contained in one variable is contained in another variable. For example, if you own a very expensive house then you probably own a very expensive car and vice versa. Thus, information on the respondent's house price is somewhat redundant, if information pertaining to car type is available. In this vein, we employ factor analysis to reduce the number of variables without an undue loss of information.

Factor analysis is of further use, in that we can also identify the dimensionality of the data. If we had 100 variables measuring only five different basic characteristics of our sample, then obviously the employment of 100 variables represents gross inefficiencies. (The money could possibly have been better spend on managing response or non-response error, for example.)

Therefore, factor analysis is used by a researcher when:

1. the researcher cannot distinguish between the dependent variable(s) and the independent variable(s);
2. the variables are metric-based;
3. a large number of variables are to be reduced or summarised into a smaller set, as in new product development, product positioning, measuring opinion leaders and opinion-seekers,[13] assessing advertising readership or establishing product/ service quality factors.

Factor analysis typically starts with a matrix of correlations between the variables of interest, as shown in Table 14.4. We note that variables X_1 and X_2 are highly correlated. This suggests 'variable redundancy'.

Table 14.4 Correlation between variables

	X₁	X₂	X₃
X₁	1	0.91	0.20
X₂	0.91	1	0.15
X₃	0.20	0.15	1

Factor analysis attempts to generate three important measures:

1. the proportion of responses (statements) variability explained by the factors, commonly labelled 'communalities';
2. a standardised score, 'eigenvalues', which is the actual response measured in terms of the number of standard deviations from the mean;
3. the correlation between each statement score and the various original variables, called 'factor loadings'. An illustration serves to explain these terms and factor analysis further.

FACTOR ANALYSIS ILLUSTRATED

A survey is conducted to examine those attributes which influence consumers in their choice of car. The researcher measured a sample of customers by means of the nine statements shown in Table 14.5 below.

Table 14.5 Customer responses

Statements	I	II	III	Communalities
I like sport cars	0.75	0.20	0.03	0.60
I insist that my car has good acceleration	0.68	0.30	0.09	0.56
I watch a lot of Grand Prix racing	0.81	–0.16	0.15	0.70
I like cars with improved heating	0.21	0.73	0.21	0.62
I like cars with leather seats	0.33	0.69	0.04	0.59
I prefer a quiet car	0.25	0.56	–0.04	0.38
I insist on a robust car	0.29	0.33	0.68	0.66
I prefer a car with a ten-year warranty	0.31	0.11	0.71	0.61
I insist on a car that rarely requires servicing	–0.18	0.08	0.62	0.42
Eigenvalues	2.11	1.61	1.43	
Percent of variance explained	23.4%	17.8%	15.8%	
Cumulative percent of variance explained	23.4%	41.2%	57.0%	

The question to be addressed here is whether these statements are measuring nine different aspects of the sample or whether the nine measurements are representative of a smaller number of more basic consumer characteristics. The data was processed by means of a factor analysis software programme (such as those in SPSS, SAS or Minitab) and some of the output is shown in Table 14.5. The computer printout demonstrates that there are only three distinct aspects being measured by the nine statements, or at least three factors account for an acceptable proportion of the variation in the sample. These three factors are as follows:

Factor 1

Each of the first three statements in Table 14.5 has a high loading or correlation with the first factor and thus these three statements are identifying a single underlying attribute of consumer demand which may be termed 'I prefer fast cars'.

Factor 2

The next three statements in the table have a high loading on the second factor. These statements are measuring 'I prefer comfortable cars'.

Factor 3

The last three statements are measuring the underling factor 'I prefer reliable cars'.

Thus the nine statements may essentially be reduced to only three. The factor loading in the table, on each of the nine statements, is high on a single factor only.

Table 14.5 also contains additional information in the form of communalities and eigenvalues. The communality is the proportion of each statement's variability that is explained by the three factors. The three factors are better at explaining the variability in some statements than in others. For example, the factors explain 70% of the variability in the statement 'I watch a lot of Grand Prix racing', but only 38% of the variability in the statement 'I prefer a quiet car'. In seven of the nine statements, the three factors explain at least 56% of the variability in these statements. The eigenvalue is the sum of the squared factor loadings for each factor.

CLUSTER ANALYSIS

This is a technique which groups or clusters objects or individuals so that objects/individuals within each group are more similar to each other than they are to objects/individuals of different groups.[14] Cluster analysis procedures search through large amounts of data and 'identify respondents who have given identical or similar answers to a certain combination of questions'. These respondents then form a cluster.[15] Cluster analysis is utilised in marketing research when:

1. the dependent variable(s) and independent variable(s) cannot be differentiated;
2. the data is metric data;

3. a large group of people or objects is to be summarised, as is the case with market segmentation studies or facilitating the selection of test markets for experimentation purposes.

Cluster analysis measures 'similarity' between respondents. This similarity is normally measured in terms of distance between respondents. One commonly used distance measure is the 'euclidean' distance.[16]

CLUSTER ANALYSIS ILLUSTRATED

Suppose we are considering the clustering of customers based on attitudes towards shopping. Suppose five attitudinal variables are employed upon which consumers are asked to express their degree of agreement using a six-point scale (1 = disagree, 2 = agree). The variables are given by:

Var. 1: I shop for bargains
Var. 2: I only buy designer brands
Var. 3: I only shop during the sales
Var. 4: I insist on a guarantee with products
Var. 5: I shop mostly at discount shops

A computer application (SPSS, SAS or Minitab etc.), on analysing the responses, would include a table of centroids for the desired number of clusters. Suppose that we specify that the desired number of clusters is two and that these centroids produced by the computer are given by Table 14.6 (each entry corresponds to the mean value of each variable for all objects/respondents in that cluster).

Table 14.6 Cluster analysis and centroids

	Var. 1	Var. 2	Var. 3	Var. 4	Var. 5
Cluster number 1	5.1	2.8	4.8	2.9	5.0
Cluster number 2	3.0	4.9	1.0	5.1	1.9

All objects/respondents have being grouped into either cluster 1 or cluster 2. We see that objects/respondents in cluster 1 have a high value on variables 1, 3 and 5, but low values on variables 2 and 4. Such objects/respondents could be termed 'shoppers concerned with price'. Alternatively, objects/respondents in cluster 2 have a high value on variables 2 and 4, but low values on variables 1, 3 and 5, and could be termed 'shoppers concerned with quality'.

Cluster Analysis at Work

Cluster analysis was used in a study in Switzerland that was investigating the area of wellness tourism. Guest clustering was based on their information about the importance of wellness components and parameters for their stay in the hotel. The cluster analysis came up with four guest segments: 'demanding health guests', 'independent infrastructure users', 'care-intensive health guests' and 'undemanding recreation guests'.

At around 40%, **demanding health guests** were the largest group, attaching great care and importance to professional competence and comprehensive wellness amenities. Women made up more than three-quarters of this group, and their average age of 48 was the lowest. One-third of these guests spent their holiday alone, and just one-quarter with a partner.

Just under one-quarter of guests, as **independent infrastructure users**, attached no great importance to guest care, information or professional know how, but greatly appreciated wellness facilities such as a whirlpool, steam bath, sauna and swimming pool. Other wellness amenities were less important. This group of independent infrastructure users was the only one with a majority of men (54%) who were usually on holiday with partners. The average age for this group was 49 and, at around 80%, the proportion of graduates or those with a higher professional qualification is exceptionally high, while the average stay of 6.5 days was by far the shortest.

Care-intensive health guests accounted for one-fifth of guests. They cited healing/therapy/convalescence as the main reason for their stay, and health promotion was another important factor for them. Consequently, they attached great importance to medical competence as well as individual care and advice. About 60% were women with an above-average proportion of singles, and the average age was around 53. At slightly over ten days, care-intensive guests had the longest stays.

Undemanding recreation guests ranked the importance of nearly all the particular wellness components and parameters lowest. At 14%, they were the smallest guest group. More than half of the guests gave recreation and relaxation as the main reasons for their stay. The wellness infrastructure, guest supervision and information were not important for this group, which appreciated a swimming pool above all else. Health promotion or convalescence was not relevant for these guests, whose most frequent objective was to enjoy themselves and let themselves be pampered. Undemanding recreation guests have the highest average age (approx 58) and the percentage of women (a good 50%) was below average. The average stay for this group of guests was just under nine days and, in an above-average number of cases, the time was spent with their partner or family members.

From the above cluster analysis, it was recommended that there needs to be a clear demarcation of the wellness concept for marketing strategies to be successful.

Reference: Mueller, Hansruedi and Kaufmann, Eveline, Lanz, 'Wellness Tourism: Market Analysis of a Special Health Tourism Segment and Implications for the Hotel Industry', *Journal of Vacation Marketing*, Vol. 7. No. 1, 2001, pp. 5-17.

MULTIDIMENSIONAL SCALING

Multidimensional scaling (MDS) is a class of procedures for describing and representing consumer attitudes, especially perceptions and preferences. In this manner, MDS attempts to identify important consumer attributes, and measure their relative importance. It results in a visual map, such representations often being called 'spatial maps'. The axes of the map are assumed to denote the underlying variables/dimensions respondents use to form perceptions and preferences. MDS is employed in a large number of applications and has been used in marketing for segmentation studies, product life-cycle examinations, vendor evaluations and media selection.

MDS CONSIDERATIONS, DIRECT VERSUS DERIVED

One issue for the researcher to consider in employing MDS is whether to utilise direct or indirect MDS. In gathering perception data, the direct MDS approach asks respondents to judge how similar or dissimilar various brands or objects are using their own criteria. Respondents are frequently required to rate all possible pairs of objects in terms of similarity on a Likert scale. Direct approaches have the advantage that the researcher does not have to identify a set of pertinent attributes. Respondents form their judgments using their own criteria.

In derived MDS approaches to collecting perception data, the respondents are required to rate these objects on a set of specified attributes/criteria. The advantage of the derived approach is that it is easy to identify clusters of respondents based on the attribute ratings. Also, the labelling dimensions, which result from implementation of MDS, may be considerably simplified when the derived approach is adopted.

Once the collected perceptual data has been input into a computer programme, three further issues are investigated. Firstly, how many dimensions underlie consumer perceptions; and secondly, what is the configuration of those perceptions, i.e. which products are perceived to be most alike and which are most dissimilar? These two questions produce a goodness-of-fit or lack-of-fit, referred to as a stress index. Thirdly, the actual attributes are identified, and can be compared to the ideal point, a point that describes the consumer's first preference (regardless of whether it is real or imagined).

MULTIDIMENSIONAL SCALING ILLUSTRATED

Suppose respondents are asked to rate, using their own criteria, five brands of soap using the following five-point Likert scale.

Table 14.7 Respondent's comparison of soap brands

	Very dissimilar			Very similar	
	1	2	3	4	5
Soap 1 versus Soap 2.					
Soap 1 versus Soap 3.					
Soap 1 versus Soap 4.					
Soap 1 versus Soap 5.					
Soap 2 versus Soap 3.					
Soap 2 versus Soap 4.					
Soap 2 versus Soap 5.					
Soap 3 versus Soap 4.					
Soap 3 versus Soap 5.					
Soap 4 versus Soap 5.					

The data from one respondent might be as follows:

Table 14.8 Similarity ratings of soap brands

	Soap 1	Soap 2	Soap 3	Soap 4	Soap 5
Soap 1	—				
Soap 2	5	—			
Soap 3	1	2	—		
Soap 4	2	3	4	—	
Soap 5	1	2	2	2	—

On supplying this similarity matrix as the basis for an MDS procedure, a typical output is given in Figure 14.4.

Figure 14.4 Typical output in MDS

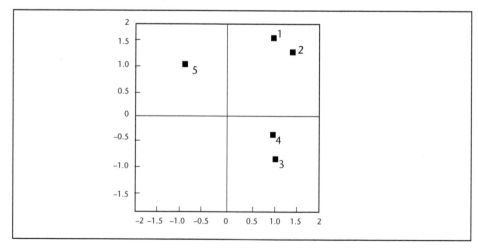

From examination of the map, we find that soaps 1 and 2 are clustered together, soaps 3 and 4 are clustered together and soap 5 is not clustered with any other soap. Suppose the respondents are shown this map and asked to label the dimensions — the horizontal and vertical axes, as they provided similarity measures based on their own dimensions/criteria. In doing so, they could label soaps 1 and 2 as 'dirt removing and pleasant smelling'; soaps 3 and 4 as 'dirt removing and failing to leave a pleasant smell' and soap 5 as 'poor dirt remover and pleasant smelling'.

MULTIVARIATE TECHNIQUES, CONCLUDING COMMENTS

Before concluding our discussion on multivariate techniques, a number of points are worthy of our attention again. The use of multivariate approaches is significantly increasing; one force fuelling this trend is the ready availability of relevant, user-friendly PC software. Coupled with this, new multivariate techniques, such as LISREL,[17, 18] are emerging and will continue too, as a result of the commercial imperative to survive and sustain competitiveness in the marketplace and marketspace. Against this background, multivariate techniques are to be treated with caution, and an eye kept on the ten commands of multivariate analysis:[19]

1. Do not be technique-oriented.
2. Consider multivariate models as information for management.
3. Do not substitute multivariate methods for researcher skill and imagination.
4. Develop non-technical communication skills.
5. Avoid the temptation to over-analyse.
6. Beware of generalisations.
7. Beware of the peculiarities of the method.
8. Start at the beginning.
9. Don't use the technique in isolation, ignoring other descriptive methods.
10. Keep an eye on the cost-benefit factors.

SUMMARY

This chapter focused upon some of the more popular multivariate data analysis techniques in marketing research, namely multiple regression analysis, discriminant analysis, factor analysis, cluster analysis and multidimensional scaling. These methods are applicable only to a certain type of variable, dependent or independent and to a certain type of data, metric or non-metric. They make extensive use of computer procedures, reflect the complex and dynamic nature of many marketing situations and are growing in popularity. When used with caution by a researcher, they can provide invaluable insights and information to assist the manager or management team with their decision-making.

KEY TERMS

Univariate analysis	Bivariate analysis
Multivariate analysis	Discriminant analysis
Discriminant axis	Communality
Dependent variable	Independent variable
Metric data	Non-metric data
Factor analysis	Centroid
Cluster analysis	Eigenvalue
Multidimensional scaling	Factor loading

QUESTIONS

1. What are multivariate techniques?
2. Provide real or hypothetical examples where multivariate analysis might be beneficial to a marketing researcher.
3. How does multiple regression analysis differ from regression analysis as described in Chapter 13?
4. What are the objectives of discriminant analysis?
5. What is factor analysis and why is it useful in the analysis of marketing research data?
6. In factor analysis, what is the difference between a factor and a factor loading? What is meant by the eigenvalue associated with each factor?
7. What is cluster analysis?
8. Describe how factor and cluster analysis differ.
9. What is meant by the term 'Multidimensional scaling'?
10. Why is the use of multivariate methods increasing?
11. Differentiate between direct and derived approaches to MDS.

PROBLEMS AND ASSIGNMENTS

1. A marketing company wishes to conduct a cluster analysis study of the fast-food industry in Ireland. What variables associated with this industry should be measured?
2. Suppose that a marketing department has collected data on the leisure equipment expenditure of 500 consumers. Members of the sample have also completed surveys measuring 30 psychological variables and 20 different demographic variables. Discuss how each of the following could contribute to analysis of such data:
   (a) Discriminant analysis.
   (b) Cluster analysis.
   (c) Factor analysis.

3. Use the Internet to go to the SPSS home page at http://www.spss.com and examine the package with respect to multivariate techniques.
4. Illustrating your answer with examples, distinguish between discriminant analysis and multiple regression analysis in respect of:
   (a) the usual or most common purpose of the technique; and
   (b) the type of variables involved.
   (*Adapted from a Marketing Institute of Ireland Examination Paper, 1996*)
5. Describe three different problems in marketing which you feel might be suited to analysis by multi-dimensional scaling. Show how you would use multi-dimensional scaling in each case. (*Adapted from a Marketing Institute of Ireland Examination Paper, 1993*)
6. An oil company has developed a multiple regression model to predict the sales of 50 of its filming stations. The variables used are:
   Y = average monthly sales in gallons;
   X_1 = square foot area of station property;
   X_2 = average daily traffic flow;
   X_3 = number of competing filling stations.
   The empirical results are shown in Table 14.9.

Table 14.9

Variable	Variable mean	Variable range	Regression coefficient	t-value
Y_1	10,000			
X_1	10,000	3,000–20,000	$b1 = 4.0$	1.3
X_2	6,000	2,500–12,500	$b2 = 4.0$	1.0
X_3	12	0 – 25	$b3 = -1000$	
$r2 = .45$			$bo = 10,000$	

   (a) What is the regression equation?
   (b) Which variable seems to be the most significant predictor?
   (c) Provide a prediction of sales given the following inputs:

   $X_1 = 5,000$
   $X_2 = 2,000$
   $X_3 = 2$

   (d) Comment on the usefulness of your prediction.
   (*Adapted from a Marketing Institute of Ireland Examination Paper, 1993*)

7. (a) Define cluster analysis and indicate some common uses of the procedure in marketing research.
   (b) Comment briefly on the options/considerations when conducting a cluster analysis in relation to the following:
      (i) Selection of a distance/similarity measure.
      (ii) Selection of a clustering procedure.
      (iii) Decisions on the number of clusters.
   (*Adapted from a Marketing Institute of Ireland Examination Paper, 1997*)

8. Illustrating your answer with examples, distinguish between discriminant analysis and multiple regression analysis in respect of:
   (a) the usual or most common purpose of the technique; and
   (b) the type of variables involved.

9. Choosing multidimensional scaling and illustrating your answer with a suitable example, discuss the method briefly under the following headings:
   (a) The basic (or most usual) purpose of the technique.
   (b) How the input data are generally obtained.
   (c) An analytical/mathematical rationale for the procedure (it is not essential to include particular mathematical models or expressions in your answers).
   (d) The type of output from the analytical method.
   (*Adapted from a Marketing Institute of Ireland Examination Paper, 1996*)

Case Study
The Irish Farmhouse Cheese Industry*

The history of Ireland's farmhouse cheeses offers the most potent proof that small-scale, high-quality artisan food producers can thrive and prosper in the modern marketplace, creating a dedicated audience for their cheese and contributing substantially to the creation of a food profile in Ireland. This quiet revolution has resulted in villages such as Durrus and areas such as Cratloe and Knockanore being known the world over by virtue of the cheeses that are produced there.

The Irish Farmhouse Cheese Market

The first Irish farmhouse cheese makers started business in 1980. At the last count in 1996, total sales of Irish farmhouse cheese amounted to 700 tonnes. Consumption of farmhouse cheese in Ireland was estimated at 600 tonnes in 2000. The definition of farmhouse cheese is variable, but generally involves small farmer producers making cheese on their farms, using either pasteurised or unpasteurised milk. The majority of producers have their own supply of milk, which allows them greater control over this raw material. Generally there is a handmade element to the process and the operation is typically small scale. In 2000 there were estimated to be about thirty-five farmhouse cheese producers in Ireland.

Establishing the Attributes

Product attributes are components or characteristics of the product. Conjoint analysis starts with the determination of relevant attributes that are believed to influence a consumer's preference (between different cheeses).

Three focus groups were conducted, the first one in Dublin. The sampling frame for this research comprised:

- All cheese eaters, with a half being Irish farmhouse cheese eaters.
- Food buyers.
- ABC1 Socio-economic group.
- Females.

The important differentiating attributes identified by the focus groups were:

1. Flavour.
2. Texture.
3. Price.
4. Nutritional and other information.
5. Pasteurisation.
6. Packaging.
7. Colour.
8. Weight.

The focus groups identified attributes such as the shape of the cheese and the convenience of the selling point to be of lesser importance. Consumers bought some cheese in wheel form, especially if they were giving the cheese as a gift to someone, but the vast majority of the farmhouse cheese was bought in wedge form, cut in small quantities from a larger wheel. It was subsequently decided to anchor all discussion of the attribute levels and conjoint analysis profile cards (discussed later) at the weight of 200 g, as this was the weight of cheese most commonly purchased. Consumers also wanted a label stating that the cheese was 'Irish farmhouse cheese'.

Determination of Attribute Levels

The next step involved ascertaining the relevant attribute levels. The focus groups identified the following attribute levels:

1. Flavour – strong and mild;
2. Texture – hard and soft;
3. Price – €1.91, €2.54 and €3.17;
4. Nutritional information – present on the label or absent;
5. Pasteurisation – pasteurised or unpasteurised;
6. Packaging – waxed wheel, cling-film wedge or vacuum-packed wedge; and
7. Colour – red or white.

Generation of Scenarios for Respondents

Having established the relevant attributes and their levels, hypothetical scenarios with different combinations of attributes were presented to individuals. The study gave rise to 288 possible combinations (2 x 2 x 3 x 2 x 2 x 3 x 2). Clearly it would have been unrealistic to ask individuals their preferences for so many scenarios. This study utilised a fractional factorial design, under SPSS Conjoint, to reduce the number of profiles to a manageable size, while at the same time maintaining orthogonality. Thus there were fewer judgments to be made by the respondents. This reduced the number of profiles to be evaluated to sixteen.

The full-profile approach was utilised as the means of presentation to the respondents. In this approach, respondents were asked to rate the full product descriptions (full product profiles or combinations of levels of all the attributes) according to preference. A rating scale was utilised over a rank scale due to possible time constraints on respondents. The scale was anchored from one to nine, with one being 'dislike extremely' and nine being 'like extremely'.

This study utilised a verbal description approach. Each verbal description of the potential farmhouse cheese was placed on a profile card. This meant that each respondent was given sixteen stimulus cards, with each card defining the levels of each of the seven attributes. Each card contained a simple sketch of either a wheel or a wedge of cheese, weighing 200 g and with a simple label stating that the cheese was 'Irish farmhouse cheese'. The sixteen conjoint profile cards were administered to 256 respondents in the Dublin area. Dublin was picked as the location for this study due to the large number of farmhouse cheese shops in the area. All respondents had to have eaten Irish farmhouse cheese at least once in the last month.

Establishing Preferences & Estimating Utilities

All 256 respondents interviewed provided a set of metric (rating) scores for the combinations of attributes. Based on these scores, the conjoint analysis procedure calculated the contribution of each product attribute to the respondent's preference. The contribution of the attribute level is termed its 'part-worth utility'. Conjoint uses the utility ranges to compute importance scores for each attribute.

Results: Conjoint analysis – Part-worths and relative importance of attributes

Table 14.10 shows the part-worth utility scores for each level of each attribute. Packaging was identified as the most important factor (24%), followed by flavour (17%), price (17%), colour (11%), nutritional information (11%), pasteurisation (10%) and finally texture (10%). Packaging was therefore more than doubly important for respondents compared to the texture/colour/nutritional information/pasteurisation of the farmhouse cheese.

Within the attributes, the utilities of each level were also investigated. For example, with packaging, the most utility was obtained from a wheel that was packaged in wax (U = 0.2766), whereas the utility of a vacuum-packed wedge was lower (U = -0.0038), but higher than a wedge wrapped in cling-film (U = -0.2728). The overall 256 respondents obtained a higher utility from a cheese made with pasteurised milk (U = 0.0495) than from a cheese made with unpasteurised milk (U = -0.0495). The remaining utilities can be read from Table 14.10. It is interesting that a price of €3.17 had the highest utility (U = 0.0300) among the price levels, compared to a price of €2.54 (U = 0.0002) and €1.90 (U = -0.0302). The latter shows that consumers in this survey were not price conscious, deriving a higher utility from farmhouse cheese that was of a higher price. If a producer were to charge €1.90 instead of €3.17, there would be a consequent loss in utility of 0.0602. Also, if a producer were to make his cheese using pasteurised milk, there would be a consequent rise in utility of 0.099 for the 256 respondents. This is interesting, as the ethos of the Irish farmhouse cheese lobby has been to preserve the use of raw milk as a constituent of farmhouse cheese.

Table 14.10 Results of conjoint analysis (*n* = 256)

Attribute	Level	Utility	Relative importance (%)
Flavour	Strong	-0.2667	17
	Mild	0.2667	
Texture	Hard	0.0506	10
	Soft	-0.0506	
Packaging	Waxed Wheel	0.2766	24
	Clingfilm Wedge	-0.2728	
	Vac-packed Wedge	-0.0038	
Pasteurisation	Pasteurised	0.0495	10
	Raw	-0.0495	
Nutritional information	Provided	0.1513	11
	Not provided	-0.1513	
Colour	Red	-0.0769	11
	White	0.0769	
Price	€1.90	-0.0302	17
	€2.54	0.0002	
	€3.17	0.0300	

Notes: Pearson's *R* = 0.991. Kendall's tau = 0.9000. These statistics show that the data fit was very good.

The conjoint analysis for the overall 256 consumers found that the ideal farmhouse cheese had the following attributes: a strong flavour, a hard texture, a wax packaged wheel made with pasteurised milk, nutritional information present on the package, a white coloured cheese and a price of €3.17 per 200 g.

Market Segmentation

A market cluster analysis was conducted to ascertain if clearly defined clusters of consumers existed. A two-cluster solution was found to have the best fit. The first cluster contained 139 respondents and the second contained 117. Each of these had different perceptions of the relative importance of the attributes and it is useful to analyse them separately and contrast the results (Tables 14.11 and 14.12 below).

Table 14.11 Importance scores for each attribute

Attribute	All consumers (n = 256) Importance score (%)	Cluster 1 (n = 139) Importance score (%)	Cluster 2 (n = 117) Importance score (%)
Flavour	17	24	34(a)
Texture	10(b)	3(b)	8
Packaging	24(a)	33(a)	23
Pasteurisation	10(b)	12	5
Information	11	13	21
Colour	11	12	2(b)
Price	17	3(b)	7

Notes: (a) most important attribute; (b) least important attribute

Table 14.12 Utility score of attributes

Attribute	All consumers (n = 256)	Cluster 1 (n = 139)	Cluster 2 (n = 117)
Flavour			
Strong	0.2667	0.2610	0.2735(a)
Mild	0.2667	-0.2610	-0.2735

Attribute	All consumers (n = 256)	Cluster 1 (n = 139)	Cluster 2 (n = 117)
Texture			
Hard	0.0506	0.0374	0.0664(a)
Soft	0.0506	-0.0374	-0.0664
Packaging			
Waxed wheel	0.2766	0.3746(a)	0.1587
Clingfilm Wedge	-0.2728	-0.3306	-0.2033
Vac-packed wedge	-0.0038	-0.0441	0.0445
Pasteurisation			
Pasteurised	0.0495	0.1241(a)	-0.0401
Raw	-0.0495	-0.1241	0.0401
Nutritional information			
Provided	0.1513	0.1391	0.1660(a)
Not provided	-0.1513	-0.1391	-0.1660
Colour			
Red	-0.0769	-0.1314	-0.0114
White	0.0769	0.1314(a)	0.0114
Price			
€1.90	-0.0302	-0.0329	-0.0269
€2.54	0.0002	0.0384	-0.0457
€3.17	0.0300	-0.0054	0.0727(a)

Notes: (a) cluster with highest utility for this attribute

Questions/Issues for Further Research

1. Outline a possible discussion guide for the focus groups on the important product attributes of Irish farmhouse cheese.
2. Do you agree with the sampling frame used for the focus groups on the differentiating attributes of Irish farmhouse cheese? Why/Why not?
3. In relation to the overall 256 consumers, determine the combination of attributes which yields the lowest utility.
4. In relation to both clusters one and two, determine the combination of attributes that yields the highest and lowest utilities.
5. What is the most important/least important attribute for both clusters one and two?
6. Analyse cluster two's preference on the issue of pasteurisation. Compare this to cluster one and the overall 256 consumers.

7. In relation to the attributes of price and packaging, compare and contrast where each cluster derives the highest utility. Compare these to the overall 256 consumers.

* This case was written by Maurice Murphy, Management and Marketing Department, Cork Institute of Technology. The case is based on a real EU study conducted across seven EU countries. It is intended to be used as a basis for class discussion rather than to illustrate either effective or ineffective handling of a research situation.

Case Study
The Irish Honey Industry*

Beekeeping in Ireland is for some an absorbing hobby and for others a valuable farm income supplement. It was estimated in 1998 that there were 2,000 beekeepers in Ireland, managing 22,000 colonies (hives) of bees. The majority of beekeepers have a small number of hives – a 1990 census of population of both colonies and beekeepers noted that 78% of beekeepers had 1–10 hives. In 1997 honey production was 198 tonnes, or nearly 11% of Irish needs, and consumption was at 1,779 tonnes. A clear deficit exists that could be made up by increased production. The EU itself only produces half its needs, with the remainder being imported from New Zealand, Mexico and Russia.

This case deals with an EU study into farmhouse foods, conducted in seven EU countries. The Irish participation involved identifying the distinguishing characteristics of Irish honey made by small producers, through conjoint analysis. For this research, 153 consumers of honey were interviewed in both Cork and Dublin.

Establishing the Attributes

A focus group was conducted with eight female consumers of honey to determine the relevant attributes that are believed to influence a consumer's preference between different honeys. The recruitment criteria was as follows:

- Female buyers and consumers of honey.
- All had to consume honey at least once a month.
- ABC1 Socio-economic group.
- Age from 30–60 years.

Three attributes were identified which were very important for consumers of any honey, but which did not differentiate between honeys. These were that a honey should be:

- Pure;
- Irish; and
- A healthy nutritional product.

It was subsequently decided to anchor all conjoint analysis profile cards with a label stating that the honey was 'Pure 100% Irish Honey'. The important differentiating attributes were:

- Texture of the honey;
- Colour of the honey;
- Source of the honey;
- Price; and
- Packaging.

Determination of Attribute Levels

Having determined relevant attributes, levels must be assigned to them. Two further focus groups were conducted, again with eight females in each group. The objective for both these groups was to identify the levels associated with the five attributes that were identified by the first focus group. These attribute levels were as follows:

- Texture – thick and runny.
- Colour – dark golden and light golden.
- Source – mass produced and made by a small scale producer.
- Price – €2.48, €2.73 and €3.11.
- Packaging – 227 g (8 oz) shaped glass jar and 454 g (1 lb) plain glass jar.

These levels were identified by the focus groups. The levels of the price were chosen in a way that the 'middle' level reflected the average price paid for a jar of honey, irrespective of the size of the jar. Price was unique among the identified attributes, in that consumers felt that there were three realistic prices that they could pay for honey. Any price below €2.48 and above €3.11 was not considered realistic for a jar of honey.

Generation of Scenarios for Respondents

Having established the relevant attributes and their levels, hypothetical scenarios with different combinations of attributes were presented to individuals. This study gave rise to 48 possible combinations (2 x 2 x 2 x 3 x 2, corresponding to texture x colour x source x price x packaging). Clearly it would have been unrealistic to ask individuals their preferences for so many scenarios. This study utilised a fractional factorial design, under SPSS Conjoint, to reduce the number of profiles to a manageable size, while at the same time maintaining orthogonality. Thus there were fewer judgments to be made by the respondents. This reduced the number of profiles to be evaluated to eight.

The full-profile approach was utilised as the means of presentation to the respondents. In this approach, respondents were asked to rate the full product descriptions (full product profiles or combinations of levels of all the attributes) according to preference. In this case the list of attributes is not long, so respondents were not expected to have difficulties in distinguishing between them. A rating scale was utilised over a rank scale due to possible time constraints on respondents. The scale was anchored from one to nine, with one being 'dislike extremely' and nine being 'like extremely'.

This study utilised a verbal description approach. Each verbal description of the potential honey was placed on a profile card. This meant that each respondent was given eight stimulus cards, with each card defining the levels of each of the five attributes. Each card contained a simple sketch of a honey jar (size was dependant on the packaging of the profile), with a simple sketch stating that the honey was 'Pure 100% Irish Honey'.

The eight conjoint profile cards were administered to 153 respondents. Respondents were chosen at random in both Cork and Dublin. The overall study involved an analysis of both commercial and small producer honey, so areas had to be chosen where both types of product were on sale. Commercial brands of honey are available in both markets. However, in Cork there are also a large number of small-scale producers with markets in the area, while Dublin consumers had less access to the products of these producers. Respondents had to have eaten honey at least once in the last month.

Establishing Preferences & Estimating Utilities

All 153 respondents interviewed provided a set of metric (rating) scores for the combinations of attributes. Based on these scores, the conjoint analysis procedure calculated the contribution of each product attribute to the respondent's preference. The contribution of the attribute level is termed its 'part-worth utility'. Conjoint uses the utility ranges to compute importance scores for each attribute.

Results: Conjoint Analysis – Part-worths and Relative Importance of Attributes

Table 14.13 shows the part-worth utility scores for each level of each attribute. Respondents overall felt that price was the most important factor (26%), closely followed by texture (25%), packaging (19%), scale of production (17%) and finally the colour of the honey (13%). Price was therefore twice as important for respondents as the colour of the honey. Price and texture accounted for just over 50% of the importance all consumers attached to the attributes of a honey. The colour of the honey was the least valued attribute.

Within the attributes, the utilities of each level were also investigated. With regard to the price of honey, €3.11 had a negative utility (U = -0.5375), while a price of €2.73 had a higher utility (U = 0.2439) and a price of €2.48 had the highest utility (U = 0.2936). A honey from a small producer had more utility (U = 0.5877) than one that was produced on a mass scale (U = -0.5877). The remaining utilities can be read from Table 14.13.

Table 14.13 Results of conjoint analysis (*n* = 153)

Attribute	Level	Utility	Relative Importance (%)
Texture	Thick	0.4801	25
	Runny	-0.4801	
Colour	Light golden	-0.0315	13
	Dark golden	0.0315	
Scale of production	Small	0.5877	17
	Mass	-0.5877	
Price	€2.48	0.2936	26
	€2.73	0.2439	
	€3.11	-0.5375	
Packaging	8 oz (227 g) shaped glass	-0.6291	19
	1 lb (454 g) plain glass	0.6291	

Pearson's R = 0.997. Kendall's tau = 1.000. p = 0.0000. These statistics show that that the data fit to the model was very good.

The utility of the price attribute shows that consumers in this survey were price conscious, deriving a higher utility from a honey of a lower price. They can also be judged as being in some way price sensitive, as they derived a higher utility from the larger 1 lb (454 g) jar than from the smaller 8 oz (227 g) shaped glass jar. The degree to which the bigger jar was preferred due to its larger size could not be determined, but certainly, from conducting the questionnaire, a lot of people preferred the larger jar as it gave them value for money. If a producer were to charge €2.73 instead of €2.48 for their honey, there would be a consequent loss in utility of 0.0497 (0.2936 – 0.2439). However, if the producer were to package his honey in a 454 g plain glass jar instead of a 227 g shaped glass jar, there would be a consequent rise in utility of 1.2582 (0.6291 + 0.6291). If this larger jar of honey was priced at €2.73 instead of €2.48, the utility would rise by 1.2085 (1.2582 – 0.0497). Alternatively, if the price was reduced from €3.11 to €2.48 and the honey was packaged in the 454 g plain glass container instead of a 227 g shaped glass jar, there would be a consequent rise in utility of 2.0893 (0.8311 + 1.2582). The implication is clear that these 153 consumers would derive a higher utility from a cheaper honey, packaged in larger jars.

The market was segmented on the attribute of scale to ascertain if clearly defined clusters of consumers existed. Scale was considered the most appropriate basis for segmentation as it would divide the respondents according to those who obtained a high utility for a honey from a small-scale producer and from a larger-scale producer. It must be remembered that the overall purpose of this EU study was to identify the reasons why consumers purchased from small-scale producers rather than purchasing mass-produced honeys. A three-cluster solution was found to have the best fit. The first cluster contained seventeen respondents, the second contained seventy-two and the third contained sixty-four.

All three clusters preferred the 454 g plain glass jar and a thick textured honey. However, differences existed with respect to the other attributes for consumers in the three clusters. For cluster one, in addition to a 454 g plain glass jar and a thick textured honey, the ideal product was also dark golden in colour, priced at €2.73 and from a small-scale producer. For cluster two, the ideal product was similar but light golden in colour. For cluster three, it was dark golden, priced at €2.48 and mass-produced. Table 14.14 shows the importance scores for all 153 consumers as well as the three clusters. Table 14.15 details the attribute levels and the utility associated with each level. None of the three clusters derived a positive utility from a price of €3.11.

Cluster one derived the highest utility of all clusters from a honey made by a small-scale producer (Table 14.15) and this attribute also contributed nearly 50% towards the importance associated with buying a honey (Table 14.14). They derived the lowest utility from a price of €2.48. Price was also one of the lowest contributors towards the importance of various honey attributes, when compared to other clusters. Though they gave a positive utility towards the 454 g plain glass jar, it was the lowest on a cross-cluster basis. Cluster one, in subsequent analysis, was found to have the highest percentage of single people and the lowest percentage of children. They also had the highest percentage of respondents working full-time and the lowest working part-time.

Though colour was the least important attribute for consumers in cluster two, they were the only consumers to derive a positive utility from a light-coloured honey. This differentiated them from the other clusters in terms of their ideal honey profile. They derived the highest utility of all three clusters from a price of €2.73 and the lowest utility from €3.11. This group of respondents, however, gave a higher utility to €2.48 than cluster one, but this utility is lower than cluster three.

Cluster three considered price as the second most important attribute when buying a honey and obtained the largest positive utility of all clusters from a price of €2.48, while obtaining the lowest utility of all clusters from a price of €2.73. They also obtained the largest positive utility from a 454 g jar, compared to the other clusters, and this is reinforced when one considers that, of all three clusters, this cluster considered packaging to have the largest importance. They were also the only cluster to derive a positive utility from a honey produced on a mass scale. Cluster three, in further analysis, were found to have the most children.

Table 14.14 Importance scores for each attribute

Attribute	All consumers (*n* = 153) Importance score (%)	Cluster 1 (*n* = 17) Importance score (%)	Cluster 2 (*n* = 72) Importance score (%)	Cluster 3 (*n* = 64) Importance score (%)
Texture	25	12	23	29 (a)
Colour	13 (b)	10 (b)	14 (b)	13
Scale of Production	17	49 (a)	20	6 (b)
Price	26 (a)	18	27 (a)	27
Packaging	19	11	16	25

Notes: (a) Most important attribute; (b) Least important attribute

Table 14.15 Utility scores of attributes

Attribute	All consumers (*n* = 153) Importance score (%)	Cluster 1 (*n* = 17) Importance score (%)	Cluster 2 (*n* = 72) Importance score (%)	Cluster 3 (*n* = 64) Importance score (%)
Texture –				
Thick	0.4801	0.3676	0.6302 (a)	0.3367
Runny	-0.4801	-0.3676	-0.6302	-0.3367
Colour –				
Light golden	-0.0315	-0.1912	0.0017	-0.0262
Dark golden	0.0315	0.1912 (a)	-0.0017	0.0262
Scale –				
Small	0.5877	2.2353 (a)	0.7691	-0.0746
Mass	-0.5877	-2.2353	-0.7691	0.0746
Price –				
€2.48	0.2936	0.1176	0.1736	0.4812 (a)
€2.73	0.2439	0.3088	0.4514	-0.0148
€3.11	-0.5375	-0.4265	-0.6250	-0.4664
Packaging –				
227 g shaped	-0.6291	-0.1176	-0.4149	-1.0181
454 g (1 lb) plain glass	0.6291	0.1176	0.4149	1.0181 (a)

Note: (a) cluster with highest utility for this attribute

Questions/Issues for Further Research

1. Outline a possible discussion guide for the focus group set up to ascertain the relevant attributes that are believed to influence a consumer's preference.
2. Outline a possible discussion guide for the focus group set up to ascertain the relevant attribute levels that are believed to influence a consumer's preference.
3. In relation to the overall 153 respondents, ascertain the product that provided the least utility.
4. For all three clusters, ascertain the profiles that provided the highest and lowest utility for consumers.
5. Do you think there is an opening for a high-class 'gourmet' honey for cluster one? Why?
6. What would be the characteristics of such a honey?
7. In relation to cluster three, comment on why the mass-produced honeys had a higher market share compared to cluster one.

* This case was written by Maurice Murphy, Management and Marketing Department, Cork Institute of Technology. The case is based on a real EU study conducted across seven EU countries. It is intended to be used as a basis for class discussion rather than to illustrate either effective or ineffective handling of a research situation.

CHAPTER 15

COMMUNICATION OF RESEARCH FINDINGS, REPORT WRITING AND PRESENTATION

CHAPTER OVERVIEW

▸ Introduction   ▸ Written Research Report Guidelines   ▸ The Contents of the Marketing Research Report   ▸ The Oral Report   ▸ Summary

INTRODUCTION

The final step in the research process is the preparation and presentation of the research report. After spending days, weeks or even months working on a project, the researcher may view the preparation of the report as just a mere formality. This is far from the truth. In marketing we frequently hear of product failure that can be attributed to poor packaging. This final phase could very well be the most important part of the research process. No matter how appropriate the research design, how proper the statistical analysis, how representative the sample, how carefully worded the questionnaire, how well the fieldwork is managed, etc., everything will be for nought if the report is confusing, poorly written and communicated ineffectively to the appropriate decision-makers. Often the research report is the only part of the research project that others will ever see. The quality of the report (written and oral presentation) is often used as a major indicator of the quality of the research itself. In fact, management's decision to undertake research in the future (or to use that research firm again!) will be greatly influenced by the perceived usefulness of the report and the presentation. The perceived quality of the research report by managers is also a primary determinant of whether the managers will use the research findings.[1] In this chapter we will discuss two vital ingredients of this communications process, the written research report and the oral presentation.

The objectives of this chapter are thus:

1. to discuss the importance of the research report;
2. to outline and explain the contents of the written research report;
3. to detail the requirements for an oral presentation.

WRITTEN RESEARCH REPORT GUIDELINES

The market research report has three primary roles: to communicate findings, to serve as a reference document, and to provide credibility for the work carried out. No two people will prepare a written report in exactly the same way. Situational differences in the personality, background and responsibility of the researcher and the manager to whom the report is addressed should conspire to give each report a unique flavour. There are, however, a series of guidelines which should be followed.

Consider the Audience

The researcher should use only words familiar to the readers and define all technical terms. The technical sophistication of the reader(s) determines their capacity for understanding methodological decisions such as sampling plan, measurement device, experimental design, analysis technique, etc. The readers of your reports are busy people, and very few of them can balance a research report, a cup of coffee and a dictionary at the one time.[2] In fact, most managers are extremely busy and are probably much less interested in the technical and logical aspects of a research problem than the researcher is. Depending on your audience, your research report may be either *technical* or *popular* in orientation. While both approaches describe the research study, its methodology, findings, conclusions and recommendations, they can differ considerably in terms of detail, writing style, use of technical terms and length of report.

The technical report is generally intended for other researchers, or for research managers. For example, the majority of articles which appear in the *Journal of Marketing Research* tend to use a format and language style that is typical of the technical report. The popular report, on the other hand, is intended for a more general audience. The writing style and complexity will tend to resemble what we find in the business section of *The Irish Times* or in a magazine such as *Business and Finance*. The report writer's difficulties in tailoring the report are often compounded by the existence of several audiences. A possible solution is to place the more technical aspects of the report in a separate section such as the appendix and to use a more balanced writing style in the main body of the report suitable for both levels of reader. Over-use of technical terms not common to the reader is likely to result in misunderstanding, suspicion and even hostility.

Address the Information Needs

A good report is designed to communicate information to decision-makers by answering the questions derived from the statement of objectives. This requires the research report-writer to be familiar with and to adhere to the study objectives. The report should reflect the interest of the reader rather than that of the researcher. The report should be built around the decision and how the resultant information is relevant to the decision. Unfortunately, researchers are often more interested in the research problem and the methodology used to solve it.

Be Complete, Concise, Accurate and Clear

No report was ever written that contained everything known on the given subject. If too much is included, there is a danger that the important points will be lost in the detail. Yet completeness is required. A report is complete when it addresses all of the questions raised in the original assignment. And although the report must be complete, it must also be concise. 'Concise writing makes maximum use of every word . . . no word in a concise discussion can be removed without impairing or destroying the function of the whole composition . . . To be concise is to express a thought completely and clearly in the fewest words possible'.[3] If something does not pertain directly to the subject, it should be omitted. One way of ensuring that the report is concise is to read the draft aloud. 'The eye can grow accustomed to the appearance of a sentence, but it is much more difficult for the tongue, lips and jaw to deal with what the eye might readily accept.'[4]

Lengthy discussions of commonly known methods should also be avoided. The writer of the research report must avoid restating the obvious or quoting numbers that the reader can easily see in a table. The challenge is to make the report complete and brief. For example, when discussing the survey method used, it is not necessary to devote page upon page to justifying your decision to use that particular method. Researchers must use their judgment in deciding what can be omitted.

Even with accurate input from the previous steps in the research process, the research report may generate inaccuracies because of carelessness in handling the data, illogical reasoning or inept phrasing.[5] Examples of inaccuracies in report writing include:

- Mathematical errors such as subtraction and addition.
- Confusion between percentages and percentage points.
- Grammatical errors in punctuation, spelling, tense, subject and verb agreement, etc.

If the report contains errors, the reader is likely to ask 'How can I be confident that they know what they are doing?' Word-processing software will not identify all errors. For important documents, two proofreaders should be used.

Clarity in report-writing is also important. Clear and logical thinking and precise expression produce clarity. The writer should make an outline of the major points. These points should be ordered logically and supporting details should be placed in their proper position. Tell the reader what you are going to do, do it and then tell them what you have done. Choose your words carefully. Don't expect to get it right first time. Few people write well enough to product a polished draft the first time. The writer should plan at least one major rewrite.

The report should be visually attractive, interesting and easy to read. Sprinkle the report with short quotes from the respondents. This can vitalise a perhaps otherwise dull report. Because the report represents the research firm (and the writer), it should convey positive professional impressions. It should have clear headings which correspond directly with the table of contents. The report should flow logically from topic to topic (corresponding to the research objectives, or questionnaire sequence).

The researcher should:

- write in the present tense and use the active voice;
- avoid jargon, slang and clichés;
- avoid 'I, we' etc. Write in the third person;
- write naturally and simply — the way you talk;
- avoid using too many difficult words or technical, complex language. Words should be chosen that provide variety and change of pace to the report;
- choose to use short words over long words that mean the same thing;
- avoid long-windedness and unnecessary complexity in sentence structure. Always prefer the simple to the complex;
- vary the length and structure of sentences;
- within a sentence keep the subject and verb together. This makes it easier for the reader to understand the message;
- use brisk, business-like English;
- the report should have a uniform style and format. Headings and subheadings with sufficient white space is important. Page after page of type is not a good idea. The typography should be varied. It is better to 'break up' the text of the report with headings, subheadings, bullets, indentations and the like. Visual aids such as tables, graphs and charts should also be built into the report.

Be Objective

Objectivity is a virtue which must at all times be maintained. Researchers should never overlook their scientific role, even though from time to time they will probably encounter situations whereby the research findings will not be easily accepted by the client. The results may not concur with the readers' judgment, accumulated industry experience or past decisions taken. The research should resist slanting the findings to conform to the expectations of management. Instead the research findings should be presented in an objective manner and their validity defended if challenged by the client.

CONTENTS OF THE MARKETING RESEARCH REPORT

Box 15.1

Title Page
1. Title
2. Client
3. Research company
4. Date of submission

Letter of Transmittal

Executive Summary
1. Concise statement of objectives
2. Concise statement of methodology
3. Concise statement of major finding(s)
4. Concise statement of conclusions and recommendations
5. Other pertinent information as required (e.g. special limitations or techniques)

Table of Contents
1. Section titles and sub-headings with page numbers
2. List of tables
3. List of figures
4. List of exhibits
5. List of appendices

Introduction
Background to the research undertaken
Problem definition and objectives

Research Methodology (Design)
a. Type of research design
b. Information needs
c. Data collection from secondary sources
d. Data collection from primary sources
e. Scaling techniques
f. Questionnaire development and pre-testing
g. Sampling techniques
h. Field work

Data Analysis
Data Analysis methodologies and techniques

Results/Findings

Limitations

Conclusions and Recommendations

Appendices
1. Questionnaire and forms
2. Statistical output
3. Other appendices as necessary, e.g. geographical map, bibliography, tables not included in findings section, instructions to field workers.

Report Format

There is no single, acceptable organisation for a report. The format chosen depends on the audience and the topic of the report. However, a general format is suggested in Box 15.1. This can be easily altered as required. It should not be thought of as a rigid outline that must always be followed. The format given here is for the most formal type of report. For less formal reports, some parts may be shorter or omitted. The general rule is to include all parts needed for effective communication in the particular circumstances and no more.

The Parts of the Report

Each of the report format items is discussed briefly in the following paragraphs.

Title Page

The title page should state a title that conveys the essence of the report, by whom the report was prepared, the name of the recipient organisation and the date of release or presentation.[6] Addresses and telephone numbers of the research firm and recipient may also be included. The title should be brief and informative but 'catchy' if possible. Some research reports are confidential and for limited distribution; in such cases, a list of people to whom the report should be circulated may be named on the title page.

Letter of Transmittal

The letter of transmittal is included in relatively formal to very formal reports. It is the 'Here it is' dimension of the report. It should be brief, to the point and should include:

1. the authorisation for the report;
2. a carbon-copy (cc) notation;
3. broad comment(s) on the report findings;
4. a reference to implementation or future related research.

Executive Summary

It is reasonable to assume that some key individuals within the recipient organisation may not have time to read the report in its entirety. The executive summary is a condensed, accurate, one- to two-page statement of what is important in the report. The summary should be written only after the rest of the report has been completed. It represents the essence of the report, and should not be viewed as a miniature of the main report. A good test of a summary is self-sufficiency. Can it stand on its own? It will rarely be broken down through the use of headings and sub-headings. If you can't hold your breath while reading it, most likely it is probably too long. As a variation, the summary may be detached from the main report and circulated by itself.

The executive summary should:

1. State the objectives of the research report.
2. Outline the nature of the decision problem.
3. Identify the methodology and key findings.
4. State conclusions.
5. State recommendations (this is optional).

Table of Contents

The table of contents lists, in order of appearance, the divisions and subdivisions of the report with page references. The purpose of a table of contents is to help readers find the particular sections of the report that are of most interest to them. All items, except title page and table of contents, are listed with page numbers in the table of contents. As a rule, front matter pages are numbered with lower-case Roman numerals (e.g. i, ii, etc). The main body uses Arabic numerals. If the report includes numerous tables, graphs and charts, they should be listed in a separate page immediately following the table of contents. This is referred to as a list of illustrations. It may comprise two separate pages, one for tables, the other for figures. Tables are words or numbers that are arranged in rows or columns. Figures are graphs, charts, pictures, maps, etc. Within each, the table or figure, the individual table or figure should be referenced by number, title description and corresponding page number(s).

Introduction

This section begins the main body of the report and bridges the gap between the table of contents and the data analysis/results sections. The introduction begins with the background information as to why the report was undertaken. In some cases, a description of the company or product involved may also be required. Reference and short review should be made to any previous related research work carried out on the decision problem. It must explain the nature of the decision problem and state explicitly the objectives of the study. Frequently this is presented as primary and secondary research objectives.

Research Methodology

The section on research methodology contained in the introduction should specify these details, e.g. 'how' the research was conducted, i.e. how the information was collected to achieve the research objectives. Enough detail must be included to document the nature of the methodology used, yet it should not be the major section of the report. Technical details should be included in the appendix. Readers must be told whether the research design was exploratory, descriptive or causal. Are the results based on secondary or primary data or both? If a primary data collection method was used, was it based on observational or survey research? If a survey, was the questionnaire administered in person or by telephone or post? An account must be given of the sampling plan. How was the population defined? What sampling frame was used? Was probability or non-probability sampling used, and which technique? How large was the sample size? How were fieldwork issues dealt with? These are all questions which must be answered by the research methodology section. It is also best to provide a brief argument as to why you chose a particular approach, e.g. postal versus telephone, probability versus non-probability, etc. However, you do not need to defend every aspect of your methodology. As mentioned earlier, readers requiring a more detailed methodology discussion should be referred to the appendix.

Data Analysis

Relatively little can be said about the analysis and interpretation methods. The results tend to show what has been done in this regard. However, it can be useful to include a brief discussion on analysis before presenting the results. You may wish to make reference to the data analysis techniques employed, including computer statistical packages, if any are used. Again, it is probably better not to get too technical at this point. A more detailed discussion of methods of analysis including raw data and calculations can be presented in the appendix.

Results/Findings

The 'results' section is the 'meat' of the report. It may comprise several chapters. It makes up the bulk of the report and is organised around the research objectives and information reeds. A combination of continuous narrative text with liberal use of relevant tables, charts, graphs, etc. tends to work best. Personal computers and graphics software packages provide a quick and low-cost means of preparing graphics of all types, both simple and sophisticated 3D. The findings must be presented in a clear, logical, organised and attractive way. It is not merely an assortment of tables, graphs and text. The findings section should not read as a series of response frequencies to questionnaire items. Greater creativity is required than that if the report is to retain the interest of the reader. Comprehensive or detailed tables and charts should be confined to the appendix. The researcher should avoid the temptation to present everything that has been learnt regardless of its bearing on the research objectives. This can be overcome by continual reference to the study objectives and by placing less pertinent findings in the appendix.

Limitations

Almost every research project has limitations. Many of these are time, budget or organisation based. Many of the research errors described in Chapter 2 are potential project limitations or caveats. The limitations section should indicate the nature of any potential weaknesses without unduly degrading the reader's credibility in the overall quality of the work. Rather than belabouring the minor weaknesses of the study, the limitations section should instead provide a realistic basis for assessing the validity of the study results. The ethical researcher does not overstate the weaknesses but instead assumes a balanced perspective. In fact, an open, frank admission of the study limitations can actually increase, rather than diminish the reader's confidence in the quality of the work undertaken.

Conclusions and Recommendations

Conclusions and recommendations are not the same. A conclusion is an opinion based on the results, while recommendations are suggestions for action. Ideally, the reader should be able to read the objectives, turn to the conclusions section and find specific conclusions relative to each objective. There are two schools of thought as to whether recommendations should be included in the report or not. One says that, because the researcher is probably not familiar with the bigger picture of the client firm, he should not include recommendations in the research report. That is seen as the job of the client's management team. Managers may prefer to determine the appropriate courses of action for themselves. Alternatively, those people from the other school feel that the researcher is in the best position to suggest a course of action. If recommendations are included in the research report, they should be practical and actionable and based on the study results. The recommendations may or may not be followed by the management team.

Appendix

The appendix should be reserved for material that is too technical or too cumbersome to place in the main body of the report. This includes materials of interest only to some readers or subsidiary materials not directly related to the objectives. The appendix will typically contain a copy of the questionnaire or observational form used, interviewer instructions, details of the sampling plan, detailed statistical tables, geographical maps, bibliography, etc. Each appendix item should be titled, referenced, explained and listed in the table of contents. The writer should not put material in the appendix if its omission from the body of the report would create gaps in the presentation.

Evaluating Research Reports

The following is a number of guidelines for evaluating research reports.[7]

Origin — what is behind the research. The report should contain a clear statement of why the research was conducted, who sponsored it, and who conducted it. Key questions:

- Does the report identify the organisations (divisions, departments) that requested the research?
- Does it contain a statement of purpose that clearly states what the research was to accomplish?
- Are the organisations that defined and conducted the research identified?

Design — the concept and the plan. The research approach, the sample, and the analysis should be described clearly and they should be appropriate for the purpose of the study. Key questions:

- Is there a complete non-technical description of the research design?
- Is the design consistent with the purpose for which the research was conducted?
- Does any aspect of the design, including the measuring instrument(s), induce any bias (particularly bias in favour of the sponsor)?
- Does the design control for patterns of sequence or timing or other external factors which might prejudice the results?
- Are the respondents capable of answering the questions raised?
- Is there a precise statement of the populations the research is to represent?
- Does the sampling frame fairly represent the population?
- Does the report describe how the data are analysed?
- Are copies of the questionnaire, field and sampling instructions, and other materials available in the appendix or on file?

Execution — collecting and handling the information. Data should be carefully collected by competent people using forms and methods appropriate for the task. Key questions:

- Does the report describe the data collection procedures including 'quality control' procedures?
- Does the report specify the proportion of the selected sample from which information was collected?
- Were those who collected the data treated in a manner that would minimise any bias they might introduce?

Stability — sample size and reliability. The sample size should be reported and it should be large enough to yield stable results. Key questions:

- Is the sample large enough to provide stable findings?
- Are sampling error limits shown (if applicable)?
- Is the calculation of sampling error, or the lack of such a calculation, explained?
- Does the treatment of sampling error make clear that it does not include non-sampling error?
- For the major findings, are the reported error tolerances based on direct analysis of the variability of the collected data?

Applicability — generalising the findings. The research report should clearly indicate the boundaries which limit the findings. Key questions:

- Does the report specify when the data were collected?
- Does the report state clearly whether its results apply beyond the direct source of the data?
- Is it clear which groups, if any, are under-represented in the data?
- If the research has limited applications, is there a statement describing who or what it represents and the times and conditions under which it applied?

Meaning — interpretations and conclusions. All assumptions and judgments involved in reaching any findings, conclusions or recommendations should be clearly specified. Key questions:

- Are the measurements described in simple and direct language?
- Does the use of the measurements make sense?
- Are the actual findings clearly differentiated from any interpretation of the findings?
- Has rigorous objectivity and candid reporting been used in interpreting research findings as evidence of caution or as predictive of future behaviour?

Candour — open reporting and disclosure. The research report should be an honest, complete description of the research process and outcome. Key questions:

- Is there a full and forthright disclosure of how the research was done?
- Have all the potentially relevant findings been presented?

THE ORAL REPORT

In addition to one or more written reports, you may also have to give an oral report of your research. While not unlike public speaking, presentation of the research report has a number of distinguishing characteristics:

- Generally a smaller group of people is involved.
- Statistics, graphics and key points make up the bulk of the presentation.

- The audience members are usually management — they want to hear only the critical elements.

As a researcher, you may be required to deliver an oral presentation at one or more stages of the research project, namely:

- The research proposal stage.
- Progress to date reports.
- Presentation of final report and research results.

Barriers to Communication

It is the listener or reader who will determine the extent to which the message is understood. What we hear, see or understand is shaped very largely by our own experience and background. In reality, many barriers to good communications exist. The main ones are as follows.[8]

1. *Language:* Some individuals may have vocabulary deficiencies due to age, education or environment. Words can also have different meanings to different people. For example, look at the possible communication difficulties that arise between Americans, English and Irish who all speak the English language. Jargon used by specialists can also cause difficulties.
2. *Perception:* Our personal feelings will often affect the way we interpret communications. Its is often difficult to separate what we hear from our feelings about the person who says it. Stereotyping would be a prime example.
3. *Listening:* Communication involves receiving as well as issuing information. Some individuals are good talkers but poor listeners, hearing only what they want to hear and disregarding any critical comments. Communication overload can also occur.
4. *Authority:* An individual's position in an organisation may be relevant. Communications from senior managers will be considered important and significant. On the other hand, research has shown that people with low status within an organisation find difficulty communicating with those who have a higher status.
5. *Distortion of message:* Lines of communication may be too long, resulting in a dilution of the information. Personality clashes may also contribute.
6. *Non-verbal communication:* Body language can be a help, but sometimes it can prove a barrier if misinterpreted. This can often arise in contacts with individuals from different cultures.
7. *Emotions:* Emotions can colour our ability to convey or receive the true message.
8. *Time:* The individual may not have been accorded sufficient time to deal with a particular communication.

A good oral presentation is as much an art as a science. Some people have a natural flair for presenting, but for the less fortunate, spoken communication is a skill that can be acquired like any other and, given time and proper tutoring, excelled at.[9]

A couple of years ago, a survey was conducted in the UK which considered man's greatest fears — anything that put the fear of God into respondents. The results surprised the researchers. From the survey it appears that man's greatest fear is not fire, not drowning, not great heights, but publicly speaking to a group of people. Yes, it appears that the one thing guaranteed to turn an otherwise rational, logical and organised individual into a quivering mass is — talking to people.[10]

The key success factor in any presentation: apply the KISS principle — Keep it short and simple. Overall, tell them what you are going to tell them, tell them, and tell them what you have told them. In other words:

- Have an opening to grab their attention.
- Have a short introduction.
- Have a body (middle section) that is logically structured.
- Have a strong close.
- Finish before you are expected to.

Some Tips for Effective Presentations

You and Your Audience

- Where are the audience members from — internal or external?
- What knowledge and experience do they have?
- Why are they attending (is attendance voluntary or compulsory)?
- What do they think of me?
- What do they think of my subject matter?
- What is the prevailing mood of the audience likely to be?
- What do they expect from me?
- What is the audience's age range and educational background?

Language

- Given that your audience has not spent as much time researching the subject area, it is reasonable to assume they will probably not be as familiar as you are with your basic ideas or concepts.
- Keep the wording of your presentation formal but also conversational. Use familiar words and have examples to explain.
- Try to avoid unnecessary abstract terms or overly theoretical examples. Keep the explanation simple and use short, precise sentences.
- Avoid slang, catchphrases and 'in jokes' which might alienate your audience.
- Avoid using jargon or inappropriate technical language.

- Be careful not to over-use certain words or phrases, for example 'like'.
- The above applies when answering questions, too.

Visual Aids

- The more commonly used visual aids include: whiteboard, flip-chart, overhead projector, slide projector, video, samples and hand-outs.
- Stick to one, or at most two kinds of visual aids, and use them only when you need them.
- By distributing samples or handouts before or during your presentation, you may end up competing with them for your audience's attention.
- It may be better not to have a prepared flipchart or OHP visible before you need it, as your audience will be looking at it rather than you.
- If you are going to write on a flipchart or board, there are three points to remember:
  — Don't talk while you write with your back to the audience. Turn and write in silence. This may also be used as a pause in the presentation.
  — Don't scribble; write slowly and legibly. Do use colours.
  — Do not mask the visual aid with your own body.
- Visual aids are not a substitute for an oral presentation. If a visual aid does not add to the content of your presentation, do not use it.
- Make sure you check that you have everything you need beforehand. Is all of the equipment working?

Body Language and Eye Contact

- Start with a smile.
- You are on show, and every move you make conveys a message to your listeners.
- Stand with both feet flat on the ground and slightly apart. This will give an impression of confidence. You will also feel steadier.
- Be prepared to make eye contact with your audience. Don't avoid eye contact as this undermines what you are saying.
- Don't talk to the one person who looks at you most — that person is probably already interested; it's the others you need to convince.
- Watch for signs of boredom — people looking at their watches, tapping feet, sighing. Use your voice, eye contact, or even a question to get them interested again.
- Identify and eliminate distracting mannerisms such as fiddling with your watch, or other accessories. Remove all coins from your pocket. Do you know what to do with your hands?

Voice

- Use your voice to add interest and emphasis to your speech. Work on your voice for volume, speed, tone and variety.

- Practise by reading a passage from a book out loud. Use a tape-recorder if you wish. Do you sound interesting?
- Nervousness on the day of the presentation can make you speed up. A good trick is to take several deep breaths before you start, or hold your breath occasionally or try speaking in an unnatural voice.

Using Notes

- Write your headings and main points on index cards. Write any visual aid prompts on these too. You can put them on the desk or table in front of you and turn them over when you have finished with each one.
- Don't read your whole presentation out. If you do, you reduce eye contact and do not properly involve the audience. You will probably sound monotonous and look impersonal and uninteresting. You also reduce audibility as your voice is directed to the ground.
- Repeat important bits.

Above all, try to RELAX and be yourself. Remember: practice makes perfect. If you fail to prepare, prepare to fail.

QUESTIONS

1. Why is the research report important?
2. Differentiate between the technical report and the popular report as applied to marketing research findings.
3. Why is it important to focus on the audience when writing a research report?
4. What is meant by the research criteria of completeness, accuracy, clarity and conciseness?
5. How do the objectives of the study relate to the writing of the report?
6. Discuss the importance of objectivity in writing a marketing research report.
7. Why is it critical to avoid spelling and grammar errors in research reports?
8. Discuss the difference between conclusions and recommendations in research reports.
9. Describe the following parts of the report: title page, table of contents, executive summary, research design, data analysis, conclusions and recommendations. What should go in each part?
10. In what circumstances is it appropriate to use the various forms of tables and charts which might be included in the body of the research report?
11. Why is the limitations and caveats section included in the report?
12. By what criteria would you evaluate an oral presentation? Develop an evaluation form.
13. What visual aids are available for oral presentations?

PROBLEMS AND ASSIGNMENTS

1. Re-phrase each of the following titles so that the communication will be on a more professional level.
   (a) 'A study of what students at UCD like and don't like about their contact lenses.'
   (b) 'A study to see if residents of Malahide own different kinds of cars than the people who live in Leixlip.'
   (c) 'Age, income, education level, and some other demographic measurements describing households owning a Whirlpool washer and dryer.'

2. Select any paragraph from this chapter, then use a thesaurus to help you rewrite it at the most complex level possible. Might there ever be any benefit from employing such language?

3. The Director of your local Chamber of Commerce asked a marketing research class to prepare a research report on members' attitudes toward the service offerings of the Chamber. Evaluate the completeness of the executive summary portion of their report, which follows:

   > To provide a foundation for a comprehensive marketing plan, the Chamber of Commerce (CC) undertook a membership survey in November 2006. Eighty-four usable surveys were returned from a stratified proportionate sampling plan of 172 CC members.
   >
   > Results showed that members were familiar with all of the services except National Safety Council materials and employers' manuals. Newsletters were found to be the most often used as well as the most important service offered by the Chamber. Government regulation and mandated employee benefits were thought to be the most threatening issues facing business, according to eleven statements about Chamber of Commerce services.

4. Observe three specific oral presentations outside of class. Consider the following:
   (a) Were there any distracting mannerisms?
   (b) What did the presenters do with their hands?
   (c) How was the audience involved, if at all?
   (d) Evaluate the visual aids used. Would you recommend the use of other visual aids?
   (e) Did you become confused or bored? Was there anything the presenter could have done differently to counteract that tendency?

5. You are giving a presentation of a marketing report related to which new advertising campaign your food product employer should run for its new low-fat snack cookies. There has been a great deal of debate among the marketing managers as to whether the product should take a 'health' position or a 'taste' position. Your research has results related to this positioning issue, as well as the test results for the copy test of ads for each position. Discuss how you would handle the following events at the presentation.

   (a) One manager keeps interrupting you to ask questions about issues that will be presented later in your report.

   (b) A professional health positioning manager argues that your whole research has far too small a sample (n = 300), has a sample that was collected improperly (you used a syndicated ad testing service mall intercept), and that the statistical test (the z test) is suspect due to the lack of an underlying normal distribution in the population. These and other similar technical arguments arose when your early results seemed to question health positioning.

   (c) A professional taste manager draws a conclusion about what the strategy and execution should be — a conclusion that uses your results improperly.

   (d) One manager states, 'I don't care what the copy testing results are. That ad will lack true impact in the marketplace. I've been in this business too long to accept that test result.'

   (e) The general manager asks what decision you would make based upon the marketing research.

6. There are a number of graphic presentation forms. Which would you suggest using to show each of the following? Why?

   (a) A comparison of changes in average annual *per capita* income for the United States and Russia from 2002–2006.

   (b) The percentage composition of average family expenditure patterns, by the major types of expenditure, for families whose heads are under 30 years compared with families whose heads are 50 years or older.

   (c) A comparison of the change between 31 December 2004, and 31 December 2005, of the share price of six major technology firms.

7. Outline a set of visual aids that you might use in an oral briefing on:

   (a) How to write a research report.

   (b) The outlook for the economy over the next two years.

   (c) The major analytical article in the latest *Business and Finance.*

8. Go to the library and try to find some research reports. How do they meet the standards set forth in this chapter?

9. Using the business section of newspapers or business magazines, find examples of good/bad table and graphic presentation. How might they be improved?

Case Study
Big Al's 10 Years On*

As 2005 drew to a close, the Big Al's marketing team was preparing for a major review of the brand early in 2006 when the brand would celebrate its tenth birthday. Big Al's was a range of frozen convenience foods developed by Kepak Convenience Foods (KCF). By any standards, it was a highly successful brand and had also contributed to the success of other brands in KCF. However, the team, Simon Walker, Managing Director, and Bláthnaid Ní Fhátharta, Big Al's Brand Manager, was acutely aware that there were many challenges in the marketplace. These challenges and opportunities would need to be addressed if the brand was to continue to thrive. An excellent track record by Big Al's and other KCF brands in the past ten years would not guarantee continued success in a changing market.

The Kepak Group

Kepak was originally established by the late Noel Keating in 1981. However, its origins were laid well before this when Noel established a butcher shop in inner-city Dublin. From this there was a natural progression from retail sales to larger contracts with institutions and then to wholesale to other butchers. This eventually led to the development of a processing operation, Kepak, in Clonee, Co. Meath. Today the business is still owned by the Keating family.

By 2005 the Kepak Group had a turnover in excess of €750 million and was divided into three separate divisions:

- Fresh Meat
- Trading
- Kepak Convenience Foods

The Fresh Meat Division slaughters, processes and packs beef and lamb for retail, food service and manufacturers of food products (see p.554 for definitions). This division accounts for 80% of group turnover and bulk supplies to customers from five processing plants in Ireland and two in the UK. Kepak is now the largest lamb processor in Europe.

The trading division, known as Agra Trading, operates globally in international sourcing and supply of meat and food products. It was acquired in 1997 and currently has a turnover of €60 million.

The third division, KCF, accounted for approximately 12% of group turnover and was continuing to grow. Its principal brands are Big Al's and Rustlers and it produces frozen and chilled meat-based products (see p.548 for definitions) at its two plants in Glasnevin, Dublin and near Blackpool in England.

The Development of Kepak Convenience Foods and its Brands

KCF had its origins in Goldstar Meats which was established by a number of independent investors in 1978. Noel Keating was one of the five founding investors. The business was established to develop a range of burger products to meet a growing demand in both food service – with businesses such as McDonald's and Burger King developing rapidly – and retail, which was in the early stages of growth.

After a difficult start-up period, the directors appointed Mr Patrick Nolan as Managing Director in 1980. Mr Nolan, who also became a shareholder, continued in that position until 1990. An interesting account of Patrick Nolan's life and career was published in the Notre Dame University business magazine (http://www. nd.edu/~ndbizmag/spring2005/feature_tears_web.shtml).

The focus of the new company was on frozen raw burgers through private label and for the food service trade. Although the burgers were branded under the Dunnes Stores, Quinnsworth and other retailer brands, Goldstar Meats did extensive below-the-line promotion, particularly in-store tastings.

The company was also innovative in its new product development, focusing on 100% beef content and on developing burger sizes such as the quarter-pounder. By the end of the 1980s, Goldstar was in a dominant market position in the Irish frozen-burger retail market as private label held 50% market share at retail level and Goldstar accounted for most of this. Birds Eye was the other major player in the market, with 35% market share. The remaining 15% was held by Findus, Green Isle, Ross and other smaller brands. By this time the other shareholders in Goldstar had been bought out and the company became a wholly owned subsidiary of Kepak. It was renamed Kepak Convenience Foods, though the Goldstar name continued to be used interchangeably, particularly in relation to the food-service sector.

In 1990 Ray Moylan, previously Marketing Manager at Goldstar, succeeded Patrick Nolan as Managing Director, and Simon Walker was recruited as Marketing Executive. Ray left the company in 2005 to pursue other business interests and Simon Walker was appointed Managing Director of the Irish operation. This resulted from the separation of the Irish and UK parts of KCF as outlined below.

1990 also saw Kepak Convenience Foods begin to develop business in the UK, again as private label, with retail customers such as Iceland, Safeway and Aldi. Around the same time, the company lost the Dunnes Stores contract when that retailer established its own burger-processing operation. At this time, Dunnes Stores would have been the largest supermarket group in Ireland, holding in excess of 20% share of the grocery market.

However, KCF continued to grow and, by 1993, 60% of its sales of frozen burgers were to the UK. However, two major events in the UK caused significant problems for the company. The first of these was a crisis caused by the sudden fall in the value of sterling when it was forced out of the European Exchange Rate Mechanism (ERM) by speculators. Sterling fell in value from an average of stg£0.90 against the Irish pound to stg£1.10. This immediately made KCF products uneconomic in the sterling currency zone. The recovery of sterling to its former levels was slow. To protect its position in this key developing market, Kepak Group acquired a burger and fresh-meat plant in Scotland, which became Kepak Buchan.

The second crisis was the identification of BSE (Bovine Spongiform Encephalopathy) or 'mad cow disease'. This was a chronic, degenerative disorder affecting the central nervous system of cattle. The disease was first detected in 1986 and peaked in the early 1990s. There was major public concern in the UK and elsewhere that the disease could be transmitted to humans through meat consumption. Burgers were seen as a particular problem as cheaper cuts of meat were often used and older animals, which were more susceptible to BSE, were also used in some burger processing. The sight of the then UK minister for agriculture virtually force-feeding a burger to his daughter live on television to demonstrate his confidence in British beef was not regarded as helpful to the cause! However, the concerns of BSE were subsequently seen to be exaggerated and the eventual impact was small. Consumer confidence returned to the industry through measures such as testing, culling of older animals and removing possible sources of infection from the food chain.

A third possible difficulty for its private label business in Ireland was also identified by Ray Moylan at this time. It was common knowledge that the major UK food retailers such as Tesco and Sainsbury were examining entry to the Irish market either by acquisition or the establishment of a green field operation. This could threaten KCF's market share as UK retailers were likely to bring their existing suppliers of private label products with them. For all these reasons, decisions were taken to develop a branded range of products, widening the range to encompass new products and processes. (Tesco did subsequently enter the Irish market through the acquisition of Quinnsworth in 1997. KCF retained contracts with Tesco, including contracts to supply meat products under the Tesco premium label, Tesco Finest. KCF continues to develop this relationship.)

KCF had always been at the forefront in process development, continually upgrading its facilities, with significant support from Enterprise Ireland, the organisation responsible for the development of indigenous Irish industry. This support enabled it to consider new areas of growth. Developing a branded range of products was the way the company saw to ensure a successful future.

The Big Al's Brand Comes to Market

Once the decision was made in mid 1994 to develop a new brand, Ray and Simon, assisted by Grey Helme as marketing partners, worked on several fronts to bring the new brand to market. Issues tackled included the name, range, packaging and promotion methods. At an early stage it was decided to stay in the frozen-food sector, though there were signs that growth in the sector as a whole was slowing. There were also major variations in growth in sub-categories of the frozen food market.

The positioning selected for the new brand was described as follows:

**'Better eating the American way from
the freezer cabinet and better value too'**

This *American Style* was perceived in Ireland as representing the home of quality convenience food. Accordingly, it was decided that the brand should have the following attributes:

- American in style.
- Descriptive of a 'type' of eating experience.
- Generous.
- Relevant to a busy lifestyle, making life easier.
- Good value for money.

The brand name Big Al's was selected as it was considered to have all of these attributes. In particular, it reflected the 'New York diner' eating experience. In designing the brand as it would appear on packaging and through promotion, the team also ensured that all of the brand's images reflected these attributes.

The initial range consisted of six products: two burger products and four chicken grill products shaped from chopped chicken pieces. At the time the company did not have crumb and batter technology to coat the chicken pieces, so the products were dusted with various spices producing Chinese, spicy and barbeque flavours. The range was successfully launched, selling IR£1 million (€1.25 million) in its first year and then building from that initial figure. The launch coincided with a significant shift from beef to poultry in the frozen convenience meat (FCM) sector as a result of the fallout from BSE. The target market for this new brand was the island of Ireland.

KCF continuously looked to develop the range. In the early stages they stayed relatively close to the original concept by developing, in 1997, larger burgers branded as Big Al's Big Eat. These were a relatively new concept on the market as the focus had previously been on smaller individual servings.

The new product development team, led by Ray Moylan, was constantly examining new and emerging trends. The team, together with production management, began to explore cooking technology with a view to developing cooked frozen-meat products, particularly burgers. The team considered that cooked frozen products represented a viable way forward for two reasons. Firstly, consumer demand for convenience was enhanced by the wide availability of microwave ovens. By 1998, over 70% of Irish households had a microwave and the rate of penetration was continuing to rise (source: CSO). Secondly, there was a growing awareness among the public of problems caused by E. coli, an infection most commonly caused by eating undercooked ground beef. There had been a number of outbreaks in the UK which had received considerable publicity.

The search for suitable technology led Kepak Convenience Foods to the USA where such products were already on the market. The team found that there was a trade-off between production efficiency and taste. They focused on the technology which gave the most succulent product through retention of moisture and best replicated the home-cooked product. The product was initially launched into the food service sector through Pierre's, part of Cuisine de France. Then, in 1998, a range branded as Big Al's Microwavers was launched into the Irish market, featuring beefburgers, barbeque-style pork ribs and chicken-breast grills. This cooking technology led the team to actively investigate the possibility of launching the Big Al's brand in the UK. The Microwavers products were suitable for microwaving to reheat in five minutes or less.

In 1999 Mandy Mullins joined the KCF commercial team as product/brand manager. Mandy brought with her a wealth of experience of marketing FMCG products. She initiated a major review of the brand in 2001. This process reexamined positioning, the purchase decision-making process, packaging and new product development. Extensive research was carried out, both qualitative and quantitative. The Big Al's brand came out well in the research with its positioning being seen as:

- Big.
- American.
- High Quality.
- Innovative.
- 'New Kid on the Block'.

The research also found that consumers were unhappy with the marketing offering of chicken products, describing them as 'bland', 'plastic', 'rubbery' and 'all minced chicken'. As a result of the research and the brand audit, the team decided to launch a new range of products containing 100% chicken breast pieces coated in a crispy batter. The products introduced to the market were as follows:

- Chicken Fillets at a weight of 110 g (largest on the market), two per box.
- Chicken Bites at a weight of 220 g, 12 bites per box, average weight 18 g (larger than any other nugget-type product).
- Chicken Tenders at a weight of 220 g, average 8 tenders per box.

This strategy again brought the Big Al's brand into direct competition with Birds Eye who were undisputed leaders in this category. Meanwhile, another major brand was about to be launched which would, at least temporarily, take much of the focus away from the Big Al's brand.

The Rustlers Brand Comes to Market

Leitrim Foods, a member of the Kepak Group, was involved in the manufacture and supply of chilled pasta to the retail trade in Ireland under the Cucina brand. The company had been experimenting with a chilled product of cooked burger and bun in a plastic container. The product was eventually branded as Rustlers. In 1999 the Leitrim Foods operation was closed, but the Rustlers product was retained and production moved to KCF's Glasnevin site. The brand was, at that stage, turning over less than €3 million at Retail Selling Price (RSP). Rustlers then came under the marketing control of the Kepak Convenience Foods team. They viewed it as having major potential for several reasons:

- Chilled cooked food was a strong growth sector.
- In research, the taste of the product exceeded expectations.
- Snacking was a growing market, particularly among 18–30-year-old males.
- Trials in the UK with Sainsbury and Somerfield, two major retail chains, had been successful.
- Other products were in the pipeline which could broaden the appeal.

The company decided to undertake a full launch of the Rustlers brand into the UK. However, the company could only support one such brand, so the planned launch of Big Al's into the UK was cancelled. This proved to be a wise decision as production on the Glasnevin site quickly reached capacity as a result of Rustlers success in the UK. The Rustlers range eventually consisted of the following five products:

Flame-Grilled Quarter-Pounder with Cheese

A premium flame-grilled quarter-pounder with cheese and tomato ketchup in a sesame-seed bun. Available in single and twin packs.

Flame-Grilled Chicken-Breast Steak Sandwich

A flame-grilled chicken-breast steak in a sesame seed bun with mayonnaise.

Flame-Grilled BBQ Ribsteak

Prime, flame-grilled pork with BBQ seasoning in a sesame seed bun and BBQ sauce.

Hot Dog

A hot dog with relish and crispy onion in a maize topped bun.

The Big One

Big 6-oz beefburger with relish and cheese in a floury bap, the XXL burger of the range.

Market research undertaken in 2002 indicated that the product reached two audiences: males aged 18–30 and budget-conscious providers with younger children. This latter group typically had the add-on products such as cheese and ketchup in the home already and therefore the Rustlers offering might not be seen by them as adding value. As a result, a new range branded as Speedy Snacks was also developed. Portion size was smaller and recommended selling price was lower than Rustlers. Promotion for this range was exclusively below the line and included price discounting, couponing and special offers such as buy one get one free (BOGOF). Speedy Snack has grown to be a €20 million brand in the UK. Unlike Rustlers, it is not sold in Ireland. The Speedy Snack range is shown below.

Flame-Grilled Beefburger

3-oz beefburger in a sesame seed bun.

Southern-Fried Chicken Burger

Chicken burger in a southern-fried coating in a sesame seed bun.

Sausage Sandwich

Traditional sausage in a soft bread roll.

All products in both ranges are cooked, microwavable and chilled.

The production of these ranges, together with Big Al's, quickly outgrew the capacity of the factory in Glasnevin and it became clear that new production capacity was required. Given the limitations of the landlocked Glasnevin site, it was agreed that this new facility should be situated in the main market. A new factory was opened in 2004, located close to Blackpool. At the same time, a new marketing team was also put in place in the UK to manage the Rustlers and Speedy Snacks brands. Together, these brands now accounted for €70 million in sales at RSP.

Big Al's from 2002 to 2005

Following the brand audit in 2001 and subsequent launch of the new chicken range, the Big Al's brand was relaunched in 2002 with the emphasis on the new 100% chicken products. The brand and product range were given a facelift with new packaging. Positioning was adjusted to the following proposition:

Big Al's provides top-quality New York diner food from your freezer.

The objective was to reinforce the 'New York diner' positioning in all communication. Another objective was to demonstrate to retailers that the company was serious about becoming a major long-term player in the frozen-foods market. A much expanded marketing spend budget of over €600,000 was made available at this time.

Research undertaken in 2003 indicated that the positioning was resonating with consumers and that the brand was now seen as a strong challenger to the category leader, Birds Eye. In order to build on this, it was decided to develop a cohesive marketing programme both above and below the line. Advertising was deemed by the team to be necessary for the following reasons:

- To build awareness for the Big Al's brand;
- To create a distinct positioning within the frozen-food category;
- To recruit new users to the brand (from other brands and into the category);
- To build on the brand positioning as outlined above;
- With the basics of product, packaging and positioning right, 'we need to tell people about the brand'.

A series of three commercials was developed on the theme of *Big Al's – New York diner food in your own home without the drama*. Filmic cues were used dramatising New York dining experiences as well as showing how Big Al's provided consumers with the ease of enjoying the real New York taste at home. The commercials themselves can be viewed and played at www.dit.ie/big-als. One of the commercials was adapted for cinema. The commercials were aired in early March and again in short bursts in May/June and in September. They were aired on RTÉ One, TV3 and UTV and on Irish services of C4, E4 and Sky. The television advertising was supported by an outdoor campaign, in-store tastings, a door-drop campaign targeting 450,000 households, a roadshow, on-pack offers and a public relations campaign.

In 2003 Big Al's Chicken Fillets and Bites were made available in larger 440 g foil bags and four new products were introduced to the market. They were:

- Poppin' Chicken
- Hot 'n' Spicy Wings
- Hot 'n' Spicy Fillet
- XXL – The 8-oz Burger

The objectives were to build on the growth in the chicken category, with a particular focus on premium products, to expand the Big Al's range and to create a new burger category targeted at males with substantial appetites.

In 2004 the TV commercials were aired again in six bursts, showing on RTÉ One and Network 2, TV3, TG4, Sky One, Sky News, Sky Sports and E4 in order to create further awareness and trial. Several themed promotions also took place throughout the year at summer, Hallowe'en and Christmas, together with more in-store tastings, online couponing as well as utilising retailer club cards.

By 2005, Big Al's brand annual sales exceeded €15 million at RSP. The range was listed in all major multiples and C-sector (convenience) stores on the island of Ireland. By late 2005 the range consisted of twenty products. As indicated, many of these have evolved over time. For example, the range originally introduced as Microwavers in 1998 was now branded as Flame Grilled. A new range of fully cooked chicken products packaged in a foil bag, as distinct from the traditional cardboard box, was also introduced in 2005. This new form of packaging was introduced to all cooked products to distinguish them from raw products. The full Big Al's range still consisted of only frozen products.

The frozen-food category in the Republic of Ireland was valued in 2004 at €303 million at RSP. This represents a small decline of 0.2% on the previous year. Within the sector there are various sub-markets with different shares of the overall category as the following chart indicates:

Figure 15.1 Sales by category in frozen food markets in 2004

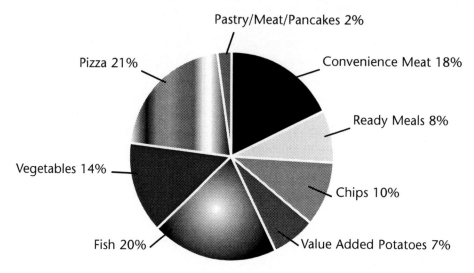

Pastry/Meat/Pancakes 2%

Pizza 21%

Convenience Meat 18%

Ready Meals 8%

Vegetables 14%

Chips 10%

Fish 20%

Value Added Potatoes 7%

Figure 15.2 Percentage change in sales between 2003 and 2004 by category

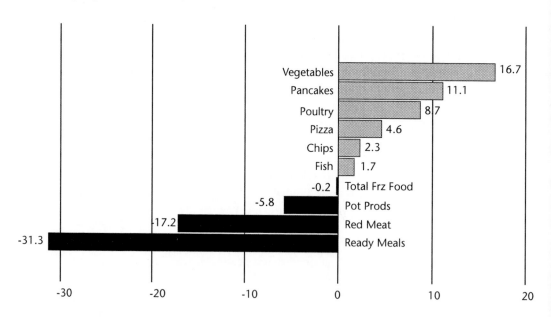

Taking frozen convenience meat as the composite sub-category in which Big Al's competed (red meat and poultry), as can be seen, it accounts for 18% of total frozen-food sales. This had moved very slightly upward on 2003, but masked a decline in frozen red meat of 17% to €12.9 million and a rise of almost 9% in poultry to €38.2 million. A key issue for the KCF marketing team was whether these changes were cyclical or whether there were other forces at work. There was also an indication of a drop in market penetration in both categories, though this was partly offset by a higher spend per visit to the store. This higher spend did not appear to be as a result of volume or price increases, rather it was caused by lower levels of in-store/on-pack price promotions.

While the market for frozen convenience meats was flat overall, Big Al's sales at retail level had grown by 9% in the same period as a result of the brand's market penetration holding up well against the trend, together with some price increases.

As a result of this growth, Big Al's share had grown to 25% in 2004 as the following chart indicates:

Figure 15.3 Market share of frozen convenience meat in 2004

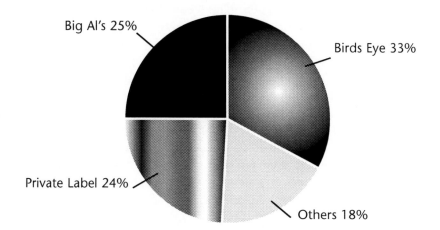

It should be noted that at least eleven brands accounted for the 'others' category. Further good news for the Big Al's brand came from tracking studies covering the quarter to May 2005 which showed that Big Al's had, for the first time, with a share of 29.1 %, just surpassed Birds Eye in the frozen convenience meats category. The Birds Eye brand was owned by Unilever. Its products were sold in the UK and Ireland and Unilever was also well represented in other categories of the frozen-food sector. It also had a number of leading brands in other markets. It had recently invested considerable resources in developing and supporting a range of frozen prepared meals with the tag line that there were no additives contained in the products. This was probably the frozen-food category's major advantage in that products such as meats and vegetables could be prepared in that way. Longer shelf life over the chilled category was also an advantage, though the chilled category would have claimed fresher taste and greater convenience as its major advantages. There were regular rumours in the trade that Unilever might consider selling off some or all of its frozen-food division to enable it to concentrate on higher growth markets (source:www.telegraph.co.uk/money and bfff.co.uk).

In addition to tracking sales, the KCF marketing team also were cognisant of the importance of brand awareness. At 74%, Big Al's was second in terms of awareness among frozen-food consumers behind Birds Eye, but well ahead of all other brands which had much lower awareness levels.

Promoting the Big Al's Brand

The Big Al's brand was strongly supported throughout Ireland with both above- and below-the-line promotional activity. While the total budget varied from year to year, usually depending on advertising production costs, an average of €750,000 was being spent annually by 2005. This budget was divided roughly equally between above and below the line, excluding production costs. Above the line focused mostly on TV advertising. Here the budget, excluding production costs, was about €300,000.

Typically €40,000 was spent on outdoor advertising, mostly on six-sheet shopperlites at locations close to point of purchase.

€11,000 was spent on print advertising, mostly on a small number of full page advertisements in *The RTÉ Guide*, a TV listings and general-interest weekly publication which was seen as matching the profile of the typical Big Al's customer. €15,000 was also spent on radio and smaller amounts on trade-press advertising. Below the line, the focus was on online couponing, in-store sampling, door drops, extra fill packs, on-pack promotions and other retailer-specific activities as detailed earlier. The brand also sponsored national BBQ week.

The marketing team regularly commissioned market research. Typically it undertook quantitative research once a year. Normally this was done through inserting questions in an omnibus survey of approximately 1,400 consumers. Usually six or seven questions were posed, depending on current issues in the marketplace. Average costs of an omnibus survey in Ireland were approximately €1,000 per question. Normally every two years a qualitative research project was undertaken. Usually this was in the form of focus groups of targeted customers.

KCF strongly encouraged its marketing partners to communicate which each other as they saw the benefits that such interaction would bring to the overall marketing of the brand. It employed an advertising agency, a sales promotion company and a packaging consultancy. The KCF marketing team meet together with all three each year for a brand planning day.

Looking to the Future

The Big Al's brand was no longer confined by production capability. This had been resolved by partnering with specialist producers that provided scale and expertise. The relatively high labour and raw material costs of locally sourced poultry had led Kepak Convenience Foods, in common with other brands, to outsource to more specialised producers and/or lower-cost producers in Ireland and overseas. This meant that the brand was no longer constrained by what could be produced in Glasnevin.

The marketing team was very clear in its positioning of the brand. It saw itself as positioned in the frozen convenience-food market in Ireland with the following proposition articulated:

Big Al's is the friend in the freezer that guides Mum to provide exciting New York diner food in the home.

The target market was mothers in the 25–45 age group and C1C2DE social class purchasing for the family. See Appendix 6 for description and size of socio-economic groups in the Republic of Ireland. In addition to the emotional point of difference outlined in the above proposition, a key rational point of difference sought by the marketing team was that the brand was to be perceived as being the best in the sector for quality and taste. Big Al's brand personality was described as friendly, warm, fun, reliable, out-going, understanding, helpful, confident, contemporary, with a can-do attitude.

Big Al's was regarded as highly important in both Kepak Convenience Foods and the wider Kepak company. It was the first brand that the company had developed from scratch and it was clear that if the team could do it successfully once they could do it again. Big Al's success had been built on the following key factors:

- Consumer and market knowledge
- Superiority in product and technology
- Investment in new product development
- Focus on sales and marketing
- Strong in-store activity
- Good trade relations

These factors had sustained the brand through its first decade. Would they be enough to see it develop in the future?

Questions

1. Evaluate the role played by market research in the development of the Big Al's brand to date.
2. Outline a strategy for the brand as it moves into its second decade.
3. What market research process and plan would you recommend in the rolling out of that strategy?

*This case study was developed by Gerry Mortimer of the Dublin Institute of Technology. It was developed as a basis for class discussion, rather than to illustrate effective or ineffective handling of an administrative situation. The author acknowledges the assistance of research student Tara Rooney in preparing this case and of Simon Walker and Blathnaid Ní Fhátharta of Kepak Convenience Foods and Niamh MacHale of An Bord Bia (Irish Food Board) in facilitating its development.

DEFINITIONS

Chilled Foods: Retail-prepared products which can be ready to eat, ready to heat or which require cooking and are stored at all stages of the chilled chain at between 0C and 5C, i.e. refrigeration standard. Typical shelf life is one to two weeks.

Food Service: The food-service industry consists of restaurants, fast-food outlets, hotels, catering and other suppliers of prepared foods to consumers.

Frozen Foods: Frozen food is either raw or cooked food, which is quick frozen to preserve the food and retain the taste and texture. It remains in a frozen state in temperatures of –20C to –40C until thawed for use or further processing. Its invention is credited to Clarence Birdseye.

APPENDIX 1

Random Digits

37751	04998	66038	63480	98442	22245	83538	62351	74514	90497
50915	64152	82981	15796	27102	71635	34470	13608	26360	76285
99142	35021	01032	57907	80545	54112	15150	36856	03247	40392
70720	10033	25191	62358	03784	74377	88150	25567	87457	49512
18460	64947	32958	08752	96366	89092	23597	74308	00881	88976
65763	41133	60950	35372	06782	81451	78764	52645	19841	50083
83769	52570	60133	25211	87384	90182	84990	26400	39128	97043
58900	78420	98579	33665	10718	39342	46346	14401	13503	46525
54746	71115	78219	64314	11227	41702	54517	87676	14078	45317
56819	27340	07200	52663	57864	85159	15460	97564	29637	27742
34990	62122	38223	28526	37006	22774	46026	15981	87291	56946
02269	22795	87593	81830	95383	67823	20196	54850	46779	64519
43042	53600	45738	00261	31100	67239	02004	70698	53597	62617
92565	12211	06868	87786	59576	61382	33972	13161	47208	96604
67424	32620	60841	86848	85000	04835	48576	33884	10101	84129
04015	77148	09535	10743	97871	55919	45274	38304	93125	91847
85226	19763	46105	25289	26714	73253	85922	21785	42624	92741
03360	07457	75131	41209	50451	23472	07438	08375	29312	62264
72460	99682	27970	25632	34096	17656	12736	27476	21938	67305
66960	55780	71778	52629	51692	71442	36130	70425	39874	62035
14824	95631	00697	65462	24815	13930	02938	54619	28909	53950
34001	05618	41900	23303	19928	60755	61404	56947	91441	19299
77718	83830	29781	72917	10840	74182	08293	62588	99625	22088
60930	05091	35726	07414	49211	69586	20226	08274	28167	65279
94180	62151	08112	26646	07617	42954	22521	09395	43561	45692
81073	85543	47650	93830	07377	87995	35084	39386	93141	88309
18467	39689	60801	46828	38670	88243	89042	78452	08032	72566
60643	59399	79740	17295	50094	66436	92677	68345	24025	36489
73372	61697	85728	90779	13235	83114	70728	32093	74306	08325
18395	18482	83245	54942	51905	09534	70839	91073	42193	81199
07261	28720	71244	05064	84873	68020	39037	68981	00670	86291
61679	81529	83725	33269	45958	74265	87460	60525	42539	25605
11815	48679	00556	96871	39835	83055	84949	11681	51687	55896
99007	35050	86440	44280	20320	97527	28138	01088	49037	85430
06446	65608	79291	16624	06135	30622	56133	33998	32308	29434

Source: *Exploring Marketing Research*, sixth edition, by William G. Zikmund. The Dryden Press. Copyright © 1997.

APPENDIX 2
Area Under the Normal Curve

z	.00	.01	.02	.03	.04	.05	.06	.07	.08	.09
0.0	.0000	.0040	.0080	.0120	.0160	.0199	.0239	.0279	.0319	.0359
0.1	.0398	.0438	.0478	.0517	.0557	.0596	.0636	.0675	.0714	.0753
0.2	.0793	.0832	.0871	.0910	.0948	.0987	.1026	.1064	.1103	.1141
0.3	.1179	.1217	.1255	.1293	.1331	.1368	.1406	.1443	.1480	.1517
0.4	.1554	.1591	.1628	.1664	.1700	.1736	.1772	.1808	.1844	.1879
0.5	.1915	.1950	.1985	.2019	.2054	.2088	.2123	.2157	.2190	.2224
0.6	.2257	.2291	.2324	.2357	.2389	.2422	.2454	.2486	.2518	.2549
0.7	.2580	.2612	.2642	.2673	.2704	.2734	.2764	.2794	.2823	.2852
0.8	.2881	.2910	.2939	.2967	.2995	.3023	.3051	.3078	.3106	.3133
0.9	.3159	.3186	.3212	.3238	.3264	.3289	.3315	.3340	.3365	.3389
1.0	.3413	.3438	.3461	.3485	.3508	.3531	.3554	.3577	.3599	.3621
1.1	.3643	.3665	.3686	.3708	.3729	.3749	.3770	.3790	.3810	.3830
1.2	.3849	.3869	.3888	.3907	.3925	.3944	.3962	.3980	.3997	.4015
1.3	.4032	.4049	.4066	.4082	.4099	.4115	.4131	.4147	.4162	.4177
1.4	.4192	.4207	.4222	.4236	.4251	.4265	.4279	.4292	.4306	.4319
1.5	.4332	.4345	.4357	.4370	.4382	.4394	.4406	.4418	.4429	.4441
1.6	.4452	.4463	.4474	.4484	.4495	.4505	.4515	.4525	.4535	.4545
1.7	.4554	.4564	.4573	.4582	.4591	.4599	.4608	.4616	.4625	.4633
1.8	.4641	.4649	.4656	.4664	.4671	.4678	.4686	.4693	.4699	.4706
1.9	.4713	.4719	.4726	.4732	.4738	.4744	.4750	.4756	.4761	.4767
2.0	.4772	.4778	.4783	.4788	.4793	.4798	.4803	.4808	.4812	.4817
2.1	.4821	.4826	.4830	.4834	.4838	.4842	.4846	.4850	.4854	.4857
2.2	.4861	.4864	.4868	.4871	.4875	.4878	.4881	.4884	.4887	.4890
2.3	.4893	.4896	.4898	.4901	.4904	.4906	.4909	.4911	.4913	.4916
2.4	.4918	.4920	.4922	.4925	.4927	.4929	.4931	.4932	.4934	.4936
2.5	.4938	.4940	.4941	.4943	.4945	.4946	.4948	.4949	.4951	.4952
2.6	.4953	.4955	.4956	.4957	.4959	.4960	.4961	.4962	.4963	.4964
2.7	.4965	.4966	.4967	.4968	.4969	.4970	.4971	.4972	.4973	.4974
2.8	.4974	.4975	.4976	.4977	.4977	.4978	.4979	.4979	.4980	.4981
2.9	.4981	.4982	.4982	.4983	.4984	.4984	.4985	.4985	.4986	.4986
3.0	.49865	.4987	.4987	.4988	.4988	.4989	.4989	.4989	.4990	.4990
4.0	.49997									

Source: *Exploring Marketing Research*, sixth edition, by William G. Zikmund. The Dryden Press. Copyright © 1997.

APPENDIX 3

Distribution of *t* for Given Probability Levels

d.f.	Level of Significance for One-Tailed Test					
	.10	.05	.025	.01	.005	.0005
	Level of Significance for Two-Tailed Test					
	.20	.10	.05	.02	.01	.001
1	3.078	6.314	12.706	31.821	63.657	636.619
2	1.886	2.920	4.303	6.965	9.925	31.598
3	1.638	2.353	3.182	4.541	5.841	12.941
4	1.533	2.132	2.776	3.747	4.604	8.610
5	1.476	2.015	2.571	3.365	4.032	6.859
6	1.440	1.943	2.447	3.143	3.707	5.959
7	1.415	1.895	2.365	2.998	3.499	5.405
8	1.397	1.860	2.306	2.896	3.355	5.041
9	1.383	1.833	2.262	2.821	3.250	4.781
10	1.372	1.812	2.228	2.764	3.169	4.587
11	1.363	1.796	2.201	2.718	3.106	4.437
12	1.356	1.782	2.179	2.681	3.055	4.318
13	1.350	1.771	2.160	2.650	3.012	4.221
14	1.345	1.761	2.145	2.624	2.977	4.140
15	1.341	1.753	2.131	2.602	2.947	4.073
16	1.337	1.746	2.120	2.583	2.921	4.015
17	1.333	1.740	2.110	2.567	2.898	3.965
18	1.330	1.734	2.101	2.552	2.878	3.992
19	1.328	1.729	2.093	2.539	2.861	3.883
20	1.325	1.725	2.086	2.528	2.845	3.850
21	1.323	1.721	2.080	2.518	2.831	3.819
22	1.321	1.717	2.074	2.508	2.819	3.792
23	1.319	1.714	2.069	2.500	2.807	3.767
24	1.318	1.711	2.064	2.492	2.797	3.745
25	1.316	1.708	2.060	2.485	2.787	3.725
26	1.315	1.706	2.056	2.479	2.779	3.707
27	1.314	1.703	2.052	2.473	2.771	3.690
28	1.313	1.701	2.048	2.467	2.763	3.674
29	1.311	1.699	2.045	2.462	2.756	3.659
30	1.310	1.697	2.042	2.457	2.750	3.646
40	1.303	1.684	2.021	2.423	2.704	3.551
60	1.296	1.671	2.000	2.390	2.660	3.460
120	1.289	1.658	1.980	2.358	2.617	3.373
∞	1.282	1.645	1.960	2.326	2.576	3.291

Source: *Exploring Marketing Research*, sixth edition, by William G. Zikmund. The Dryden Press. Copyright © 1997.

APPENDIX 4

Chi-Square Distribution

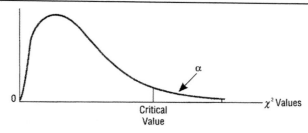

Critical
Value

Degrees of Freedom (d.f.)	Area in Shaded Right Tail (α)		
	.10	.05	.01
1	2.706	3.841	6.635
2	4.605	5.991	9.210
3	6.251	7.815	11.345
4	7.779	9.488	13.277
5	9.236	11.070	15.086
6	10.645	12.592	16.812
7	12.017	14.067	18.475
8	13.362	15.507	20.090
9	14.684	16.919	21.666
10	15.987	18.307	23.209
11	17.275	19.675	24.725
12	18.549	21.026	26.217
13	19.812	22.362	27.688
14	21.064	23.685	29.141
15	22.307	24.996	30.578
16	23.542	26.296	32.000
17	24.769	27.587	33.409
18	25.989	28.869	34.805
19	27.204	30.144	36.191
20	28.412	31.410	37.566
21	29.615	32.671	38.932
22	30.813	33.924	40.289
23	32.007	35.172	41.638
24	33.196	36.415	42.980
25	34.382	37.652	44.314
26	35.563	38.885	45.642
27	36.741	40.113	46.963
28	37.916	41.337	48.278
29	39.087	42.557	49.588
30	40.256	43.773	50.892

Example of how to use this table: In a chi-square distribution with 6 degrees of freedom (*d.f.*), the area to the right of a critical value of 12.592—i.e., the α area—is .05.

Source: *Exploring Marketing Research,* sixth edition, by William G. Zikmund. The Dryden Press. Copyright © 1997.

APPENDIX 5

Critical Values of $F_{v_1 v_2}$ for $\alpha = .05$

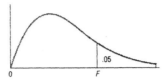

v_1 = Degrees of Freedom for Numerator

v_2 = Degrees of Freedom for Denominator

	1	2	3	4	5	6	7	8	9	10	12	15	20	24	30	40	60	120	∞
1	161	200	216	225	230	234	237	239	241	242	244	246	248	249	250	251	252	253	254
2	18.5	19.0	19.2	19.2	19.3	19.3	19.4	19.4	19.4	19.4	19.4	19.4	19.5	19.5	19.5	19.5	19.5	19.5	19.5
3	10.1	9.55	9.28	9.12	9.01	8.94	8.89	8.85	8.81	8.79	8.74	8.70	8.66	8.64	8.62	8.59	8.57	8.55	8.53
4	7.71	6.94	6.59	6.39	6.26	6.16	6.09	6.04	6.00	5.96	5.91	5.86	5.80	5.77	5.75	5.72	5.69	5.66	5.63
5	6.61	5.79	5.41	5.19	5.05	4.95	4.88	4.82	4.77	4.74	4.68	4.62	4.56	4.53	4.50	4.46	4.43	4.40	4.37
6	5.99	5.14	4.76	4.53	4.39	4.28	4.21	4.15	4.10	4.06	4.00	3.94	3.87	3.84	3.81	3.77	3.74	3.70	3.67
7	5.59	4.74	4.35	4.12	3.97	3.87	3.79	3.73	3.68	3.64	3.57	3.51	3.44	3.41	3.38	3.34	3.30	3.27	3.23
8	5.32	4.46	4.07	3.84	3.69	3.58	3.50	3.44	3.39	3.35	3.28	3.22	3.15	3.12	3.08	3.04	3.01	2.97	2.93
9	5.12	4.26	3.86	3.63	3.48	3.37	3.29	3.23	3.18	3.14	3.07	3.01	2.94	2.90	2.86	2.83	2.79	2.75	2.71
10	4.96	4.10	3.71	3.48	3.33	3.22	3.14	3.07	3.02	2.98	2.91	2.85	2.77	2.74	2.70	2.66	2.62	2.58	2.54
11	4.84	3.98	3.59	3.36	3.20	3.09	3.01	2.95	2.90	2.85	2.79	2.72	2.65	2.61	2.57	2.53	2.49	2.45	2.40
12	4.75	3.89	3.49	3.26	3.11	3.00	2.91	2.85	2.80	2.75	2.69	2.62	2.54	2.51	2.47	2.43	2.38	2.34	2.30
13	4.67	3.81	3.41	3.18	3.03	2.92	2.83	2.77	2.71	2.67	2.60	2.53	2.46	2.42	2.38	2.34	2.30	2.25	2.21
14	4.60	3.74	3.34	3.11	2.96	2.85	2.76	2.70	2.65	2.60	2.53	2.46	2.39	2.35	2.31	2.27	2.22	2.18	2.13
15	4.54	3.68	3.29	3.06	2.90	2.79	2.71	2.64	2.59	2.54	2.48	2.40	2.33	2.29	2.25	2.20	2.16	2.11	2.07
16	4.49	3.63	3.24	3.01	2.85	2.74	2.66	2.59	2.54	2.49	2.42	2.35	2.28	2.24	2.19	2.15	2.11	2.06	2.01
17	4.45	3.59	3.20	2.96	2.81	2.70	2.61	2.55	2.49	2.45	2.38	2.31	2.23	2.19	2.15	2.10	2.06	2.01	1.96
18	4.41	3.55	3.16	2.93	2.77	2.66	2.58	2.51	2.46	2.41	2.34	2.27	2.19	2.15	2.11	2.06	2.02	1.97	1.92
19	4.38	3.52	3.13	2.90	2.74	2.63	2.54	2.48	2.42	2.38	2.31	2.23	2.16	2.11	2.07	2.03	1.98	1.93	1.88
20	4.35	3.49	3.10	2.87	2.71	2.60	2.51	2.45	2.39	2.35	2.28	2.20	2.12	2.08	2.04	1.99	1.95	1.90	1.84
21	4.32	3.47	3.07	2.84	2.68	2.57	2.49	2.42	2.37	2.32	2.25	2.18	2.10	2.05	2.01	1.96	1.92	1.87	1.81
22	4.30	3.44	3.05	2.82	2.66	2.55	2.46	2.40	2.34	2.30	2.23	2.15	2.07	2.03	1.98	1.94	1.89	1.84	1.78
23	4.28	3.42	3.03	2.80	2.64	2.53	2.44	2.37	2.32	2.27	2.20	2.13	2.05	2.01	1.96	1.91	1.86	1.81	1.76
24	4.26	3.40	3.01	2.78	2.62	2.51	2.42	2.36	2.30	2.25	2.18	2.11	2.03	1.98	1.94	1.89	1.84	1.79	1.73
25	4.24	3.39	2.99	2.76	2.60	2.49	2.40	2.34	2.28	2.24	2.16	2.09	2.01	1.96	1.92	1.87	1.82	1.77	1.71
30	4.17	3.32	2.92	2.69	2.53	2.42	2.33	2.27	2.21	2.16	2.09	2.01	1.93	1.89	1.84	1.79	1.74	1.68	1.62
40	4.08	3.23	2.84	2.61	2.45	2.34	2.25	2.18	2.12	2.08	2.00	1.92	1.84	1.79	1.74	1.69	1.64	1.58	1.51
60	4.00	3.15	2.76	2.53	2.37	2.25	2.17	2.10	2.04	1.99	1.92	1.84	1.75	1.70	1.65	1.59	1.53	1.47	1.39
120	3.92	3.07	2.68	2.45	2.29	2.18	2.09	2.02	1.96	1.91	1.83	1.75	1.66	1.61	1.55	1.50	1.43	1.35	1.25
∞	3.84	3.00	2.60	2.37	2.21	2.10	2.01	1.94	1.88	1.83	1.75	1.67	1.57	1.52	1.46	1.39	1.32	1.22	1.00

Source: *Exploring Marketing Research*, sixth edition, by William G. Zikmund. The Dryden Press. Copyright © 1997.

APPENDIX 6

Socio Economic Groups in the Republic of Ireland

Adults

Social Group	Total		Male		Female	
	'000	%	'000	%	'000	%
AB	438	13.3	247	15.1	191	11.4
C1	881	26.7	396	24.3	485	29.1
C2	776	23.5	426	26.1	350	21.0
DE	891	27.0	382	23.4	509	30.5
F1	241	7.3	136	8.3	105	6.3
F2	74	2.2	45	2.8	29	1.7
Total	3301	100	1632	100	1669	100

Source JNRS/Lansdowne 2005

Social Class – Definitions:

A	Upper/Middle Class
B	Middle Class
C1	Lower Middle Class
C2	Skilled Working Class
D	Other Working Class
E	Lowest Level of Subsistence
F1	Large Farmers (50 + Acres)
F2	Small Farmers (50 - Acres)

REFERENCES

Chapter 1

1. Fahy, J., Moloney, S. and McAleer, S., 2003, *Marketing in the 21st Century – A Study of Marketing Practice and Performance in Ireland*, UL/IMI Centre for Marketing Studies, Ireland.
2. Quinn, Feargal, *Crowning the Customer, How to Become Customer-Driven*, Dublin: O'Brien Press, 1990, 57.
3. Barabba, V. and Zaltman, G., *Hearing the Voice of the Market, Competitive Advantage through Creative Use of Market Information*, Harvard Business School Press, 1991.
4. Interview with John Casey, Chief Executive, The Marketing Institute of Ireland, 1996.
5. The Market Research Society (UK), *Definition of Market Research*, www.marketresearch.org.uk, 1998.
6. American Marketing Association, *Definition of Marketing Research*, Chicago, 1988.
7. Boyd, H., Westfall, R. and Stasch, S., *Marketing Research, Text and Cases*, 5th edition, Illinois: Irwin, 1981, 29–35.
8. Baker, Michael, *Research for Marketing*, London, UK: Macmillan, 1995.
9. Irish Trade Advertisement, *MII Newsletter*, March 1998.
10. 'Duty free promises huge liqueur sales', *Sunday Tribune*, 1st December 1996.
11. McCraith, Joe, 'Critical Incident Research', *MII Newsletter*, March/April, Vol. 9 No. 2, 1996, 6–7.
12. 'Cheesestrings Tackle UK Market After Successful Granada Test', *IMJ*, October 1996, 8.
13. 'Goodfella's Market Slice', *Sunday Business Post*, 23rd December 1994.
14. 'HB to Launch New Corporate Identity', *Irish Media Journal*, November 1997.
15. Harrison, B., 'In Cod's Name, What's Happened to Capt. Birdseye?', *The Irish Times*, June 1998.
16. Bank of Ireland Customer Satisfaction Survey, 1997.
17. 'Goodfella's Pizza', *MII Newsletter*, 1997; and Marketing Institute of Ireland, *Yearly Diary*, 1996, 74.
18. Interview with Roger Jupp, *LMR*, 1996.
19. Brophy, M., *IMJ*, April 1997, 50.
20. *MII Newsletter*, March/April 1996, Vol. 9 No. 2, 16–17.
21. Laitin, J. and Klaperman, B., 'The Brave New World of Marketing Research, Market Research Forum', *Medical Marketing and Media*, July 1997.
22. O'Donoghue, Redmond, presentation to National University of Ireland, Galway, 27 February 2004.
23. *Galway Independent*, 1 March 2006.
24. der Vegt, Van, 'We are Drowning in Data but We Lack Information', *Marketing and Research Today*, May, Vol. 27 No. 2, 1998, 73–100; *Irish Media Journal*, April 1997, 50.

25. *Irish Medical Journal*, December 1999.
26. *Ibid.*

Chapter 2

1. 'Does Colour Make a Difference?', *IMJ*, April 1996, 18.
2. Marketing Institute of Ireland, 1996, *Yearly Diary*, 74.
3. 'Omega 3 Research Beneficial', *CEX*, 20th January 1996.
4. Syedain, H., 'Cadbury: Sweet Dreams', *Management Today*, September 1989, 4.
5. *Irish Independent*, 30th May 1996.
6. 'Gilbey's Targets Wine Buyers', *Sunday Business Post*, 1st September 1996.
7. Curtis, J., 'Giving Birth to the Male Pill (Branding Contraceptives)', *Marketing*, 25th September 1997, 30–2.
8. Daly, Dr. Aidan, Marketing Department, NUI, Galway, 2003.
9. *IMJ*, February 1997, 6.
10. Gray, R., 'Keeping up With the Kids (Researching Children's Tastes)', *Marketing*, 24th April 1997, 26–8.
11. Quinn, F., *Crowning the Customer*, Dublin: O'Brien Press, 1990.
12. Harper, T., 'Quantitative Research', in *Perspectives on Marketing Management in Ireland*, edited by Mary Lambkin and Tony Meenaghan, Dublin: Oak Tree Press, 1994, 369–80.
13. Domegan, C., 'An Evaluation of AnCO's Distance Learning Package for Marketing Managers', MBS dissertation, UCD, 1984.
14. Thornton, A., 'The Use of Conjoint Analysis in the Cheese Industry in Ireland', unpublished MBS thesis, UCD, 1984.
15. Malhotra, Naresh K. and Peterson, Mark, 'Marketing Research in the New Millennium: Emerging Issues and Trends', *Marketing Intelligence and Planning*, Vol. 19, No. 4, pp. 216–232, 2001.
16. Burke, Rangaswammy and Gupta, 1999.
17. Edmondson, B. 'The Wired Bunch', *American Demographics*, June 1997.
18. Mann, C. and Stewart, P., *Internet Communication and Qualitative Research – A Handbook for Researching Online*, Sage Publications, London, 2000.
19. Zigmund, W.G., *Exploring Marketing Research*, Thomas South Western, 2002.
20. Sparks, J. R. and Hunt, S. D., 'Marketing Researcher Ethical Sensitivity: Conceptualisation, Measurement and Exploratory Investigation', *Journal of Marketing*, Vol. 62 No. 2, 1998, 92–110.
21. Irish Marketing Surveys, 'Thank You' leaflet 20, 21 Upper Pembroke Street, Dublin, 1997.
22. The Market Research Society, 'Code of Conduct', 2003, at www.marketresearch.org.uk.
23. www.esomar.org
24. Nancarrow, C., Pallister, J. and Brace, I. 'A New Research Medium, New Research Populations and Seven Deadly Sins for Internet Researchers', *Qualitative Marketing Research: An International Journal*, Vol. 4, No. 3, 2001, 136–49.
25. *Ibid.*
26. 'Marketing Research, Business Studies', *Business and Finance*, 14th November 1991.

Chapter 3

1. Gibson, L. D., 'Defining Marketing Problems', *Marketing Research*, Vol. 10 No. 1, 1998, 5–13.
2. Adapted from discussions with Martin MacBride, Managing Director, Envision Marketing, Belfast.
3. Assael, H., *Consumer Behaviour and Marketing Action*, 4th Edition, Boston, USA: PWS-Kent, 1992.
4. Murrary, J., and O'Driscoll, A., *Managing Marketing*, Dublin: Gill & Macmillan, 1993, 131–45.
5. 'How to Develop and Use Marketing Information and Planning Systems', Van Mayros, Seminar in MkIS, MII, Dublin, December 1991.
6. 'Aer Arran, Flying High', DMP Programme, NUI, Galway, Unpublished study, 1995.
7. Piercy, Nigel, *Market-led Strategic Change*, London: Butterworth Heinemann, 1992.
8. Barrett, Ciara, 'Marketing Information Systems — An Investigation into the Uses and Management of Marketing Information by Irish Award-winning Companies', unpublished MBS thesis, NUI, Galway, 1997.
9. O'Connor, J., and Galvin, E., 'Marketing and Information Technology — the Strategy, Application and Implementation of IT in Marketing', London: Pitman, 1997.
10. Baker, Michael Thomas, 1991, 'Research for Marketing', UK: Macmillan.
11. Milliken, J., 'Qualitative Research and Marketing Management', *Management Decision*, Vol.39, No.1, 2001, 71–8; Zimmerman, A. and Szenberg, M., 'Implementating International Qualitative Research: Techniques and Obstacles', *Qualitative Market Research: An International Journal*, Vol.3, No.3, 2000, 158–64.
12. Dickens, J., 'The Fresh Cream Cakes Market: the use of qualitative research as part of a consumer research programme', 4–43, in *Applied Marketing and Social Research*, edited by U. Bradley, England: Van Norstrand Reinhold Company Ltd, 1982.
13. Barnes, J., 'Strategic Marketing Information', MII Seminar, Autumn 1994.
14. Harper, Tom, 'Quantitative Research', in *Perspectives on Marketing Management in Ireland*, edited by Mary Lambkin and Tony Meenaghan, Dublin: Oak Tree Press, 1994, 369–80.
15. Briks, D., 'Market Research', 238–67; and Meidan, A., and Moutinho, L., 'Quantative Methods in Marketing Research', 268–302, in *The Marketing Book*, 3rd Edition, Michael Baker, Butterworth-Heinemann, 1995.
16. CAO Annual Report, 2003.
17. Council of Directors, 'Some Factors Affecting the Flow of Students to the Institutes of Technology to 2010', 2002.
18. Hampton, Gerald, 'Gap Analysis of College Student Satisfaction as a Measure of Professional Service Quality', *Journal of Professional Services Marketing*, Vol. 9(1), 115–128, 1993.

Chapter 4

1. Williams, Jane, 'Marketing Research', talk given at MII West of Ireland Regional function, Ardilaun Hotel, Galway, October 1995.
2. Bond, C., 'Complementary Forces: Databases and Marketing Research', *Marketing*, January 1997, 29.

3. Nielson, Monica, *Tourism Marketing In Ireland*, GMIT, Dublin Road, Galway, 1998.

4. Adapted from 'Marketing Sources of information', written by Jim Ward for the 1984 AnCO Distance Learning package, *Marketing Management*.

5. Central Statistics Office, *Guide to CSO Publications and Information Services*, April, Dublin and the CSO web site, http://www.cso.ie, 2002.

6. Kompass, http://www.kompass.ie.

7. Burke, R.R., 'Rethinking Marketing Research in the Digital World', 1999.

8. Malhotra, N.K. and Peterson, M., 'Marketing Research in the New Millennium: Emerging Issues and Trends', *Marketing Intelligence and Planning*, Vol. 19, 2001.

9. Burke, R.R., *op. cit.*

10. AC Nielsen at http://acnielsen.com/ie/ieoffc.htm

11. Fourth International Conference on Grey Literature: New Frontiers in Grey Literature – GreyNet, Grey Literature Network Service. Washington DC USA, 4–5 October 1999.

Chapter 5

1. From glossary of *Principles of Marketing*, Brassington and Pettitt, Pittman Publishing, 1997.

2. 'Prospecting for That Research Gold', *Marketing*, 23rd May 1996.

3. *Irish Independent*, 30th May 1996.

4. *MII News*, March/April, Vol. 8 No. 3, 1995, 3.

5. *Sunday Tribune*, 21st April 1996.

6. Penny, Richard, 'Using the Right Method', *Sunday Tribune*, 21st April 1991, 31.

7. O'Leary, Phelim, 'Qualitative Research: Where it's at, Where it's Going', *Irish Marketing Review*, Vol. 6, 1993.

8. Gulledge, Larry, 'Satisfaction Measures', *Marketing News*, Vol. 30 No. 22, 21st October 1996.

9. Darling, Eleanor, 'Banking Leaves Nothing to Chance', *BusinessPlus*, April 1998.

10. McLoughlin, Damien and Feely, Finola, 'Successful Brand Name Selection: Finches Soft Drinks', *Irish Marketing Review*, 31st August 1996.

11. 'The Name Game', *Marketing*, 22nd August 1996.

12. Lyons, Madeline, Goodfella's launch £350,00 ad blitz, SBP, 1995.

13. *The Irish Times*, 18th September 1996.

14. *MII News*, January/February 1996, Vol. 9 No. 1, 7.

15. 'The Big Pint', SBP, 13th April 1997.

16. Greenbaum, Thomas, 'Using Focus Groups Effectively in Packaging Research', *Marketing News*, Vol. 29 No. 12, 5th June 1995.

17. Bristol and Fern, 'Exploring the Atmosphere Created by Focus Group Interviews', *Journal of Marketing Research Society*, Vol. 38 No. 2, April 1996.

18. Moran, William T., 'The Science of Qualitative Research', *Journal of Advertising Research*, 26, June–July 1986, RC-16.

19. Calder, Bobby, 'Focus Groups and the Nature of Qualitative Marketing Research', *Journal of Marketing Research*, 14, August 1977, 353–64.

20. Krueger, Richard, *Focus Groups, A Practical Guide*, Sage publications, 1988.

21. Calder, Bobby, *op. cit.*

22. *Irish Marketing & Advertising Journal*, Vol. 27, No. 8.

23. Nelson, James E. and Frontczak, Nancy, 'How Acquaintanceship and Analyst Can Influence Focus Group Results', *Journal of Advertising*, 17, 1988, 41–8.
24. 'Marketing', *The Wall Street Journal*, 13th January 1992, B1.
25. Sykes, W., 'Validity and Reliability in Qualitative Market Research: a Review of the Literature', *Journal of the Market Research Society*, 32, 3 1990, 289–328.
26. Fern, Edward F., 'The Use of Focus Groups for Idea Generation: The Effects of Group Size, Acquaintanceship, and Moderator on Response Quantity and Quality', *Journal of Marketing Research*, 19, February 1982, 1–13.
27. McQuarrie, Edward F., 'New Books in Review', *Journal of Marketing Research*, February 1989, 121–4.
28. Greenbaum, Thomas, 'Focus Groups by Video', *Marketing News*, Vol. 130 No. 16, 29th July 1996.
29. Greenbaum, Thomas L., 'Focus Groups Research Is Not A Commodity Business', *Marketing News*, Vol. 27 No. 5l, 1st March 1993, 4.
30. Grinchaunas, Richard and Siciliano, Tony, 'Focus Groups Produce Verbatims, Not Facts', *Marketing News*, Vol. 27 No. 1, 4th January 1993, FG-19.
31. See John M. Hess, 'Group Interviewing', in R. L. King (ed.), *New Science of Planning*, Chicago: American Marketing Association, 1968, 4.
32. Darling, Eleanor, *op. cit.*
33. Heckman, J., 'Turning the Focus Online; Web snares ever-more qualitative research', *Marketing News*, American Marketing Association, 28th February 2000, 15.
34. Sweet, C., 'Designing and Conducting Virtual Focus Groups', *Qualitative Market Research: An International Journal*, Vol. 4, No 3, 2001, 130–5.
35. Mann, C. and Stewart, F., *Internet Communication and Qualitative Research – A Handbook for Researching Online*, Sage Publications, London, 2000.
36. Montoya-Weiss M.M., Massey A.P. and Clapper D.L., 'On-line focus groups: conceptual issues and a research tool', *European Journal of Marketing*, Vol. 32, No. 7/8, 1998, 713-23.
37. Sweet, C., *op. cit.*
38. Mann and Stewart 2001. *op. cit.*
39. McGrath, J. and Hollingshead, A., *Groups Interacting with Technology*, Sage Publications, 1993.
40. Chakrapani, C. (ed) *Marketing Research: State of the Art Perspectives*, American Marketing Association and the Professional Marketing Research Society, Mc Graw-Hill, 2000.
41. Bowers, D.K., 'FAQs on Online Research', *Marketing Research*, Vol. 10, Issue 4, 1998, 45–8.
42. Malhotra, N., *Marketing Research: An Applied Orientation*, Prentice Hall, 1999.
43. Sokolow, H., 'In-Depth Interviews Increasing in Importance', *Marketing News*, 13th September 1985, 26.
44. Knox, M. Z., 'In-Depth Interviews Can Reveal What's In a Name', *Marketing News*, 3, January 1986, 4.
45. Hazel, Kahan, 'One-on-Ones Should Sparkle Like The Gems They Are', *Marketing News*, 3rd September 1990, 8–9.
46. *MII News*, January/February 1995, Vol. 8 No. 1, 1.

47. Proctor, Tony, *Essentials of Marketing Research*, Pitman Publishing, 1997, 165.
48. Greenbaum, Thomas L., 'Focus Groups vs One-on-Ones: The Controversy Continues', *Marketing News*, 2nd September 1991, 16.
49. Penny, Richard, *op. cit.*
50. Mitchell, Vincent Wayne, 'Getting the Most from In-Depth Interviews', *Business Marketing Digest*, Vol. 18 No. 1, First quarter, 1993, 63–70.
51. Greenbaum, Thomas L., *op. cit.*
52. Hollander, Sharon L., 'Projective Techniques Uncover Real Consumer Attitudes', *Marketing News*, 4th January 1988, 34.
53. Kassarjian, H. H., 'Projective Methods', in R. Ferber (ed.), *Handbook of Marketing Research*, New York: McGraw-Hill, 1974, 3.85–3.100.
54. Lindzey, G., 'On the Classification of Projective Techniques', *Psychological Bulletin*, 1959, 158–68.
55. McLoughlin, Damien and Feely, Finola, *op. cit.*
56. O'Leary, Phelim, *op. cit.*
57. O'Leary, Phelim, *op. cit.*
58. Haire, Mason, 'Projective Techniques in Marketing Research', *Journal of Marketing*, April 1950, 649/652.
59. O'Leary, Phelim, *op. cit.*

Chapter 6

1. Oppenheim, A. N., *Questionnaire Design and Attitude Measurement*, NY: Basic Books, 1996.
2. Seymour, Harry, 'Conducting and Using Customer Surveys', *Marketing News*, 23rd September 1996, Vol. 30 No. 20, 8.
3. Sudman, Seymour, *Reducing the Cost of Surveys*, Chicago: Aldine, 1967.
4. Proctor, Tony, *Essentials of Marketing Research*, Pitman Publishing, 1997, 99.
5. DuPont, Thomas D., 'Do Frequent Mall Shoppers Distort Mall-Intercept Results?', *Journal of Advertising Research*, Vol. 27 No. 4, August/September 1987, 45–51.
6. Tyebjee, Tyzoon T., 'Telephone Survey Methods: The State of the Art', *Journal of Marketing Research*, Summer 1979, 69; Howard Gershowitz, 'Entering the 1990s: The State of Data Collection — Telephone Data Collection', *Applied Marketing Research*, Vol. 30 No. 2, Second Quarter 1990, 16–19.
7. Gates, Roger and Brobst, Bob, 'RAN-DIAL: A Program for Generating Random Telephone Numbers in Interviewer Usable Form', *Journal of Marketing Research*, 14, May 1977, 240–2.
8. Czaja, Ronald, Blair, Johnny and Sebestik, Jutta P., 'Respondent Selection in a Telephone Survey: A Comparison of Three Techniques', *Journal of Marketing Research*, 19th August 1982, 381–5; and O'Rourke, Diane, and Blair, Johnny, 'Improving Random Respondent Selection in Telephone Interviews', *Journal of Marketing Research*, 20, November 1983, 428–32.
9. *Your Opinion Counts*, 14. See also Jolene M. Struebbe, Jerome B. Kernan, and Thomas J. Georgan, 'The Refusal Problem in Telephone Surveys', *Journal of Advertising Research*, June–July 1986, 29–37.
10. Reported by Survey Sampling Inc., March 1993.

11. Becker, Emil, 'Automated Interviewing has Advantages', *Marketing News*, January, 2, Vol. 29 No. 1.

12. Berdie, Douglas, 'Reassessing the Value of High Response Rates to Mail Surveys', *Marketing Research*, September 1989, 52–63; Jean Charles Chebat and Ayala Cohen, 'Response Speed in Mail Surveys: Beware of Shortcuts', *Marketing Research*, Spring 1993, 20–5; and Robert J. Sutton and Linda L. Zeits, 'Multiple Prior Notifications, Personalization, and Reminder Surveys', *Marketing Research*, December 1992, 14–21.

13. Kanuk, Leslie and Berenson, Conrad, 'Mail Surveys and Response Rates: A Literature Review', *Journal of Marketing Research*, November 1975, 440–53; Lee Harvey, 'Factors Affecting Response Rates to Mailed Questionnaires: A Comprehensive Literature Review', *Journal of the Market Research Society (UK)*, July 1987, 341–53.

14. Parker, Charles D. and McCrohan, Kevin F., 'Increasing Mail Survey Response Rates: A Discussion of Methods and Induced Bias', in John Summey, R. Viswanathan, Ronald Taylor, and Karen Glynn (eds.), *Marketing Theories and Concepts For Era of Change*, Atlanta: Southern Marketing Association, 1983, 254–6.

15. Darling, Eleanor, 'Banking Leaves Nothing to Chance', *BusinessPlus*, April 1998.

16. See, for example, Stephen W. McDaniel and Perry Werille, 'Do Topic Differences Affect Survey Non-Response?', *Journal of the Marketing Research Society*, Vol. 29 No. 1, January 1987, 55–66.

17. Brennan, Mike, Hoek, Janet and Aistridge, Craig, 'The Effect of Monetary Incentives on the Response Rate and Cost Effectiveness of a Mail Survey', *Journal of Market Research Society*, Vol. 33 No. 3, 229–41.

18. Darling, Eleanor, *op. cit.*

19. Kanuk and Berenson, 'Mail Surveys', 450. Reprinted from the *Journal of Marketing Research*, American Marketing Association.

20. Boyer, K.K., Olson, J.R., Calantone, R.J. and Jackson, E.C., 'Print Versus Electronic Surveys: A Comparison of Two Data Collection Methodologies', *Journal of Operations Management*, Vol. 292, 2001, 1–17.

21. Information Week , 15th October 2001, 26.

22. Mann and Stewart, *op. cit.*

23. Klassen, R.D. and Jacobs, J., 'Experimental Comparison of Web, Electronic and Mail Survey Technologies in Operations Management', *Journal of Operations Management*, 19, 2001, 713–728.

24. Miller, T.W. 'Can We Trust The Data Of Online Research?', *Business and Management Practices*, Vol. 13, No. 2; Summer 2001, 26–32.

25. Klassen, R.D. and Jacobs, J., *op. cit.*

26. Coupey, E., *Marketing and the Internet*, Prentice Hall Inc, New Jersey, 2001.

27. Zubey, M.L., Wagner, W. and Otto, J.R., 'Conjoint analysis of voice over IP attributes', *Internet Research: Electronic Networking Applications and Policy*, Vol. 12, No. 1, 2002, 7–15.

28. Bowers, D.K. 'FAQs on Online Research', *Marketing Research*, Vol. 10, Issue 4, 1998, 45–8.

29. Vehovar, V., Manfreda, K.L. and Batagelj, 'Sensitivity of Electronic Commerce Measurement to the Survey Instrument', *International Journal of Electronic Commerce*, Vol. 6, No. 1, 2001, 31–51.

30. Nancarrow, C., Pallister, J. and Brace, I., 'A New Research Medium, New Research Populations and Seven Deadly Sins for Internet Researchers', *Qualitative Marketing Research: An International Journal*, Vol. 4, No. 3, 2001, 136–49.

31. Mann and Stewart, *op. cit.*

32. Zikmund, W.G., *op. cit.*

33. Kumar, V., Aaker, D.A. and Day, G.S., *Essentials of Marketing Research*, John Wiley & Sons, New York, 1999.

34. *Ibid.*

35. Grossnickle, J. and Raskin, O. 'What's Ahead On the Internet', *Marketing Research*, Vol. 13, Issue 2, 2001, 8–13.

36. Mann and Stewart, *op. cit.*

37. Miller, T.W., *op. cit.*

38. Boyer *et al*, *op. cit.*

39. Ranchhod, A., and Zhou, F., 'Comparing Respondents of eMail and Mail Surveys: Understanding the Implications of Technology', *Marketing Intelligence & Planning*, Vol. 19, No. 4, 2001, 254–62.

40. Boyer *et al*, *op. cit.*

41. Bowers, D.K., *op. cit.*

42. Addis, Robin, 'Understanding Your Customers and Finding New Ones', *Business and Finance*, October 1990, 14–18.

43. *MII News*, March/April 1996, Vol. 9 No. 2, 14.

44. Sainsbury, R., Ditch, J. and Hutton, S., 'Computer Assisted Personal Interviewing', *Social Research Update*, University of Surrey, March 1993.

45. Zikmund, William, G., *Exploring Marketing Research*, 6th Edition, Dryden Press, 1997, 206.

46. Aaker and Day, *Marketing Research*, 4th Edition, Wiley Publications, 139.

47. Miller, T.W. and Dickson, P.R., 'On-Line Market Research', *International Journal of Electronic Commerce*, Vol. 5, No 3, 2001, 139–67.

48. Mann and Stewart, *op. cit.*

49. Sweet, C., *op. cit.*

50. Boyer *et al*, *op. cit.*

51. Harper, Tom, 'Quantitive Research', in *Perspectives on Marketing Management in Ireland*, Mary Lambkin and Tony Meenaghan (eds.), Dublin, Oak Tree Press, 1994, 369–80.

52. Lansdowne Market Research Promotional Material.

53. 'Market Research in Ireland', *Business and Finance*, 16th September 1993.

54. Chisnall, Peter, *Marketing Research*, 5th Edition, McGraw-Hill, 229.

55. Harper, Tom, *op. cit.*

56. 'Omnibus Surveys', *Irish Marketing & Advertising Journal*, Vol. 27, No. 9, 2001, 44.

57. Mason, Jennifer, *Qualitative Researching*, Sage Publications, 1996.

58. 'The Magic of Mystery Shopping', *Marketing*, 17th October 1996, 41–3.

59. 'Does Colour Make a Difference?', *IMJ*, April 1996, 18–20

60. Wiedmann, K.P., Buxel, H. and Walsh, G., 'Customer profiling in e-commerce: Methodological aspects and challenges', *Journal of Database Marketing*, Vol. 9, No. 2, 2002, 170–84.

61. Kozinets, J., 'The Field Behind the Screen: Using Netnography for Marketing Research in Online Communities', *Journal of Marketing Research*, Winter 2002, 61.
62. *Ibid.*

Chapter 7

1. Campbell, D., and Stanley, J., 'Experimental and Quasi-Experimental Designs for Research', Chicago: Rand McNally, 1966.
2. Hunt, Shelby, D., *Marketing Theory, The Philosophy Of Marketing Science*, Irwin, 1983, 120–5.
3. Wiener, R.S., 'Experimentation in the 21st Century: The Importance of External Validity', *Journal of the Academy of Marketing Science*, Vol. 27, No. 3, 1999, 349–58.
4. Rothlisberger, F., and William, J., *Management and the Worker, An Account of a Research Program Conducted by the Western Electric Company, Hawthorne Works, Chicago*, Harvard University Press, 1939.
5. Fox, M., and Phua, K., 'Using Medicaid Claims Data to Evaluate a Large Physician Fee Increase', *Health Services Research*, Vol. 29, No. 3, 1994, 315–29.
6. *Irish Marketing Journal*, April 1999, Vol. 25, No. 10.
7. Thornton, Sarah, 'Sales Promotion and Experimental Designs', unpublished MBS thesis, NUI, Galway, 1997.
8. Domegan, Christine, 'An Evaluation Study of AnCO's Open Learning Marketing Management Programme', UCD, 1984, 28.
9. Rothlisberger, F., and William, J., *op. cit.*
10. Churchill, G.A., 'Marketing Research Methodological Foundations', 6th Edition, London: Dryden Press, 216.
11. Weiner, J., 'Consumer Electronics Marketer Uses Conjoint Approach to Configure its New Product and Set the Right Price', *Marketing Research*, Vol. 6 No. 3, 1996, 7–11.
12. Almquist, E. and Wyner, G., 'Boost Your Marketing ROI with Experimental Design', *Harvard Business Review*, October 2001, 135–41.
13. Adapted from Tull, S., and Hawkins, D., *Marketing Research, Measurement and Method*, 5th Edition, Macmillan, 207.
14. 'Guinness Test Market Range of Premium Beers', *IMJ*, November 1997.
15. 'Mars Celebrate', *IMJ*, November 1997.
16. 'World Stella Test Marketed', *Factfinder*, 31st August 1997.
17. Yarbrough, J., 'Fill 'er up', *Sales and Marketing Management*, Vol. 148 No. 9, 1996, 126.
18. 'Beamish Red Ahead of Expectations in UK', *Factfinder*, 31st March 1997.
19. 'Baileys Test Two New Line Extensions', *Drinks Industry Ireland*, 2005.
20. 'No Frontiers', *Licencing World*, 2004.
21. IDL Launches Cork Crimson', *Drinks Industry Ireland*, 2005.
22. *Irish Marketing and Advertising Journal*, Vol. 27, No. 10, October 31st–November 30th 2001, 15.
23. *Irish Marketing and Advertising Journal*, April 1998, Vol. 24, No. 4.
24. Klassen, R.D. and Jacobs, J., 'Experimental Comparison of Web, Electronic and Mail Survey Technologies in Operations Management', *Journal of Operations Management*, 19, 2001, 713-728.

25. Hayes, Dermot J., Shogren, Jason F., Fox, John A. and Kliebenstein, James B., 'Test Marketing New Food Products Using a Multi-Trial Nonhypothetical Experimental Auction with Market Discipline', *Psychology and Marketing* 13 (1996), pp. 365–379.
26. Bases Worldwide, 'Simulated Test Marketing' at http://www.bases.com/stm.htm, 1998.
27. Cohen, S., and Gadd, M., 'Virtual Reality Shopping Simulation for the Modern Marketer', in the 48th ESOMAR Marketing Research Congress, ' Making the Decision', The Hague, 17th–20th September 1995, 269–83.
28. Burke, Raymond R., *Virtual Shopping Breakthrough in Marketing Research*, HBR March/April, 1996, 120–31
29. Clancy, K. J., and Shulman, R. S., 'Test for Success', *Sales and Marketing Management*, 1995, 111–14.
30. Kleinschmidt, E. J., and Cooper, R. G., 'The Impact of an International Orientation on Product Innovation', *European Journal of Marketing*, Vol. 22 No. 10, 1988, 56.
31. Phillips, A., 'Developing a Rounder Tea', *Marketing and Research Today*, Vol. 19 No. 1, 1991, 3–14.

Chapter 8

1. Seymour, Harry, 'Conducting and Using Customer Surveys', *Marketing News*, 23rd September 1996, Vol. 30 No. 20, 8.
2. Malhotra, Naresh K., *Marketing Research, An Applied Orientation*, 1993, Prentice Hall, 318–19.
3. Haller, Terry, *Danger: Marketing Researcher at Work*, Westport, Conn: Quorum Books, 1983, 149.
4. Jones, S., 'Listening to Complexity', *Journal of the Market Research Society*, January 1981, 26–39; and McDonald, C., 'Coding Open-Ended Answers with the Help of a Computer', *Journal of the Market Research Society*, January 1982, 9–27.
5. Krosnick, Jon A., and Alwin, Duane F., 'An Evaluation of a Cognitive Theory of Response-Order Effects in Survey Measurement', *Public Opinion Quarterly*, Summer 1987, 201–19; and Payne, S. L., *The Art of Asking Questions*, Princeton, NJ: Princeton University Press, 1951, 141.
6. Morgan, Fred W., 'Judicial Standards for Survey Research: An Update and Guidelines', *Journal of Marketing*, 54, January 1990, 59–70; and Peterson, R. A., and Kerin, R. A., 'The Quality of Self-Report Data: Review and Synthesis', in Ben Enis and Kenneth Roering (eds.), *Annual Review of Marketing 1981*, Chicago: American Marketing Association, 1981, 5–20.
7. Omura, G. S., 'Correlates of Item Nonresponse', *Journal of the Market Research Society*, October 1983, 321–30; and Presser, S., 'Is Inaccuracy on Factual Survey Items Item-Specific or Respondent-Specific?', *Public Opinion Quarterly*, Spring 1984, 344–55.
8. Payne, S. L., *The Art of Asking Questions*, Princeton NJ: Princeton University Press, 1951, 41.
9. Boyd, Harper W., Jr., Westfall, Ralph and Stasch, Stanley F., *Marketing Research: Text and Cases*, 7th Edition, Homewood, IL.: Richard D. Irwin, 1989, 277.
10. Smith, Tom W., 'That Which We Call Welfare by Any Other Name Would Smell Sweeter. An Analysis of the Impact of Question Wording on Response Patterns', *Public Opinion Quarterly*, Spring 1987, 75–83.
11. Payne, *op. cit.*

12. Boyd, Harper W., Jr., Westfall, Ralph and Stasch, Stanley F., *op. cit.*
13. See, for example, George F. Bishop, 'Experiments with the Middle Response Alternative in Survey Questions', *Public Opinion Quarterly*, Vol. 51, Summer 1985, 220–32; or Clinton B. Schertizer and Jerome B. Kernan, 'More on the Robustness of Response Scales', *Journal of the Marketing Research Society*, Vol. 27, October 1985, 262–82.
14. Mayer, Charles S., and Piper, Cindy, 'A Note on the Importance of Layout in Self-Administered Questionnaires', *Journal of Marketing Research*, 19, August 1982, 390–1.
15. 'Mailing List Brokers Sell More than Names to Their Many Clients', *The Wall Street Journal*, 19th February 1974, 1, 18; and Bob Davis, 'Baby-Goods Firms See Direct Mail as the Perfect Pitch for New Moms', *The Wall Street Journal*, 29th January 1986, 31.
16. Leeuw, E. and Hox, J., 'The Effect of Computer Assisted Interviewing', *JMRS*, Vol. 37 No. 4, 1995.
17. Normally pretests are done individually, but a focus group could be used. See Steven A. Long, 'Pretesting Questionnaires Minimizes Measurement Error', *Marketing News*, Vol. 25 No. 11, 27th May 1991.
18. Hunt, Shelby D., Sparkman, Richard D. Jr., and Wilcox, James B., 'The Pretest in Survey Research: Issues and Preliminary Findings', *Journal of Marketing Research*, 19, May 1982, 265–75.
19. Kiecker p. Nelson 'Do interviewers follow telephone survey instructions?', *JMRS*, April 1996, Vol. 38 No. 2, 161– 76(16).

Chapter 9

1. Gordon Allport, 'Attitudes' in C. A. Murchinson (ed.), *A Handbook of Social Psychology*, Worchester, MA.: Clark University Press, 1935, 798–844.
2. Neelankavil, J. P., O'Brien, J. V. and Rashjain, R., 'Techniques to Obtain Market-related Information from Very Young Children', *Journal of Advertising Research*, June/July 1985, 41–7. See also M. C. Macklin, 'Do Children Understand TV Ads?', *Journal of Advertising Research*, February/March 1983, 63–70.
3. McDaniel, Carl Jr., Gates, Roger, *Contemporary Marketing Research*, 3rd Edition, West Publishing Company, 1996, 355.
4. See Churchill, Gilbert A. Jr., 'A Paradigm for Developing Better Measures of Marketing Constructs', *Journal of Marketing Research*, 16, February 1979, 64–73, for a procedure that can be used to construct scales having construct validity. See J. Paul Peter, 'Construct Validity: A Review of Basic Issues and Marketing Practices', *Journal of Marketing Research*, 18, May 1981, 133–45
5. Perreault, William D. Jr., and Leigh, Laurence E., 'Reliability of Nominal Data Based on Qualitative Judgments', *Journal of Marketing Research*, 25, May 1989, 135–48; Peter J. Paul, 'Reliability: A Review of Psychometric Basics and Recent Marketing Practices', *Journal of Marketing Research*, 16, February 1979, 6–17.
6. Grigg, A. O., 'Some Problems Concerning the Use of Rating Scales for Visual Assessment', *Journal of the Market Research Society*, January 1980, 29–43; and L. W. Friedman and H. H. Friedman, 'Comparison of Itemised vs Graphic Rating Scales', *Journal of the Market Research Society*, July 1986, 285–90. For a different view see S. I. Lampert, 'The Attitude Pollimeter: A New Attitude Scaling Device', *Journal of Marketing Research*, November 1979, 578–82.

7. Cose, Eli P. II, 'The Optimal Number of Response Alternatives for a Scale: A Review,' *Journal of Marketing Research*, November 1980, 407–22.

8. Friedman, H. H. and Leefer, J. R., 'Label Versus Position in Rating Scales', *Journal of the Academy of Marketing Science*, Spring 1981, 88–92.

9. Dickson, John and Albaum, Gerald, 'A Method for Developing Tailor-Made Semantic Differentials for Specific Marketing Content Areas', *Journal of Marketing Research*, 14, February 1977, 87–91.

10. Malhotra, Naresh K., 'A Scale to Measure Self-Concepts, Person Concepts and Product Concepts', *Journal of Marketing Research*, 18, November 1981, 456–64.

11. Friedman, H. H. and Leefer, J. R. 'Label Versus Position in Rating Scales', *Journal of the Academy of Marketing Science*, Spring 1981, 88–92. R. I. Haley and P. B. Case, 'Testing Thirteen Attitude Scales for Agreement and Brand Discrimination', *Journal of Marketing*, Fall 1979, 20–32.

12. Likert, Rensis, 'A Technique for Measuring of Attitudes', *Archives of Psychology*, 140.

13. Riecken, G. and Samli, A. C., 'Measuring Children's Attitudes Toward Television Commercials: Extension and Replication', *Journal of Consumer Research*, June 1981, 57–61.

14. See Jacob Jacoby and Michael S. Matell, 'Three Point Likert Scales Are Good Enough', *Journal of Marketing Research*, November 1971, 495–506; Roger Best, Del I. Hawkins, and Gerald Albaum, 'The Effort of Varying Response Intervals on the Stability of Factor Solutions of Rating Scale Data', in *Advances in Consumer Research*, Vol. VII, Jerry Olson (ed.), San Francisco: ACR, 1979, 539–54.

15. Roberts, Mary Lou and Wortzel, Lawrence H., 'New Lifestyle Determinants of Women's Food Shopping Behaviour', *Journal of Marketing*, Summer 1979, 28–39.

16. Osgood, Charles E., Sici, George J., and Tannenbaum, Percy H., *The Measurement of Meaning*, University of Illinois Press, Urbana, 1957.

17. Malhotra, Naresh K., 'A Scale to Measure Self-Concepts, Person Concepts and Product Concepts', *Journal of Marketing Research*, 18, November 1981, 456–64.

18. Andrews, F. M., 'Construct Validity and Error Components of Survey Measures', *Public Opinion Quarterly*, Summer 1984, 432.

19. Anderson, R. C. and Scott, E. A., 'Supermarkets: Are they really alike?', *Journal of Retailing*, Autumn 1970.

20. Another way to avoid the halo effect is to have subjects rate each stimulus on the same attribute and then move to the next attribute. See Bob T. W. Wu and Susan Petroshius, 'The Halo Effect in Store Image Management', *Journal of the Academy of Marketing Science*, Vol. 15 No. 1, 1987, 44–51.

21. Wirtz, J., 'Improving the measurement of customer satisfaction: a test of three methods to reduce Halo', *Managing Service Quality*, Vol. 11, No. 2, 2001, 99–112.

22. Garg, Rajendar K., 'The Influence of Positive and Negative Wording and Issue Involvement on Responses to Likert Scales in Marketing Research', *Journal of the Marketing Research Society*, Vol. 37 No. 3, July 1996, 234–46.

23. Menezes, Dennis and Elbert, Nobert F., 'Alternative Semantic Scaling Formats for Measuring Store Image: An Evaluation', *Journal of Marketing Research*, February 1979, 80–7.

24. Hawkins, Del I., Albaum, Gerald, and Best, Roger, 'Stapel Scale or Semantic Differential in Marketing Research?', *Journal of Marketing Research*, August 1974, 318–22.

Chapter 10

1. http:/www.Insightsc.ie, 2002.
2. Rodger, Leslie, *Statistics for Marketing*, McGraw-Hill Marketing Series, 1984.
3. Churchill, Gilbert A., *Marketing Research Methodological Foundations*, 6th Edition, The Dryden Press, 574–651, 2002
4. Williams, Jane, 'The Sampling Process', 61–96, in *Business Research Methods, Strategies, Techniques and Sources*, T. Brannick and W. Roche (eds.), Dublin: Oak Tree Press, 1997.
5. CSO, Census of Population, 1996, Preliminary Report, Commentary, 5.
6. Weiers, Ronald, *Marketing Research*, 2nd Edition, Prentice-Hall International.
7. Furrer, Q. and Sudharshan, D., 'Internet Marketing Research: Opportunities and Problems', *Qualitative Market Research: An International Journal*, Vol.4, Issue 3, 2001, 123–29.
8. Wyner, G., 'Representation, Randomization and Realism', *Marketing Research*, American Marketing Association, Vol.13, No.3, 4–6.
9. Williams, Jane, *op. cit.*
10. Furrer, Q. and Sudharshan, D., *op. cit.*
11. Rodger, Leslie, *op. cit.*
12. Hague, P. and Harris, P., *Sampling and Statistics*, the Marketing Research Series, Kogan Page, 1993.
13. Maisel, R. and Persell C., *How Sampling Works*, New York: Pine Forge, 1996.
14. CSO, *Household Budget Survey, 1994–1995, Volume 1, Detailed Results for all Households*, Appendix 4, 215–24.
15. Whyte, M.A.,'Leading Edge Internet Marketing Strategy in Ireland', Unpublished MBS thesis, Department of Marketing, NUI, Galway, 1997.
16. *The Irish Times and MRBI Ltd*, 'Fianna Fáil expected to lead next government', 7th June 1997 and 'FF and PDs close to gaining majority, new poll reveals', 31st May 1997.
17. *Sunday Business Post*, 28th May 2002.
18. Harper, Tom, 'Quantitative Research' in *Perspectives on Marketing Management in Ireland*, Mary Lambkin and Tony Meenaghan (eds.), Dublin: Oak Tree Press, 1994, 369–80.
19. Wilson, Alan and Laskey, Nial, 'Internet Based Marketing Research: A Serious Alternative to Traditional Research Methods?', *Marketing Intelligence and Planning*, Vol. 21, No. 2, 2003, pp. 79–84.
20. Opperman, M. (1995), 'Email Surveys – Potential and Pitfalls', *Marketing Research*, Vol. 7, No. 3, p. 28.
21. Litvin, S.W. and Kar, G.H., 'E-surveying for Tourism Research: Legitimate Tool or a Researcher's Fantasy?' *Journal of Travel Research*, Vol. 39, No. 3, 2001, p. 308.
22. Dommeyer, C.J. and Moriarty, E., 'Comparing Two Forms of an Email Survey: Embedded vs Attached', *Journal of the Market Research Society*, Vol. 42, No. 1, 2000, pp. 39–50.
23. Shachtman, 'Web Enhances Market Research, Database and Research: But Issues such as Recruiting Representative Sample Remain', *Advertising Age*, 18 June 2001.
24. Elder and Incalcatera, 'Pushing the Envelope', in Brookes, R. (ed.), 'Marketing Research in a .com Environment', *ESOMAR Monograph*, Vol. 10, Amsterdam, 2000.

25. Gunter, B., Nicholas, D. Huntington, P. and Williams, P. 'Online verses Offline Research: Implications for Evaluating Digital Media', Aslib Proceedings, Vol. 54, 2002, pp. 229–239.

26. 'Does Internet Research Work?', *International Journal of Market Research Society*, Vol. 40, No. 4, 2000.

27. Miller, T.W., *op. cit.*

28. Shachtman, 'Web enhances market research; Database and Research: But issues such as recruiting representative sample remain', *Advertising Age*, 18th June 2001, 18.

29. Elder and Incalcatera, 'Pushing the Envelope' in Brookes, R. (ed.), *Marketing Research in a .com Environment*, ESOMAR Monograph Volume 10, Amsterdam, 2000

30. Strauss, J. and Frost, R., *eMarketing*, 2nd Edition, Prentice Hall, 2001.

31. Miller, T.W. and Dickson, P.R., *op. cit.*

32. Bowers, D.K., *op. cit.*

33. Jarvis, S. 'Opt-in can't be stressed enough online; You should say that again', *Marketing News*, American Marketing Association, 21, 2001, 6.

34. http://zdnet.com.com/2100-1105-886030.html

35. *Marketing Research in the New Millennium*, 2001.

36. Nancarrow *et al*, op.cit.; Felson, L., 'Netting limitations; Online researchers' new tactics for tough audiences; Keeping mix in the mix' , *Marketing News*, American Marketing Association, 26th February 2001, 43.

37. Neilson, M., Health Farms of Ireland Association, 2001.

Chapter 11

1. Rodger, Leslie, *Statistics for Marketing*, McGraw-Hill, 1984.

2. Kish, Leslie, *Survey Sampling*, New York: John Wiley & Sons, Inc., 1965.

3. Zikmund, William, *Exploring Marketing Research*, 6th Edition, Dryden Press, 1997.

4. *Ibid*

Chapter 12

1. Aaker, David and Day, George, *Marketing Research*, 4th Edition, John Wiley & Sons, Inc., 1990, 431.

2. Keller, Wouter J., 'Trends in Survey Data Processing', *Journal of Market Research Society*, Vol. 35 No. 3, July 1993.

3. Aaker, David and Day, George, *op. cit.* See also, D. W. Stewart, 'Filling the Gap; A Review of the Missing Data Problem', *An Assessment of Marketing Thought and Practice*, American Marketing Association, 1982, 395–9, and Malhotra, Naresh K., 'Analysing Marketing Research Data with incomplete information on the Dependent Variable', *Journal of Marketing Research*, 24, February 1987, 74–84.

4. For a further discussion of coding see also, Philip S. Sidel, 'Coding', in Robert Ferber (ed.), *Handbook of Marketing Research*, New York: McGraw-Hill, 1974, pp. 2–178–2–199.

5. Malhotra, Naresh, K., *Marketing Research, An Applied Orientation*, Prentice-Hall, 1993, 487.

6. For a detailed discussion on fundamental statistics, see Richard I. Levin, *Statistics for Management*, Englewood Cliffs, New Jersey: Prentice-Hall, 1987, or any business statistics textbook.

7. For an excellent discussion on this, see Keane, John G., 'Questionable Statistics', *American Demographics*, Vol. 7 issue 6, June 1985, 18–21.

8. For an excellent discussion on creating graphics presentations see, Gus Venditto, 'Twelve Tips for Better Presentations', *PC Magazine*, 28th January 1992, 253–60

9. This discussion of charts is taken from the Excel Spreadsheet Software package.

Chapter 13

1. Bowles, B. and Blyth, B., 'How Do You Like Your Data; Raw, Al dente or Stewed?', *Journal of the Market Research Society*, Vol. 19 No. 1, 1997, 165–74.

2. Davis, E. J., 'Statistical Tests', Appendix 3, 351–64, in *The Marketing Research Process*, 4th Edition, by M. Crimp and L. T. Wright, Prentice-Hall, 1995.

3. Groebner, D. and Shannon, P., *Business Statistics, A Decision-Making Approach*, 3rd Edition, Merrill, 1989.

4. Downie, N. M. and Heath, R. W., *Basic Statistical Methods*, Harper & Row International, 1974.

5. Janpi, G. K., *100 Statistical Tests*, Sage Publications, 1993.

6. Berenson, M. and Levine, D., *Basic Business Statistics, Concepts and Applications*, Prentice-Hall, 1996.

Chapter 14

1. Hair, J., Anderson, R., Tatham, R., and Black, W., *Multivariate Data Analysis*, 5th Edition, Prentice-Hall International, 1998.

2. Hooley, Graham and Hussey, Michael, *Quantative Methods in Marketing*, London: Dryden Press, 1995.

3. Sharma, Subhash, 'Applied Multivariate Techniques', USA: John Wiley, 1996.

4. Fornell, C. and Zinkhan, G, 1987, 'Classification Schemes for a new generation of multivariate Analysis', American Marketing Association Winter Education Conference, 295–9.

5. Diamantopoulos, A. and Schilegelmilch, B., *Taking the Fear out of Data Analysis*, London: The Dryden Press, 1997.

6. Hair, J., Anderson, R., Tatham, R. and Black, W., *op. cit.*

7. Sharma, Subhash, *op. cit.*

8. Hair, J., Anderson, R., Tatham, R. and Black, W., *op. cit.*

9. Green, P.E. and Krieger, A.M., 'Segmenting Markets with Conjoint Analysis', *Journal of Marketing*, Vol. 55, 1991, 20–31; Green, P.E. and Srinivasan, V., 'Conjoint Analysis in Consumer Research: Issues and Outlook', *Journal of Consumer Research*, 5, 1978, 103–123; Green, P.E. and Srinivasan, V., 'Conjoint Analysis in Marketing: New Developments with Implications for Research and Practise'. *Journal of Marketing*, 54 4, 1990, 3–19; Green, P.E. and Wind, Y. 'New Way to Measure Consumers' Judgements', *Harvard Business Review*. July–August 1975; Hair, J.F., Anderson, R.E., Tatham, R.L. and Black, W.C., *Multivariate Data Analysis*, 5th Edition, Prentice Hall, New Jersey, 1998.

10. Boyd, H., Westfall, R. and Stasch, S., *Marketing Research, Text and Cases*, 5th Edition, USA: Richard Irwin, Inc., 1981.
11. Sharma, Subhash, *op. cit.*
12. Johnson, D., Foreword, 'Some Observations on, and Developments in, the Analysis of Multivariate Survey Data', *Journal of Market Research Society*, Vol. 38 No. 4, 1996, 447.
13. Flynn, L., Goldsmith, R. and Eastmann, J., 'Opinion Leaders and Opinion Seekers, Two New Measurement Scales', *Journal of Academy of Marketing Science*, Vol. 24 No. 2, 1996, 137–47.
14. Inglis, J. and Johnson, D., 'Some observations on, and developments in, the analysis of multivariate survey data', *Journal of Market Research Society*, Vol. 12 No. 2, 1970, 449–71.
15. Boyd, H., Westfall, R. and Stasch, S., *op. cit.*
16. Churchill, G., *Marketing Research, Methodological Foundations*, 5th Edition, Chicago: Dryden Press, 921.
17. Diamantopoulous, A., 'Modelling with LISTREL: A Guide for the Uninitiated', in Hooley, Graham and Hussey, Michael, *Quantitative Methods in Marketing*, London: Dryden Press, 1995, 105–36.
18. Mountinho, I., Goode M. and Davis, F., *Quantitative Analysis in Marketing Management*, England: John Wiley, 1998.
19. Hooley, Graham and Hussey, Michael, *op. cit.*

Chapter 15

1. Deshpande, Rohit and Zaltman, Gerald, 'A Comparison of Factors Affecting Researcher and Manager Perceptions of Market Research Use', *Journal of Marketing Research*, 21, February 1984, 37.
2. Britt, S. H. 'The Writing of Readable Research Reports', *Journal of Marketing Research*, May 1971, 265.
3. Gallagher, William J., *Report Writing for Management*, Massachusetts: Addison-Wesley Publishing Company, Inc., 1969, 87.
4. *Ibid.*, 84.
5. See Gallagher, *Report Writing*, 80–3, for a number of examples that display some of the inaccuracies that may arise. The examples are particularly interesting because they have been extracted from actual company reports.
6. Resta, Paul, E., *The Research Report*, NY: An American Book Company, 1972, 5.
7. Tull and Hawkins, *Marketing Research*, 4th Edition, New York: Macmillan, 1987.
8. Lawlor, Kevin, 'Communicate or Die', *Business and Finance*, 12th October 1995.
9. Hayes, Stephen, 'Making Effective Presentations', *Marketing, Running Your Business*, June/July 1996.
10. *Ibid.*

INDEX